Auditing Concepts and Applications

A RISK-ANALYSIS APPROACH

To the student: A study guide is available to supplement this textbook. Entitled *Study Guide to Accompany Auditing Concepts and Applications: A Risk-Analysis Approach, Second Edition,* and containing outlines and review questions/answers, this supplement may be useful in enhancing your understanding of the text material. If your bookstore does not presently stock the study guide, the store manager can order it for you.

SECOND EDITION

Auditing Concepts and Applications

A RISK-ANALYSIS APPROACH

Larry F. Konrath

UNIVERSITY OF TOLEDO

WEST PUBLISHING COMPANY

Minneapolis / St. Paul • New York • Los Angeles • San Francisco

Copyediting: Publication Support Services
Composition: Carlisle Communications
Cover Design: Paul Konsterlie
Cover Photo: Bob Cunningham/Photo Resource
Text Design: Rick Chafian
Art: Ambos Company

Production, Prepress, Printing and Binding by West Publishing Company

WEST'S COMMITMENT TO THE ENVIRONMENT

In 1906, West Publishing Company began recycling materials left over from the production of books. This began a tradition of efficient and responsible use of resources. Today, up to 95 percent of our legal books and 70% of our college and school texts are printed on recycled, acid-free stock. West also recycles nearly 22 million pounds of scrap paper annually—the equivalent of 181,717 trees. Since the 1960s, West has devised ways to capture and recycle waste inks, solvents, oils, and vapors created in the printing process. We also recycle plastics of all kinds, wood, glass, corrugated cardboard, and batteries, and have eliminated the use of styrofoam book packaging. We at West are proud of the longevity and the scope of our commitment to our environment.

CIA examinations material from *Standards for the Professional Practice of Internal Auditing* by The Institute of Internal Auditors. Copyright 1978 by The Institute of Internal Auditors, Inc., 249 Maitland Avenue, Altamonte Springs, Florida 32701 U.S.A. Reprinted with permission.

Material from Uniform CPA Examination, Questions, and Unofficial Answers, copyright 1982, 1983, 1984, 1985, 1986, 1987, 1988, 1989 by American Institute of Certified Public Accountants, Inc., is reprinted or adapted with permission.

Library of Congress Cataloging-in-Publication Data

Konrath, Larry F.
   Auditing concepts and applications : a risk-analysis approach /
Larry F. Konrath.—2nd ed.
     p.   cm.
   Includes index.
   ISBN 0-314-01099-8
   1. Auditing. I. Title.
HF5667.K62 1993
657'.45—dc20
                                                    92-17895
                                                 ∞ CIP

Contents

Preface   *xvii*

1 AN OVERVIEW OF AUDITING   2

Definition of Auditing   *4*
Independent Auditing vs. Internal Auditing   *6*
Audits by Governmental Organizations   *8*
    General Accounting Office   8
    Defense Contract Audit Agency   8
    Internal Revenue Service   9
How Auditing Differs from Accounting   *9*
Why Independent Auditing is Necessary   *10*
Requirements for an Effective Audit   *11*
How Evidence is Evaluated   *12*
How the Auditor's Findings are Communicated   *12*
The Audit Process-An Overview   *14*
    Audit Planning   14
    Interim Audit   18
    Final Audit   19
    Audit Report   19
Key Terms   *19*
Review Questions   *20*
Multiple Choice Questions   *20*
Essay Questions and Problems   *22*

2 PROFESSIONAL RESPONSIBILITY   28

Introduction   *30*
Definition of Quality   *31*
    Generally Accepted Auditing Standards   33
    Attestation Standards   36
    Statements on Standards for Consulting Services   37
    Statements on Responsibilities in Tax Practice   38
    Code of Professional Conduct   38

Maintenance of Quality   *48*
  Self-Regulation and the Expectations Gap   48
  The AICPA, State Boards of Accountancy and Quality
    Maintenance   51
  Division for CPA Firms   52
  Securities and Exchange Commission   52
  AICPA Quality Control Standards Committee   53
  The Courts   55
Key Terms   *55*
Review Questions   *55*
Multiple Choice Questions   *56*
Essay Questions and Problems   *59*

3   AUDITORS' LEGAL LIABILITY   66

Introduction   *68*
Types of Liability   *68*
  Ordinary Negligence vs. Gross Negligence   68
  Gross Negligence vs. Fraud   71
Sources of Auditor Liability   *72*
  Common Law   74
  Statutory Law   76
  Racketeer Influenced and Corrupt Organizations Act (RICO)   79
Summary of Sources and Types of Auditor Liability   *80*
Liability for Unaudited Statements   *80*
Preventing Legal Actions   *81*
Dealing with Liability   *82*
Key Terms   *83*

APPENDIX   *83*
Legal Cases Involving Auditors   *83*

Review Questions   *91*
Multiple Choice Questions   *92*
Essay Questions and Problems   *96*

4   AUDIT EVIDENCE   104

Introduction   *106*
Characteristics of Audit Evidence   *106*
  Factual vs. Inferential Evidence   106
  Underlying Accounting Data and Corroborating Information   106
  Sufficiency and Competence of Evidence   107
Audit Objectives   *107*
  Audit of the Information System   107
  Audit of Transactions and Balances—Substantive Testing   110
Audit Evidence and Related Auditing Procedures   *114*
  Physical Evidence   115
  Confirmation   116

Documentary Evidence   116
Mathematical Evidence   118
Analytical Evidence   118
Hearsay Evidence   120
Materiality and Audit Evidence   *121*
Individual Item Materiality   122
Aggregate Materiality   122
Relationship Among Audit Risk, Audit Evidence, and Materiality   *125*
Audit Programs   *127*
Developing Audit Programs   128
Documentation of Audit Programs   130
Audit Workpapers   *131*
Working Trial Balance   131
Lead Schedules   131
Supporting Schedules   131
How Audit Workpapers are Interconnected   133
Guidelines for Preparing Adequate Audit Workpapers   136
Initial vs. Recurring Audits   *137*
Key Terms   *138*
Review Questions   *139*
Multiple Choice Questions   *139*
Essay Questions and Problems   *142*

5   AUDIT RISK ANALYSIS   *150*

Introduction   *151*
Audit Risk Defined   *153*
Components of Audit Risk   *153*
Inherent Risk   153
Control Risk   154
Detection Risk   154
Quantifying Audit Risk   *155*
Analysis of Inherent Risk   *157*
Preliminary Phases of Audit Planning   158
Study of the Business and Industry   159
Analytical Procedures   167
Classifying the Warning Signs   *171*
Indicators of Possible Material Financial Statement Errors   171
Indicators of Forces Affecting Earnings or Liquidity   171
Indicators of Possible Disclosure Requirements   172
Indicators of Audit Complexity   172
Indicators of Possible Management Dishonesty   172
Risk Analysis Matrix   *173*
Incorporating Inherent Risk Analysis into the Audit   *177*
Risk Driven vs. Procedures Driven Audits   177
Preliminary Audit Programs   178
Time Budgets and Staff Scheduling   179
Preaudit Conference   180

Key Terms *182*
Review Questions *183*
Multiple Choice Questions *183*
Essay Questions and Problems *186*

6   INTERNAL CONTROL STRUCTURE: CONCEPTS *196*

Introduction *198*
Internal Control Structure Defined *198*
The Control Environment *198*
    Management Philosophy and Operating Style 200
    Organizational Structure 200
    Audit Committees 200
    Personnel Policies and Procedures 200
    Communicating Assignment of Authority and Responsibility 201
    Internal Audit Function 201
    External Influences 202
The Accounting System *202*
    *Chart of Accounts, Accounting Manuals, and Standard Journal
      Entries 202*
    Documentation of Transactions 203
    Review of Transactions 203
    Method of Transaction Processing 204
Control Procedures *204*
    Competence of Personnel 204
    Policy and Procedures Manuals 205
    Planning, Budgeting, and Performance Reporting 205
    Decentralized Operations and the Need for Accountability 205
    Asset Safeguards 205
    Periodic Inventories and Cash and Securities Counts 206
Internal Control Structure Policies and Procedures Relevant
  to an Audit *207*
    Existence or Occurrence 208
    Completeness 211
    Rights and Obligations 212
    Valuation or Allocation 214
    Presentation and Disclosure 216
Inherent Limitations of Control Structure *217*
    Collusion 217
    Management Override 217
    Temporary Breakdown 219
    Environmental Changes 219
Internal Control for a Small Business *220*
Key Terms *222*
Review Questions *222*
Multiple Choice Questions *223*
Essay Questions and Problems *225*

7 INTERNAL CONTROL STRUCTURE: ASSESSMENT OF CONTROL RISK 230

The Reason for the Auditor's Assessment of Control Risk 232
The Auditor's Approach to Assessing Control Risk 232
    Obtain an Understanding of the Control Structure 232
    Document Understanding 236
    Reduce the Assessed Level of Control Risk through Control
        Testing 241
    Assess Control Risk and Document Conclusions 243
Design Substantive Audit Programs 243
    Adjusting Materiality Thresholds Based on Risk
        Analysis 243
    Qualitative Approach to Designing Substantive Tests 245
    Quantitative Approach to Designing Substantive Tests 245
Summary of Audit Risk Assessment 246
Communication of Reportable Conditions 248
Key Terms 249
Review Questions 249
Multiple Choice Questions 251
Essay Questions and Problems 255

APPENDIX 264
Transaction Cycles and Related Control Tests 264
Revenue Cycle 265
    Sales 265
    Cash Receipts 270
Expenditure Cycle 275
    Purchases 275
    Payments to Vendors 280
    Payroll 283
    Production 290
Financing and Investing Cycle 295
    Borrowing from Others 295
    Lending to Others 296
    Acquisitions and Disposals of Financial Assets 298
    Capital Stock and Dividend Transactions 299

8 INTERNAL CONTROL AND EDP 302

Need for a Different Auditing Approach 305
    Auditing Around vs. Through the Computer 305
    Audit Objectives vs. Audit Approach 305
Types of EDP Accounting Systems 306
    Processing Systems 306
    File Systems 309
    Hardware Configurations 310

Kinds of EDP Controls   *312*
   General Controls   314
   Application Controls   316
   User Controls   318
Techniques for Testing EDP-Based Controls   *319*
   Understanding the System   319
   Controls Testing to Reduce the Assessed Level of Control Risk   321
   Auditing Through the Computer to Test Controls   323
EDP and Audit Risk Implications   *329*
   Factors Affecting Control Risk   329
   How Mitigated   330
   Managing Detection Risk   334
Key Terms   *336*
Review Questions   *337*
Multiple Choice Questions   *337*
Essay Questions and Problems   *342*

APPENDIX   *348*
Effective Writing in Auditing   *348*
Need for Consideration   *348*
How to Plan a Written Document   *349*
   Identify Reader(s) and Information Content   349
   Prepare an Outline   349
How to Compose a Written Document   *351*
   Facilitate the Reader's Task   351
   Maintain a Logical Order   351
   Use Headings and Subheadings   351
   Repeat Main Ideas   351
   Clarity and Conciseness are Important   352
Computer Assisted Writing   *354*
   Word Processors   354
   Grammar Checkers   354
   Outliners   354
   Data Bases   355
How to Answer Essay Questions   *355*
Summary   *354*
Practice Case-Reportable Conditions Letter   *356*
Suggested Solution to Practice Case   *359*
Solution Notes   *365*

9 EDP AND SUBSTANTIVE AUDIT TESTING: AUDITING WITH THE COMPUTER   366

Advantages of Auditing with the Computer   *368*
How to Audit with the Computer   *370*
   Generalized Audit Software   370
   Custom-Designed Programs   370
   Microcomputer Packages   370

Microcomputer Packages and Substantive Audit Testing   *371*
   Analytical Procedures   371
   Electronic Workpaper Files   374
   Accounts Receivable Aging Analysis   374
   Property, Plant, and Equipment   381
   Audit of Investment Portfolios   381
   Other Substantive Testing Applications   381
   Budget and Time Summary   385
Expert Systems in Auditing   *385*
Key Terms   *388*
Computer Audit Practice Case   *388*
Review Questions   *389*
Multiple Choice Questions   *389*
Essay Questions and Problems   *391*

10 STATISTICAL SAMPLING FOR TESTING CONTROL PROCEDURES 396

Sampling Applications in Auditing   *399*
How Sampling can Assist in Control Testing   *399*
   Forms of Control Testing   399
   Sampling to Test Controls Leaving Documentation   400
Statistical vs. Nonstatistical Sampling   *400*
Statistical Sampling and Audit Judgment   *401*
Statistical Sampling for Control Testing   *402*
   Sampling for Attributes   402
   Choice of Sampling Method   402
   Calculating the Sample Size   403
   Case Study   405
   Summary of Steps in Applying Attribute Sampling   416
Statistical Sampling and Audit Risk Implications   *416*
   Review of Audit Risk and Reason for Quantifying   416
   How to Quantify Control Risk   417
   How to Quantify Inherent Risk   418
   How to Quantify Detection Risk   419
Extended Example   *420*
Key Terms   *425*
Computer Audit Practice Case   *425*
Review Questions   *426*
Multiple Choice Questions   *426*
Essay Questions and Problems   *430*

11 STATISTICAL SAMPLING FOR SUBSTANTIVE TESTING 436

Introduction   *438*
Approaches to Variables Sampling   *439*
Mean per Unit   *439*

Calculating Sample Size   *441*
   Equation for MPU Sample Size   *443*
Raw Materials Inventory Example   *444*
Drawing the Sample and Evaluating Sample Results   *446*
Difference Estimation   *448*
   Reasons for Using and Conditions to be Met   *448*
   Steps in Applying   *449*
   Accounts Receivable Example   *450*
Probability Proportional to Size Sampling   *452*
   Advantages of PPS   *452*
   Steps in Applying   *453*
   Application Involving Plant Asset Additions   *454*
Computer Assisted Sampling   *458*
Key Terms   *460*
Computer Audit Practice Case   *460*
Review Questions   *460*
Multiple Choice Questions   *461*
Essay Questions and Problems   *463*

12 SUBSTANTIVE AUDIT TESTING: REVENUE CYCLE   472

Introduction   *474*
Review of the Audit Process   *474*
Overview of Substantive Testing   *475*
   Timing of Substantive Testing   *475*
   Cost/Benefit and Substantive Testing   *476*
   Analytical Procedures and Substantive Testing   *476*
   Audit Objectives, Evidence, and Procedures   *477*
   Emphasis and Direction of Substantive Testing   *477*
Auditing the Revenue Cycle   *479*
   Sales Transactions and Accounts Receivable Balances   *481*
   Cash Receipts Transactions and Cash Balances   *489*
Audit Risk Analysis and the Revenue Cycle   *495*
   Inflated Sales or Fictitious Accounts Receivable   *495*
   Inadequate Loan Loss Reserves   *496*
   Early Revenue Recognition   *498*
   Proof of Cash   *499*
Key Terms   500
Computer Audit Practice Case   *501*
Review Questions   501
Multiple Choice Questions   502
Essay Questions and Problems   504

APPENDIX   510
Auditing Objectives and Procedures: Revenue Cycle   510

13 SUBSTANTIVE AUDIT TESTING: EXPENDITURE CYCLE 514

Purchases, Production, and Inventory *516*
 Summary of Processing Steps 516
 Audit Objectives 517
 Audit Evidence and Procedures 519
 Summary Audit Program 526
Plant Assets *527*
 Audit Objectives 527
 Audit Evidence and Procedures 529
 Summary Audit Program 532
Intangible Assets *532*
 Audit Objectives 532
 Audit Evidence and Procedures 534
 Summary Audit Program 535
Current Liabilities *536*
 Audit Objectives 536
 Audit Evidence and Procedures 537
 Summary Audit Program 538
Audit Risk Analysis and the Expenditure Cycle *539*
 Idle Capacity 540
 Abnormal Inventory Increase 541
 High Technology Industry 541
 Significant Increase in Plant Asset Additions 541
 Existence of Related Parties 542
Key Terms *542*
Computer Audit Practice Case *543*
Review Questions *543*
Multiple Choice Questions *543*
Essay Questions and Problems *545*

APPENDIX *554*
Audit Objectives and Procedures: Expenditure Cycle *554*

14 SUBSTANTIVE AUDIT TESTING: FINANCING AND INVESTING CYCLE 562

Types of Transactions in Financing and Investing Cycle *565*
 Investing Transactions 565
 Borrowing Transactions 565
 Stockholders' Equity Transactions 565
Summary of Processing Steps in Financing and Investing Cycle *566*
Investing Transactions *567*
 Audit Objectives 567
 Audit Evidence and Procedures 568
 Summary Audit Program 572

Borrowing Transactions *573*
    Audit Objectives 573
    Audit Evidence and Procedures 573
    Summary Audit Program 577
Stockholders' Equity Transactions *577*
    Audit Objectives 577
    Audit Evidence and Procedures 579
Audit Risk Analysis and the Financing and Investing Cycle *579*
    Search for Related Party Transactions 579
    Loan Defaults and Violations of Restrictive Covenants 582
    Disposal of a Segment 582
Completing the Audit *582*
    Analytical Procedures as Part of Audit Review 583
    Further Materiality Considerations 583
    Subsequent Events 584
    Statement of Cash Flows 585
    Workpaper Review 586
    Open Items 586
    Auditor/Client Conference 587
    Communication with Audit Committee 588
    Client Representation Letter 588
    Communication of Internal Control Structure Related
    Matters 592
Key Terms *595*
Computer Audit Practice Case *595*
Review Questions *595*
Multiple Choice Questions *596*
Essay Questions and Problems *599*

APPENDIX *605*
Audit Objectives and Procedures: Financing and Investing Cycle *605*

15 AUDIT REPORTS *610*

Nature of the Audit Report *613*
Components of the Audit Report *614*
    Title and Addressee 614
    Introductory Paragraph 614
    Scope Paragraph 615
    Opinion Paragraph 615
    Signature and Date 615
Kinds of Audit Opinions *617*
    Unqualified 617
    Qualified 617
    Adverse 617
    Disclaimer 620
Divided Responsibility *621*
Explanatory Paragraph: Unqualified Opinion *625*

Departure from Designated Principle 625
Material Uncertainty 626
Ability of Entity to Continue as a Going Concern 628
Change in Accounting Principle 632
Emphasis of a Matter 633
Other Topics Affecting Audit Reports 633
Updating the Audit Report 633
Subsequent Discovery of Facts Existing at the Date of the Audit Report 635
The Meaning of ''Present Fairly in Accordance with GAPP'' 639
Other Information in Documents Containing Audited Financial Statements 639
Supplemental Information Required by FASB 642
Related Party Transactions 642
Omitted Procedures Discovered After the Date of the Audit Report 643
Key Terms 643
Computer Audit Practice Case 644
Review Questions 644
Multiple Choice Questions 644
Essay Questions and Problems 649

16 OTHER ACCOUNTING SERVICES AND REPORTS 656

Attestation Standards 658
Attestation Defined and Levels of Assurance 658
Preconditions for Attestation Services 658
Attestation Standards as Contrasted with Auditing Standards 658
Audited Statements Prepared on a Basis Other than GAAP 661
Unaudited Statements 662
Public Entity 662
Compilations and Reviews 663
Lack of Independence 666
Agreed-Upon Procedures 666
Letter for Underwriters 667
Reporting on Internal Control 668
Review of Interim Financial Information 670
CPA's Association with Prospective Financial Statements 673
Compilation of Prospective Financial Statements 675
Examination of Prospective Financial Statements 675
Applying Agreed-Upon Procedures to Prospective Financial Statements 675
Table Summarizing Other Services 677
Key Terms 680
Review Questions 680
Multiple Choice Questions 681
Essay Questions and Problems 684

17 OPERATIONAL AND COMPLIANCE AUDITING 688

Introduction   *690*
Operational Auditing   *691*
   Operational Auditing Defined   691
   Management Auditing—A Special Type of Operational Audit   691
   Evolution of Internal Auditing   691
   Operational Auditing Today   693
   Operational Audit Approach   693
   Summary   706
Compliance Auditing   *706*
   Compliance Auditing Defined   706
   Responsibility Under GAAS   707
   Yellow Book Responsibility   707
   Single Audit Act Responsibility   707
   Responsibility Under Circular A-133   708
   Compliance Auditing and Audit Risk   708
Key Terms   *710*
Review Questions   *710*
Multiple Choice Questions   *711*
Essay Questions and Problems   *715*

APPENDIX   *722*
Standards for the Professional Practice of Internal Auditing   *722*

**Trim Lawn Manufacturing Corporation—
An EDP Audit Practice Case   *725***

Answers to Selected Multiple Choice Questions   *779*

Glossary   *787*

Index   *807*

Preface

Auditing has changed more in the last five years than in the preceding forty years. Audit objectives, as well as the audit approach have shifted dramatically to accommodate more demanding user expectations. To cope with these changes, students need to gain a conceptual understanding of auditing. Like the earlier edition, therefore, the primary goal of *Auditing Concepts and Applications*, Second Edition, is to provide the senior level accounting student with a sound conceptual foundation. To this end, the text emphasizes meeting user expectations through audit risk analysis, application of audit judgment, and ethical considerations in auditing. A secondary goal is to provide the student with an effective means for preparing to take the auditing part of the Certified Public Accountant examination. Therefore, the book is well-documented with relevant materials from pronouncements by the American Institute of Certified Public Accountants (AICPA).

To emphasize the importance of the "risk-driven" audit, the textbook introduces audit risk early by devoting an entire chapter to audit planning and risk analysis (Chapter 5). After developing the topic in Chapter 5, the text refines and integrates risk analysis into the remaining chapters as appropriate. The textbook examines risk relative to all aspects of the audit, from audit planning through internal control evaluation, substantive audit testing, and the audit reporting decision.

To offer full coverage of audit risk, the textbook assigns much of the systems detail—internal control procedures; EDP systems, controls and flowcharts; data processing materials—to well-organized and useful chapter appendices. Since many senior level accounting students have had a course in accounting information systems (AIS), assignment of systems detail to appendices reduces unnecessary topic redundancy between the systems and auditing courses. For those who have not had a prior systems course, the appendix following Chapter 7 should provide adequate background information.

CHANGES IN SECOND EDITION

Although the second edition of *Auditing Concepts and Applications* retains and builds upon the risk analysis framework developed in the first edition, significant changes have been made. Some of the changes expand upon topics already covered; some add new topics. Other changes improve readability and provide for greater flexibility of coverage. The following paragraphs describe the major changes.

Operational and Compliance Auditing Chapter

The second edition adds a new chapter on operational and compliance auditing (Chapter 17). CPAs are becoming increasingly involved in compliance audits of state and local governmental units, as well as other not-for-profit entities receiving federal financial assistance. Operational auditing, as performed by internal auditors and the General Accounting Office, has also become an increasingly important aspect of effective resource utilization in both the public and private sectors of the economy. Chapter 17 addresses both of these topics and includes an operational auditing case study culminating in an audit report.

Materiality Coverage

The second edition emphasizes the importance of materiality in audit planning and review. To this end, the textbook introduces the topic in Chapter 4 and presents an approach to developing individual item and aggregate materiality thresholds. To illustrate how the approach might be implemented, a materiality workpaper is included. Also, end-of-chapter problems permit the student to consider materiality issues and calculate thresholds. Chapter 4 also contains an exhibit emphasizing the relationship among materiality, audit risk, and audit evidence.

Increased Use of Cases

The first edition of this textbook used cases to illustrate various aspects of audit risk. The revised edition expands on this feature by introducing several new cases—some in the body of the chapter, and some as end-of-chapter materials. Included among the new cases are MiniScribe, Chambers Development, Crazy Eddie, Hughes Aircraft, Lincoln Savings, Orion Pictures, E.F. Hutton, and Bank of Credit & Commerce International (BCCI).

Added Questions and Exhibits

The second edition of *Auditing Concepts and Applications* also increases the number of multiple choice questions, essay questions, and problems as end-of-chapter materials. This should add to flexibility of coverage as well as enhance student understanding of the materials. Since all the multiple choice questions, as well as many of the essay questions, are taken from past CPA and CIA examinations, students should find them helpful in preparing for these professional examinations.

To increase clarity and understanding of the more complex auditing concepts, the second edition includes several new exhibits. An audit process flowchart is introduced in Chapter 1, for example, and provides an overview of an independent financial audit from start to finish. This flowchart is then reproduced and expanded upon in later chapters to provide perspective regarding where the chapter subject matter fits within the audit process. A set of flowcharts has also been added to the substantive testing chapters (Chapters 12–14). Like the audit process flowcharts, the goal is to enhance understanding and provide perspective. The flowcharts summarize the processing steps and highlight internal control features for the transaction cycle subsets covered in the respective chapters.

Writing Ability

An appendix entitled ''Effective Writing in Auditing'' appears following Chapter 8. The purpose of this appendix is to help accounting students and accounting practitioners improve their writing ability. It is also designed to help CPA candidates become more effective in answering essay questions on the exam. A case is presented at the end of the appendix. This case entails writing a reportable conditions letter (a letter describing significant deficiencies in internal control) and gives students an opportunity to apply the concepts and suggestions offered in the appendix.

As an added benefit, the appendix should help students complete Module I of the Trim Lawn audit practice case. Module I requires the student to prepare a narrative describing the results of his or her analysis of audit risk and justify the chosen risk levels. This narrative should be clear and complete, and should flow logically. The guidelines contained in the appendix will facilitate the process.

Other Changes

Although the changes described above are the most significant, the following revisions have also been made:

Ethical Coverage

Chapter 2 incorporates the *Code of Professional Conduct*, as amended in May, 1991. While the first edition placed heavy emphasis on ethics, the revision accents the topic even more and stresses the need for CPAs to maintain a ''spirit'' of proper ethical behavior.

Racketeer Influenced and Corrupt Organizations Act

In the legal liability chapter (Chapter 3), a section describing the Racketeer Influenced and Corrupt Organizations Act (RICO) has been added. A RICO case, *ESM vs. Alexander Grant*, has also been added to the appendix following Chapter 3.

Internal Control for Small Businesses

Chapter 6 includes more discussion of internal control for a small business. Small businesses have unique control needs; this section of the chapter addresses those needs.

EDP Auditing

Chapters 8 and 9, the EDP auditing chapters, have been updated to incorporate advances in this area. Some of the topics added include a section on electronic data interchange (EDI), expert systems applications in auditing, and relational data bases as an alternative to electronic spreadsheets for handling large volumes of data.

Audit Reports

The audit reports, presented in Chapter 15 for illustrative purposes, have been updated to include more recent audits. Most of the reports are for actual audits and were extracted from the National Automated Accounting Research System (NAARS) data base.

Audit Report Decision Flowchart

In addition to the more recent audit reports, Chapter 15 also includes an audit reporting flowchart. This flowchart clarifies the decision process used by the auditor in deciding on the form of audit report to issue under varying circumstances.

Flowcharting Problems

Flowcharting problems have been added in Chapters 7 and 8. These problems provide students an opportunity, if they have not already done so in their AIS course, to study an internal control narrative and graphically present it in the form of a flowchart.

LEARNING AIDS AND PEDAGOGICAL TOOLS

EDP Audit Practice Case

The appendix following Chapter 17 contains a computer audit practice case, Trim Lawn Manufacturing Corporation. The practice case is divided into fifteen modules which parallel related chapter topics. A diskette containing partially completed audit workpapers accompanies the case. The diskette is available to adopters free of charge from West Educational Publishing. The modules, which may be assigned individually or severally, at the instructor's option, begin following Chapter 9. They continue at the end of succeeding chapters, ending with Chapter 15.

The practice case enables the student to discover how much of the typical financial audit can be automated by auditing with the computer. In addition, the student obtains a hands-on exposure to computer auditing. The materials are sufficiently menu-driven that excessive amounts of computer time are not consumed in completing the exercises. At the same time, however, the student is required to assess audit risk, analyze data, apply auditing procedures, and evaluate the results — all with the aid of the computer. These materials make *Auditing Concepts and Applications* unique in the market and add an exciting dimension to the study of auditing.

The second edition incorporates certain changes in Trim Lawn to make the case even more useful as a learning device. First, several of the modules now require the student to consider the issue of materiality. In Module I, for example, the student is asked to calculate materiality thresholds; and in Module XIV the student must analyze the proposed audit adjustments and reclassifications to determine which meet the materiality thresholds.

To provide instructor choice as to which Trim Lawn solutions material will be provided to students, the second edition has removed the adjusted working trial balance, the audit adjustments workpaper, and the completed audit report from the "student diskette." These are now included only on the "instructor diskette."

For students wishing to complete the case without using a computer, a workbook is available, at a nominal charge, from West Educational Publishing. The workbook contains the same partially completed audit workpapers that are included on the diskette.

Audit Objectives and Procedures Matrices

Matrices, providing integrated framework for analysis, are included in appendices following Chapters 12–14.

The matrix approach helps to reinforce students' understanding of substantive audit testing, and, more importantly, provides a framework for developing sound audit programs built around careful risk analysis and formulation of specific objectives.

Use of Cases

To bring the material alive and to emphasize the importance of audit risk analysis in auditing, the text makes liberal use of case examples. Extensive reference to cases involving auditors serves to reinforce the student's mastery of concepts by relating the concept to an actual company. Some of the cases are incorporated into the chapters, while others are included as end-of-chapter materials. All of the cases are based on actual events, and are structured to contrast what should have been done with what actually was done.

The Expectation Gap and the Auditor

The 1977 report of the Commission on Auditors' Responsibilities first identified what was later referred to as the "expectation gap." In this report, the Commission stated:

> It is vital to the economy that users of information have confidence in auditors. Such confidence is dependent on mutual understanding as to the appropriate responsibilities of auditors and a belief by users that such responsibilities are being fulfilled . . . The expectation gap is at the heart of the criticism of the profession. Only when this gap is narrowed and reasonable levels of expectation are established as guidelines for professional conduct will the litigious environment in which we exist be sharply narrowed.[1]

The many recent cases presented in *Auditing Concepts and Applications* illustrate the continuing seriousness of the expectation gap. The only way to effectively narrow the gap is for auditors to perform *risk based* audits—the approach developed and emphasized in this textbook.

---

[1]Commission on Auditors' Responsibilities, "Report of Conclusions," New York, AICPA, 1977.

Illustrations

The book makes extensive use of diagrams, tables, and listings to facilitate the learning process. Control flowcharts and listings of necessary documents, records, and functions appended to the control chapters facilitates easy review of control techniques without unnecessarily cluttering the chapter on control structure concepts.

Coverage of AICPA Professional Standards

The standards issued by the American Institute of Certified Public Accountants, referred to as *AICPA Professional Standards*, are given comprehensive coverage throughout the text as they impact given subject areas.

Chapter Organization

Careful attention has been given in *Auditing Concepts and Applications*, Second Edition to chapter organization in order to maintain maximum clarity and completeness. The study of auditing is organized into five major categories. Chapters 1 through 3 describe the *environment of auditing*; chapters 4 through 7 present a *conceptual approach to auditing*; chapters 8 through 11 address *computer and statistical applications in auditing*; chapters 12 through 14 cover the topic of *substantive audit testing*; and chapters 15 through 17 discuss *audit reports and other accounting services*.

Chapter Outline, Overview, and Study Objectives

At the beginning of each chapter an outline, an overview, and a listing of study objectives are presented to introduce the reader to the major topics to be covered and to identify the major concepts to be learned from studying the chapter.

Key Terms and Glossary

A list of key terms is provided at the end of each chapter and serves as additional reinforcement of the learning process. Although auditing is related to accounting, it is not the same. The auditing student encounters many new terms as well as familiar terms with a different connotation.

A complete glossary at the end of the textbook supplements the list of key terms and helps the student learn the language of auditing.

End-of-Chapter Materials

Essay as well as multiple choice questions from past CPA exams are provided at the end of each chapter, along with end-of-chapter review questions and applicable parts of the Trim Lawn computer audit practice case. These materials serve the dual purpose of solidifying the learning process and providing the student with questions important to CPA exam preparation. The multiple choice questions are especially effective in reviewing the contents of the SASs, a major component of the auditing part of the CPA exam. Answers to selected multiple-choice questions, along with reasons for correct and incorrect choices, are provided at the end of the textbook.

SUPPLEMENTS

Materials available to supplement this textbook include an *Instructor's Manual,* a *Study Guide,* a computerized *Test Bank,* and a diskette containing *Lecture Outlines.* In addition, for those completing the Trim Lawn case without using a computer, a *Workbook* of partially completed audit workpapers is available. The *Test Bank* contains nearly 1,000 multiple choice questions from past CPA and CIA examinations. It is computerized and compatible with *WESTEST.* It is also available in printed form. The *Instructor's Manual* includes the following:

1. Answers to end-of-chapter materials (review questions, multiple choice questions, essay questions, and problems). For CPA exam and CIA exam questions, the official answers are provided. For multiple choice questions, the answers are accompanied by narrative supporting correct choices and reasons for incorrect choices.

2. Useful outlines for preparing lectures on the topics presented in each chapter.

3. Printout of solutions to the Trim Lawn Manufacturing audit practice case modules.

4. An instructor's diskette containing completed worksheets for the Trim Lawn Manufacturing audit practice case.

5. Transparency masters highlighting important chapter topics.

6. Teaching suggestions at the beginning of each chapter, as appropriate, and for the Trim Lawn Manufacturing audit practice case.

The *Study Guide* includes the following materials which the students will find useful in mastering the topics covered in the textbook:

1. A review, in expanded outline form, of key points covered in each chapter.

2. True/false, multiple choice, and matching questions highlighting major chapter topics.

3. Answers to questions, including reasons for true/false and multiple choice answers.

ACKNOWLEDGMENTS

The author would like to thank the American Institute of Certified Public Accountants and the Institute of Internal Auditors for their generosity in granting permission to quote extensively from the professional literature, as well as for granting permission to use past professional examination questions as a major part of the end-of-chapter materials. Thanks also go to the AICPA and to Mead Data Central for granting permission to reproduce certain audit reports contained in the NAARS data base.

The author gratefully acknowledges the valuable advice of the many persons who reviewed the textbook drafts. Special thanks go to the following persons: Ronald Abraham, University of Northern Iowa; Urton Anderson, University of Texas–Austin; Edmund J. Boyle, University of Rhode Island; Suzanne N. Cory, St. Mary's University of San Antonio; George A. Fiebelkorn, Marymount University; Stephen R. Goldberg, Purdue University; Randall L. Hahn, Southern Illinois

University–Carbondale; Charles F. Klemstine, University of Michigan; Fred E. Krause, Ferris State University; Jake Landas, Mankato State University; William H. Love, University of Wisconsin–Stevens Point; Rick Miller, Olivet Nazarene University; Kathleen D. Mills, University of Tulsa; Kathy S. Moffeit, Southwest Texas State University; Jane F. Mutchler, Pennsylvania State University; Herbert A. O'Keefe, Georgia Southern College; Evelyn R. Patterson, University of Michigan; Michael A. Pearson, Kent State University; Marshall K. Pitman, University of Texas–San Antonio; and Stephen D. Willits, Bucknell University.

A special note of thanks also goes to Arnis Burvikovs and Susanna Smart, whose editorial advice has greatly enhanced the value of this textbook. I would also like to acknowledge the production and marketing staff at West Publishing for the fine job of producing and promoting the book.

Finally, I would like to thank my wife Charn, and my children Kris and Jenny for all their encouragement. They, perhaps more than I, believed that I could write a good textbook.

Auditing Concepts and Applications

A RISK-ANALYSIS APPROACH

1

An Overview of Auditing

CHAPTER OUTLINE

I. Auditing defined
   A. Management's assertions about economic actions and events
   B. Correspondence between assertions and established criteria
   C. Systematic and objective collection of evidence
   D. Evaluation of evidence for sufficiency and competence
   E. Communication of results in an audit report

II. Independent vs. internal auditing
   A. Three types of internal auditing
   B. Independent auditing limited to financial auditing
   C. Reporting responsibility
   D. Employee (internal) vs. independent contractor

III. Audits by government organizations
   A. General Accounting Office audits various agencies and programs for efficiency and effectiveness
   B. Defense Contract Audit Agency audits defense contracts for the government
   C. Internal Revenue Service audits taxpayers

IV. How auditing differs from accounting
   A. Accounting collects, summarizes, reports, and interprets data
   B. Auditing gathers and evaluates evidence supporting financial statements
   C. Generally accepted accounting principles represent the standard used by the auditor in evaluating fairness

V. Reasons for independent audits
   A. Conflict of interest
   B. Quality of financial statements

VI. Requirements for an effective audit
   A. Understanding of the company and industry
   B. Comprehensive knowledge of GAAP
   C. Solid grasp of internal control concepts
   D. Expert command of evidence gathering and evaluation methods

VII. Evaluation of evidence
   A. Sufficiency and competence
   B. Reasonable rather than absolute assurance

VIII. Communication of auditor's findings
   A. Audit report
      1. Introductory paragraph
      2. Scope paragraph
      3. Opinion paragraph
   B. Conditions necessary for an unqualified opinion

IX. The audit process
  A. Audit planning
    1. Preliminary arrangements
    2. Audit risk analysis
    3. Audit field work planning
  B. Interim audit
  C. Final audit
    1. Inventory observation
    2. Tests of transactions and balances
  D. Audit report

OVERVIEW

Chapter 1 provides a broad audit perspective through a basic audit model or framework that will be expanded upon in subsequent chapters. The chapter begins with a definition of auditing and a discussion of the components contained in the definition. The requirements for an effective audit are then addressed in terms of necessary auditor training and proficiency.

The need for independent auditing is considered, and internal auditing is contrasted with independent auditing. Auditing is then differentiated from accounting, and GAAP is identified as the connecting link between the two disciplines.

The ensuing sections of the chapter deal with the collection and evaluation of audit evidence and the communication of the auditor's findings within the context of the standard audit report.

The final section of the chapter provides an overview of the audit process. This overview should be studied carefully inasmuch as it provides the focal point for much of the discussion in the remaining chapters of the text.

STUDY OBJECTIVES

After reading this chapter, you should be able to:

1. Define auditing;

2. Identify the attributes of a successful auditor and explain why these skills are necessary;

3. Differentiate between internal and independent auditing and between accounting and auditing;

4. Provide a broad overview of how audit evidence is collected and evaluated;

5. Describe the standard audit report, the types of departures from the standard report, and the reasons for such departures;

6. Enumerate and explain the steps in the audit process.

DEFINITION OF AUDITING

Auditing is a form of **attestation.** Attestation, in a general sense, refers to an "expert" communicating a conclusion about the reliability of someone else's assertion. For example, an antique expert might attest to the genuineness of a *Duncan Phyfe* table; or an art expert might attest to the authenticity of a Matisse painting. A food expert might attest to the composition of ingredients in a newly introduced health food product. In a narrower sense, attestation has been defined by the American Institute of Certified Public Accountants (AICPA) as "a written communication that expresses a conclusion about the reliability of a written assertion that is the responsibility of another party."[1] As stated above, auditing is a form of attestation and has been defined in different ways by different sources. The definition given by the American Accounting Association is the most comprehensive and provides an effective means for introducing and initially exploring the topic. **Auditing** may be defined as:

> A systematic process of objectively obtaining and evaluating evidence regarding assertions about economic actions and events to ascertain the degree of correspondence between those assertions and established criteria and communicating the results to interested users.[2]

Assertions, as used in this definition, are the assertions or *representations* of management as to the fairness of the financial statements. Each line of a financial statement represents some form of underlying substance. The term "Inventories" on the balance sheet, for example, represents the investment in goods for use in manufacturing or resale. Financial statements, in other words, are symbolic of the assets, liabilities, ownership equity, revenues, and expenses portrayed by them.

The job of the auditor is to determine whether these representations are indeed fair; that is, to "ascertain the degree of correspondence between the assertions and established criteria." For financial reporting purposes, the *established criteria* are the body of "generally accepted accounting principles" (GAAP) as contained in the Statements of Financial Accounting Standards (SFASs), Accounting Principles Board Opinions (APBOs), Accounting Research Bulletins (ARBs), and other sources.

To evaluate fairness, the auditor must gather audit evidence either supporting or refuting the assertions. For this purpose, **evidence** consists of "the underlying accounting data and all corroborating information available to the auditor."[3]

The evidence must be gathered *objectively*. Most audits are performed on a test basis. This means that the auditor examines only a portion of the transactions and events that occurred during the period covered by the audit. In order for the samples to be representative of the respective populations tested, the auditor must be careful not to introduce any bias into the selection process. For example, assume the auditor

---

[1]Auditing Standards Board, Accounting and Review Services Committee, and the Management Advisory Services Executive Committee, *Professional Standards,* New York: AICPA, Section AT 100.01.

[2]Committee on Basic Auditing Concepts, *A Statement of Basic Auditing Concepts,* Sarasota, Florida: American Accounting Association, 1973, p. 2.

[3]Auditing Standards Board, *AICPA Professional Standards*, New York: American Institute of Certified Public Accountants, Section AU 326.14.

wishes to gain satisfaction concerning the existence of a client's surplus parts inventory by selecting a sample of the inventory and physically inspecting it. Assume further that both the auditor and the client's main warehouse are located in Phoenix and that the client has a smaller warehouse, also containing surplus parts, in Houston. The auditor, given the distance involved, may find it inconvenient to include the Houston warehouse in the total population of surplus parts to be sampled; but, if the test count of surplus parts is limited to the main Phoenix warehouse, the sample will not have been objectively obtained and the results cannot be rationally extended to the population.

Auditing is a *systematic process,* consisting of a series of *sequential* steps that test the information system and test transactions and balances. The **information system** produces the data appearing on the financial statements. A reliable system produces reliable financial statements. The auditor **tests the information system** before testing the substance of transactions and balances (substantive testing). A strong system increases the level of auditor confidence and decreases the extent of transaction and balances testing (see Figure 1.1).

The auditor must evaluate the evidence gathered. In order to satisfy the definition, the evidence must be sufficient and competent. *Sufficient* means that "enough" evidence was examined; this is a function of the professional judgment of the auditor. The auditor is not guaranteeing the accuracy of the financial statements, but is expressing an opinion as to their fairness. The question is, "How much evidence is adequate to support this opinion?" The answer to this question is not easily obtained and often requires an auditor with much training and experience.

To be *competent,* evidence must be both *valid* and *relevant.* Validity is similar to reliability and is enhanced by an effective information system. Relevance must always relate to the audit objectives. Examining the surplus parts inventory, for example, helps satisfy the existence of inventory, but it does not provide a great deal of evidence concerning proper valuation of that inventory. Similarly, inspecting documents in support of recorded transactions is relevant for the purpose of locating errors in recorded transactions; but, this procedure is not relevant in identifying

FIGURE 1.1   Major Steps in The Systematic Process of Auditing

(A) Planning → (B) System Testing → (C) Substantive Testing → (D) Audit Report

(B) **Test the Information System**
1. Study the system
2. Determine the nature, timing, and extent of substantive tests to be performed

(C) **Test Transactions and Balances**
1. Examine transactions and balances
2. Evaluate fairness of financial statement components

transactions that have been omitted from the accounts. Tracing from documents forward to the accounts is a more effective procedure for detecting omissions.

The auditor *communicates* the results to interested users. The communication process is referred to as **attestation** and its mechanism is the **audit report.** The audit report is included with the financial statements in the annual report to stockholders. It describes the scope of the audit and the findings of the auditor. The findings are expressed in the form of an opinion concerning the fairness with which the statements present the firm's financial position, results of operations, and cash flows. Interested users are typically the stockholders and creditors of the client company, but may also include labor unions, regulatory agencies, and others, including the general public.

GENERALLY ACCEPTED AUDITING STANDARDS

Figure 1.2 contains the ten generally accepted **auditing standards** (GAAS) that must be observed by the auditor in conducting the examination. The standards define the quality of independent auditing. The first three **general standards** relate to the characteristics of the auditor. The three **field work standards** relate to the conduct of the examination. The **reporting standards** provide the framework for communicating the results of the examination to interested users. These standards are addressed more fully in Chapter 2.

INDEPENDENT AUDITING VS. INTERNAL AUDITING

Up to this point, auditing has been considered only in the form of external or **independent auditing.** Its main features are that it is conducted by auditors who are independent of management and represent third-party users (e.g., stockholders and creditors), and it is limited to the auditee's financial statements; therefore, it is referred to as *financial auditing*.

Internal auditing (discussed more fully in Chapter 17) is just as important as independent auditing, yet is different in many significant respects. The major difference between internal auditing and independent auditing is that internal auditing serves management while independent auditing serves third-party financial statement users. They are similar in that both involve collecting and evaluating evidence relating to assertions.

The Institute of Internal Auditors defines internal auditing as '' . . . an independent appraisal function established within an organization to examine and evaluate its activities as a service to the organization.''[4] Oriented towards activities and programs, three distinct types of internal auditing can be identified, each possessing unique characteristics. These three types of internal auditing and their definitions are as follows:

1. **Operational auditing.** An operational audit is a future-oriented, independent, and systematic evaluation performed by the internal auditor for management of

---

[4]Institute of Internal Auditors, *Standards for the Professional Practice of Internal Auditing,* Orlando, FL, 1978.

FIGURE 1.2   Generally Accepted Auditing Standards

General Standards
1. The examination is to be performed by a person or persons having adequate technical training and proficiency as an auditor.
2. In all matters relating to the assignment, an independence in mental attitude is to be maintained by the auditor or auditors.
3. Due professional care is to be exercised in the performance of the examination and the preparation of the report.

Standards of Field Work
1. The work is to be adequately planned, and assistants, if any, are to be properly supervised.
2. A sufficient understanding of the internal control structure is to be obtained to plan the audit and to determine the nature, timing, and extent of tests to be performed.
3. Sufficient competent evidential matter is to be obtained through inspection, observation, inquiries, and confirmation to afford a reasonable basis for an opinion regarding the financial statements under examination.

Standards of Reporting
1. The report shall state whether the financial statements are presented in accordance with generally accepted accounting principles.
2. The report shall identify those circumstances in which such principles have not been consistently observed in the current period in relation to the preceding period.
3. Informative disclosures in the financial statements are to be regarded as reasonably adequate unless otherwise stated in the report.
4. The report shall either contain an opinion regarding the financial statements, taken as a whole, or an assertion to the effect that an opinion cannot be expressed. When an overall opinion cannot be expressed, the reasons therefor should be stated. In all cases where an auditor's name is associated with financial statements, the report should contain a clear-cut indication of the character of the auditor's examination, if any, and the degree of responsibility taken.

Source: Auditing Standards Board, *Codification of Statements on Auditing Standards,* New York: American Institute of Certified Public Accountants, 1991, Section AU 150.02.

the operational activities controlled by top-, middle-, and lower-level management for the purposes of improving organizational profitability and increasing the attainment of the other organizational objectives.

2. **Management auditing.** A management audit is a future-oriented, independent, and systematic evaluation of the activities of all levels of management performed by the internal auditor for the purposes of improving organizational profitability and increasing the attainment of other organizational objectives.

3. **Financial auditing.** A financial audit is a historically oriented, independent evaluation performed by the internal auditor or the external auditor for the purposes of attesting to the fairness, accuracy, and reliability of the financial data.[5]

As can be seen from the definition, internal auditing is broader in scope than independent auditing. Independent auditing is concerned exclusively with the financial statements prepared principally for external users. The internal auditor, by contrast, is concerned with all kinds of financial and other data generated for both internal and external users. The internal auditor is also engaged in evaluating the efficiency of operations (operational auditing) and the effectiveness of management (management or performance auditing).

Another feature differentiating independent and internal auditing is reporting responsibility. The external auditor represents the stockholders and reports to them. The internal auditor, by contrast, is an employee of the entity being audited and does not possess the same degree of independence as the external auditor. To compensate for lack of external independence, an important measure of the quality of internal auditing is the level within the organization to which the internal auditor reports (internal independence). A rule of thumb is that the internal auditor must report to a level sufficiently high that the audit findings will be implemented. Today, more and more companies are having their internal auditors report directly to the audit committee of the board of directors, thus providing maximum internal independence. Ordinarily, the **audit committee** consists mainly of outside directors having no management ties to the organization.

AUDITS BY GOVERNMENT ORGANIZATIONS

Several federal agencies perform a significant number of audits. These include the General Accounting Office (GAO), the Defense Contract Audit Agency (DCAA), and the Internal Revenue Service (IRS).

General Accounting Office

The most frequent application of management auditing may be found in the work of the **GAO.** This federal agency reports directly to Congress on the efficiency, effectiveness, and compliance of other government agencies, projects, and functions. GAO auditors have frequently evaluated the effectiveness of management in their reports and have on occasion recommended substantial decreases in the level of funding or even discontinuance of various agencies and programs. GAO also has a set of standards governing the conduct of their examinations, but these standards are considered beyond the scope of this book.

Defense Contract Audit Agency

DCAA examines the records of entities fulfilling defense contracts for the federal government. The major goals of such examinations are to determine that only those

---

[5]Institute of Internal Auditors, Research Report 19, *An Evaluation of Selected Current Internal Auditing Terms,* Orlando, Florida: 1975, pp. vii–viii.

FIGURE 1.3   Auditors and Types of Auditing—Areas of Audit Emphasis

	Independent Auditors	Internal Auditors	Governmental Auditors
Operational Auditing – Efficiency	Nominal	Primary	Primary
Management Auditing – Effectiveness	None	Nominal	Primary
Financial Auditing – Fairness	Primary	Primary	Nominal
Compliance Auditing – Conformity	Secondary	Primary	Primary

costs pertaining to the fulfillment have been charged to the contracts and that the entities have conformed to the contract terms. This type of auditing is referred to as **compliance auditing.** As more fully discussed in Chapter 17, independent auditors also engage in compliance auditing when examining the financial records of state and local governmental units receiving federal financial assistance.

Internal Revenue Service

IRS audits affect individuals as well as businesses. Also a form of compliance auditing, IRS audits are designed to measure compliance with the federal tax laws.

The matrix in Figure 1.3 depicts the relationship of the types of auditing to classes of auditors.

HOW AUDITING DIFFERS FROM ACCOUNTING

Accounting students who have not yet studied the subject frequently think of auditing as another accounting course. Although auditing and accounting are related, they are distinct from one another. Accounting involves collecting, summarizing, reporting, and interpreting financial data. Auditing, by contrast, utilizes the theory of evidence—much the same as does the legal profession—to verify the overall reasonableness (fairness) of the financial statements presented. As shown in Figure 1.4, generally accepted accounting principles are the link between accounting and auditing. In assembling financial statements, accountants determine the best means for measuring, classifying, disclosing, and reporting financial information by referring to appropriate GAAP. In evaluating fairness of financial presentation, auditors use GAAP as the standard. Auditors, therefore, must be expert in accounting matters. The central thrust of auditing, however, is the collection and evaluation of evidence.

FIGURE 1.4   Accounting and Auditing Contrasted

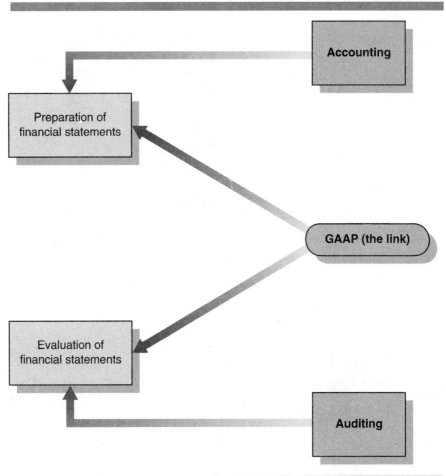

WHY INDEPENDENT AUDITING IS NECESSARY

Professions cannot exist without wide public acceptance, and independent auditing is no exception. Over the years, society has perceived a need for audits of publicly held companies, which has developed as a result of the separation of ownership and management. A conflict of interest may be assumed to exist between management and stockholders regarding the financial statements. Management, knowing that it is being evaluated by the stockholders on the basis of the financial statements, desires to present the results of its stewardship in the most favorable light. The stockholders, on the other hand, are interested in financial statements that portray as closely as possible the true financial position, results of operations, and cash flows. Given these divergent attitudes toward financial reporting, the role of the independent auditor as impartial attestor evolved.

As an expert in the application of generally accepted accounting principles, the independent auditor further enhances the quality of financial reporting. The proper selection and application of GAAP have become increasingly complex over the years, given new types of transactions and new rules of accounting and disclosure pertaining to them. For this reason, the need for the professional auditor, knowledgeable in GAAP, has become more and more apparent to investors and creditors.

REQUIREMENTS FOR AN EFFECTIVE AUDIT

In order for an audit to be completed within the framework just discussed, certain attributes are required of the auditor. First, the auditor must have a thorough *understanding of the company or the institution and the industry* of which it is a part. As auditors have learned painfully from numerous legal actions filed against them by stockholders and creditors, complex transactions must be thoroughly understood if the auditor is to detect material errors and ensure adequate disclosure in the financial statements. In one case, known widely as the *Bar Chris case* (see Chapter 3), the substance of certain sale and leaseback transactions involving the construction and sale of bowling establishments was not apparent to the auditor. This enabled Bar Chris to prematurely recognize profit on many of these transactions. As a result, net income, assets, and stockholders' equity were materially overstated in the financial statements included in the annual report to stockholders.[6]

Auditing requires a thorough understanding of a company and its industry. Here auditors discuss performance characteristics of a new Goodyear tire with a driver at the company's test track.

---

[6]Federal Securities Law Report, *Escott et al v. Bar Chris Construction Corp. et al.*, 283 F. Supp. 643 (S.D.N.Y. 1968).

The auditor must also have a *comprehensive knowledge of GAAP* in order to audit effectively. The body of GAAP is the standard by which fairness of financial presentation is judged by the auditor. Therefore, the auditor who is to rationally formulate an opinion on the financial statements must be able to recognize material departures from GAAP, including errors in recording transactions and events as well as inadequate disclosure. In satisfying this need, most auditing firms have extensive libraries containing SFASs, APBOs, ARBs, SEC pronouncements, and other sources of GAAP, as well as staff training programs to keep personnel informed of current developments in GAAP.

A solid *grasp of concepts of internal control structure* and a careful review and evaluation of the underlying structure are also necessary ingredients to an effective audit. As discussed more fully in Chapter 6, internal control structure is the set of policies and procedures designed by management to enhance the reliability of financial records and safeguard assets. The more effective the control structure is in achieving these goals, the more confidence the auditor can place in it for preventing and detecting material errors. For this reason, in designing audit programs for testing transactions and balances, the auditor assesses the quality of internal control structure policies and procedures. The more effective the structure, the lower is the probability of material errors and irregularities affecting the financial statements. This, in turn, leads to reduced need for examination of transactions and balances.

In addition to understanding the company, GAAP, and internal control, the auditor must also be *knowledgeable in the area of evidence gathering and evaluation.* The definition states that auditing is a "systematic process of . . . obtaining and evaluating evidence." In conducting the examination, the auditor has the opportunity of choosing among alternative forms of evidence and alternative means for gathering evidence. Some auditing procedures may be more costly to apply than others. Some auditing procedures may be more effective in meeting specific objectives. Certain forms of evidence are more reliable under conditions of effective internal control. In deciding among alternative ways of satisfying audit objectives, therefore, the auditor must be able to exercise sound judgment based upon an understanding of the characteristics of audit evidence. These characteristics will be addressed more fully in Chapter 4.

HOW EVIDENCE IS EVALUATED

Generally accepted auditing standards require that the auditor gather sufficient competent evidential matter as a basis for the audit opinion.[7] Sufficiency of evidence is a matter of audit judgment. Reasonable rather than absolute assurance as to freedom from material error is required. And, the most effective means for assuring sound audit judgment are the training and experience of the auditor.

Although some guidelines are provided in the professional standards (notably Auditing Standards, Section 326), deciding whether the evidence is competent under the circumstances likewise is subject to the seasoned judgment of the auditor. Some forms of evidence are, by their very nature, more competent than others. Examining an inventory for the existence of items, for example, produces more

---

[7] Auditing Standards Board, *AICPA Professional Standards,* Section AU 326.01.

reliable evidence than a client response to a question regarding their existence. The internal control structure also has an impact on competence. The more reliable the structure, the more valid is the transaction evidence produced by it.

Evaluating audit evidence is a topic for further discussion throughout the text as audit testing is related to transaction cycles. These guidelines are introduced here simply to provide an overview and will be reinforced in Chapter 4, as part of the more exhaustive examination of audit evidence, audit procedures, and audit programs.

HOW THE AUDITOR'S FINDINGS ARE COMMUNICATED

The auditor's findings are communicated through the audit report. Exhibit 1.1 illustrates the standard audit report form recommended by the American Institute of Certified Public Accountants (AICPA).[8] This report contains three main components: an introductory paragraph, a scope paragraph, and an opinion paragraph.

EXHIBIT 1.1   Standard Audit Report

Report of Independent Auditors

To: Board of Directors and Stockholders
      ABC Corporation

We have audited the accompanying balance sheet of ABC Corporation as of December 31, 1993, and the related statements of income, retained earnings, and cash flows for the year then ended. These financial statements are the responsibility of the Company's management. Our responsibility is to express an opinion on these financial statements based on our audit.

We conducted our audit in accordance with generally accepted auditing standards. Those standards require that we plan and perform the audit to obtain reasonable assurance about whether the financial statements are free of material misstatement. An audit includes examining, on a test basis, evidence supporting the amounts and disclosures in the financial statements. An audit also includes assessing the accounting principles used and significant estimates made by management, as well as evaluating the overall financial statement presentation. We believe that our audit provides a reasonable basis for our opinion.

In our opinion, the financial statements referred to above present fairly, in all material respects, the financial position of ABC Corporation as of December 31, 1993, and the results of its operations and its cash flows for the year then ended in conformity with generally accepted accounting principles.

Gibson and Keller, CPAs
March 2, 1993

---

[8]*Ibid.*, Section AU 508.08.

The introductory paragraph states that management is responsible for preparing the financial statements, and the auditors are responsible for expressing an opinion as to fairness of that presentation. The scope paragraph tells what the auditor did in terms of whether the examination was conducted in accordance with generally accepted auditing standards. The opinion paragraph contains the auditor's findings in terms of whether the financial statements are presented fairly in accordance with generally accepted accounting principles.

The standard audit report, containing no exceptions, is rendered only under circumstances involving no material restrictions on the scope of the audit and no material departures from generally accepted accounting principles. Material scope restrictions and departures from GAAP necessitate modifying the audit report.

Any material restrictions on the scope of the examination, for which the auditor is not able to obtain satisfaction by alternate means, would ordinarily cause the auditor to take exception in the audit report. These exceptions, termed *qualifications,* are usually explained in a separate paragraph of the audit report. Depending on the severity of the restriction, the auditor may have to *disclaim* an opinion on the grounds that insufficient evidence was obtained to support rendering an opinion.

A material departure from GAAP may result in either a *qualified* or *adverse* audit opinion, depending on how significantly the financial statements are affected by the departure. Failure to properly account for costs under a pension plan may result in a qualified opinion; whereas failure to capitalize financing leases, when virtually all plant assets are leased, may lead to an adverse opinion. The adverse opinion states that, in the opinion of the auditor, the financial statements do not fairly present the financial position, results of operations, and cash flows.

An explanatory paragraph must be added to the audit report when an inconsistency has occurred during the period under audit. A change in accounting principle represents an **inconsistency,** and an explanatory paragraph must be added whenever there is a material change in an accounting principle. The purpose for the consistency paragraph is to alert the reader to the change, because it may materially affect the comparability of financial data among the periods presented in the annual report.

An explanatory paragraph must also be added under conditions of material *uncertainty.* Because of pending litigation, violations of restrictive covenants in loan agreements, liquidity problems, or other factors, the auditor may conclude that uncertainty regarding the ultimate outcome of these conditions is sufficient to warrant adding a paragraph highlighting that uncertainty. Whether included for an inconsistency or an uncertainty, the explanatory paragraph does not represent a qualification of the auditor's opinion.

To summarize the discussion, the following conditions may be cited as necessary to warrant an unqualified audit opinion:

1. No material scope restrictions occurred for which the auditor was not able to obtain satisfaction by alternate means (other forms of evidence); and

2. The financial statements contain no material departures from GAAP (including adequacy of disclosure).

An explanatory paragraph is required to bring material inconsistencies or uncertainties to the reader's attention. More extensive coverage of the audit report is provided in Chapter 15.

THE AUDIT PROCESS—AN OVERVIEW

Figure 1.5 summarizes the audit process in chronological fashion. The following paragraphs discuss the various steps shown in the diagram. The model will be refined in subsequent chapters as audit planning, control structure testing, substantive testing, and audit reporting are explored in depth.

Audit Planning

Preliminaries

The audit process usually begins with preliminary arrangements being made with the client. General information questions concerning the operations of the entity, its organizational structure, its control structure (including the control environment, the

FIGURE 1.5   The Audit Process

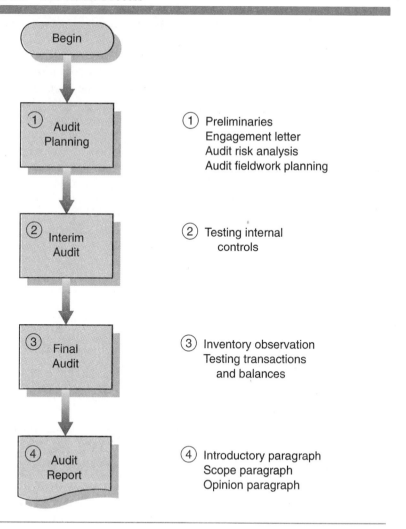

accounting system, and control procedures), and the existence of electronic data processing (EDP) applications should be raised during the preliminaries. This exercise is important if the auditor is to gain a working knowledge of the entity. It should also help in planning the audit to identify those high risk areas requiring special attention.

In a more procedural sense, certain aspects of the audit need to be discussed with the client well in advance of their implementation. For example, if the auditor expects to utilize client personnel, the client must be informed in order to plan for available time. Much of the detailed audit work may be delegated by the auditor to the appropriate client employees as long as audit judgment decisions are not delegated. Such delegation of parts of the workload enables the auditor to concentrate more heavily on the judgmental portions of the audit. From a cost-benefit point of view, delegating work to the client's staff also reduces the fee charged the client.

If the client has significant inventories of materials or merchandise, the preliminary arrangements should also include discussion of inventory taking procedures. Such matters as how the inventory is to be counted, provision for the presence of the auditors during the inventory, and provision of copies of the inventory taking instructions to the auditors, at least, need to be sketched out at this time.

The preliminary arrangements discussed earlier are especially important in an initial engagement as contrasted with a recurring one. In a recurring engagement, many of the arrangements are already understood by the client and the auditor. Under these circumstances, the preliminaries, for the most part, consist of identifying significant changes that have occurred since the last audit and that will impact the conduct of the examination.

A final note before leaving the preliminaries relates to the question of acceptance or continuance of clients. During these discussions with the client, the auditor may discover that he or she does not possess the technical expertise to conduct the audit; or the auditor may conclude that management integrity is sufficiently lacking as to preclude acceptance; or perhaps the auditor discovers that certain mutual relationships preclude the necessary independence between the auditor and the client. If for any reason the auditor concludes that an examination is not feasible, the client should be so informed and the engagement declined.

Engagement Letter

Whether an initial or recurring audit, an **engagement letter** should be signed by both the client and the auditor. Exhibit 1.2 illustrates a common form of engagement letter. It summarizes the agreement of the parties formulated during the preliminaries, and states very clearly the mutual understanding of the nature of the engagement. Its main function is to provide written evidence of agreement concerning the examination. Misunderstandings between auditor and client regarding the nature of the engagement may be more easily resolved given the engagement letter. Engagement letters are recommended regardless of the nature of the appointment and are not limited solely to audit engagements.

Audit Risk Analysis

Before performing tests of transactions and balances, the auditor should gain a thorough understanding of *the client's business and the industry* of which it is a part,

EXHIBIT 1.2   Engagement Letter

Mr. Howard Hill   September 6, 1993
ABC Corporation
2000 Expressway Drive North
Toledo, Ohio 43617

Dear Mr. Hill:

In accordance with the agreement reached in our conference on September 4, 1993, we are to perform an audit of the balance sheet of the ABC Corporation as of December 31, 1993, and of the related statements of income, retained earnings, and cash flows for the fiscal year then ended. The audit report will be mailed to you and the Board of Directors. We are also to prepare the federal and state income tax returns for the fiscal year ending December 31, 1993.

Our audit will be made in accordance with generally accepted auditing standards and, accordingly, will include such tests of the accounting records and such other auditing procedures as we consider necessary to enable us to express an opinion regarding your financial statements. Although generally accepted auditing standards require that we plan and perform the audit to obtain reasonable assurance that the financial statements are not materially misstated, the audit cannot be relied upon to disclose all errors, defalcations, and other similar irregularities.

Our audit will include a study and review of your company's internal accounting control structure. The purpose of the study and review of the internal accounting control system is to determine the scope of our audit engagement and is not performed to detect all errors in the processing of information. On the basis of our study and review of the internal accounting control structure, we will make suggestions, where appropriate, for improving the structure. If we should discover material weaknesses in the design or the execution of the system, we will disclose these weaknesses to you in writing before the conclusion of the audit.

Based on our discussion with your personnel and the predecessor auditor and a preliminary review of your accounting records, we estimate the cost of the audit engagement, including the preparation of the related tax returns, will be approximately $75,000. It should be recognized that the estimated fee could be affected by unusual circumstances we cannot foresee at this particular time. However, if we should encounter such problems, we will immediately contact you to discuss the implications of the new developments.

We appreciate the opportunity to serve your company. Do not hesitate to contact us if you have questions about the engagement or desire other professional services.

If the terms designated in this letter are satisfactory, please sign in the space provided below and return the duplicate copy of the letter to us.

Sincerely,
James Gibson, CPA

Accepted by: _____
Title: _____
Date: _____

and *the existing internal control structure* as it affects the assertions contained in the financial statements. A major trend in auditing, created by the rising incidence of cases alleging auditor negligence, has been the increased attention given by auditors to risk analysis. **Audit risk** may be defined as the probability of rendering an unqualified opinion on financial statements that are materially misstated. In order to adequately assess risk exposure, the auditor needs to understand the entity, the industry, and the economic substance of all significant transactions. The auditor also needs to obtain a sufficient understanding of the client's internal control structure policies and procedures to permit planning the audit.

Auditors must be alert to attempts by managements to deliberately misstate the financial position and results of operations. Termed **management misrepresentation fraud,** these attempts have been prompted by such diverse factors as increasing competition and the need to maintain earnings growth, liquidity problems and the attempt to conceal violations of restrictive covenants in loan agreements, a declining industry (farm machinery manufacturing, for example) and efforts to mask uncertainty about continued existence, and dishonesty in management (fabricating earnings and assets through fraudulent transactions). The possibility of management misrepresentation fraud is a principal factor in audit risk. Analysis of the business and industry, along with study and evaluation of the internal control structure, collectively represent the most significant part of audit risk analysis and assessment. These topics are addressed more fully in chapters 5 and 6, respectively.

Audit Field Work Planning

Before the "audit team" can actually begin the field work (that part of the audit performed mainly on the client's premises), some preliminary **audit field work** planning needs to be done. First, preliminary audit programs needs to be formulated. **Audit programs** are collections of audit procedures to be applied to meet specified audit objectives. At this stage in the examination, the programs will be based on the preliminaries, the analysis of business and industry, and the auditor's understanding of the control structure as discussed earlier. Further testing of the control procedures, as will be discussed later, may lead to subsequent modification of the audit programs.

Once the preliminary programs have been formulated, the "in-charge" (senior) auditor is in a position to determine the number of people needed to conduct the various phases of the audit. A *time budget* is usually prepared at this point, and it contains extensive detail concerning each phase and the number of hours of assistant, senior, manager, and partner time required.

After the time budget has been prepared and people selected for the audit, a **pre-audit conference** with the audit team may be held to discuss significant aspects of the audit. Such matters as assignment of audit tasks, high risk areas, information regarding the nature of the entity to be audited, and a general description of the internal control structure should be covered during the pre-audit conference. EDP accounting applications and the possible need for EDP audit specialists should also be considered at this time.

Traditionally, audit field work (the actual application of auditing procedures) has been conducted in two major phases:

1. The **interim audit,** consisting of further testing of the client's control structure for the purpose of lowering the assessed risk level; and

2. The **final audit,** during which most of the audit of transactions and balances is performed.

The nature, timing, and extent of transaction and balance testing depends primarily on the nature of the business and industry and the quality of the existing internal controls, as determined in the audit planning and further control testing phases.

In recent years, certain changes in the environment have begun to alter the traditional approach to the interim audit phase. Instead of testing the internal control procedures during a single interim time period, auditors are applying these tests, along with testing selected transactions, at frequent intervals throughout the year. This is sometimes referred to as **"continuous" auditing.** Continuous auditing is especially applicable to those clients with sophisticated EDP accounting applications. Many of these systems do not retain permanent records of the "audit trail" (the means by which the auditor is able to follow a transaction from its source to the general ledger accounts). By testing both control procedures and transactions frequently during the year, the auditor is able to locate and substantiate controls and transactions before the "audit trail" is lost.

Inventory Observation

If the client has significant amounts of inventory and takes a physical inventory at or near year end, the independent auditor will plan to be present to observe the physical inventory. The main purpose for observing the inventory and conducting test counts is to gain satisfaction concerning its existence.

Tests of Transactions and Balances

Most of the tests of transactions and balances are performed during the final audit, preferably at or close to year end. These procedures are referred to as **substantive tests** because the auditor examines evidence representing the substance underlying the transactions. They include, but are not limited to, confirming accounts receivable with customers, determining the overall fairness of the inventory values assigned by the client, determining that amounts recorded as accrued and prepaid are correct, and searching for unrecorded liabilities. Added control testing may also be necessary at this time if significant changes in the manner in which transactions are processed have occurred since the interim audit.

During both the interim and final audit phases, all audit work of assistants should be supervised by the in-charge auditor. At the completion of the final audit phase, the audit manager is usually called in to perform an overall review of the audit.

Audit Report

The audit report is the final step in the audit process. It summarizes the scope of the audit and presents the auditor's findings in the form of an audit opinion. The audit report has been briefly discussed in this chapter and will be covered more exhaustively in Chapter 15.

KEY TERMS

Assertions	Financial auditing
Attestation	General Accounting Office (GAO)
Audit committee	General standards
Audit evidence	Inconsistency
Audit field work	Independent auditing
Auditing	Information system
Audit planning	Information system testing
Audit program	Interim audit
Audit report	Internal auditing
Audit risk	Management auditing
Audit standards	Management misrepresentation fraud
Compliance auditing	Operational auditing
Continuous auditing	Pre-audit conference
Defense Contract Audit Agency (DCAA)	Reporting standards
Engagement letter	Substantive testing
Field work standards	Transaction testing
Final audit	

REVIEW QUESTIONS

1. Financial statements have been referred to as "symbolic representations." Explain.
2. How does the auditor ascertain the degree of correspondence between management's assertions and established criteria?
3. What is meant by "systematically and objectively" obtaining evidence?
4. How does the auditor decide when evidence is sufficient and competent?
5. What is the communication mechanism used by the auditor?
6. How does internal auditing differ from independent auditing?
7. Name the governmental agencies involved in audits and briefly describe their respective audit activities.
8. How does auditing differ from accounting?
9. How is auditing related to accounting?
10. How does the audit enhance the quality of the financial statements?
11. Why is an understanding of the business and industry of the client necessary for an effective audit?
12. In addition to an understanding of the business and industry, what are the other requirements for an effective audit?
13. Differentiate between the scope and opinion paragraphs of the standard audit report.

14. What conditions are necessary for an unqualified opinion?
15. What is an "engagement letter" and why is it recommended prior to rendering of professional services by CPAs?
16. What function is served by the audit program?
17. Who participates in the pre-audit conference and what topics should be covered?
18. What distinguishes the interim audit from the final audit?
19. Why must the auditor test the information system prior to testing transactions and balances?
20. What purpose is served by the ten generally accepted auditing standards?
21. Define attestation. In what way(s) is auditing a form of attestation?

MULTIPLE CHOICE QUESTIONS FROM CPA EXAMINATIONS

1. An auditor who accepts an audit engagement and does not possess the industry expertise of the business entity should
   a. Engage financial experts familiar with the nature of the business entity.
   b. Obtain a knowledge of matters that relate to the nature of the entity's business.
   c. Refer a substantial portion of the audit to another CPA who will act as the principal auditor.
   d. First inform management that an unqualified opinion cannot be issued.

2. Which of the following statements relating to the competence of evidential matter is always true?
   a. Evidential matter gathered by an auditor from outside an enterprise is reliable.
   b. Accounting data developed under satisfactory conditions of internal control are more relevant than data developed under unsatisfactory conditions of internal control.
   c. Oral representations made by management are not valid evidence.
   d. Evidence gathered by auditors must be both valid and relevant to be considered competent.

3. With respect to the auditor's planning of a year-end examination, which of the following statements is always true?
   a. An engagement should not be accepted after the fiscal year end.
   b. An inventory count must be observed at the balance sheet date.
   c. The client's audit committee should not be told of the specific audit procedures that will be performed.
   d. It is an acceptable practice to carry out substantial parts of the examination at interim dates.

4. Those procedures specifically outlined in an audit program are primarily designed to
   a. Gather evidence.
   b. Detect errors or irregularities.
   c. Test internal systems.
   d. Protect the auditor in the event of litigation.

5. A typical objective of an operational audit is for the auditor to
   a. Determine whether the financial statements fairly present the entity's operations.
   b. Evaluate the feasibility of attaining the entity's operational objectives.
   c. Make recommendations for improving performance.
   d. Report on the entity's relative success in maximizing profits.

6. If the auditor believes there is a minimal likelihood that resolution of an uncertainty will have a material effect on the financial statements, the auditor would issue a(an)
   a. "Except for" opinion.
   b. Adverse opinion.
   c. Unqualified opinion.
   d. "Subject to" opinion.

7. When, in the auditor's judgment, the financial statements are not presented fairly in conformity with generally accepted accounting principles, the auditor will issue a(an)
   a. Qualified opinion.
   b. Special report.
   c. Disclaimer of opinion.
   d. Adverse opinion.

8. In which of the following circumstances would an adverse opinion be appropriate?
   a. The auditor is not independent with respect to the enterprise being audited.
   b. A material uncertainty regarding litigation exists.
   c. The statements are not in conformity with APB Opinion No. 8 regarding pension plans.
   d. A client-imposed scope limitation prevents the auditor from complying with generally accepted auditing standards.

9. The primary purpose of the auditor's study and evaluation of internal control is to provide a basis for
   a. Determining whether procedures and records that are concerned with the safeguarding of assets are reliable.
   b. Constructive suggestions to clients concerning improvements in internal control.
   c. Determining the nature, extent, and timing of audit tests to be applied.
   d. The expression of an opinion.

10. The scope and nature of an auditor's contractual obligation to a client ordinarily is set forth in the
    a. Management letter.
    b. Scope paragraph of the auditor's report.
    c. Engagement letter.
    d. Introductory paragraph of the auditor's report.

ESSAY QUESTIONS AND PROBLEMS

1.1 A CPA, serving as independent auditor, is asked by the controller of the client company how his role differs from that of the accountant. The auditor responds that he is indeed an accountant, but that his role as auditor is much broader, and transcends accounting.

Required:
a. Explain how auditing differs from accounting.
b. How is auditing similar to the practice of law? How does it differ?
c. Why is it necessary for an auditor to also be an accountant?

1.2 At the annual stockholders' meeting, the following question was raised by one of the minority shareholders and directed to the independent auditors: "Inasmuch as our company already has an internal audit staff, why is it necessary to be audited by outside CPAs? After all, the internal auditors know much more about the company's operations and are much more familiar with the personnel and the accounting system. It would appear that the internal auditors could do the job more effectively and at considerably less cost than the outside CPAs.''

Required:
a. Respond to the shareholder's question.
b. How does the independent auditor fulfill a public need?

1.3 Chill and Will, CPAs, have accepted an engagement to audit the financial statements of Walker, Inc., a large wholesale hardware distributor. While discussing the preliminary arrangements with Walker's controller, Bill Chill, the partner in charge of the Walker audit, requested that certain workpaper analyses and other audit field work tasks be assigned by the controller to Walker's staff. ''Wait a minute,'' replied Stan Gordon, Walker's controller. ''I thought we were paying you to do the audit. My people have better things to do than help you earn your fee.''

Required:
a. Respond to the concerns of the controller.
b. In assigning specific tasks to the client's employees, what factors must the independent auditor consider?

1.4 During a staff training session, the participants were asked to identify characteristics of audit evidence, and explain how each characteristic assists the auditor in conducting the examination.

Required:
a. Identify the necessary characteristics of audit evidence.
b. Give an example of a type of audit evidence.
c. Discuss how that particular piece of evidence might help you in formulating an opinion on the financial statements.
d. How would you evaluate your evidence in terms of the characteristics just identified in (a)?

1.5 The firm of Darl Shank, CPAs, has just accepted an engagement to audit Toys, Inc., a small manufacturer of specialty toys. Susan Shore has been selected as the in-charge auditor for the engagement, and John Beach will be her assistant. In planning the audit field work, Shore makes the following assignments of audit tasks:

	Susan Shore	*John Beach*
Interim audit	Perform tests of cash receipts transactions and cash receipts balances.	Perform tests of internal control over cash disbursements.
Final audit	Perform tests of cash disbursements transactions and inventory balances	Perform tests of internal control over cash receipts

Required:
a. Identify the steps to be followed in completing an audit.
b. What is meant by the term ''systematic process'' as contained in the definition of auditing?
c. Explain the strengths and weaknesses in Shore's audit planning.

1.6 Feiler, the sole owner of a small hardware business, has been told that the business should have financial statements reported on by an independent CPA. Feiler, having some bookkeeping experience, has personally prepared the company's financial statements and does not understand why such statements should be examined by a CPA. Feiler discussed the matter with Farber, a CPA, and asked Farber to explain why an audit is considered important.

Required:

a. Describe the objectives of an independent audit.
b. Identify five ways in which an independent audit may be beneficial to Feiler. (AICPA adapted)

1.7 *Part a.* The first generally accepted auditing standard of field work requires, in part, that "the work is to be adequately planned." An effective tool for the auditor in adequately planning the work is an audit program.

Required:

What is an audit program, and what purposes does it serve?

Part b. Auditors frequently refer to the terms *standards* and *procedures*. Standards deal with measures of the quality of the auditor's performance. Standards specifically refer to the ten generally accepted auditing standards. Procedures relate to those acts that are performed by the auditor while trying to gather evidence. Procedures specifically refer to the methods or techniques used by the auditor in the conduct of the examination.

Required:

List at least two types of procedures that an auditor would use during an examination of financial statements. For example, a type of procedure that an auditor would frequently use is the observation of activities and conditions. Do not discuss specific accounts. (AICPA adapted)

1.8 The auditor should obtain a level of knowledge of the entity's business, including events, transactions, and practices that will enable the planning and performance of an examination in accordance with generally accepted auditing standards. Adhering to these standards enables the auditor's report to lend credibility to financial statements by providing the public with certain assurances.

Required:

a. How does knowledge of the entity's business help the auditor in the planning and performance of an examination in accordance with generally accepted auditing standards?
b. What assurances are provided to the public when the auditor states that the financial statements "present fairly . . . in conformity with generally accepted accounting principles?" (AICPA adapted)

1.9 An important measure of the quality of the internal auditing function concerns the level within the organization to which the internal auditor reports. A "rule of thumb" is that the internal auditor must report to a sufficiently high level that his/her findings will be implemented.

Required:

a. How does reporting to a higher level within the organization improve the chances for the internal auditor's findings to be implemented?

b. Today, many companies have their internal auditors report directly to the audit committee of the board of directors. How does this practice enhance the effectiveness of internal auditing?

1.10 In addition to financial auditing, the internal auditor is also engaged in evaluating the efficiency of operations (operational auditing) and the effectiveness of management (management or performance auditing).

Required:
a. Distinguish among the terms *financial auditing, operational auditing,* and *management auditing.*
b. Briefly describe the role of the General Accounting Office (GAO) in the performance of management audits.
c. The Internal Revenue Service and the Defense Contract Audit Agency perform ''compliance'' audits. Explain how this type of auditing differs from financial and operational auditing.

1.11 As used in the definition of auditing, *assertions* are representations of management as to the fairness of the financial statements. Each line item on the financial statements, therefore, represents management's assertions concerning such matters as existence and proper valuation of recorded assets, liabilities, revenues, and expenses. For each of the following balance sheet components, state how you would satisfy yourself as to existence and valuation (i.e., what evidence you might gather to gain reasonable assurance).

a. Inventories of finished goods
b. Marketable equity securities
c. Accounts receivable

1.12 Prior to the release of their 1988 annual report to stockholders, General Motors (GM) stated (*Wall Street Journal,* January 5, 1989) that the company would report record earnings for 1988. Roger Smith, then GM's Chief Executive Officer, stated that the figure would '' . . . surpass the old net income record of $4.52 billion or $14.27 per share reported in 1984.'' Mr. Smith referred to the increase as further evidence of the turnaround he said GM had accomplished after three years of declining earnings. He cited ''cost cutting'' as the major factor accounting for the recovery.

Financial analysts, however, remained skeptical as to the claim of an earnings record. They said GM had more conservative accounting procedures in 1984 and some estimated that 1988 earnings would be closer to $8 per share if 1984 accounting principles were applied. Others argued that GM artificially inflated profits by boosting production in the fourth quarter.

The audited financial statements, included in GM's 1988 annual report to stockholders, reported per share earnings of $12.33, considerably below the figure announced by Smith prior to the audit.

Required:
a. How does the above case demonstrate the adversarial relationship between corporate managements and their stockholders?
b. In what way does the case support a need for independent auditing?
c. How can a ''production boost'' in the fourth quarter ''artificially inflate'' earnings?

1.13 The firm of Young and Shaw, CPAs, has just accepted a new audit client, Jiles Enterprises, Inc. The firm has been engaged as of June 1, 1993 to perform the audit for the fiscal year ending September 30, 1993. Donald Beavers has been assigned as the in-charge senior auditor for the engagement and has completed a preliminary study of the company, preparatory to developing preliminary audit programs and performing the first phase of the interim audit. The information documented in the preliminary study was gathered by discussions with client personnel, including the corporate controller, observation of company personnel, and studying company policy manuals and accounting manuals, as well as industry trade data. Some of Beavers' findings follow.

> Jiles Enterprises, incorporated in 1965, manufactures and sells household furniture and business furniture, such as desks, chairs, file cabinets, and computer tables. In addition, the company recently acquired a restaurant chain selling and servicing franchises on a nationwide scale. The company was previously audited by Howell & Bates, CPAs. Although Beavers hasn't yet contacted the previous auditors, Daryl McIntire, Jiles' controller, stated the reason for the change in auditors was the failure of Howell & Bates to provide needed management services, such as help with the new on-line computer system that Jiles hopes to install in the next year. In questioning McIntire about Jiles' control structure, Beavers couldn't seem to elicit specific information—only a general assurance by the controller that the structure is "sound." The accounting system appears somewhat dated and transactions are entered in batches rather than on-line. Also, the company does not maintain perpetual inventory records. Beavers finds this somewhat surprising in view of Jiles' size (1992 sales of $8.5 million and net assets of $12.6 million). Jiles does not have an internal audit staff and the accounting department seems small relative to the volume of transactions processed.

Required:

a. What is the significance of obtaining information during the preliminary phase of an audit engagement?

b. Identify any concerns you have, based on Beavers' preliminary study of Jiles. Discuss how your concerns might impact the conduct of the Jiles 1993 audit. Use the following format in answering this part of the question:

CONCERN   *AUDIT IMPACT*

2

Professional Responsibility

CHAPTER OUTLINE

I. **Introduction**

II. **Definition of quality**
   A. Professional standards
      1. Generally Accepted Auditing Standards
         a. General standards
         b. Field work standards
         c. Reporting standards
      2. Attestation Standards
      3. Statements on Standards for Accounting and Review Services
      4. Statements on Standards for Consulting Services
      5. Statements on Responsibilities in Tax Practice
   B. Code of Professional Conduct
      1. Principles
      2. Rules
         a. Rule 101: Independence
         b. Rule 102: Integrity and Objectivity
         c. Rule 201: General Standards
         d. Rule 202: Compliance with Standards
         e. Rule 203: Accounting Principles
         f. Rule 301: Confidential Client Information
         g. Rule 302: Contingent Fees
         h. Rule 501: Acts Discreditable
         i. Rule 502: Advertising
         j. Rule 503: Commissions and Referral Fees
         k. Rule 505: Form of Practice and Name

III. **Maintenance of quality**
   A. Self-regulation and the expectations gap
   B. AICPA, state boards of accountancy, and quality maintenance
   C. Division of CPA Firms
   D. Securities and Exchange Commission
   E. AICPA Quality Control Standards Committee
   F. The courts

OVERVIEW

The means for achieving and maintaining quality in the rendering of auditing and accounting services by CPAs are explored in this chapter. Providing services at a level of competence expected by the recipients of those services is necessary if CPAs are to maintain their status as a profession.

High quality in auditing is defined by the ten Generally Accepted Auditing Standards (GAAS) and the Statements on Auditing Standards (SASs) promulgated by the American Institute of Certified Public Accountants (AICPA). The Attestation Standards, Statements on Consulting Services, Statements on Responsibilities in Tax Practice, and Statements on Standards for Accounting and Review Services set quality guidelines for other accounting services. Like the auditing standards, these other statements and standards are also issued by the AICPA. Although the standards establish acceptable levels of quality, the Code of Professional Conduct establishes acceptable levels of conduct by the CPA. All of these pronouncements are presented and discussed in the first part of the chapter.

Maintaining quality of service requires a mechanism for monitoring the activities of CPAs in rendering professional services, and for invoking disciplinary action in those situations involving substandard performance. The AICPA, the Securities and Exchange Commission, the various state boards of accountancy, and the courts are all instrumental in monitoring performance by CPAs and in imposing discipline where appropriate. The second part of the chapter discusses maintenance of quality and utilizes these bodies as a focal point.

STUDY OBJECTIVES

After reading this chapter, you should be able to:

1. Identify and discuss the following sources defining the quality of services rendered by CPAs:
    Generally Accepted Auditing Standards (GAAS)
    Statements on Auditing Standards (SASs)
    Attestation Standards
    Statements of Standards for Accounting and Review Services (SSARSs)
    Statements on Standards for Consulting Services (SSCSs)
    Statements on Responsibilities in Tax Practice (TXs)
    Code of Professional Conduct (through principles and rules)

2. Define the ''expectations gap'' and recognize the importance of quality control in any attempt to narrow the gap.

3. Recognize the means by which the profession regulates itself and maintains the necessary level of quality in rendering auditing and accounting services.

4. Identify the organizations and agencies involved in monitoring the activities of the profession and in invoking disciplinary action:
    AICPA (through its Trial Board, Quality Control Standards Committee, and Professional Oversight Board monitoring CPA firms)
    SEC (through the Office of the Chief Accountant and the SEC reporting requirements)
    State boards of accountancy (through CPA certification, licenses to practice, and continuing professional education requirements)
    The courts

INTRODUCTION

The accounting profession, like any other profession, exists only through wide public acceptance. Public acceptance of the professions means that society perceives a need which can best be met by highly trained professionals.

In the case of auditing, the perceived need is for the independent attest function. Third-party users need to have the financial statements audited by accounting experts who are highly trained in evidence gathering and evaluation methods and who are also independent of the statement preparers (management). The attest function, as performed by the independent auditor, adds this needed dimension to the financial statements in the form of enhanced relevance and reliability.

Independent auditing maintains its professional status by striving for consistency of quality and by maintaining independence from management. If the quality of the attest function were to significantly deteriorate, or if auditors were perceived as not being independent, auditing could be reduced to a status below that of a profession.

The alleged "audit failures" involving a number of financial institutions such as Lincoln Savings & Loan Association, Bank of Credit & Commerce International (BCCI), United American Bank of Knoxville, Penn Square, and E.S.M. Government Securities, have caused the public to ask "Where were the auditors?" As a result of these and other cases, the House Energy and Commerce Oversight and Investigations Subcommittee, a congressional committee, has been conducting hearings into the status of the accounting profession. The Moss and Metcalf House and Senate committees, respectively, also conducted hearings in the 1970s. In addition to questioning audit quality, these investigations and hearings have raised the related issue of whether the auditing profession is capable of regulating itself in terms of quality maintenance or whether the standard setting and enforcement functions should be transferred to the public sector.

In response to these concerns, the AICPA, the American Accounting Association (AAA), the Financial Executives Institute (FEI), the Institute of Internal Auditors (IIA), and the Institute of Management Accountants (IMA) jointly sponsored the National Commission on Fraudulent Financial Reporting. The purpose of the Commission was to study the financial reporting system in the United States, identify causal factors that can lead to fraudulent reporting, and recommend steps to reduce its incidence. The results of this study were published in a Report of the Commission released in 1987. Referred to as the "**Treadway Report**," after James Treadway, Chairman of the Commission, the study contains recommendations that are likely to influence the performance of CPAs for many years to come.[1] The more immediate impact of the study is evidenced by the 1988 and 1990 revisions to the Code of Professional Conduct and the Bylaws of the AICPA, and the release of nine new statements on auditing standards by the Auditing Standards Board. These revisions are significant, and are briefly described in the following paragraphs. They are also incorporated, as appropriate, throughout the text.

The revised Code of Conduct provides for a more positive approach to accountants' ethical behavior. A new set of principles and rules replaces the rules and

---

[1]National Commission on Fraudulent Financial Reporting, *Report of the National Commission on Fraudulent Financial Reporting,* New York: October, 1987.

interpretations contained in the former code. Further, the new code was broadened to encompass all services rendered by CPAs. Prior to 1988, the code covered mainly audit services. The new bylaws add three new requirements for AICPA members. First, members must be enrolled in quality maintenance programs approved by the AICPA. Second, the bylaws impose continuing professional education requirements on AICPA members. Third, prospective CPAs desiring membership in the AICPA must, by the year 2000, complete 150 hours of baccalaureate education prior to sitting for the CPA examination. The nine new SASs, among other matters, produce significant changes in the auditor's study and evaluation of internal control and in the form of the standard audit report.

In addition to a high quality of performance, the auditing profession must demonstrate to the public it serves that it is independent of the management of audited companies. Cases alleging auditor complicity in the application of questionable accounting practices and inadequate disclosure have occurred over time, causing questions of auditor independence to surface. These cases have involved such distortions as early revenue recognition, fictitious receivables, failure to disclose the existence of related parties and related party transactions, and loans not secured by adequate collateral. Many of the cases are discussed in Chapter 3 on legal liability.

How does auditing achieve and maintain the level of quality needed to preserve its professional status? Figure 2.1 summarizes the existing **quality control** structure covering auditing and other accounting services rendered by CPAs and forms a basis for the discussion that follows. Two aspects of quality control are depicted in Figure 2.1. The upper part lists the sources that *define* quality performance, and the lower portion identifies the organizations and the structure that provides a means for *maintaining* quality.

Notwithstanding the efforts of the AICPA and other bodies, however, quality of service will only be achieved and maintained to the extent that CPAs, individually and collectively, assume a positive approach to ethical behavior and strive to abide by the *spirit,* as well as by the *letter* of the professional standards.

DEFINITION OF QUALITY

The AICPA has provided a framework for defining the acceptable quality of independent audits and other services rendered by CPAs. The standards and Code of Professional Conduct listed at the top of Figure 2.1 constitute this framework. Figure 2.2 goes a step further by categorizing the kinds of services performed by CPAs and the source of AICPA standards defining quality. Note that a separate set of standards has been promulgated for each type of service. In addition to the standards, the Code of Conduct establishes acceptable levels of conduct and covers all services rendered by CPAs.

The auditing and attestation standards, the Statements on Auditing Standards (SASs), considered interpretations of the standards, and the Code of Conduct are all binding on members of the profession. They are enforceable by the AICPA, as well as the respective state boards of accountancy. The consequences of violation will be addressed in the second part of the chapter dealing with maintenance of quality, but now we turn to these standards and code of conduct.

FIGURE 2.1   **Achieving and Maintaining Professional Status**

Definition of Acceptable Quality

Generally Accepted Auditing Standards (GAASs)
Statements on Auditing Standards (SASs)
Statements on Standards for Attestation Engagements
Statements on Standards for Accounting and Review Services (SSARSs)
Statements on Standards for Accountants' Services on
     Prospective Financial Information
Statements on Responsibilities in Tax Practice (TXs)
Statements on Standards for Consulting Services (SSCSs)
AICPA Code of Professional Conduct: principles, rules, and interpretations

Maintenance of Quality

Securities and Exchange Commission
   Office of the Chief Accountant:
      Monitors Auditing Standards Board
      Investigates alleged audit failures
   Change in auditors (Form 8-K)

State Boards of Accountancy
   CPA certificate
   License to practice
   Continuing Professional Education requirements

Courts
   Liability for negligence
   Criminal liability

American Institute of Certified Public Accountants
   Bylaws:
      Continuing professional education requirement
      Quality Review Division
      150-hour CPA requirement
   Trial Board
   Quality Control Standards Committee
     (Statements on Quality Control Standards)
   Division of CPA Firms
     Quality maintenance
     Peer review
     Public Oversight Board (POB)
       Monitors SEC Practice Section of Division for CPA Firms

FIGURE 2.2   Range of CPAs' Services and Definition of Quality

Service	Quality Defined (Source)	C O D E O F C O N D U C T
Auditing	Auditing Standards SASs	

Other attest services:
  Financial projections
  Financial forecasts
  Pro forma statements
  Reports on internal control
	Attestation Standards
	  Statements on Standards for
	  Attestation Engagements
	  (SSAEs)	

Compilations and reviews	Statements on Standards for
	  Accounting and Review Services
	  (SSARs)	

Consulting engagements	Statements on Standards for
	  Consulting Services
	  (SSCSs)	

Tax services	Statements on Responsibilities in
	  Tax Practice
	  (TXs)	

PROFESSIONAL STANDARDS

Generally Accepted Auditing Standards (GAAS)

The ten auditing standards promulgated by the AICPA were briefly described in Chapter 1 (See Figure 1.2). The auditing standards establish a required level of quality for examining professional practice; auditing procedures are the means of attaining that level. These are set by the AICPA.[2]

General Standards

The three **general standards** relate to the character and competence of the auditor.

1. The examination is to be performed by a person or persons having adequate technical training and proficiency as an auditor.

2. In all matters relating to the assignment, an independence in mental attitude is to be maintained by the auditor or auditors.

3. Due professional care is to be exercised in the performance of the examination and the preparation of the report.

---

[2]Auditing Standards Board, *AICPA Professional Standards*. New York: AICPA, Section AU 150.02.

Adequate technical **training and proficiency as an auditor** assures clients that CPAs are able to adequately perform the services for which they represent themselves. If a client's accounting system contains complex EDP applications, for example, the auditor must have an adequate understanding of computers and computer processing to permit examination of the system and the related financial data flowing through the system. An auditor who undertakes to examine the financial statements of a client in a previously unfamiliar industry must attain a level of understanding of the transactions and accounting practices unique to that industry to afford a basis for successful completion of the audit.

Auditor independence means that auditors must be independent of management if they are to adequately serve the interests of financial statement users. Auditor independence has two aspects: **independence in fact,** and **independence in appearance.** Auditor independence is discussed more fully in the ethics section of this chapter.

Due audit care refers to the auditor's exercise of professional judgment during the conduct of an examination. Determining when evidence is sufficient or competent, categorizing an internal control weakness or a financial statement error as material, deciding on the form of audit report to render in the circumstances—all these areas require the exercise of audit judgment. The standard of due audit care requires that the "prudent auditor" apply such judgment in a conscientious manner, carefully weighing the relevant factors before reaching a decision.

Due care also suggests that the auditor make a reasonable effort to ensure that the financial statements are free from material error. This aspect of due audit care is the concept most frequently cited by the courts in cases alleging auditor negligence. In these cases, the courts tend to address the question as to whether the auditor performed the examination with a reasonable degree of diligence and whether the auditor possessed the level of skill required by the profession in order to carry out the engagement.

In the case of *Escott v. Bar Chris Construction Corporation* (See Chapter 3), the court held that the auditors did not exercise due care in the conduct of the examination. In this case, the auditors failed to gain an adequate understanding of certain complex sale and leaseback transactions entered into by Bar Chris. These transactions related to the construction, sale, leasing, and operation of bowling centers, the main activity of Bar Chris. Failure to comprehend the nature of these rather complex transactions, together with failure to identify certain related party transactions, resulted in material undetected errors in the financial statements. Assets and income were overstated as a result, and related party transactions were improperly classified on the balance sheet. The court, in finding the auditors guilty of negligence, stated that the in-charge senior auditor did not follow some of the steps set forth in the written audit programs and, most important, was "too easily satisfied with glib answers to his questions."[3]

Due audit care does not require the auditor to make perfect judgment decisions in all cases, but it does require that the examination be completed with a reasonable degree of diligence by persons possessing the average skills required by the profession.

---

[3]*Escott et al. v. Bar Chris Construction Corp. et al.*, 283 F. Supp. 643 (S.D.N.Y. 1968).

Standards of Audit Field Work

Whereas the general standards deal with the character and competence of the auditor, the **field work standards** are concerned with the audit process.

1. The work is to be adequately planned and assistants, if any, are to be properly supervised.

2. A sufficient understanding of the internal control structure is to be obtained to plan the audit and to determine the nature, timing, and extent of tests to be performed.

3. Sufficient competent evidential matter is to be obtained through inspection, observation, inquiries, and confirmations to afford a reasonable basis for an opinion regarding the financial statements under examination.

Adequate **planning and supervision** are required if the audit is to proceed in a systematic fashion. Audit planning encompasses such tasks as making arrangements with the client concerning the timing of the audit field work and use of the client's staff in completing certain phases of the examination. Planning also involves preparation of a time budget estimating the hours required to complete the various parts of the audit, obtaining an understanding of the business, and developing audit programs. The pre-audit conference, as described in Chapter 1, is also part of audit planning.

To ensure an adequate quality of auditing, assistants must be properly supervised. The in-charge senior auditor is the direct line supervisor on the engagement. To ensure adequate supervision, the senior must assign to assistants only those audit tasks which the assistants are capable of performing. Also, the senior must be prepared to answer questions raised by the assistants in the performance of their assigned tasks. Finally, and perhaps most important, the senior must carefully review the workpapers prepared by the assistants, making certain that they are complete and conclusive in all material respects.

Proper *study and evaluation of internal accounting control* is needed because virtually all independent financial audits are **test-based audits.** This means that the auditor examines a sampling of transactions rather than all of the transactions consummated by the client during the period under audit. In determining the extent, as well as the nature and timing of such tests, the auditor must determine the effectiveness of existing internal control structure policies and procedures as they affect the reliability of the assertions contained in the financial statements. An effective control structure requires less substantive testing of transactions and balances than a weak structure. Internal control concepts, as well as the auditor's approach to study and evaluation of internal control, are more fully addressed in chapters 6-8.

Sufficient competent evidential matter is that standard which comes closest to addressing the application of auditing procedures, but it does not constrain the auditor in the selection of which procedures to apply in particular circumstances. Instead, the standard, along with Statement on Auditing Standards (SAS) No. 31, identifies the various types of evidence available to the auditor, and offers guidelines for the auditor to follow in judging *sufficiency* and *competence* of evidential matter. Sufficiency and competence of evidential matter were described in Chapter 1.

Standards of Reporting

The four **reporting standards** relate to the attest function—the end result of the audit.

1. The report shall state whether the financial statements are presented in accordance with generally accepted accounting principles.

2. The report shall identify those circumstances in which such principles have not been consistently observed in the current period in relation to the preceding period.

3. Informative disclosures in the financial statements are to be regarded as reasonably adequate unless otherwise stated in the report.

4. The report shall either contain an expression of opinion regarding the financial statements, taken as a whole, or an assertion to the effect that an opinion cannot be expressed. When an overall opinion cannot be expressed, the reasons therefore should be stated. In all cases where an auditor's name is associated with financial statements, the report should contain a clear-cut indication of the character of the auditor's examination, if any, and the degree of responsibility he is taking.

Specifically, these standards require the auditor to determine whether the financial statements are essentially in accordance with generally accepted accounting principles (GAAP), and whether informative disclosures are adequate. Additionally, the standards require that the auditor either formulate an opinion regarding the financial statements taken as a whole, or disclaim an opinion and give a reason for the disclaimer. These four standards are addressed at length in Chapter 15.

As stated previously, the ten standards, along with the related statements on auditing standards (SASs), must be adhered to in the conduct of the audit. The SASs are considered interpretations of the standards, and auditors must justify any material departures from them. Although the standards have just been discussed, the SASs are covered throughout the text, as appropriate to specific topics.

Attestation Standards

Many nonaudit services (e.g., special compliance engagements, reviews, and reports on internal control structure) require some form of attestation (opinion) by the accountant. To provide for maintenance of a standard quality in the performance of these services, the AICPA has established eleven **attestation standards** (See Figure 16.1). The standards, which are fully addressed in Chapter 16, do not supersede the ten generally accepted auditing standards. Rather, they complement them and make explicit certain preconditions for the performance of nonaudit attest services.

Statements on Standards for Accounting and Review Services

In lieu of an audit, nonpublic clients may request the CPA to *compile* or perform a *review* of the financial statements. These engagements are significantly less in scope than an audit. They consist mainly of reading the financial statements, inquiry and analytical procedures, and do not entail study and evaluation of internal control nor such auditing procedures as confirmation, physical examination, observation, calculation, and reconciliation.

In order to achieve consistency in the rendering of such services, the AICPA, in 1977, established the Accounting and Review Services Committee. Equivalent to the Auditing Standards Board, the Accounting and Review Services Committee issues **Statements on Standards for Accounting and Review Services** (SSARSs). These statements establish the framework and define acceptable quality for performing compilations and reviews. Like the SASs, the SSARs are binding upon the profession, and the CPA must be prepared to justify departures from them. Compilations and reviews, along with the related SSARSs, are discussed more fully in Chapter 16.

Statements on Standards for Consulting Services

CPAs are frequently asked by their clients to render consulting services. These services have become quite diverse and may assume the form of analyzing an accounting system, reviewing a profit plan, installing a computer system, analyzing a merger proposal, providing staff for computer programming services, selling packaged training programs, and other areas in which the CPA possesses expertise. These services are collectively referred to as CPA **consulting services** and are governed by the **Statements on Standards for Consulting Services** (SSCSs) issued by the AICPA Management Advisory Services Executive Committee.

In performing consulting services for audit clients, the CPA must exercise care that independence is not compromised. This is best achieved by avoiding situations in which the CPA is required to make management decisions that might impair objectivity. SSCS No. 1, issued by the Committee in 1991, defines CPA consulting and provides guidelines for effectively performing consulting services without compromising independence. The following six areas of consulting services are identified and defined in the statement:

1. *Consultations,* in which the practitioner's function is to provide counsel in a short time frame;
2. *Advisory services,* in which the practitioner's function is to develop findings, conclusions, and recommendations for client consideration and decision making;
3. *Implementation services,* in which the practitioner's function is to put an action plan into effect;
4. *Transaction services,* in which the practitioner's function is to provide services related to a specific client transaction;
5. *Staff and other support services,* in which the practitioner's function is to provide appropriate staff . . . to perform tasks specified by the client; and
6. *Product services,* in which the practitioner's function is to provide the client with a product and associated professional services in support of the installation, use, or maintenance of the product.[4]

---

[4]See *AICPA Professional Standards,* New York: AICPA, Sections MS 11.01-31.15.

SSCSs are included under Rule 202 of the Code of Professional Conduct, thus making them binding on members. Departures from the provisions of the SSCSs must be justified in the same manner as departures from GAAS and the related SASs.[5]

Statements on Responsibilities in Tax Practice

The **Statements on Responsibilities in Tax Practice** (TXs) issued by the Committee on Federal Taxation of the AICPA are also covered under Rule 202 of the Code of Conduct. As such, they provide guidance for CPAs in performing tax services and representing clients in tax matters before the Internal Revenue Service. They also provide the necessary framework for ensuring compliance with Rule 102 of the Code of Conduct, which covers knowing misrepresentation of facts and subordination of judgment.

Since its inception in 1964, the committee has issued several TXs, covering such issues as the circumstances under which the CPA may sign a return as preparer, appropriate actions when a client refuses to answer questions on a return, knowledge of errors in returns, and the CPA's approach when representing the client in administrative proceedings before the Internal Revenue Service.[6]

In addition to Rule 102 of the Code of Conduct, the CPA must also comply with IRS Circular 230, which defines practice before the IRS. A CPA may practice before the IRS upon filing a declaration that he or she is licensed as a CPA and authorized to represent the client. The CPA must then conform to the standards of conduct contained in Circular 230 when representing clients in tax matters.

Code of Professional Conduct

The second part of the framework dealing with the quality of auditing is the AICPA **Code of Professional Conduct.** The code, containing principles and rules of conduct, governs the CPA's performance of the various services rendered by the profession. The principles provide a framework for the rules. The rules are binding upon the CPA, whether engaged in auditing or other professional accounting services such as tax practice or management consulting services. Departures from the rules of conduct must be justified by the member committing such violations. Material departures are subject to deliberations by the Professional Ethics Division and the Trial Board of the AICPA, and may lead to suspension or revocation of membership in the AICPA.

In addition to principles and rules, the Executive Committee of the Professional Ethics Division, from time to time, issues "interpretations" and "ethics rulings." The interpretations and rulings, like the statements on auditing standards, represent further clarification of the principles and rules of conduct. Like the SASs, departures from the interpretations and rulings must be justified by the CPA.

The following paragraphs address the principles and rules of conduct as contained in the Code. Although interpretations and ethics rulings are not covered

---

[5]*Ibid.*

[6]*Ibid.*, Sections TX 101.01-201.13.

extensively in this chapter, the student may wish to study the AICPA Professional Standards for further understanding of these important ingredients of quality control. Some of the cases presented at the end of this chapter require further research into the interpretations and rulings to enhance this understanding. We might note as one moves down the hierarchy of the Code from principles to rules to interpretations to ethics rulings, the general concepts are transformed into specific examples of proper and improper conduct. For example, Article III of the Principles addresses the question of *integrity* and states that " . . . members should perform all professional responsibilities with the highest sense of integrity." Rule 102 goes a step further in defining objectivity and integrity as requiring freedom from "conflicts of interest, misrepresentation of facts, and/or subordination of judgment to others." Interpretation 102.03 clarifies what is meant by "conflicts of interest" as it pertains to public accounting services, and Ethic Ruling 191.001-002 states that a member accepting "more than a token gift from a client would create a conflict of interest."[7]

Principles

Article I: Responsibilities In carrying out their responsibilities as professionals, members should exercise sensitive professional and moral judgments in all their activities.

Article II: The Public Interest Members should accept the obligation to act in a way that will serve the public interest, honor the public trust, and demonstrate commitment to professionalism.

Article III: Integrity To maintain and broaden public confidence, members should perform all professional responsibilities with the highest sense of integrity.

Article IV: Objectivity and Independence A member should maintain objectivity and be free of conflicts of interest in discharging professional responsibilities. A member in public practice should be independent in fact and appearance when providing auditing and other attestation services.

Article V: Due Care A member should observe the profession's technical and ethical standards, strive continually to improve competence and the quality of services, and discharge professional responsibility to the best of the member's ability.

Article VI: Scope and Nature of Services A member in public practice should observe the Principles of the Code of Professional Conduct in determining the scope and nature of services to be provided.[8]

In rendering attestation and other services, CPAs must always promote the public interest which they are to serve. Public trust should never be subordinate to personal gain. These principles provide a framework for ensuring an appropriate level of services rendered by CPAs. The principles of objectivity, independence, integrity, and due care strongly suggest that the CPA perform competently and diligently. As stated previously, CPAs must strive continually to conform to the *spirit* of these principles if public confidence in the profession is to be maintained.

---

[7]*AICPA Professional Standards,* Vol. 2, New York, NY: AICPA, Section ET 191.001-002.

[8]AICPA, *Code of Professional Conduct,* New York: AICPA, 1991.

Rules

The **rules of conduct** presented in the following paragraphs flow from the preceding principles. The bylaws of the AICPA require adherence to the rules. Where appropriate, interpretations of the rules are also included.

The first rule, dealing with independence, encompasses review services, reports on examinations of prospective financial statements, and reports on attest engagements, as well as audit engagements. Earlier codes of conduct contemplated that independence should apply to audit engagements only.

Rule 101
Independence

A member in public practice shall be independent in the performance of professional services as required by standards promulgated by bodies designated by Council.

Interpretation 101-1. Independence shall be considered to be impaired if, for example, a member had any of the following transactions, interests, or relationships:

A. During the period of a professional engagement or at the time of expressing an opinion, a member or a member's firm
  1. Had or was committed to acquire any direct or material indirect financial interest in the enterprise.
  2. Was a trustee of any trust or executor or administrator of any estate if such trust or estate had or was committed to acquire any direct or material indirect financial interest in the enterprise.
  3. Had any joint, closely held business investment with the enterprise or with any officer, director, or principal stockholders thereof that was material in relation to the member's net worth or to the net worth of the member's firm.
  4. Had any loan to or from the enterprise or any officer, director, or principal stockholder of the enterprise.

B. During the period covered by the financial statements, during the period of the professional engagement, or at the time of expressing an opinion, a member or a member's firm
  1. Was connected with the enterprise as a promoter, underwriter or voting trustee, as a director or officer, or in any capacity equivalent to that of a member of management or of an employee.
  2. Was a trustee for any pension or profit-sharing trust of the enterprise.

The above examples are not intended to be all-inclusive.[9]

In order to fairly represent the users of his/her services, the CPA must be independent of the client's management. Such independence encompasses two facets—independence in fact, and independence in appearance. Independence in fact involves a state of mind. The CPA must be independent in mental attitude in all matters relating to the engagement. Independence in appearance relates to how financial statement users perceive independence. If a CPA were to serve simultaneously as auditor and member of the client's board of directors, users might well regard the dual capacity of auditor and board member as a conflict of interest and

---

[9]*Ibid.*

a compromising of independence. The CPA may be able to perform this dual role while remaining objective in all matters relating to the engagement (state of mind); but the second aspect of the rule (appearance) has been violated.

The appearance of independence would also be impaired were the CPA to have a material direct financial interest in or a loan from a company that he or she is auditing. Making management decisions, such as hiring the new controller, supervising client office personnel, approving vouchers for payment, and preparing reports would also impair independence.

In the performance of any professional service, a member shall maintain objectivity and integrity, shall be free of conflicts of interest, and shall not knowingly misrepresent facts or subordinate his or her judgment to others.[10]

Rule 102
Integrity and
Objectivity

Although Rule 101 relates to auditing and other attest services, Rule 102 is broader and covers other services rendered by CPAs such as management consulting and tax services. Independence is not so critical in the rendering of these other services. Indeed, in performing tax services and when dealing with the taxing authorities, the auditor is allowed to be an advocate of the client, representing the client's interests.

The CPA, however, must not knowingly agree to false representations of the client; nor should the CPA simply carry out the wishes of management. Instead, an attitude of striving to provide honest and professional service to the client must be maintained.

The Statements on Standards for Consulting Services and the Statements on Responsibilities in Tax Practice, discussed earlier, provide further clarification of these issues.

A member shall comply with the following standards and with any interpretations thereof by bodies designated by Council.

Rule 201
General Standards

A. Professional competence. Undertake only those professional services that the member or the member's firm can reasonably expect to be completed with professional competence.

B. Due professional care. Exercise due professional care in the performance of professional services.

C. Planning and supervision. Adequately plan and supervise the performance of professional services.

D. Sufficient relevant data. Obtain sufficient relevant data to afford a reasonable basis for conclusions or recommendations in relation to any professional services performed.[11]

---

[10]*Ibid.*

[11]*Ibid.*

These standards are applicable to all public accounting services rendered by CPAs. They are similar to, but should not be confused with, the general and field work auditing standards.

Competence includes technical qualifications, the ability to supervise and evaluate work performed, and the ability to exercise sound judgment. The CPA does not, however, assume responsibility for infallibility of knowledge or judgment.

Rule 202
Compliance with
Standards

A member who performs auditing, review, compilation, management advisory, tax, or other professional services shall comply with standards promulgated by bodies designated by Council.[12]

This rule makes it mandatory for CPAs who are members of the Institute to abide by *all of the standards* issued by the various bodies so designated by the Institute that govern the practice of public accounting. In prior versions of the Code, Rule 202 applied only to auditing services.

Rule 203
Accounting
Principles

A member shall (1) not express an opinion or state affirmatively that the financial statements or other financial data of any entity are presented in conformity with generally accepted accounting principles or (2) state that he or she is not aware of any material modifications that should be made to such statements or data in order for them to be in conformity with generally accepted accounting principles, if such statements or data contain any departure from an accounting principle promulgated by bodies designated by Council to establish such principles that has a material effect on the statements or data taken as a whole. If, however, the statements or data contain such a departure and the member can demonstrate that due to unusual circumstances the financial statements or data would otherwise have been misleading, the member can comply with the rule by describing the departure, its approximate effects, if practicable, and the reasons why compliance with the principle would result in a misleading statement.[13]

Rule 203 makes the accounting principles binding upon the CPA in the same manner as Rule 202 requires adherence to the professional standards. Since 1973, the "body designated by Council" has been the Financial Accounting Standards Board (FASB). Prior to that date, the Accounting Principles Board (1959–1973) and the Committee on Accounting Procedure (prior to 1959) had such principle setting authority. Thus, FASB Statements of Financial Accounting Standards and those Accounting Principles Board Opinions and Accounting Research Bulletins that have not been superseded by action of the FASB constitute GAAP and are covered by Rule 203.

Except for unusual circumstances causing the financial statements to be otherwise misleading, the CPA may not agree with material departures from such

---

[12]*Ibid.*

[13]*Ibid.*

principles. ''Unusual circumstances'' is a matter of professional judgment. Circumstances that may justify a departure include new legislation or the evolution of a new form of business transaction. The existence of conflicting industry practices would not ordinarily justify a departure.

When, in an audit, the CPA agrees that application of the principle would cause the financial statements to be materially misleading, the departure must be disclosed in the auditor's report on the financial statements. This is usually presented in a fourth paragraph, following the opinion paragraph (see Chapter 15), wherein the monetary effects of the departure must be set forth, where practicably determinable.

More recently, a Governmental Accounting Standards Board (GASB) has been established by the Financial Accounting Foundation and is responsible for issuing pronouncements on government accounting standards. In evaluating fairness of financial presentation for state and local government units, therefore, the auditor must consider the pronouncements of the GASB to be the top hierarchy of generally accepted accounting principles.[14]

A member in public practice shall not disclose any confidential information without the specific consent of the client.

**Rule 301
Confidential Client
Information**

This rule shall not be construed (1) to relieve a member of his or her professional obligations under rules 202 and 203, (2) to affect in any way the member's obligation to comply with a validly issued and enforceable subpoena or summons, (3) to prohibit review of a member's professional practice under AICPA or state CPA society authorization, or (4) to preclude a member from initiating a complaint with or responding to any inquiry made by a recognized investigative or disciplinary body.

Members of a recognized investigative or disciplinary body and professional practice reviewers shall not use to their own advantage or disclose any member's confidential client information that comes to their attention in carrying out their official responsibilities. However, this prohibition shall not restrict the exchange of information with a recognized investigative or disciplinary body or affect, in any way, compliance with a validly issued and enforceable subpoena or summons.[15]

The purpose of Rule 301 is to encourage clients to provide the CPA access to all information which is necessary to the successful completion of an engagement. The rule achieves this end by requiring the CPA to respect the confidentiality of such information. The information obtained during an engagement must not be disclosed to third parties unless it is necessary to the fairness of financial presentation or unless it is requested by the courts in cases involving clients. An exception to the confidentiality requirement is also included in order to provide for access to information by other CPAs during peer reviews of engagement workpapers.

An interesting contrast to the U.S. Code of Conduct is the British practice of providing for confidential contacts between independent auditors and certain regulatory bodies. In the audit of the Bank of Credit & Commerce International (BCCI), for example, Price Waterhouse was able to establish contact with the Bank of

---

[14]*AICPA Professional Standards, op. cit.*, Section AU 411.06.

[15]AICPA, *Code of Professional Conduct.*

England as the auditors were uncovering evidence of fraud. In the U.S. such a practice would be considered a breach of confidentiality. Britain's 1987 Banking Act provides that "if a bank's management doesn't act to remedy a problem after being alerted by its auditors, then the auditors must go directly to the Bank of England."[16]

Rule 302
Contingent Fees

A member in public practice shall not

(1) Perform for a contingent fee any professional services for, or receive such a fee from, a client for whom the member or the member's firm performs
    (a) an audit or review of a financial statement; or
    (b) a compilation of a financial statement when the member expects, or reasonably might expect, that a third party will use the financial statement and the member's compilation report does not disclose a lack of independence; or
    (c) an examination of prospective financial information; or
(2) Prepare an original or amended tax return or claim for a tax refund for a contingent fee for any client.[17]

If a CPA were to base the fee for *attest services* on engagement results, independence and objectivity would be impaired in appearance, if not in fact. A fee, for example, based on a multiple of final audited net income or earnings per share figures, would bias the auditor to favor those audit adjustments affecting income in the direction of increasing the audit fee. For this reason, such arrangements constitute violations of Rule 302 and are prohibited for audit and other attest engagements.

The rule is not meant, however, to prevent the setting of fees according to the complexity of the engagement. Often, especially in initial audits, the fee quoted by the CPA is adjusted as the result of discovered weaknesses in internal accounting control that were not contemplated in the initial setting of the fee. Such adjustments should be provided for in the engagement letter. Also, under a "consent agreement" between the AICPA and the Federal Trade Commission (FTC), completed in August, 1990, CPAs are permitted to accept contingent fees and referral commissions relating to *nonattest engagements*.[18]

Rule 501
Acts Discreditable

A member shall not commit an act discreditable to the profession.[19]

Professional status can be achieved and maintained only through public acceptance, and requires a level of conduct commensurate with such status. Although the rule itself is silent as to what specifically constitutes a discreditable act, the bylaws of the AICPA identify situations leading to membership suspension or termination. These include committing a felonious crime, failure to file an income tax return, or filing or assisting in preparing a fraudulent return for a client.

---

[16]*Wall Street Journal,* July 12, 1991.

[17]AICPA, *Code of Professional Conduct.*

[18]See *The Journal of Accountancy,* October, 1990, page 35.

[19]AICPA, *Code of Professional Conduct.*

A member in public practice shall not seek to obtain clients by advertising or other forms of solicitation in a manner that is false, misleading, or deceptive. Solicitation by the use of coercion, over-reaching, or harassing conduct is prohibited.[20]

Prior to 1978, advertising was prohibited by the Code of Conduct. In 1977, the U.S. Supreme Court ruled that the American Bar Association could not prohibit advertising by lawyers. The AICPA then amended Rule 502 to similarly permit advertising by accountants.

Although most of the advertising has been quite subdued, the AICPA Board of Directors, in 1981, adopted a policy statement reading in part as follows:

> The Board believes that members should exercise appropriate restraint if they elect to engage in the commercial practices of advertising and solicitation. Such self-restraint can be exercised through the application of common sense, good taste, moderation and individual responsibility. This exercise of self-restraint contributes to adherence to technical and ethical standards and, as a result, serves the public interest.

The Board's concern in this regard was that excesses in advertising and solicitation might jeopardize adherence to technical and ethical standards.

Advertising that is informative and objective is encouraged under Rule 502. Examples of informative and objective content, contained in Interpretation 502-1, permit inclusion of such information as names, addresses, telephone numbers, services offered, educational and professional attainments, and statements of policy or position related to the practice of public accounting. Examples of deceptive advertising, contained in Interpretation 502-2, include statements which imply false expectations, self-laudatory statements, comparisons with other CPA firms, or testimonials or endorsements. Under the 1990 AICPA/FTC consent agreement referred to previously, however, the AICPA can no longer prohibit members from engaging in "self-laudatory advertising, comparative advertising, testimonial advertising," or advertising that some members may believe is "undignified" or "lacking in good taste." In summary, Rule 502 encourages advertising that is informational but, given the consent agreement, cannot prohibit other forms of advertising that might be considered misleading.

A. Prohibited Commissions

A member in public practice shall not, for a commission, recommend or refer to a client any product or service, or for a commission recommend or refer any product or service to be supplied by a client, or receive a commission, when the member or the member's firm also performs for that client

(a) an audit or review of a financial statement; or

(b) a compilation of a financial statement when the member expects, or reasonably might expect, that a third party will use the financial statement and the member's compilation report does not disclose a lack of independence; or

(c) an examination of prospective financial information.

---

[20]*Ibid.*

This prohibition applies during the period in which the member is engaged to perform any of the services listed above and the period covered by any historical financial statements involved in such listed services.

B. Disclosure of Permitted Commissions

A member in public practice who is not prohibited by this rule from performing services for or receiving a commission and who is paid or expects to be paid a commission shall disclose that fact to any person or entity to whom the member recommends or refers a product or service to which the commission relates.

C. Referral Fees

Any member who accepts a referral fee for recommending or referring any service of a CPA to any person or entity or who pays a referral fee to obtain a client shall disclose such acceptance or payment to the client.[21]

The members of a profession represent themselves as capable of providing services at a level of quality commensurate with that typified by the profession. Accordingly, CPAs have traditionally obtained new clients through the recommendations of other clients and associates. Such recommendations have generally been based on the quality of service rendered by the CPA. Obtaining clients through referral commissions removes some of the incentive for increasing the quality of services provided to clients and, instead, permits growth through such devices as referral commissions and fee splitting. For this reason, the AICPA has seen fit to discourage such practices relating to audits and other attest engagements, as well as for tax services and compilations where third party use of the financial statements is expected. Here again, however, the AICPA/FTC consent agreement permits CPAs to accept contingent fees in performing nonattest engagements, and permits the acceptance of referral fees and product recommendation commissions generally.[22]

**Rule 505
Form of Practice
and Name**

A member may practice public accounting in any organizational form permitted by the laws of the state in which the firm is located.

A member shall not practice under a firm name that is misleading. Names of one or more past partners or shareholders may be included in the firm name of a successor partnership or corporation. Also, a partner or shareholder surviving the death or withdrawal of all other partners or shareholders may continue to practice under such name which includes the name of past partners or shareholders for up to two years after becoming a sole practitioner.

A firm may not designate itself as ''Members of the American Institute of Certified Public Accountants'' unless all of its partners or shareholders are members of the Institute.[23]

---

[21]*Ibid.*

[22]*The Journal of Accountancy,* October, 1990, page 35.

[23]AICPA, *Code of Professional Conduct.*

Prior to 1969, CPAs were not permitted to incorporate. Corporations provide for limited liability to their stockholders, while unlimited liability was traditionally considered a condition of public sanction in the professions. In 1992, however, the AICPA membership voted to amend Rule 505 to permit CPA firms to organize themselves in any manner permitted by the state in which they practice. Thus, under this amendment, if state law permits, a firm can organize itself as a general corporation or a limited liability company. As a general corporation or limited liability company, the individual partners' liability in firm negligence actions will be limited rather than unlimited as heretofore. The major impetus behind this amendment was the devastating effects the "litigation explosion" has had on the personal assets of partners whose firms were being sued for negligence allegedly committed by other partners in the firm.[24]

EXHIBIT 2.1   AICPA Council Resolution Permitting Professional Corporations or Associations

RESOLVED, that the characteristics of a professional corporation as referred to in Rule 505 of the Code of Professional Ethics are as follows:

1. *Ownership.* All shareholders of the corporation or association shall be persons engaged in the practice of public accounting as defined by the Code of Professional Ethics. Shareholders shall at all times own their shares in their own right and shall be the beneficial owners of the equity capital ascribed to them.

2. *Transfer of Shares.* Provision shall be made requiring any shareholder who ceases to be eligible to be a shareholder to dispose of all of his shares within a reasonable period to a person qualified to be a shareholder or to the corporation or association.

3. *Directors and Officers.* The principal executive officer shall be a shareholder and a director, and to the extent possible, all other directors and officers shall be certified public accountants. Lay directors and officers shall not exercise any authority whatsoever over professional matters.

4. *Conduct.* The right to practice as a corporation or association shall not change the obligation of its shareholders, directors, officers, and other employees to comply with the standards of professional conduct established by the American Institute of Certified Public Accountants.

5. *Liability.* The stockholders of professional corporations or associations shall be jointly and severally liable for the acts of a corporation or association, or its employees—except where professional liability insurance is carried, or capitalization is maintained, in amounts deemed sufficient to offer adequate protection to the public. Liability shall not be limited by the formation of subsidiary or affiliated corporations or associations each with its own limited and unrelated liability.

Source: AICPA bylaws and implementing resolutions of council as amended January 8, 1990.

---

[24]See *The Journal of Accountancy,* October, 1991, page 45.

With regard to firm name, the AICPA/FTC consent agreement now permits CPAs to practice under names that might otherwise be considered "misleading" under Rule 505. Such designations as "Quality CPA Services," or "Suburban Tax Services" are now permissible under the agreement as long as there are no falsehoods or deceptions.[25]

MAINTENANCE OF QUALITY

Although the standards and ethics define the quality of services rendered by CPAs, some mechanism is needed for monitoring professional practice. Such monitoring is necessary to ensure that the defined level of quality is maintained. If CPAs are to account for departures from the standards and ethics, a means must exist for identifying those departures. The Securities and Exchange Commission, the AICPA, and the various state boards of accountancy have all played significant roles in maintenance of quality control (see Table 2.1).

Traditionally the monitoring mechanism has been housed mainly within the AICPA. Internal enforcement of the standards and ethics by the AICPA is referred to as **self-regulation.**

Self-Regulation and the Expectations Gap

For self-regulation to prevail, users must perceive a level of quality of services rendered by CPAs that equals their expectations. A disparity between users' and CPAs' perceptions of CPA services, especially regarding the attest function, is referred to as the **expectations gap.** (See Figure 2.3)

TABLE 2.1   Means of Enforcing Standards

AICPA TRIAL BOARD

Admonish members who have violated standards or rules

Suspend or expel from membership

Develop quality control standards through the Quality Control Standards Committee

STATE BOARDS OF ACCOUNTANCY

Suspend or revoke certificate

Suspend or revoke license

Impose continuing professional education requirements

SEC OFFICE OF THE CHIEF ACCOUNTANT

Investigate audit failures

Monitor peer review

Review changes in auditors

---

[25]*The Journal of Accountancy,* October, 1990.

FIGURE 2.3 The Expectations Gap

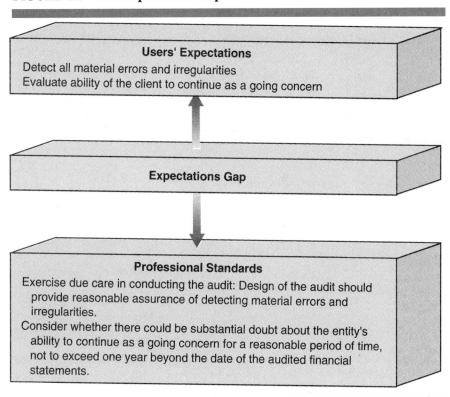

The independent auditor's responsibility for detecting fraud is one of the major areas contributing to the expectations gap relating to auditing. Most financial statement users believe that an unqualified audit opinion means that the auditor has detected all material errors and/or irregularities that may have occurred during the period under audit. Statements on auditing standards, however, are at variance with this view, and hold the auditor responsible only for exercising due care in the conduct of the examination.[26] Management override of the control structure and other forms of management misrepresentation may occur and be so cleverly concealed that the exercise of due audit care fails to detect the financial statement errors produced by such means.

Such recent cases as Lincoln Savings, Crazy Eddie, and Miniscribe, all involving significant financial statement misrepresentations not detected by the independent auditors, have tended to widen the expectations gap.

Another area of differing perceptions of auditor responsibility concerns the ability of a company to continue as a going concern. Most users believe that an unqualified audit opinion provides the company with a "clean bill of health." When the company later files for bankruptcy or otherwise gets into financial difficulty, users question why the auditors did not detect such conditions and cover them in the

---

[26] *AICPA Professional Standards, op. cit.*, Section AU 316.01-08.

Auditors must meet and abide by the generally accepted auditing standards, which set a required level of quality for the profession.

audit report. Until recently, however, the professional standards did not require the auditor to search for evidential matter relating to the entity's continued existence and otherwise report on "financial health." In an effort to narrow the expectations gap in this area, the AICPA recently adopted an SAS relating to continuation. Specifically, the SAS requires the auditor to consider whether the results of the audit indicate that substantial doubt exists as to the entity's ability to continue as a going concern for a period not to exceed one year. If such doubt does exist, an explanatory paragraph must be added following the opinion paragraph of the audit report.[27]

The appointment of audit committees by most public companies has also helped to narrow the expectations gap by providing the auditor with a means for resolving disputes with management. An audit committee is a committee of the board of directors consisting mainly of outside directors—those not having management positions in the company—thus helping to assure independence from management. Among other duties, the audit committee is responsible for overseeing the internal control structure and arbitrating disagreements between the auditors and management. Such disagreements usually concern accounting measurement or disclosure issues that could result in a qualified audit opinion or a change in auditors if not resolved.

Recent changes in the Institute's bylaws have also been made in an effort to reduce the number of so-called audit failures, and to further narrow the expectations gap. Members of the AICPA must enroll in an Institute-approved practice moni-

---

[27]*Ibid.*, Section AU 341.

toring program. A division has been established to conduct the quality review program for the AICPA, and to conduct reviews of firms enrolled in the program.[28] Another change in the Institute's bylaws requires members to complete continuing professional education requirements as established by Council.[29] In addition, persons applying for AICPA membership after the year 2000 must have completed a five-year accountancy program.[30]

Efforts such as these taken by the AICPA recognize the increasing risk of public regulation of the profession if the expectations gap is permitted to widen further. Public regulation is usually thought of as a decline in the governing power of the AICPA and assumption of regulatory authority by the SEC or some other agency established by Congress.

The following paragraphs discuss other means employed by the Institute in its efforts to maintain the quality of professional services rendered by CPAs. The impact of the Securities and Exchange Commission, Congress, and the courts on quality control are also considered.

The AICPA, the State Boards of Accountancy, and Quality Maintenance

Provision is made in the bylaws of the AICPA for disciplining members who are found by the Trial Board to be in violation of the Rules of Conduct of the Code of Professional Conduct. Such disciplinary action may take the form of admonishment, suspension, or expulsion from membership within the Institute. Given the broad coverage of Rule 202 of the Code, virtually all forms of auditing, accounting, and consulting services rendered by CPAs fall within this regulatory mechanism; departures from any of the respective standards exposes the CPA to the threat of a hearing before the Trial Board and the possibility of such disciplinary action.

The CPA is also subject to the requirements of the board of accountancy of the state in which he or she is licensed to practice. Such regulatory powers are most critical to the CPA in that the legal right to practice as a CPA is obtained by a license granted by the state board. In order to retain and periodically renew this license, the CPA must abide by the state laws which govern the practice of accountancy.

In addition to the newly-enacted AICPA continuing education requirement, many of the states have also prescribed continuing professional education requirements. The purpose of the continuing education requirements is to encourage CPAs to keep abreast of changes occurring within the profession, and to provide the best possible service to their clients.

Violations of the state licensing statutes are subject to varying degrees of disciplinary action, including suspension or revocation of the CPA certificate, and/or suspension or revocation of the CPA's license to practice.

---

[28]*Code of Professional Conduct,* Bylaws of the American Institute of Certified Public Accountants, Section 2.2.3.

[29]*Ibid.,* Section 2.3.3.

[30]*Ibid.,* Section 2.2.4.

Division for CPA Firms

In 1977, the AICPA created the **Division for CPA Firms** for the purpose of promoting quality and consistency in the rendering of professional services. The Division is comprised of two sections: the SEC Practice Section and the Private Companies Practice Section. Firms with clients who are subject to SEC filing requirements enroll in the **SEC Practice Section,** while those with only non-SEC clients seek membership in the **Private Companies Practice Section.** Although membership in the Private Practice Section is voluntary, CPA firms with public clients must enroll in the SEC Practice Section. The conditions for membership in both sections include agreement to participate in peer review, conform to specified continuing professional education requirements, and to maintain adequate levels of liability insurance.

Peer reviews are to be performed every three years. Such reviews are conducted by other CPAs who are members of the Division. The review consists mainly of examining the documentation supporting audits and other accounting services rendered by the firm being reviewed. Whether a CPA is performing an audit or rendering other professional services, all work must be fully documented. Documentation, in the form of appropriately indexed workpapers, is the only evidence of the CPA's adherence to professional standards. In cases involving alleged negligence, these workpapers may be the CPA's principal defense.[31]

The continuing professional education requirement consists of 120 hours of credit every three years. Division members practicing in states lacking mandatory continuing professional education for licensing purposes are still required to undertake formal professional development to maintain membership in the Division.

The SEC Practice Section is supervised by the **Public Oversight Board** (POB) of the AICPA. The majority of POB members are not accountants. The Board may recommend that the executive committee of the Section impose sanctions for failure to maintain compliance with membership requirements. Such sanctions assume the forms of corrective measures to be implemented by the firm in violation, required continuing professional education, special peer review, and suspension and/or expulsion from membership in the Section.

Securities and Exchange Commission (SEC)

The SEC possesses broad authority over the accounting profession in terms of the power to set accounting and auditing standards and the authority to take disciplinary action where requirements are violated. The SEC derives its authority from the 1933 Securities Act and the 1934 Securities and Exchange Act. These acts require that the securities of most publicly held companies be registered with the Commission, and that the financial statements accompanying the registration statement be audited by independent CPAs.

The **Chief Accountant of the SEC** conducts investigations of alleged audit failures and is empowered to impose sanctions as considered necessary. These sanctions typically take the form of temporarily prohibiting the CPA from accepting

---

[31]Audit workpapers are discussed and illustrated in Chapter 4.

new SEC clients (usually for six months to one year). Required special peer review or continuing professional education or both may also be invoked by the Chief Accountant as disciplinary measures.

In addition to the investigative and disciplinary powers just described, the Chief Accountant also has the authority to monitor the activities of the Financial Accounting Standards Board and the Auditing Standards Board, as well as the peer review program of the SEC Practice Section of the Division for CPA Firms.

The SEC must be notified when a company changes auditors. Such notification must include the reason for the change and any disagreements with the former auditors in the previous two years. In addition, the former auditors must submit a response letter, either agreeing or disagreeing with the company's version of why the change occurred, and past disagreements. In addition, SAS 7 requires that the new auditor attempt to communicate with the former auditor. Referred to as **communication with predecessor auditor,** such communication may be instituted only with the prospective client's permission. Discussions with the predecessor auditor would, among other matters, include the reason for the change in auditors, any major disagreements between the former auditors and the management of the client firm, integrity of management, and any other factors having a significant impact on audit risk.[32]

Although the SEC is given broad regulatory authority under the securities laws, the Commission has opted to permit the profession to regulate itself through the various means described earlier. Such self-regulation efforts of the profession, however, are under continuous review by the SEC. For this reason, the threat of public regulation exists and will continue to exist as long as questions arise concerning the ability of the accounting profession to regulate itself. Chapter 3 describes more fully the SEC's impact on the auditing profession.

AICPA Quality Control Standards Committee

AICPA professional standards require firms to install and implement quality control systems. Failure to do so constitutes a violation of GAAS.[33] A system of quality control is defined as " . . . the policies adopted and procedures established to provide the firm with reasonable assurance of conforming with professional standards."[34] Moreover, as described earlier, the bylaws of the Institute require members to be enrolled in practice monitoring programs. Firms, therefore, need to establish quality control policies and procedures which will provide reasonable assurance of conformance with generally accepted auditing standards (GAAS). These policies and procedures should also apply to other accounting and review services for which professional standards have been established.

In 1979, Statement of Quality Control Standards No. 1 (SQCS-1), *System of Quality Control for a CPA Firm,* was issued by the AICPA Quality Control Standards Committee. The Statement provides quality control guidelines relating to specific areas. These guidelines and areas are set forth in Table 2.2.

---

[32]*AICPA Professional Standards, op. cit.,* Section AU 315.03-07.

[33]*Ibid.,* Section QC 10.02.

[34]*Ibid.,* Section QC 10.03.

TABLE 2.2   Quality Control Guidelines

1. *Independence* to insure that objectivity will be maintained in performing audit and other attest engagements;

2. *Assignment of personnel* such that engagements will be completed by persons having the necessary technical competence;

3. *Consultation* with appropriate specialists and experts as necessary;

4. *Supervision* at all levels to assure that work performed meets appropriate firm quality standards;

5. *Hiring* practices that provide reasonable assurance of employing individuals who will perform competently;

6. *Professional development* policies to keep personnel abreast of changes affecting the profession;

7. *Advancement and promotion* of firm personnel to provide reasonable assurance that positions within the firm will be occupied by competent persons;

8. *Acceptance and continuance* of clients to minimize the likelihood of association with clients whose managements lack integrity;

9. *Inspection* policies to assure that the procedures relating to other elements of quality control are being effectively applied.

Source: *AICPA Professional Standards,* 1991, Section QC 10.07.

Accounting firms use various means in conforming to these guidelines. In helping to ensure independence, for example, the firm might elect to distribute a list of clients and have staff members sign a statement of independence. Advance planning can help in assigning qualified personnel to engagements. Most firms designate specific persons as experts in areas such as auditing, taxation, and management advisory services. This provides a mechanism for obtaining answers to technical questions that arise during engagements. Requiring all workpapers to be reviewed by supervisory or technical personnel supports the supervision guideline. Providing minimum qualifications for hiring of personnel, establishing continuing education requirements, and evaluating the performance of staff members help to ensure quality maintenance in hiring, development, and promotion of personnel within the firm.

To ensure that the firm does not associate with clients whose managements lack integrity, present clients should be reviewed for continuance and prospective clients should be reviewed for acceptance. In reviewing prospective clients for acceptance, the auditor may make inquiries of predecessor auditors, bankers, attorneys, and other business associates.

The pronouncements of the Quality Control Standards Committee are not a part of the official pronouncements of the Auditing Standards Board; nor are they covered under Rule 202 of the Code of Conduct. They must be followed, however, by members of the Division for CPA Firms, and they are recommended by the AICPA for voluntary adoption by of all CPA firms.

The Courts

In addition to the quality maintenance means described in the preceding paragraphs, the courts have also played an important role in maintaining the quality of auditing and other services performed by CPAs. This role is addressed in Chapter 3.

KEY TERMS

Attestation standards
Auditor independence
Chief Accountant of the SEC
Communication with predecessor auditor
Consulting services
Code of Professional Conduct
Continuing professional education
Division for CPA Firms
Due audit care
Expectations gap
Field work standards
General standards
Generally Accepted Auditing Standards (GAAS)
Independence in fact vs. appearance
Peer review
Planning and supervision

Private Companies Practice Section
Public Oversight Board
Quality control
Reporting standards
Rules of conduct
SEC Practice Section
Self-regulation
Statements on Auditing Standards (SASs)
Statements on Responsibilities in Tax Practice (TX)
Statements on Standards for Accounting and Review Services
Statements on Standards for Consulting Services
Test-based audit
Treadway report
Training and proficiency as an auditor

REVIEW QUESTIONS

1. How does the audit function enhance the quality of the financial statements?
2. Describe the framework which defines the quality of independent auditing.
3. Differentiate between auditing standards and auditing procedures.
4. List and briefly describe each of the ten Generally Accepted Auditing Standards.
5. What is meant by "due audit care"?
6. The ten Generally Accepted Auditing Standards, along with the related Statements on Auditing Standards, must be adhered to in the conduct of an audit. The Code of Professional Conduct, however, is applicable to all services rendered by CPAs. Explain why.
7. Distinguish between independence "in fact" and "in appearance."
8. Why is independence not so critical in rendering tax and management consulting services as in the performance of an audit?
9. The attestation standards serve a different purpose than the auditing standards. Explain.
10. Explain the significance of Rule 202 — Compliance with Standards of the Code of Conduct.

11. Rule 203 makes the accounting principles binding upon the auditor in the same manner as Rule 202 requires adherence to the auditing standards. Explain how.

12. How do Rules 202 and 203 impact Rule 301 — Confidential Client Information?

13. What purpose is served by the Statements on Standards for Accounting and Review Services?

14. In what way do the Statements on Responsibilities in Tax Practice differ from the SASs, SSARSs, and SSCSs?

15. How does the so-called "expectations gap" relate to quality control?

16. How does the Division for CPA Firms promote quality control?

17. Describe the function of the Public Oversight Board.

18. What role does the SEC play in the maintenance of quality in auditing?

19. What are the duties of the Chief Accountant of the SEC relative to independent audits?

20. Describe the role of the AICPA Quality Control Standards Committee. What authority do their pronouncements have?

MULTIPLE CHOICE QUESTIONS FROM CPA EXAMINATIONS

1. Which of the following statements best describes the primary purpose of Statements on Auditing Standards?
   a. They are guides intended to set forth auditing procedures which are applicable to a variety of situations.
   b. They are procedural outlines which are intended to narrow the areas of inconsistency and divergence of auditor opinion.
   c. They are authoritative statements, enforced through the code of professional ethics, and are intended to limit the degree of auditor judgment.
   d. They are interpretations which are intended to clarify the meaning of "generally accepted auditing standards."

2. The AICPA Code of Professional Conduct recognizes that the reliance of the public, the government, and the business community on sound financial reporting imposes particular obligations on CPAs. The code derives its authority from
   a. Public laws enacted over the years.
   b. General acceptance of the code by the business community.
   c. Requirements of governmental regulatory agencies such as the Securities and Exchange Commission.
   d. Bylaws of the American Institute of Certified Public Accountants.

3. A CPA, while performing an audit, strives to achieve independence in appearance in order to
   a. Reduce risk and liability.
   b. Become independent in fact.
   c. Maintain public confidence in the profession.
   d. Comply with the generally accepted standards of field work.

4. The AICPA Code of Professional Conduct states that a CPA shall not disclose any confidential information obtained in the course of a professional engagement except

with the consent of the client. This rule should be understood to preclude a CPA from responding to an inquiry made by

   a. An investigative body of a state CPA society.

   b. The trial board of the AICPA.

   c. A CPA-shareholder of the client corporation.

   d. An AICPA voluntary quality review body.

5. Which of the following should an auditor obtain from the predecessor auditor prior to accepting an audit engagement?

   a. Analysis of balance sheet accounts.

   b. Analysis of income statement accounts.

   c. All matters of continuing accounting significance.

   d. Facts that might bear on the integrity of management.

6. The least important evidence of a CPA firm's evaluation of its system of quality controls would concern the CPA firm's policies and procedures with respect to

   a. Employment (hiring).

   b. Confidentiality of audit engagements.

   c. Assigning personnel to audit engagements.

   d. Determination of audit fees.

7. Williams & Co., a large international CPA firm, is to have an "external peer review." The peer review will most likely be performed by

   a. Employees and partners of Williams & Co. who are not associated with the particular audits being reviewed.

   b. Audit review staff of the Securities and Exchange Commission.

   c. Audit review staff of the American Institute of Certified Public Accountants.

   d. Employees and partners of another CPA firm.

8. An audit independence issue might be raised by the auditor's participation in management consulting services engagements. Which of the following statements is most consistent with the profession's attitude toward this issue?

   a. Information obtained as a result of a management consulting services engagement is confidential to that specific engagement and should not influence performance of the attest function.

   b. The decision as to loss of independence must be made by the client based upon the facts of the particular case.

   c. The auditor should not make management decisions for an audit client.

   d. The auditor who is asked to review management decisions is also competent to make these decisions and can do so without loss of independence.

9. Which one of the following is not a pronouncement of an authoritative body designated by the AICPA Council to establish accounting principles, pursuant to the AICPA Code of Professional Conduct?

   a. AICPA Statements of Position.

   b. AICPA Accounting Principles Board Opinions.

   c. FASB Interpretations.

   d. FASB Statements of Financial Accounting Standards

10. The exercise of due professional care requires that an auditor

   a. Examine all available corroborating evidence.

   b. Critically review the judgment exercised at every level of supervision.

   c. Reduce control risk below the maximum.

   d. Attain the proper balance of professional experience and formal education.

11. Which of the following is the authoritative body designated to promulgate attestation standards?

   a. Auditing Standards Board.

   b. Governmental Accounting Standards Board.

   c. Financial Accounting Standards Board.

   d. General Accounting Office.

12. A CPA firm evaluates its personnel advancement experience to ascertain whether individuals meeting stated criteria are assigned increased degrees of responsibility. This is evidence of the firm's adherence to which of the following prescribed standards?

   a. Quality control.

   b. Human resources.

   c. Supervision and review.

   d. Professional development.

13. A CPA firm should establish procedures for conducting and supervising work at all organizational levels to provide reasonable assurance that the work performed meets the firm's standards of quality. To achieve this goal, the firm most likely would establish procedures for

   a. Evaluating prospective and continuing client relationships.

   b. Reviewing engagement working papers and reports.

   c. Requiring personnel to adhere to the applicable independence rules.

   d. Maintaining personnel files containing documentation related to the evaluation of personnel.

14. The authoritative body designated to promulgate standards concerning an accountant's association with unaudited financial statements of an entity that is *not* required to file financial statements with an agency regulating the issuance of the entity's securities is the

   a. Financial Accounting Standards Board.

   b. General Accounting Office.

   c. Accounting and Review Services Committee.

   d. Auditing Standards Board.

15. On completing an audit, Larkin, CPA, was asked by the client to provide technical assistance in the implementation of a new EDP system. The set of pronouncements designed to guide Larkin in this engagement is the Statements on

   a. Auditing Standards.

   b. Standards for Consulting Services.

   c. Quality Control Standards.

   d. Standards for Accountants' EDP Services.

16. A CPA owes a duty to

   a. Provide for a successor CPA in the event death or disability prevents completion of an audit.

   b. Advise a client of errors contained in a previously filed tax return.

   c. Disclose client fraud to third parties.

   d. Perform an audit according to GAAP so that fraud will be uncovered.

ESSAY QUESTIONS AND PROBLEMS

2.1 Daniels and Joel, CPAs, assigned Laura Peterson, a newly promoted senior staff person, as auditor in charge of the initial examination of Newell, Inc., a small construction firm. As the audit progressed, Peterson discovered some rather complex contracts accounted for on a percentage of completion basis. Although she wasn't sure whether the profits should have been recognized in this manner, the controller of Newell assured her that these contracts did indeed constitute sales and that the profits had been properly booked in accordance with GAAP. Peterson accepted the controller's assurances with some reluctance and an unqualified audit opinion accompanied the financial statements of Newell, Inc. Shortly thereafter, Newell filed for bankruptcy and Daniels and Joel were sued for negligence by the minority stockholders. The contracts that had concerned Peterson were, in reality, sale and leaseback transactions, followed by subleasing and extensive discounting of notes with banks and factors. Title to most of the properties resulting from the projects had remained with Newell and the profits, therefore, should not have been recognized. When asked by Mr. Daniels why she had not detected the fictitious nature of the profits, Peterson replied that, due to the level of complexity involved, she simply did not understand the economic substance of the transactions in question.

Required:
   a. Identify any standards and ethics which, in your opinion, have been violated in this case. Explain why you feel the standard or rule in question had not been observed.
   b. What should Peterson have done after examining the contracts?
   c. What should the audit manager (Peterson's supervisor in this instance) have done upon examining Laura's workpaper supporting the contracts?

2.2 Ray, the owner of a small company, asked Holmes, a CPA, to conduct an audit of the company's records. Ray told Holmes that an audit was to be completed in time to submit audited financial statements to a bank as part of a loan application. Holmes immediately accepted the engagement and agreed to provide an auditor's report within three weeks. Ray agreed to pay Holmes a fixed fee plus a bonus if the loan was granted.

   Holmes hired two accounting students to conduct the audit and spent several hours telling them exactly what to do. Holmes told the students not to spend time reviewing the controls, but instead, to concentrate on proving the mathematical accuracy of the ledger accounts and summarizing the data in the accounting records that support Ray's financial statements. The students followed Holmes' instructions and after two weeks gave Holmes the financial statements which did not include footnotes. Holmes reviewed the statements and prepared an unqualified auditor's report. The report, however, did not refer to generally accepted accounting principles.

Required:
Briefly describe each of the generally accepted auditing standards and indicate how the action(s) of Holmes resulted in a failure to comply with each standard.
   Organize your answer as follows:

Brief description of   Holmes' actions resulting in
Generally Accepted   failure to comply with Generally
Accepted Auditing Standards   Accepted Auditing Standards

(AICPA adapted)

2.3 Savage, CPA, has been requested by an audit client to perform a non-recurring engagement involving the implementation of an EDP information and control system. The client requests that in setting up the new system and during the period prior to conversion to the new system, that Savage

a. counsel on potential expansion of business activity plans.
b. search for and interview new personnel.
c. hire new personnel.
d. train personnel.

In addition, the client requests that during the three months subsequent to the conversion, Savage

a. supervise the operation of the new system.
b. Monitor client-prepared source documents and make changes in basic EDP generated data as Savage may deem necessary without concurrence of the client.

Savage responds that he may perform some of the services requested, but not all of them.

Required:
Which of these services may Savage perform and which of these services may Savage not perform? Explain. (AICPA adapted)

2.4 For each of the following situations, indicate whether or not auditor independence has been impaired. Explain your reasoning in each case.

a. During the course of the examination, the auditor discovers a major defalcation and brings it to the attention of the client. Detection by the auditor brings the thefts to a halt and results in substantial savings to the client. As a reward, the client offers to send the auditor and his family to Bermuda on an all-expense-paid vacation.
b. After retiring from the CPA firm, John Lawson, former senior partner, accepts an appointment to the board of directors of Little, Inc., the largest of his former firm's audit clients. In addition, Mr. Lawson, as recognition for his years of service, is granted an office in the firm's suite and the right to receive calls through the firm's switchboard. He is also retained by the firm as a paid consultant.
c. Joseph Norton, CPA, audits the financial statements of Orga, Inc., a local wholesale distributor of heating and air conditioning equipment. Norton's brother-in-law (his wife's brother) is the vice-president and sales manager of Orga. Norton's brother-in-law also owns stock in the company.
d. Jones and Farland, CPAs, have financed the purchase of the building housing their firm's offices by issuing a first mortgage to First Farmers' Savings Association, an audit client.

2.5 In examining the financial statements of Falls Manor, Inc., a major leasing company, the auditor discovers that gross profits, recognized from certain sales-type leases, include contingent rentals yet to be realized. The controller, upon inquiry, explains that the lessees in question have consistently earned adequate revenues to more than cover the contingent rentals included in the "gross lease payments receivable" account. Further, he asserts that not to include the contingent rentals in the sales price would make the financial statements materially misleading.

Required:
a. Under what circumstances may an auditor agree to a departure from a principle "promulgated by the body designated by Council?"
b. Assuming that you are the auditor in this case, how would you respond to the controller's assertion?
c. If you agree to the company's accounting treatment, what effect would this have on your audit report? What effect would it have if you do not agree?

2.6 Three weeks after the audit report has been released to the stockholders, James Jones, CPA and auditor of Client, Inc., learns that Client, Inc. has engaged in certain related party transactions that may be in violation of the law. These transactions are not clearly disclosed in the recently released financial statements. Moreover, based on the newly discovered information, Jones concludes that the reported profits of Client, Inc. are materially overstated by the inclusion of such transactions.

Jones decides to approach the client and request that the stockholders be notified that the financial statements and audit report are no longer to be relied upon, and that revised financial statements and audit report will be forthcoming. The client refuses to comply on the grounds that the financial statements are fairly presented in all material respects. Jones is told by the president of Client, Inc. that the transactions are not illegal and that the parties are not directly related. Moreover, he informs Jones that any information concerning such transactions, conveyed by Jones to the stockholders, will be considered a violation of auditor-client confidentiality.

Required:
a. Discuss the requirements of Rule 301 dealing with confidential client information.
b. If you were Jones, what would you do in this case? Explain why you would assume the position which you have elected.

2.7 In 1977, the AICPA created the Division for CPA Firms for the purpose of promoting quality and consistency in rendering professional services. The Division is comprised of two sections.

Required:
a. Identify and describe the two sections comprising the Division.
b. How is the quality of service enhanced through such a mechanism?
c. What is the function of the Public Oversight Board and how does its role promote quality of professional services?

2.8 The Securities and Exchange Commission possesses broad authority over the accounting profession, in terms of the power to set accounting and auditing standards and the authority to take disciplinary action where requirements are violated.

Required:

a. Where does the SEC derive such authority?

b. To what extent has the SEC exercised its authority?

c. Through what means does the SEC monitor the accounting profession's efforts at "self-regulation?"

d. Discuss the role of the Chief Accountant of the SEC as it affects the accounting profession.

2.9 Statements on Auditing Standards No. 25 requires accounting firms to establish quality control policies and procedures. To assist the firms in this endeavor, the AICPA Quality Control Standards Committee was established.

Required:

a. What authority do the pronouncements of the Quality Control Standards Committee have with respect to the CPA?

b. Discuss the purpose of Statement on Quality Control Standards No. 1. Briefly describe its contents.

c. What are the implications to an accounting firm for failure to establish quality control policies?

2.10 Match the following terms with their definitions:

a. Chief Accountant of the SEC

b. Division for CPA Firms

c. Due audit care

d. Expectations gap

e. Field work standards

f. Peer review

g. Reporting standards

h. SEC Practice Section

i. General standards

j. Rules of conduct

   1. Monitors the activities of the accounting profession
   2. Relate to the attest function
   3. The process whereby one accountant or firm reviews the work of another accountant or firm
   4. The major parts of the Code of Professional Conduct
   5. The auditor must perform the examination at a reasonable level of skill and with a reasonable degree of care
   6. That part of the Division of CPA Firms consisting of firms with SEC clients
   7. The disparity between auditor and user perceptions of the role of the independent audit
   8. A body, consisting of two sections, established by the AICPA for the purpose of promoting self-regulation
   9. Relate to the character and competence of the auditor
   10. Relate to the audit process

2.11 You are a newly hired assistant auditor in the firm of Stumble & Fall, CPAs. On your first audit you have been assigned to the sales and accounts receivable transaction cycle. Two matters trouble you about your assignment:

a. The audit program calls for examining accounts receivable at an interim date instead of at year end. Based upon what you learned in your auditing course, you think this is improper and you so inform the in-charge senior auditor. She tells you to follow the audit program as written.

b. The engagement time budget allows six hours for the examination of documentation for 200 sales transactions. Despite working as fast as you can, you have completed only 45 in five hours. Given your previous encounter with the in-charge auditor, you do not want to bother her again. You are considering the following alternative courses of action:

    1. Completion of the remaining transactions as called for in the audit program, regardless of the time involved;

    2. Completion of as many sales transactions as you can in the six hours allowed;

    3. Examination of all 200 sales transactions but in much less detail than followed to date;

    4. Coming in on Saturday (without pay) to complete the assigned work.

You know that audit efficiency is valued highly in your firm and you don't want to look bad in comparison to the assistant who did the work last year.

Required:
Discuss the proper course of action to take in the present situation. Refer to the Code of Conduct as appropriate.

2.12 You have two clients, Hickory and Dickory. Hickory is considering a monetary advance to Dickory as part of a long-term contractual arrangement. It is not public knowledge, but you know that Dickory is in very "shaky" financial condition. While the advance and long-term contract would be very good for Dickory and might save that company, you think that this undertaking would be a big mistake for Hickory, given the risks involved. You wonder whether you should inform Hickory of the potential danger.

Required:
Should you inform Hickory? Justify your answer by referring to the appropriate section(s) of the Code of Conduct.

2.13 As an independent auditor, one often becomes aware of matters not known by the general public. For example, the following two situations have recently arisen:

a. The assistant controller of Client A has told you that he would like to change jobs. You know that Client B wishes to replace its controller and has asked your firm to make recommendations. This would be a good promotion for the assistant controller and you think he would be capable. However, you are concerned about fairness to Client A if you inform the assistant controller of the Client B job, particularly since the job is not known to the general public.

b. The controller of Client C thinks he is underpaid. Based on what you know from similar clients, he is. He has asked you, as a friend, to tell him what you think a fair salary would be.

Required:
For each of the above situations, identify the course of action that you believe is appropriate relative to the Code of Conduct. Cite appropriate principles, rules, and interpretations to support your position.

2.14 Steve Julian of Harpers and Ferry, CPAs, is the in-charge senior auditor for the Ralph's Wholesale Appliances audit and has been associated with this audit as assistant auditor and then in-charge senior for five years. This is his third year as in-charge senior on the audit. Julian is an outgoing individual and is very popular among the employees and management of Ralph's. Moreover, he is a very competent auditor and, by offering suggestions from time to time, has helped the client improve its control structure significantly over his years of participation on the audit. In appreciation for Julian's contributions to Ralph's and in celebration of Julian's approaching marriage, Stan Schroeder, Ralph's president, presents him with an expensive entertainment center taken from the inventory of the company. Before accepting the gift, Julian decided to consult with Marjory Helfing, the Harpers and Ferry partner responsible for the Ralph's Wholesale Appliances audit.

Required:

May Julian accept the gift? Support your response by reference to rules and interpretations of the *Code*.

2.15 John Hinton, CPA, has several small clients for whom he provides bookkeeping services. The clients submit source documents to Hinton for processing on Hinton's computer. The source documents consist of sales invoices, vendors' invoices, payroll time cards, check stubs, and remittance advices. Hinton's staff enter the documents into the computer where they are recorded and the results stored for monthly printout of journals, ledgers, payroll summaries, earnings records, and financial statements. Hinton also prepares various federal, state, and local tax returns for the clients, such as sales tax returns, payroll tax returns, and federal, state, and local income tax returns.

Hedley Jewlers, one of the clients, has applied to the bank for a long-term loan and the bank has requested audited financial statements. Hedley requests Hinton to perform the audit.

Required:

May Hinton perform the audit, given that he renders bookkeeping services to Hedley? Support your answer by reference to appropriate rules, interpretations, and/or ethics rulings pertaining to the Code of Professional Conduct.

2.16 Paul Olscamp, CPA, is a partner in the firm of Olscamp, Nelson, and Biddle, CPAs. Although most of the firm's clients are nonaudit, involving such services as compilation and review, management consulting, and tax advice and return preparation, a few audits are performed. During an annual fund-raising event eliciting the participation of business and professional persons from various sectors, Olscamp was asked by the president of one of the local banks if his firm would be interested in conducting the annual audit of the bank. None of the firm's present audit clients are banks or other kinds of financial intermediaries. Olscamp does recall, however, when he was working for a "Big Six" accounting firm several years ago (before striking out on his own), participating as a senior auditor on a savings and loan bank audit. Moreover, his firm has an extensive library of research materials that Olscamp might consult in preparing for such an engagement. If the firm accepts the engagement, the interim work will need to begin within the next month or two.

Required:

Will Olscamp violate the Code of Professional Conduct or the auditing standards by accepting the engagement? Be specific in referring to parts of the Code and auditing standards to support your position.

3

Auditors' Legal Liability

CHAPTER OUTLINE

I. **Types of liability**
A. Ordinary negligence vs. gross negligence
B. Gross negligence vs. fraud—intent

II. **Sources of liability**
A. Common law
B. Statutory law
C. Racketeer Influenced and Corrupt Organizations Act (RICO)

III. **Liability for unaudited statements**
A. Exercise of due care
B. Adherence to compilation and/or review standards and attestation standards
C. Engagement letter to define services

IV. **Prevention of legal actions**
A. Allocation of resources to high audit risk areas
B. Insistence on proper treatment of discovered errors
C. Utilization of audit committee
D. Supervision of assistants' work
E. Independence from time pressures
F. Communication with predecessor auditors
G. Review of clients for acceptance

V. **Dealing with liability**
A. Adequate documentation
B. Adequate liability insurance

VI. **Appendix: Legal cases involving auditors**

OVERVIEW

This chapter defines and illustrates various aspects of legal liability confronting auditors. The chapter begins by identifying and discussing *types* of liability. This is followed by a similar consideration of *sources* of auditor liability. The relationship between types and sources of liability is then addressed and finally summarized in the form of a relational exhibit (Table 3.1). Key cases are used to clarify the nature of auditor liability.

Following consideration of auditor liability, the CPA's liability for unaudited statements is described and illustrated. The 1136 Tenants case is used as a focal point for the discussion.

The chapter concludes by enumerating means for preventing legal actions and for dealing with liability as it confronts the CPA. Risk analysis and the exercise of due audit care are the most effective preventatives. Adequate audit documentation, on the other hand, is the best defense in the event of legal action against the CPA.

STUDY OBJECTIVES

After reading this chapter, you should be able to:

1. Identify and define the sources and types of auditor liability and relate them one to another;

2. Describe the key cases illustrating specific sources and types of auditor liability; and

3. Develop a plan for preventing legal actions, and dealing with liability that does arise.

INTRODUCTION

In addition to the AICPA, the SEC, and the various state boards of accountancy, the courts have also played a role in maintaining the quality of auditing. This role begins when clients or third parties sue auditors for negligence or fraud. During the proceedings, lawyers and judges often consider the meaning of such auditing and accounting concepts as "due care," "present fairly," "related parties," "GAAP," "independence," "internal control," and "sufficiency and competence of evidence." These deliberations result in conclusions which are either in agreement or at variance with existing pronouncements (SASs and SFASs). If the court's findings do not agree, the Auditing Standards Board or the Financial Accounting Standards Board may wish to reconsider the matters dealt with by the court. The result may be a new SAS or SFAS or a reaffirmation of existing pronouncements. In the Continental Vending Machine Corporation case, for example (see appendix following this chapter), the judge instructed the jury to look beyond GAAP, if necessary, in determining whether the financial statements were fairly presented.[1] Auditors had heretofore been accustomed to using GAAP as the framework within which to evaluate fairness. SAS 5, "The Meaning of Present Fairly in Conformity with Generally Accepted Accounting Principles in the Independent Auditor's Report," issued as a result of this case, reaffirmed GAAP as the appropriate framework for judging fairness.

Clients may sue their auditors for failing to detect employee fraud. Stockholders and creditors may sue because they relied on audited financial statements that contained material errors and were injured by such reliance.

This chapter defines the sources and types of auditor liability, presenting actual cases to illustrate some of the more common causes for legal actions against auditors. The chapter concludes by suggesting ways of preventing and dealing with legal actions. An appendix, identifying and discussing the more significant auditor liability cases, follows the chapter.

Types of Liability

Auditors may be found guilty of ordinary negligence, gross negligence, or fraud in actions relating to the examination of financial statements. **Ordinary negligence** actions allege that the auditor failed to exercise *reasonable care*. **Gross negligence** means that the auditor failed to exercise *minimum care*. **Fraud** actions allege *intent to deceive,* and accuse the auditor of complicity in misrepresenting financial position and/or results of operations. Figure 3.1 is a diagrammatic representation of auditor liability.

Ordinary Negligence vs. Gross Negligence

Ordinary negligence, failure to exercise reasonable care, occurs when an auditor fails to detect an error or irregularity that application of generally accepted auditing standards may or may not have uncovered. *Gross negligence,* failure to exercise minimum care, occurs when material errors or irregularities that should have been

---

[1]*U.S. v. Simon et al.,* 425 F. 2d 796 (2d Cir. 1969).

FIGURE 3.1   Types of Auditor Liability

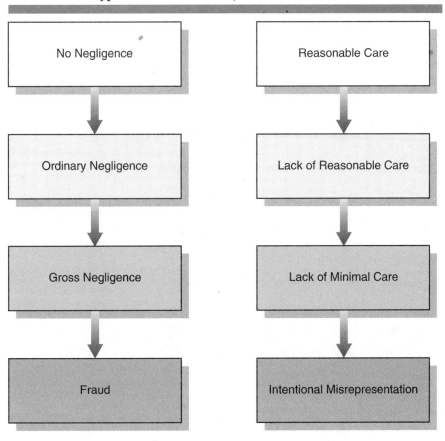

detected by the application of GAAS go undetected. Two concepts are helpful in differentiating between auditor liability for ordinary and gross negligence— *materiality* and *internal control*.

The more material the error, the greater the likelihood of detection by the auditor. The application of standard auditing procedures (as described in subsequent chapters), for example, should alert the auditor to material amounts of fictitious sales recorded by the client at year end to inflate earnings. Failure to detect this type of intentional misstatement, referred to as *management misrepresentation fraud*, might be interpreted as gross negligence in a legal action brought against the auditor.

A similar misstatement of earnings might be effected by understating several expense accounts, each by a small amount. Assume that none of the misstatements is material by itself, but the aggregate effect on income is material. The application of standard audit procedures, in this instance, is not likely to disclose unusual abnormalities. The probability of detection by the auditor, therefore, is much less. Under these circumstances, failure to detect may be construed by the courts as ordinary negligence, given the material aggregate effect on income, but not gross negligence.

Internal accounting control, as it relates to auditing, is also helpful in distinguishing between ordinary and gross negligence. As defined in Chapter 1, internal accounting control is that part of the information system designed to enhance the reliability of financial records and safeguard assets. Errors may occur within the system due to control weaknesses. Under generally accepted auditing standards, material control weaknesses should be identified by the auditor and tests of transactions and balances should be extended in those areas. Thus, one might expect the auditor to detect significant financial statement errors that occur because of major control weaknesses.

Errors may also result from conditions existing outside the control structure through such means as collusion (employees working together to circumvent the structure) and management override of the control structure (see Figure 3.2). These

FIGURE 3.2   Auditor Liability as Related to Internal Control

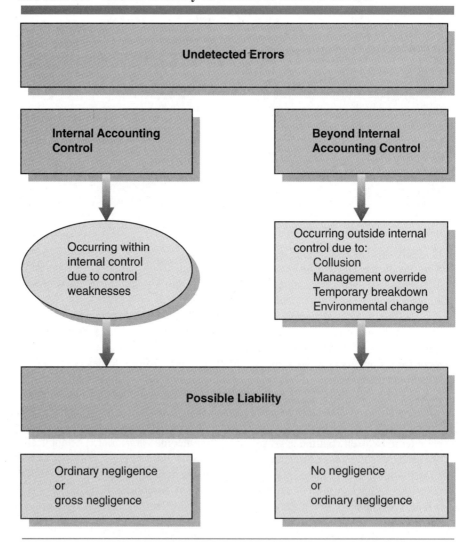

errors are much more difficult for auditors to detect, given enhanced concealment means. For this reason, plaintiffs' allegations of negligence are more difficult to sustain under such circumstances.

To summarize, material errors occurring within the control structure, due to significant weaknesses, are more likely to be detected in the course of the audit than those occurring outside the structure. This is because auditors expand their tests of transactions and balances under conditions of weak internal accounting control. Therefore, as a generality, one might postulate that failure to detect ''inside control'' errors is more indicative of gross negligence than failure to detect ''outside control'' errors.

In the case of *Cenco v. Seidman & Seidman,* a $25 million inventory fraud, which had been well concealed by management, was not detected by the auditors. Clearly, this is an example of management override, the resulting fraud occurring outside the internal control structure. The court, in this case, found the auditors not guilty. In his decision, the judge stated that the auditors cannot be expected to detect misrepresentation fraud when management turns the company ''into an engine of theft against outsiders.''[2]

Gross Negligence vs. Fraud

Fraud means intentional deceit. A charge of fraud, therefore, accuses the auditor of complicity in the deception. In the Continental Vending Machine Corporation case, the auditors were charged and convicted of knowingly drawing up and certifying a false and misleading financial statement of Continental Vending for the year ending September 30, 1962.[3]

In the National Student Marketing Corporation case, the auditors were also found guilty of fraud. In this case, material overstatements of 1968 earnings were concealed. The concealment was effected by a combination of 1969 write-offs and reductions in the 1968 earnings of certain pooled companies. Also, in order to alleviate the 1968 effect, the company reversed a deferred tax credit. The court concluded that the concealment was known to the auditors, and therefore, they were directly involved in the misrepresentation.[4]

Negligence does *not* involve deceit. The auditor may have failed to do what should have been done to detect the error or irregularity; but he/she did not intentionally contrive with the client to deceive third-party financial statement users. The courts have defined different levels of negligence. The distinction between ordinary and gross negligence was described above. Negligence may be so flagrant, however, as to border on deceit. The courts have termed this level of negligence as **constructive fraud.** If the auditor ignores that which is obvious, or if the auditor has no reason to believe that the financial statements are fairly presented and renders an unqualified audit opinion, the court will likely find the auditor guilty of reckless misconduct and interpret the negligence as constructive fraud. In the *Ultramares v. Touche* case (see appendix), for example, the auditors were found not guilty of intentional deceit. In finding them guilty of negligence, however, the court held that

---

[2]*Cenco, Incorporated v. Seidman & Seidman* (1982).

[3]*U.S. v. Simon et al.*

[4]U.S. Ct. Appeals, 2nd Circuit, 1975, F. 2d.

TABLE 3.1   Summary of Types of Auditor Liability

NO NEGLIGENCE

Audit conducted in accordance with generally accepted auditing standards
Management override of internal control
Fraud well concealed
Collusive fraud

ORDINARY NEGLIGENCE

Undetected errors occurring outside internal control
Material management misrepresentation which is concealed by spreading the misstatements over several financial statement components

GROSS NEGLIGENCE

Material management misrepresentation not well concealed
Material errors and/or irregularities occurring within internal control
Analysis of relationships among financial statement components should have aroused suspicions

CONSTRUCTIVE FRAUD

Willful disregard of facts
Application of generally accepted auditing standards should have disclosed
Reckless misconduct
No sound reason to believe the financial statements were fairly presented

FRAUD

Intentional deceit
Auditor complicity

negligence might be so gross as to be construed as fraud. In this case, the auditors failed to detect significant overstatements of assets effected through unsupported penciled postings to accounts receivable in the general ledger. Instead of investigating the added postings, the auditors accepted the numbers without any form of verification.[5]

Table 3.1 summarizes the various types of auditor liability by relating the level of liability to the characteristics associated with it. Figure 3.3 presents a flowchart identifying the types and levels of auditor liability.

SOURCES OF AUDITOR LIABILITY

The two sources of auditor liability are *common law* and *statutory law*. Under common law, auditors are liable to their clients for breach of contract. They are also subject to civil liability to third parties. Under statutory law, auditors may be held liable for violating the provisions of the Securities Act of 1933 and the Securities Exchange Act of 1934. In addition, auditors may be subject to civil liability under the Racketeer Influenced and Corrupt Organizations Act of 1970. These five subsets of sources are discussed in the following paragraphs.

---

[5]*Ultramares v. Touche,* 255 N.Y. 170, 174 N.E. 441 (N.Y. Ct. App. 1931).

FIGURE 3.3 Legal Liability Flowchart

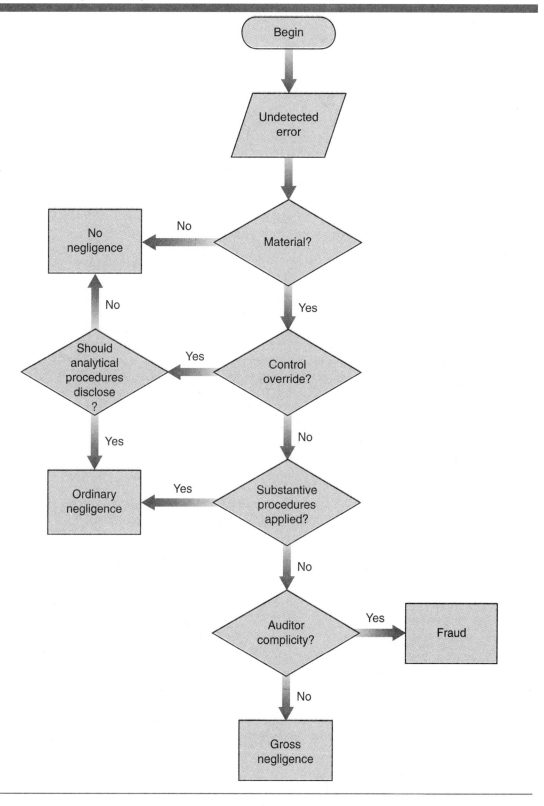

Common Law

Contractual Liability to Client

The CPA has an agreement with the client to perform, for consideration, whatever services are described in the engagement letter. This agreement (contract) is breached whenever one or both parties violate the provisions. Under contract law, auditors have **contractual liability** to their clients for ordinary negligence, gross negligence, and fraud. Failure to detect employee fraud is the most common cause for actions brought by clients against their auditors. Liability does not extend to third parties. This limitation of liability under contract law is known as **privity of contract.**

An exception to the rule of privity is made when a third party is a primary beneficiary and is specifically known to the auditor to be relying on the financial statements. Two cases illustrating the extension of privity are the Rusch Factors and Rhode Island Hospital Trust cases (see appendix). In the Rusch Factors case, the plaintiff had placed reliance on audited financial statements for the purpose of making a loan to a company that failed shortly after the loan was made. In finding for the plaintiff, and thereby extending privity, the court held as follows: "This court holds that an accountant should be liable in negligence for careless financial misrepresentations relied upon by *actually foreseen and limited classes of persons*. According to the plaintiff's complaint in the instant case, the defendant knew that his certification was to be used for, and had as its very aim and purpose, the reliance of potential financiers of the Rhode Island corporation. The defendant's motion is, therefore, denied."[6]

The Rhode Island Trust case is similar to Rusch Factors in that the auditors knew that the bank (Rhode Island Trust) was relying on the financial statements in deciding whether to expand and extend the company's existing line of credit. The financial statements contained material misrepresentations in the form of leasehold improvements which did not exist. The "additions" to the asset accounts were in fact operating expenses that had been capitalized in order to inflate earnings. The auditors had attempted to satisfy themselves as to the existence of the facilities by examining underlying documentation, but the documentation was deficient and the auditors did not examine the facilities. As in the Rusch Factors case, the auditors were held liable for the plaintiff's damages.[7]

---

[6]*Rusch Factors, Inc. v. Levin*, 248 F. Supp. 85 (D.R.H. 1968).

[7]*Rhode Island Hospital Trust National Bank v. Swartz*, 455 F. 2d, 847 (4th Cir. 1972).

Privity is important in these cases because if privity is extended to the known third party, the auditor can be held liable for ordinary negligence. Under common law, as discussed below, third parties may hold auditors liable for fraud and gross negligence, but not for ordinary negligence.

If a client sues the auditor for failure to detect fraud, the burden of proof is on the plaintiff (client) to demonstrate that failure to detect resulted from auditor negligence. The auditor, in turn, may plead the defense of contributory negligence by the client. **Contributory negligence,** an assertion that the client's own negligence gave rise to the fraud, is a particularly strong defense if the fraud occurs at a high level in the organization or involves management override of the control structure. In the *Cenco v. Seidman & Seidman* case, cited earlier, the auditors were found not guilty for failure to detect inventory fraud perpetrated by management.[8] In a similar case, *Cedars of Lebanon Hospital v. Touche,* the auditors were sued by the new management for failure to detect massive embezzlements committed by their predecessors. The court ruled in this case that management cannot sue an auditor for failing to detect a fraud which management itself perpetrated.[9]

Civil Liability to Third Parties Under Common Law

Under common law, no contractual relationship exists between the auditors and third parties. Privity is extended, however, when the third party is specifically identified and known by the auditor to be relying on the financial statements. This means that auditors are not generally liable to third parties for ordinary negligence. They are liable, however, for gross negligence and fraud. These distinctions between contractual liability to clients and **civil liability** to third parties are most clearly described in the case of *Ultramares v. Touche* (see appendix). In this case, the judge held that, ''If liability for negligence exists, a thoughtless slip or blunder, the failure to detect a theft or forgery beneath the cover of deceptive entries, may expose accountants to a liability in an indeterminate amount for an indeterminate time to an indeterminate class.''[10] The court also held, however, that negligence might be so gross as to constitute constructive fraud, in which instance the auditor could be held liable to third parties.[11]

---

[8]*Cenco, Incorporated v. Seidman & Seidman.*

[9]*Cedars of Lebanon Hospital Corporation v. Touche Ross & Co.* (1982).

[10]*Ultramares v. Touche.*

[11]*Ibid.*

Like contract law, in civil liability actions the burden of proof is placed upon the third party to demonstrate that reliance was placed on financial statements that were materially misstated and that injury resulted from such reliance.

Statutory Law

The Securities Act of 1933 and the Securities Exchange Act of 1934 are the two primary sources of auditor liability under statutory law, referred to as **statutory liability.** The 1933 Act covers new securities offerings, while the 1934 Act establishes recurring reporting requirements for public companies once their securities have been registered with the SEC.

The 1933 Act

In registering a new securities offering, a company must file a registration statement and prospectus with the SEC. The prospectus must be furnished to purchasers of the securities, and includes much of the information contained in the registration statement. Materials accompanying the statement are to include audited balance sheets, income statements, and statements of cash flows for the last three years. In addition, an unaudited balance sheet and income statement within 90 days of the filing date must be included if 90 days prior to the filing date falls after the latest audit.

The registration process begins with the company filing the registration statement. The statement is reviewed by the Division of Corporate Finance and a letter of comments is issued, setting forth deficiencies in the statement. Upon receiving the letter of comments, the company makes the necessary corrections and additions and resubmits the statement. Upon final review, the SEC declares the registration effective, whereupon the securities may be issued by the underwriters.

To illustrate the above process, assume the following dates:

- Most recent audited balance sheet: December 31, 1992
- Filing date of registration statement: September 30, 1993
- Effective date of registration statement: November 30, 1993

Given these assumptions, the registrant must include the December 31, 1991 and 1992 audited balance sheets, and audited statements of income and cash flows for the years ending December 31, 1990, 1991, and 1992. In addition, an unaudited balance sheet as of a date no earlier than June 30, 1993, and an unaudited income statement and statement of cash flows for the partial year must be included.

The 1933 Act is the most stringent in terms of potential auditor liability. Under this Act, liability is increased in the following ways:

1. The burden of proof shifts from the third party to the auditor to demonstrate due care, that is, that the auditor had reasonable grounds for believing the statements were presented fairly;
2. The auditor is liable to injured third parties for ordinary as well as gross negligence; and
3. Auditor liability extends to the effective date of the registration statement.

In view of item 3, the auditor should extend the subsequent events review to the effective date of the registration statement. As defined and discussed in Chapter 14, the subsequent events review requires that the auditor search for events, occurring after the balance sheet date, that may require adjustment or disclosure in the financial statements being audited. In the present case, the review should extend through November 30, 1993.

Inasmuch as the underwriters usually request a **comfort letter,** the auditor will likely apply certain limited procedures to the unaudited data, in addition to searching for subsequent events up to the effective date of the registration statement. As described and illustrated in Chapter 16, the comfort letter is usually addressed to the underwriters. It is dated as of the effective date of the registration statement and provides limited assurance with respect to:

1. Adequacy of disclosure concerning events occurring subsequent to the date of the most recent audited balance sheet; and

2. Unaudited data included in the interim financial statements.

Escott v. Bar Chris Construction Corporation is an example of a case brought under Section 11 of the Securities Act of 1933 (see appendix). The auditors were found guilty of negligence in this case.[12] Bar Chris was in the business of constructing bowling alleys. They used the percentage of completion method in accounting for the contracts. Upon completion, the alleys were sold to bowling proprietors, who made a down payment and financed the balance. Bar Chris sold the notes to a factor, receiving the proceeds minus a ''holdback'' for loss reserve purposes. The holdback was refunded to Bar Chris in proportion to collections by the factor. In one case, Bar Chris sold a bowling alley to a factor, who then leased it back to a wholly owned subsidiary of Bar Chris.

The legal action was brought by purchasers of the company's 5.5% convertible debenture bonds. The plaintiffs alleged that their injuries were caused by the auditors' negligence in expressing an unqualified opinion on financial statements that were materially false and misleading. The financial statements in question were for the year ended December 31, 1960, and were included in the registration statement that Bar Chris had filed with the SEC, pursuant to selling the debentures. Income, earnings per share, and current assets had all been overstated by approximately 16%, due to the recognition of gross profit not yet earned or realized. In addition, the financial statements failed to disclose unpaid officers' loans and customers' delinquencies on installment contracts. Shortly after issuing the bonds, the company filed under Chapter XI of the Bankruptcy Act.

In finding for the plaintiffs, the court held that the auditors had not exercised due care in the conduct of their audit. Moreover, the opinion of the court found the auditors lacking due diligence in conducting the ''S-1 review'' **(subsequent events review)** covering the period extending to the effective date of the registration statement.[13]

---

[12]*Escott et al. v. Bar Chris Construction Corp. et al.,* 283 F. Supp. 643 (S.D.N.Y. 1968).
[13]*Ibid.*

The 1934 Act

The Securities Exchange Act of 1934 requires companies whose securities are registered with the SEC to file quarterly and annual reports with the Commission. The quarterly reports (Form 10-Q) include unaudited financial statements and the annual report (Form 10-K) includes audited financial statements. In addition, special events, such as changes in principal stockholders and changes in auditors, must be promptly reported (Form 8-K).

Much of the financial statement information in Form 10-K is identical to the information contained in the annual report to shareholders. Given the concept of **"integrated disclosure,"** as defined by the SEC, this information may be "incorporated by reference" in Form 10-K.[14] This has greatly simplified SEC reporting requirements.

Prior to the 1976 U.S. Supreme Court decision in the case of *Ernst & Ernst v. Hochfelder* (see appendix), the auditor's liability under Rule 10b-5 of the 1934 Act was thought to be generally the same as under common law. Given this interpretation, the auditor was considered liable for gross negligence and fraud, but not for ordinary negligence. *Ernst & Ernst v. Hochfelder* changed this interpretation significantly. The decision in this case sets a precedent requiring the plaintiff to prove **scienter** — intent to deceive — in order for the auditors to be held liable under 10B-5.[15]

Ernst & Ernst (now Ernst & Young) was being sued in this case by customers of First Securities Company of Chicago, a small brokerage firm and a client of Ernst & Ernst. The customers had invested in a fraudulent securities scheme perpetrated by Leston Nay, president of First Securities. Nay had induced the customers to invest in certain nonexistent escrow accounts with the promise of above normal interest rates. The investors were instructed to make all checks payable to Nay, who insisted on opening his own mail. The suit charged that Ernst & Ernst should have detected the internal control deficiency allowing Nay to open his own mail and, further, should have notified the SEC of the deficiency. In finding for the auditors in this case, the court held: "When a statute speaks so specifically in terms of manipulation and deception, and of implementing devices and contrivances — the commonly understood terminology of intentional wrongdoing — and when its history reflects no more expansive intent, we are quite unwilling to extend the scope of the statute to negligent conduct.[16] This decision has been interpreted to mean that auditors are liable only for fraud (intentional deceit) under 10B-5. The Supreme Court, however, did not address the question of whether reckless conduct produces negligence so gross as to constitute fraud. Cases brought subsequent to Hochfelder have more explicitly addressed that question.

Another important difference between the 1933 and 1934 acts relates to burden of proof. Under the Securities Act of 1933, the burden of proof rests upon the auditor to demonstrate due care in performing the audit. Under the Securities Exchange Act of 1934, however, the burden shifts back to the plaintiff for proving negligence by the auditor.

---

[14]Incorporation by reference directs the reader's attention to information included in the annual report to shareholders rather than reporting such information in Form 10-K.

[15]*Ernst & Ernst v. Hochfelder,* 425 U.S. 185, 96 S Ct. 1375, 47 L Ed 2d 668 (1976).

[16]*Ibid.*

Racketeer Influenced and Corrupt Organizations Act

In addition to contractual and civil liability under common law and liability under the Securities Acts enforced by the SEC, auditors have more recently become liable to third parties under the Racketeer Influenced and Corrupt Organizations Act (RICO), a 1970 bill passed by Congress as an effort to eradicate "organized crime" in the United States. Although not intended to impact such noncriminal elements as legitimate businesses and practicing professionals, CPAs have experienced significant repercussions following the bill's enactment. The provision of the bill most affecting CPAs results from Congress' inability to define "organized crime," and, instead listing a variety of activities categorized as "criminal." In addition to murder, kidnapping, extortion, hijacking, and arson, criminal activities, as defined in the Act, encompass mail fraud, wire fraud, and fraud in the sale of securities. Moreover, as the bill was going to the floor of the House of Representatives for a vote, the drafters added a rider that permits private parties to bring civil actions under its provisions and to collect *treble damages and attorneys' fees*. Referred to as "civil RICO," this has perhaps been the most devastating provision of the bill affecting CPAs.

To be found guilty under RICO, one must have engaged in a "pattern of racketeering activity." As defined in the statute, however, a "pattern" may be established if the defendant has been accused (not necessarily found guilty) of committing any of the listed acts twice within a 10-year span. This, of course, exposes virtually all CPA firms with public clients to real and potential liability under the act.[17] For example, assume that a CPA firm has been accused of scienter (intentional deceit) at least twice in a 10-year period for having rendered an unqualified opinion on financial statements containing material misrepresentations (this would include all of the "big six" accounting firms). Assume further that the firm was exonerated in each instance. A third accusation by an allegedly injured party within that same 10-year period could be invoked under civil RICO, and, given the potential award of treble damages and lawyers' fees, this would seem the most likely approach for the plaintiff.

✳ The case of *ESM Government Securities v. Alexander Grant & Co.* was prosecuted under civil RICO in 1986. The ESM Group was formed in 1977 as a holding company for ESM Government Securities. ESM Government Securities had been formed in 1975. Using a series of intercompany transactions resulting in receivables and payables, losses from securities trades were concealed. Moreover, an Alexander Grant partner was accused of being a party to the concealment, having known about the fraudulent transactions since 1978. As a result of the misrepresentations, investors in ESM, including municipalities such as Toledo, Ohio, and thrift institutions such as Home State Savings Bank of Cincinnati, lost millions of dollars from temporary investments of funds in the firm. The case against Grant was ultimately settled out of court for an amount reportedly in excess of $50 million.[18]

Efforts are presently underway to amend the Act to remove the availability of civil RICO from "ordinary commercial transactions," but would retain its provisions relative to "major white collar frauds."[19]

---

[17]For an excellent overview of RICO, see *Journal of Accountancy,* December, 1985, pp. 102–108.

[18]See *Journal of Accountancy,* June 1985, pp. 8–18.

[19]See *Journal of Accountancy,* June 1991, p. 31.

SUMMARY OF SOURCES AND TYPES
OF AUDITOR LIABILITY

Auditors are liable to their clients, under contract law, for ordinary negligence, gross negligence, and fraud. Under common law, auditors are liable to third parties for gross negligence and fraud. Additionally, they are liable for ordinary negligence to specifically identified third parties known to be relying on the financial statements. Under the Securities Act of 1933, auditors are liable to third-party purchasers of securities for ordinary negligence, gross negligence, and fraud. Moreover, the 1933 Act requires the auditor to prove due care and extends liability to the effective date of the registration statement. Under the Securities Exchange Act of 1934, auditors are liable to third parties for fraud but not for negligence. The profession remains uncertain as to whether reckless conduct will be construed as fraud in future cases brought under 10B-5 of the 1934 Act. Moreover, the 1934 Act shifts the burden of proof back to the plaintiff for proving either fraud or constructive fraud on the part of the auditor.

Under civil RICO, CPAs may be charged with fraud where unqualified opinions were rendered on financial statements that were intentionally and significantly misrepresented. Table 3.2 summarizes the sources and types of auditor liability.

LIABILITY FOR UNAUDITED STATEMENTS

CPAs must exercise due care, regardless of the type of service performed. For unaudited financial statements, due care is exercised by adhering to those standards designed to maintain the quality of unaudited statements. These standards are addressed in Chapter 16. Further, a CPA who is aware of material errors or irregularities in unaudited financial statements has a duty to inform the owners.

In addition to defining the accountant's liability for unaudited financial statements, the 1971 case of *1136 Tenants Corporation v. Max Rothenberg & Co.* demonstrates the need for reaching a clear understanding with the client regarding the type of service to be performed. In this case, 1136 Tenants Corporation owned a cooperative apartment complex and retained Max Rothenberg & Co., a CPA firm,

TABLE 3.2   Sources and Types of Auditor Liability

Sources	Ordinary Negligence	Gross Negligence	Fraud
COMMON LAW			
Contractual Liability	X	X	X
Civil Liability (To Third Parties)		X	X
STATUTORY LAW			
1933 Act	X	X	X
1934 Act		X	X
CIVIL RICO			X

to prepare financial statements. While preparing the statements, the accountants noted that documentation supporting certain disbursements was missing. They did not try to locate the missing documents. Moreover, they did not notify the client of the "missing invoices." The invoices, in fact, never existed. Indeed, Riker, the managing agent for the apartment complex, had embezzled over $1 million and concealed the embezzlement with fraudulent journal entries debiting operating expenses and crediting cash. In deciding for the plaintiffs, the Appellate Division of the Supreme Court of New York stated: "Even if a firm of certified public accountants was hired only to perform "write-up" services for owners of (an) apartment building, when accountants became aware that material invoices purportedly paid by the manager of the building were missing, the accountants were negligent in failing to inform owners of the building of that fact."[20] Given the lack of a formal engagement letter and the fact that the accountants had performed some limited auditing procedures, the court was also unclear as to whether the defendants were retained to prepare audited or unaudited statements. This further weakened the accountants' due care defense.

SAS 26, *Association with Financial Statements,* was issued as the direct result of 1136 Tenants. The Accounting and Review Services Committee was also formed, and Statements on Standards for Accounting and Review Services, Number 1, *Compilation and Review of Financial Statements,* was issued following this case.[21]

PREVENTING LEGAL ACTIONS

The best approach to preventing lawsuits is to remove the basis for legal actions. Allocating resources to areas of high audit risk helps to ensure that material errors and irregularities are detected by the auditor.

Detection, by itself, however, is not enough. Auditors must also follow through to determine that material errors detected by the auditors have been corrected by the client. Otherwise, injury by third parties relying on materially misstated financial statements will result. Auditor insistence on proper treatment in financial statements of discovered errors and irregularities, including footnote disclosure of related-party transactions, are significant in preventing third-party injury.

Chapter 5 presents an approach to risk analysis that supports these efforts. The approach evaluates audit risk by analyzing the business and industry to gain a better understanding of transactions and events consummated by the client, noting unusual relationships among accounting data that may be indicative of financial statement errors, and studying and evaluating the internal control structure to determine its effectiveness and to aid in audit planning. These audit risk elements are then considered collectively in planning the audit and designing procedures for testing transactions and balances (substantive audit testing). This approach provides a systematic means for detecting errors and reduces the overall audit risk of

---

[20]*1136 Tenants Corporation v. Max Rothenberg & Co.,* 36 App. Div. 2d, 30 N.Y. 2d 804, 319 N.Y.S. 2d 1007 (1971).

[21]The attestation standards and the statements on standards for accounting and review services collectively define the quality of unaudited financial statements. These standards, along with the various forms of nonaudit services performed by CPAs, are addressed fully in Chapter 16.

expressing an unqualified opinion on financial statements that are materially misstated. Other measures that can help in preventing legal actions include the following:

1. Utilize the audit committee of the board of directors wherever possible. The audit committee, composed of nonmanagement board members, typically has responsibility for monitoring the internal control structure and arbitrating disputes arising between the independent auditors and management.

2. Carefully supervise assistants and thoroughly review their work. Audit personnel who are new to the engagement do not possess the knowledge of the business and may not readily recognize questionable transactions and other unusual circumstances.

3. Don't submit to "time pressure" during the audit. Clients sometimes press the auditors to finish the engagement earlier than warranted by existing conditions. Early completion reduces the cost to the client and minimizes disruption of the client's staff. It may also prevent the auditor from detecting significant financial statement errors because of failure to apply necessary auditing procedures.

4. For initial audits, communicate with predecessor auditors (in accordance with Section AU 315 of the AICPA Professional Standards) and carefully consider whether to accept the engagement. Auditors should not be associated with the financial statements of entities whose managements lack integrity. Such association is in violation of the code of professional conduct and also increases the risk of undetected errors or irregularities in the financial statements.

5. Review clients annually for continuance for the same reasons just cited.

6. Always observe the spirit of ethical behavior and make a positive effort to serve the interests of third-party users of audited financial statements. Be particularly conscious of Rule 102, which requires the CPA to *"maintain objectivity and integrity, be free of conflicts of interest, and not knowingly misrepresent facts or subordinate his or her judgment to others."*

DEALING WITH LIABILITY

Regardless of the extent of due care, the auditor can never be absolutely assured that all material errors have been detected and properly reflected in the financial statements. The audit is, after all, test based and, therefore, includes some risk of material errors occurring and going undetected. For this reason, even the most diligent auditor may be sued by third parties who have been injured by relying on materially misstated financial statements. Therefore, auditors need to be prepared to defend themselves in the event of legal actions brought by clients or third parties.

The best defense is demonstration of due care in the conduct of the audit, which is best evidenced by thorough documentation of the audit. Workpapers that are particularly helpful in establishing due care include the following:

1. Documentation of discovered control weaknesses and the thought processes leading to modification of substantive audit programs in light of the weaknesses;

2. Engagement letter clearly setting forth the nature of the services to be performed by the CPA; and

3. Evidence that the work of assistants was properly reviewed, and that all unanswered questions were cleared prior to issuing the audit report.

Audit workpapers are addressed more fully in Chapter 4.

In addition to the due care defense, auditors should also plan for adequate liability insurance as protection in the event of lawsuits. Most firms are finding the cost of such insurance increasingly burdensome in light of the mounting incidence of third party legal actions against auditors. Yet, some form of insurance is necessary, given the magnitude of settlements being awarded.

KEY TERMS

Civil liability
Comfort letter
Constructive fraud
Contractual liability
Contributory negligence
Fraud
Gross negligence
Integrated disclosure
Minimum care
Ordinary negligence

Privity of contract
Reasonable care
Racketeer Influenced and Corrupt
   Organizations Act
Scienter
Securities Act of 1933
Securities Exchange Act of 1934
Statutory liability
Subsequent events review

APPENDIX

LEGAL CASES INVOLVING AUDITORS

CASES UNDER COMMON LAW

McKesson & Robbins, Inc. (1938)

Although settled out of court, this 1930's case marked the beginning of the auditing standards and SASs. The case involved sizable amounts of fictitious inventories and accounts receivable. Documentation supporting purchases, receipts of goods, sales, and shipments had been fabricated. As a result, assets and income were overstated by $19 million and $18 million, respectively, in the audited financial statements. Accepted auditing procedures at the time did not include inventory observation or direct correspondence with customers of the client. For this reason, the CPAs were not aware of the fraud and issued an unqualified opinion on the statements. Shortly thereafter, the fraud was discovered by the treasurer of McKesson & Robbins, and trading in the stock was halted. The SEC conducted an investigation and asked for the president's resignation. The investigation resulted in statements by both the SEC and the AICPA (then the American Institute of Accountants) addressing audit deficiencies existing at that time, and recommending observation of inventories and confirmation of receivables.

Ultramares v. Touche (op. cit.) (1931)

The Ultramares case established that auditors are not liable to unknown third-party users for ordinary negligence. The court did hold, however, that auditors may be held liable for gross negligence which the judge equated with "constructive fraud."

In this case, the firm of Touche, Niven & Co. had been retained by Fred Stern & Co. to prepare and certify the company's December 31, 1923 balance sheet. The balance sheet reflected assets and liabilities approximating $2.5 million and $1.5 million, respectively. In fact, the company was insolvent, and their liabilities exceeded assets by $200,000.

The auditors were held negligent in not examining documentation supporting penciled debit postings to accounts receivable in the general ledger. These unsupported entries, posted after the regular month-end postings had been completed, represented fictitious sales. Other factors, according to the court decision, should also have alerted the auditors to material errors and fraud by Stern & Co.

The plaintiff, Ultramares, had made numerous loans to the company on the basis of the certified balance sheet. Fred Stern & Co. subsequently collapsed and declared bankruptcy on January 2, 1925.

Although deciding in favor of the plaintiffs (Ultramares), the court did uphold the doctrine of privity. In the words of Justice Cardozo, who wrote the court's opinion: "If liability for negligence exists, a thoughtless slip or blunder, the failure to detect a theft or forgery beneath the cover of deceptive entries, may expose accountants to a liability in an indeterminate amount for an indeterminate time to an indeterminate class." The court then declared that constructive fraud exists if the plaintiffs can prove gross negligence. The court found the defendants guilty of gross negligence in this case. The auditors, according to the decision, should have further investigated the added postings to accounts receivable. Instead, they accepted the numbers without any form of verification.

Rusch Factors, Inc. v. Levin (1968)

This case further clarified the Ultramares decision by extending privity to specifically identified third parties known by the auditor to be relying on the audited financial statements. In 1963, the plaintiff, a New York banker and factor, had made substantial loans to a Rhode Island corporation. Leonard Levin, a CPA, had issued an unqualified opinion on the financial statements that were, in fact, materially misstated. Rusch Factors loaned more than $300,000 to the corporation on the basis of those statements. The company subsequently went into receivership, and Rusch recovered only a portion of the loans.

The court held that "An accountant should be liable in negligence for careless financial misrepresentation relied upon by actually foreseen and limited classes of persons." Inasmuch as the plaintiffs proved negligence, the court found for the plaintiffs.

Rhode Island Hospital Trust National Bank v. Swartz (1972)

This case is similar to Rusch Factors in holding auditors liable to known third parties in negligence actions. Rhode Island Hospital Trust National Bank had extended and enlarged a line of credit to a company on the basis of reported increases in earnings per share. The increases, as later established, were gained by debiting operating expenses to leasehold improvements accounts. The leasehold improvements were ostensibly related to port facilities used by the company in grain handling opera-tions. The improvements, in fact, did not exist, and documentation supporting the debits was lacking.

Although the auditors disclaimed an opinion on the financial statements, the court found them negligent in not clearly explaining the reasons for the disclaimer. The reasons given by the auditors were as follows: "Additions to fixed assets in 1963 were found to include principally warehouse improvements and installation of machinery and equipment. . . . Practically all of this work had been done by em-ployees . . . complete detailed cost records were not kept of these improvements and no exact determination could be made as to the actual cost of said improve-ments." The court held that the auditors should have addressed the question of existence, as well as valuation, in citing reasons for the disclaimer. The auditors were therefore found guilty of ordinary negligence and privity was extended to Rhode Island Trust as a specifically identified third party.

CASES UNDER STATUTORY LAW

Escott v. Bar Chris Construction Corporation (1968)

This case involved a civil action brought under the Securities Act of 1933. The securities being registered consisted of 15-year convertible subordinated debenture bonds. The case is meaningful in that it emphasizes the significance of gaining a thorough understanding of the business and industry in which the client operates. It also demonstrates the importance of exercising due diligence in conducting the S-1 (subsequent events) review.[22]

Bar Chris was in the business of constructing, selling, leasing, and occasion-ally operating bowling establishments. The company financed some of the sales, but often sold the notes to a factor in order to satisfy immediate cash needs. Given the overbuilding of bowling establishments in the 1960s, Bar Chris began to encounter difficulties in collecting from its customers, and ultimately filed under the Bank-ruptcy Act.

The court action brought against the auditors by third-party purchasers of the debentures alleged lack of due care in performing the audit, and lack of due dili-gence in performing the S-1 review. Assets and income were found to be overstated because of incorrect application of the percentage of completion method, and re-cording transfers to related parties as sales. Other transactions with related parties were found to be improperly classified on the December 31, 1960 balance sheet. The unaudited financial statements, covering the 1961 period prior to the filing date, were also deemed misstated.

The court found the auditors guilty of negligence, both in the performance of the audit and in the conduct of the S-1 review. With respect to the audit, the court

---

[22]Remember that, under the 1933 Act, auditors are liable for both ordinary and gross negligence and liability extends to the effective date of the registration statement.

held that the auditors depended too heavily on oral responses to their questions and did not further corroborate the answers. Concerning the S-1 review, the auditor's review program was considered adequate, but the court held that it was not properly carried out. In ruling on the due diligence question, the judge stated:

> There had been a material change for the worse in Bar Chris's financial position. That change was sufficiently serious so that the failure to disclose it made the 1960 figures misleading. Beradi (the senior auditor on the engagement) did not discover it. As far as results were concerned, his S-1 review was useless.
>
> Accountants should not be held to a standard higher than that recognized in their profession. I do not do so here. Beradi's review did not come up to that standard. He did not take some of the steps which the written (audit) program prescribed. He did not spend an adequate amount of time on a task of this magnitude. Most important of all, he was too easily satisfied with glib answers to his inquiries.
>
> This is not to say that he should have made a complete audit. But there were enough danger signals in the materials which he did examine to require some further investigation on his part. Generally accepted accounting (auditing) standards required such further investigation under these circumstances. It is not always sufficient merely to ask questions.

Fischer v. Kletz (The "Yale Express" Case)
266 F. Supp. 180 (S.D.N.Y. 1967)

Yale Express demonstrates the importance of auditor follow-up when facts are later discovered that, if known at the time the audit report was released, might have affected the auditor's opinion. The subsequently discovered facts, in this case, related to accounts receivable reported on the year-end audited balance sheet. A substantial portion of the receivables were determined to be fictitious. This discovery was made by management advisory personnel who were engaged to perform systems work following the audit engagement. The management advisory services people promptly reported their findings to the audit staff. The auditors notified Yale Express management, but neither management nor the auditors took further action.

Yale Express was engaged in trucking and freight forwarding services. Its 1963 financial statements showed a profit of $1.14 million. Had the statements been adjusted for the fictitious receivables, a loss of $1.2 million would have been reflected. In conjunction with its 1964 audit report, the auditors mentioned the 1963 loss. Yale Express filed for bankruptcy in May, 1965. Upon discovering the 1963 loss, purchasers of Yale's securities sued the auditors for deceit under Rule 10b-5 of the Securities Exchange Act of 1934.

Although settled out of court, this case demonstrates the importance of the auditor's responsibility to third parties. At that time, there were no auditing pronouncements dealing with information discovered subsequent to the audit report date. As a result of Yale Express, Statement on Auditing Procedure 41, entitled "Subsequent Discovery of Facts Existing at the Date of the Auditor's Report," was released by the AICPA. This SAP was later incorporated into Statement on Auditing Standards No. 1.

United States v. Simon (Continental Vending Machine Corporation Case)
425 F. 2d, 796 (2d Cir. 1969)

The stockholders of Continental Vending, like those of Yale Express, alleged that the auditors engaged in willful deceit by expressing an unqualified opinion on financial statements that were materially misleading. In contrast to Yale, however, this case involved disclosure standards rather than measurement standards.

Harold Roth was president and chief executive officer of Continental Vending. He was also president of Valley Commercial Corporation, a wholly owned subsidiary of Continental. He was the controlling stockholder in both companies, and used them to channel funds to his own personal use. Such diversions were concealed by extensive movements (''laundering'') of the funds. Continental issued notes to Valley and Valley discounted the notes at various banks. The proceeds were then transferred by Valley to Continental, whereupon Continental made advances to Valley. Finally, Valley made loans to Harold Roth from the advances received from Continental (see Figure 3A.1).

FIGURE 3A.1   Continental Vending Scheme

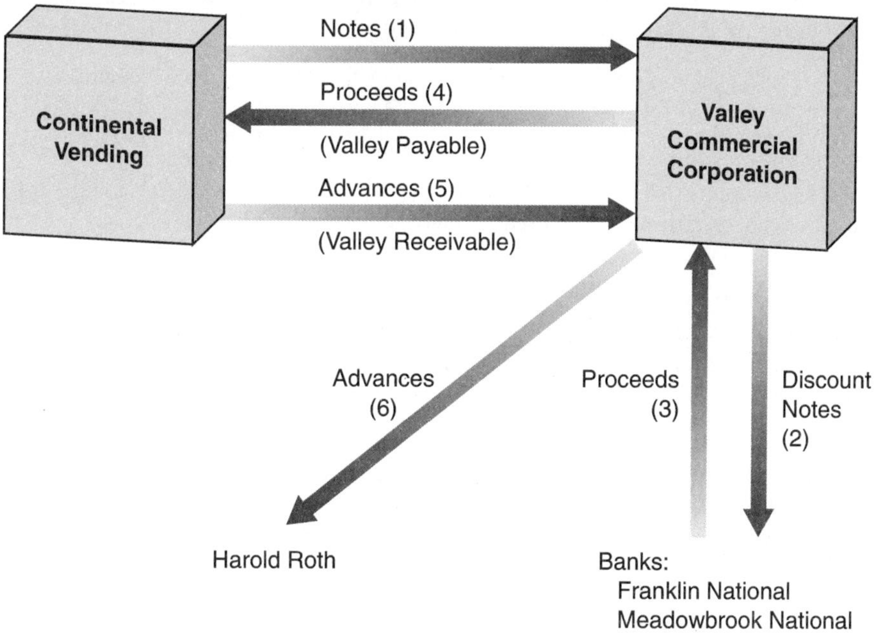

9/30/62:

Valley payable: $1.03 million (50% of current liabilities)

Valley receivables: $3.5 million
(secured mainly by Continental stock pledged as collateral by Harold Roth)

At the fiscal year end, September 30, 1962, the amount payable to Valley was $1.03 million, and the amount receivable from Valley was $3.5 million. By the date of the audit report, the auditors had learned that Valley was unable to meet its obligation to Continental. Shortly after release of the 1962 financial statements and audit report, Continental collapsed and trading in the company's securities was halted by the SEC.

The defendants in this case, two audit partners and a manager, were prosecuted for allegedly participating in a conspiracy to defraud Continental's stockholders. The action was brought under Section 32 of the Securities Exchange Act of 1934. They were convicted in 1968 and the judge imposed prison terms. They received a presidential pardon in 1973.

A central question surrounding the Continental Vending case is that of "legal form vs. economic substance" of transactions. Although technically a loan to an affiliate, secured by collateral, the receivable was, in fact, an advance to an officer. Moreover, the loan was uncollectible, inasmuch as it was secured by Continental's own stock and Roth was unable to pay. A sort of "catch 22" existed with regard to collectibility of the receivable. Since Roth was unable to pay, collectibility became dependent on the collateral. However, given the magnitude of the receivable, relative to total assets, the value of the collateral (Continental stock) was dependent on the collectibility of the receivable.

Note 2 to the consolidated financial statements described the receivable as follows:

> The amount receivable from Valley Commercial Corp. (an affiliated company of which Mr. Harold Roth is an officer, director and stockholder) bears interest at 12% a year. Such amount, less the balance of the notes payable to that company, is secured by the assignment to the company of Valley's equity in certain marketable securities. As of February 15, 1963, the amount of such equity at current market quotations exceeded the net amount receivable.

Although expert witnesses from other "big eight" accounting firms testified that the note constituted adequate disclosure, the government argued that the note did not clearly reflect the substance of the transactions. Instead, they presented the following as preferred wording of the footnote:

> The amount receivable from Valley Commercial Corp. (an affiliated company of which Mr. Harold Roth is an officer, director and stockholder), which bears interest at 12% a year, was uncollectible at September 30, 1962, since Valley had loaned approximately the same amount to Mr. Roth who was unable to pay. Since that date, Mr. Roth and others have pledged as security for the repayment of his obligation to Valley and its obligation to Continental (now $3,900,000 against which Continental's liability to Valley cannot be offset) securities which, as of February 14, 1963, had a market value of $2,978,000. Approximately 80% of such securities are stock and convertible debentures of the Company.

Continental's Board of Directors had not been informed of the loans, and when they did learn of them, they disapproved.

A significant result of the Continental Vending case was the issuance by the Auditing Standards Board of Statement on Auditing Standards 6, "Related Party

Transactions." This statement (later superseded by SAS 45) defines the auditor's responsibility for identifying and auditing transactions similar to the Continental-Valley-Roth transactions. Moreover, it requires the auditor to insist upon adequate disclosure of the substance of such transactions.

United States v. Natelli
F. 2d.f (2d Cir. 1975)

Referred to as National Student Marketing (NSM), this is another case in which the auditors were charged with intentional deceit under Section 32 of the Securities Exchange Act of 1934. National Student Marketing Corporation was engaged in developing advertising for clients wishing to market their products on college campuses. Based on increased earnings, the price of the company's stock had increased dramatically within a six-month period. NSM was taking advantage of the favorable market performance by using its stock to acquire other companies.

Demonstrating to the auditors that most of the revenue producing effort was expended "up front" in identifying media, developing layout, and producing the ads, NSM recognized revenue upon completion of these activities. Given the time lag between completion of production and appearance of the ads in the media, revenue was frequently recognized in one year, while the ads actually appeared in a subsequent year. This method of revenue recognition is acceptable, provided firm contracts with clients exist and the revenue has been substantially earned. In the absence of written contracts, however, 1968 commitments totalling $1.7 million were booked as revenue. The auditors agreed with this only to discover that approximately $1 million of these revenues were written off in 1969. In fact, the amounts written off represented nonexistent 1968 contracts.

In adjusting for the "error" the auditors allegedly agreed to the following plan:

- Charged to 1969 earnings $350,000
- Subtract from 1968 sales of pooled companies $678,000

In addition, the auditing firm's tax department recommended a reversal of a tax deferral in the amount of $189,000, thus changing the income effect from ($210,000) to ($21,000). The apparent reason for such "spreading" of the adjustments was to avoid any breakdown in merger negotiations taking place in 1969 between NSM and prospective pooling candidates. Such a significant downward adjustment of previously reported 1968 earnings would have materially increased the number of NSM shares to be given up in exchanges.

In light of these circumstances, the court found the auditors guilty of conspiring with NSM management in misrepresenting the 1968 financial statements and intentionally concealing the errors.

Ernst & Ernst v. Hochfelder
425 U.S. 185 (1976)

More than any other case to date, the Hochfelder case clearly defines the auditor's liability under Section 10B-5 of the Securities and Exchange Act of 1934. The Supreme Court decided in this case that auditors are not liable for negligence, but only for fraud under the Act. Cases decided subsequent to Hochfelder indicate that reckless conduct on the part of auditors may yet be construed as fraud. Although auditors had never been held liable for ordinary negligence under 10B-5, the courts had begun to lean towards a liberal definition of gross negligence. The Supreme Court decision in Hochfelder served to halt this trend.

Ernst & Ernst, the auditors of First Securities Corporation of Chicago, a small brokerage firm, was sued by investors in nonexistent escrow accounts. The plaintiffs charged that the auditors should have notified the Midwest Stock Exchange of a weakness in internal accounting control. The weakness allegedly permitted the chief executive officer of First Securities to misappropriate escrow funds during the period 1942–1966.

In addition to being CEO of First Securities, Leston Nay also owned 92% of the stock in the corporation. Nay had induced friends and associates to invest in certain "escrow accounts" that promised to pay higher than normal rates of return. He requested that the investors make the checks payable to him in order to promote flexibility in investing in those accounts promising the highest rates of return. The monies were never invested. Instead, Nay misappropriated the funds.

Nay concealed the fraud by insisting that all of his mail be placed on his desk unopened, even if he happened to be absent at the time. In this way, no one but Nay and the investors knew that the checks were payable to Nay. The fraud was never discovered, and only came to light as a result of a letter written by Nay shortly before his suicide.

The plaintiffs asserted that Ernst & Ernst was negligent in not detecting and reporting the "mail rule" to the SEC as a material weakness in internal control. Ernst & Ernst responded by stating that the mail rule was not relevant to internal control and that First Securities, in fact, had an adequate system of internal control. The fraud perpetrated by Nay was actually made possible through management override—not from any weakness in the control structure.

The trial court decided for Ernst & Ernst and dismissed the case. Upon appeal, the trial court's decision was reversed. This prompted Ernst & Ernst to appeal to the U.S. Supreme Court, which found for the auditors on the basis of "no scienter (i.e., no intent), no liability."

Cases subsequent to *Ernst & Ernst v. Hochfelder,* notably *McLean v. Alexander* (420 F. Supp. 1057, 1976), have modified the Supreme Court decision somewhat by holding auditors liable under 10B-5 for reckless conduct. The court stated in this regard that the auditor's conduct in preparing the client's financial statements amounted to reckless and knowing misbehavior. The court further described the auditors' actions as "far more than mere negligence" but falling "short of a preconceived actual intent to defraud."

CASE BROUGHT UNDER THE RACKETEER INFLUENCED AND CORRUPT ORGANIZATIONS ACT

ESM Government Securities v. Alexander Grant & Co. (1986)

Although only one of many, this case is probably the most significant of those against CPA firms charging criminal activity under the Racketeer Influenced and Corrupt Organizations Act (RICO). Alexander Grant & Co. (now Grant Thornton), a CPA firm and auditors of ESM, was charged with complicity in a scheme to defraud savings and loan institutions and municipalities out of millions of dollars of their temporary investments in ESM. Among the municipalities so affected was the city of Toledo, Ohio, and among the thrift institutions was Home State Savings Bank of Cincinnati, which advanced an estimated $150 million in unsecured loans to ESM.

ESM Government Securities and ESM Securities, Inc., formed in 1975, were related brokerage firms licensed by the Securities and Exchange Commission and the National Association of Securities Dealers. They purportedly invested funds for thrifts and municipalities in various types of government and other securities offering relatively high rates of return. In 1976, ESM Financial Group was formed and in 1977, the ESM Group was formed to be holding companies for the other two firms. By recording fictitious transactions between the brokerage firms and the holding companies, losses incurred by ESM Government Securities were transferred to ESM Financial. The transactions were supported by false documentation purporting loans by Government to Financial. Not only were the losses thus concealed, but ESM Government was also able to accrue interest on the fictitious loans. Moreover, the partner in charge of the ESM audit, a young and ambitious CPA, allegedly accepted "bribes" from ESM management in return for aiding in concealing the fraud.

In 1984, ESM collapsed and charges were filed against several of the parties involved, including Alexander Grant & Co. Although never tried in court, the out of court settlement with Alexander Grant was reportedly in excess of $50 million. The CPA firm partner involved in the fraud was ultimately terminated and subsequently prosecuted by the state of Florida.

REVIEW QUESTIONS

1. The AICPA has contributed to the maintenance of audit quality by promulgating auditing standards and a code of conduct. The courts have similarly furthered the quality of auditing. Discuss how, citing specific cases in support of your answers.
2. Differentiate between ordinary negligence and gross negligence in terms of the following:
   a. due care
   b. materiality
   c. internal control
3. Give two examples of errors occurring outside internal control.
4. How did the *Cenco v. Seidman & Seidman* case further clarify the auditor's liability for negligence?
5. Differentiate between gross negligence and fraud.
6. What is the principal difference, in terms of auditor liability, between the court's findings in the Bar Chris case and the Continental Vending Machine Corporation case?
7. Identify the sources of auditor liability and the subsets within each source.
8. Define "privity of contract."
9. Under what conditions does privity extend to injured third parties?
10. How does the Rhode Island Trust case further define the concept of privity?

11. What is the major difference, in terms of auditor liability, between contract law and common law?

12. How do the reporting requirements differ between the Securities Act of 1933 and the Securities Exchange Act of 1934?

13. How is the auditor's liability more extensive under the 1933 Act?

14. Why do auditors find it necessary to extend the subsequent events review to the effective date of the registration statement for filings under the 1933 Act?

15. Define the following terms
    a. 10-K
    b. integrated disclosure
    c. incorporation by reference
    d. 10-Q

16. What major point of law concerning auditor liability emerged from the *Ernst & Ernst v. Hochfelder* case?

17. Define the auditor's liability under civil RICO. Why do auditors consider this law unduly oppressive?

18. Briefly summarize the major sources and types of auditor liability.

19. What constitutes due care when CPAs are associated with unaudited financial statements?

20. How can legal actions against auditors be best prevented?

21. Legal actions which do arise require that the auditor demonstrate due care in the conduct of the examination. How can auditors, during the conduct of their examinations, ensure an adequate due care defense?

MULTIPLE CHOICE QUESTIONS FROM CPA EXAMINATIONS

1. Doe and Co., CPAs, issued an unqualified opinion on the 1983 financial statements of Marx Corp. These financial statements were included in Marx's annual report and form 10-K filed with the SEC. Doe did not detect material misstatements in the financial statements as a result of negligence in the performance of the audit. Based upon the financial statements, Fitch purchased stock in Marx. Shortly thereafter, Marx became insolvent, causing the price of the stock to decline drastically. Fitch has commenced legal action against Doe for damages based upon section 10(b) and rule 10b-5 of the Securities Exchange Act of 1934. Doe's best defense to such an action would be that
   a. Fitch lacks privity to sue.
   b. The engagement letter specifically disclaimed all liability to third parties.
   c. There is no proof of scienter.
   d. There has been no subsequent sale for which a loss can be computed.

2. Dexter and Co., CPAs, issued an unqualified opinion on the 1983 financial statements of Bart Corp. Late in 1984, Bart determined that its treasurer had embezzled over $1 million. Dexter was unaware of the embezzlement. Bart has decided to sue Dexter to recover the $1 million. Bart's suit is based upon Dexter's failure to discover the missing money while performing the audit. Which of the following is Dexter's best defense?
   a. That the audit was performed in accordance with GAAS.
   b. Dexter had no knowledge of the embezzlement.

   c. The financial statements were presented in conformity with GAAP.

   d. The treasurer was Bart's agent and as such had designed the internal controls which facilitated the embezzlement.

3. Rhodes Corp. desired to acquire the common stock of Harris Corp. and engaged Johnson & Co., CPAs, to audit the financial statements of Harris Corp. Johnson failed to discover a significant liability in performing the audit. In a common law action against Johnson, Rhodes at a minimum must prove

   a. Gross negligence on the part of Johnson.

   b. Negligence on the part of Johnson.

   c. Fraud on the part of Johnson.

   d. Johnson knew that the liability existed.

4. If a stockholder sues a CPA for common law fraud based upon false statements contained in the financial statements audited by the CPA, which of the following is the CPA's best defense?

   a. The stockholder lacks privity to sue.

   b. The CPA disclaimed liability to all third parties in the engagement letter.

   c. The contributory negligence of the client.

   d. The false statements were immaterial.

5. In a common law action against an accountant, the lack of privity is a viable defense if the plaintiff

   a. Bases his action upon fraud.

   b. Is the accountant's client.

   c. Is a creditor of the client who sues the accountant for negligence.

   d. Can prove the presence of gross negligence that amounts to a reckless disregard for the truth.

6. Locke, CPA, was engaged by Hall, Inc., to audit Willow Company. Hall purchased Willow after receiving Willow's audited financial statements, which included Locke's unqualified auditor's opinion. Locke was negligent in the performance of the Willow audit engagement. As a result of Locke's negligence, Hall suffered damages of $75,000. Hall appears to have grounds to sue Locke for

	Breach of Contract	Negligence
a.	Yes	Yes
b.	Yes	No
c.	No	Yes
d.	No	No

7. To recover in a common law action based upon fraud against a CPA with regard to an audit of financial statements, the plaintiff must prove among other things

   a. Privity of contract.

   b. Unavailability of any other cause of action.

   c. That there was a sale or purchase of securities within a six month period that resulted in a loss.

   d. Reliance on the financial statements.

8. DMO Enterprises, Inc. engaged the accounting firm of Martin, Seals, and Anderson to perform its annual audit. The firm performed the audit in a competent, nonnegligent manner and billed DMO for $16,000, the agreed fee. Shortly after delivery of the audited financial statements, Hightower, the assistant controller, disappeared, taking with him $28,000 of DMO's funds. It was then discovered that

Hightower had been engaged in a highly sophisticated, novel defalcation scheme during the past year. He had previously embezzled $35,000 of DMO's funds. DMO has refused to pay the accounting firm's fee and is seeking to recover the $63,000 that was stolen by Hightower. Which of the following is correct?

a. The accountants cannot recover their fee and are liable for $63,000.

b. The accountants are entitled to collect their fee and are not liable for $63,000.

c. DMO is entitled to rescind the audit contract and thus is not liable for the $16,000 fee, but it cannot recover damages.

d. DMO is entitled to recover the $28,000 defalcation, and is not liable for the $16,000 fee.

9. In which of the following statements concerning a CPA firm's action is scienter or its equivalent absent?

a. Reckless disregard for the truth.

b. Actual knowledge of fraud.

c. Intent to gain monetarily by concealing fraud.

d. Performance of substandard auditing procedures.

10. Hall purchased Eon Corp. bonds in a public offering subject to the Securities Act of 1933. Kosson and Co., CPAs, rendered an unqualified opinion on Eon's financial statements which were included in Eon's registration statement. Kosson is being sued by Hall based upon misstatements contained in the financial statements. In order to be successful, Hall must prove

	Damages	Materiality of the Misstatement	Kosson's Scienter
a.	Yes	Yes	Yes
b.	Yes	Yes	No
c.	Yes	No	No
d.	No	Yes	Yes

11. One of the elements necessary to recover damages if there has been a material misstatement in a registration statement filed pursuant to the Securities Act of 1933 is that the

a. Plaintiff suffered a loss.

b. Plaintiff gave value for the security.

c. Issuer and plaintiff were in privity of contract with each other.

d. Issuer failed to exercise due care in connection with the sale of the securities.

12. The registration requirements of the Securities Act of 1933 are intended to provide information to the SEC to enable it to

a. Evaluate the financial merits of the securities being offered.

b. Ensure that investors are provided with adequate information on which to base investment decisions.

c. Prevent public offerings of securities when management fraud or unethical conduct is suspected.

d. Assure investors of the accuracy of the facts presented in the financial statements.

13. Which of the following are exempt from the registration requirements of the Securities Act of 1933?

a. Bankers' acceptances with maturities at the time of issue ranging from one to two years.

b. Participation interests in money market funds that consist wholly of short-term commercial paper.

c. Corporate stock offered and sold only to residents of the state in which the issuer was incorporated and is doing all of its business.

d. All industrial development bonds issued by municipalities.

14. The registration of a security under the Securities Act of 1933 provides an investor with

a. A guarantee by the SEC that the facts contained in the registration statement are accurate.

b. An assurance against loss resulting from purchasing the security.

c. Information on the principal purposes for which the offering's proceeds will be used.

d. Information on the issuing corporation's trade secrets.

15. Mix and Associates, CPAs, issued an unqualified opinion on the financial statements of Glass Corp. for the year ended December 31, 1989. It was determined later that Glass' treasurer had embezzled $300,000 from Glass during 1989. Glass sued Mix because of Mix's failure to discover the embezzlement. Mix was unaware of the embezzlement. Which of the following is Mix's best defense?

a. The audit was performed in accordance with GAAS.

b. The treasurer was Glass' agent and, therefore, Glass was responsible for preventing the embezzlement.

c. The financial statements were presented in conformity with GAAP.

d. Mix had *no* actual knowledge of the embezzlement.

16. A CPA firm issues an unqualified opinion on financial statements not prepared in accordance with GAAP. The CPA firm will have acted with scienter in all the following circumstances *except* where the firm

a. Intentionally disregards the truth.

b. Has actual knowledge of fraud.

c. Negligently performs auditing procedures.

d. Intends to gain monetarily by concealing fraud.

17. Which one of the following, if present, would support a finding of constructive fraud on the part of a CPA?

a. Privity of contract.

b. Intent to deceive.

c. Reckless disregard.

d. Ordinary negligence.

18. Burt, CPA, issued an unqualified opinion on the financial statements of Midwest Corp. These financial statements were included in Midwest's annual report and Form 10-K filed with the SEC. As a result of Burt's reckless disregard for GAAS, material misstatements in the financial statements were not detected. Subsequently, Davis purchased stock in Midwest in the secondary market without ever seeing Midwest's annual report or Form 10-K. Shortly thereafter, Midwest became insolvent and the price of the stock declined drastically. Davis sued Burt for damages based on Section 10(b) and Rule 10b-5 of the Securities Exchange Act of 1934. Burt's best defense is that

a. There has been *no* subsequent sale for which a loss can be computed.

b. Davis did *not* purchase the stock as part of an initial offering.

c. Davis did *not* rely on the financial statements or Form 10-K.

d. Davis was *not* in privity with Burt.

19. Gold, CPA, rendered an unqualified opinion on the 1987 financial statements of Eastern Power Co. Egan purchased Eastern bonds in a public offering subject to the Securities Act of 1933. The registration statement filed with the SEC included the financial statements. Gold is being sued by Egan under Section 11 of the Securities Act of 1933 for the misstatements contained in the financial statements. To prevail, Egan must prove

	Scienter	*Reliance*
a.	No	No
b.	No	Yes
c.	Yes	No
d.	Yes	Yes

ESSAY QUESTIONS AND PROBLEMS

3.1 Herbert McCoy is the chief executive officer of McCoy Forging Corporation, a small but rapidly growing manufacturing company. For the past several years, Donovan & Company, CPAs, had been engaged to do compilation work, a systems improvement study, and to prepare the company's federal and state income tax returns. In 1992, McCoy decided that due to the growth of the company and requests from bankers, it would be desirable to have an audit. Moreover, McCoy had recently received a disturbing anonymous letter which stated: "Beware, you have a viper in your nest. The money is literally disappearing before your very eyes! Signed: A friend."

McCoy believed that the audit was entirely necessary and easily justifiable on the basis of the growth and credit factors mentioned above. He decided he would keep the anonymous letter to himself.

Therefore, McCoy, on behalf of McCoy Forging, engaged Donovan & Company, CPAs, to render an opinion on the financial statements for the year ended June 30, 1993. He told Donovan he wanted to verify that the financial statements were "accurate and proper." He did not mention the anonymous letter. The usual engagement letter providing for an audit in accordance with generally accepted auditing standards was drafted by Donovan & Company and signed by both parties.

The audit was performed in accordance with GAAS. The audit did not reveal a clever defalcation plan by which Harper, the assistant treasurer, was siphoning off substantial amounts of McCoy Forging's money. The defalcations occurred both before and after the audit. Harper's embezzlement was discovered in October 1993. Although the scheme was fairly sophisticated, it could have been detected had additional checks and procedures been performed by Donovan & Company. McCoy Forging demands reimbursement from Donovan for the entire amount of the embezzlement, some $20,000 of which occurred before the audit and $25,000 after. Donovan has denied any liability and refuses to pay.

Required:
  a. In the event McCoy Forging sues Donovan & Company, will it prevail in whole or in part?
  b. Might there be any liability to McCoy Forging on McCoy's part, and if so, under what theory? (AICPA adapted)

3.2 Perfect Products Co. applied for a substantial bank loan from Capitol City Bank. In connection with its application, Perfect engaged William & Co., CPAs, to audit its financial statements. William completed the audit and rendered an unqualified opinion. On the basis of the financial statements and William's opinion, Capitol granted Perfect a loan of $500,000.

  Within three months after the loan was granted, Perfect filed for bankruptcy. Capitol promptly brought suit against William for damages, claiming that it had relied to its detriment on misleading financial statements and the unqualified opinion of William.

  William's audit workpapers reveal negligence and possible other misconduct in the performance of the audit. Nevertheless, William believes it can defend itself against liability to Capitol based on the privity defense.

Required:
  a. Explain the privity defense and evaluate its application to William.
  b. What exceptions to the privity defense might Capitol argue? (AICPA adapted)

3.3 James Danforth, CPA, audited the financial statements of the Blair Corporation for the year ended December 31, 1992. Danforth rendered an unqualified opinion on February 6, 1993. The financial statements were incorporated into Form 10-K and filed with the Securities and Exchange Commission. Blair's financial statements included as an asset a previously sold certificate of deposit (CD) in the amount of $250,000. Blair had purchased the CD on December 29, 1992, and sold it on December 30, 1992, to a third party who paid Blair that day. Blair did not deliver the CD to the buyer until January 8, 1993. Blair deliberately recorded the sale as an increase in cash and other revenue, thereby significantly overstating working capital, stockholders' equity, and net income. Danforth confirmed Blair's purchase of the CD with the seller and physically observed the CD on January 5, 1993.
  a. Assume that on January 18, 1993, while auditing other revenue, Danforth discovered that the CD had been sold. Further assume Danforth agreed that in exchange for an additional audit fee of $20,000, he would render an unqualified opinion on Blair's financial statements (including the previously sold CD).
    1. The SEC charges Danforth with criminal violations of the Securities Exchange Act of 1934. Will the SEC prevail? Include in your discussion what the SEC must establish in this action.
    2. Assume the SEC discovers and makes immediate public disclosure of Blair's action with the result that no one relies, to his detriment, on the audit report and financial statements. Under these circumstances, will the SEC prevail in its criminal action against Danforth?
  b. Assume that Danforth performed his audit in accordance with generally accepted auditing standards and exercised due professional care, but did not discover Blair's sale of the CD. Two weeks after issuing the unqualified opinion, Danforth discovered that the CD had been sold. The day following this

discovery, at Blair's request, Danforth delivered a copy of the audit report, along with the financial statements, to a bank which in reliance thereon made a loan to Blair that ultimately proved uncollectible. Danforth did not advise the bank of his discovery.

Required:

If the bank sues Danforth for the losses it sustains in connection with the loan, will it prevail? (AICPA adapted)

3.4 Arm Watchband Company manufactures a full line of expansion watch bands, including platinum, gold, and a medium-priced silver. With the skyrocketing prices of precious metal and booming sales, Arm is bursting at the seams with cash and extremely valuable inventory. Dutch, the controller of Arm, noted some irregularities which aroused his suspicion that there might be some embezzlement of company funds. He therefore instituted a full-fledged internal audit of the company's books and records, examined all accounting procedures, and took other appropriate steps necessary to assure himself that nothing was amiss. The only thing unearthed by this was a $300 discrepancy in petty cash which had apparently been stolen.

Dutch talked to Wheeler, the president of Arm, and told him his fears. He also suggested that in addition to the regular annual audit performed by Rice & Campbell, CPAs, that they be engaged to perform a full-fledged defalcation audit. This was authorized by Wheeler and the engagement letter for the audit in question clearly reflected this understanding.

Rice & Campbell performed the normal annual audit in their usual competent, nonnegligent manner. The special defalcation audit revealed additional shortages in petty cash. The method was determined and the culprit was exposed and dismissed. Nothing else was revealed despite the fact that the customary procedures for such an audit were followed. Ten months later, Schultz, the warehouse supervisor, was caught by another employee substituting inexpensive copies of the watchbands for the genuine Arm items.

The copies were remarkably similar to the originals in appearance. In fact, it would take a precious metals expert to tell the difference based upon a careful visual examination. The packaging was the same since Schultz had access to the packaging materials, including the seals which were used in an attempt to provide greater security and detect theft. Schultz always placed the boxes of the copies at the bottom of the inventory supplies. Despite this fact, one such carton had been shipped to a leading department store several months ago, but the substitution of copies for the originals had not been detected.

Required:

Would Rice & Campbell be liable for failure to detect the defalcation scheme in question? (AICPA adapted)

3.5 The common stock of Wilson, Inc. is owned by 20 stockholders who live in several states. Wilson's financial statements as of December 31, 1992 were audited by Doe & Co., CPAs, who rendered an unqualified opinion on the financial statements.

In reliance on Wilson's financial statements, which showed net income for 1992 of $1,500,000, Peters, on April 10, 1993, purchased 10,000 shares of Wilson Stock for $200,000. The purchase was from a shareholder who lived in another state. Wilson's financial statements contained material misstatements. Because

Doe did not carefully follow GAAS, it did not discover that the statements failed to reflect unrecorded expenses which reduced Wilson's actual net income to $800,000. After disclosure of the corrected financial statements, Peters sold his shares for $100,000, which was the highest price he could obtain.

Peters has brought an action against Doe under federal securities law and under common law.

Required:
a. Will Peters prevail on his federal securities law claims?
b. Will Peters prevail on his common law claims? (AICPA adapted)

3.6 Able Corporation decided to make a public offering of bonds to raise needed capital. On June 30, 1992, it publicly sold $2.5 million of 12% debentures in accordance with the registration requirements of the Securities Act of 1933.

The financial statements filed with the registration statement contained the unqualified opinion of Baker & Co., CPAs. The statements overstated Able's net income and net worth. Through negligence, Baker did not detect the overstatements. As a result, the bonds, which originally sold for $1,000 per bond, have dropped in value to $700.

Ira is an investor who purchased $10,000 of the bonds. He promptly brought an action against Baker under the Securities Act of 1933.

Required:
Will Ira prevail on his claim under the Securities Act of 1933? Give the reasons for your conclusions. (AICPA adapted)

3.7 Mason & Dilworth, CPAs, were the accountants for Monrad Corporation, a closely held corporation. Mason & Dilworth had been previously engaged by Monrad to perform certain compilation and tax return work. Crass, Monrad's president, indicated he needed something more than the previous type of services rendered. He advised Walker, the partner in charge, that the financial statements would be used internally, primarily for management purposes, and also to obtain short-term loans from financial institutions. Walker recommended that a review of the financial statements be performed. Walker did not prepare an engagement letter.

In the course of the review, Walker indicated some reservations about the financial statements. Walker indicated at various stages that "he was uneasy about certain figures and conclusions," but that "he would take the client's word about the validity of certain entries since the review was primarily for internal use in any event and was not an audit."

Mason & Dilworth did not discover a material act of fraud committed by management. The fraud would have been detected had Walker not relied wholly on the representations of management concerning the validity of certain entries about which he had felt uneasy.

Required:
a. What is the role of the engagement letter when a CPA has agreed to perform a review of a closely held company? What points should be covered in a typical engagement letter which would be relevant to the parties under the facts set forth above?
b. What is the duty of the CPA in the event suspicious circumstances are revealed as a result of the review?

c. What potential liability does Mason & Dilworth face and who may assert claims against the firm? (AICPA adapted)

3.8 Arthur & Doyle, CPAs, served as auditors for Dunbar Corp. and Wolfe Corp., publicly held corporations listed on the American Stock Exchange. Dunbar recently acquired Wolfe Corp. pursuant to a statutory merger by issuing its shares in exchange for shares of Wolfe. In connection with that merger, Arthur & Doyle rendered an unqualified opinion on the financial statements and participated in the preparation of the pro forma unaudited financial statements contained in the combined prospectus and proxy statement circulated to obtain shareholder approval of the merger and to register the shares to be issued in connection with the merger. Dunbar prepared a form 8-K (the current report with unaudited financial statements) and Form 10-K (the annual report with audited financial statements) in connection with the merger. Shortly thereafter, financial disaster beset the merged company which resulted in large losses to the shareholders and creditors. A class action suit on behalf of the shareholders and creditors has been filed against Dunbar and its management. In addition, it names Arthur & Doyle as codefendants, challenging the fairness, accuracy, and truthfulness of the financial statements.

Required:
As a result of the CPAs having expressed an unqualified opinion on the audited financial statements of Dunbar and Wolfe and as a result of having participated in the preparation of the unaudited financial statements required in connection with the merger, indicate and briefly discuss the various bases of the CPAs' potential liability to the shareholders and creditors of Dunbar under:
a. The federal securities acts.
b. Common law (AICPA adapted).

3.9 Cherrylawn Acres is a large condominium complex located in the Traverse Bay area of northern Michigan. Residential units have been sold primarily to retired individuals and those contemplating retirement. Jack Sloan was hired by the Cherrylawn Owners' Association to manage the complex, comply with the various employment and tax laws, and issue annual financial statements to the homeowners. Diller & Dollar, CPAs, were engaged by the association to review (not audit) the financial statements prepared by Sloan's accountant. An engagement letter was not drafted by the CPAs.

While reviewing the accounts, Jimmy Dollar, Harold Dollar's son and newly hired assistant accountant, was unable to locate invoices supporting disbursements to several vendors for condominium repairs. Not knowing whether to pursue the matter further, he prepared a workpaper entitled "Missing Invoices" and placed it in the current workpaper file. He later asked his father what to do about the missing invoices. Harold Dollar replied that nothing need be done inasmuch as the firm was engaged to review the financial statements, and not to conduct an audit. A review, he reminded his son, consists primarily of analyzing relationships among financial statement components and inquiring of management, and does not involve the application of procedures normally associated with an audit. "Furthermore," he said, "we're going to disclaim an opinion, anyway, on the basis that the numbers are strictly management's representations."

Shortly after releasing the financial statements, Sloan informed the Cherrylawn Owners' Association that he had found another position and would be resigning as manager effective immediately. The following week (Sloan had already left the country), creditors began to request payment of allegedly significant balances owing them and the bank notified the association of a $10,000 overdraft that needed to be settled immediately. Alarmed at this sudden liquidity crisis (Sloan had told the association prior to his departure that the complex was in sound financial condition and that the owners should be contemplating temporary investment sources for excess funds and possibly rebating maintenance fees to the condominium owners), the association requested that Diller & Dollar conduct an investigation of whatever events had contributed to the current problems. The CPAs discovered that Sloan had been embezzling funds and concealing the thefts by recording fraudulent disbursements. The fraud had been perpetrated over a number of years and had become so significant that Sloan felt he couldn't "cover it" any longer. This threat of exposure led to his resignation and self-imposed exile.

The association subsequently filed an action against Diller & Dollar for recovery of $1.3 million, the best estimate of loss from Sloan's embezzlement. The action alleges that Diller & Dollar were negligent in failing to discover the fraud. Diller & Dollar responded that they were not engaged to conduct an audit examination, notwithstanding the absence of an engagement letter supporting their position. Upon subpoena of Dollar's workpapers, lawyers for the plaintiffs discovered the workpaper entitled "Missing Invoices."

Required:
a. Who should prevail in this case? Give reasons for your answer.
b. What does this case demonstrate as to the importance of an engagement letter?
c. What is the responsibility of a CPA when his/her suspicions are aroused during an engagement? How does this responsibility differ as to type of engagement?

3.10 Doyle & Boyle, CPAs, had been auditing Wiley Willy Distributors for many years. They rendered an unqualified opinion on Wiley's financial statements for the current year ended December 31, 1993. The audited financial statements reflected a net income of $1.4 million and earnings per share of $3.50.

Roger Boyle, the partner in charge of the audit, was aware that Wiley had applied to First State Bank in January, 1993 to expand the company's line of credit from $4 million to $6 million, and to extend the current due date from 1/15/94 to 1/15/95. First State agreed on the condition that Wiley increase 1993 audited earnings per share to at least $3.20 (1992 earnings per share had been $2.60). Boyle had so informed the in-charge senior, Alice Cooper, and instructed her to be alert to any attempt to fabricate the needed earnings increase. Cooper, in turn, had relayed this information to the audit team during the pre-audit conference that precedes each Doyle & Boyle audit.

At the beginning of 1993, Wiley decided to expand the capacity of its Duluth warehouse by constructing a major addition. In the process of verifying debits to "Construction in Progress" relating to the addition, John Burke, one of the staff auditors assigned by Cooper, was unable to locate invoices supporting many of the charges appearing on "Construction Work Order A1016," the work order pertaining to the Duluth warehouse addition. Upon inquiry, John Deft, the corporate controller, told Burke that the invoices had been sent to Duluth for verification purposes and would be returned to headquarters by March 15 (well after the completion of audit field work). Cooper said not to worry inasmuch as the addition had not been completed by the 1993 year end. The team would examine the invoices during the 1994 interim audit.

Based on the audited financial statements, First State expanded and extended the line of credit as agreed. Shortly thereafter, Wiley became insolvent and filed for bankruptcy under Chapter 11. The line of credit expansion had been used to fight a hostile takeover. Moreover, the trustee in bankruptcy learned that the Duluth warehouse addition never existed. Instead, the debits to ''Construction in Progress'' were really operating expenses which had been fraudulently capitalized in order to achieve the earnings increase necessary to effect the line of credit adjustments. First State Bank sued Wiley Distributors, Inc. and also brought action against Doyle & Boyle for negligence in not detecting the fraud.

Required:
a. What sources and types of liability confront the auditors in the present case?
b. Do you think the auditors were negligent? Support your answer.
c. Does privity extend to First State Bank? Explain why.

4

Audit Evidence

CHAPTER OUTLINE

I. **Characteristics of audit evidence**
   A. Factual vs. inferential evidence
   B. Underlying accounting data and corroborating information
   C. Sufficiency and competence of evidence

II. **Audit objectives**
   A. Audit of information system (identify high audit risk areas)
   B. Audit of transactions and balances
      1. Existence or occurrence
      2. Completeness
      3. Rights and obligations
      4. Valuation or allocation
      5. Presentation and disclosure

III. **Audit evidence and related auditing procedures**
   A. Physical evidence
   B. Confirmation evidence
   C. Documentary evidence
   D. Mathematical evidence
   E. Analytical evidence
   F. Hearsay evidence

IV. **Materiality and audit evidence**
   A. Individual item materiality
   B. Aggregate materiality
   C. Aggregate materiality workpaper

V. **Relationship among audit evidence, audit risk, and materiality**

VI. **Audit programs**
   A. Outline of procedures to follow
   B. Developed for each transaction cycle
      1. Revenue cycle
      2. Expenditure cycle
      3. Financing and investing cycle
   C. Nature, timing and extent of auditing procedures

VII. **Audit workpapers**
   A. Documentation of the audit
   B. Permanent file
   C. Current file

VIII. **Initial v. recurring audits**

OVERVIEW

Chapter 4 provides an audit framework which will be used as a focal point in subsequent discussions of audit testing. The framework consists of two sets of audit objectives: one set supporting the audit of the information system, and the other set supporting the audit of transactions and balances.

Following the discussion of audit objectives, the chapter addresses various forms of audit evidence and the auditing procedures used in gathering the respective types of evidence. Audit evidence and procedures are also related to the audit objectives as an integral part of the coverage. The chapter then focuses on the concept of materiality and the interrelationship among materiality, audit risk, and audit evidence.

Audit programs are then defined and related to the audit planning standard. If audit evidence is to be gathered in a systematic fashion, audit programs must be developed in light of risk and materiality considerations, and subsequently modified on the basis of further testing of internal control and other information obtained during the course of the audit.

The concluding section of Chapter 4 introduces the student to audit workpapers and the need for complete documentation of the audit. Workpapers are classified as to "permanent" file workpapers and "current" file workpapers. Each classification is defined and illustrations of audit workpapers are presented and discussed.

STUDY OBJECTIVES

After reading this chapter, you should be able to:

1. Develop a framework, in terms of objectives, evidence, and procedures, for conducting an independent financial audit;
2. Identify and describe the various forms of audit evidence, the procedures for gathering such evidence, and how to relate the evidence and procedures to the audit objectives;
3. Incorporate materiality considerations into the gathering and evaluation of audit evidence;
4. Define audit programs and understand the need for them, how they are prepared, and how they are classified;
5. Understand the relationship among risk, materiality, and evidence and how this interrelationship is reflected in the development of audit programs;
6. Understand the nature and purpose of audit workpapers and know the difference between the "current" and "permanent" file workpapers;
7. Recognize the attributes of the complete audit workpaper, and know why each is important to adequate documentation of the audit;
8. Differentiate between the nature, timing, and extent of audit procedures applied in an initial audit versus a recurring audit.

INTRODUCTION

The third standard of audit field work requires that "sufficient competent evidential matter is to be obtained through inspection, observation, inquiries, and confirmations to afford a reasonable basis for an opinion regarding the financial statements under examination."[1] To satisfy this standard, the auditor must first identify **audit objectives** for the engagement. The kinds of **audit evidence** and procedures necessary to meet the objectives are then selected. The audit plan containing the specified objectives and procedures is referred to as an **audit program.**

Chapter 4 begins by addressing the characteristics of audit evidence. This is followed by a discussion of audit objectives. Next, various forms of audit evidence and procedures are identified and described. Auditor consideration of materiality is discussed relative to gathering and evaluating audit evidence. Audit programs and audit workpapers are then considered within the combined framework of planning, materiality, and the need to document the audit process.

CHARACTERISTICS OF AUDIT EVIDENCE

Factual vs. Inferential Evidence

Audit evidence consists of those facts and inferences that influence the auditor's mind with respect to financial presentation. **Factual evidence** is direct and, therefore, is generally considered to be stronger than inferential evidence. Noting the existence of inventory through observation is an example of factual evidence. By looking at the inventory, the auditor may directly conclude that it exists. **Inferential evidence,** in contrast, does not lend itself to direct conclusions. Noting what appear to be excessive quantities of particular stock items, for example, may lead the auditor to suspect that the inventory is obsolete. This is inferential evidence. It is not conclusive or direct evidence. The auditor only infers obsolescence. Additional evidence, either supporting or refuting the initial inference as to obsolescence, may be obtained through inquiry of client personnel and tests of inventory turnover.

Underlying Accounting Data and Corroborating Information

Section 326 of the Codification of Statements on Auditing Standards describes evidential matter supporting the financial statements as consisting of "the underlying accounting data and all corroborating information available to the auditor."[2] **Underlying accounting data** include the books of original entry, ledgers, and supporting work sheets. **Corroborating information** includes such documentation as canceled checks, bank statements, sales invoices, vendors' invoices, vouchers, time cards, requisitions, purchase orders, bills of lading, and shipping orders. It also includes evidence developed by the auditor, such as confirmations, calculations, observation, and reconciliations.

---

[1]Auditing Standards Board, *AICPA Professional Standards,* New York: AICPA, Section AU 150.02.
[2]*Ibid.,* Section AU 326.14.

Sufficiency and Competence of Evidence

Evidence must be both sufficient and competent. To be **sufficient,** evidence must be adequate to support the auditor's opinion on the financial statements. Sufficiency is a matter of audit judgment and is usually based on materiality and the adequacy of the existing internal control structure. The auditor will generally require greater amounts of evidence for major account balances and transaction classes. Plant asset additions for a manufacturing entity, for example, will be audited more intensely than miscellaneous expenses.

The stronger the internal control structure policies and procedures, the more reliable is the accounting data produced by that structure. Under these conditions, the auditor may examine a smaller number of transactions or test count a smaller proportion of inventory than under conditions of weak internal control.

To be **competent,** evidence must be both valid and relevant.[3] **Validity** relates to the conditions under which the evidence was gathered. A sales invoice produced under conditions of satisfactory internal control possesses greater validity than one produced under conditions of weak internal control. **Relevance** relates to specific audit objectives. Observing the taking of the physical inventory, for example, provides evidence concerning existence of the inventory, but it is not relevant to determining ownership.

Figure 4.1 summarizes the qualities of audit evidence as just described. Note the importance of internal control in determining both sufficiency and competence of evidential matter.

AUDIT OBJECTIVES

Before determining the kinds of audit evidence to gather and the procedures to be applied in a particular engagement, the auditor must clearly identify the appropriate audit objectives. Audit objectives may be classified into two categories: audit of information system and audit of transactions and balances.

Audit of the Information System

The objectives in an **audit of the information system** consist of two parts:

1. Understanding the business and the industry of which it is a part; and
2. Understanding the existing internal control structure.

Understand the Business and the Industry

Effective allocation of audit resources requires that the auditor have a clear understanding of the client's business and the industry of which it is a part. Understanding the business and industry enables the auditor to concentrate audit resources in those areas of high audit risk.

---

[3]*Ibid.,* Section AU 326.19.

FIGURE 4.1   Factors Influencing the Quality of Audit Evidence

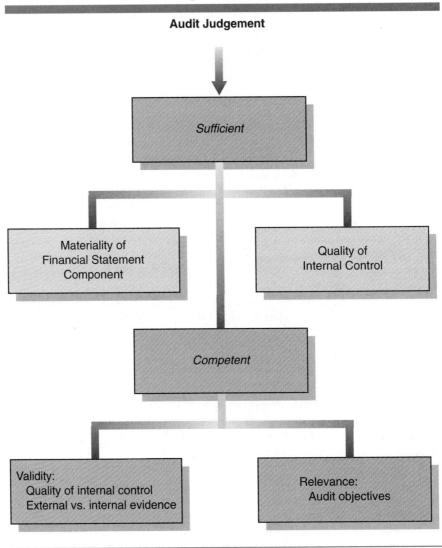

Audit risk is defined as "the risk that the auditor may unknowingly fail to appropriately modify his(her) opinion on financial statements that are materially misstated."[4] Such misstatements may be the result of errors; or they may be intentional.

Analysis of the business and industry assists in audit risk assessment by directing the auditor's attention toward areas suggesting intentional misstatements by management. The analysis is also helpful in identifying factors which may question

[4]*Ibid.*, Section AU 312.02.

the ability of the entity to continue as a going concern.[5] Finally, study of the client's business and industry can help to identify complex transaction areas contributing to higher probabilities of recording errors.

In addition to business and industry analysis, the auditor also assesses the probability of unintentional errors in the financial statements by studying and evaluating the internal accounting control structure. Such study and evaluation, referred to as *assessment of control risk,* is described below and discussed at length in Chapters 7 and 8.

Some of the specific risk areas which may be identified by analyzing the nature of the client's business are the following:

1. **Competition within the industry.** Today's so-called high tech industries are very competitive. Within this environment, companies may be "pressured" by the financial community to maintain earnings growth. The auditor must be alert, under these conditions, to the possibility of early revenue recognition or unjustified deferral of costs as means for misrepresenting earnings growth.

2. **Declining industry.** The airline industry has suffered in recent years following deregulation and declining demand. Competition has increased due to deregulation and, at the same time, given international terrorism and cost cutting efforts by businesses, demand for air travel slackened markedly. The problem has been so severe that companies such as Pan Am and Eastern Airlines have gone out of business. Circumstances such as these raise the question of whether other companies in the industry can survive in the face of increasing competition and declining demand. When auditing companies in declining industries, the auditor needs to ascertain specifically how the client is dealing with the situation and assess the degree of uncertainty prevailing in each case. High uncertainty may require an explanatory paragraph in the audit report or, perhaps, another basis of accounting if the going concern assumption is not appropriate in the circumstances.

3. **Idle capacity.** Frequently, companies or entire industries (steel, for example) experience idle capacity due to declining demand, increased competition from imports, or some combination of factors. Within such an environment, the auditor must determine that inventories are not excessive (suggesting possible obsolescence). Even where the inventories are not deemed excessive, the auditor must determine that they do not contain excessive amounts of fixed overhead more appropriately charged to current operations as a capacity loss.

4. **Related parties.** Shell companies, subsidiaries, executives, and their families are all examples of related parties. The economic substance of transactions with related parties is sometimes at variance with legal form. The auditor, under such circumstances, must ensure that economic substance takes precedence.[6] To il-

---

[5]SAS 59 requires the auditor to consider whether the aggregate results of all audit procedures performed during planning, performance, and evaluation indicate that there could be substantial doubt about the entity's ability to continue as a going concern for a reasonable period of time, not to exceed one year beyond the date of the audited financial statements. If such doubt exists, the auditor is required to add an explanatory paragraph following the opinion paragraph in the audit report (see Chapter 15).

[6]*AICPA Professional Standards, op. cit.,* Section AU 334.02.

lustrate, assume that a series of transactions are represented by a manufacturing client as sales with revenues recognized at the point of sale. Careful examination of these and similar transactions, however, reveal that the sales were made to an affiliated company, set up by the client as a distributor. Although a sale in legal form, the substance of the transactions is such that revenue should be deferred and recognized only when realized through transactions with third parties external to the economic entity.

Given the magnitude of related-party transactions, the professional standards. require that audit procedures be applied for the purpose of identifying related parties and related-party transactions and ensuring proper disclosure of the economic substance of these transactions.

Understand the Existing Internal Control Structure

The auditor studies the internal control structure in order to identify types of potential misstatements and assess control risk. A strong control structure reduces the probability of material errors. This, in turn, leads to a reduction in the quantity of audit evidence necessary to satisfy the objectives.

In studying internal controls, the auditor must obtain an understanding of each element of the structure. SAS 55 identifies the elements as the *control environment*, the *accounting system*, and the *control procedures*.[7] The auditor's understanding of the control structure is then used to

1. Identify the types of potential misstatements;

2. Consider the factors that may affect the risk of material misstatement; and

3. Design substantive tests (of transactions and balances).[8]

Significant weaknesses in the internal control structure may be likened to those areas of high audit risk discussed in the preceding section. Both types of environment pose a threat in terms of potential errors in the financial statements. Both, therefore, suggest the need for additional audit resources in order to adequately manage the associated audit risk.

Chapters 5 through 7 deal more extensively with the subjects of audit planning, risk analysis, and internal control study and evaluation. The current discussion is presented solely for the purpose of providing a basis for relating audit objectives to forms of audit evidence and audit procedures.

Audit of Transactions and Balances— Substantive Testing

With an understanding of the business and industry and the internal control structure, the auditor can proceed with the **audit of transactions and balances.** Figure 4.2 summarizes the following discussion and provides a framework for relating auditing procedures to various forms of audit evidence and audit objectives. Note that audit evidence is a function of audit objectives; and auditing procedures are

---

[7]*Ibid.*, Section AU 319.

[8]*Ibid.*

FIGURE 4.2   Audit Objectives, Evidence, and Procedures

Audit Objectives:

Audit of Information System
Business and Industry
Internal Accounting Control
Audit of Transactions and Balances – Substantive Testing
Existence or occurence – errors of commission
Completeness – errors of omission
Rights and Obligations
Valuation or Allocation
Presentation and Disclosure

Audit Evidence:

Physical   Sufficient
Confirmation   Competent
Documentary   Valid and Relevant
Mathematical
Analytical
Hearsay

Audit Procedures:

Observe inventory taking
Confirm accounts receivable
Vouch plant asset additions
Calculate accrued interest
Compare gross profit with prior year
Inquire as to contingent liabilities

dependent upon the nature and amount of evidence needed to satisfy the specific examination objectives. The procedures should therefore flow logically from the objectives.

Auditing objectives and procedures are not necessarily related on a one-to-one basis. Some audit procedures satisfy many objectives. In other audit applications, a combination of procedures may be required to satisfy a single objective.[9]

Substantive audit testing consists of examining evidence in support of the items appearing on the financial statements. Inasmuch as the nature, timing, and extent of substantive audit tests are dependent on the nature of the business and the quality of existing internal control, the systems objectives necessarily precede the transactions and balances objectives in Figure 4.2.

In the third paragraph of the standard audit report, the auditor expresses an opinion as to the fairness with which the financial statements present the financial

---

[9]*Ibid.*, Section AU 326.10.

position, results of operations, and cash flows. Five specific audit objectives have been identified by the auditing profession as necessary in order to support fairness of financial presentation:

1. Existence or occurrence;
2. Completeness;
3. Rights and obligations;
4. Valuation or allocation;
5. Presentation and disclosure.[10]

These objectives are now considered in terms of how they support such fairness.

Existence or Occurrence

The financial statements contain management's representations concerning assets, equities (used hereafter to mean liabilities and ownership equity), revenues, expenses, gains, and losses. The auditor must, through substantive audit testing, determine that all of the assets, equities, revenues, expenses, gains, and losses represented in the statements exist at the balance sheet date or occurred during the period being audited. Inclusion of nonexistent items results in overstatements of such components and are referred to as **errors of commission.**

Auditors ordinarily consider audit risk involving errors of commission to be most critical in the areas of assets and revenues, given the past tendencies of some companies to inflate income by overstating these components of the financial statements.

Completeness

Just as assets and revenues are more often overstated than understated, liabilities and expenses are more frequently understated than overstated. Errors resulting in understatements of financial statement components are referred to as **errors of omission.** In both cases, the result is overstatement of net assets and net income. To this end, most audit programs contain procedures for identifying unrecorded liabilities, as well as procedures dealing with possible asset overstatements.

The completeness objective is more difficult to satisfy than the existence objective. In determining existence, the auditor has a starting point—the representations contained in the financial statements. In ascertaining completeness (omissions), on the other hand, the auditor must begin the search from outside the statements. The auditor, in other words, must determine whether any material transactions or events have occurred during the period under audit that are not reflected in the financial statements.

Rights and Obligations

In addition to existence and completeness, the auditor must ascertain that the assets are owned by the client (**rights**) and that the liabilities are those of the client (**obligations**). Inventories held by the client under consignment arrangements, for

---

[10]*Ibid.*, Section AU 326.03.

example, exist but are not owned by the client. The auditor must determine, therefore, that "inventories" as represented on the balance sheet do not contain significant amounts of consigned inventories.

In examining recorded liabilities, the auditor may discover that the client has recorded operating leases as capital leases. This results in reporting a liability on the balance sheet that is not an obligation of the client.

Valuation or Allocation

In assessing fairness of financial statement presentation, the auditor must determine **valuation**—that assets and equities are properly valued in accordance with GAAP. Reporting inventories or plant assets at current or constant dollar cost, for example, represents a departure from GAAP and would ordinarily lead to an adverse audit opinion.

The auditor must also be satisfied that **allocations** are within GAAP. Prime costing, for example, under which only materials and direct labor are included in manufactured inventories as product costs, whereas overhead is charged to expense, is also a violation of GAAP. Other allocation areas include interest during construction, ordinary vs. extraordinary repairs, depreciation and amortization policies, and treatment of past service cost under pension plans.

Presentation and Disclosure

Presentation of components within the financial statements relates mainly to proper classification. **Disclosure** is ordinarily associated with the footnotes to the financial statements.

With regard to classification, the auditor must determine that the distinctions between current and noncurrent and between operating and nonoperating have been properly observed in the balance sheet and income statement respectively. Significant classification errors can materially distort liquidity and profitability ratios.

Concerning footnotes, the auditor must be satisfied that disclosure is adequate in order to make the financial statements not misleading. In the Continental Vending Machine Corporation case, for example, the court held that the footnote describing the Valley Commercial Corporation receivable was deficient in that it did not adequately describe either the nature of the transactions involved or the collateral securing the loans.[11]

The main theme associated with the five objectives discussed above is that the financial statements are the representations of management;[12] and the job of the auditor is to gather evidence which will be useful in testing the five hypotheses (as the objectives might be labeled) for acceptance or rejection.

Another way of viewing the relationship between management's assertions and audit objectives is in terms of **account** and underlying **substance.** The financial statements (accounts) might be viewed as being symbolic of the actual substance underlying them. The line item labeled *inventories,* for example, represents the investment in the substance called *inventories;* the *accounts receivable* component

---

[11]*U.S. v. Simon et al.,* 425 F. 2d, 796 (2d Cir. 1969).

[12]*AICPA Professional Standards, op. cit.,* Section AU 326.03.

TABLE 4.1   Account: Substance

Account	Substance (as evidenced by)
Cash in bank	Bank statement, canceled checks, deposit tickets
Marketable securities	Securities in vault or in safekeeping, brokers' advices
Inventories	Goods in warehouses, out on consignment
Accounts receivable	Customers' records of amounts owing to client, shipping documents
Notes receivable	Makers' notes payable
Property, plant, and equipment	Plant assets at various locations, vendors' invoices
Accounts payable	Vendors' records of accounts receivable, vendors' invoices, vendors' statements
Notes payable	Payees' notes receivable
Capital stock	Records maintained by registrar and transfer agent
Sales revenue	Sales invoices, shipping documents, cash register tapes
Operating expenses	Vendors' invoices, canceled checks
Wages and salaries expense	Payroll summaries, time cards, clock cards, canceled checks, personnel records

of the balance sheet likewise symbolizes the amounts owing the client by trade customers of the company. Referring to the financial statement components as accounts, one might describe the job of the auditor as one of determining that the "accounts" are, in all material respects, representative of the underlying "substance" to which they relate. Table 4.1 supports such a framework by including some examples of "accounts" and related "substance."

AUDIT EVIDENCE AND RELATED AUDITING PROCEDURES

Figure 4.2 classifies **audit evidence** into six types:

1. Physical evidence;
2. Evidence obtained through confirmation;
3. Documentary evidence;
4. Mathematical evidence;
5. Analytical evidence;
6. Hearsay evidence.

Each of these forms of evidence, together with the related auditing procedures, are considered in the following paragraphs. While all of these forms of evidence are used for substantive testing purposes (i.e., audit of transactions and balances), some of the forms also support the information systems set of objectives (internal control study and evaluation and study of the business and industry). The ensuing discussion differentiates between evidence and procedures supporting each category of audit objectives.

Physical Evidence

Physical evidence consists of everything that can be counted, examined, observed, or inspected; it provides, through **direct evidence,** primary support for the existence objective. The auditor counts cash on hand at year end and traces it to the cash receipts record and bank statement in order to determine that cash receipts transactions have been recorded in the proper accounting period. The auditor examines securities held by the client for the purpose of determining that the line item "marketable securities" fairly represents the underlying substance.

The auditor observes the taking of the physical inventory. The client takes the inventory. The auditor tests the client's physical counts and compares them with the recorded amounts in order to gain satisfaction concerning the existence of recorded inventories.

Observing the functioning of the internal control structure is a further example of physical evidence. This set of audit procedures supports the systems set of audit objectives. The procedures are applied prior to substantive testing as a basis for determining the nature, timing, and extent of tests to be applied in the circumstances. The extent of inventory test counting, for example, is a function of the quality of internal control over purchases and inventories.

If the client has made significant acquisitions of plant assets during the year, the auditor may wish to inspect major additions, at least on a test basis. As with inventories and marketable securities, the purpose of this set of procedures is to determine that the assets, as represented in the accounts, actually exist.

Inventory observation: Physical evidence of existence.

Confirmation

Confirmation consists of obtaining evidence of existence, ownership, or valuation directly from third parties, *external* to the client. The most common example of this form of evidence relates to trade accounts receivable. In confirming accounts receivable, the auditor typically sends a copy of the client-prepared customer statement to the customer and requests that the customer reply directly to the auditor concerning agreement or disagreement with the balance appearing on the statement. The strength of this form of evidence lies in the fact that it is obtained directly by the auditor from the third-party source.

In addition to confirming accounts receivable, many other forms of confirmation are utilized in the normal audit. Notes receivable and notes payable are confirmed with the makers and payees respectively; inventories out on consignment are confirmed with the consignee; goods in public warehouses, as well as securities in safekeeping, are confirmed with the respective agents.

The *lawyer's letter* obtained by the auditor directly from the client's outside legal counsel is also a form of confirmation. The purpose of this letter is to provide evidence regarding pending litigation and the possible need for journal entries or footnotes relating to asserted and unasserted claims. The lawyer's letter is described more completely in Chapter 13.

Documentary Evidence

Documentary evidence consists of the accounting records and all of the underlying documentation supporting the transactions and events recorded in these records. Some examples are the following:

1. Ledgers and journals;
2. Supporting workpapers;
3. Purchase orders, requisitions, receiving reports, vendors' invoices, and vouchers;
4. Sales orders, sales invoices, shipping orders, bills of lading, and freight bills;
5. Time cards, clock cards, employee earnings records, and payroll summaries;
6. Inventory tags and listings;
7. Cash receipts listings, remittance advices, cash register tapes, and deposit tickets;
8. Canceled checks and bank statements;
9. Correspondence;
10. Contracts;
11. Insurance policies;
12. Minutes of meetings;
13. Tax returns; and
14. Monthly financial statements.

Documentary evidence is *internal* as contrasted with evidence obtained through confirmation. Moreover, unlike physical evidence, much of it is *inferential* rather than factual in that conclusions often cannot be drawn directly from the evidence. Notwithstanding these weaker qualities, documentary evidence plays a significant role in the conduct of most audits. Documentation constitutes an integral element of the so-called audit trail. The **audit trail** consists of that stream of evidence that enables the auditor to trace a transaction or event forward from its inception to the appropriate ledger account(s)—or, conversely, backward from the ledger account to the inception of the transaction or event. This act of two-way tracing is referred to as **vouching** of transactions and events and represents a very important phase of any audit program (see Figure 4.3). Inasmuch as the document provides evidence of transaction inception, adequate documentation is imperative to effective vouching.

The auditor's study and evaluation of internal control is closely related to the importance of documentary evidence. The degree of confidence that the auditor places in the internal documentation of transactions and events is a function of the quality of the related controls over such documentation. For example, if internal control over sales and cash receipts is strong, the auditor can rely more heavily on sales invoices, bills of lading, cash receipts listings, and the accounts receivable subsidiary ledger (i.e., the internal documentation) and will need to confirm a smaller proportion of customers' accounts than if internal control were weak.

Some parts of the audit would not be feasible in the absence of adequate documentation. Such transactions as plant asset additions, payroll, cash receipts, and cash disbursements require documentation if they are to be examined and evaluated by the auditor.

FIGURE 4.3   Vouching—A Two-Way Process

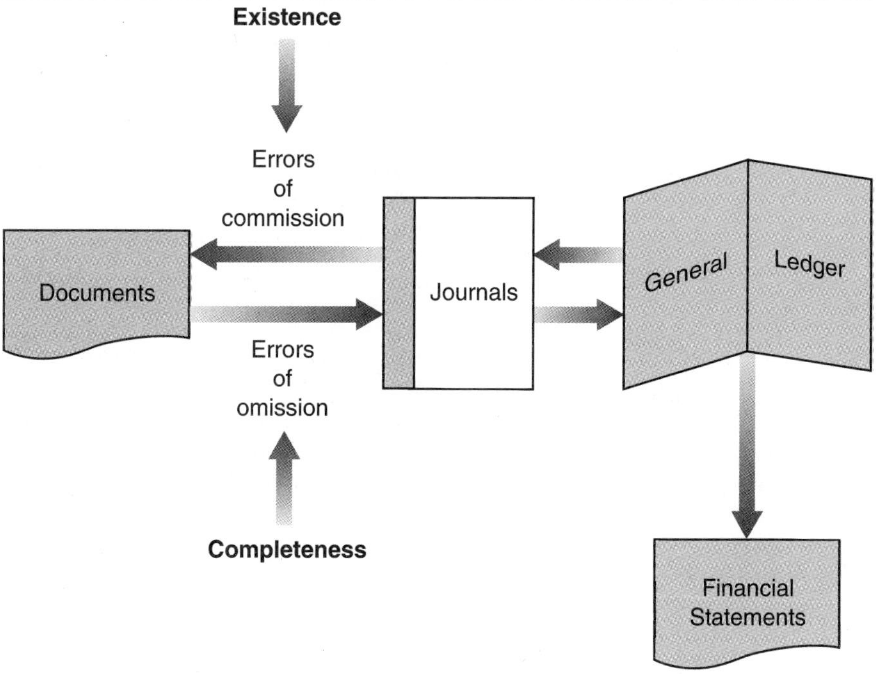

Mathematical Evidence

Mathematical evidence consists of calculations, recalculations, and reconciliations performed by the auditor. In auditing the client's final inventory amounts, for example, extensions (price $\times$ quantity) and footings of inventory listings must be tested. These tests produce mathematical evidence. Mathematical evidence is a *direct* form of audit evidence in that the auditor performs the computations on the data.

An important category of mathematical evidence relates to allocations and accruals. The following are examples of allocations and accruals tested through calculation or recalculation as part of the audit:

1. Interest receivable and payable;
2. Depreciation;
3. Income, property, excise, and payroll taxes;
4. Product warranty;
5. Accrued payroll;
6. Gain or loss on disposals of plant assets, marketable securities, and other assets.

In evaluating the reasonableness of accounting estimates developed by management, as required by SAS 57, the auditor may utilize one or more of the following approaches:

1. Review and test the process used by management to develop the estimate, or
2. Develop an independent expectation of the estimate to corroborate the reasonableness of management's estimate, or
3. Review subsequent events or transactions occurring prior to the completion of field work.[13]

The second choice results in a form of mathematical evidence. The auditor, for example, may recalculate warranty expense, net realizable value of inventories, the allowance for loan losses, or potential losses on purchase commitments.

Reconciliations, given that they involve numerous computations, may also be categorized as mathematical evidence. Examples include bank reconciliations, agreeing subsidiary ledgers to control accounts, and reconciling inter- and intracompany accounts of those clients with subsidiaries and/or divisions.

Analytical Evidence

Analytical procedures are substantive tests of financial information performed by studying and comparing relationships among data.[14] They must be applied during the planning stages of the audit, *prior* to applying the main body of substantive testing procedures.[15] They must also be applied at the end of audit field work as part of the overall audit review.[16] In the first instance, the objective is to identify areas

---

[13]*Ibid.,* Section AU 342.

[14]*Ibid.,* Section AU 329.02.

[15]*Ibid.,* Section AU 329.04.

[16]*Ibid.*

of high audit risk. Such high risk areas are suggested by unusual relationships within or between periods being audited. Having identified significant abnormalities, the auditor should plan to apply substantive procedures more intensively to these areas. The changes in relationships may have been caused by a change in the environment; or errors may have been made in recording or classifying data. In either case, the auditor must determine the cause and suggest corrections for any material errors discovered in the process.

As part of the overall review phase, the auditor evaluates the reasonableness of audited transactions and balances. Having audited the finished goods inventory, for example, the auditor may elect to apply the gross profit method in arriving at an estimate of the ending inventory using historic gross profit rates. Proximity of the audited and estimated inventories will lend added assurance to the auditor concerning the final audited inventory figures. Wide disparity, on the other hand, will form a basis for further examination.

Some examples of analytical procedures are the following:

1. *Compare major components of the monthly financial statements with the same period of the prior year and investigate significant variations*. If the gross profit rate, for example, has increased significantly during the current year, this could be the result of a change in product mix or a cost reduction program—or it could reflect inflated inventories caused by failing to relieve the inventory accounts for goods sold at year end. This analytical procedure is ordinarily applied as part of the audit planning stage.

2. *Compare sources of revenue and expense and investigate new sources and disappearance of prior sources*. Sources of miscellaneous revenue and expense may vary from year to year. Investigating these changes, together with comparison of amounts, may be the only procedure applied to these accounts. If the amounts have not materially changed in relation to the other income statement components, and if the sources are the same as the prior year, the auditor may properly conclude that miscellaneous revenues and expenses are fairly stated.

3. *Examine performance reports and investigate significant variations from the budget*. If sales have fallen materially short of budget expectations, two concerns face the auditor. First, if production was not curtailed in the face of declining sales, there may be a problem of inventory overstock and possible obsolescence. Second, if production was cut back, an abnormal volume or capacity variance is probable, and the auditor must determine that the variance has been accounted for as a charge to the current period's operations and not treated as either a deferred charge or as a part of inventory cost on the balance sheet. Applying these analytical procedures should lead the auditor to discover the cause and effect of all significant budget variations. This is another example of a set of analytical procedures applied during the planning stages of an audit.

4. *Compare key ratios and percentages with industry averages*. Profit margin, return on total assets, return on net assets, inventory turnover, and accounts receivable turnover are some of the "key ratios and percentages" to be included in this type of review. Significant differences between the client and the industry averages may be due to the unique nature of the client's operations. Alternatively, the variations could be the result of intentional or unintentional errors in

recording or classifying data. This set of analytical procedures may be applied during the overall review stage of the audit, as well as during audit planning.

Application of analytical procedures is perhaps the most effective means for the auditor to become initially aware of material omissions from the accounting records. As noted earlier, one of the objectives of substantive audit testing is to detect material errors of omission as well as errors of commission. Errors of omission are generally more difficult to detect because, unlike errors of commission, there is no convenient starting point for testing a hypothesis. If the auditor suspects that accounts receivable are inflated (error of commission), confirmation of accounts selected from the subsidiary ledger should reveal any significant errors. If, on the other hand, significant amounts of sales revenue have gone unrecorded, analytical procedures, by disclosing the decrease, will direct the auditor's attention to the possibility of omitted revenues. In the absence of analytical procedures, the chances for detecting this type of error are substantially lessened.

To summarize, analytical procedures serve two functions for the auditor. First, they assist the auditor in detecting unusual relationships that suggest possible errors in recording or classifying data. Labeled *high audit risk areas,* audit resources may then be allocated accordingly. Second, they enable the auditor to evaluate the reasonableness of final audited transactions and balances during the overall review stages of the examination.

Hearsay Evidence

Hearsay (oral) evidence consists of answers to questions posed by the auditor to client personnel. Hearsay is the weakest form of audit evidence in that it must be further corroborated. It is, however, applied extensively by the auditor throughout the examination. During the study and evaluation of internal control, for example, the auditor questions client personnel concerning duties and responsibilities, as well as the specific workings of internal control procedures.

In addition to questions regarding internal control, the auditor also inquires about contingent liabilities, inventory obsolescence, consignments, contracts, commitments, guarantees of indebtedness, related parties, illegal acts, and subsequent events. Like analytical procedures, hearsay evidence often leads the auditor toward areas requiring further investigation.

Sometimes the questions are suggested as a result of applying analytical procedures. For example, a significant decrease in inventory turnover should lead to the questioning of inventory and production personnel concerning inventory obsolescence. Similarly, a decrease in accounts receivable turnover suggests that the auditor question the credit manager as to changes in credit terms or the existence of doubtful accounts.

Some Concluding Observations

Some observations might be made at this point concerning the various forms of audit evidence just discussed. First, some forms of evidence are more *reliable* than others. Physical, mathematical, and confirmation evidence, for example, are direct forms of audit evidence in that the auditor obtains the evidence directly through observation, calculation, or formal inquiry of third parties. Documentary and hearsay evidence, on the other hand, are **indirect** forms of evidence and therefore not so conclusive as the former types.

Although certain forms of evidence are more reliable than others, other forms of evidence may be more **relevant** in terms of specific audit objectives. Documentary evidence, for example, is frequently the only means available to the auditor for the purpose of determining proper valuation or allocation. For these reasons, all of the audit evidence forms considered are significant, and all of the forms are used to greater or lesser degrees in most financial audits.

A second observation concerns how the evidence is gathered by the auditor. Some of the evidence discussed in this chapter may be gathered by computer-assisted means. Testing inventory footings and extensions, reconciling subsidiary ledger and control accounts, and applying analytical procedures can all be automated and extended with the aid of computers. This topic will be more fully explored in Chapter 9.

MATERIALITY AND AUDIT EVIDENCE

Materiality has been defined as that amount of misstatement that would affect the decisions of a reasonably intelligent user of the financial statements.[17] In deciding materiality, the auditor should consider the impact of possible misstatements on those profitability and liquidity measures typically applied by investors and creditors in making investing and lending decisions. Net operating income as a percent of net sales, gross profit margin, net income as a percent of operating assets, net income as a percent of stockholders' equity, inventory turnover, accounts receivable turnover, earnings per share, times interest earned, current ratio, quick ratio, and net working capital are examples of ratios and percents that the auditor should consider when establishing materiality levels. Inasmuch as these ratios and percentages are based on both balance sheet and income statement components, materiality considerations should give equal weight to both statements. Materiality and its influence on sufficiency and competence of audit evidence is considered in the following paragraphs.

Establishing appropriate materiality levels and identifying areas of audit emphasis vary with different engagements and is a matter of audit judgment. To illustrate, assume two separate audit clients: one is a wholesale distributor and the other is a service organization. One would expect a greater proportion of audit resources to be dedicated to the audit of inventory balances for the wholesale distributor, given the relative materiality of investment in inventories. In contrast, primary emphasis might be given to testing the appropriateness of revenue recognition for the service client. Proper timing of revenue recording relative to earning and realization is of utmost importance to fairly stating assets and income for service organizations.

The auditor should consider materiality in both the planning and overall evaluation phases of the audit—that is, at the beginning and at the end of the audit. In the planning stages, preliminary judgments about materiality levels are made. These judgments are typically based on the smallest aggregate level of errors or irregu-

---

[17]*Ibid.*, Section AU 312.06.

larities that could be considered material to any one of the financial statements. These levels are hereafter referred to as *materiality thresholds*. For example, if a $100,000 error is considered material to net income, while a $200,000 error is material to financial position, the auditor should select $100,000 as the appropriate materiality threshold.[18]

Consideration of materiality in the evaluation phase of the audit differs from the planning stage in two respects. First, materiality thresholds may change between the planning and evaluation stages. Using the above example, assume that proposed audit adjustments developed during the course of the field work have lowered net income by $300,000. If the original $100,000 materiality threshold was derived by applying a percentage to unaudited net income, that threshold has now decreased and the auditor must question the sufficiency of audit evidence in light of the revised materiality level. This would suggest that if, during the audit planning phase, the auditor suspects earnings overstatement, lower materiality thresholds should be set to prevent underauditing.

Materiality judgments during the evaluation phase also differ from audit planning due to qualitative factors arising during the implementation of audit programs. Examples of qualitative factors that impact materiality judgments are illegal payments, irregularities, and contingencies. To illustrate, a small illegal payment, discovered during the audit of transactions and balances may be insignificant by itself; but it could result in fines, lawsuits, or court injunctions producing subsequent expenditures or loss of revenues in substantial amounts. Irregularities, likewise, may be immaterial in quantitative terms, but raise major questions regarding management integrity. Contingencies may be material in a qualitative sense in that they affect the disclosure assertion rather than the quantitative assertions of completeness, existence, and valuation.

The auditor cannot very readily anticipate all of the qualitative materiality factors during the audit planning phase and build them into the audit programs. Rather, he/she must consider them individually as they arise during substantive audit testing and evaluate their overall financial statement implications during audit evaluation.

Individual item materiality concerns the impact of a single error or irregularity on the financial statements. Along with individual item materiality, the auditor must also consider **aggregate materiality**—the total effect of two or more errors, each of which, by itself, is not material. Assume that the magnitude of classification errors between the repairs and maintenance accounts and the plant asset accounts is immaterial in the judgment of the auditor. Assume further, however, that the auditor discovers classification errors between other asset and expense accounts. If each account is misstated to some degree, the aggregate effect on total operating expenses and net income could well be significant. To ensure proper consideration of aggregate materiality, the auditor should set a second materiality threshold measure. This level is then used for selecting misstatements to be included as *potential* audit adjustments. A special audit workpaper should be prepared for accumulating these adjustments. The auditor will refer to this workpaper in the evaluation phase for gauging the aggregate impact of the individual misstatements. If the individual item materiality threshold, for example, is $100,000, the auditor may elect to accumu-

---

[18]If an error affects the balance sheet only, the higher balance sheet threshold may be used in deciding whether or not an audit reclassification entry is appropriate.

late, in a separate audit workpaper, errors less than $100,000 and greater than $10,000 (the aggregate materiality threshold) for later aggregate evaluation. If the combined effect of the potential adjustments equals or exceeds the individual item materiality threshold ($100,000), the auditor should present these adjustments, as well as the individual item adjustments, to the client for posting and inclusion in the audited financial statements. Exhibit 4.1 illustrates some of the considerations involved in aggregate materiality determinations.

EXHIBIT 4.1   Aggregate Materiality Workpaper

WP Z
Prepared by:
Reviewed by:

Brandt Manufacturing
Aggregate Materiality
12/31/93

Individual item materiality threshold (firm policy):
  2% of net income
  1% of net assets
  Qualitative considerations:
    Intent
    Volume of transactions
Brandt Manufacturing—Unaudited:
  Net income . . . .$5 million
  Net assets. . . . .$30 million
Materiality thresholds as related to Brandt:
  As related to net income $100,000
  As related to net assets. $300,000
Individual item materiality for Brandt Manufacturing audit:
  For audit adjustment purposes $100,000
  For balance sheet reclassification purposes $300,000
Aggregate materiality as based on audit risk assessment:
  For high control risk and/or business risk environments,
      firm policy is to set aggregate materiality threshold
      at 1% of individual item materiality
  For low risk environments, firm policy is to set the level
      at 15% of individual item materiality
  Risk assessment for Brandt (see control and business risk
      assessment workpapers at Index 1-A):
        Control risk . . . . .Medium
        Business risk . . . . .Low

(continued)

EXHIBIT 4.1   *(continued)*

Based on firm policy and the Brandt assessment, aggregate materiality is set at $10,000 (10% of individual item materiality, given the approximation to a low risk environment). Therefore, any error greater than $10,000 and lower than $100,000 will be documented on this workpaper as a proposed audit adjustment. If the proposed adjustments aggregate more than $100,000, they will be presented to Brandt management along with the other audit adjustments. (See workpaper Z-1 for list of adjustments and conclusions.)

WP Z-1
Prepared by:
Reviewed by:

Brandt Manufacturing
Aggregate Materiality
Possible Audit Adjustments
12/31/93

WP Ref.	Description	Income Effect
D-1	Product development costs incorrectly capitalized as intangible assets	$ 23,500
L-3	Understatement of estimated product warranty liability	$ 44,600
E-1	Added depreciation on disposals of machinery and equipment	$ 63,200
	Total	$131,300

Inasmuch as these possible adjustments, each greater than $10,000 and less than $100,000, sum to an amount exceeding the individual item materiality threshold, they should be presented to the client as audit adjustments. They have, therefore, been transcribed to the "Audit Adjustments" workpaper (see WP X).

Whether the aggregate materiality threshold is $10,000 or some other amount higher or lower than $10,000 is a function of the auditor's preliminary judgments concerning audit risk. As a general rule, the more misstatements the auditor expects, the lower should be the aggregate materiality threshold. For example, if the auditor perceives, during the audit planning phase, that transactions are processed accurately and in accordance with GAAP, the aggregate materiality threshold will be set higher than if he/she suspects numerous processing errors. If expectations subsequently change as the audit progresses, the threshold should be raised or lowered as appropriate. A preliminary expectation of few errors, for example, followed by subsequent discovery of numerous errors should lead to a decrease in the aggregate materiality threshold. Revising aggregate materiality thresholds is considered more specifically in Chapter 7 as part of the auditor's assessment of control risk.

For auditing purposes, materiality must be applied to transactions as well as balances. A bank account, for example, may have become inactive during the period under audit, with only a nominal balance remaining at year end. Suppose, however, that prior to inactivating the account and during the year under audit, a large volume of cash receipts and disbursements transactions were processed through this account. Were the auditor to consider materiality in light of balances only, this account would receive inadequate audit attention. When the concept of materiality is extended to transactions as well as balances, a more rational allocation of audit resources results. The trend in auditing toward the audit of transaction cycles and away from exclusive examination of account balances has supported such an expansion of the materiality concept.

Auditors may also differentiate between balance sheet and income statement materiality. Income statement materiality thresholds are generally based on the auditor's judgment as to what constitutes a material misstatement of net income. Balance sheet materiality, on the other hand, relates to classification errors within the balance sheet that have no impact on net income. As an example, the auditor may need to decide whether to reclassify credit balances in trade accounts receivable as current liabilities. Inasmuch as net income and net assets are not affected, balance sheet thresholds are usually set at higher levels than income statement thresholds.

A final point regarding materiality considerations in auditing relates to discovered vs. projected error. If the auditor examines only a portion of transactions relating to a given balance sheet or income statement class, detected errors must be extended to the population represented by the evidence examined. An audit of a sampling of debits to repairs and maintenance expense, for example, may detect $20,000 of capital expenditures erroneously charged to expense. When projected to the population of debits to the account, however, the auditor may project a $150,000 overstatement of repairs expense for the period under audit. Although the detected errors aggregating $20,000 are not significant when compared with a $100,000 materiality threshold, the projected error of $150,000 becomes substantial when extended to the population. Statistical sampling procedures, as discussed in Chapters 10 and 11, provide a means for systematically projecting errors discovered in audited samples to the related populations.

RELATIONSHIP AMONG AUDIT RISK, AUDIT EVIDENCE, AND MATERIALITY

The preceding paragraphs discussed the concepts of audit risk, audit evidence, and materiality. In addition to gaining a thorough understanding of these three concepts, the auditor should also recognize the direct relationship that exists among them. This relationship is presented diagrammatically in Figure 4.4. In developing a rational audit approach that conforms to the ''due care'' concept as stated in Rule 201 of the *Code of Professional Conduct,* the auditor must first evaluate audit risk, after which materiality thresholds can be set and the nature, timing, and extent of audit evidence can be determined.

FIGURE 4.4   Relationship Among Audit Evidence, Audit Risk, and Materiality

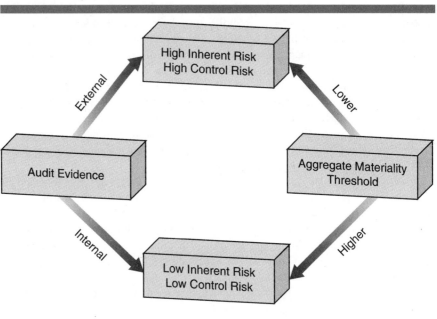

As stated previously, the auditor tests the information system to evaluate audit risk. This requires a study of the business and industry of which the client is a part, and a study and evaluation of existing internal control policies and procedures. Audit risk related to the various aspects of the business and industry is referred to as *inherent risk* and is defined and explained more fully in Chapter 5. Audit risk related to weaknesses in the internal control structure is referred to as *control risk* and is the subject of Chapters 6 through 8. Although the entire risk analysis process is discussed at length in Chapters 5 through 8, this chapter has introduced the student to those essentials of audit risk analysis necessary for an understanding of the relationship among evidence, risk, and materiality. Such an understanding, in turn, will provide a sound foundation for the topics comprising the remainder of this textbook.

Referring to Figure 4.4, if, for example, inherent risk is high because of auditor suspicion of intentional management misrepresentation of financial position and/or results of operations, aggregate materiality levels must be reduced and the auditor cannot rely as heavily on internal evidence. The reason for reducing aggregate materiality levels under such conditions is the increased probability of several accounts or transaction classes being misrepresented in order to effect concealment of the misrepresentation. The reason for obtaining greater amounts of external evidence is because internal documentation may have been fabricated.

If control risk is high, the probability of numerous unintentional errors is increased, and aggregate materiality levels must be decreased accordingly. Weak internal control also lowers the validity (reliability) of internal documentation and suggests that the auditor rely more heavily on external evidence, such as confirmations, physical inspection, calculations, and reconciliations.

AUDIT PROGRAMS

The first standard of audit field work states that ''The work is to be properly planned and assistants, if any, are to be properly supervised.''[19] As part of ''proper planning,'' the auditor develops programs for the conduct of the audit. An audit program is an outline of procedures to be followed in performing an audit, and is usually classified as to transaction cycles. A **transaction cycle** consists of a group of related transactions affecting essentially the same set of general ledger accounts. By focusing on transaction cycles rather than just account balances in assessing risk and applying substantive procedures, the auditor obtains greater assurance of testing all of management's assertions contained in a given set of financial statements. The following transaction cycles are used throughout this textbook as a framework for audit testing:

1. **Revenue cycle**
   a. Sales revenue and accounts receivable balances
   b. Cash receipts from customers and cash balances

2. **Expenditure cycle**
   a. Purchases, operating expenses, depreciation expense, and plant asset balances
   b. Payments to vendors and accounts payable balances
   c. Payroll
   d. Production and inventory balances

3. **Financing and investing cycle**
   a. Borrowing from others, interest expense, and liability balances
   b. Lending to others, interest revenue, and notes receivable balances
   c. Acquisitions and disposals of financial assets
   d. Capital stock and dividend transactions

In the appendix following Chapter 7, this format will be used to categorize tests of internal control structure policies and procedures affecting transactions and balances. Similarly, in the appendices following Chapters 12, 13, and 14, the format will be used to illustrate substantive tests of transactions and balances.

Exhibit 4.2 contains a partial program for the audit of cash receipts. Some auditing firms utilize standard audit programs classified by type of client (i.e., manufacturing, merchandising, commercial banks, life insurance companies, hospitals, colleges and universities, etc.). Other firms tailor the programs specifically to the client. Whether standard or tailored, the procedures included in the program should relate to specified audit objectives and should reflect varying degrees of audit risk and the relationship this has to forms of evidence and aggregate materiality levels.

---

[19]*AICPA Professional Standards, op. cit.,* Section AU 150.02.

EXHIBIT 4.2   Partial Audit Program

A.B. Smith, Inc.
Partial Audit Program
Cash Receipts

Audit Workpaper Reference	Procedure	Auditor	Date
	Evaluate internal controls relating to the processing and recording of cash receipts and modify audit program accordingly.		
	Count and list cash on hand at year end		
	Trace year-end cash count to cutoff bank statement		
	Identify sources of miscellaneous cash receipts and investigate any changes for proper approval and authenticity		
	Vouch nonrecurring cash receipts transactions in excess of $1,000 by examining remittance advice and receipted deposit ticket		
	Reconcile bank accounts		
	Obtain cutoff bank statement and trace reconciling items to cutoff statement		
	Confirm bank balances		

Developing Audit Programs

The nature, timing, and extent of auditing procedures to be applied (i.e., the content of the audit programs) depends on the following:

1. Study and evaluation of existing internal controls;
2. Materiality of account balance or volume of transactions;
3. Nature of the client's activities;
4. Cost/benefit.

Study and Evaluation of Internal Controls

Audit programs should be reflective of the quality of the client's internal controls. For this reason, as noted previously, the study and evaluation of internal accounting control must precede substantive testing of transactions and balances, if the collection and evaluation of audit evidence is to proceed in a systematic manner.

The stronger the internal control structure, the lower is the probability of errors in processing transactions and events. Under these circumstances, the auditor may justifiably reduce the extent of substantive testing that would otherwise be necessary. For example, if purchases of goods are fully documented and properly approved, if the perpetual inventory records are reliable, and if the physical inventory is carefully planned and taken by the client, the auditor may limit test counts and comparisons of inventory to a few major items plus a small sample of the remainder.

Materiality of Transactions and Balances

Heavier concentrations of audit resources are needed for the more significant categories of transactions and balances. Materiality was defined previously as the amount of misstatement that would affect the decisions of a reasonably intelligent financial statements user and was related to the various measures used by financial analysts and others in gauging an entity's liquidity and profitability. Preliminary audit programs for each transaction cycle subset should reflect those materiality considerations discussed previously in terms of individual item and aggregate materiality thresholds.

Nature of the Client's Activities

Audit programs must be tailored to fit the unique characteristics of the entity being examined. An audit program for a commercial bank, for example, differs significantly from one developed for a manufacturing client. For the bank, extensive audit resources are concentrated in the areas of loans receivable, loan loss reserves, and tests for solvency and liquidity. These are the areas of highest audit risk. In auditing the manufacturer, on the other hand, more attention will be devoted to inventories, purchases, manufacturing operations, and the cost accounting system.

Overall audit objectives such as existence, completeness, rights and obligations, valuation, and disclosure are the same, regardless of the nature of the auditee. The more specific subsets of objectives, however, must relate more closely to the unique operations of the entity. In examining the financial statements of the commercial bank, for example, the auditor will view the valuation objective as most critical to loans receivable. In auditing a manufacturing client, on the other hand, the auditor applies the valuation objective mainly to inventories and plant assets.

Cost/Benefit

Some auditing procedures are more costly to apply than others. To illustrate, in auditing inventories for existence, the cost involved in visiting the locations of inventories stored off the premises exceeds the cost of confirming the existence of those inventories by corresponding directly with the custodian. Although cost should not be an overriding factor in addressing questions of sufficient, competent evidential matter, neither should it be ignored. A good rule regarding **cost/benefits** is the following: Given two or more sets of audit procedures, each of which is satisfactory in attaining the specified audit objectives, the auditor should select the least costly from among the sets.

To summarize the preceding discussion, audit programs need to be modified in light of existing internal control, the nature of the entity's activities, materiality of balances and transactions, and cost where audit objectives can be attained by alternative means. Procedures may need to be added, procedures may need to be deleted, or, procedures may need to be modified in nature or extent of application.

Documentation of Audit Programs

A final observation with respect to audit programs concerns documentation. The audit workpapers should fully document the thought processes leading to the procedures contained in the final audit programs. If the nature of the entity's activities produces conditions of high audit risk leading to modification of audit programs, it is not enough to simply modify the programs. Rather, a description of the conditions, together with the *underlying rationale for modifying the programs,* should be clearly set forth in the workpapers. This type of documentation provides effective evidence that the auditors have exercised due care in the conduct of the examination.

FIGURE 4.5   Audit Workpaper Files

Current File: *(Workpapers applicable exclusively to current period under audit)*

Working trial balance
Lead schedules
Supporting schedules
Audit Adjustments
Reclassification entries
Audit report
Financial statements and footnotes
Internal accounting control questionnaires, flowcharts, and
    conclusions resulting from study and evaluation of control structure
Audit programs (substantive testing procedures)

Permanent File: *(Workpapers of ongoing significance)*

Analysis of business and industry
Organization charts
Charts of accounts
Copies of contracts
Corporate charter and bylaws
Excerpts from minutes of meetings
Labor-management agreement
Information concerning related parties
Accounting systems information
Duties and composition of internal audit staff
Descriptions of complex business transactions and/or unique accounting
    treatments
Copies of pension plans, stock option plans, and employee bonus and profit
    sharing plans
Analyses of capital and retained earnings
Descriptions of tax temporary differences and method of calculating change
    in deferred taxes

AUDIT WORKPAPERS

The collection and evaluation of audit evidence are documented in the form of **audit workpapers.** Audit workpapers are the principal record of the evidence that the auditor has gathered and evaluated in support of the audit opinion.[20] Given the expanded use of microcomputers in documenting the implementation of audit programs, most audit workpapers are now in printed rather than handwritten form. For this reason, the workpapers presented in this textbook are printed.

Figure 4.5 lists the contents of the audit workpaper files. Audit workpapers which have ongoing significance are placed in the **permanent file.** A copy of a long-term capital lease agreement containing a contingent rental clause, for example, is relevant to future audits as well as the current year's audit, and would, therefore, be contained in the permanent file. Copies of contracts, articles of incorporation, and narrative descriptions of the client's principal activities are other examples of workpapers contained in the permanent file.

Those audit workpapers which support only the period being examined are classified as **current file** workpapers. The working trial balance, as well as the results of audit tests, comprise the major part of the current file. These workpapers are considered in the ensuing paragraphs.

Working Trial Balance

The focal point of the current file is the **working trial balance.** Exhibit 4.3 illustrates a balance sheet working trial balance. A similar workpaper is prepared for the income statement accounts. The working trial balance might be likened to a table of contents found at the beginning of a book. Each line corresponds to a line item on the financial statements (in this instance, the balance sheet of Bold, Inc.).

Lead Schedules

Exhibit 4.4 presents a **lead schedule** for cash. A lead schedule lists all of the general ledger accounts comprising single line items on the financial statements. A lead schedule, of course, is not necessary where the financial statement line item consists of only one account. In this case, three accounts make up the line item "Cash" on the 12/31/93 Bold, Inc. balance sheet. In addition to listing the accounts, the lead schedule also summarizes the audit adjustments affecting the accounts. Note the index numbers in the second column of Exhibit 4.4. These numbers—subsets of the lead schedule index—are the workpaper references of the supporting workpapers. To complete the link to the current file workpapers, the page number of the working trial balance on which the lead schedule total appears is listed below that figure.

---

[20]*Ibid.,* Section AU 339.01.

EXHIBIT 4.3 Working Trial Balance

Bold, Inc.
Working Trial Balance — Balance Sheet
12/31/93

	General Ledger 12/31/92	General Ledger 12/31/93	Adjustments	Reclassifications	Audited Financial Statements 12/31/93	Workpaper Reference
ASSETS						
Cash	$ 75,000	$ 86,268	$ 421		$ 86,689	A
Trade Receivables	$ 240,000	$ 280,000	($515)		$ 279,485	B
Inventories	$ 300,000	$ 400,000			$ 400,000	C
Total Current Assets	$ 615,000	$ 766,268			$ 766,174	
Property, Plant, and Equipment (Net)	$1,200,000	$1,300,000			$1,300,000	D
Other Assets	$ 20,000	$ 20,000			$ 20,000	E
Total Assets	$1,835,000	$2,086,268	($94)		$2,086,174	
LIABILITIES AND STOCK-HOLDERS' EQUITY						
Notes Payable— Short-Term	$ 50,000	$ 60,000			$ 60,000	F
Accounts Payable	$ 150,000	$ 230,000	($ 90)		$ 229,910	G
Accrued Expenses	$ 70,000	$ 80,000			$ 80,000	H
Total Current Liabilities	$ 270,000	$ 370,000			$ 369,910	
Notes Payable— Long-Term	$ 150,000	$ 150,000			$ 150,000	I
Total Liabilities	$ 420,000	$ 520,000			$ 519,910	
Common Stock	$ 600,000	$ 600,000			$ 600,000	J
Retained Earnings	$ 815,000	$ 966,268	($4)		$ 966,264	K
	$1,835,000	$2,086,268	($94)		$2,086,174	

EXHIBIT 4.4 Lead Schedule

WP A

Prepared by: lk
Reviewed by: cbs

Bold, Inc.
Cash Lead Schedule
12/31/93

Account	Index	G/L	AJEs	Adjusted Balance
Petty Cash 101	A-2	$ 5,000.00		$ 5,000.00
City Bank 102	A-1	$61,268.00	$421.00	$61,689.00
City Bank—				
Payroll 103	A-3	$20,000.00		$20,000.00
		$86,268.00	$421.00	$86,689.00
				WTB 1

Supporting Schedules

The **supporting schedule** workpapers are perhaps the most important component of the current file. Exhibit 4.5 illustrates a supporting workpaper; in the present case, this is the workpaper containing the reconciliation of the City Bank account of Bold, Inc. The substantive tests performed by the auditor, together with the results of those tests and the auditor's conclusions, are contained in the supporting schedule workpapers. The tests, the results, and the conclusions constitute the body of "sufficient, competent evidential matter" supporting the auditor's opinion on the financial statements. If, at a future point in time, the auditor needs to demonstrate that due care was exercised in the conduct of the audit, the supporting audit workpapers are the single most important source of that evidence.

How Audit Workpapers are Interconnected

The workpaper reference column in the working trial balance (see Exhibit 4.3) tells the reader where, in the current workpaper file, to find the related lead schedule that describes the contents of the line item. The lead schedule for "cash," for example, is to be found at Workpaper A in the current file (see Exhibit 4.3). The lead schedule, in turn, is linked to the supporting schedules and is also cross-referenced to the working trial balance. This rather extensive referencing and cross-referencing found in most audit workpapers (see Figure 4.6) is for the purpose of facilitating effective review by those in charge of the audit field work. Lead schedule numbers appear in the working trial balance; supporting schedule numbers, as well

EXHIBIT 4.5   Supporting Schedule

WP A-1   Prepared by: lfk Date: 1/20/94
                                                   Reviewed by: cbs Date: 2/5/94

Bold, Inc.
Bank Reconciliation City Bank - A/C #102
12/31/93

Balance per bank		$62,765.18 *
Add deposit in transit		$ 1,452.20 &
		$64,217.38
Deduct outstanding checks:		
2345	$ 87.10 &	
2853	$ 232.90 &	
2857	$ 17.20 &	
2866	$ 619.75 &	
2867	$1,100.00 &	
2868	$ 472.19 &	
		$ 2,529.14
Adjusted balance		$61,688.24
Balance per ledger		$61,267.69 !
AJE 12: Bank collection		$ 515.00 x
		$61,782.69
AJE 13: December bank charges		($4.45)#
AJE 14: To correct error on check		
#2802		($90.00)~
Adjusted balance		$61,688.24

WP A

EXPLANATION OF AUDIT LEGENDS:
* Agreed to bank confirmation
& Traced to January bank statement
! Compared with ledger balance
Examined debit memo
~ Examined cash disbursements entry
x Examined bank credit memo

FIGURE 4.6   Linking of Audit Workpapers through Cross-Referencing

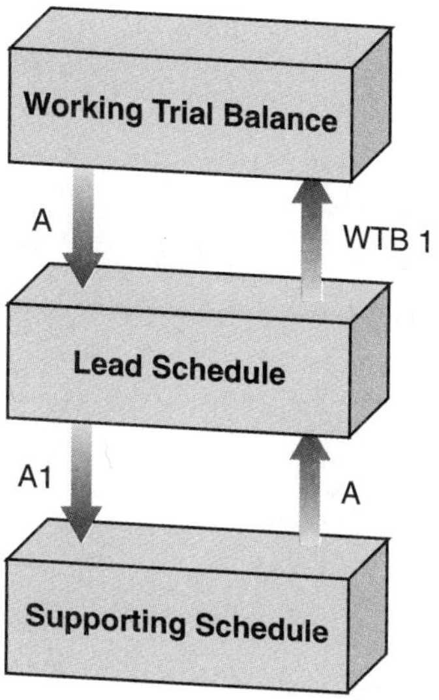

as working trial balance page numbers, appear in the lead schedule; and lead schedule numbers appear in the supporting schedules. Such a system of **indexing** permits the reviewer to proceed from working trial balance to lead schedule to supporting schedule and vice versa.

Within the working trial balance itself, the first column of numbers represents the previous year's audited financial statement balances, as taken from last year's working trial balance. These balances are compared, by the auditor, with the general ledger balances at the previous year end in order to determine that all of last year's agreed upon audit adjustments were posted by the client. The second column of numbers in Exhibit 4.3, entitled 12/31/93, are the company's current year end unaudited general ledger balances. These numbers, of course, are the numbers which are the subject matter for the current year's audit.

The *adjustments* column contains the effects of **audit adjustments** on the financial statement line items. The underlying details supporting these adjustments may be found in the supporting schedule workpapers (see Exhibit 4.5, for example) and also in the audit adjustments workpaper (Exhibit 4.6). The audit adjustments are journal entries proposed by the auditor to the client. The purpose of the entries is to correct the financial statements for material errors discovered during the examination. Inasmuch as the financial statements are the representations of management, the client must agree to the adjustments before they are actually posted to the general ledger accounts and incorporated into the financial statements.

The *reclassifications* column contains **audit reclassifications,** the entries necessary to ensure proper presentation of items in the financial statements. Significant credit balances in trade accounts receivable, for example, should be reclassified as current liabilities. Similarly, current installments of long-term liabilities, as well as bank overdrafts, should be reclassified as current liabilities if material in amount. These

EXHIBIT 4.6   Audit Adjustments

Bold, Inc.
Audit Adjustments
12/31/93

AJE 12

City Bank 102	$515.00	
Notes Receivable		$515.00

To record collection of non-interest
note by the bank.

AJE 13

Miscellaneous Expenses	$ 4.45	
City Bank 102		$ 4.45

To record December bank charge
not recorded by client.

AJE 14

Accounts Payable	$ 90.00	
City Bank 102		$ 90.00

To correct error in recording
Check No. 2802:
   Recorded as $890
   Should be $980

reclassifications are not posted by the client to the accounts. Therefore, they are displayed in a column separate from the audit adjustments in the working trial balance.

The final column of numbers represents the audited figures which are to appear on the financial statements. The analyses supporting the fairness of these numbers may be found in the workpapers indicated in the *workpaper reference* column.

Guidelines for Preparing Adequate Audit Workpapers

Some guidelines for the preparation of audit workpapers particularly directed at supporting schedules are noted at this point. Using Exhibit 4.5 as a reference, in the upper section, note where the workpaper number, the preparer's initials, the reviewer's initials, and the dates of preparation and review appear. The workpaper number facilitates location of the workpaper by those wishing to review it. The preparer's initials fixes responsibility for the preparation of the workpaper, and the reviewer's initials indicate that the workpaper has been reviewed and by whom the review was made.

The workpaper heading identifies the client, the account being examined (name and number), and the balance sheet date. Although each supporting workpaper corresponds to an account in the general ledger, it is not necessary for each account or financial statement line item to be supported by a workpaper. Materiality of the balance, the volume of transactions processed through the account, and associated audit risk determine whether the amounts involved warrant a supporting workpaper. Those procedures performed, however, do need to be documented. In the absence of a supporting workpaper, this documentation may appear on the lead schedule, or even on the appropriate line of the working trial balance.

The analysis contained in the body of the supporting schedule workpaper must be complete and self-contained in order to provide adequate evidence of due audit care. To be self-contained, the workpaper should clearly display the following:

1. The composition of the balance or transactions;

2. The auditing procedures performed;

3. The findings of the auditor;

4. The auditor's evaluation, conclusions, and recommended adjustments, if any; and

5. An explanation of all audit legends.

Adherence to these guidelines for workpaper preparation provides assurance that anyone reviewing the workpaper will be able to clearly identify the procedures performed by the auditor and the rationale supporting the auditor's conclusions and recommendations. As stated earlier, the audit workpapers provide the only source for determining whether the auditor gathered ''sufficient competent evidence supporting the audit opinion.'' Faced with the prospect of possible litigation involving auditor negligence, adequate workpaper documentation is considered imperative by auditing firms and practitioners.

In addition to affording effective review and possible legal protection, complete and properly indexed audit workpapers also facilitate future audits of the same client. The previous year's audit workpaper files provide an effective starting point for new staff members assigned to the audit for the first time. In order to familiarize themselves with the client, the staff members may review last year's workpapers together with the permanent file. In addition, many firms hold a pre-audit conference following this review. The purpose of the **pre-audit conference** is to gather together all those assigned to the audit and discuss the essential characteristics of the client, including areas of high audit risk. The major components of the audit and tentative staff assignments are also covered during the pre-audit conference.

INITIAL VS. RECURRING AUDITS

A final word with regard to audit evidence and audit workpapers concerns initial vs. recurring audits. An **initial audit** is a first-time examination, whereas a **recurring audit** is a repeat examination of the same client for the following year. Generally, the nature, timing, and extent of audit evidence is not the same for an initial audit as for a recurring audit. In an initial audit, the *study and evaluation of internal control* and the *study of the business and industry* require more time because the auditor is not familiar with the client's control structure and operations. In a recurring audit, the auditor is looking for significant changes in the control structure and operations, but is familiar with the essential characteristics.

In order to determine fairness of *real account balances,* the auditor in an initial audit must begin at the origin of the respective balances. For such assets as machinery and equipment, buildings, autos and trucks, and other plant assets, this usually involves examining several years' transactions. In a recurring examination, the auditor must obtain evidence regarding the ending inventory; in an initial audit, the *beginning inventory,* as well as the ending inventory, must be examined if the auditor is to express an opinion on the income statement. If the auditor cannot obtain satisfaction regarding the beginning inventory, a disclaimer of opinion is in order.

In conforming to the generally accepted auditing standards relating to audit reports, the auditor must determine that accounting principles have been *applied consistently* in the current year relative to the preceding year. If material changes in principle application have occurred in the year under examination, the auditor must add an explanatory paragraph following the opinion paragraph of the audit report. In an initial, as contrasted with a recurring audit, this involves examining the previous year as well as the current year, at least to the extent of identifying the accounting principles applied in both years.

In the event a new client was previously audited by another CPA, communication with the predecessor auditor, as discussed in Chapter 2, greatly facilitates the evidence gathering problems for an initial audit. If the client has never been audited, however, the task is much more extensive.

KEY TERMS

Account	Direct evidence
Aggregate materiality	Errors of commission
Audit adjustments	Errors of omission
Audit evidence	Expenditure cycle
physical	Factual evidence
confirmation	Financing and investing cycle
documentary	Indexing
mathematical	Indirect evidence
analytical	Individual item materiality
hearsay	Inferential evidence
Audit objectives	Initial audit
existence	Lead schedules
completeness	Materiality
rights and obligations	Permanent file
valuation or allocation	Pre-audit conference
presentation and disclosure	Recurring audit
Audit of information systems	Relevance
Audit of transactions and balances	Revenue cycle
Audit program	Substance
Audit reclassifications	Substantive audit testing
Audit risk	Sufficient evidence
Audit trail	Supporting schedules
Audit workpapers	Transaction cycle
Competent evidence	Underlying accounting data
Corroborating information	Validity
Cost/benefit	Vouching
Current file	Working trial balance

1. Differentiate between factual and inferential evidence, giving an example of each.
2. Describe the two aspects of competence as related to audit evidence.
3. How does the auditor determine when sufficient evidence has been obtained?
4. How does an understanding of the client's business promote effective auditing?
5. Why must the systems objectives be considered prior to substantive testing?
6. Identify the specific objectives related to the audit of transactions and balances.
7. Differentiate between the audit objectives of existence and completeness.
8. Why is the completeness objective generally more difficult to satisfy than the existence objective?
9. How does the valuation objective relate to GAAP?
10. What is meant by "correspondence between 'accounts' and related 'substance?' "
11. Name the primary objective served by the gathering of physical evidence. Give three examples of physical evidence.
12. What is the major form of confirmation evidence obtained by the auditor?
13. What is the principal factor determining the strength of documentary evidence?
14. Define the *audit trail*.
15. How is the audit procedure referred to as vouching related to the audit trail?
16. Mathematical evidence consists of calculations, recalculations, and reconciliations. Give an example of each.
17. How does the application of analytical procedures assist the auditor in learning of major omissions from the financial statements?
18. Differentiate between individual item materiality and aggregate materiality.
19. How does the expected number of errors affect aggregate materiality?
20. Why is the relationship among materiality, risk, and audit evidence an important ingredient in the development of audit programs?
21. Define the term *transaction cycle* as used in auditing.
22. Differentiate between "standard" and "tailored" audit programs.
23. What factors should the auditor consider when developing audit programs?
24. Differentiate between the "current" and the "permanent" audit workpaper files.
25. In what way is the working trial balance like a table of contents found at the beginning of a book?
26. What is a "lead" schedule? What is a "supporting" schedule? How are they linked together? Give an example of each.
27. What are the components of a complete workpaper?
28. What is the major function of audit workpapers?

MULTIPLE CHOICE QUESTIONS FROM CPA EXAMINATIONS

1. Which of the following best describes the primary purpose of audit procedures?
   a. To detect errors or irregularities.
   b. To comply with generally accepted accounting principles.
   c. To gather corroborative evidence.
   d. To verify the accuracy of account balances.

2. Which of the following statements relating to the competence of evidential matter is always true?
   a. Evidential matter gathered by an auditor from outside an enterprise is reliable.

b. Accounting data developed under satisfactory conditions of internal control are more relevant than data developed under unsatisfactory internal control conditions.

c. Oral representations made by management are not valid evidence.

d. Evidence gathered by auditors must be both valid and relevant to be considered competent.

3. As a result of analytical review procedures, the independent auditor determines that the gross profit percentage has declined from 30% in the preceding year to 20% in the current year. The auditor should

a. Document management's intentions with respect to plans for reversing this trend.

b. Evaluate management's performance in causing this decline.

c. Require footnote disclosure.

d. Consider the possibility of an error in the financial statements.

4. The auditor will most likely perform extensive tests for possible understatement of

a. Revenues.

b. Assets.

c. Liabilities.

d. Capital.

5. In the context of an audit of financial statements, substantive tests are audit procedures that

a. May be eliminated under certain conditions.

b. Are designed to discover significant subsequent events.

c. May be either tests of transactions, direct tests of financial balances, or analytical tests.

d. Will increase proportionately with the auditor's reliance on internal control.

6. Those procedures specifically outlined in an audit program are primarily designed to

a. Gather evidence.

b. Detect errors or irregularities.

c. Test internal systems.

d. Protect the auditor in the event of litigation.

7. Audit evidence can come in different forms with different degrees of persuasiveness. Which of the following is the least persuasive type of evidence?

a. Vendor's invoice.

b. Bank statement obtained from the client.

c. Computations made by the auditor.

d. Pre-numbered client invoices.

8. Which of the following elements ultimately determines the specific auditing procedures necessary under the circumstances to afford a reasonable basis for an opinion?

a. Auditor judgment.

b. Materiality.

c. Relative risk.

d. Reasonable assurance.

9. To test for unsupported entries in the ledger, the direction of audit testing should be from the

a. Ledger entries.

b. Journal entries.

    c. Externally generated documents.

    d. Original source documents.

10. Analytical procedures may be classified as being primarily

    a. Compliance tests.

    b. Substantive tests.

    c. Tests of ratios.

    d. Detailed tests of balances.

11. In testing the existence assertion for an asset, an auditor ordinarily works from the

    a. Financial statements to the potentially unrecorded items.

    b. Potentially unrecorded items to the financial statements.

    c. Accounting records to the supporting evidence.

    d. Supporting evidence to the accounting records.

12. Which of the following statements concerning evidential matter is correct?

    a. Competent evidence supporting management's assertions should be convincing rather than merely persuasive.

    b. An effective internal control structure contributes little to the reliability of the evidence created within the entity.

    c. The cost of obtaining evidence is *not* an important consideration to an auditor in deciding what evidence should be obtained.

    d. A client's accounting data *cannot* be considered sufficient audit evidence to support the financial statements.

13. A basic premise underlying the application of analytical procedures is that

    a. The study of financial ratios is an acceptable alternative to the investigation of unusual fluctuations.

    b. Statistical tests of financial information may lead to the discovery of material errors in the financial statements.

    c. Plausible relationships among data may reasonably be expected to exist and continue in the absence of known conditions to the contrary.

    d. These procedures *cannot* replace tests of balances and transactions.

14. An auditor ordinarily uses a working trial balance resembling the financial statements without footnotes, but containing columns for

    a. Reclassifications and adjustments.

    b. Reconciliations and tickmarks.

    c. Accruals and deferrals.

    d. Expense and revenue summaries.

15. The current file of an auditor's working papers most likely would include a copy of the

    a. Bank reconciliation.

    b. Pension plan contract.

    c. Articles of incorporation.

    d. Flowchart of the internal control procedures.

16. Which of the following circumstances is most likely to cause an auditor to consider whether a material misstatement exists?

    a. Transactions selected for testing are *not* supported by proper documentation.

    b. The turnover of senior accounting personnel is exceptionally low.

    c. Management places little emphasis on meeting earnings projections.

    d. Operating and financing decisions are dominated by several persons.

ESSAY QUESTIONS AND PROBLEMS

4.1 a. Auditing procedures are the means used by the auditor in gathering audit evidence. Using the classification of audit evidence presented in Chapter 4, identify the type of evidence produced by each of the following procedures:

1. Examined vendor's invoice supporting debit to "machinery and equipment."
2. Reconciled payroll bank account.
3. Recalculated accrued interest on short-term notes receivable.
4. Observed the taking of the client's physical inventory.
5. Mailed confirmations to a sampling of the client's customers.
6. Compared "sales," "cost of goods sold," and "gross profit" with prior year and investigated material changes for cause.
7. Inquired of credit manager as to collectibility of certain customers' accounts receivable.
8. Examined and listed marketable securities held for the client by a local bank.
9. Mailed letters to consignees requesting verification of goods held by them.
10. Obtained letter of audit inquiry from the client's outside legal counsel.
11. Traced a sampling of postings from customers' accounts in the subsidiary ledger to sales invoices and credit memos. Also traced a sample of invoices and credit memos to the subsidiary ledger.

   b. For each of the procedures contained in 4.1 a., identify the audit objective or objectives served by the resulting evidence.

4.2 The *audit trail* is defined as "the stream of evidence which enables the auditor to trace a transaction or event forward from its inception to the appropriate ledger account(s)—or, conversely, backward from the ledger account to the inception of the transaction or event." For each of the following specific audit objectives, indicate the recommended direction of vouching (i.e., from documents to ledger accounts, or from ledger accounts to documents):

   a. To obtain satisfaction that all shipments of merchandise have been billed to the respective customers of the client.
   b. To determine that all billings to customers are supported by shipments of merchandise.
   c. To vouch additions to plant and equipment by examining underlying documentation.
   d. To gain assurance that credits to vendors' accounts in the accounts payable subsidiary ledger are supported by documentation evidencing receipt of goods or services.
   e. To determine that vendors' invoices have been posted to the proper account.

4.3 Application of analytical procedures is perhaps the most effective means for the auditor to become initially aware of material omissions from the accounting records. Explain how each of the following applications of analytical procedures assists in identifying material omissions:

   a. Comparison of the current year's sales, cost of sales, and gross profit by months with those of the preceding year.
   b. Comparison of amounts and sources of miscellaneous revenue with the prior year.

    c. Calculation of accounts payable turnover and comparison with prior year.

    d. Calculation of accounts receivable turnover and comparison with prior year.

    e. Comparison of return on operating assets with the industry average.

4.4 Explain why each of the following situations is or is not a proper application of the concept of cost/benefit in auditing:

    a. For clients with material amounts of inventory, the auditor is generally required to observe the client's taking of the physical inventory, if feasible. Assume that H. Terrell, CPA, has a client with inventory located at two branch locations in addition to its headquarters location. Given the distances involved, the lack of audit personnel, and the fact that the branch inventories collectively represent only 30% of the total, Terrell decides to restrict inventory observation to the headquarters location only.

    b. In auditing marketable securities, the objectives of existence and ownership are of major importance. ABC, Inc., an audit client, has significant holdings of securities, both in a vault on the premises and in safekeeping with the trust department of a distant bank. The auditor decides to examine the securities on the premises; but, due to the cost of traveling to the distant location and the lack of correspondent auditors in that area, the existence and ownership of the securities in safekeeping will be determined by confirmation rather than by physical examination.

4.5 Identify all of the deficiencies in the Exhibit 4.7 audit workpaper analyzing additions to *Machinery and Equipment*.

EXHIBIT 4.7   Problem 4.5 Workpaper

	W.P. Index_____	
	Prepared by_____	
	Date_____	
	Reviewed by_____	
	Date_____	

Oblak, Inc.
Machinery and Equipment
December 31, 1993

Date	Description	Amount
12/31/92	Balance per General Ledger	$134,985
1993	Additions	57,630
1993	Disposals	(42,650)
12/31/93	Balance per General Ledger	$149,965
12/31/93	Balance per General Ledger (as above)	$149,965
	Audit adjustment to correct disposal	(12,350)
12/31/93	Adjusted Balance	$137,615

4.6 In auditing the "Leasehold Improvements" account of Diahold, Inc., the auditor becomes concerned about the magnitude of the dollar amount of debits to the account relative to the previous year. This concern is heightened in light of the auditor's knowledge of a commitment given the client by a local bank. The essence of the commitment is that a significant loan will be granted the client only if earnings per share equals or exceeds $3.50.

Required:
a. Discuss *sufficiency* and *competence* as these terms relate to audit evidence.
b. Why, do you suppose, the bank commitment "heightens the auditor's concern?"
c. In the case of the "Leasehold Improvements" account as just described, what are the major audit objectives? What kinds and amounts of evidence should the auditor collect in order to allay his or her concerns?

4.7 The audit process consists broadly of two parts: audit of the information system and audit of transactions and balances. The systems portion of the audit involves analysis of the business and industry and study and evaluation of internal control, and should precede the audit of transactions and balances.

Required:
a. Why is it necessary that the systems audit be performed first?
b. How does the outcome of the systems audit impact the audit of transactions and balances?

4.8 In analyzing the business activities of Jewel, Inc., a small computer manufacturer, Gerry Dell, CPA and auditor of Jewel, discovered that, due to declining sales volume in the face of increased competition, Jewel has been unable to maintain minimum cash balances as required by a major loan agreement. Moreover, a significant fourth quarter loss appears imminent. Due to the probable magnitude of the loss, Jewel will probably sustain a loss for the year. This will be the first time in its five-year history that Jewel has suffered a loss; and the effect on its stock price is expected to be material. This prospect is especially bleak in that Jewel was planning a public stock issue as a means for dealing with its severe liquidity problems.

In analyzing the computer industry generally, Dell has discovered that many small computer manufacturers have failed during the past five years. At the present time, Jewel is one of the few remaining members of an increasingly competitive industry. Jewel's management, however, assures Dell that they are prepared to actively compete and anticipate no problems in effecting their stock issue.

Required:
a. Based on this information, what specific audit risk factors present themselves?
b. Discuss the effects the analysis may have on Gerry Dell's audit programs.

4.9 In auditing transactions and balances, audit objectives are classified as follows:
a. Existence or occurrence;
b. Completeness;
c. Rights and obligations;
d. Valuation or allocation;
e. Presentation and disclosure.

Additionally, evidence is classified as to:
a. Physical evidence;
b. Confirmation evidence;

c. Documentary evidence;
d. Mathematical evidence;
e. Analytical evidence;
f. Hearsay evidence.

Assume that you are auditing the Country Bank, a first-time audit client. Country Bank is a small bank in a rural community, and its largest asset is its loan portfolio. Most of these loans are to farmers and farm suppliers (e.g., grain elevators and farm equipment dealers). A few significant loans have also been made to local builders. Nearly all of the loans are variable rate; that is, the interest rate moves up or down in the same direction as the market rate of interest. Most of the farmers in the area served by the bank have been "hit by hard times" as interest rates continued to increase while the prices of farm products declined. Many are presently in default on loan payments to the bank. Although a significant number of the loans are secured by first and second mortgages on the farms, the collateral may not be adequate in light of severe declines in the price of farmland.

Required:
a. Audit risk analysis is necessary to the effective allocation of audit resources. Explain why.
b. In view of this analysis, what are the critical audit objectives in the examination of the Country Bank? Be specific.
c. What kinds of audit evidence would you gather in support of the objectives just identified? Again, be specific.

4.10 Assume that during the audit planning phase for a client that manufactures machine tools, the auditor sets materiality thresholds based on the following unaudited balances:

Total assets ....$3.0 million
Net income ....$0.5 million
Liabilities ....$1.0 million
Current assets..$1.0 million
Current liabilities ....$0.5 million
Net working capital..$0.5 million

Required:
a. Assuming the auditor considers misstatements of net assets of 5% or more and misstatements of net income of 10% or more to be material, determine the individual item materiality threshold to be used for audit planning purposes. How would this threshold change if, based on past experience with this client, the auditor suspects significant amounts of earnings inflation?
b. During the implementation of audit programs developed on the basis of (a) above, the auditor discovered the following errors:
   1. The allowance for doubtful accounts is understated by approximately $50,000;
   2. Nonreimbursable research and development expenditures totalling $100,000 were debited to a noncurrent asset account titled "deferred development costs";
   3. The liability for product warranty is understated by approximately $100,000.

Draft the audit adjustments suggested by the above errors. What impact do the adjustments have on the materiality threshold set in Part (a)? What are the auditing implications, if any, of the possible change in materiality threshold?

4.11 Dodd, CPA, audited Adams Company's financial statements for the year ended December 31, 1992. On November 5, 1993, Adams notified Dodd that it was changing auditors and that Dodd's services were being terminated. On November 5, 1993, Adams invited Hall, CPA, to make a proposal for an engagement to audit its financial statements for the year ended December 31, 1993.

Required:

a. What procedures concerning Dodd should Hall perform before accepting the engagement?

b. What additional procedures should Hall consider performing during the planning phase of this audit? (After acceptance of the engagement that would *not* be performed during the audit of a continuing client.) (AICPA adapted)

4.12 Janney Manufacturing manufactures and sells a complete line of power tools and small hand tools to wholesale distributors and to retail hardware stores throughout the United States. The company has five plants serving the northeast, the southeast, the midwest, the southwest, and the west coast respectively. Cottrell and Cochran, Janney's auditors, in planning the 1991 audit, used the following unaudited amounts in setting materiality thresholds:

Sales revenue . . . .$135 million
Cost of goods sold . . . .$ 85 million
Operating expenses . . . .$ 20 million
Net financing expense . . . .$ 6 million
Current assets . . . .$100 million
Noncurrent assets . . . .$200 million
Current liabilities . . . .$ 35 million
Noncurrent liabilities . . . .$ 50 million

Misstatements equal to or exceeding 4% of net assets and 5% of net income, either individually or in the aggregate, are considered by the auditors to be material. Any misstatement equal to or exceeding 1/2% of net assets and net income will be subject to aggregate materiality consideration during the audit evaluation and review phase occurring at the end of audit field work.

Required:

a. What factors might the auditors have considered in setting the above materiality percentages? Using the selected percentages, determine the dollar amounts of materiality thresholds for balance sheet and income statement purposes.

b. The audit team discovered the following errors during the audit:

1. An invoice from Janney's legal counsel for 1991 legal services, $180,000, was not recorded until 1992.

2. 1992 sales in the amount of $3 million were recorded in 1991. The goods were properly included in the ending inventory.

3. That portion of Janney's mortgage note which is payable in 1992, $10 million, has been included in long-term liabilities.

4. Janney had not recorded any adjustment for product warranty for 1991. Based on past experience, the auditors decided that 1/2% of net sales is an appropriate percentage for determining the provision.

5. Janney incorrectly capitalized the roof replacement for two of its plants during 1991. The combined amount of the expenditures was $800,000.

Record the necessary audit adjustments (include only those that meet the individual or aggregate materiality thresholds set by the auditors). How does the auditor guard against overlooking the impact of aggregate materiality? Address this question in terms of its relevance during audit planning, audit program implementation, and audit review. In addressing the impact of aggregate materiality during the review stages of the audit, consider the effect of audit adjustments on the materiality thresholds set in the planning stages of the audit.

4.13 Your firm, L.L. Means, CPAs, has accepted a new audit client, Laughlin & Kline Manufacturers (hereafter referred to as L&K). You will be in charge of the audit field work for this engagement. The company's fiscal year ends August 31, 1992. L&K had previously been audited by the firm of Dodd & Smith, CPAs. Prior to acceptance of the engagement, Paul Sharpe, the L.L. Means partner responsible for the audit, obtained permission from the management of L&K and communicated with Dodd & Smith concerning their experience with the client. Sharpe provided you with the following information obtained from his conference with Jennifer Louden, the Dodd & Smith partner previously in charge of the L&K audit:

1. L&K manufactures and sells proprietary and ethical drugs in the United States, Canada, Mexico, and portions of Europe.

2. Increasing competition and continued regulation by the Food and Drug Administration (FDA) have placed a severe strain on the company's liquidity and profitability.

3. Management has been quite aggressive in maximizing reported income and earnings per share in light of the "profit squeeze." Louden indicated that the 1991 audit resulted in downward adjustments of income in the amount of $2.4 million or 40%.

4. Louden also indicated an unwillingness on the part of L&K management to accept audit adjustments readily and lack of an audit committee of the board of directors made the auditors' task all the more difficult.

5. Internal control structure policies and procedures in most transaction cycle subsets are adequate, but inventory control is weak and recently computerized perpetual inventory records are not very accurate. Moreover, the company does not have an internal audit staff and bank accounts are not reconciled on a regular basis.

In examining the company's annual reports for the past three years, you note a pattern of declining earnings. You also note that the auditors added two explanatory paragraphs to the 1991 audit report. The first expressed doubt as to the ability of L&K to continue as a going concern. The second referred the reader to a footnote describing a lawsuit by users of a subsequently banned L&K drug used by arthritis sufferers and found by the FDA to be a possible cause of cancer.

L&K's audited 1991 net income was $3.6 million, down from $4.5 million in 1990. The 1992 unaudited net income is $5.2 million. Audited net assets at August 31, 1991 totaled $120 million and unaudited net assets at August 31, 1992 were $123 million.

Required:

a. Using Figure 4.4 and the related chapter discussion as a focal point, discuss the types of audit evidence you might emphasize in the L&K audit and the types of audit evidence you might deemphasize.

b. Within the same framework as (a), what are your thoughts about the appropriate levels of materiality?

c. Assume the following L.L. Means policy regarding materiality thresholds:
Individual item materiality:

2% of net income

1% of net assets

Aggregate materiality:

  For high control risk and/or business risk environments 3% of individual
    item materiality

  For low risk environments 20% of individual item materiality

For environments falling between these extremes, the auditor should select an appropriate level between the above levels.

  Referring to Exhibit 4.1, the "aggregate materiality workpaper," and the related chapter discussion, set what you consider reasonable dollar thresholds for the following:

1. Individual item for income statement purposes

2. Individual item for balance sheet reclassification purposes

3. Aggregate materiality

Justify the levels you consider appropriate.

5

Audit Risk Analysis

CHAPTER OUTLINE

I. **Audit risk defined**

II. **Components of audit risk**
  A. Inherent risk
  B. Control risk
  C. Detection risk

III. **Quantifying audit risk**

IV. **Analysis of inherent risk**
  A. Preliminary phases of audit planning
  B. Study of the business and industry
  C. Analytical procedures

V. **Classifying the "warning signs"**
  A. Indicators of financial statement errors
  B. Indicators of forces affecting earnings or liquidity
  C. Indicators of possible disclosure requirements
  D. Indicators of audit complexity
  E. Indicators of possible management dishonesty

VI. **Risk analysis matrix**

VII. **Incorporating inherent risk analysis into the audit**
  A. Risk-driven audits vs. procedures-driven audits
  B. Preliminary audit programs reflecting results of risk analysis
  C. Impact of risk analysis on audit time budgets and staff scheduling
  D. Risk analysis and the pre-audit conference

OVERVIEW

Audit risk analysis was addressed briefly in Chapter 1 as part of the overall audit process. Figure 1.5 portrayed the process diagrammatically. This figure is now reproduced as Figure 5.1 with emphasis on that part of the process—inherent risk analysis—addressed in Chapter 5. To provide perspective regarding location of chapter subject matter in the overall audit process, the figure is also presented at the beginning of subsequent chapters as appropriate. Each reproduction is color coded to indicate that part of the audit process to be covered in the respective chapters.

Chapter 4 related audit risk to audit evidence and materiality. The current chapter examines risk in greater depth as a means for reducing the incidence of so-called audit failures, narrowing the "expectations gap," and generally increasing audit effectiveness.

The chapter begins by defining audit risk and subdividing it into its three components: inherent risk, control risk, and detection risk. A means for quantifying audit risk is then presented to promote consistency in analyzing such risk. The remainder of the chapter develops an approach to analyzing inherent risk. The audit functions of planning, study of the business and industry, and analytical procedures provide the structure for inherent risk analysis. Control concepts and control risk assessment are covered in Chapters 6 and 7.

Cases are presented to emphasize the importance of heeding the "warning signs" revealed by risk analysis. Although the cases are based on events that actually occurred, names and details have been changed to protect the identities of the clients and auditors. In addition to demonstrating the significance of risk analysis, the cases also permit the student to assume the role of senior auditor and experience typical audit judgment situations.

A risk analysis matrix, matching "warning signs" with "sources of information," is provided following this discussion. The purpose of the matrix is to ensure that all major risk areas are taken into account during the audit planning phase.

The chapter concludes by demonstrating how the results of inherent risk analysis serve as an input to modifying audit programs, developing time budgets, and scheduling audit staff for the engagement.

STUDY OBJECTIVES

After reading this chapter, you should be able to:

1. Define audit risk.
2. Define the three components of audit risk.
3. Quantify audit risk as a joint probability of the components.
4. Describe inherent risk analysis in terms of audit planning, study of the business and industry, and analytical procedures.
5. Identify the sources of information available to the auditor in analyzing inherent risk.
6. Identify "warning signs" providing evidence of inherent risk.
7. Understand how audit risk analysis affects the development of audit programs.
8. Recognize the impact of risk analysis on audit time budgets and staff scheduling.

FIGURE 5.1   The Audit Process

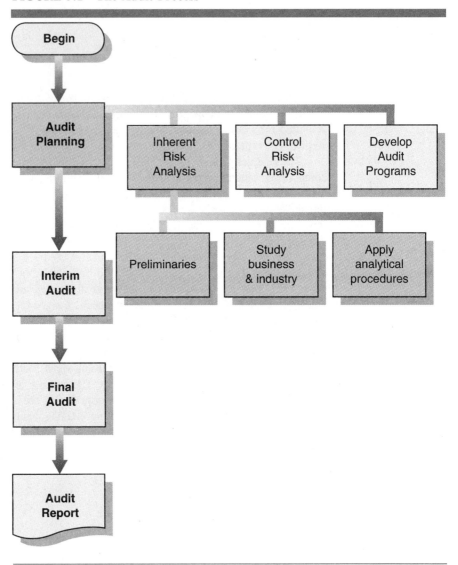

Audit risk analysis was mentioned briefly in Chapter 1 as part of the audit process overview. It was addressed again in Chapter 4 to emphasize the relationship among audit risk, audit evidence, and materiality. The relationship was represented diagrammatically in Figure 4.4; and examples were used to demonstrate that, as inherent risk and/or control risk increase, aggregate materiality thresholds need to be reduced and the auditor cannot place as much reliance on internal evidence. The current chapter continues the discussion of audit risk in greater depth with particular emphasis on how to achieve more effective allocation of audit resources through audit planning and risk analysis.

AUDIT RISK DEFINED

Audit risk has been defined as "the risk that the auditor may unknowingly fail to appropriately modify his (her) opinion on financial statements that are materially misstated."[1] Materiality was considered in Chapter 4. Material misstatements may be the result of errors or irregularities or both. **Errors** are unintentional mistakes; these were classified in Chapter 4 as errors of *omission,* and errors of *commission.* In testing for errors of omission, the auditor is concerned with management's assertion of completeness. Errors of commission relate to the existence or occurrence assertion. Errors can be minimized through effective internal control, a topic addressed in Chapter 6.

Irregularities are intentional and may involve misappropriation or management misrepresentation. **Misappropriation** is the fraudulent transfer of assets from the firm to one or more dishonest employees. The transfer is either preceded or followed by some form of concealment. For example, a dishonest employee might misappropriate unrecorded customer remittances and attempt to conceal the transfer by writing off the customer's account by charging it to the allowance for doubtful accounts. Management **misrepresentation** consists of deliberate attempts by management to misstate the financial statements by "omitting significant information from the records; recording transactions without substance; or intentionally misapplying accounting principles."[2]

SAS 53 assigns the independent auditor the responsibility for designing the audit to provide reasonable assurance of detecting errors and irregularities that are material to the financial statements.[3] SAS 47 requires that audit risk and materiality be considered both in *planning* the audit and in *evaluating* the audit results.[4] As discussed in Chapter 4, the levels of materiality may be the same at both points in the audit. If, however, in the process of evaluating audit evidence, the materiality thresholds are lowered below those set at the planning stage, the auditor should "reevaluate the sufficiency of auditing procedures which have been applied."[5]

The following paragraphs expand on the definitions of audit risk and audit risk analysis and explain how risk analysis can reduce the probability of material undetected errors in the financial statements.

COMPONENTS OF AUDIT RISK

Audit risk can be viewed as comprising the following components: inherent risk, control risk, and detection risk.

Inherent Risk

Inherent risk relates to the "susceptibility of an account balance or class of transactions to error that could be material. . . . assuming that there were no related

---

[1]Auditing Standards Board, *AICPA Professional Standards,* New York: AICPA, Section AU 312.02.

[2]*Ibid.,* Section AU 316.

[3]*Ibid.,* Section AU 316.

[4]*Ibid.,* Section AU 312.08.

[5]*Ibid.,* Section AU 312.15.

internal . . . controls.''[6] Inherent risk is often increased by unique characteristics of the business or industry, which can contribute to audit complexity and uncertainty, thereby increasing the likelihood of undetected errors or irregularities in the financial statements. Clients operating in such industries as oil and gas exploration and casualty insurance, for example, given specialized accounting treatment relating to income determination, present greater audit *complexity* than the more typical manufacturing, merchandising, or service clients. The existence of related parties, leases, and other complicated contracts and agreements also contribute to audit complexity.

Clients in declining industries present a higher audit risk than clients in stable or thriving industries. Audits of these clients may raise questions of *uncertainty* regarding the ability to continue as a going concern. Depending on the degree of uncertainty, the audit report may need to be modified. Clients in industries experiencing business declines also present a higher risk of management misrepresentation. Pressures to maintain stable earnings in the face of a business downturn may lead management to change to accounting principles that maximize earnings per share, or to classify ordinary losses as extraordinary. Violations of restrictive covenants in loan agreements (e.g., minimum cash balance and/or working capital requirements) are also more likely if diminishing revenues have given rise to liquidity problems.

Control Risk

Control risk is the risk that material errors or irregularities are not prevented or detected by the internal control structure.[7] Failure to adequately review transactions; inadequate documentation; unlimited access to negotiable securities, cash, and inventories; and lack of perpetual inventory records are examples of control weaknesses that contribute to errors in the financial statements. SAS 55 requires the auditor to assess control risk.[8] An approach to evaluating control risk is presented in Chapters 6 and 7.

Together, inherent risk and control risk determine the probability of the financial statements containing material errors.[9] As discussed in Chapter 4, these risk elements also affect the validity of internal audit evidence. Before determining the nature, timing, and extent of substantive audit testing to be performed, the auditor must carefully analyze these two risk factors.

Detection Risk

Detection risk is the risk that errors or irregularities that are not prevented or detected by the control structure are not detected by the independent auditor.[10] Chapters 11 through 14 discuss how detection risk can be reduced through the application of substantive audit procedures.

---

[6]*Ibid.*, Section AU 312.20.

[7]*Ibid.*

[8]*Ibid.*, Section AU 319.

[9]*Ibid.*, Section AU 312.20.

[10]*Ibid.*

QUANTIFYING AUDIT RISK

Audit risk analysis directly confronts inherent risk, control risk, and detection risk. It is an audit approach that attempts to identify those areas presenting the highest probability of material errors or irregularities, and those areas of greatest audit complexity. Once identified, audit risk must be evaluated and audit resources allocated more liberally to those areas presenting the highest risk.

The **expectations gap,** as described in Chapter 2, recognizes a disparity between the perceptions of users and auditors of the responsibility for error detection. Many, if not most, financial statement users expect the auditor to detect virtually all errors and irregularities having a material impact on the financial statements, regardless of how they occurred or how they were concealed. By increasing the detection probability, effective audit risk analysis enables the auditor to better meet user expectations.

A means for quantifying audit risk is presented in this section. Although auditors do not necessarily quantify audit risk for each engagement, the concept of quantification enhances one's understanding of the risk components and provides a consistent approach to risk analysis.

Audit risk can be viewed as a joint probability of inherent risk, control risk, and detection risk. The following equation expresses this interpretation of audit risk:

$$AR = IR \times CR \times DR$$

where

$$AR = \text{overall audit risk}$$
$$IR = \text{inherent risk}$$
$$CR = \text{control risk}$$
$$DR = \text{detection risk}$$

Overall *audit risk* should be set low by the auditor inasmuch as the complement of this risk factor forms the basis for the audit opinion. If, for example, audit risk is set at 5 percent, the auditor's opinion will be expressed with 95 percent confidence that the financial statements are not materially misstated by errors or irregularities. A good rule of thumb is to set the overall audit risk ≤ 10 percent.

Conservatism would suggest that inherent risk be set initially at 100 percent. One may reasonably assume, in other words, that in the absence of internal control, the probability of occurrence of material errors or irregularities is 100 percent. This is not an unreasonable assumption when one considers what might happen if transactions are not properly approved, bank accounts are not reconciled, assets are not adequately safeguarded, and transactions lack documentation.

Control risk will be assessed on the basis of the auditor's study and evaluation of internal control. As stated earlier, this phase of risk analysis is covered in Chapters 6 and 7.

Detection risk is the controllable variable in the equation, and it is a function of the auditor's evaluation of inherent risk and control risk. Detection risk is set by the auditor so that the joint probability of the three risk elements produces the desired overall audit risk. The level of detection risk is inversely related to the extent of substantive audit testing to be performed under the circumstances.

Given the equation expressing audit risk as a joint probability, and given, too, that detection risk is controllable through increasing or decreasing substantive audit testing, the equation may be rearranged so that the controllable (dependent) variable (detection risk) is on the left side of the equation and the uncontrollable (independent) variables are on the right side. This may be accomplished by dividing both sides of the equation by $IR \times CR$. The equation may now be expressed as:

$$DR = \frac{AR}{IR \times CR}$$

If IR is assumed to be 100 percent, then the equation may be shortened to

$$DR = \frac{AR}{CR}$$

Assume the following percentages have been determined by the auditor:

AR = 10 percent (set low because it forms the basis for the audit opinion)

CR = 30 percent, based on study and testing of internal control

Therefore,

$$DR = .1/.3 = 33 \text{ percent}$$

If study and testing of internal controls had revealed weaker controls than indicated earlier, CR may have been assessed at, say, 60 percent rather than 30 percent. Detection risk would then decrease to 16⅔ percent, requiring a substantial increase in the amount of substantive testing in order to compensate for weaker controls and yet maintain the overall audit risk at the specified 10 percent.

The detection risk percentage, together with materiality thresholds set by the auditor, will be used in Chapter 11 to calculate a sample size for substantive testing purposes.

The analysis of inherent risk, as will be discussed, enables the auditor to *reduce inherent risk below 100 percent*. By concentrating audit resources in the high risk areas, the probability of undetected errors decreases. Both inherent risk analysis and control risk analysis, therefore, affect the nature, timing, and extent of substantive audit testing.

Figure 5.2 summarizes this discussion of errors, irregularities, and audit risk analysis, and sets the course for the discussion that follows. As indicated in Figure 5.2, inherent risk is covered in this current chapter. The audit planning phases involving inherent risk analysis are:

- Preliminary phase of audit planning;
- Study of the business and industry; and
- Analytical procedures.

Control risk is covered in Chapters 6 and 7, which deal collectively with the auditor's understanding and testing of internal control. Detection risk is addressed in Chapters 11 through 14 as part of the discussion of substantive audit testing.

FIGURE 5.2   Audit Planning and Risk Analysis

I. Factors Contributing to Audit Risk
   A. *Errors*
      1. Commission
      2. Omission
   B. *Irregularities*
      1. Misappropriation
      2. Misrepresentation

II. Components of Audit Risk
   A. Inherent Risk:
      Unique characteristics of the business or industry that contribute to audit complexity and uncertainty
   B. Control Risk:
      Risk that errors or irregularities will not be prevented or detected by the control structure
   C. Detection Risk:
      Risk that errors or irregularities not prevented or detected by the control structure will not be detected by the independent audit

III. Audit Risk Analysis

Risk Component	*Audit Phase*	*Chapter*
Inherent Risk	Audit planning	5
	Study of the business and industry	
	Analytical procedures	
Control Risk	Further testing of selected controls	6–8
Detection Risk	Substantive audit testing (as modified based on analysis of inherent risk and control risk)	11–14

ANALYSIS OF INHERENT RISK

Inherent risk, as defined earlier, is the probability of errors and/or irregularities occurring in the absence of internal control. Inherent risk may be compounded or mitigated by unique characteristics of the business and industry. These character-istics can contribute to audit complexity and uncertainty, and can influence the incidence of material errors and/or irregularities in the financial statements. The following paragraphs demonstrate how the auditor can manage inherent risk through analysis. Inherent risk analysis is considered within the context of the preliminary phases of audit planning, study of the business and industry, and analytical proce-dures.

Preliminary Phase of Audit Planning

Audit planning, as described in Chapter 1, culminates in the formulation of preliminary audit programs. An audit program, as defined in Chapter 4, is an outline of procedures to be followed in performing the audit. The audit programs reflect the auditor's assessment of inherent risk and control risk. Control risk assessment is addressed in Chapter 7. Inherent risk assessment will now be discussed.

The preliminary phase of audit planning facilitates inherent risk analysis in the following ways:

Inquiry of Client Personnel Assists in Identifying Risk Areas

The audit planning phase affords the auditor the opportunity to question client personnel concerning the entity organization. Such questioning should direct the auditor's attention to some of the higher risk areas. For example, the auditor may learn that the existence of excess capacity, combined with strong competition from imports, has placed a "squeeze" on profits. These conditions should make the auditor alert to possible earnings inflation through early revenue recognition, expense deferral, or some combination of these means. The increased probability of misrepresentation should also cause the auditor to lower aggregate materiality thresholds and consider the merits of obtaining greater amounts of external relative to internal evidence.

The preliminary discussions between auditor and client also facilitate early identification of areas of high audit complexity. Such early identification affords the auditor an opportunity to modify audit programs accordingly, make audit team additions or changes, and plan for effective coverage of these areas. Examples of complex transactions requiring special attention are leases containing contingent rental clauses, modification of an existing pension plan, an "in substance defeasance" related to long-term debt, and inventories requiring special expertise for counting or valuation.

On-line, real time electronic data processing systems also present complex auditing issues related to internal control evaluation and substantive audit testing. Some of the systems are so complex as to require the use of computer audit specialists. Inasmuch as the computer audit specialists are in limited supply within the firm, early identification of need permits more effective audit planning and scheduling.

Use of Client Personnel Enables the Auditor to Concentrate on High Risk Areas

Part of audit planning involves arrangements between the auditor and client concerning use of client personnel on the engagement. By using client personnel in a judicious manner, the auditor is able to devote more time to areas of high audit risk. Virtually any audit task, short of audit judgment decision making, may be assigned to client personnel, provided the auditor reviews and verifies their work on at least a test basis. The auditor should, of course, use employees capable of performing the assigned tasks.

The Client Acceptance Decision as Part of Risk Analysis

As part of the preliminary planning phase, the auditor may determine that inherent risk is so high as to preclude acceptance of the audit engagement. The exercise of due audit care, as required by the *Code of Professional Conduct,* may not be possible in an environment of management dishonesty and widespread misrepresentation. The quality control guidelines issued by the AICPA Quality Control Standards Committee (see Chapter 2) include a provision for **client acceptance:** evaluating new clients for acceptance and periodically reviewing existing clients for continuance. The policies and procedures adopted for this purpose should provide reasonable assurance that the firm will not be associated with clients whose management lacks integrity.

Study of the Business and Industry

Careful analysis of the client's business and the industry of which it is a part provides an effective means for the auditor to gain a better understanding of the client's organization and operations. This, in turn, assists the auditor in identifying those transaction areas posing the greatest threat of material error. In the process of studying the organizational structure and conducting preliminary discussions with the client's management personnel, the auditor already has some grasp of the nature of the client's organization and its operations. A more penetrating study is needed, however, now that the client has been accepted.

Study of the business and industry also enables the auditor to identify complex transaction areas and more clearly differentiate between the form and substance of transactions. The Bar Chris case (cited in Chapter 3) involved highly complex sale and leaseback transactions that the company had treated as sales in the ordinary course of business. Accordingly, revenue was recognized upon signing of the leases. Although legally (i.e., in form) these were sales, in substance the criteria for revenue recognition were not met and, therefore, the revenue was recognized prematurely. The court determined in this case that the in-charge auditor did not have a thorough understanding of the substantive nature of these transactions and found the auditors negligent for (among other things) not recommending deferral of the revenue.

Classifying Business and Industry Information

Sources of information which should be consulted by the auditor in studying the client's business and industry are listed in Figure 5.3.

The information to be gathered from these sources may be classified as follows:

1. Information concerning the economy;
2. Information concerning the industry;
3. Information concerning the business.

The procedures to be applied in obtaining the necessary information are discussed in the following paragraphs.

FIGURE 5.3   Sources of Business and Industry Information

1. The permanent file (if a recurring audit) and last year's current file
2. Correspondence files and minutes of directors' meetings
3. Prior year's financial statements and related footnotes
4. AICPA industry audit and accounting guides
5. Industry publications describing the nature of the industry and economic, political, and other events affecting the industry at the time of the audit
6. Government publications relating to the industry, including those containing industry statistics and economic factors affecting the industry (many such publications are available through the Government Printing Office)
7. Tax laws unique to the industry
8. Annual reports of other companies in the industry
9. Discussions with predecessor auditor (if a new client was previously audited by another CPA firm)
10. Credit reports from such sources as Dunn & Bradstreet and commercial banks
11. Corporate manuals such as accounting manuals, and chart of accounts and policy procedures manuals
12. Computer data bases containing industry information (e.g., NEXIS, COMPACT DISCLOSURE, etc.)

Information Concerning the Economy

Familiarity with current economic conditions promotes risk analysis in several ways. A downturn in the economy, for example, may create problems in collecting customer accounts receivable and suggest increased audit time be devoted to the allowance for uncollectible accounts.

Many of the savings and loan failures occurring in the 1980s were the result of accepting risky loans during the more prosperous times immediately following government deregulation of the industry and preceding the recession years. Faced with these portfolios, auditors began to concentrate their resources on evaluating portfolio quality, and devoted particular attention to the adequacy of loan loss reserves. Case 5.1, involving United Bank of Seattle, emphasizes the auditor's need for understanding the impact of economic conditions on the client's business.[11]

---

[11]This is the first of four cases presented in Chapter 5 to illustrate the importance of audit risk analysis. Although the proper course of action for the auditor to have taken might seem obvious, one needs to recognize that only the pertinent factors in the cases have been isolated for illustrative purposes. In the actual situation, the auditors may have been faced with several issues requiring the exercise of audit judgment as to the adequacy of audit evidence supporting existence, completeness, valuation, classification, and disclosure. One must also recognize that most facts seem more obvious when viewed *ex post facto*—that is, hindsight is 20/20. The auditor, however, is in an *ex ante facto* position and must evaluate the adequacy of audit evidence and the cost-benefit trade-off of gathering additional evidence.

United Bank of Seattle

Case Description

George Brenner, CPA and senior auditor for Jackson, Brewster, and Hampton, CPAs, was the in-charge auditor for the 1993 examination of United Bank of Seattle. His audit team consisted of a semi-senior auditor and three assistants. Brenner and his team began the final audit on January 4, 1994 and completed the examination on January 26.

United Bank had experienced rapid growth in its loan portfolio from 1990 to 1992. Most of these loans were related to the Seattle Sesquicentennial held at that time. Moreover, nearly half of the loans were to friends and relatives of Lauren Knox, chief executive of United Bank and chairman of the Sesquicentennial. By 1993, most of these loans were found to be uncollectible, given the heavy losses suffered by the Sesquicentennial sponsors. As a result, the bank was insolvent.

Knox and his brother operated several banks besides United Bank. To conceal the gravity of the situation from the auditors and bank examiners, Knox attempted to transfer problem loans to some of these other banks before the auditors arrived.

What Would You Do?

Industry analysis should have alerted the auditors to the abnormal portfolio growth of United Bank and the heavy concentration of Sesquicentennial loans. The existence of significant related-party transactions should also have raised a "red flag" for the auditors and examiners. Related parties in this case included not only friends and relatives to whom loans had been made, but also the other banks operated by the Knox brothers, as well as the Sesquicentennial Committee, inasmuch as Lauren Knox was chairman.

Such warning signs as the above should have caused the auditors to concentrate heavily on analysis of the loan portfolio for quality and collectibility. Critical attention should also have been given to the loan loss reserves, which, in this instance, proved quite inadequate.

Federal bank examiners were on the premises during much of the audit, investigating the loan portfolio and applying selected solvency measures. These means enabled the examiners to detect many of the more significant problem loans and determine the inadequacy of the loan loss reserves. Given the circumstances of this case, the auditors should have questioned the examiners as to any findings concerning loan quality.

What Was Done?

Brenner and his team applied standard audit procedures in this case without concentrating audit resources on loan quality. Judgment regarding the adequacy of the loan loss reserve was applied essentially in terms of a percentage of outstanding loans. As a result, the problem loans were not identified and the auditors issued a "clean" opinion. Moreover, the federal examiners reported that, notwithstanding their common presence on the premises for two weeks in January 1994, neither Brenner nor any member of the audit team questioned them concerning their investigation and findings.

Consequences

On February 14, 1994, shortly after the auditors had issued their opinion on United Bank's financial statements, the bank was found to be insolvent and was closed by the state banking commissioner. The auditors were later sued for negligence for not disclosing the problem loans.

Another sector affected by economic conditions in the 1970s and early 1980s was the farm equipment manufacturing industry. Many of these companies verged on bankruptcy as a result of changing economic conditions in the farming industry. High debt service payments, combined with declining crop and livestock revenues, forced the farmers to retain old equipment rather than replace it with new equipment. As a result, new equipment sales declined drastically. Faced with such a serious decline in revenue and experiencing large inventories of farm equipment and heavy debt service on outstanding loans, the farm equipment manufacturers were forced into debt restructuring agreements and other means for survival. Recently, Deere & Co. announced that, due to the continued slump in its farm and construction equipment businesses, it planned to eliminate 2,100 jobs and take a charge of about $120 million to cover the cost of the early retirements. The auditors, under these circumstances, should consider this information as a further sign of audit risk and be particularly alert as to proper valuation of inventories and accounts receivable. Economic slumps of this nature increase the probability of inventory overstocking and uncollectible receivables.

National Harvester Company, a farm equipment manufacturer, is used in Case 5.2 to illustrate the added inherent risk posed by this type of economic environment and the kind of audit approach needed to cope with it.

CASE 5.2

National Harvester Company

Case Description

National Harvester Company, for years a leader in the manufacture of farm equipment, had seen its revenues and profits grow steadily during the 1950s and 1960s. Low interest rates, combined with stable farm commodity prices, had prompted farmers to acquire more land. In acquiring the additional land, the farmer typically made a small down payment and financed the balance through variable rate loans with local banks. Given increased demand, relative to supply, farmland prices climbed rapidly. Many farmers became wealthy (at least "on paper") as a result. As farmers tilled more acres, they acquired more and bigger farm equipment. Tractors, combines, corn pickers, and "six-bottom" plows were in heavy demand. National Harvester, as was typical in the industry, financed many, if not most, of such purchases by farmers.

As long as interest rates were low and commodity prices stable, the farmers were able to meet the debt service payments on their land and equipment loans. When interest rates began to rise sharply in the 1970s, however, and commodity prices began to decrease, the typical leveraged farmer faced a liquidity crisis. The result was inability to pay the higher interest on loans, decreased demand for farmland, falling land prices, and foreclosures by banks.

National Harvester, along with other farm equipment manufacturers, also experienced mounting liquidity problems as equipment sales declined and farmers defaulted on their equipment loans. As a result, the company filed under Chapter 11 shortly after the 1980 financial statements were released.

Compounding the liquidity problems, National Harvester had not adjusted production quickly enough in light of decreased demand. As a result, the 1980 financial statements reported inventories containing significant amounts of obsolete equipment. Had this equipment been adjusted to net realizable value, the reported profit of $1.2 million would have been transformed into a loss of $2.3 million.

What Would You Do?

The "economic doom" surrounding this industry should have raised significant uncertainty questions in the minds of the auditors. Moreover, the steadily mounting inventories should have alerted them to the increased risk of obsolescence. This, in turn, should have led to increased audit concentration in the areas of inventories, notes receivable, and long-term liabilities.

What Was Done?

Susan Trimline, a four-year senior auditor for DeNutt & Stevens, CPAs, had been in charge of the 1980 audit of National. Harry Mack was the manager, and William DeNutt was the partner in charge. Five weeks of audit field work culminated in an unqualified opinion issued on February 16, 1981.

Instead of utilizing a risk analysis approach, Trimline and her audit team conducted the standard examination. They did not examine loan collateral and did not evaluate collectibility beyond applying standard percentages to outstanding receivables. These were the same percentages, incidentally, used during the years when farmers were prosperous and National's loan losses were insignificant. Moreover, the auditors applied standard procedures to test the costing of the inventories and did not test extensively for obsolescence. As a result, they took no exception to management's reporting of the inventories at full cost.

Consequences

Shortly after the company declared bankruptcy, the stockholders and creditors of National Harvester sued the auditors for negligence. In finding the auditors guilty, the court held that study of the business and industry should have prompted the auditors to concentrate audit resources on examining inventories for obsolescence and loan collateral for adequacy.

Under such circumstances, auditors have become increasingly aware of these outside forces that significantly affect a client's ability to continue as a going concern. For the farm equipment manufacturers, the economic conditions affecting the farming industry should have prompted the auditors to raise questions concerning excessive inventories and possible losses from obsolescence.

Auditors have also become more alert to the higher than normal probability of violations of restrictive covenants in loan agreements during economic downturns. Failure to maintain working capital at the level stated in the loan agreement is a common violation. A client who violates restrictive covenants in a loan agreement is considered to be in default and may be required to liquidate the loan and any accrued interest on demand. Auditors, therefore, must read the loan agreements carefully in order to identify the relevant covenants and determine compliance. This procedure becomes particularly critical for clients experiencing financial difficulty.

In addition to raising questions of valuation and disclosure, economic downturns often produce uncertainty concerning the ability of a client to continue as a going concern. For this reason, auditors, under such circumstances, may wish to add an explanatory paragraph to the audit report (discussed in Chapter 15).

Information Concerning the Industry

Certain characteristics of the client's industry can also assist in inherent risk analysis. First, an awareness as to whether the industry is growing, declining, or stable provides the auditor with a benchmark for comparing the client's reported performance with the industry norm. If, for example, the client is reporting a significant increase in earnings while the industry is experiencing a decline, the auditor needs to be skeptical concerning the fairness of reported earnings.

Second, the auditor must be aware of cyclical or seasonal factors unique to the industry. A textbook publisher, for example, should ordinarily not experience high revenues in June, ice cream sales should not peak in February, revenues from the sale of bicycles are usually low in January, and tax service revenues are not expected to be high in July. High reported revenues during traditionally low revenue months should alert the auditor to possible revenue inflation.

Case 5.3, involving a major toy manufacturer, illustrates the importance of seasonal analysis and the need to allocate audit resources to areas of high audit risk, as revealed by the analysis. In this case, the company reported the heaviest sales of the year in December, which is traditionally the slowest month.

CASE 5.3

Highbell Toy Company

Case Description

Highbell Toy Company was one of the largest toy manufacturers in the United States. Over the years, the company had experienced considerable success and steadily increasing profits. Expanded product lines, however, coupled with increasing severity of competition within the industry, had begun to put a "squeeze" on Highbell's profitability and liquidity.

In 1991, while the toy industry was suffering substantial losses in sales, Highbell found itself especially threatened. Unless additional financing could be obtained, the company faced the prospect of a cash flow crisis and possible loan defaults.

In the opinion of Highbell's management, however, additional financing could not be obtained unless the 1991 income statement showed an increase in profit over the preceding year. To effect such an increase, Highbell's controller, in collusion with the marketing vice-president, fabricated a substantial amount of fictitious December sales. Sales orders, shipping orders, bills of lading, and invoices were prepared for nonexistent sales. The customers were real, but the sales and shipments were not.

As an illustration of management's desperate attempts at profitability, the company purported to have shipped over $2 million of toys during the last Saturday in December. This would have been virtually impossible, given Highbell's shipping facilities at that time!

What Would You Do?

Study of business and industry data, in this case, should have revealed to the auditors that December is traditionally the slowest month for toy manufacturers. Further analysis should also have disclosed the declining trend in the toy industry and the fact that other manufacturers were suffering losses in 1991. The auditors should have become suspicious of Highbell's reported increase in earnings under these circumstances. Such findings should have prompted the auditors to concentrate on the audit of sales revenue and accounts receivable, possibly increasing the proportion of customers' accounts confirmed at year end.

What Was Done?

Frank Blazer, a CPA, was in his fourth year as a senior auditor for Lugibill and Associates, CPAs. Although this was his first year as in-charge auditor for the Highbell engagement, he had been a member of the audit team for the two preceding Highbell audits. His audit team consisted of two semi-senior auditors and four assistants. Jack Glublow, audit manager, was in charge of the overall review of the Highbell audit.

Although Blazer and his audit team confirmed customers' accounts receivable as of year end, they failed to discover the fraud. Several of Highbell's larger customers, including We are Toys and Q Mart, returned confirmation requests with significant exceptions. Although Sally George, one of the semi-senior auditors, tried to clear the exceptions, she had little success. Most of the exceptions related to the fictitious shipments for which the customers had no record. A meeting with Blazer, Jack Glublow, and Harley Frawd, Highbell's controller, led to a decision by the audit team to rely on the internal documentation. The auditors, in other words, elected to ignore the exceptions if Highbell's documentation supported the charges appearing on the customer statements accompanying the confirmation requests. The documentation, of course, consisted of the fictitious sales orders, bills of lading, and invoices.

Consequences

Based on the fraudulent 1991 financial statements, Highbell was able to obtain additional financing in the form of new bank loans and extensions of existing loans. Within a year, however, the company found itself in difficulty once more and was forced into receivership because of failure to meet interest payments on the loans. A special investigation, ordered by a trustee appointed by the creditors, disclosed the 1991 fraud. The auditors were sued and the court found them grossly negligent for not discovering the fictitious sales.

The auditor should ascertain whether the client's industry is labor or capital intensive. Increasing labor costs, along with burgeoning technology, have prompted U.S. manufacturers to become increasingly automated. A capital intensive, or highly automated, industry enjoys greater operating leverage due to high fixed costs relative to variable costs. This causes earnings to increase rapidly once the breakeven point has been reached; but companies in these industries also face higher risk during periods of declining revenues, inasmuch as certain fixed costs remain stable regardless of the level of activity achieved. Under conditions of excess capacity, therefore, auditors must be alert to the increased probability of excessive amounts of fixed costs in ending inventories. In the presence of under-utilization, the auditor needs to devote greater attention to analysis of overhead rates and the extent of capacity loss for the year.

The auditor should also be alert to the degree of competition within an industry, and how successfully the client is meeting the challenge posed by competitors' actions. An intensely competitive industry may suggest questions concerning inventory valuation. Large amounts of inventory carried at full cost, for example, may pose a valuation problem at a time when competition is forcing the industry to lower prices.

Companies in the so-called high tech industries face a greater risk of product obsolescence than companies in other industries. Auditors examining the financial statements of these companies, therefore, should be aware of the increased probability of inventory overstatement resulting from such obsolescence.

Auditors frequently encounter accounting practices that are unique to the client's industry. Under such circumstances, the auditor needs to determine whether the practice is in accordance with GAAP. The fact that other companies in the industry are applying the same accounting treatment to a particular class of transactions, or to a particular category of assets or equities, does not necessarily qualify the application as being in accordance with GAAP. Material departures from SFASs, APBs, and other official pronouncements are assumed to be violations of GAAP, unless the client can demonstrate that application of GAAP would make the financial statements materially misleading.

A company engaged in manufacturing custom-made refrigeration equipment for ships and hospitals, decorating hotels and casinos, and building food-service systems used a method referred to as ''cost to cost percentage of completion accounting.'' Under this method profits were recognized in proportion to the amount of money spent on materials regardless of whether the materials had been used in existing projects. This practice was clearly at variance with GAAP in that revenues were recognized prior to having been either earned or realized. In one instance, the company borrowed $4 million to finance deck planking, most of which was still in the form of trees growing in forests at the time revenue was recognized.

The Client's Business

In addition to gaining familiarity with the client's industry and economic conditions as they affect the industry, the auditor must gain a thorough understanding of the client's business operations, the kinds of transactions occurring, how the transactions are processed and recorded, and any other characteristics of the business that affect audit risk. Inquiry of client personnel and discussions with predecessor auditors are means commonly utilized for obtaining business information.

If the client is new and was previously audited by other CPAs, an attempt should be made by the new auditor to communicate with the predecessor auditor. The purpose for such communication is to learn more about the nature of the client's business and to elicit information from the predecessor auditor concerning management integrity and possible disagreements between the predecessor auditor and management. Such communication usually assumes the form of discussions and examination of audit reports and the audit workpapers of the predecessor. SAS 7 requires that the successor auditor attempt to communicate with the predecessor, but only with the client's permission.[12] If the client will not grant permission, the auditor should generally decline the engagement.

In a recent case, a brokerage firm had overstated its assets by $45 million, when in reality the firm was insolvent and soon thereafter declared bankruptcy. Inasmuch as the former auditors would not agree to the questionable asset valuation, the brokerage firm switched auditors. The rendering of an unqualified opinion by the successor auditors shortly before bankruptcy proceedings began raises a question as to whether or not the communication process required by SAS 7 was attempted in this case.

In addition to the preliminary discussions with the client and consultation with predecessor auditors, other means of gaining familiarity with the client's business include visiting major locations and talking with personnel; reviewing the prior year's financial statements and audit report (noting particularly any scope limitations or uncertainties); obtaining and reviewing tax returns, policy and procedures manuals, and company forms and documents.

Analytical Procedures

Analytical procedures, by highlighting abnormalities, provide another important mechanism for identifying high audit risk areas. As discussed in Chapter 4, the most frequently applied analytical procedures include the following:

1. Compare major components of the monthly financial statements with the same period of the prior year and investigate significant variations;
2. Compare sources of revenue and expense and investigate new sources or disappearance of previous sources;
3. Examine performance reports and investigate significant variations from budget; and
4. Compare key ratios and percentages with industry averages.

Although analytical procedures do not provide conclusive evidence, they do comprise a powerful means for identifying abnormalities caused by material errors or irregularities. As applied in the audit planning stage, they also provide a basis for lowering materiality thresholds where significant earnings inflation is indicated. Moreover, by utilizing computers along with spreadsheet and statistical software, auditors are able to apply analytical procedures to a much greater extent than before. A recent application of the use of analytical procedures to assist in risk assessment involves the use of regression analysis to predict account balances and to evaluate

---

[12]*AICPA Professional Standards, op.cit.,* Section AU 315.03.

differences between predicted and reported balances. If, for example, the auditor wishes to predict cost of sales by month in the period under audit, he/she might use regression analysis to determine the historical rate of change in cost of sales that is dependent on changes in sales. If reported and predicted sales differ markedly, the regression model can be further utilized to quantitatively evaluate the significance of the difference.[13]

As a further example of analytical procedures to assist in risk assessment, assume that the auditor discovers, by dividing cost of goods sold for the year by the ending inventory, that inventory turnover has declined and that the ending inventory appears to be significantly higher than normal. The auditor may decide, under such circumstances, to extend the amount of test counting during inventory observation or to perform additional tests for obsolescence.

Returning to the Highbell Toy Company case and the recording of fictitious December sales, application of analytical procedures would have revealed a material change relative to the prior year, as well as a monthly sales pattern significantly at variance with the industry norm. This, in turn, should have alerted the auditors to the increased probability of management misrepresentation and caused them to place less reliance on internal evidence (sales orders, sales invoices, and bills of lading).

In another case, a company obtained millions of dollars in loans to finance a large inventory of computers purportedly for lease to a major multinational conglomerate. The computers, in fact, did not exist, and the loans, therefore, were obtained fraudulently. Again, application of analytical procedures should have revealed a significant change in the year-end inventory level, thus prompting further investigation as to cause.

Case 5.4 illustrates the importance of analytical procedures in identifying high inherent risk conditions. In this case, a substantial increase in leasehold improvements, accompanied by a sharp decline in the percentage of operating expenses to sales, should have aroused the auditors' suspicions.

CASE 5.4

Johnson Grain Handlers

Case Description

Johnson Grain Handlers, a midwestern company, was a principal exporter of corn, wheat, and soybeans. Dock space was leased at Duluth and Chicago. Grain handling facilities had been constructed by the company and were carried in the accounts as leasehold improvements. In 1990, Johnson expanded its operations to include Toledo and Cleveland. At the same time, the company decided to construct improved handling facilities at all locations to provide for more efficient loading of bulk grain.

In January, 1990, Johnson's management requested National Illinois Bank of Chicago to increase an existing line of credit to help finance the expansion. The bank initially turned down the application, but later reversed their decision on the basis

---

[13]For an excellent discussion of the use of regression analysis in audit risk assessment, see Campbell, Robert J. and Rankin, Larry J., *The Ohio CPA Journal,* Volume 49, No. 3, Autumn 1990, pp. 7–12.

of Johnson's assurance that increased profitability would result from the improved handling facilities.

During 1990, as predicted, the company's reported income and earnings per share increased by 25 percent. The increase was effected primarily through significant decreases in operating expenses relative to gross revenues. Shortly after the financial statements were released, however, the company defaulted on its line of credit and was unable to meet further interest and principal payments. An investigation later determined that the reported increase in profits was fictitious and resulted from capitalizing operating expenses as leasehold improvements. The purported improvements did not exist.

What Would You Do?

Application of analytical procedures should have revealed the decrease in operating expenses as a percent of gross revenues. The decline in operating expenses and the significant additions to leasehold improvements should have prompted the auditors to devote particular audit emphasis to these areas. Inasmuch as Johnson self-constructed the facilities, the auditors should have been alert to possible overapplication of labor and overhead to the jobs. Careful examination of the leasehold improvements accounts should also have assisted in disclosing the misclassifications.

What Was Done?

Larry Latchkey, a CPA, was considered by the partners of Hansen & Co., CPAs, to be one of the most promising senior auditors the firm had hired in the past several years. Although with the firm for only two years, Latchkey had been assigned to the 1990 Johnson Grain Handlers engagement as the in-charge auditor. Alice Powell, a first year assistant, was assigned the task of performing an analytical review for the twelve months ended December 31, 1990. Although she noticed the substantial increase in profitability, she was informed by Johnson's chief accountant that new and more effective cost control measures had been instituted in 1990. She made a note of this in the audit workpapers and proceeded to complete the application of analytical procedures.

In testing additions to the leasehold improvements accounts, Latchkey encountered difficulty locating adequate documentation. Cost records supporting labor and overhead application did not exist. Upon inquiry, Josh Make, Johnson's controller, informed Latchkey that materials invoices for the improvements were held by the internal auditors at the construction locations. Labor and overhead application had been estimated and recorded by monthly journal entries. Given the lack of documentary support, Latchkey relied on "appraisal reports" supplied by Johnson's management as evidence of the carrying amounts of the additions.

Larry did not perceive the connection between the lack of documentation and the results of Powell's analytical review. Moreover, he elected not to visit the locations to verify existence of the improvements.

An unqualified opinion was rendered on the company's 1990 financial statements.

Consequences

Following Johnson's failure, National Illinois Bank brought action against Hansen & Co., CPAs, alleging negligence in not detecting the fraud perpetrated by Johnson's management. The auditors' defense of due care did not "stand up."

Instead, the court held that the auditors should not have relied on the appraisal reports alone, but, in light of significant changes revealed by the application of analytical procedures, should have persisted in examining evidence of the charges to the leasehold improvements accounts.

Figure 5.4 summarizes the three phases of inherent risk analysis as described in the preceding paragraphs. A means for classifying the identified risk factors follows.

FIGURE 5.4   Inherent Risk Analysis

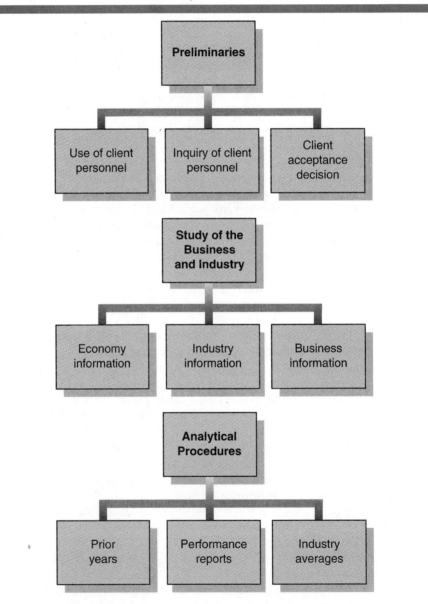

CLASSIFYING THE WARNING SIGNS

During the preliminary audit planning phase, the study of the business and industry, and the application of analytical procedures, the auditor should document all factors, referred to hereafter as **warning signs,** that are indicative of significant audit risk. Such documentation should be incorporated into the audit workpaper file and serve as input to setting materiality thresholds and designing audit programs.

The warning signs so identified can be classified as follows:

1. Indicators of possible material financial statement error;
2. Indicators of forces impacting earnings or liquidity;
3. Indicators of possible disclosure requirements;
4. Indicators of audit complexity; and
5. Indicators of possible management dishonesty.

Indicators of Possible Material Financial Statement Errors

Perhaps the most important of the warning signs, these indicators raise serious questions regarding fairness of financial presentation. Such factors as abnormal ratios or trends and related-party transactions should generally lead to further investigation, given the high probability of error caused by such occurrences.

Of somewhat lesser importance, but possible error indicators nevertheless, are such factors as IRS audits in progress and compensation or stock options tied to reported performance over which management has control. Significant errors discovered by an IRS audit may be indicative of financial statement errors, and if the errors relate to prior financial statements, a prior period adjustment is in order. Moreover, an IRS audit in progress at the date of the audit report may require an explanatory paragraph pending resolution of the matters involved.

Compensation or stock option plans tied to reported earnings always carry the risk that managers having control over the accounting process may be inclined to maximize their own compensation by selecting accounting principles that maximize reported earnings. Therefore, auditors must be particularly alert to the increased probability of earnings overstatement under such circumstances.

Indicators of Forces Affecting Earnings or Liquidity

Certain factors over which management has little or no control can often produce a severe ''squeeze'' on earnings or liquidity. Intense competition from imports, a sluggish economy along with excess capacity, government regulations, highly inflexible debt agreements, high technology causing a threat of product obsolescence, and dependence on a single product or a small number of products or customers are representative of this class of warning signs. Auditors need to consider these factors in audit planning for two reasons. First, asset valuation questions and possible violations of debt agreements may require audit adjustments or special footnote disclosures. Second, the present and projected impact on working capital may be so significant as to produce doubt whether the entity can continue as a going concern. Under such circumstances, the auditor must consider whether to add an explanatory paragraph to the audit report directing the reader's attention to the uncertainty.

Indicators of Possible Disclosure Requirements

During discussions with the client and study of the business and industry, the auditor may discover circumstances requiring disclosure in the form of footnotes to the financial statements. An IRS audit or litigation in progress represent possible loss contingencies, and—depending upon materiality, measurability, and degree of uncertainty—may require footnote disclosure or even accrual of the loss.

The existence of related parties and related-party transactions may also be discovered during this phase of the audit. If the transactions are material, footnote disclosure is required. Such disclosures must identify the related party and the nature of the relationship, as well as the type and volume of transactions involved.

Indicators of Audit Complexity

Study of the client's business and industry may reveal conditions creating higher than normal audit complexity. Certain types of inventory, for example, may require special expertise for valuation; or the auditor may discover that a major part of the client's accounting system is on-line, posing complex EDP audit questions. Early identification of such conditions permits the auditor to retain specialists well in advance and otherwise modify audit programs in consideration of the complexities involved. In these cases, an appraiser may be needed for inventory valuation and a computer audit specialist may be required for assistance in evaluating computer controls and in performing substantive audit tests.

Discovery of unique accounting practices utilized by the client in recording and reporting significant classes of transactions may also produce conditions of high audit complexity—especially if the unique practices are also used by other companies in the industry and appear to be at variance with GAAP. Under these circumstances, the auditor must determine whether the "departure from a principle promulgated by the body designated by Council" can be justified on the basis that conformity to the principle designated by Council would make the financial statements materially misleading, or whether the principle is being inappropriately applied. The complexities presented by the application of unique practices usually require that extended audit procedures be applied to the transaction cycles affected. In this regard, early identification permits more effective audit planning, both in terms of the nature and extent of the procedures to be applied.

Indicators of Possible Management Dishonesty

Warning signs that cause the auditor to question management integrity must be taken seriously and pursued vigorously. The auditor must determine whether the suspicions aroused by such warning signs have validity and, if so, whether, under the circumstances, the auditor can continue to be associated with the financial statements. Additionally, the auditor has a responsibility to communicate illegal acts, as well as other findings of this nature, to the audit committee of the client's board of directors.[14]

---

[14]*AICPA Professional Standards, op.cit.,* Section AU 317.

Examples of warning signs raising questions concerning management integrity include the following:

1. Increasing interest by management in earnings-per-share effects of accounting alternatives;
2. Indications of personal financial difficulty of senior management;
3. A complex corporate structure not warranted by corporate size;
4. High turnover rate in key management positions;
5. Material transactions with related parties;
6. Large or unusual transactions at year end;
7. Progressive deterioration in the quality of earnings.[15]

RISK ANALYSIS MATRIX

Table 5.1 incorporates the discussion contained in the preceding pages into a Risk Analysis Matrix, matching *warning signs* with the *sources of information* available to the auditor for identifying the warning signs.

The permanent audit workpaper file contains much of the information referenced in the matrix and, for this reason, can be very helpful to the auditor in analyzing inherent risk. The existence of related parties and types of related-party transactions, compensation or stock option plans tied to reported earnings, debt agreements, nature of operations and competition, EDP applications, unique inventories requiring special expertise for valuation, the corporate structure, and unique industry accounting practices—all these are contained in the permanent file. New staff persons assigned to the audit for the first time should be asked to review the permanent file along with the prior year's current file in order to gain some familiarity with the client's operations preparatory to engaging in the audit field work.

Both internal and external documents also contain information essential to effective inherent risk analysis. Correspondence files and minutes of directors' meetings may reveal related parties and related-party transactions. These sources may also disclose possible loan defaults, as well as authorization of new loan agreements. Directors' minutes frequently discuss earnings performance and liquidity problems, both of which are of interest to the auditor in analyzing risk.

AICPA audit and accounting guides, along with industry publications, shed light on unique accounting practices and particular audit complexities that might be encountered due to the unique characteristics of the industry of which the client is a part. To the extent the client has experienced difficulties in obtaining credit or in meeting the terms of existing debt agreements, the reports of such credit agencies as Dunn & Bradstreet will reflect the relevant conditions and circumstances.

---

[15]With respect to the last warning sign (number 7), "quality of earnings" relates to the accounting principles applied by the entity. Principles that produce early revenue recognition or excessive deferral of costs are viewed by the financial statement users as reducing the quality of reported earnings through possible overstatement, as contrasted with reported earnings resulting from the application of more conservative accounting practices.

TABLE 5.1 Risk Analysis Matrix

WARNING SIGN	SOURCE OF INFORMATION					
	Mgmt. Inquiry 1	Auditor's Workpapers 2	Internal Documents 3	External Documents 4	Predecessor Auditor	Analytical Procedures
I. INDICATORS OF POSSIBLE MATERIAL FINANCIAL STATEMENT ERROR						
a. IRS audit	x		x		x	
b. Related party transactions	x	x	x		x	
c. Abnormal ratios or trends						x
d. Compensation or stock options tied to reported performance over which management has control	x	x	x		x	
e. Inventory increase without comparable sales increase						x
II. INDICATORS OF EXTERNAL OR INTERNAL FORCES AFFECTING EARNINGS OR LIQUIDITY						
a. Import competition	x	x	x		x	
b. Sluggish economy or excess capacity	x		x		x	x
c. Government regulations affecting the company or industry	x	x	x	x	x	
d. Highly inflexible debt agreements	x	x	x		x	
e. Narrowing profit margins due to declining sales volume, cost increases, etc.			x		x	x
f. Decreasing working capital causing liquidity squeeze			x			x
g. High technology industry causing threat of product obsolescence	x	x		x	x	
h. Reduction in sales order backlog					x	x

TABLE 5.1 *(continued)*

	SOURCE OF INFORMATION					
WARNING SIGN	*Mgmt. Inquiry 1*	*Auditor's Workpapers 2*	*Internal Documents 3*	*External Documents 4*	*Predecessor Auditor*	*Analytical Procedures*
i. Slowdown in customer collections						x
j. Difficulty in obtaining credit			x	x	x	
k. Dependence on a single product or small number of products or customers	x	x		x	x	
l. Rapidly growing or declining industry		x		x	x	
III. INDICATORS OF POSSIBLE DISCLOSURE REQUIREMENTS						
a. IRS audit	x		x			
b. Pending litigation	x		x		x	
c. Existence of related parties and related-party transactions	x	x	x		x	
IV. INDICATORS OF AUDIT COMPLEXITY						
a. Inventories requiring special expertise for valuation	x	x	x	x	x	
b. Complex EDP applications	x	x	x		x	
c. Unique industry accounting practices	x	x	x	x	x	
d. Prior year's audit report qualified for uncertainty or scope limitation		x	x		x	
e. Ineffective board of directors or audit committee	x	x	x		x	
V. INDICATORS OF POSSIBLE MANAGEMENT DISHONESTY						
a. Indications of control override		x			x	x
b. Increasing interest in management in EPS effects of accounting alternatives	x	x	x		x	

(continued)

TABLE 5.1 *(continued)*

| | Source of Information | | | | | |
Warning Sign	Mgmt. Inquiry 1	Auditor's Workpapers 2	Internal Documents 3	External Documents 4	Predecessor Auditor	Analytical Procedures
c. Indications of personal financial difficulty of senior management	x		x		x	
d. Proxy contests	x		x		x	
e. Complex corporate structure not warranted by corporation's size		x	x		x	
f. High turnover rate in key positions	x	x	x		x	
g. Frequent change of auditors or legal counsel	x	x	x		x	
h. Material transactions with related parties	x	x	x		x	
i. Large or unusual transactions at year-end			x			x
j. Client pressure to complete audit in unusually short time		x			x	
k. Management reluctance to provide auditors with clear explanations	x	x			x	
l. Progressive deterioration in the "quality" of earnings		x	x		x	x
m. Existence of significant litigation, especially between shareholders and management	x		x		x	
n. Significant tax adjustments by IRS, especially if a regular occurrence	x	x	x		x	
o. Unmarketable collateral	x	x	x		x	

TABLE 5.1 *(continued)*

Key To Sources:

1. Management inquiry:
   a. Preliminary discussions with management
   b. Discussions during tour of major locations
2. Auditor's workpapers:
   a. Permanent file
   b. Current file (last year)
3. Internal documents:
   a. Correspondence files and minutes of meetings
   b. Prior financial statements and audit report
   c. Accounting manuals
   d. Policy and procedures manuals

   e. Company forms and documents
   f. List of stockholders (if small or closely held company)
4. External documents:
   a. AICPA audit and accounting guides
   b. Industry trade publications
   c. Government publications
   d. Moody's, Standard & Poor's, Robert Morris Associates
   e. Credit reports (Dunn & Bradstreet, banks, etc.)

In summary, the matrix, although not meant to be exhaustive, contains the major warning signs and sources of information that are significant in analyzing inherent risk. Use of this type of matrix, therefore, ensures that all major risk areas are taken into account during the audit planning phase.

INCORPORATING INHERENT RISK ANALYSIS INTO THE AUDIT

Risk-Driven vs. Procedures-Driven Audits

In 1988, the General Accounting Office (GAO) completed a review of the quality of audits of savings and loan associations in the Dallas Federal Home Loan Bank District. The GAO study focused on 11 audits of savings and loans (S&Ls) that failed during the 1985–87 period. The GAO concluded that 6 of the 11 audits were substandard in not adequately assessing and dealing with audit risk.[16] The lesson to be learned from this study is that if auditors are to narrow the expectations gap and fulfill their responsibility for detecting material errors and irregularities, audits must be "risk driven." A **risk-driven audit** is one that carefully analyzes audit risk, sets materiality thresholds based on audit risk analysis, and develops audit programs that allocate a larger proportion of audit resources to high risk areas. A **procedures-driven audit,** on the other hand, utilizes standard audit programs regardless of varying levels of audit risk. This approach has two major weaknesses. First, it results in over-auditing in low risk areas and under-auditing in high risk areas. Second, procedures-driven audits, by not concentrating resources in high risk areas, greatly increase the probability of undetected errors and irregularities. The findings in the GAO report referred to above indicate that some, if not most, of the S&L audits covered in the report were procedures driven.

---

[16]United States General Accounting Office, Report to the Chairman, Committee on Banking, Finance, and Urban Affairs, House of Representatives, *CPA Audit Quality,* February, 1989.

Inasmuch as procedures-driven audits are unacceptable in today's financial environment, the thrust of this and the ensuing chapters will be in the direction of careful analysis of audit risk and the development of audit programs that fully account for assessed risk.

Preliminary Audit Programs

Based on the discussions with the client, the auditor's study of the client's business and industry, application of analytical procedures, and study of internal control structure (as described in Chapter 7), **preliminary audit programs** may be designed. These programs should reflect the auditor's assessment of inherent risk and control risk and their impact on detection risk.

Figure 5.5 is an expansion of the audit risk equation presented previously, and provides guidance for relating the auditor's assessment of inherent risk and control risk to varying levels of detection risk. Regarding inherent risk, for example, a decline in accounts receivable turnover may be the result of a weakness in the credit and collection function, or it may be indicative of inflated accounts receivable. Detection risk, therefore, should be set at a relatively low level, and the audit program for sales and accounts receivable, under these circumstances, should be extended—particularly in the areas of evaluating the adequacy of the allowance for doubtful accounts and confirmation of accounts receivable. If accounts receivable are materially inflated, extending the confirmation process (external evidence) should detect the overstatements. Increased attention to sales transactions recorded at year-end may likewise detect the recording of next year's sales during the current year. The auditor may even elect to confirm the more significant of these recorded transactions. Such confirmation reflects the need to rely more heavily on external (confirmation) evidence relative to internal (documentary) evidence when management misrepresentation is suspected.

If the declining receivables turnover is the result of a weakening of the credit and collection function, the probability of uncollectible accounts increases, and the analysis of the allowance for doubtful accounts should be expanded accordingly. Such expansion might assume the form of extended analysis of subsequent collections of year-end accounts receivable.

The procedures cited in the above illustration are not unique. They are, however, selected and applied by the auditor based on the unique characteristics of the client being audited. The problem areas, revealed by audit risk analysis, prompted an expansion of the procedures beyond the degree normally applied, and also impacted the form of audit evidence. The lesson to be learned is the necessity for the auditor to vary the nature or timing, as well as the extent of audit procedures in order to adequately deal with identified audit risk. As another example, a material decline in "revenue from scrap sales" might prompt the auditor to confirm the nonexistence of transactions with the client's scrap dealers; a procedure that would not be applied under ordinary circumstances.

A final point needs to be considered relative to preliminary audit programs. As discussed in Chapter 4, a major factor considered by the auditor in the design of audit programs is the potential for misstatement as revealed by the study and testing of the client's internal control structure. At this stage in the audit process, however, testing of internal control policies and procedures has not yet been completed. The

FIGURE 5.5   Determining the Required Level of Detection Risk for Planning and Substantive Audit Tests

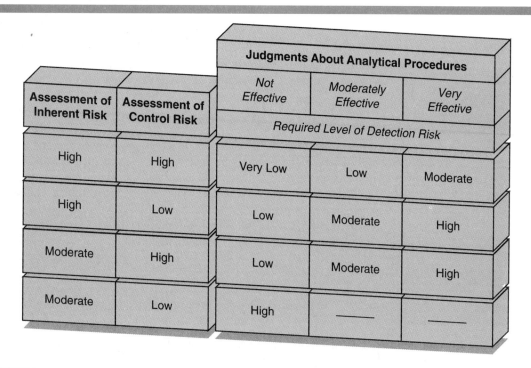

Assessment of Inherent Risk	Assessment of Control Risk	Judgments About Analytical Procedures		
		Not Effective	Moderately Effective	Very Effective
		Required Level of Detection Risk		
High	High	Very Low	Low	Moderate
High	Low	Low	Moderate	High
Moderate	High	Low	Moderate	High
Moderate	Low	High	——	——

Source: Adapted from Auditing Standards Board, *Control Risk Audit Guide* draft, May, 1989.

auditor, during the audit planning phase, will have obtained a basic understanding of the client's internal control structure and will have made a preliminary assessment of control risk. This assessment is subject to further modification, however, if the auditor decides to test the controls. (This process is covered at length in Chapter 7.) For this reason, the programs developed upon completion of audit planning are referred to as *preliminary audit programs*. The programs, as modified after testing of the control structure, are referred to as *final audit programs*. Recalling the sequence of audit steps leading to the rendering of the audit report, they are as follows:

1. Audit *planning* and risk assessment;
2. Modification of assessed control risk through testing;
3. *Conducting* the audit through substantive audit testing;
4. Preparation of the audit *report*.[17]

---

[17]This sequence is not rigid. Analytical procedures, for example, are substantive audit procedures, not withstanding application during both the audit planning and review phases. Moreover, control weaknesses overlooked during the internal control study and evaluation phase may come to light during substantive testing and require further audit program modification at that point.

In simplified terms, the auditing model may now be expressed as:

- PLAN
- CONDUCT
- REPORT

The current file of audit workpapers, as described in Chapter 4, should provide ample evidence of completing these three phases of the audit.

Time Budgets and Staff Scheduling

Having reached a preliminary assessment of inherent and control risk and having designed preliminary audit programs in light of this assessment, the auditor may now prepare a **time budget** and determine audit staff needs for the engagement. Exhibit 5.1 illustrates an audit time budget. The time budget estimates the hours required to complete each phase of the audit. It is broken down as to audit area and level of staff person (e.g., assistant, senior auditor, manager, partner). The timing of need (i.e., interim audit, inventory observation, and other year-end procedures, final audit) should also be included in the time budget in order to facilitate staff scheduling.

The time budget is usually prepared by the in-charge auditor, subject to review by the manager or audit partner. Factors to be considered in its preparation are the following:

1. Nature of the audit client;
2. Assessment of inherent risk;
3. Preliminary assessment of control risk (subject to modification resulting from further testing of controls);
4. Prior year's time budget and its relationship to actual time (if a recurring audit);
5. Staff members having previous audit experience with the client; and
6. Required expertise.

Once the time budget has been prepared, personnel may be assigned to the audit. In scheduling people, the firm should take into account the degree of participation by the client's employees.

As various parts of the audit are completed, the actual times should be posted to the time budget and compared with the projected times. Such comparison serves two purposes. First, it serves as input into the preparation of next year's time budget. Second, to the extent overruns result from weaknesses in the client's accounting system, the added hours may be considered chargeable and included in the client billing. If the additional hours, however, are the result of using inexperienced audit staff personnel, the client should not be expected to pay for those hours.

Pre-audit Conference

Given its significance and complexity, most of the inherent risk analysis, including the preliminary discussions with the client, will be performed by the in-charge auditor, with the possible participation of the audit manager. Once this phase of the

EXHIBIT 5.1 Time Budget

Jones and Journey, Inc.
Time Accounting and Budget
December 31, 1994

Audit Area	Staff Assistant 1	Staff Assistant 2	InCharge Senior	Manager	Partner	Typing and Proofreading	Budgeted Hours	Actual Hours	Explanation of Variance
Cash	30		2				32	28	
Accounts receivable		60	5				65	110	See WP 20: Many exceptions to con-firmation requests
Inventory	30	30	5				65	96	See WP 30: Failure to achieve proper cutoff
Plant assets	20		10				30	33	
Investments			5				5	7	
Other assets			5				5	3	
Accounts payable	10	10	3				23	22	
Long-term debt and equity			10				10	20	Debt restructuring required more audit hours
Revenue and ex-pense ac-counts			5				5	7	
Payroll	10		5				15	12	
Pension, profit sharing, etc.			20				20	23	
Planning, review and super.			25	10	5		40	38	
Reports				10	5		15	15	
Taxes	20		5		3		28	26	
Support staff						8	8	7	
	120	100	105	20	13	8	366	447	

The pre-audit conference: A time to focus on audit risk.

audit has been completed, along with the time budget and staff scheduling, a **pre-audit conference** should be convened by the in-charge auditor. All persons involved in the audit field work should be included in the conference. The purpose of the pre-audit conference is to increase the effectiveness of the audit by discussing the results of risk analysis with the staff members associated with the audit. The nature of the client's business, the organizational structure, major locations of operations, and key features of the accounting system and control procedures should also be covered during the pre-audit conference.

Of major importance during the conference is the identification of warning signs detected during audit planning and risk analysis, making certain that the persons assigned to the audit are fully aware of the high risk areas associated with their respective assignments.

KEY TERMS

Analytical procedures
Audit planning
Audit risk
Audit risk analysis
Client acceptance
Control risk
Detection risk
Errors
Expectations gap
Inherent risk

Irregularities
Misappropriation
Misrepresentation
Pre-audit conference
Preliminary audit programs
Procedures-driven audit
Risk-driven audit
Time budget
Warning signs

REVIEW QUESTIONS

1. Differentiate between errors and irregularities. Identify and define the types of errors and irregularities.
2. Define the following terms:
   a. audit risk
   b. inherent risk
   c. control risk
   d. detection risk
3. In what way is materiality related to audit risk?
4. State audit risk in equation form.
5. Which of the audit risk components is controllable by the auditor?
6. Why is overall audit risk set low?
7. Restate the audit risk equation in a form more useful to the auditor. Why is this form of the equation more useful?
8. Assuming that overall audit risk is set at 5 percent and control risk is estimated at 30 percent, calculate the detection risk percentage (assume inherent risk = 100 percent).
9. At what point in the audit process does the auditor deal with inherent risk? Control risk?
10. How does audit planning assist in analyzing inherent risk?
11. What are the three phases of inherent risk analysis? How does each class assist in inherent risk analysis?
12. Name three sources of business and industry information.
13. SAS 7 requires the successor auditor to request permission from the client to communicate with the predecessor auditor. How does such communication assist in audit risk analysis?
14. Discuss analytical procedures in terms of their audit risk analysis features.
15. What are ''warning signs'' and how are they useful to the auditor?
16. Name the five classes of warning signs of importance to the auditor, giving two examples of each class.
17. Warning signs that cause the auditor to question management integrity must be taken seriously and pursued vigorously. Explain.
18. Differentiate between ''preliminary'' and ''final'' audit programs.
19. What is the purpose of the audit time budget?
20. How does the ''pre-audit conference'' increase the effectiveness of the audit?
21. Differentiate between ''risk-driven'' audits and ''procedures-driven'' audits.
22. Name and briefly define the three steps in the auditing model.

MULTIPLE CHOICE QUESTIONS FROM CPA EXAMINATIONS

1. What is the responsibility of a successor auditor with respect to communicating with the predecessor auditor in connection with a prospective new audit client?
   a. The successor auditor has no responsibility to contact the predecessor auditor.
   b. The successor auditor should obtain permission from the prospective client to contact the predecessor auditor.

    c. The successor auditor should contact the predecessor regardless of whether the prospective client authorizes contact.

    d. The successor auditor need not contact the predecessor if the successor is aware of all available relevant facts.

2. Which of the following ratios would be the least useful in reviewing the overall profitability of a manufacturing company?

    a. Net income to net worth.

    b. Net income to working capital.

    c. Net income to sales.

    d. Net income to total assets.

3. Which of the following would be least likely to be comparable between similar corporations in the same industry line of business?

    a. Earnings per share.

    b. Return on total assets before interest and taxes.

    c. Accounts receivable turnover.

    d. Operating cycle.

4. The auditor notices significant fluctuations in key elements of the company's financial statements. If management is unable to provide an acceptable explanation, the auditor should

    a. Consider the matter a scope limitation.

    b. Perform additional audit procedures to investigate the matter further.

    c. Intensify the examination with the expectation of detecting management fraud.

    d. Withdraw from the engagement.

5. If management refuses to furnish certain written representations that the auditor believes are essential, which of the following is appropriate?

    a. The auditor can rely on oral evidence relating to the matter as a basis for an unqualified opinion.

    b. The client's refusal does not constitute a scope limitation that may lead to a modification of the opinion.

    c. This may have an effect on the auditor's ability to rely on other representations of management.

    d. The auditor should issue an adverse opinion because of management's refusal.

6. Which of the following situations would most likely require special audit planning by the auditor?

    a. Some items of factory and office equipment do not bear identification numbers.

    b. Depreciation methods used on the client's tax return differ from those used on the books.

    c. Assets costing less than $500 are expensed even though the expected life exceeds one year.

    d. Inventory is comprised of precious stones.

7. Which of the following is ordinarily designed to detect possible material dollar errors on the financial statements?

    a. Compliance testing.

    b. Analytical review.

    c. Computer controls.

    d. Post-audit working paper review.

8. Patentex developed a new secret formula that is of great value because it resulted in a virtual monopoly. Patentex has capitalized all research and development costs associated with this formula. Greene, a CPA who is examining this account, will probably
   a. Confer with management regarding transfer of the amount from the balance sheet to the income statement.
   b. Confirm that the secret formula is registered and on file with the county clerk's office.
   c. Confer with management regarding a change in the title of the account to "goodwill."
   d. Confer with management regarding ownership of the secret formula.

9. Having determined that accounts receivable increased due to slow collections in a "tight money" environment, the CPA would be likely to
   a. Increase the balance in the allowance for bad debts account.
   b. Review the going concern ramifications.
   c. Review credit and collection policy.
   d. Expand tests of collectibility.

10. As the acceptable level of detection risk decreases, an auditor may change the
    a. Timing of substantive tests by performing them at an interim date rather than at year end.
    b. Nature of substantive tests from a less effective to a more effective procedure.
    c. Timing of tests of controls by performing them at several dates rather than at one time.
    d. Assessed level of inherent risk to a higher amount.

11. The element of the audit planning process most likely to be agreed upon with the client before implementation of the audit strategy is the determination of the
    a. Timing of inventory observation procedures to be performed.
    b. Evidence to be gathered to provide a sufficient basis for the auditor's opinion.
    c. Procedures to be undertaken to discover litigation, claims, and assessments.
    d. Pending legal matters to be included in the inquiry of the client's attorney.

12. Which of the following audit risk components may be assessed in nonquantitative terms?

	Inherent Risk	Control Risk	Detection Risk
a.	Yes	Yes	No
b.	Yes	No	Yes
c.	No	Yes	Yes
d.	Yes	Yes	Yes

13. Which of the following statements best describes an auditor's responsibility to detect errors and irregularities?
    a. The auditor should study and evaluate the client's internal control structure, and design the audit to provide reasonable assurance of detecting all errors and irregularities.
    b. The auditor should assess the risk that errors and irregularities may cause the financial statements to contain material misstatements, and determine whether

the necessary internal control procedures are prescribed and are being followed satisfactorily.

   c. The auditor should consider the types of errors and irregularities that could occur, and determine whether the necessary internal control procedures are prescribed and are being followed.

   d. The auditor should assess the risk that errors and irregularities may cause the financial statements to contain material misstatements, and design the audit to provide reasonable assurance of detecting material errors and irregularities.

14. The acceptable level of detection risk is inversely related to the
   a. Assurance provided by substantive tests.
   b. Risk of misapplying auditing procedures.
   c. Preliminary judgment about materiality levels.
   d. Risk of failing to discover material misstatements.

15. An auditor assesses control risk because it
   a. Indicates where inherent risk may be the greatest.
   b. Affects the level of detection risk the auditor may accept.
   c. Determines whether sampling risk is sufficiently low.
   d. Includes the aspects of nonsampling risk that are controllable.

16. The third standard of field work states that sufficient competent evidential matter is to be obtained through inspection, observation, inquiries, and confirmations to afford a reasonable basis for an opinion regarding the financial statements under audit. The substantive evidential matter required by this standard may be obtained, in part, through
   a. Flowcharting the internal control structure.
   b. Proper planning of the audit engagement.
   c. Analytical procedures.
   d. Auditor working papers.

17. Analytical procedures used in planning an audit should focus on identifying
   a. Material weaknesses in the internal control structure.
   b. The predictability of financial data from individual transactions.
   c. The various assertions that are embodied in the financial statements.
   d. Areas that may represent specific risks relevant to the audit.

18. Which of the following comparisons would be most useful to an auditor in evaluating the results of an entity's operations?
   a. Prior year accounts payable to current year accounts payable.
   b. Prior year payroll expense to budgeted current year payroll expense.
   c. Current year revenue to budgeted current year revenue.
   d. Current year warranty expense to current year contingent liabilities.

ESSAY QUESTIONS AND PROBLEMS

5.1 a. In applying analytical procedures, a common practice is to compare monthly income statement components with the preceding year. What is the purpose for such comparisons?

   b. Jerry Jewel, staff auditor for Holmes and Associates, CPAs, discovers during the application of analytical procedures that Harry's Short and Small Clothing

Store, an audit client, experienced a significant decline in inventory turnover during the current year. What might have caused the decrease? What steps might Jewel take to pursue the matter further? How might this discovery affect the audit program? Be specific in terms of audit area affected and possible added procedures.

5.2 Audit risk and materiality should be considered when planning and performing an examination of financial statements in accordance with generally accepted auditing standards. Audit risk and materiality should also be considered together in determining the nature, timing, and extent of auditing procedures and in evaluating the results of those procedures.

Required:
a. 1. Define audit risk.
   2. Describe its components of inherent risk, control risk, and detection risk.
   3. Explain how these components are interrelated.
b. 1. Define materiality.
   2. Discuss the factors affecting its determination.
   3. Describe the relationship between materiality for planning purposes and materiality for evaluation purposes.
   (AICPA adapted)

5.3 For each of the following situations explain how audit risk has been increased and how such risk may be reduced through the modification of audit programs (i.e., what kinds of auditing procedures should be applied in each case in order to keep audit risk within acceptable bounds?).
a. While conducting a study of the business, Susan Phelps, the in-charge auditor on the newly acquired Milson audit, discovers that Milson owns 60 percent of the stock of Jellio, Inc., and that Jellio has never been audited.
b. Hofley International Paper Company, an audit client of Redman & Associates, CPAs, completed construction of three highly automated paper mills during the current year. Funding of the construction required some rather unique financing arrangements, including sale and leaseback of two of the mills. Much of Hofley's present paper production is being transferred to the new, more efficient mills.
c. International Deere, a farm equipment manufacturer, follows a policy of guaranteeing the indebtedness of farm operators purchasing International Deere farm equipment. Given the significance of some of the loans, International has seen fit to require collateral in the form of second mortgages on some of the farms owned by the purchasers. In light of depressed land and commodity prices, combined with increased liquidity problems faced by the operators, a significant portion of the loans are in danger of default.
d. In applying analytical procedures to the financial data of International Deere, Colin Moore, a newly-assigned assistant auditor, discovers that Deere's net profit margin has remained at approximately 12 percent, while the industry, for the most part, has been suffering losses.

5.4 The Board of Directors of Unicorn Corp. asked Tish & Field, CPAs, to audit Unicorn's financial statements for the year ended December 31, 1992. Tish & Field explained the need to make an inquiry of the predecessor auditor and requested permission to do so. Unicorn's board refused to honor the request on the grounds that relations with the predecessor had deteriorated so significantly that Tish & Field would receive biased and defamatory information from the predecessor.

Required:

a. What is the purpose of the communication between the successor and predecessor auditors?
b. How does such communication aid in assessing audit risk?
c. What position should Tish & Field assume in the present situation? How should they respond to Unicorn's refusal to permit communication with the predecessor?

5.5 During the course of an audit engagement an independent auditor gives serious consideration to the concept of *materiality*. This concept is inherent in the work of the independent auditor and is important for planning, modifying, and implementing audit programs. It underlies the application of all the generally accepted auditing standards, particularly the standards of field work and reporting.

Required:

a. Briefly describe what is meant by the independent auditor's concept of materiality.
b. What are some common relationships and other considerations used by the auditor in judging materiality?
c. Identify how the planning and execution of an audit program might be affected by the independent auditor's concept of materiality.
   (AICPA adapted)

5.6 Analytical procedures are substantive tests that are extremely useful in the initial audit planning stage as well as part of the overall review at the close of audit field work.

Required:

a. Explain why analytical procedures are considered substantive tests.
b. Explain how analytical procedures may be useful in the initial audit planning stage.
c. Explain how analytical procedures may be useful in the overall review stage.
d. Identify the analytical procedures that one might expect a CPA to utilize during an audit performed in accordance with generally accepted auditing standards.
   (AICPA adapted)

5.7 For each of the following cases, identify the warning sign and explain how audit risk is increased by the condition and explain how the audit program should be modified, given the circumstances.

a. During the examination of a rural bank, the auditors discover a significant number of loans secured by farmland and farm equipment. Farmland prices, as well as farm commodity prices, have experienced sharp declines during the two-year period preceding the audit.
b. Due to an increasingly tight working capital position, one of your audit clients has applied to a local bank for an increase in an existing line of credit. The bank has agreed to the increase, provided the company can achieve a 15 percent increase in the current year's earnings per share over the preceding year.
c. A large distributor of school supplies an audit client reported an unusually large volume of sales in June, the last month of its fiscal year.

d. One of your clients is a wholesale distributor of computers and computer accessories. During a tour of the warehouse, you notice a large inventory of recently discontinued personal computers.

e. A client engaged in processing molasses recognizes revenue upon completion of the production process on the basis that a ready market exists for the product.

5.8 Your firm has recently accepted Handco, Inc. as an audit client. You have been assigned as the in-charge auditor and are in the process of conducting a preliminary review. During inquiry and the application of analytical procedures, you discover several aspects of the company, some of which may affect the audit programs to be developed for the Handco audit. The company is a large, diversified manufacturer of toys, hardware, and building supplies. Moreover, they have recently acquired a company which manufactures dog food and pet supplies, having accounted for the acquisition as a pooling of interests. Most of the manufactured building supplies are sold to home builders, and Handco has been guaranteeing loans by local banks to the home builders to finance purchases from Handco. Handco was previously audited by Epworth and Associates, a local CPA firm. They have decided to retain your firm because they are anticipating a public offering of securities within the next couple of years, and your firm is more widely known and already has several public clients.

In applying analytical procedures, you note that the firm's profit margin appears to be significantly higher than the industry average in the building supplies area, while inventory turnover is substantially lower.

Required:

a. What questions are raised by the narrative which, in your opinion, might have an impact on the audit programs to be developed for the Handco audit?

b. What kinds of audit procedures would you apply in addressing the questions just identified?

5.9 Although analytical procedures do not provide conclusive evidence, they do constitute a powerful means for identifying abnormalities caused by material errors or irregularities. For each of the following "abnormalities," indicate the type of error or irregularity that might have occurred and how you would resolve your doubts. Organize your answers as to the type of error or irregularity and the audit procedure(s) to be applied.

a. December, 1991 sales are 20 percent higher than December, 1990 sales.

b. Revenue from scrap sales has declined by 30 percent this year.

c. Inventory turnover has declined from 3.5 to 2.0 during the current year, while sales have increased by 10 percent.

d. Although production has declined by 40 percent in the current year, an insignificant volume variance appears in the general ledger.

e. Accounts receivable turnover decreased from 12 to 7 during the current year, while sales increased by 25 percent.

f. In past years, the company has had substantial amounts of inventory out on consignment. Although management has informed us that the consignment arrangements have been discontinued, inventory turnover has declined significantly during the current year.

g. Repairs and maintenance expense, as a percent of sales, has increased from 5 percent to 15 percent during the current year.

5.10 The audit time budget, broken down as to audit area and level of staff member, estimates the hours required to complete each phase of the audit.

Required:
a. What is the purpose of the time budget?
b. What factors affect its preparation?
c. How does the time budget also serve as a performance report?
d. What are the possible causes of unfavorable time variances?

5.11 Parker is the in-charge auditor with administrative responsibilities for the upcoming annual audit of FGH Company, a continuing audit client. Parker will supervise two assistants on the engagement and will visit the client before the field work begins.

Parker has started the planning process by preparing a list of procedures to be performed prior to the beginning of field work.

The list includes:

1. Review correspondence and permanent files.

2. Review prior years' audit working papers, financial statements, and auditor's reports.

3. Discuss with CPA firm personnel responsible for audit and nonaudit services to the client matters that may affect the examination.

4. Discuss with management current business developments affecting the client.

Required:
Complete Parker's list of procedures to be performed prior to the beginning of field work.   (AICPA adapted)

5.12 Analytical procedures consist of evaluations of financial information made by a study of plausible relationships among both financial and nonfinancial data. They range from simple comparisons to the use of complex models involving many relationships and elements of data. They involve comparisons of recorded amounts or ratios developed from recorded amounts, to expectations developed by the auditors.

Required:
a. Describe the broad purposes of analytical procedures.
b. Identify the sources of information from which an auditor develops expectations.
c. Describe the factors that influence an auditor's consideration of the reliability of data for purposes of achieving audit objectives.
(AICPA adapted)

5.13 Hanlon, Inc. manufactures and sells personal computers. Manufacturing operations are conducted at the company's sole plant in Hoopshire, New Hampshire, where general offices are also located. Products are distributed nationally through such retail outlets as Abcess III and Computer Country. Many large discount chains also handle the Hanlon Computers. The firm has just completed its seventh year of operations. Your firm has audited Hanlon since its inception seven years ago. Financial statements for the past three years, along with certain industry data, are presented Exhibits 5.2 and 5.3. One of the first companies to manufacture personal computers, Hanlon experienced substantial growth during the first five

EXHIBIT 5.2   Problem 5.13 Balance Sheets

Hanlon, Inc.

	UNAUDITED 12/31/X7	AUDITED 12/31/X6	AUDITED 12/31/X5
Cash in bank—general	$ 4,000	12,000	53,000
Cash in bank—payroll	4,000	4,000	8,000
Petty cash	500	500	500
Notes receivable—current	8,000	6,000	10,000
Accounts receivable—trade	300,000	150,000	220,000
Allowance for doubtful accounts	(12,000)	(12,000)	(15,000)
Interest receivable	600	400	500
Investments—current	7,000	2,000	6,000
Raw materials and purchased parts inventories	270,000	80,000	100,000
Goods in process	4,500	12,000	30,000
Finished goods inventory	300,000	180,000	266,000
Prepaid expenses—current	8,000	5,900	7,800
Plant assets—net	1,620,000	1,210,000	1,200,000
Intangible assets—net	350,000	115,000	120,000
Other assets	7,000	4,000	6,000
Total assets	$2,871,600	1,769,800	2,012,800
Notes payable—trade	$ 2,000	7,000	3,000
Accounts payable—trade	199,086	113,586	120,000
Taxes payable	8,000	6,000	20,000
Accrued liabilities	5,800	6,500	7,800
Mortgage note payable—current	200,000	200,000	147,000
Note payable—10%—current	100,000		
Note payable—10%—due 19X9	900,000		
Mortgage note payable—8%	400,000	520,000	720,000
Common stock—no par	300,000	300,000	300,000
Additional paid—in capital	120,000	120,000	120,000
Retained earnings	636,714	496,714	575,000
	$2,871,600	1,769,800	2,012,800

years of its existence. As more companies entered the field, however, Hanlon's earnings began to decline. By its sixth year, Hanlon was struggling with severe cash flow problems and the threat of a net loss. The liquidity problems were temporarily averted by negotiating a $1 million term loan with the Hoopshire National Bank and Trust Company. The loan bears interest at 10 percent, and is payable in $100,000 annual installments, beginning in 19X8.

EXHIBIT 5.3   Problem 5.13 Income Statement

| | Hanlon, Inc.
for the years ending | | |
	UNAUDITED 12/31/X7	AUDITED 12/31/X6	AUDITED 12/31/X5
Sales	$1,800,000	1,300,000	2,860,000
Cost of goods sold	800,000	620,000	1,700,000
Gross profit	1,000,000	680,000	1,160,000
Operating expenses	600,000	488,954	520,000
Income before income taxes	400,000	191,046	640,000
Income taxes	180,000	154,332	250,000
Net income	220,000	36,714	390,000
Retained earnings—BOY	496,714	575,000	300,000
Total	716,714	611,714	690,000
Dividends	80,000	115,000	115,000
Retained earnings—EOY	$ 636,714	496,714	575,000
Selected Industry Averages:			
Inventory turnover	3.00		
Accounts receivable turnover	10.00		
Profit margin	5.00%		
Debt: equity ratio	50.00%		
Current ratio	2:1		

Required:

a. Copy the comparative financial statements and add columns for expressing balance sheet amounts as a percent of total assets, and income statement amounts as a percent of sales.

b. Compute the following ratios for each of the three years:

   1. Inventory turnover

   2. Accounts receivable turnover

   3. Profit margin

   4. Debt: Equity ratio

   5. Current ratio

c. Enter the given industry averages for these ratios and

   1. Compare company and industry

   2. Compare current and prior years

   3. Identify areas requiring further investigation

   4. Identify possible causes of disparities cited in 3.

5.14 In 1988, as other computer disk drive companies were laying off hundreds of employees, MiniScribe Corp. announced its thirteenth consecutive record-breaking quarter, a trend that had caused the company's stock price to quintuple over a two-year period. Under the direction of Quentin Thomas Wiles, otherwise known as "Dr. Fix-It," the company had been "resurrected from the dead" and appeared to have made a miracle recovery. Wiles, who took over ailing MiniScribe in 1985, immediately cut the workforce by 20 percent and reorganized the company into separate divisions to "promote accountability." As a further effort to enhance accountability, Mr. Wiles held quarterly "dash meetings" during which division managers were required to defend their "dash books," a term used to describe the rigid plans under which the managers were held accountable. On occasion, during the dash meetings Mr. Wiles would fire managers who had not met their budget. The purpose of such public berating and firings was to demonstrate to all the managers that Dr. Fix-It was in complete control of the company.

By late 1986, Mr. Wiles had become so committed to "hitting the number" — meeting the budgeted sales figure — that it became a company-wide obsession. The dash meetings were almost totally consumed by discussing sales objectives and defending sales variances.

Although volume continued to increase, the 1988 record earnings picture was somewhat clouded by a sudden three-month increase in accounts receivable from $109 million to $173 million, a 59 percent increase, and a 55 percent increase in inventories from $93 million to $141 million. The inventory increase was particularly troublesome to Coopers & Lybrand, MiniScribe's auditors, because disk drives can become obsolete from one quarter to the next.

Required:

a. What warning signs are presented in this case? What kinds of audit evidence and procedures might have led the auditors to identify the warning signs? Organize your answer as follows:

   Warning Sign   *Audit Procedures for Identifying*

b. Having become aware of the inventory and accounts receivable increases, what kinds of audit evidence and procedures should the auditors apply in resolving their suspicions concerning possible overvaluation of inventory and receivables?

5.15 The following quote is from an article appearing in the 10/29/90 issue of the *Wall Street Journal:*

> Hughes Aircraft Co., faced with cost overruns on a fixed-price contract to develop a radar system for the F-15 jet fighter, improperly charged expenses to other government pacts, a government audit alleged.

The Air Force audit team had discovered that Hughes had charged $21.4 million of development costs of the radar system to a contract with Grumman Corp. for an advanced F-14 radar and to a contract with Northrop Corp. for the B-2 bomber's radar. These costs should have been charged to the F-15 project under the control of prime contractor McDonnell Douglas Corp. Hughes' motive, as alleged by the auditors, was to reduce losses on the F-15 contract, a fixed price contract that was already in a cost overrun condition, by charging the costs to other projects that would permit reimbursement.

Hughes had created a system whereby all development costs, regardless of whether directly related to a specific contract, were charged to a "common pool" and subsequently charged out to contracts. Hughes rebutted that the auditors were incorrect in their allegations of wrongdoing in that many, if not most, of the development costs were general in nature and therefore applicable to all of the contracts jointly and should not have been charged to single contracts as maintained by the Air Force auditors. The government report stated, however, that while Grumman and Northrop had agreed that certain components in their radar systems would be identical to those used in others, the decision to distribute these costs and the ratio for the distribution were made internally by Hughes with no input from the contractors or the appropriate government offices.

Required:
a. One of the factors increasing inherent risk is audit complexity. How does audit complexity relate to the Hughes Aircraft Company case?
b. How might auditors be alerted to a situation such as that described in this case? In other words, what sounds the "warning whistle?"
c. Having been alerted to a possible error or irregularity, how should the auditors proceed in gathering evidence to resolve their suspicions? To answer this question, recall the various forms of audit evidence and types of procedures described in Chapter 4.

6 Internal Control Structure: Concepts

CHAPTER OUTLINE

I. **Internal control structure defined**

II. **Control environment**
   A. Management philosophy and operating style
   B. Organizational structure
   C. Audit committees
   D. Personnel policies and procedures
   E. Communicating assignment of authority and responsibility
   F. Internal audit function
   G. External influences

III. **Accounting system**
   A. Chart of accounts, accounting manuals, and standard journal entries
   B. Documentation of transactions
   C. Review of transactions
   D. Method of transaction processing

IV. **Control procedures**
   A. Competence of personnel
   B. Policy and procedures manuals
   C. Planning, budgeting, and performance reporting
   D. Decentralized operations and need for accountability
   E. Asset safeguards
   F. Periodic inventories, cash, and securities counts

V. **Internal control structure policies and procedures relevant to an audit**
   A. Those that relate to financial statement assertions of management
      1. Existence or occurrence
      2. Completeness
      3. Rights and obligations
      4. Valuation or allocation
      5. Presentation and disclosure
   B. Of particular concern to the auditor

VI. **Inherent limitations of the control structure**
   A. Collusion
   B. Management override
   C. Temporary breakdown
   D. Environmental changes

VII. **Internal control for a small business**

OVERVIEW

Chapter 5 described an approach to evaluating inherent risk by incorporating audit risk analysis into the planning phase. Chapter 6 discusses concepts affecting the internal control structure; and Chapter 7 goes a step further, showing how the auditor can assess control risk through studying and evaluating the firm's internal control structure.

Chapter 6 begins by defining control structure and describing its three components: control environment, accounting system, and control procedures. The chapter goes on to identify and discuss those aspects of the control structure that are relevant to a financial statement audit.

Inasmuch as the auditor's direct concern is with management's assertions contained in the financial statements, the ensuing discussion emphasizes control elements relating to those assertions: existence or occurrence, completeness, rights and obligations, valuation or allocation, and presentation and disclosure.

Given their impact on the independent audit, limitations inherent in all control structures are covered at length in the chapter. Inherent limitations give rise to opportunities for errors and irregularities, even in situations in which the auditor assesses control risk at a relatively low level. Such limitations require the auditor to perform minimum substantive tests, regardless of internal control effectiveness.

The chapter concludes with a discussion of internal control as modified to meet the needs of small businesses. The owner/manager, under these conditions, needs to assume a more active role in defining and achieving control objectives.

STUDY OBJECTIVES

After reading this chapter, you should be able to:

1. Define internal control structure and describe its three components

2. Identify those control elements relevant to a financial statement audit, and classify them as to management's assertions regarding financial statement presentation

3. Understand the need for a minimum audit given the limitations inherent in any control structure

4. Identify the ingredients for effective internal control for a small business, and understand how this differs from the control structure found in larger entities

Chapter 5 described an approach to evaluating *inherent risk* as part of audit planning, and Figure 5.1 provided perspective relative to where inherent risk analysis fits into the overall audit process. Chapters 6, 7, and 8 explain how to assess *control risk* by obtaining an adequate understanding of an entity's internal control structure. Figure 6.1 shows where control risk analysis fits into the process. Control risk assessment, like inherent risk assessment, is considered part of the overall planning phase of the audit.[1] Once inherent and control risk have been established, the auditor can set *detection risk* accordingly.[2]

Chapter 6 defines internal control structure and discusses control structure concepts. These concepts should assist the auditor in obtaining an understanding of a given client's structure. Chapter 7 discusses the auditor's approach to assessing control risk as a basis for designing substantive tests. Chapter 8 examines the impact of electronic data processing on the auditor's consideration of control risk.

INTERNAL CONTROL STRUCTURE DEFINED

The Auditing Standards Board (hereafter referred to as ASB) of the AICPA has defined **internal control structure** as ''the policies and procedures established to provide reasonable assurance that specific entity objectives will be achieved.''[3] ASB further describes internal control structure as having three components, all of which are important to effective control:

1. *Control Environment.* The collective effect of various factors on establishing, enhancing, or mitigating the effectiveness of specific policies and procedures. Perhaps the most important single factor is the attitude of management and the board of directors relative to designing and implementing effective control policies and procedures.

2. *Accounting Systems.* The methods and records established to identify, assemble, analyze, classify, record, and report an entity's transactions and to maintain accountability for the related assets and liabilities.

3. *Control Procedures.* Policies and procedures in addition to the control environment and accounting system that management has established to provide reasonable assurance that specific entity objectives will be achieved.[4]

THE CONTROL ENVIRONMENT

Certain environmental factors have an impact on how closely an entity adheres to its policies and how well it follows established procedures. SAS 55 collectively refers to these factors as the **control environment,** some of which are discussed in the following paragraphs.

---

[1]Auditing Standards Board, *AICPA Professional Standards,* New York: AICPA, Section AU 319.

[2]Chapter 5 presented a way of quantifying audit risk in equation form. After the auditor has established inherent risk and control risk, detection risk is set such that the overall audit risk objective can be achieved.

[3]Auditing Standards Board, *AICPA Professional Standards, op. cit.,* Section 319.

[4]*Ibid.*

FIGURE 6.1   The Audit Process

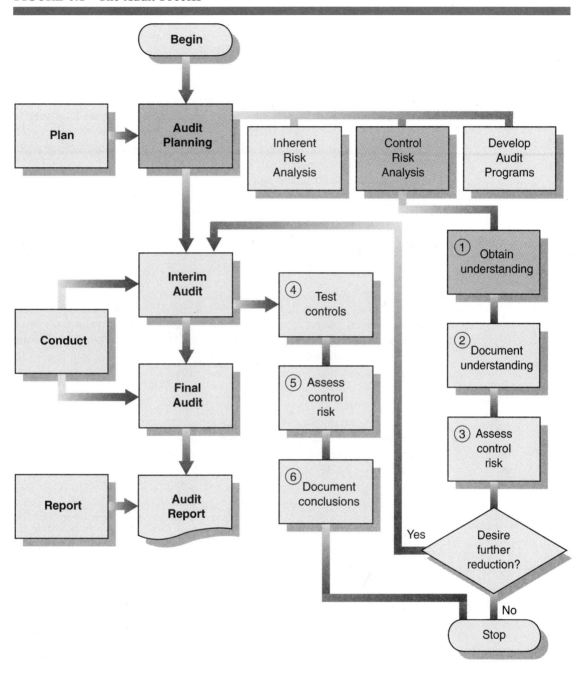

Management Philosophy and Operating Style

Management's attitude toward control can have a significant impact on control effectiveness. To this end management must be strongly supportive of internal control and must communicate that support throughout the organization. An organizational awareness that top management takes internal control seriously helps to maximize the effectiveness of the accounting system and control procedures.

A management operating style that supports proper ethical behavior also enhances control. If an entity's personnel perceive that management conducts itself in accordance with proper ethical standards, such conduct will tend to reflect itself throughout the organization. Proper ethical behavior, in turn, minimizes the probability that financial statements will be intentionally inaccurate.

Management establishment and support of a system of planning, budgeting, and performance reporting throughout the entity will also strengthen the control structure. Such a system enables the firm to define objectives more clearly, identify departures from established goals on a more timely basis, and take corrective action promptly.

Organizational Structure

An organizational structure that provides for clearly defined lines of authority significantly enhances control. Careful attention to organizational structure and fixing of responsibility provides a basis of accountability for actions—an important component of effective control.

Audit Committees

Another environmental factor that enhances the control structure is a strong and responsible audit committee. The audit committee of the board of directors is generally composed primarily of board members who are not part of the entity's management. Significant among the duties of the audit committee are to monitor the control structure and arbitrate disputes between management and the independent auditors. Being independent of management, the audit committee is best able to act as liaison.

Many companies also have their internal audit staffs report directly to the audit committee. This helps the committee to better discharge its responsibility for monitoring the control structure. It also helps to expedite the correction of serious control structure weaknesses.

Personnel Policies and Procedures

A centralized, efficient human resources function enhances control by placing the right people in the right jobs and training them properly to perform their assigned tasks. Clear and complete job descriptions, effective training programs, well-defined hiring policies, and entry and exit interviews are important aspects of this area of the control environment. In addition, an adequate program of employee benefits can contribute greatly to achieving objectives by maintaining employee morale at a high level.

Communicating Assignment of Authority and Responsibility

If entity objectives are to be achieved and policies and procedures are to be followed, management must clearly communicate lines of authority and responsibility throughout the organization. Such devices as policy manuals, organization charts, and meetings and conferences help to enhance this aspect of the control environment. Careful supervision and a system of performance reporting are also important in communicating authority and responsibility.

Internal Audit Function

Effective internal auditing is vital to a strong control environment. As discussed in Chapter 1, internal auditing transcends traditional financial auditing by examining and assessing the efficiency, effectiveness, and policy compliance for all units within the organization. If goals are not being met or policies and procedures are not being followed, the internal auditors can assist the units to take the proper corrective action.

To be effective, internal auditors must be competent and objective. As discussed earlier, objectivity is strengthened by having the internal auditors report to the highest levels of management and, preferably, to the audit committee of the board of directors. Competent internal auditing, with audit findings reported to a sufficiently high level, has proven beneficial in maximizing an entity's control structure effectiveness.

Internal auditing: A critical component of the control environment.

External Influences

Certain environmental factors outside the direct confines of the organization may also affect the firm's control structure. Some may strengthen controls, while other factors may place a strain on the control structure. The constant threat of an Internal Revenue Service audit of past tax returns, for example, strengthens present financial controls and promotes compliance with tax laws. The existence of related parties and related-party transactions are factors that could weaken existing controls. Newly enacted government regulations requiring the entity to reduce emissions or clean up waste deposits may place added strains on profitability and encourage inflation of earnings.

A possible future federal law under present consideration would require both independent auditors and management to report on an entity's internal control structure in the annual report to shareholders. If enacted, this law should further strengthen the control environment for publicly held companies, inasmuch as information regarding any material weaknesses will be available to the public.

THE ACCOUNTING SYSTEM

The entity's accounting system is an important component of the overall control structure. An effective accounting system can strengthen the control structure by ensuring that all transactions completed by an entity possess the following characteristics:

1. The transaction supports effective allocation of the firm's resources;
2. The transaction is within the confines of firm policy;
3. The transaction has been properly approved;
4. The transaction has been adequately reviewed;
5. The transaction has been recorded in accordance with GAAP;
6. Any assets resulting from the transaction are appropriately safeguarded.

An adequate accounting system begins with the execution of transactions or events, and encompasses proper recording and control over resulting assets. The system is concerned with the flow of transactions and must provide reasonable assurance as to proper recording and adequate accountability. Some important aspects of accounting systems that support an effective control structure are described in the following paragraphs.

Chart of Accounts, Accounting Manuals, and Standard Journal Entries

A *chart of accounts* is a listing of account numbers and titles for all accounts appearing in the general ledger, as well as in the detail ledgers. An *accounting manual* describes the kinds of transactions affecting each of the accounts. These two devices, when combined with transaction review, promote proper recording of transactions and events. The accounting manual is particularly useful as a reference when recording transactions that are unusual in nature.

A set of **standard journal entries** for recurring month-end transactions and events provides reasonable assurance that material adjustments are not overlooked in preparing monthly, quarterly, or annual financial statements. The standard entries may be numbered (for example, Standard Entry No. 1 may be for monthly depreciation of plant assets and No. 2 may be for bad debts) and prewritten, except for amounts. Month-end accruals of taxes, product warranty, and interest are other examples of possible standard journal entries. Entries to cost production and sales might also be recorded monthly through standard journal entries.

Transaction Documentation

Proper **transaction documentation** is the starting point in establishing a well defined "audit trail." An **audit trail** provides evidence of proper approval, review, and recording of transactions and events. By providing evidence supporting the initial capturing of a transaction, proper documentation, like standard journal entries, can prevent transactions from being inadvertently missed in the recording process (errors of omission). Strict documentation requirements also increase the difficulty for employees to record fictitious transactions (errors of commission). To this end, documents should be prenumbered, access to unused documents should be limited, and the numeric sequence of used documents should be periodically examined.

Documentation should be provided as necessary for each step in a cycle of transactions. Expenditure transactions, for example, should require requisitions, purchase orders, receiving reports, vendor's invoices, and disbursement vouchers as a condition for payment. Revenue transactions should require customers' orders, sales orders, sales invoices, shipping orders, and bills of lading as necessary documentation.

Review of Transactions

The accounting system should provide for review and approval of each step in a transaction cycle. That is, transactions should be reviewed before, during, and after processing. Examples of control techniques providing evidence of proper approval and review are the following:

1. Requisitions should be signed by those requesting goods or services, and approved as appropriate by supervisors;
2. Purchase orders should be signed by the purchasing agent;
3. Receiving reports, the document evidencing receipt of goods, should be signed or initialled by the persons inspecting and counting incoming goods;
4. Vendors' invoices should be compared with purchase orders and receiving reports, and the covering voucher should be signed or initialled by the person performing such comparisons;
5. Check signers should review all documentation for completeness and accuracy before signing and mailing disbursement checks.

When combined with transaction documentation, proper **transaction review** assists in preventing unauthorized transactions.

Documentation and review also aid in detecting unintentional errors which might have been committed in completing the various steps in the transaction cycle. Using the customer order and invoicing part of the revenue cycle as an illustration, some of the errors which might be detected by applying the above procedures are the following:

1. Incorrect selling prices used in pricing customer orders;
2. Types and quantities on sales invoice not in agreement with customer order;
3. Extension errors (price times quantity) committed in completing the sales invoice;
4. Account recording errors made in determining credits to various revenue accounts.

Method of Transaction Processing

The method of data processing used to capture and record transactions and events also has an impact on control structure. As will be described in Chapter 8, an on-line real-time processing system does not typically provide the sharply defined audit trail produced by a manual or batch processing system. Other types of controls, therefore, must compensate for lack of more traditional controls. Password security over access to computer data bases and the editing of transactions as they are being input into EDP systems are examples of such alternate controls. The impact of EDP on control structure is more fully addressed in Chapter 8.

CONTROL PROCEDURES

In addition to the control environment and the accounting system, other policies and procedures are necessary if entity objectives are to be achieved. Collectively referred to as **control procedures,** these other aspects of the control structure are described in the following paragraphs.

Competence of Personnel

To a greater or lesser extent, depending on the level of automation of the data processing system, people perform control functions. For example, people review transactions, determine account distribution (debits and credits) for given transactions and events, prepare documents, record transactions, prepare monthly financial statements, determine the need for adjusting entries, determine financial statement disclosure needs, compare assets with recorded accountability, prepare bank reconciliations, prepare budgets and performance reports, and take corrective action based on variance analysis.

An effective control structure requires procedures for ensuring that the people performing these functions possess the necessary competence and are doing their work efficiently and effectively. Detailed job descriptions, proper attention to hiring policies, and effective training programs greatly assist in matching people with jobs. An internal audit staff reviewing operations and submitting audit findings also strengthens the personnel aspect of the entity's control structure. By identifying weaknesses and assisting operating units to improve their efficiency or effectiveness, the internal auditors are often the foundation of the control structure.

Policy and Procedures Manuals

Carefully written policies and procedures and communication of these throughout the organization contribute to attaining the firm's control objectives. Regardless of the thoroughness with which management considers and sets policy, communication through **policy and procedures manuals** is vital to effective implementation and adherence.

Planning, Budgeting, and Performance Reporting

Strategic planning is vital to establishing long-range goals and objectives. To maximize the probability of attaining the goals, strategic planning should be accompanied by the following:

1. Communication of long-range plans throughout the organization as necessary;
2. A system of participatory budgeting that breaks the long-range objectives into annual profit plans representing intermediate term goals and objectives;
3. A system of standard costing and variance analysis to effect short-term control over costs and revenues;
4. A system of performance reporting comparing actual with budgeted performance; and
5. Provision for corrective action where significant variations from budgets occur.

Decentralized Operations

In decentralized organizations, procedures must be established for making divisional heads accountable for their actions. Attention to divisional budgeting, followed by meetings with the executive committee to discuss performance, can greatly assist in controlling operations at the divisional level.

Asset Safeguards

Procedures for safeguarding the firm's assets are also necessary for effective control. Examples of **asset safeguards** include policies relating to asset management and the investment of funds, limiting access to valuable and portable assets, background investigation and bonding of employees in positions of trust, insurance coverage, and environmental management. In addition to limiting access to valuable and portable assets, the control procedures should also limit access to documents authorizing the use or disposition of assets and should also fix responsibility over custody of assets and documents.

Limited access controls over portable and valuable assets, such as inventory, small tools, negotiable securities, and cash receipts, and assigning responsibility over the custody of each class of these assets serves two control functions. First, the assets are physically protected by limitation of access. Second, fixing responsibility for custody in a single person provides **accountability controls** for the safety of those assets.

Limiting access to assets without limiting access to documents authorizing the use or disposition of assets does not constitute adequate physical control. Assume, for example, that a company has installed limited access controls over merchandise in the warehouse, has fixed responsibility over merchandise, and prohibits shipments without a properly approved shipping order. These controls will be effective only if unused shipping order forms are also under physical control. If access to shipping orders is unlimited, goods may be removed from the warehouse through fabricated shipping orders. For this reason, all documents authorizing the use or disposition of assets (e.g., shipping orders, sales invoices, vouchers, disbursement checks, and receiving reports) should be placed under the same physical control as the assets to which they relate. Some of the specific control techniques classified as asset safeguards follow.

Limited Access Controls

1. Secure areas for merchandise, small tools, supplies, securities, and so on;
2. Cash registers with locked-in tapes;
3. Limited access to unused documents and proper cancellation of used documents;
4. Daily intact deposits of cash receipts;
5. Limited access to computers, access codes to terminals, disk files, and elements of data bases (as discussed in Chapter 8);
6. Dual access to negotiable securities and other valuable portable assets (unauthorized removal could occur only through collusion under these circumstances).

Accountability Controls

1. Prelisting incoming cash receipts for later comparison with the daily cash receipts journal entry and bank deposit ticket;
2. Prenumbered documents and fixed responsibility;
3. Periodic accounting for the numeric sequence of used documents;
4. Imprest funds for petty cash and payroll accounts and fixed responsibility for custodianship;
5. Recording serial numbers and affixing tags with recorded numbers to assets not having serial numbers to prevent removal and temporary substitution of similar assets;
6. Bonding employees in positions of trust.[5]

Periodic Inventories, Cash, and Securities Counts

The asset safeguards discussed provide a means for establishing accountability over assets and documents. An effective control structure, however, must also include provision for the monitoring of such accountability through **periodic inventories and comparisons** of assets and equities with recorded accountability. Periodic

---

[5]Bonding serves a dual purpose. First, it compensates the firm in the event of loss. Second, some companies consider bonding to be a psychological deterrent against theft in that the bonded employee would have to contend with the bonding company should misappropriation be suspected.

inventories and cash and securities counts provide the means for effective monitoring of accountability and represents yet another set of prevention and detection controls.

The term *inventories,* as used within the context of these controls, is broader than that usually considered. Determining the quantity or dollar amount of any *substance underlying* an *account balance* is considered inventorying within the present meaning. Comparing the details of creditors' statements with the respective accounts in the accounts payable subsidiary ledger and comparing the total with the general ledger control account, for example, would constitute an inventory and comparison.

The following are typical of the inventories and comparisons to be found in an effective set of control procedures:

1. Perpetual inventory records and periodic counts and comparisons;
2. Subsidiary ledgers for such general ledger accounts as accounts receivable, accounts payable, investments, and plant assets and periodic comparisons of subsidiary ledgers with the control account in the general ledger and the underlying substance (customer exceptions to monthly statements, monthly creditors' statements, examination of securities, and periodic inspection of plant assets);
3. Monthly bank reconciliations;
4. Daily cash register audit (counting cash in registers and comparing with cash register tapes, then forwarding cash register tapes to the person responsible for comparing cash receipts with entry and deposit);
5. Comparison of deposit slip with cashbook entry and prelisting.

The asset safeguards discussed earlier included locked-in cash register tapes and prelistings of incoming mail cash receipts. Assigning control over the tapes and prelistings to an individual not having access to cash receipts or accounting records and requiring daily comparisons with the bank deposit ticket and cashbook entry provides an effective means to determine that all cash receipts are properly recorded and deposited in the bank intact. The prelistings and tapes establish accountability; the comparison monitors the effectiveness of accountability so established.

The preceding discussion of control structure elements encompassed a broad spectrum of entity goals and policies and procedures for attaining them. The following paragraphs narrow the focus to those control policies and procedures of interest to the independent auditor.

INTERNAL CONTROL STRUCTURE POLICIES AND PROCEDURES RELEVANT TO AN AUDIT

Relate to Management Assertions

The independent auditor is interested only in those aspects of control that affect the financial statements. Controls that enhance the reliability of the financial statements may be **prevention controls**—e.g, separation of record keeping from asset custody—or **detection controls**—e.g., monthly bank reconciliations. Prevention controls avoid errors and irregularities while detection controls, recognizing that errors will occur even under ideal conditions, provide for a "double-check" to locate significant occurrences after the fact.

The ASB, in SAS 55, refers to these aspects as "internal control structure policies and procedures relevant to an audit" and defines them as "the policies and procedures embodied in an entity's internal control structure that pertain to the entity's ability to record, process, summarize, and report financial data consistent with management's assertions embodied in the financial statements or that pertain to data the auditor uses to apply auditing procedures to financial statement assertions."[6] **Management's assertions** concerning data contained in the financial statements were identified in Chapter 4 as:

1. Existence or occurrence;

2. Completeness;

3. Rights and obligations;

4. Valuation or allocation; and

5. Presentation and disclosure.

Table 6.1 presents a matrix which matches the necessary control structure elements with these assertions, and it may be regarded as an overview of the independent auditor's concern with control structure. The components of the matrix are discussed in the following paragraphs.

Existence or Occurrence

Management's assertions pertaining to the **existence or occurrence** of financial statement components purport that all assets and equities appearing on the financial statements exist as of the balance sheet date and that all revenues, expenses, gains, and losses appearing on the income statement occurred during the period covered by the statement. The independent auditor is interested in the degree to which the three components of the entity's control structure prevent or detect material errors of existence or occurrence (errors of commission).

The Control Environment.

A history of management integrity and concern for proper financial reporting is an important ingredient for preventing errors of commission. Regardless of the existence of other control structure elements, lack of management integrity or a disinterested attitude toward control can negate them and cause the entire structure to be ineffective.

Management communication of control structure support also helps to prevent errors of commission. If personnel recognize that management is serious about control, they in turn will be more serious about performing the control functions assigned to them. Documents will be more carefully reviewed, account distribution errors will be less frequent, and necessary month-end adjustments will be more reliable.

---

[6]Auditing Standards Board, *AICPA Professional Standards, op. cit.,* Section 319.

**TABLE 6.1   Control Structure—Management Assertions Matrix
(Policies and Procedures Relevant to an Audit)**

CONTROL STRUCTURE COMPONENT	MANAGEMENT ASSERTION				
	Existence or Occurrence	*Completeness*	*Rights and Obligations*	*Valuation or Allocation*	*Presentation and Disclosure*
Control Environment	Management integrity Management support of control structure Internal auditing	Management integrity Management support of the control structure Internal auditing	Management integrity Management support of the control structure Review of documents by legal counsel and internal auditors	Management integrity Management support of the control structure Adequate level of competence within controller and internal audit staffs	Management integrity Management support of the control structure Regular discussions with legal counsel regarding disclosure needs Review by internal auditors Review by audit committee
Accounting System	Transaction documentation Separation of accounting and custodial functions	Journal vouchers and checklists of recurring adjustments Monthly reconciliations	Transaction documentation Transaction review Chart of accounts and accounting manuals	Transaction documentation Transaction review Journal vouchers and checklists for recurring adjustments	Accounting manuals coverage of disclosure requirements Transaction documentation Transaction review
Control Procedures	Budgeting and performance reporting system Asset safeguards	System of standard costs and variance analysis Asset safeguards Prenumbered documents Personnel training	Access controls Separation of consigned goods	Standard costs and variance analysis Monthly aging of accounts receivable Periodic analysis of investment portfolio Statement review and timely attention to customer and creditor exceptions	Review of legal counsel correspondence by controller Review of subsidiary ledgers for possible classification issues

The existence of internal auditing also assists in preventing and detecting errors of commission. Periodic review of transactions and events, examination of underlying documentation, and comparison of assets with recorded accountability enable the internal auditor to detect errors in the processing and recording of transactions. Knowledge that their work will be reviewed by the internal auditors also increases employee diligence and discourages errors and irregularities involving commission.

The Accounting System

A well-designed accounting system should provide for both prevention and detection of errors of commission. By requiring complete documentation and evidence of review and approval for all transactions and events, the system provides an effective means for auditing and reconstructing transactions that have occurred. Completeness of documentation, when combined with internal auditing, minimizes the probability of erroneous or fictitious journal entries.

The accounting system should also provide for separation of functional responsibilities such that accounting and custodial functions are not combined. Accounting personnel who have access to cash or negotiable securities, for example, may be inclined to misappropriate assets and conceal the misappropriation by recording and posting fictitious journal entries. Charging a customer's account against the allowance for doubtful accounts, for example, might conceal the misappropriation of that customer's remittance. Such transfer and concealment is much easier to effect when a single employee has access to both the cash remittance and the customers' ledger.

Similarly, computer programmers should not have access to computer files and should not be permitted to process transactions and update master files. Strict password security should be maintained in on-line real-time systems and responsibility should be fixed for defined elements of data bases.[7]

Control Procedures

A system of budgeting, standard costs, and variance analysis, by isolating unusual data for follow-up, can be very effective in preventing and detecting erroneous or fictitious data. This set of controls becomes especially important in decentralized firms where divisional heads are fully accountable to the home office on a periodic and recurring basis. To provide maximum utility from the standard cost system, many firms require frequent meetings between divisional and headquarters personnel. During these meetings, discussions will take place concerning significant variances and corrective actions being taken to correct out-of-control conditions. Such a system of accountability tends to increase divisional attentiveness to proper transaction processing and discourages intentional misstatements.

Proper asset safeguards prevent irregularities involving commission. If limited access and accountability controls are functioning properly, employees will be unable to misappropriate assets and conceal such misappropriation through fabricated journal entries and other forms of account alteration.

---

[7]These topics are discussed more fully in Chapter 8.

The assertion of **completeness** states that all assets and equities that exist and belong to the entity appear on the entity's balance sheet and that all revenues, expenses, gains, and losses that have occurred during the period appear on the entity's income statement. To the extent this assertion has not been met, *errors of omission,* as defined in Chapter 4, are said to be present. The following paragraphs describe how the three control structure components assist in the prevention or detection of errors of omission.

The Control Environment

A framework within which top management strongly supports transaction documentation, review, and approval and communicates this support throughout the organization is an effective means for preventing and detecting errors of omission. For maximum effectiveness, an active and competent internal audit staff should be established, preferably reporting to the audit committee of the board of directors. Attention by the internal auditors, for example, to related parties and possible related-party transactions, and the application of analytical procedures may lead to discovery of significant omissions involving unrecorded liabilities. Limiting access to computer files and programs also prevents errors of omission through inadvertent or intentional alteration or destruction of computer files. Similarly, effective separation of duties among computer programmers, systems analysts, and computer operators helps prevent unrecorded transactions as a means for concealing misappropriations.

The Accounting System

In addition to requiring that all transactions and events be fully documented, the accounting system can aid in preventing and detecting errors of omission by incorporating the following features:

1. A system of standard journal entries or checklists for ensuring that all necessary monthly, quarterly, and year-end adjustments are recorded;
2. Careful review of the general ledger trial balance by responsible accounting personnel for needed monthly and year-end adjustments;
3. Reconciliation of all bank accounts, as well as subsidiary ledgers and controlling accounts, on a monthly basis.

Control Procedures

An effective system of budgeting, standard costs, and variance analysis assists in detecting material errors of omission. A properly functioning system should highlight abnormalities that arise when significant transactions or events go unrecorded. Proper asset safeguards that prevent unrecorded assets from being misappropriated also help to reduce the probability of omissions. Cash registers with locked-in tapes and limited access, secure areas for inventories and small tools, and negotiable securities held in safekeeping are controls which protect assets from being improperly transferred prior to recording.

Extensive training of persons charged with the responsibility for capturing transactions at origin also helps in preventing omissions. Such training should emphasize the need for transaction documentation, review, and approval. Use of prenumbered documents, limited access to documents, and periodic accounting for used documents should also be stressed as part of such employee training.

Rights and Obligations

Management's assertions regarding **rights and obligations** state that all assets appearing on the balance sheet are property rights owned by the firm and that all liabilities are obligations of the firm as of the balance sheet date. The control structure elements that strengthen these assertions are described in the following paragraphs.

The Control Environment

Management integrity and support of proper financial reporting is critical to an environment conducive to full disclosure of the firm's rights and obligations. Cases abound in which management intentionally misrepresented financial position by reflecting leased, consigned, or otherwise unowned assets in the financial statements. The purpose for such asset inflation may have been to obtain needed financing by misrepresenting financial position to potential lenders, or it may have been to conceal asset shortages by temporarily substituting similar but unowned assets for those misappropriated. Case 6.1 illustrates a situation in which a dishonest treasurer was able to misappropriate large amounts of cash from the sale of securities and conceal the misappropriation through substitution.

CASE 6.1

Larson Hospital Supply

Case Description

Larson Hospital Supply, located in Yuma, Arizona, was the principal distributor of surgical equipment and hospital supplies for the hospitals located in Yuma and the surrounding area. Annual sales were approximately $10 million and net income for the latest fiscal year was $2.3 million. Chalmers and Pierson, CPAs, had been auditing the financial statements of Larson for the past several years. Judy Riemsnyder, a newly appointed senior auditor, was placed in charge of the 1992 audit for the first time.

Lars Nielson, the corporate treasurer, was responsible for managing Larson's rather sizeable investment portfolio. In order to provide maximum flexibility, Larson placed its accounts at the various brokerage houses in Nielson's name. All purchases and sales were authorized by Nielson, and checks for sales proceeds were written to the order of Lars Nielson and mailed to him % Larson Hospital Supply. Brokers' advices and other correspondence from brokers were similarly mailed directly to Nielson. The investment ledger supporting the portfolio was maintained by Nielson. The general ledger was maintained by Hubert Pompano, Larson's controller.

Given the weaknesses in control over purchases and sales of securities, Lars Nielson misappropriated $350,000 of proceeds from the sale of securities over a period of two years ending with the close of the 1992 fiscal year. Nielson effected the defalcations by depositing checks from brokerage firms into his own bank accounts and destroying the brokers' advices. In the absence of brokers' advices, Pompano had not recorded the sales. To maintain correspondence between the investment ledger and the general ledger control account, Nielson did not credit the investment ledger for the fraudulent sales. Prior to the annual audits, Nielson would transfer cash and securities from his personal accounts with brokers to the company accounts to cover the year-end discrepancies between the accounts with brokers and investment ledger.

What Would You Do?

Study of the internal control structure should have clearly revealed the weaknesses in this area of the investment cycle. Upon discovery, the auditors should have

1. Notified senior management and the board of directors of the weakness and recommended appropriate separation of duties. Nielson, as corporate treasurer, should have been responsible for authorizing purchases and sales of securities and for custody over all proceeds arising from sales and investment income. The accounts, however, should have been in the name of Larson Hospital Supply, and all brokers' advices mailed directly to Pompano, the corporate controller. The investment ledger should have been maintained by the controller's office rather than by the treasurer.

2. Extended their substantive procedures by examining all securities as of year end. In the process of inspecting securities in the brokerage offices, the auditors should have compared descriptions and serial numbers with the investment ledger. Such comparison would have revealed the fraudulent substitution of borrowed securities for those sold and not credited in the investment ledger. Review of dividends and interest should also have disclosed that certain securities, as represented in the investment ledger, were no longer earning income. Comparison with Standard & Poor's or Moody's dividend reporters would have contradicted the absence of income on the securities.

What Was Done?

Neither Riemsnyder nor her predecessor on the Larson audit extended their substantive audit procedures. They did confirm the balances with brokers; but, as long as the totals agreed with the investment ledger, no further procedures were applied and the shortages were not detected. Riemsnyder did include the control weaknesses in her reportable conditions letter to senior management and the board of directors and recommended the improvements just suggested.

Instances have also occurred in which expenses and liabilities have been overstated for the purpose of minimizing net income and earnings per share. The motivation for such "management fraud" is often to evade income taxes or avoid remitting monies to "greedy" parent companies.

Unintentional errors in reflecting rights and obligations may also occur. Complex issues involving ownership are often associated with various forms of contracts and agreements. The internal control environment, therefore, should provide that these documents be examined carefully by the entity's legal counsel and internal auditors. Examination of contracts, leases, loan agreements, and related-party transactions by legal counsel helps to identify and define the assets and obligations arising from the transactions. Systematic review of these documents by the internal audit staff helps to ensure that the resulting assets and obligations are properly reflected and disclosed in the financial statements. Particular attention should be directed toward such agreements as:

1. Leases containing contingent rental clauses; and
2. Franchises, patents, and licensing agreements calling for varying royalty payments.

The Accounting System

By requiring complete documentation of all transactions and events, the accounting system can help to prevent errors in recording rights and obligations. In addition to documentation, proper review of transactions in manual systems or input editing in EDP systems helps in properly reflecting rights and obligations in the accounting records.

A common error involving ownership relates to goods received on consignment. Title to such merchandise rests with the consignor. The accounting system, therefore, should provide for coding receiving documents related to consignments in, or otherwise "flagging" these goods to avoid erroneous recording as purchases. A chart of accounts and accounting manuals describing proper treatment for consigned goods, accompanied by effective transaction review, should also assist in preventing recording errors relating to consignments.

Control Procedures

In addition to the control environment and accounting system, certain other control procedures can help in ensuring proper reporting of rights and obligations. First, asset safeguards that prevent misappropriation remove the need to effect concealment through such means as substitution. Limiting access to cash and negotiable securities as well as data bases, and fixing custodial responsibility for such assets are examples of safeguard controls. Proper identification and segregation of goods received on consignment should prevent erroneous recording of these goods as assets in the inventory accounts. In addition to specially coded receiving reports, as discussed earlier, physical separation in the storage area should also be required by the control procedures.

Valuation or Allocation

Valuation or allocation of assets and equities in accordance with GAAP is critical to fairness of financial reporting. Particular care should be exercised, therefore, in designing a control structure that will provide reasonable assurance of proper valuation.

The Control Environment

As for preceding assertions, management support of proper accounting and reporting is vital to the valuation assertion. Complex valuation issues such as the following surface on a recurring basis and must be carefully considered for proper recording in accordance with GAAP:

1. Net realizable value of inventories and accounts receivable;
2. Estimated product warranty liability;
3. Pension liability;
4. Discounted value of financing leases.

Careful consideration of these issues by the controller's staff and review by the internal auditors help to ensure proper recording. Review of major transactions by the audit committee can also assist in resolving disputed valuation issues such as inventory obsolescence and adequacy of the allowance for doubtful accounts. Situations in which the valuation questions are particularly complex (leases and pensions, for example) may prompt the entity to contact the independent auditors for advice as to proper recording and reporting in conformity with GAAP.

The Accounting System

The accounting system supports valuation by providing for effective documentation of transactions and events in conjunction with review by persons competent in resolving complex accounting issues. Such review should begin at the point of transaction input. A chart of accounts and accounting manuals may serve as reference aids for determining proper valuation, but should not be considered substitutes for competent personnel. Standard journal entries and checklists supporting monthly and annual adjustments also support proper valuation and allocation within the financial statements.

Control Procedures

An effective system of budgeting, standard costs, and variance analysis is an important set of control procedures for monitoring the valuation process. Careful attention to establishing standards provides greater assurance that inventories will be valued in accordance with GAAP. Recurring analysis of significant variances, in turn, helps isolate valuation errors and assists in assuring that high cost goods are reflected at net realizable value. Other control procedures that support proper valuation are the following:

1. Monthly accounts receivable aging analysis and adjustment of the allowance for doubtful accounts;
2. Segregation of slow-moving and obsolete inventory for special treatment as to valuation;
3. Monthly analysis of the investment portfolio and adjustment of securities to lower of cost or market;
4. Systematic comparison of creditors' statements with the accounts payable subsidiary ledger and clearing of exceptions; and

5. Timely attention to customer exceptions and issuance of credit or debit memos as appropriate.

Presentation and Disclosure

Aspects of the control structure supporting **presentation and disclosure** are concerned with ensuring proper classification and adequacy of footnote disclosure within the financial statements.

Control Environment

Like the preceding assertions, management support of the control structure is vital to meeting this set of assertions. Management awareness of the need for full and fair disclosure and a commitment to achieving proper classification and disclosure within the financial statements provide insurance against intentional irregularities.

Periodic discussion with legal counsel concerning possible footnote needs also supports adequacy of disclosure. Financial review by the internal audit staff and reports to the audit committee are effective in detecting classification and disclosure errors. In addition to the report from the internal auditors, the audit committee should review the monthly, quarterly, and annual financial statements for possible questions concerning presentation and disclosure.

Accounting System

Accounting manuals should provide detailed coverage of recurring classification and disclosure issues. In conjunction with after-the-fact review of unusual transactions by the controller, this aspect of the accounting system strongly supports the presentation and disclosure assertion. Adequacy of transaction documentation is also important for determining how transactions are to be classified and whether added disclosure is needed.

Control Procedures

In addition to those provided by the control environment and the accounting system, control procedures for ensuring proper presentation and adequacy of disclosure are the following:

1. Plant assets removed from production and awaiting disposal should be physically separated and accounting should be notified that such assets have been removed from operations. Such assets, if material in amount, should be classified as other assets on the balance sheet, and further depreciation should not be taken with respect to them. If disposal is not contemplated in the near future, the assets should be reduced to estimated net realizable value and a loss recognized as appropriate;

2. Copies of correspondence with legal counsel should be forwarded to the controller for review as to possible disclosure needs; and

3. The accounts receivable subsidiary ledger should be reviewed monthly and the following balances, if material, should be reclassified: receivables from officers and employees and credit balances in customers' accounts.

INHERENT LIMITATIONS

An internal control structure, regardless of how carefully designed and implemented, contains certain **inherent limitations.** This is why the structure is said to provide "reasonable" rather than "absolute" assurance of preventing and detecting errors and irregularities. This is also why the independent auditor must perform a **minimum audit** (i.e., perform some substantive testing) no matter how effective the control structure. The inherent limitations are classified and discussed in the following paragraphs.

Collusion to Circumvent Control

Adequate separation of functional responsibilities provides reasonable assurance against a single individual both perpetrating and concealing an irregularity; but this class of controls can be circumvented by **collusion,** involving two or more individuals working together to effect the misappropriation and concealment. A person having custody over incoming cash receipts, for example, might conspire with a person responsible for processing and recording those receipts. Together, these individuals can effect a fraudulent diversion of cash receipts accompanied by concealment. Concealment might assume the form of failure to record the cash receipts, overstating discounts, recording fictitious returns, writing off accounts receivable, or some combination of these or other possible means.

Management Override

The accounting system and related control procedures may be collectively referred to as an *arm of management*. As such, the controls are as effective or as ineffective as management wishes them to be. They cannot be expected, therefore, to prevent or detect irregularities perpetrated by those members of management responsible for monitoring the control structure.

Management override may assume the form of either misrepresentation or misappropriation. Misappropriation, the fraudulent transfer of assets accompanied by concealment, was discussed earlier. Although misappropriation of assets by lower level employees can be effectively prevented through documentation, limited access, and separation of duties, misappropriation by members of top management cannot be prevented, given the opportunity for override. Case 6.2 illustrates how an effective control system breaks down under conditions of management override.

CASE 6.2

Maples of Singapore Hospital

Case Description

Maples of Singapore Hospital, with 1200 beds, was one of the largest hospitals in the Atlanta metropolitan area. It was considered by other hospitals in the region to be one of the best managed and most competitive health care institutions. The ''management team'' consisted of Wade Holloway, chief executive officer, Nolan Tuckerman, vice-president and chief operating officer, Jack Hanlan, controller, and Georgiann Bartells, treasurer. Gerald Smile & Associates, CPAs, had been performing the annual audit of Maples for several years, the latest having been the fiscal year ending June 30, 1991.

For as long as Smile & Associates had been auditing Maples, the management team had conspired to perpetrate material defalcations of monies received from insurers and patients. The frauds primarily involved inflating insurance claims. Claims for actual patients were padded and claims for nonexistent patients were filed. The frauds involved millions of dollars annually, and had been cleverly concealed through false documentation—all properly approved by the management team.

The frauds were discovered after Hanlan became ill and was temporarily replaced by Jason Drew, assistant controller. Not having been included in the conspiracy, Drew became suspicious upon reviewing insurance claims for patients alleged to be in rooms known by Drew to be vacant on the dates referenced in the claims. Drew had visited Hanlan on the dates in question and had specifically noted the unusual vacancy rate on Hanlan's floor. Upon questioning Tuckerman, Drew was told that he must be mistaken and not to pursue the matter further. Being confident of his facts, Drew took the matter to Wade Holloway, who also tried to convince him that he was wrong.

Finding no other avenue open to him, Mr. Drew contacted one of the outside members of the board of directors. An emergency board meeting was called, and Holloway admitted the fraud when confronted by the board. An investigation was then conducted by Smile & Associates, who later estimated the defalcation at $35 million over a five-year period.

Holloway, Tuckerman, Hanlan, and Bartells were all terminated, prosecuted by the state of Georgia and sentenced to terms in prison. Smile & Associates were sued by the new hospital administrators for negligence in not detecting the defalcations. Although the lower court found them guilty, the court of appeals reversed the decision, stating that, ''Auditors cannot be expected to detect defalcations perpetrated and concealed by top management. Moreover, the management of an entity should not be able to recover damages for losses sustained as a result of their own frauds. In the present case, the management of Maples of Singapore Hospital had turned the institution into an engine of fraud.''

What Would You Do?

Cases of this nature fairly defy detection by the auditors. Top management override of the internal control creates the illusion of smooth operation of the system and authenticity of fictitious and falsified transactions. The appeals court was correct in its observation that auditors should not be expected to detect this type of fraud.

Misrepresentation occurs when management attempts to intentionally misstate financial position or results of operations. The early revenue recognition method used by the custom-made refrigeration equipment manufacturer (see Chapter 5) is an example of misrepresentation fraud.

Temporary Breakdown of the System

The functioning of the accounting system and related control procedures is as effective as the performance of the people administering the controls. People cannot be expected to perform the control functions in a consistent manner at all times. Misunderstanding, mistaken judgment, carelessness, distraction, or fatigue are some factors causing **temporary breakdown** of the structure. A significant extension (price times quantity) error on the face of a vendor's invoice may go undetected; a shipment of merchandise may never get billed to a customer; an unauthorized disbursement may be made because the check signer did not adequately review the accompanying documentation. These "control failures" are certain to happen occasionally, whenever people are charged with administering control functions.

Chapter 8 offers a means for minimizing the incidence of temporary breakdowns through effective computer controls. Computers, unlike people, perform programmed functions in a consistent manner. Therefore, if properly programmed to perform comparisons, recalculations, and reconciliations, the magnitude of temporary control breakdowns can be dramatically reduced.

Environmental Changes Not Accompanied by Revised Controls

Companies operating in a dynamic environment must adapt to change in order to survive and remain competitive. Examples of **environmental changes** affecting the control structure include acquiring other companies, opening branches in other locations, and adding and dropping divisions, departments, or product lines. Frequently, when these changes occur the accounting system and other control procedures do not adapt immediately to the new environment. Until they do, errors or irregularities may occur. A company, for example, may require that all incoming cash receipts be prelisted and that the prelisting be compared to the daily deposit ticket received from the bank. A newly opened branch may have temporarily overlooked this requirement and failed to prelist cash receipts or otherwise maintain proper accountability over cash. The situation may go undetected until the internal auditors arrive from the home office and inform the branch manager of the "gap" in control.

A related type of change occurs when the environment remains stable while the accounting system changes. Computerizing a portion of the accounting system, for example, may result in a temporary loss of control—or it may result in temporary control redundancy. Assume that a manual payroll system provides for double-checking pay rates, hours, and withholdings. Assume further that the company replaces the manual system with a computerized payroll system. The new system may include programmed routines for verifying rates, hours, and withholdings, in which case the manual checking becomes unnecessary. Retaining the manual controls beyond the normal "debugging" stage would result in control redundancy.

A more serious matter presents itself, however, if the manual checking were eliminated and the new system did not contain the verification routines. For this reason, most companies require that EDP systems be operated alongside the manual systems until the EDP system is functioning adequately and all controls are in place and working.

INTERNAL CONTROL FOR A SMALL BUSINESS

Small firms, given personnel constraints, cannot justify many of the accounting system features and control procedures found in larger entities. Separation of functional responsibilities, for example, present in large entities, are not found in smaller businesses due to the added personnel cost needed to effect such separation. In addition, smaller companies cannot afford to maintain the internal audit staffs found in larger businesses. Given these constraints, compensating controls are needed to achieve adequate control in a cost-effective manner. Active participation by the owner or manager is usually the best form of compensating control. Such active involvement should include at least the following functions:

1. *Examine all documentation before signing checks, and mail checks directly upon signing.* The owner/manager's knowledge of the business should enable him/her to recognize documents that are fabricated, altered, or otherwise not representative of transactions consummated by the entity. Also, by mailing signed checks directly, the owner/manager is preventing accounting personnel from having access to financial assets (signed disbursement checks) for possible misappropriation and concealment.

2. *Mail customer statements directly after careful review.* The purpose for reviewing customer statements is to identify significant past due balances for follow-up with customers. Whether the past due balances are the result of lapping[8] or actually are delinquent accounts, the owner/manager's review and follow-up should reveal the cause. Moreover, knowledge of the owner/manager's review and follow-up policy should discourage accounting personnel from fraudulently lapping customer's remittances and should encourage vigorous collection policies.

3. *Examine purchase orders before submission to vendors.* By examining purchase orders before they are forwarded to vendors, the owner/manager can support those control objectives related to buying goods and services of adequate quality, at the best price, and in quantities that satisfactorily balance order cost and carrying cost. Recurring purchases from the same vendor, given the availability of several vendors, purchases in small quantities, given high costs of shipping, and prices that are obviously excessive are some of the problem areas mitigated by careful examination of purchase orders.

4. *Apply analytical procedures and investigate unusual relationships.* By requiring budgets, along with monthly financial statements and performance reports, the owner/manager can apply analytical procedures similar to those discussed in Chapter 4. This, in turn, should enable him/her to identify significant abnormalities and investigate them for cause. Ratios and percentages of particular interest include gross profit rates, budget variances, current and quick ratios, accounts receivable turnover, inventory turnover, and times interest earned. Whether significant declines are the result of deteriorating economic condi-

---

[8]Lapping is a form of concealment whereby current customer remittances are credited to customers whose previous remittances have been misappropriated. Lapping is discussed in Chapter 12.

tions, increased competition, errors, or irregularities, by investigating for cause and following up for correction, the owner/manager is able to achieve effective control.

5. *Control cash receipts and compare with daily deposit ticket obtained from the bank.* To ensure that all incoming cash receipts are deposited intact, the owner/manager should require the following:

    a. Incoming checks should be restrictively endorsed by someone not having access to accounting records (e.g., the owner/manager's secretary or a receptionist) and listed for later comparison with the deposit ticket;

    b. Cash registers should be audited by the owner/manager or the person responsible for incoming checks;

    c. The cash register tapes and sales slips should be forwarded to the accountant;

    d. Checks and cash register receipts should be deposited by the person endorsing checks and auditing the cash registers, and the receipted deposit ticket should be forwarded to the owner/manager;

    e. The owner/manager should compare the deposit ticket total for agreement with the cash receipts entry, and the sum of the cash register tapes and the listing of checks received by mail.

6. *Reconcile bank account or have account reconciled by someone other than the cashier or bookkeeper.* As a further control to detect errors or irregularities relating to cash, the owner/manager should reconcile the bank account monthly, or assign this task to someone not having access to either cash receipts or accounting records.

7. *Approve all write-offs of customer accounts.* To guard against premature write-offs of otherwise collectible accounts, or to prevent dishonest employees from writing off accounts to conceal misappropriated remittances, the owner/manager should contact customers and/or collection agencies prior to approving write-offs of presumably uncollectible accounts.

8. *Test count inventory periodically and compare with perpetual records.* Significant disparities between physical inventories and perpetual inventory records may result from either inventory shortages or inadequate perpetual records. Whatever the cause, the result is loss of inventory control. By recurring test counts and comparisons, the owner/manager can quickly detect shortages and investigate for cause. This practice should also strengthen inventory accounting by encouraging the person(s) maintaining the perpetual records to exercise care in minimizing errors.

9. *Review payroll checks prior to signing and perform an occasional surprise distribution of payroll checks.* In a small business, the owner/manager should be familiar with his/her labor force, as well as normal working hours and rates of pay. By reviewing payroll checks before signing, he/she should be able to identify errors and irregularities relating to hours, rates of pay, fictitious employees, and/or terminated employees remaining on the payroll. If the number of employees is too great for ready recognition, the owner/manager can compensate for lack of familiarity by occasionally distributing checks and retaining unclaimed checks for follow-up.

10. *Retain an independent CPA for recurring review of the accounting system and related financial statements.* Although small businesses are not typically audited by independent CPAs, reviews are quite common. Further defined in Chapter 16, a review, although lesser in scope than an audit, does provide limited assurance regarding the financial statements. Moreover, although the CPA is not required to study and evaluate internal control as part of a review, significant control weaknesses should be sufficiently obvious to the trained professional, enabling him/her to so inform the owner/manager.

In essence, the owner or manager, in performing the above functions, is acting in the capacity of internal auditor, thus strengthening the control environment and providing compensating controls in the absence of separation. Systematic application of these procedures requires little of the owner or manager's time, while providing much needed control of the firm's assets and accounting system.

KEY TERMS

Accountability controls	Management's assertions
Accounting systems	Management override
Asset safeguards	Minimum audit
Audit trail	Periodic inventories and comparisons
Collusion	Policy and procedures manuals
Completeness	Presentation and disclosure
Control environment	Prevention controls
Control procedures	Rights and obligations
Detection controls	Standard journal entries
Environmental changes	Temporary breakdown
Existence or occurrence	Transaction documentation
Inherent limitations	Transaction review
Internal control structure	Valuation or allocation
Limited access controls	

REVIEW QUESTIONS

1. Define *internal control structure*.
2. Identify the three components of control structure.
3. How can an effective accounting system strengthen the firm's control structure?
4. What are some of the aspects of accounting systems which support a sound control structure?
5. Discuss the importance of management support of the control structure.
6. How does the firm's method of data processing affect control?
7. An effective control structure is said to have both prevention and detection aspects. Explain how.
8. How does functional separation of duties make concealment of misappropriation more difficult?

9. What aspects of the control environment help to ensure that assets and equities will be properly valued?
10. Differentiate between access controls and accountability controls.
11. Why must access to documents, as well as assets, be limited?
12. How does fixing responsibility enhance control?
13. Give three examples of "periodic inventories and comparisons."
14. Why is a minimum audit necessary, notwithstanding an effective control structure?
15. How does the internal control structure differ in a small entity as opposed to a large one?

MULTIPLE CHOICE QUESTIONS FROM CPA EXAMINATIONS

1. In general, a material internal accounting control weakness may be defined as a condition in which material errors or irregularities may occur and not be detected within a timely period by
   a. An independent auditor during the control testing phase of the study and evaluation of internal accounting control procedures.
   b. Employees in the normal course of performing their assigned functions.
   c. Management when reviewing interim financial statements and reconciling account balances.
   d. Outside consultants who issue a special-purpose report on internal control.

2. Control procedures are not designed to provide reasonable assurance that
   a. Transactions are executed in accordance with management's authorization.
   b. Irregularities will be eliminated.
   c. Access to assets is permitted only in accordance with management's authorization.
   d. The recorded accountability for assets is compared with the existing assets at reasonable intervals.

3. In a properly designed set of control procedures, the same employee should not be permitted to
   a. Sign checks and cancel supporting documents.
   b. Receive merchandise and prepare a receiving report.
   c. Prepare disbursement vouchers and sign checks.
   d. Initiate a request to order merchandise and approve merchandise received.

4. A client erroneously recorded a large purchase twice. Which of the following internal control procedures would be most likely to detect this error in a timely and efficient manner?
   a. Footing the purchases journal.
   b. Reconciling vendors' monthly statements with subsidiary payable ledger accounts.
   c. Tracing totals from the purchases journal to the ledger accounts.
   d. Sending written quarterly confirmations to all vendors.

5. Which of the following control procedures may prevent failure to bill customers for some shipments?
   a. Each shipment should be supported by a prenumbered sales invoice that is accounted for.
   b. Each sales order should be approved by authorized personnel.

    c. Sales journal entries should be reconciled to daily sales summaries.

    d. Each sales invoice should be supported by a shipping document.

6. Of the following statements about a firm's internal accounting control structure, which one is correct?

    a. The maintenance of the internal control structure is an important responsibility of the internal auditor.

    b. Administrative controls relate directly to the safeguarding of assets and the systems of authorization and approval.

    c. Because of the cost-benefit relationship, internal accounting control procedures may be applied on a test basis in some circumstances.

    d. Internal accounting control procedures reasonably ensure that collusion among employees cannot occur.

7. Alpha Company uses its sales invoices for posting perpetual inventory records. Inadequate internal accounting controls over the invoicing function allow goods to be shipped that are not invoiced. The inadequate controls could cause an

    a. Understatement of revenues, receivables, and inventory.

    b. Overstatement of revenues and receivables, and an understatement of inventory.

    c. Understatement of revenues and receivables, and an overstatement of inventory.

    d. Overstatement of revenues, receivables, and inventory.

8. In a properly designed accounts payable system, a voucher is prepared after the invoice, purchase order, requisition, and receiving report are verified. The next step in the system is to

    a. Cancel the supporting documents.

    b. Enter the check amount in the check register.

    c. Approve the voucher for payment.

    d. Post the voucher amount to the expense ledger.

9. Sound internal accounting control procedures dictate that defective merchandise returned by customers should be presented to the

    a. Purchasing clerk.

    b. Receiving clerk.

    c. Inventory control clerk.

    d. Sales clerk.

10. For effective internal control purposes, which of the following individuals should be responsible for mailing signed checks?

    a. Receptionist.

    b. Treasurer.

    c. Accounts payable clerk.

    d. Payroll clerk.

11. Which of the following internal control procedures most likely addresses the completeness assertion for inventory?

    a. Work in process account is periodically reconciled with subsidiary records.

    b. Employees responsible for custody of finished goods do *not* perform the receiving function.

    c. Receiving reports are prenumbered and periodically reconciled.

    d. There is a separation of duties between payroll department and inventory accounting personnel.

12. Which of the following factors are included in an entity's control environment?

	Audit committee	Internal Audit function	Organizational structure
a.	Yes	Yes	No
b.	Yes	No	Yes
c.	No	Yes	Yes
d.	Yes	Yes	Yes

ESSAY QUESTIONS AND PROBLEMS

6.1 Dunbar Camera Manufacturing, Inc., produces high-priced precision motion picture cameras in which the specifications of component parts are vital to the manufacturing process. Dunbar buys valuable camera lenses and large quantities of sheetmetal and screws. Screws and lenses are ordered by Dunbar and billed by the vendors on a unit basis. Sheetmetal is ordered by Dunbar and is billed by the vendors on the basis of weight. The receiving clerk is responsible for documenting the quality and quantity of merchandise received. A preliminary review of the internal control structure indicates that the following procedures are being followed:

Receiving Report: Properly approved purchase orders, which are prenumbered, are filed numerically. The copy sent to the receiving clerk is an exact duplicate of the copy sent to the vendor. Receipts of merchandise are recorded on the duplicate copy by the receiving clerk.

Sheetmetal: The company receives sheetmetal by railroad. The railroad independently weighs the sheetmetal and reports the weight and date of receipt on a bill of lading (waybill) which accompanies all deliveries. The receiving clerk only checks the weight on the waybill to the purchase order.

Screws: The receiving clerk opens cartons containing screws, then inspects and weighs the contents. The weight is converted to number of units by means of conversion charts. The receiving clerk then checks the computed quantity to the purchase order.

Camera Lenses: Each camera lens is delivered in a separate corrugated carton. Cartons are counted as they are received by the receiving clerk and the number of cartons are checked to purchase orders.

Required:
   a. Explain why the internal control procedures, as they apply individually to receiving reports and the receipt of sheetmetal, screws, and camera lenses, are adequate or inadequate. Do not discuss recommendations for improvements.
   b. What financial statement distortions may arise because of the inadequacies in Dunbar's control structure and how may they occur? (AICPA adapted)

6.2 You have been engaged by the management of Alden, Inc. to review internal control over the purchase, receipt, storage, and issue of raw materials. You have prepared the following comments that describe Alden's procedures.

   Raw materials, which consist mainly of high-cost electronic components, are kept in a locked storeroom. Storeroom personnel include a supervisor and four clerks. All are well trained, competent, and adequately bonded. Raw materials are removed from the storeroom only upon written or oral authorization of one of the production foremen.

There are no perpetual inventory records; hence, the storeroom clerks do not keep records of goods received or issued. To compensate for the lack of perpetual records, a physical inventory count is taken monthly by the storeroom clerks who are well supervised. Appropriate procedures are followed in making the inventory count.

After the physical count, the storeroom supervisor matches quantities counted against predetermined reorder levels. If the count for a given part is below the reorder level, the supervisor enters the part number on a materials requisition list and sends this list to the accounts payable clerk. The accounts payable clerk prepares a purchase order for a predetermined reorder quantity for each part and mails the purchase order to the vendor from whom the part was last purchased.

When ordered materials arrive at Alden, they are received by the storeroom clerks. The clerks count the merchandise and agree the counts to the shipper's bill of lading. All vendors' bills of lading are initialed, dated, and filed in the storeroom to serve as receiving reports.

Required:

Describe the weaknesses in internal control and recommend improvements in Alden's procedures for the purchase, receipt, storage, and issue of raw materials. Organize your answer sheet into two columns: *Weakness,* and *Recommended Improvements.* (AICPA adapted)

6.3 The Jameson Co. produces a variety of chemical products for use by plastics manufacturers. The plant operates on two shifts, five days per week, with maintenance work performed on the third shift and on Saturdays as required.

An audit conducted by the staff of the new corporate internal audit department has recently been completed and the comments on inventory control were not favorable. Audit comments were directed particularly to the control of raw material ingredients and maintenance materials.

Raw material ingredients are received at the back of the plant, signed for by one of the employees of the batching department, and stored near the location of the initial batching process. Receiving tallies are given to the supervisor during the day, who then forwards them to the inventory control department at the end of the day. The inventory control department calculates ingredient usage using weekly reports of actual production and standard formulas. Physical inventories are taken quarterly. Purchase requisitions are prepared by the inventory control department and rush orders are frequent. In spite of the need for rush orders, the production superintendent regularly gets memos from the controller stating that there must be excess inventory because the ingredient inventory dollar value is too high.

Maintenance parts and supplies are received and stored in a storeroom. There is a storeroom clerk on each operating shift. Storeroom requisitions are to be filled out for everything taken from the storeroom; however, this practice is not always followed. The storeroom is not locked when the clerk is out because of the need to get parts quickly. The storeroom is also open during the third shift for the maintenance crews to get parts as needed. Purchase requisitions are prepared by the storeroom clerk and physical inventory is taken on a cycle count basis. Rush orders are frequent.

Required:

a. Identify the weaknesses in Jameson Company's internal control procedures used for ingredients inventory and maintenance material and supplies inventory. Then, recommend improvements to be instituted for each of these areas.

b. What procedures would the internal auditors use to identify the weaknesses in Jameson Company's inventory control? (AICPA adapted)

6.4 The following functions are enhanced by the presence of certain internal control procedures:

a. Error prevention
b. Error detection
c. Irregularity prevention
d. Irregularity detection

For each of the following specific controls, indicate by appropriate letter or letters the function(s) served by the control:

1. Prelisting incoming cash receipts

2. Monthly bank reconciliations

3. Cash disbursements not made without properly approved voucher supported by necessary documentation

4. Time cards approved by supervisor at the end of each day

5. Account distributions, appearing on the face of vouchers, are double-checked by a second person

6. Pay rates, hours, extensions, and withholdings are reviewed prior to distribution of payroll checks

7. Detailed job descriptions have been written for all clerical positions

8. Custody of accounting records is separate from custody of cash and negotiable securities

9. Receiving reports required for all incoming goods, including sales returns

10. Chart of accounts and accounting manuals

11. All documents are prenumbered

12. All inventories in physically secured areas

13. Responsibility for physical control over inventories fixed in the stores manager

14. Daily intact deposits of cash receipts

15. Inventories periodically ''spot-checked'' and compared with perpetual records

6.5 Trapan Retailing, Inc. has decided to diversify operations by selling through vending machines. Trapan's plans call for the purchase of 312 vending machines which will be situated at 78 different locations within one city and the rental of a warehouse to store merchandise. Trapan intends to sell only canned beverages at a standard price.

Management has hired an inventory control clerk to oversee the warehousing functions and two truck drivers who will periodically fill the machines with merchandise and deposit cash collected at a designated bank. Drivers will be required to report to the warehouse daily.

Required:

What internal controls should the auditor expect to find in order to ensure the integrity of the cash receipts and warehousing functions? (AICPA adapted)

6.6 C. R. Jones, a CPA who has been engaged to examine the financial statements of Ajax, Inc., is about to commence an assessment of Ajax's internal accounting control structure and is aware of the inherent limitations that should be considered.

Required:

a. What are the objectives of control structure that are relevant to a financial audit?
b. What are the reasonable assurances that are intended to be provided by the internal accounting control structure?
c. When considering the potential effectiveness of any accounting control structure, what are the inherent limitations that should be recognized? (AICPA adapted)

6.7 The Art Appreciation Society operates a museum for the benefit and enjoyment of the community. During hours when the museum is open to the public, two clerks, who are positioned at the entrance, collect a $5 admission fee from each nonmember patron. Members of the Art Appreciation Society are permitted to enter free of charge upon presentation of their membership cards.

At the end of each day, one of the clerks delivers the proceeds to the treasurer. The treasurer counts the cash in the presence of the clerk and places it in a safe. Each Friday afternoon, the treasurer and one of the clerks deliver all cash held in the safe to the bank and receive an authenticated deposit slip that provides the basis for the weekly entry in the cash receipts journal.

The board of directors of the Art Appreciation Society has identified a need to improve the internal control over cash admission fees. The board has determined that the cost of installing turnstiles, sales booths, or otherwise altering the physical layout of the museum will greatly exceed any benefits that may be derived. However, the board has agreed that the sale of admission tickets must be an integral part of its improvement efforts. Smith has been asked by the board of directors of the Art Appreciation Society to review the internal controls over cash admission fees and provide suggestions for improvement.

Required:

Indicate weaknesses in existing internal control over cash admission fees, which Smith should identify, and recommend one improvement for each of the weaknesses identified. Organize your answer into two columns: *Weakness* and *Recommendation*. (AICPA adapted)

6.8 Jeanetta Pond joined Amex Metals as assistant controller in March, 1985 after having been with Kramer and Fox, CPAs, for six years. At the end of her employment with the accounting firm, Pond was the in-charge auditor on several engagements, including the Amex Metals audit. She progressed in the company even faster than anticipated by Amex management and assumed the title of controller in 1989 following the former controller's retirement. As corporate controller, Pond was in charge of the accounting system, encompassing the internal as well as the external reporting functions. She was considered by Bart Bleaker, Amex's chief executive officer, as a "very loyal, devoted employee, who earned a lot of trust from us." She had also earned the highest respect from her former employer and continuing independent auditors of Amex, the firm of Kramer and Fox.

Acting on an anonymous tip, however, Amex Metals officials became suspicious about their controller's life style, and became concerned that she was living well beyond her $65,000-a-year salary. Of particular interest was the $250,000 houseboat recently purchased by Pond and moored at the private lake that was part of the subdivision where she lived, and the 911 Porsche turbo-charged automobile, also recently acquired. The anonymous tipster informed Mr. Bleaker that Ms. Pond had paid cash for both the boat and the automobile.

Mr. Bleaker, after discussing the matter with his executive staff, decided to engage Kramer and Fox to conduct a special audit of the books to determine if the company's financial assets were secure. Gretchen Havens, the in-charge auditor for the Amex engagement (Pond's replacement), was placed in charge of the special investigation. She and her audit team quickly discovered that at least $700,000 was missing. Upon being informed of the finding, Mr. Bleaker asked for and received a court freeze on Ms. Pond's assets.

The amount had been misappropriated over a period of eleven months, from mid-1990 to mid-1991, and equaled the company's first-half profits for 1991. The fraud had been perpetrated by overbuying from Amex suppliers and subsequently returning the excess and requesting a refund. Ms. Pond had opened an account with a local bank in the name of the company and for which she was the sole signatory — i.e., only she could withdraw funds from the account. She then deposited the unrecorded refund checks in this account and drew checks on the account to fund her personal purchases. To conceal the overstatement in the account "receivable from vendors" set up as excess inventory was returned to the suppliers, Ms. Pond debited various operating expense accounts. In this manner, none of the expenses appeared to be "out of line" and the auditors would have a difficult time detecting the fraud.

Required:

a. What kinds of controls are needed to prevent and/or detect this type of misappropriation?
b. What responsibility do you think the independent auditors have for detecting misappropriation of this nature?

6.9 A company uses expensive metals in manufacturing its products. Production is highly efficient, but large amounts of scrap metal are generated. The company sells the scrap to a large scrap metal dealer who counts it, picks it up, and sends the company a check. The storage place is physically secure and personnel record, on blank forms, what and how much is sold based on the purchaser's record. The total quantity of scrap sales for each quarter is reviewed for reasonableness and comparison to prior periods.

Required:

Identfy three strengths and six weaknesses in the internal control over scrap metal. (IIA adapted)

7

Internal Control Structure: Assessment of Control Risk

CHAPTER OUTLINE

I. **Reason for the auditor's assessment of control risk**
   A. Required for audit planning
   B. As a basis for constructive suggestions

II. **The auditor's approach to assessing control risk**
   A. Obtain understanding of the control structure
   B. Document understanding
   C. Reduce the assessed level of control risk through control testing
      1. Decide whether to test controls
      2. Select form of control testing
   D. Assess control risk and document conclusions

III. **Design of substantive audit programs**
   A. Adjusting materiality thresholds based on risk analysis
   B. Qualitative approach to designing substantive tests
   C. Quantitative approach to designing substantive tests

IV. **Summary of audit risk assessment**

V. **Communication of reportable conditions**
   A. Examples of reportable conditions
   B. Form of communication

VI. **Appendix: Transaction cycles and related control tests**

OVERVIEW

Chapter 7 presents the auditor's approach to assessing control risk through the study and evaluation of control structure policies and procedures relevant to an audit. To assess control risk, the auditor must first obtain an understanding of the client's control structure sufficient to identify the types of potential material misstatements of financial statement components. Such understanding may be gained through study of the organizational structure, inquiry, and observation. The understanding must also be documented. Documentation may assume the form of narrative memoranda, internal control flowcharts, internal control checklists or questionnaires, or some combination of these.

Based on the initial understanding, the auditor may decide to assess control risk at or below the maximum level. In addition, the auditor may elect to test certain controls as a means for further reducing the assessed level of control risk. Control testing may be in the form of transaction reprocessing, added observation, document examination and testing, or some combination of these. Whenever control risk is assessed below the maximum level, the auditor must document the basis for such assessment.

The assessment of control risk, combined with the assessment of inherent risk (Chapter 5), form the basis for setting detection risk and designing substantive audit programs. Risk assessment will affect the nature, timing, and extent of the procedures incorporated into such programs. Any reportable conditions identified by the auditor during the assessment of control risk must be communicated to the client's audit committee. Such communication may be written or oral.

STUDY OBJECTIVES

After reading this chapter, you should be able to:

1. Explain the reason for the auditor's assessment of control risk
2. Describe an approach to assessing control risk
3. Differentiate between an initial understanding of the design and implementation of internal control and control testing for operating effectiveness
4. Determine the need for additional testing of the control structure
5. Develop the methodology for additional testing of the control structure
6. Develop the necessary documentation of the auditor's understanding of a client's control structure.
7. Develop the necessary documentation supporting an assessed level of control risk below the maximum level
8. Describe both a quantitative and a qualitative approach to the design of substantive audit procedures after having assessed inherent risk and control risk
9. Understand the meaning of "reportable conditions" and how and to whom to report them.

THE REASON FOR THE AUDITOR'S ASSESSMENT OF CONTROL RISK

The second standard of audit field work requires that the auditor obtain a sufficient understanding of a client's control structure to plan the audit and to determine the nature, timing, and extent of tests to be performed. Chapter 5 defined the three components of audit risk and presented an approach to assessing *inherent risk,* as part of the overall audit process. The essence of this part of the audit model involved a thorough study of the company and industry and application of analytical procedures. In order to complete the planning phase of the audit, the auditor needs to assess *control risk.* The ensuing paragraphs address the auditor's assessment of control risk through study and evaluation of control structure policies and procedures relevant to an audit. Figure 7.1 shows, in diagram form, where control risk assessment fits into the overall audit process. Note that if the auditor decides to perform control tests, control risk assessment extends from audit planning into the interim audit phase.

In addition to providing a basis for developing substantive audit programs, study of the control structure serves as a basis for offering constructive suggestions to the client concerning control weaknesses. Referred to as "reportable conditions," they are considered in the concluding section of this chapter.

THE AUDITOR'S APPROACH TO ASSESSING CONTROL RISK

Control risk is the risk that a material misstatement that could occur in a financial statement assertion will not be prevented or detected on a timely basis by the entity's internal control structure policies or procedures.[1] Figure 7.2 presents a flowchart that summarizes the auditor's approach to assessing control risk and defines the **assessed level of control risk.** The flowchart serves as a focal point for the ensuing discussion.

Obtain an Understanding of the Control Structure

In order to plan the audit, the auditor needs to obtain an understanding of the **design and implementation** of the client's internal controls. Only those **control structure** policies and procedures having an impact on the assertions contained in the financial statements, however, are of concern to the auditor in assessing control risk.

The auditor's goal in studying the client's control structure policies and procedures is to obtain sufficient evidence to identify the types of potential material misstatements of financial statement components, and the risks associated with each. Accordingly, for each of the transaction cycles identified in Chapter 4 (revenue cycle, expenditure cycle, financing and investing cycle) the auditor should:

1. Consider the types of errors or irregularities that could occur in the absence of necessary controls;

2. Determine the control structure policies and procedures necessary to prevent or detect those errors or irregularities;

---

[1]*AICPA Professional Standards,* New York: AICPA, Section AU 312.02.

FIGURE 7.1   The Audit Process

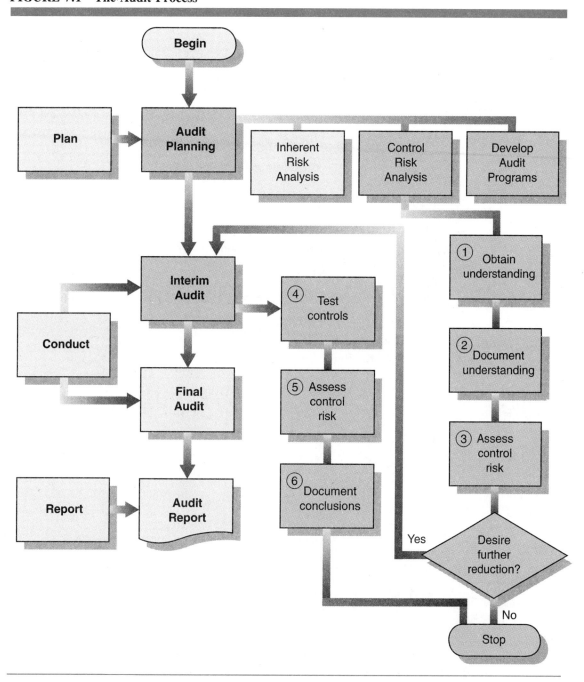

FIGURE 7.2   Control Risk Assessment Flowchart (SAS 55)

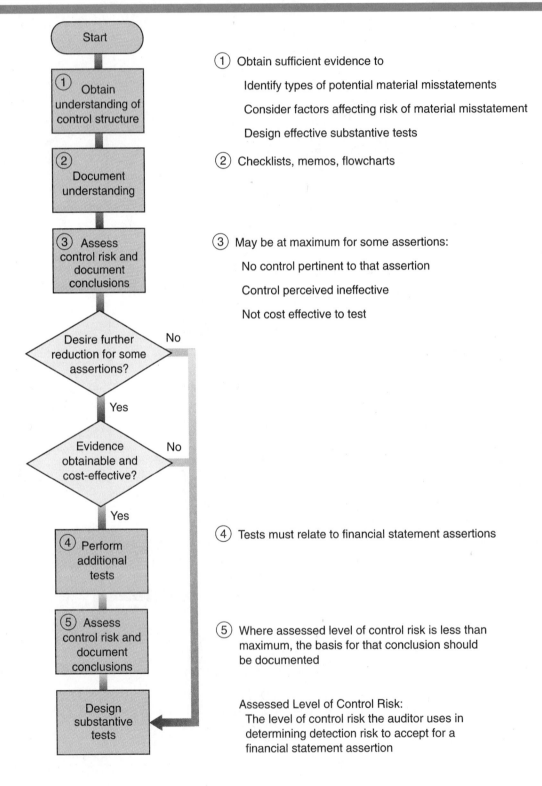

3. Determine whether the necessary policies and procedures have been designed and whether they have been placed in operation;

4. Identify weaknesses (potential errors and irregularities not covered by control policies and procedures);

5. Design substantive audit programs to reflect the weaknesses identified in 4; and

6. Communicate weaknesses identified as reportable conditions to the audit committee.

Much of the auditor's understanding of the client's control structure policies and procedures will have been gained during the initial planning phases of the audit. Certain aspects of the control structure, such as the following, for example, may be evaluated by the auditor at this point:

1. Management support of the control structure;

2. Communication of firm policy;

3. Competence and objectivity of the internal audit staff;

4. Separation of functional responsibilities;

5. Competence of persons performing accounting functions and control procedures;

6. Quality of the budgeting and performance reporting system;

7. Existence of asset safeguards which provide limited access to assets and accountability through fixing of responsibility.

Evidence concerning these aspects may have been obtained by either or both of the following means during the initial planning phases of the audit:

1. Study of the organizational structure as a basis for rational inquiry. The auditor needs to identify the persons involved in the performance of various accounting and control procedures. For a recurring audit, much of the information will already be available in prior working papers, but should still be verified as up-to-date and accurate. For an initial audit, study of the business and industry, as described in Chapter 5, should provide the answers.

2. Inquire of management about necessary controls and whether those controls exist. The focal point of such questioning should be the various classes of transactions and the methods by which the transactions are authorized, executed, and recorded. The means of data processing should also be determined, along with management's methods for supervising the system.

Based on the initial understanding, the auditor may decide to assess control risk at the **maximum level** for some assertions and **below maximum** for others. The assessed level of control risk may also vary by transaction cycles. For those assertions assessed at maximum, a *primarily substantive audit approach* is suggested. Emphasis on substantive testing requires that the auditor examine a larger proportion of transactions and balances than under conditions of lower than maximum control risk.

As an alternative to assessing control risk on the basis of the initial understanding, the auditor may wish to lower the assessed level of control risk further through *control testing*. This, in turn, will enable the auditor to further reduce the amount of substantive testing related to the affected transaction cycles and assertions. While the initial understanding of internal control provides evidence of proper design and implementation, control testing enables the auditor to further evaluate the *operating effectiveness* of the controls. Operating effectiveness provides increased evidence as to proper functioning of controls during the period under audit. Whether or not control testing is undertaken depends upon the auditor's perception of control effectiveness and the cost-effectiveness of control testing. The auditor may decide not to perform added tests because the overall internal control structure design is perceived to be *inadequate* (i.e., the controls have already been perceived ineffective); discovery during the initial planning phase, for example, that bank accounts have not been properly reconciled during the year is convincing evidence as to the weakness of this control, and the auditor would ordinarily not elect to test the control for operating effectiveness. The auditor may decide not to test a control after concluding that further testing is not *cost-effective* (i.e., the cost of control testing exceeds the cost savings associated with reduced substantive testing). A few major plant asset additions occurring during the year, for example, may be more effectively audited through examination of the assets and underlying purchase documentation (a primarily substantive audit approach) than by testing control policies and procedures covering plant asset additions.

In audits of small businesses, given the combining of functional responsibilities and the lack of an internal audit staff, auditors frequently follow a primarily substantive audit approach. That is, the auditor will obtain an understanding of those controls that do exist, but will then assess control risk at maximum and apply substantive audit procedures extensively. Even in the presence of controls, substantive testing may be more cost-effective, given the relatively small volume of transactions consummated by a small business. In other words, examining virtually 100% of the entity's transactions may be less costly than testing controls for the purpose of reducing substantive testing.

Document Understanding

Regardless of the decision to test further, the auditor must fully *document* his or her understanding of the control structure policies and procedures obtained through whatever means.[2] Documentation may assume the form of internal control checklists, internal control flowcharts, or internal control memoranda.

The **internal control memorandum** (see Exhibit 7.1) consists of a narrative description of a transaction cycle, together with a statement describing control strengths and weaknesses. The processing of cash receipts, sales transactions, payroll, purchases and vouchering, and cash disbursements might each be the subject of an internal control memorandum. Together, the various memoranda would constitute the documentation of the auditor's understanding of the internal control structure policies and procedures.

The advantage of the memorandum approach lies in its rigor of analysis and the control structure understanding such rigor promotes. This means of control structure analysis, however, does not readily lend itself to quick review and ready comprehension by someone other than the author of the memorandum. The narrative form

---

[2]*Ibid.*

EXHIBIT 7.1   Internal Control Memorandum—Sales Processing

> Prenumbered sales orders, including evidence of proper credit approval, are based on customer orders, approved by the regional sales manager, received from the regional sales offices via remote terminals, and reviewed by one of the three product managers. These orders are sent to accounting for a completeness review, including evidence of credit approval. After reviewing the orders, accounting prepares an input recording form. The recording form contains customer number, sales representative number, stock number, and quantity of each stock item ordered by the customer. The recording forms are then forwarded daily to EDP where they form the basis for entry into the system. A copy of the sales order is forwarded by EDP to shipping to trigger processing of the shipment to the customer. The computer prepares the sales invoice set after editing the order for the customer number, existence of customer credit approval, customer credit limit vs. existing customer balance, stock number, and availability of products. As part of the sales processing, the computer inserts the customer's name and address, product descriptions and prices, and extensions and footings. Terms of payment and discount availability are also determined by the computer and included on the invoice. For each order processed, the computer records the transaction, including costing the sale, and updates the accounts receivable and inventory modules. EDP then forwards the invoice sets to accounting where they are filed awaiting notification from shipping that the goods were shipped to the customer. Upon receipt of the shipping order and signed bill of lading from shipping, accounting reviews all documents (sales invoice, sales order, shipping order, and bill of lading) for completeness and agreement, and mails the invoice to the customer.

of documentation, if not presented in combination with internal control flowcharts as described later and in the appendix to this chapter, does not quickly convey a clear image of the structure. This is especially critical when new people are assigned to the audit for the first time, and wish to review the control structure policies and procedures relevant to the audit engagement. The memorandum, by itself, also presents a problem for the audit manager in reviewing the audit field work.

The **internal control questionnaire** and the **internal control checklist** supplement the memo as part of the documentation of the auditor's understanding of control structure. A partial internal control questionnaire is presented as Exhibit 7.2. As used in an actual audit, the questionnaire is quite extensive and detailed and could consist of several pages. Checklists are illustrated in the appendix to this chapter. Questionnaires and checklists attempt to cover all pertinent control points in a given transaction cycle, and they are designed to readily identify weaknesses in control structure. In the questionnaire, questions are usually worded such that "yes" answers denote strengths and "no" answers identify weaknesses. The advantage of the questionnaire-checklist approach lies in its thoroughness of coverage. Virtually every aspect of the transaction cycle being analyzed is covered. Moreover, these devices are easy to apply and portray control weaknesses clearly to whomever is reviewing the documentation. A possible disadvantage is the tendency toward cursory review, given the ease of completing the questionnaire or checklist. New or inexperienced auditors who may not comprehend the reasons for including certain

**EXHIBIT 7.2   A Partial Internal Accounting Control Questionnaire
for Processing Sales Orders and Shipping Goods**

Question	Yes	No	Remarks
Processing Sales Orders:			
Are prenumbered sales order forms used in preparing sales orders?			
Is proper credit approval noted on sales order form?			
Are prices on customer order compared with authorized price list?			
Are customer orders properly approved for quantities, shipping, and discount terms?			
Shipping Goods:			
Are properly approved and prenumbered sales orders required in order for goods to leave the warehouse?			
Are prenumbered bills of lading used?			
Are bills of lading signed by the carrier evidencing shipment?			
Invoicing Customers:			
Do copies of the sales order and bill of lading go to accounting?			
Are sales invoices prepared only on the basis of properly approved sales orders and bills of lading?			

questions or points are often assigned the task of administering parts of the questionnaire or verifying the existence of points contained in checklists. If not carefully instructed and supervised, lack of full understanding may result in failure to detect inconsistencies in responses to questions and result in serious control weaknesses that are not revealed in the questionnaire-checklist process.

The **internal control flowchart** (see Figure 7.3) is another means for documenting the auditor's understanding of control structure. The internal control flowchart lends itself to easy review of the accounting system and the control procedures applied during the processing and review of transactions and events. By presenting the processing steps pictorially in terms of actions, documents, and people performing the control procedures, it provides persons examining the flowchart for the first time with a quick and easy method for grasping the essential features of how transactions and events are processed and for identifying the major control strengths and weaknesses associated with each transaction cycle subset.

The use of flowcharting in the design of EDP systems may be cited as a reason for the growing use of internal control flowcharts by auditors. The flowchart has enhanced understanding of accounting systems and transaction processing in the same fashion that it facilitated development and comprehension of complex EDP systems. Many of the EDP system flowcharts, with slight modification, can be

FIGURE 7.3 Internal Control Flowchart for Sales Orders and Inventory

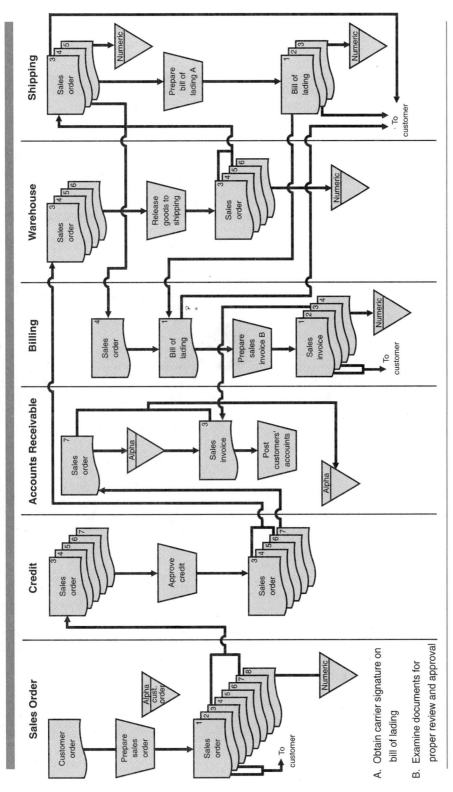

readily converted to internal control flowcharts, thereby reducing the auditor's time invested in control structure description and documentation. Automated flowcharting techniques contained in computer software packages are also reducing the time required in preparing flowcharts while expanding the depth of analysis.

In developing internal control flowcharts, certain rules should be observed to promote consistency among flowcharts. First, standard symbols should be used to represent the various actions, documents, and flows depicted in the flowchart (see Figure 7.4). Second, the flowchart should proceed from left to right and from top to bottom. Third, narrative should be kept to a minimum. The flowchart, if properly

FIGURE 7.4   Standard Flowcharting Symbols

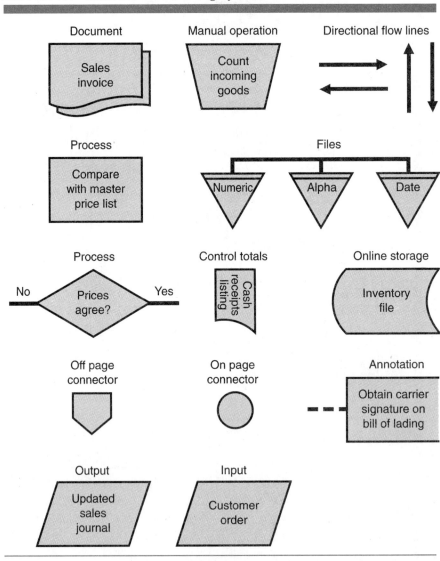

prepared, should be adequately descriptive of the system without the need for extensive narration. Further, the internal control memorandum, described earlier, already contains necessary narrative to fully supplement the pictorial flowchart description. Brief narrative descriptions are occasionally necessary, however, apart from the memorandum. Such narrative should be identified by annotation within the flowchart and presented outside the main body (see Figure 7.3).

Internal control memoranda, internal control questionnaires and checklists, and internal control flowcharts, as described, all have unique merits and shortcomings. For this reason, auditors generally prefer to use a combination of the approaches. The flowchart approach, with its ease of review, together with a questionnaire or checklist for thoroughness of coverage, provide an effective combination. The memorandum approach can provide an in-depth analysis and documentation of a modified transaction cycle where significant changes have been made by the client. Some CPAs follow the practice of performing an in-depth analysis of a control structure segment (e.g., control structure policies and procedures for a given transaction cycle) each year. The analysis, in the form of flowcharts and detailed narrative memoranda, is then placed in the permanent file and updated in subsequent years as the control structure changes.

The appendix to this chapter presents examples of checklists and flowcharts categorized by transaction cycle. To repeat, the purpose of the documentation is to provide evidence of compliance with the second field work standard. This standard requires that the auditor obtain an understanding of the control structure policies and procedures sufficient to plan the audit and to afford a basis for designing substantive audit procedures.

In determining the design and implementation of a client's control structure policies and procedures, the auditor needs to identify the necessary control points. A **control point** exists wherever an error or irregularity could occur in the capturing and processing of data and wherever assets need to be safeguarded against loss from theft or other causes. Prenumbered documents, for example, together with required approvals and reviews and evidence of the same, provide reasonable assurance that only properly approved transactions will occur and that such transactions will be documented at the point of occurrence (control over the capturing of data). Assigning competent persons to tasks involving cost allocation and account distributions and installing a system of double-check provide assurance concerning the processing of data and are examples of **accuracy controls.** Restricted access, cash registers, and separation of duties provide asset protection and are examples of **safeguard controls.** Inasmuch as accuracy and safeguard controls directly support the financial statement assertions, concentration on these controls is a cost-effective approach to studying control structure.

Reduce the Assessed Level of Control Risk through Control Testing

If the auditor decides that the assessed level of control risk can be further reduced through cost-effective means, added tests should be designed for this purpose. Three approaches to added testing are reprocessing, further observation, and document testing.

Reprocessing

The auditor may determine whether transactions are being properly executed and recorded by introducing hypothetical transactions into the system. Referred to as **reprocessing,** the transactions are designed by the auditor to test the system's ability to identify and correct errors in the capturing and processing of data. Hypothetical sales transactions, for example, may contain incorrect selling prices, new customers without credit approval, customers exceeding credit limits, sales invoices without attached shipping orders, and extension or footing errors. Similar transaction sets can be designed for expenditure, production, payroll, and financing and investing transactions.

Having designed a set of hypothetical transactions that violate all significant controls within a given transaction cycle, the auditor next introduces the transactions into the client's system and observes the results of processing. Based on such testing, the auditor may conclude that certain controls, indicated in the questionnaire or flowcharts as existing, are either missing or ineffective; or, compensating controls, not revealed in the initial understanding, may be discovered.

Reprocessing as a means of control testing is particularly useful in an electronic data processing environment. For this reason, this approach is considered again in Chapter 8 *Internal Control and EDP.*

Observation

In addition to, or in place of reprocessing, the auditor may further test control structure policies and procedures by more observation of the control functions. Observation may be particularly appropriate for clients with complex EDP systems. Transaction documentation is often less extensive in these systems, requiring the auditor to apply alternate means for testing the design and operating effectiveness of certain controls. These alternate means may take the form of observing transaction processing at the input stage. The auditor may elect to perform such observations at numerous points throughout the year under audit.

Document Examination and Testing

Where extensive documentation does exist, the auditor may elect to test controls by examining documents supporting selected transactions which occurred during the period under audit. The objective of **document examination and testing** is to determine whether the necessary controls were functioning as intended. Documents supporting disbursements, for example, might be examined for the following control features:

1. Proper review and approval of prices, quantities, and vendors;
2. All necessary documentation (requisition, purchase order, receiving report, vendor's invoice) attached to voucher;
3. Types of goods and quantities appearing on the receiving report agree with quantities on vendor's invoice;
4. Prices on vendor's invoice agree with prices appearing on the purchase order;
5. Account distributions (debits and credits) are correct;
6. Extensions (quantity times price) and footings (total of extended amounts) are correct.

Documents supporting sales, cash receipts, payroll, and production transactions and events are similarly examined for proper execution and recording. A listing of all necessary control points and careful definition of what constitutes an error are very important prerequisites to selecting and examining documents for control testing purposes.

The details concerning selection and examination of documents for control testing purposes are covered in Chapter 10. In particular, the chapter illustrates the application of statistical sampling in selecting documents for examination and evaluating sampling results.

The results of the auditor's control testing—whether obtained through reprocessing of transactions, observation, or document testing and examination—must be fully documented. Such documentation is a necessary part of the overall evidence describing the thought processes leading to the design of substantive tests, and this is especially critical where the auditor plans to assess control risk below the maximum level.

Assess Control Risk and Document Conclusions

The auditor's *assessed level of control risk* is defined by SAS 55 as "that level of control risk used by the auditor in determining the detection risk to accept for a financial statement assertion, and, accordingly, in determining the nature, timing, and extent of substantive tests."[3] SAS 55 further states that this level "may vary along a range from maximum to minimum as long as the auditor has obtained evidential matter to support that assessed level."[4] As indicated in Figure 7.2, if the auditor assesses control risk at maximum for a given set of assertions, he/she need only document an understanding of the control structure. If control risk is assessed below maximum, however, the auditor must also document the basis for such reduction. Moreover, the auditor cannot assess control risk below maximum without obtaining an understanding of the operating effectiveness of the control structure policies and procedures related to that set of assertions. Inasmuch as operating effectiveness is best defined by performing control tests, most auditors hesitate to assess control risk below maximum without having performed control tests.

DESIGN SUBSTANTIVE AUDIT PROGRAMS

Adjusting Materiality Thresholds Based on Risk Analysis

As discussed in Chapter 4, the nature, timing, and extent of substantive audit testing is a function of *materiality* and *risk*. Having set materiality thresholds and having assessed inherent risk and control risk, the auditor now has the information necessary to design substantive audit programs. In approaching program design, the auditor should observe the following guidelines:

1. Allocate proportionately more audit resources to areas of high audit risk as evidenced by the auditor's study of the business and industry and application of

---

[3]*Ibid.*

[4]*Ibid.*

analytical procedures (inherent risk), and study and evaluation of internal control structure (control risk).

2. Material account balances and transactions should generally receive more substantive audit attention than less material areas.

3. If, based on the study of the business and application of analytical procedures, the auditor suspects earnings inflation, individual item materiality thresholds should be decreased below those amounts based on unaudited income and the auditor should place less emphasis on internal relative to external evidence (see Chapter 4 and Figure 4.4).

4. For transaction cycle subsets where internal control is weak and numerous errors are expected, aggregate materiality thresholds—materiality levels for including smaller errors in an audit workpaper for later audit adjustment consideration—should be set low relative to those applicable to strong internal control subsets. The purpose is to lower the probability of overlooking numerous small errors which, in the aggregate, could exceed the individual item threshold. Also, as in (3) above, the auditor should obtain greater amounts of external relative to internal evidence in satisfying specific audit objectives.

Assume an auditor initially assesses internal control as satisfactory and sets aggregate and individual item materiality thresholds, based on satisfactory internal control, at $20,000 and $200,000 respectively. Errors of $200,000 or greater will be considered material and incorporated into proposed audit adjustments. Errors ranging between $20,000 and $200,000 will be accumulated in an audit workpaper for later evaluation as to aggregate materiality. Errors less than $20,000 will generally be ignored. Assume further that, after obtaining an understanding and performing control tests for a given internal control subset, the auditor lowers the assessment of control from satisfactory to weak. The resulting increase in the assessed level of control risk suggests a need to decrease the aggregate materiality threshold level. The underlying rationale is as follows. Under weak internal control, errors are more likely to have occurred and, given more numerous errors, the probability of errors less than $20,000 aggregating $200,000 or more (the individual item threshold) increases. The auditor, therefore, should consider lowering the aggregate level in proportion to the number of errors anticipated. Given an assumption of satisfactory internal control, an aggregate threshold of $20,000, and an individual item level of $200,000, the auditor expects ten or fewer errors aggregating $200,000 or less. Discovering internal control to be weak, the auditor may elect to lower the threshold to $10,000 (assuming the error incidence expectation has increased from ten or fewer to twenty or fewer). This will result in documenting a greater number of smaller errors, and in turn, lowers the probability of ignoring small errors which, in the aggregate, exceed the $200,000 individual item threshold.

In designing substantive audit programs based on risk assessment and materiality considerations, the auditor generally needs to modify the nature, timing, and/or extent of audit procedures contained in the programs. In determining the necessary modifications, the auditor may adopt a qualitative or quantitative approach or some combination of these. As described in the following paragraphs, the auditor typically utilizes a qualitative approach in modifying the nature and timing of audit procedures, and a quantitative approach in altering the extent of audit procedures.

Qualitative Approach to Designing Substantive Tests

The results of risk analysis may suggest a need for modifying the nature or timing of audit procedures for a given transaction cycle subset. As discussed in Chapter 4 and illustrated in the Highbell Toy case (Case 5.3), if internal control is weak, suggesting numerous errors, or if the auditor suspects management misrepresentation, less emphasis should be placed on internal relative to external evidence. Thus, the nature of audit evidence is altered on the basis of inherent and control risk analysis. In the Highbell case, the auditors should have pursued confirmation evidence (external) instead of relying on sales and shipping documents (internal). As another example, if the auditor suspects that unrecorded revenues from scrap sales have been misappropriated, internal documents in the form of sales invoices and remittances advices possess limited validity. For this reason, the auditor may decide to mail confirmations to the client's scrap buyers, requesting verification of scrap purchases by the buyers. This is not a standard procedure in the ordinary financial audit; but, circumstances such as those cited here and in the Highbell case frequently suggest altering the *nature* of auditing procedures.

Ordinarily trade accounts receivable, due to materiality and difficulty of "working forward" to year end, are confirmed by the auditor as of the client's balance sheet date. Under conditions of excellent internal control over sales and cash receipts, however, the auditor may consider confirming the accounts receivable at an interim date (change in *timing* of audit procedures). Interim application of substantive audit procedures is cost-effective in that it reduces the time required, following year end (the auditor's "busy season"), to complete the final audit.

The application of principal substantive procedures (e.g., accounts receivable confirmation and inventory observation) at an interim date does increase audit risk. The degree of incremental risk is a function of the time interval beginning with the interim date and ending with the balance sheet date (i.e., the longer the interval, the greater the increase in audit risk).[5] For this reason, these procedures should not be applied at interim dates, except under the following conditions:

1. Internal control is excellent;
2. The auditor can identify substantive tests to cover the remaining period; and
3. The costs savings resulting from interim application are not exceeded by the cost of substantive tests to cover the remaining period.[6]

Quantitative Approach to Designing Substantive Tests

Inherent and control risk analysis may also suggest modifying the *extent* of substantive auditing procedures to be applied. Chapter 5 presented the audit risk equation as:

$$AR = IR \times CR \times DR$$

Chapter 5 then presented a means for assessing inherent risk (IR) based on a study of the business and industry and application of analytical procedures. Overall audit

---

[5]*Ibid.*, Section AU 313.

[6]*Ibid.*

risk (AR) is set low because it is the basis for the auditor's opinion. An approach to assessing control risk (CR) by evaluating those elements of the control structure relating to the financial statement assertions has been presented in this chapter. Having set three of the four equation components, the auditor can determine detection risk by solving for DR. For example, assume the following values for the equation components:

$$IR = 70\%$$
$$CR = 50\%$$
$$AR = 10\%$$

DR can be solved as follows:

$$DR = \frac{AR}{IR \times CR} = .10/(.70 \times .50) = .2857 = 29\%$$

The detection risk of 29 percent may be used as input for determining the number of items to be included in a sample drawn for the purpose of evaluating the reasonableness of a specific financial statement component. To expand upon this example, assume that during document examination, the auditor discovered that repairs and maintenance expenses were charged to various plant asset accounts or vice versa. In addition, the client did not correctly calculate and account for gains and losses on disposals. Under these circumstances, control risk might be assessed at 100 percent rather than 50 percent as initially set. The resulting detection risk would then be calculated as 14 percent (.10/(.70 × 1.00)) rather than 29 percent. A lower detection risk percentage, as input into the sample size equation, will produce a larger sample size. Stated differently, the weaker the internal control structure the more extensive the substantive testing must be in order to maintain overall audit risk at a predetermined level. This approach to calculating sample size is explored in greater depth in Chapter 11.

SUMMARY OF AUDIT RISK ASSESSMENT

Figure 7.5 summarizes the auditor's approach to risk assessment as presented in Chapters 5 to 7. The combination of inherent risk and control risk determines the probability of material misstatements in the financial statements. This, in turn, enables the auditor to set detection risk accordingly and design substantive audit programs as appropriate.

A feature from the risk assessment summary presented in Figure 7.5 should be emphasized. The point to be noted is the degree to which *management attitude and character* affect both inherent and control risk. In assessing inherent risk, for example, the auditor's assessment of management integrity (character) is important for estimating the probability of management misrepresentation. If management is perceived to be dishonest, the chances for intentional misstatement of financial position and/or results of operations are increased significantly. In evaluating control risk, on the other hand, the auditor ascertains management support of internal control (attitude) as a major input in assessing the probability of material financial statement errors. If the auditor concludes that management is strongly committed to sound internal control, the probability of material financial statement errors is greatly reduced. Stated differently, if the auditor concludes that management is

FIGURE 7.5   Audit Risk Assessment Summary

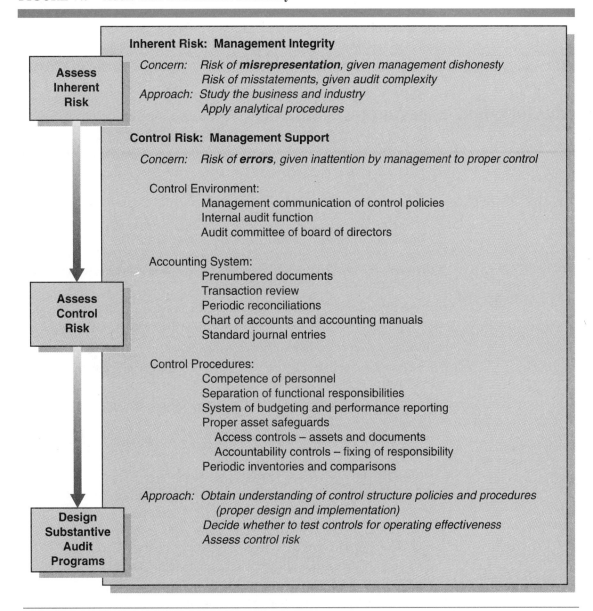

honest and committed to sound internal control, the chances for both misrepresentation and material errors are greatly reduced. If, on the other hand, the auditor perceives management to be dishonest, significant misstatements are likely even under conditions of sound internal control.

To summarize the preceding discussion, the auditor determines the nature, timing, and extent of substantive audit procedures after having set individual item and aggregate materiality thresholds, and after having assessed inherent risk and control risk. Clear and complete documentation of these determinations, together with the judgment processes leading to the decisions, should be included in the audit work-papers. Such documentation provides evidence of compliance with the second standard of field work, which requires the auditor to obtain an understanding of the client's control structure sufficient to plan the audit and design substantive audit programs.

COMMUNICATION OF REPORTABLE CONDITIONS

SAS 60 requires the auditor to communicate reportable conditions to the audit committee or to individuals with a level of authority and responsibility equivalent to an audit committee in organizations that do not have one.[7] **Reportable conditions** are defined as:

> . . . matters coming to the auditor's attention that, in his(her) judgment, should be communicated to the audit committee because they represent significant deficiencies in the design or operation of the internal control structure, which could adversely affect the organization's ability to record, process, summarize, and report financial data consistent with the assertions of management in the financial statements.[8]

Reportable conditions may relate to the control environment, the accounting system, or to control procedures. Examples of reportable conditions include the following:

1. Inadequate overall internal control structure design;
2. Absence of appropriate segregation of duties consistent with appropriate control objectives;
3. Absence of appropriate reviews and approvals of transactions, accounting entries, or systems output;
4. Inadequate procedures for appropriately assessing and applying accounting principles;
5. Inadequate provisions for safeguarding of assets;
6. Absence of other control techniques considered appropriate for the type and level of transaction activity;
7. Evidence that a system fails to provide complete and accurate output consistent with objectives and current needs because of design flaws;
8. Evidence of failure of identified controls to prevent or detect misstatements of accounting information;
9. Evidence that a system fails to provide complete and accurate output consistent with the entity's control objectives because of the misapplication of control procedures;
10. Evidence of failure to safeguard assets from loss, damage, or misappropriation;
11. Evidence of intentional override of the internal control structure by those in authority to the detriment of the overall objectives of the system;

---

[7]*Ibid.*, Section AU 325.

[8]*Ibid.*

12. Evidence of failure to perform tasks that are part of the internal control structure, such as reconciliations not prepared or not prepared in a timely manner;

13. Evidence of willful wrongdoing by employees or management;

14. Evidence of manipulation, falsification, or alteration of accounting records or supporting documents;

15. Evidence of intentional misapplication of accounting principles;

16. Evidence of misrepresentation by client personnel to the auditor;

17. Evidence that employees or management lack the qualifications and training to fulfill their assigned functions;

18. Absence of a sufficient level of control consciousness within the organization;

19. Failure to follow up and correct previously identified internal control structure deficiencies;

20. Evidence of significant or extensive undisclosed related-party transactions;

21. Evidence of undue bias or lack of objectivity by those responsible for accounting decisions.[9]

Although the communication may be written or oral, written communication of reportable conditions is preferred. Moreover, whether written or oral, the auditor must document the reportable conditions in the audit workpapers. An illustration of the recommended wording of a written communication of reportable conditions is contained in Exhibit 7.3.

KEY TERMS

Accuracy controls
Assessed level of control risk
   Maximum
   Below maximum
Control point
Design and implementation of control structure policies and procedures
Document examination as a means of control testing
Internal control checklist
Internal control flowchart

Internal control memorandum
Internal control questionnaire
Observation as a means of control testing
Operating effectiveness of control structure policies and procedures
Reportable conditions
Reprocessing as a means of control testing
Safeguard controls
Understanding of control structure

REVIEW QUESTIONS

1. Define and give an example of a *control point*.
2. Define *reprocessing*. What is the purpose for this procedure?
3. What is meant by the *auditor's understanding of a client's control structure?*

---

[9]*Ibid.*

EXHIBIT 7.3   Reportable Conditions Communication

To: Mr. James Brosley
     Chair, Audit Committee
     ABC Corporation

Subject: Reportable conditions resulting from the 1992 audit

In planning and performing our audit of the financial statements of the ABC Corporation for the year ended December 31, 1992, we considered its internal control structure in order to determine our auditing procedures for the purpose of expressing our opinion on the financial statements and not to provide assurance on the internal control structure. However, we noted certain matters involving the internal control structure and its operation that we consider to be reportable conditions under standards established by the American Institute of Certified Public Accountants. Reportable conditions involve matters coming to our attention relating to significant deficiencies in the design or operation of the internal control structure that, in our judgment, could adversely affect the organization's ability to record, process, summarize, and report financial data consistent with the assertions of management in the financial statements.

The conditions which we consider to be material weaknesses in ABC Company's internal control structure are as follows:

1. Sales invoices and bills of lading forms are not prenumbered, a condition that precludes verifying that all shipments have been billed or that all billed orders have been shipped. We recommend that these forms be prenumbered, that security be maintained over unused forms, and that used documents be effectively canceled, and that numeric sequence be periodically accounted for.

2. Statements are not mailed to customers on a monthly basis. As a result, analysis of unpaid balances in terms of specific invoices is difficult. Moreover, the company does not perform a monthly aging analysis of customer balances and, as a result, follow-up and collection of past due accounts is somewhat lax. We recommend a policy of monthly statements and monthly accounts receivable aging analysis to enhance the reliability of recorded balances, to facilitate evaluation of uncollectibility, and to improve the follow-up and collection of past due accounts.

This report is intended solely for the information and use of the audit committee (board of directors, board of trustees, or owners in owner-managed enterprises), management, and others within the organization (or specified regulatory agency or other specified third party).

Dual & Chase

February 18, 1993

---

4. How does the auditor obtain an initial understanding of a client's control structure policies and procedures?

5. What kind of documentation is required relative to the auditor's understanding of a client's control structure?

6. How does testing of control structure policies and procedures help in the design of substantive audit procedures?

7. Under what circumstances might an auditor decide not to test the control structure beyond obtaining an initial understanding?

8. Identify alternative means for testing of the control structure policies and procedures relevant to an audit.

9. Differentiate between errors of omission and errors of commission.

10. Differentiate between misrepresentation and misappropriation.

11. Give an example of how a control structure weakness may lead to an expansion of substantive audit procedures.

12. What is meant by *reportable conditions?* What purpose is served by the letter communicating internal control related matters to the audit committee?

13. What is meant by *assessed level of control risk?*

14. Summarize the steps involved in the auditor's approach to obtaining an understanding of control structure policies and procedures and assessing control risk.

15. How does an internal control flowchart assist in evaluating the controls within a given transaction cycle?

16. Describe how the memorandum, questionnaire or checklist, and flowchart approaches might be used in combination to provide an effective means for studying and evaluating a client's control structure.

17. Explain how management characteristics affect both inherent risk and control risk.

18. Define the term "primarily substantive audit" and describe the conditions suggesting a primarily substantive audit.

MULTIPLE CHOICE QUESTIONS FROM CPA AND CIA EXAMINATIONS

1. During the audit, the independent auditor identified the existence of a material weakness in the client's control procedures and orally communicated this finding to the client's senior management and audit committee. The auditor should
   a. Consider the material weakness a scope limitation and therefore disclaim an opinion.
   b. Document the matter in the working papers and consider the effects of the weakness on the audit.
   c. Suspend all audit activities pending directions from the client's audit committee.
   d. Withdraw from the engagement.

2. The auditor's review of the client's internal control structure policies and procedures is documented in order to substantiate
   a. Conformity of the accounting records with generally accepted accounting principles.
   b. Compliance with generally accepted auditing standards.
   c. Adherence to requirements of management.
   d. The fairness of the financial statement presentation.

3. Which of the following is not an auditing procedure that is commonly used in performing control tests?
   a. Inquiring.
   b. Observing.
   c. Confirming.
   d. Inspecting.

4. After obtaining an understanding of a client's control structure policies and procedures, the auditor might decide to
   a. Increase the extent of control and substantive testing in areas where the internal control structure is strong.
   b. Reduce the extent of control testing in areas where the control structure is strong.
   c. Reduce the extent of both substantive and control testing in areas where the control structure is strong.
   d. Design and apply expanded substantive testing in areas where the control structure policies and procedures are weak.

5. Which of the following is the correct order of performing the auditing procedures A through C, defined as follows?

   A = Examine and test documents supporting transactions and events.

   B = Study organizational structure, inquire of management, and observe as a basis for obtaining an understanding of the client's control structure policies and procedures.

   C = Design substantive audit procedures.

   a. ABC.
   b. ACB.
   c. BAC.
   d. BCA.

6. A well-prepared flowchart should make it easier for the auditor to
   a. Prepare audit procedure manuals.
   b. Prepare detailed job descriptions.
   c. Trace the origin and disposition of documents.
   d. Assess the degree of accuracy of financial data.

7. Based on a study and evaluation completed at an interim date, the auditor concludes that no significant internal control structure weaknesses exist. The records and procedures would most likely be tested again at year end if
   a. Control tests were not performed by the internal auditor during the remaining period.
   b. The internal control structure provides a basis for designing substantive audit procedures.
   c. The auditor used nonstatistical sampling during the interim period control testing.
   d. Inquiries and observations lead the auditor to believe that conditions have changed.

8. The auditor may observe the distribution of paychecks to ascertain whether
   a. Payrate authorization is properly separated from the operating function.
   b. Deductions from gross pay are calculated correctly and are properly authorized.
   c. Employees of record actually exist and are employed by the client.
   d. Paychecks agree with the payroll register and the time cards.

9. In a study and evaluation of the control structure policies and procedures, the completion of a questionnaire is most closely associated with which of the following?
   a. Tests of control.
   b. Substantive tests.
   c. Obtaining an initial understanding of the structure.
   d. Review of the structure design.

10. After obtaining an initial understanding of the control structure policies and procedures, the auditor who wishes to assess control risk below the maximum level should next
    a. Obtain additional understanding through further testing, document such understanding, and also document basis for reducing assessment of control risk below the maximum level.
    b. Perform control tests to provide reasonable assurance that the internal control procedures are being applied as prescribed.
    c. Complete the review of the system to determine whether the accounting control procedures are suitably designed.
    d. Design substantive tests that contemplate reliance on the control structure.

11. During consideration of the internal control structure in a financial statement audit, an auditor is *not* obligated to
    a. Search for significant deficiencies in the operation of the internal control structure.
    b. Understand the internal control environment and the accounting system.
    c. Determine whether the control procedures relevant to audit planning have been placed in operation.
    d. Perform procedures to understand the design of the internal control structure policies.

12. The primary objective of procedures performed to obtain an understanding of the internal control structure is to provide an auditor with
    a. Evidential matter to use in reducing detection risk.
    b. Knowledge necessary to plan the audit.
    c. A basis from which to modify tests of controls.
    d. Information necessary to prepare flowcharts.

13. Which of the following is *not* a reason an auditor should obtain an understanding of the elements of an entity's internal control structure in planning an audit?
    a. Identify types of potential misstatements that can occur.
    b. Design substantive tests.
    c. Consider the operating effectiveness of the internal control structure.
    d. Consider factors that affect the risk of material misstatements.

14. When control risk is assessed at the maximum level for all financial statement assertions, an auditor should document the auditor's

	Under-standing of the entity's internal control structure elements	*Conclusion that control risk is at the maximum level*	*Basis for concluding that control risk is at the maximum level*
a.	Yes	No	No
b.	Yes	Yes	No
c.	No	Yes	Yes
d.	Yes	Yes	Yes

15. After obtaining an understanding of an entity's internal control structure, an auditor may assess control risk at the maximum level for some assertions because the auditor
    a. Believes the internal control policies and procedures are unlikely to be effective.

    b. Determines that the pertinent internal control structure elements are *not* well documented.

    c. Performs tests of controls to restrict detection risk to an acceptable level.

    d. Identifies internal control policies and procedures that are likely to prevent material misstatements.

16. After obtaining an understanding of an entity's internal control structure and assessing control risk, an auditor may next

    a. Perform tests of controls to verify management's assertions that are embodied in the financial statements.

    b. Consider whether evidential matter is available to support a further reduction in the assessed level of control risk.

    c. Apply analytical procedures as substantive tests to validate the assessed level of control risk.

    d. Evaluate whether the internal control structure policies and procedures detected material misstatements in the financial statements.

17. The objective of tests of details of transactions performed as tests of controls is to

    a. Detect material misstatements in the account balances of the financial statements.

    b. Evaluate whether an internal control structure policy or procedure operated effectively.

    c. Determine the nature, timing, and extent of substantive tests for financial statement assertions.

    d. Reduce control risk, inherent risk, and detection risk to an acceptably low level.

18. An auditor uses the knowledge provided by the understanding of the internal control structure and the assessed level of control risk primarily to

    a. Determine whether procedures and records concerning the safeguarding of assets are reliable.

    b. Ascertain whether the opportunities to allow any person to both perpetrate and conceal irregularities are minimized.

    c. Modify the initial assessments of inherent risk and preliminary judgments about materiality levels.

    d. Determine the nature, timing, and extent of substantive tests for financial statement assertions.

19. An auditor uses the knowledge provided by the understanding of the internal control structure and the final assessed level of control risk primarily to determine the nature, timing, and extent of the

    a. Attribute tests.

    b. Compliance tests.

    c. Tests of controls.

    d. Substantive tests.

20. A weakness in internal control over recording retirements of equipment may cause an auditor to

    a. Trace additions to the ''other assets'' account to search for equipment that is still on hand but *no* longer being used.

    b. Select certain items of equipment from the accounting records and locate them in the plant.

    c. Inspect certain items of equipment in the plant and trace those items to the accounting records.

  d. Review the subsidiary ledger to ascertain whether depreciation was taken on each item of equipment during the year.

21. Reportable conditions are matters that come to an auditor's attention which should be communicated to an entity's audit committee because they represent
  a. Material irregularities or illegal acts perpetrated by high-level management.
  b. Significant deficiencies in the design or operation of the internal control structure.
  c. Flagrant violations of the entity's documented conflict of interest policies.
  d. Intentional attempts by client personnel to limit the scope of the auditor's field work.

22. Miller Retailing, Inc. maintains a staff of three full-time internal auditors who report directly to the controller. In planning to use the internal auditors to provide assistance in performing the audit, the independent auditor most likely will
  a. Place limited reliance on the work performed by the internal auditors.
  b. Decrease the extent of the tests of controls needed to support the assessed level of detection risk.
  c. Increase the extent of the procedures needed to reduce control risk to an acceptable level.
  d. Avoid using the work performed by the internal auditors.

23. Flowcharting as a means of internal control evaluation provides the following advantage over the use of questionnaires and descriptive narratives:
  a. Ease of preparation.
  b. Comprehensive coverage of controls.
  c. Simplicity.
  d. Ease in following information flow.

ESSAY QUESTIONS AND PROBLEMS

7.1 Cassandra Corporation, a manufacturing company, periodically invests large sums in marketable equity securities. The investment policy is established by the investment committee of the board of directors, and the treasurer is responsible for carrying out the investment committee's directives. All securities are stored in a bank safety deposit vault.

The independent auditor's internal control questionnaire with respect to Cassandra's investments in marketable equity securities contains the following three questions:

  1. Is investment policy established by the investment committee of the board of directors?
  2. Is the treasurer solely responsible for carrying out the investment committee's directives?
  3. Are all securities stored in a bank safety deposit vault?

Required:

In addition to these three questions, what questions should the auditor's internal control questionnaire include with respect to the company's investments in marketable equity securities? (AICPA adapted)

FIGURE 7.6 Flowchart of Credit Sales Activities for Problem 7.2

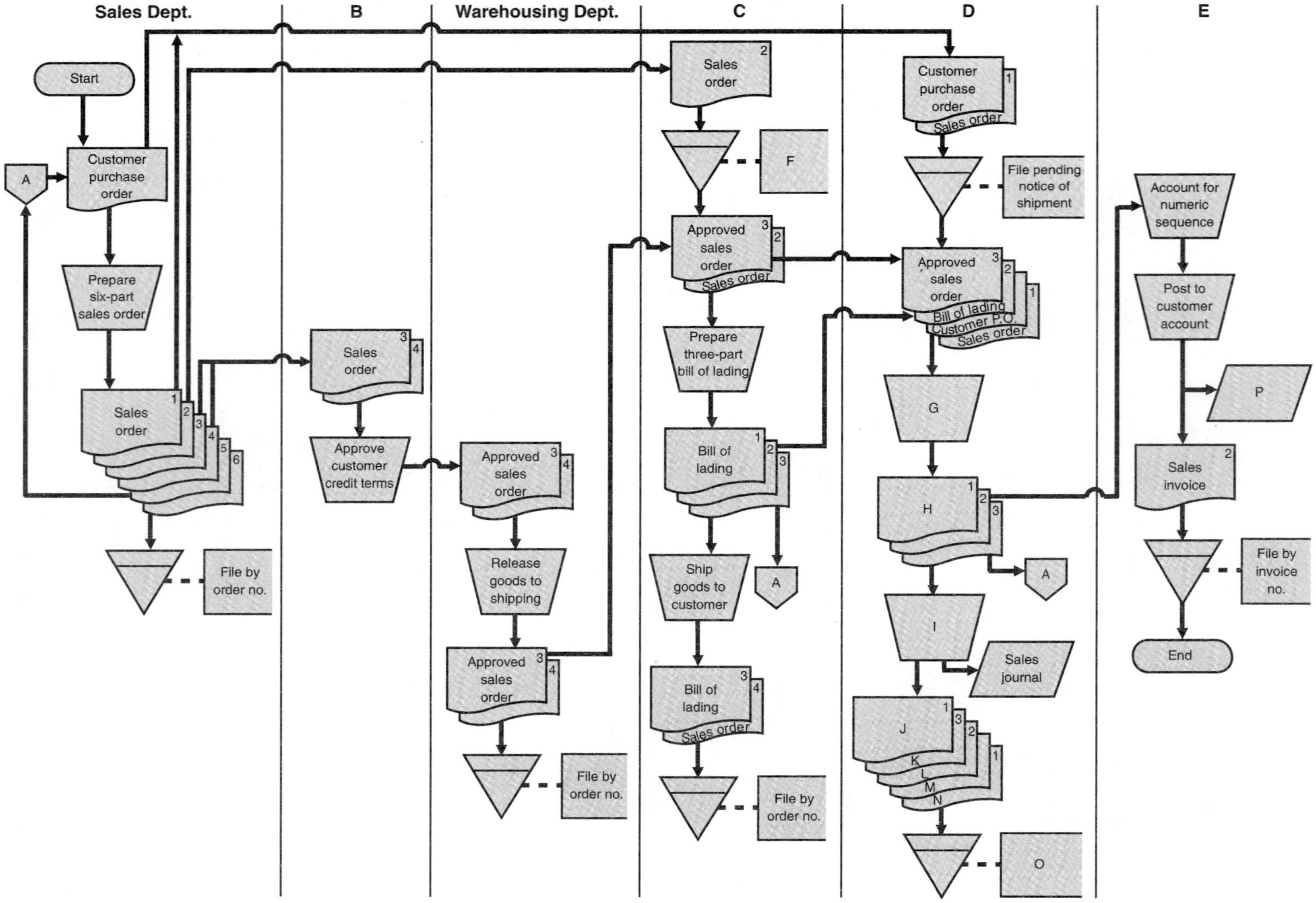

7.2 While auditing the Top Manufacturing Corporation, the auditor prepared a flow-chart (Figure 7.6) of credit sales activities. In this flowchart, Code Letter *A* represents customer.

Required:

Indicate what each of the code letters *B* through *P* represents. Do not discuss adequacies or inadequacies in the control structure. (AICPA adapted)

7.3 A CPA's audit working papers contain a narrative description of a segment of the Croyden Factory, Inc. payroll system and an accompanying flowchart:

"The internal control system with respect to the personnel department is functioning well and is not included in the accompanying flowchart (Figure 7.7).

"At the beginning of each work week, payroll clerk No. 1 reviews the payroll department files to determine the employment status of factory employees, then prepares time cards and distributes them as each individual arrives at work. This payroll clerk, who is also responsible for custody of the signature stamp machine, verifies the identity of each payee before delivering signed checks to the foreman.

At the end of each work week, the foreman distributes payroll checks for the preceding work week. Concurrent with this activity, the foreman reviews the current week's employee time cards, notes the regular and overtime hours worked on a summary form, and initials the time cards. The foreman then delivers all time cards and unclaimed payroll checks to payroll clerk No. 2."

Required:

a. Based upon the narrative and flowchart, what are the weaknesses in the control structure policies and procedures?

b. Based upon the narrative and flowchart, what inquiries should be made with respect to clarifying the existence of possible additional weaknesses in the control structure?

Note: Do not discuss the internal control structure as it relates to the personnel department. (AICPA adapted)

7.4 During the pre-audit conference for Quicko, Inc., the senior auditor described for the new staff people assigned to this year's audit the essential characteristics of Quicko's internal control structure. Except for the payroll cycle, where controls have been found severely lacking, the auditors have been reasonably satisfied with the controls within the other cycles. In the past, the controls over cash receipts have been evaluated as excellent.

Within the payroll area, material errors and irregularities can readily occur. Supervisors do not review time cards prepared by employees; pay rates, hours, extensions, and withholdings are not reviewed independently. Paychecks, after being signed, are returned to department supervisors for distribution.

Required:

a. What alternatives are available to auditors for dealing with weak internal control structure subsets? What possible effects might the absence of payroll controls have on the financial statements in this case?

b. What steps should the auditor take if, based on the initial review, controls are thought to be adequate?

c. Although the control procedures relating to cash receipts have been excellent in the past, they should be reevaluated again this year.

FIGURE 7.7 Factory Payroll System for Problem 7.3

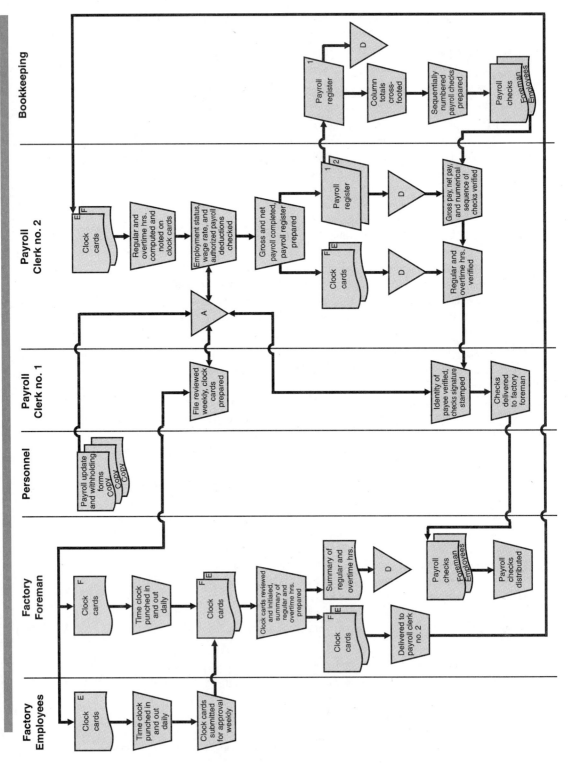

1. Why is it necessary for the auditors to study and evaluate internal control each year?
2. Why is a minimum audit necessary notwithstanding excellent controls?

7.5 a. A vital part of an effective internal control structure is documentation. Explain why.
b. List the essential documents, along with their specific control aspects, for each of the following transaction areas: sales orders and invoicing, cash receipts, purchases and cash disbursements.
c. Explain how control testing varies depending on the visibility of the audit trail.

7.6 Jordan Harris, a CPA, has been engaged to audit the financial statements of the Spartan Drug Store, Inc. Spartan is a medium-sized retail outlet that sells a wide variety of consumer goods. All sales are for cash or check. Cashiers use cash registers to process these transactions. There are no receipts by mail and there are no credit card or charge sales.

Required:

Construct the "Processing Cash Collections" segment of the internal control questionnaire on "Cash Receipts" to be used as a basis for understanding the internal control structure for the Spartan Drug Store, Inc. Each question should elicit either a yes or no response. Do not discuss the internal controls relating to cash sales. (AICPA adapted)

7.7 The overall purpose of the auditor's review of internal control structure policies and procedures is to obtain sufficient knowledge and understanding about the control environment, the accounting system, and the internal control procedures to aid the auditor in assessing control risk so that such assessment can be used in designing substantive audit procedures.

Required:

a. What knowledge should the auditor obtain from the initial understanding phase of the control structure study and evaluation? How does the auditor obtain this knowledge?
b. Upon completion of the initial phase, what possible conclusions may the auditor reach and how would each affect the auditor's substantive tests?
c. What is the appropriate extent of the auditor's documentation of the review of control structure? (AICPA adapted)

7.8 Internal control structure policies and procedures relevant to an audit consist of policies and procedures embodied in an entity's internal control structure that pertain to the entity's ability to record, process, summarize, and report financial data consistent with management's assertions embodied in the financial statements or that pertain to data the auditor uses to apply auditing procedures to financial statement assertions.

Required:

a. What is the purpose of the auditor's study and evaluation of control structure?
b. What are the objectives of the initial understanding phase in the study of control structure?
c. How is the auditor's understanding of the control structure documented?
d. Under what conditions should the auditor seek a further understanding of a client's control structure? (AICPA adapted)

FIGURE 7.8 Flowchart of Raw Materials Purchasing for Problem 7.9

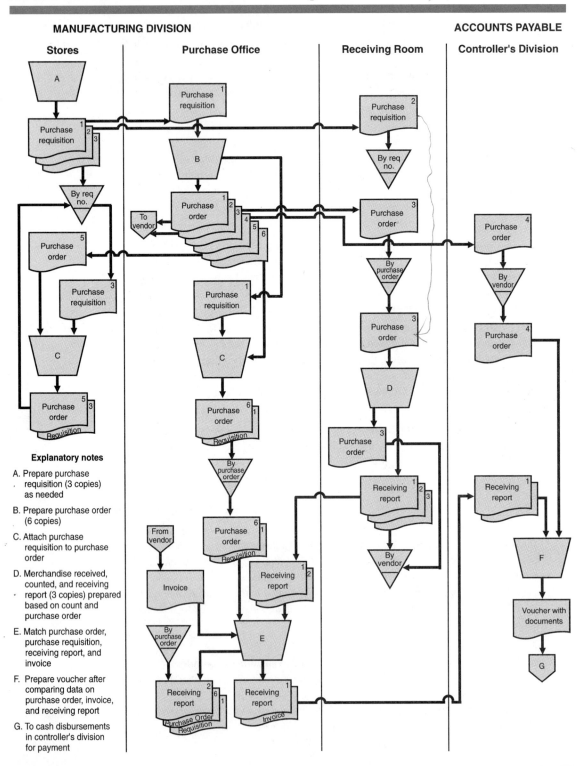

7.9 Rhonda Anthony, a CPA, prepared the accompanying flowchart in Figure 7.8 that portrays the raw materials purchasing function of one of Anthony's clients, a medium-sized manufacturing company, from the preparation of initial documents through the vouchering of invoices for payment in accounts payable. The flowchart was a portion of the work performed on the audit engagement to evaluate internal control.

Required:

Identify and explain the accounting systems and control procedures weaknesses evident from the flowchart. Include the internal control weaknesses resulting from activities performed or not performed. All documents are prenumbered. (AICPA adapted)

7.10 A partially completed charge sales systems flowchart is in Figure 7.9. The flowchart depicts the charge sales activities of the Bottom Manufacturing Corporation.

A customer's purchase order is received and a six-part sales order is prepared from it. The six copies are initially distributed as follows:

Copy No.1 - Billing copy to billing department.
Copy No. 2 - Shipping copy to shipping department.
Copy No. 3 - Credit copy to credit department.
Copy No. 4 - Stock request copy to credit department.
Copy No. 5 - Customer copy to customer.
Copy No. 6 - Sales order copy filed in sales order department.

When each copy of the sales order reaches the applicable department or destination, it calls for specific internal control procedures and related documents. Some of the procedures and related documents are indicated on the flowchart. Other procedures and documents are labeled letters *a* to *r*.

Required:

List the procedures or the internal documents that are labeled letters *c* to *r* in the flowchart of Bottom Manufacturing Corporation's charge sales system.

Organize your answer as follows (note that an explanation of the letters *a* and *b* which appear in the flowchart are entered as examples):

Flowchart Symbol Letter	Procedures or Internal Document
a	Prepare six-part sales order.
b	File by order number.

(AICPA adapted)

7.11 An auditor is required to obtain a sufficient understanding of each of the elements of the entity's internal control structure to plan the audit of the entity's financial statements and to assess control risk for the assertions embodied in the account balance, transaction class, and disclosure components of the financial statements.

Required:

a. Identify the elements of an entity's internal control structure.
b. For what purposes should an auditor's understanding of the internal control structure elements be used in planning an audit?
c. Explain the reasons why an auditor may assess control risk at the maximum level for one or more assertions embodied in an account balance.
d. What must an auditor do to support assessing control risk at less than the maximum level when the auditor has determined that controls have been placed in operation? (AICPA adapted)

FIGURE 7.9 Flowchart of Credit Sales for Problem 7.10

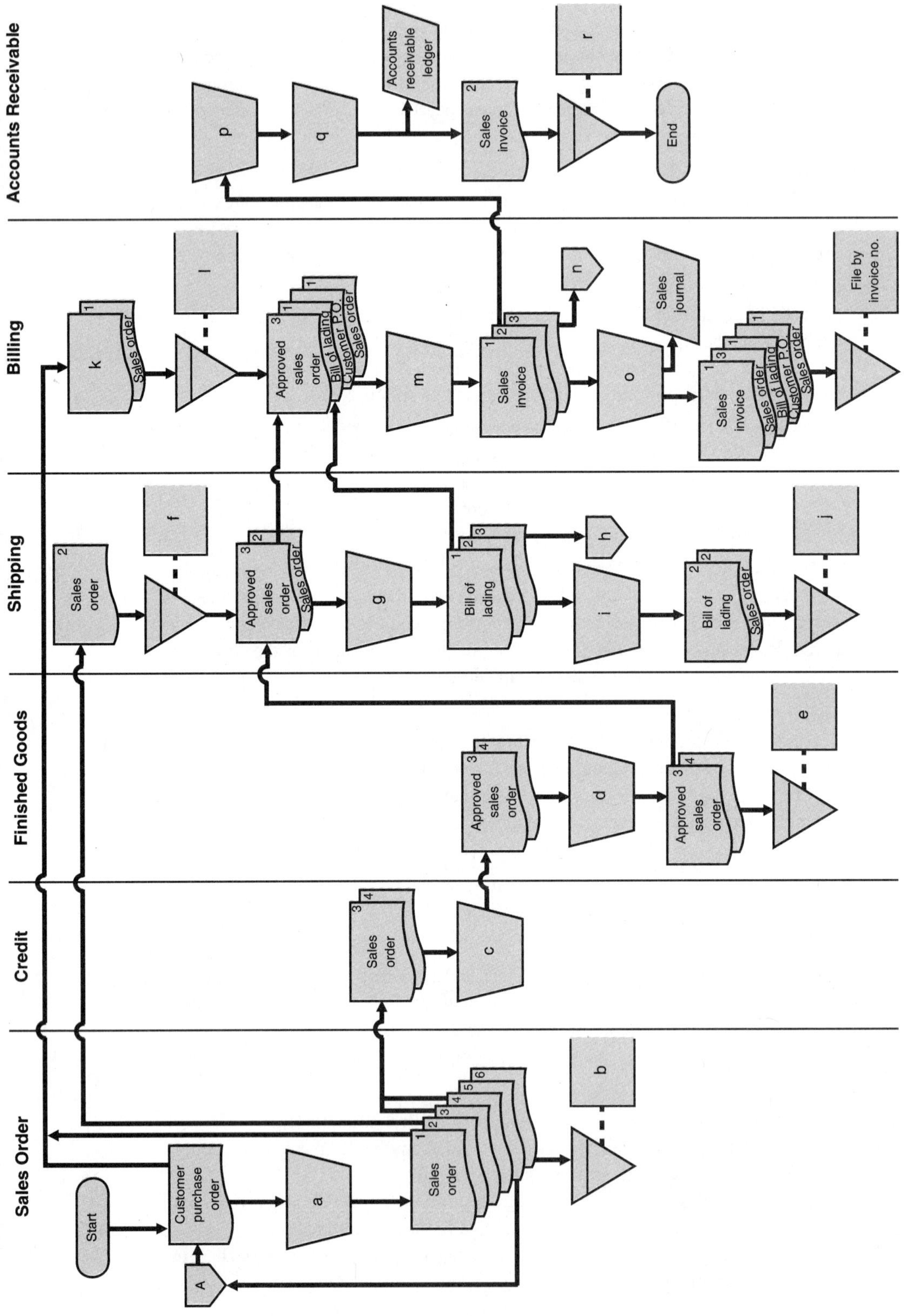

7.12 A CPA's audit working papers include the narrative description below of the cash receipts and billing portions of the internal control structure of Parktown Medical Center, Inc. Parktown is a small health care provider that is owned by a publicly held corporation. It employs seven salaried physicians, ten nurses, three support staff in a common laboratory, and three clerical workers. The clerical workers perform such tasks as reception, correspondence, cash receipts, billing, and appointment scheduling and are adequately bonded. They are referred to in the narrative as "office manager," "clerk #1," and "clerk #2."

Most patients pay for services by cash or check at the time services are rendered. Credit is not approved by the clerical staff. The physician who is to perform the respective services approves credit based on an interview. When credit is approved, the physician files a memo with the billing clerk (clerk #2) to set up the receivable from data generated by the physician.

The servicing physician prepares a charge slip that is given to clerk #1 for pricing and preparation of the patient's bill. Clerk #1 transmits a copy of the bill to clerk #2 for preparation of the revenue summary and for posting in the accounts receivable subsidiary ledger.

The cash receipts functions are performed by clerk #1, who receives cash and checks directly from patients and gives each patient a prenumbered cash receipt. Clerk #1 opens the mail and immediately stamps all checks "for deposit only" and lists cash and checks for deposit. The cash and checks are deposited daily by the office manager. The list of cash and checks, together with the related remittance advices, are forwarded by clerk #1 to clerk #2. Clerk #1 also serves as receptionist and performs general correspondence duties.

Clerk #2 prepares and sends monthly statements to patients with unpaid balances. Clerk #2 also prepares the cash receipts journal and is responsible for the accounts receivable subsidiary ledger. No other clerical employee is permitted access to the accounts receivable subsidiary ledger. Uncollectible accounts are written off by clerk #2 only after the physician who performed the respective services believes the account to be uncollectible and communicates the write-off approval to the office manager. The office manager then issues a write-off memo that clerk #2 processes.

The office manager supervises the clerks, issues write-off memos, schedules appointments for the doctors, makes bank deposits, reconciles bank statements, and performs general correspondence duties.

Additional services are performed monthly by a local accountant who posts summaries prepared by the clerks to the general ledger, prepares income statements, and files the appropriate payroll forms and tax returns. The accountant reports directly to the parent corporation.

Required:

Based on the information in the narrative:

a. Prepare an internal control flowchart that portrays the revenue cycle (billing and cash receipts) for Parktown Medical Center.

b. Based on the narrative and your completed flowchart, describe the reportable conditions and one resulting misstatement that could occur and not be prevented or detected by Parktown's internal control structure concerning the cash receipts and billing function. Do *not* describe how to correct the reportable conditions and potential misstatements. Use the format illustrated on next page.

Reportable condition

There is no control to
verify that fees are recorded
and
billed at authorized rates
and terms.

(AICPA adapted)

Potential misstatement

Accounts receivable
could be overstated and
uncollectible accounts
understated because of the
lack of controls.

APPENDIX

Transaction Cycles and Related Control Tests

Internal control structure concepts were discussed in Chapter 6. Chapter 7 addressed the auditor's approach to obtaining an understanding of control structure policies and procedures relevant to an audit. Under certain conditions, the auditor may elect to test controls to obtain knowledge about the operating effectiveness of certain controls and possibly reduce the assessed level of control risk below the maximum level. This appendix presents an in-depth analysis of the main control features and related tests associated with further exploration of control structure. The following transaction cycles, as described in Chapter 4, provide the framework for discussion:

1. Revenue cycle
   a. Sales revenue and accounts receivable balances
   b. Cash receipts from customers and cash balances
2. Expenditure cycle
   a. Purchases, operating expenses, depreciation expense, and plant asset balances
   b. Payments to vendors and accounts payable balances
   c. Payroll
   d. Production and inventory balances
3. Financing and investing cycle
   a. Borrowing from others, interest expense, and liability balances
   b. Lending to others, interest revenue, and notes receivable balances
   c. Acquisitions and disposals of financial assets
   d. Capital stock and dividend transactions

The format used in discussing control features and control testing is as follows:

1. The transactions within each type are described;
2. Documents associated with the transactions are identified;
3. A flowchart is presented that depicts the documents, people, and actions associated with the transactions;

4. The major control features are considered within the framework of the control concepts discussed in the body of Chapter 6;

5. Procedures are recommended for testing those controls the auditor wishes to study for operating effectiveness;

6. Design of substantive audit procedures is considered in light of the understanding obtained.

REVENUE CYCLE
Sales

Transactions

Sales transactions, as considered here, are limited to *sales to customers on account*. Cash sales are considered in the next section, along with collections from customers on account.

TABLE 7A.1 Control Principles and Techniques: Revenue Cycle for Sales Transactions

Control Principle	Control Feature	Control Principle	Control Feature
Competence of personnel	Approving credit Aproving write-offs of customer accounts Preparing sales invoices Recording sales and accounts receivable Approving returns and allowances	Recording in accordance with GAAP	Chart of accounts and accounting manual Account distribution on face of document Review of account distributions
Separation of duties	Processing sales orders Approving credit Shipping Billing Issuing credit memos Accounting	Assets safeguards	Limited access to finished goods Limited access to documents Fixed responsibility for custody over goods and documents

Execution in accordance with authorization	Adequate documentation
	  Customer order
	  Sales order
	  Sales invoice
	  Shipping order
	  Billing of lading signed by carrier
	  Credit memo
	Documents prenumbered
	System of reviews and approvals and evidence of same on face
		Periodic inventories and comparisons	Subsidiary accounts receivable ledger agreed to control account on a monthly basis
			Monthly statements to customers
			Clear exceptions to customer statements
			Perpetual inventory records
			Periodic test counts and comparisons with perpetual records
			Annual physical inventory and adjustment of perpetual records (after investigating significant shrinkages)

FIGURE 7A.1 Sales Flowchart

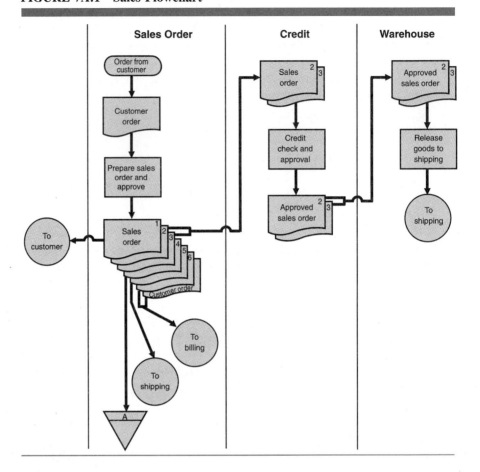

Documents

The following documents are commonly associated with account sales to customers:

1. Customer order: The order transmitted by the customer to the salesperson, indicating the type and quantity of product(s); prices, payment terms, shipping date, and means of transport may also appear on the customer order.
2. Sales order: A formalization of the customer order, the sales order, in addition to the information appearing on the customer order, contains evidence of credit check and approval.
3. Bill of lading: Evidence of shipment of goods, the bill of lading identifies the carrier, the customer, type of goods, and shipping date.
4. Sales invoice: The sales invoice is the billing rendered to the customer; the information in the preceding documents is presented together with extended amounts (price × quantity) of the charges.

Control Features and Internal Control Flowchart

Table 7A.1 lists the main control features applicable to the processing of sales transactions. Figure 7A.1 incorporates the control features into a flowchart portraying a suitable set of control procedures covering sales processing. The purpose of

266

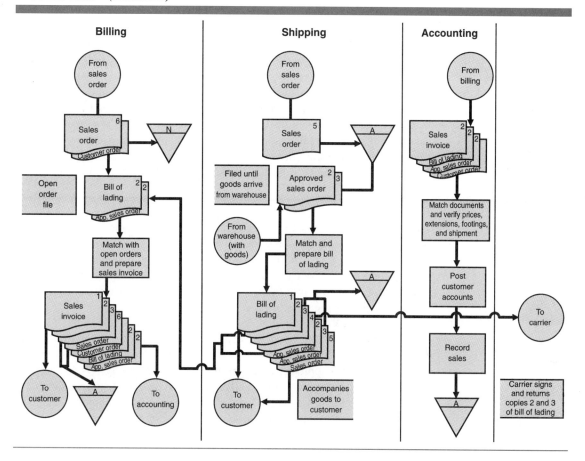

the flowchart is to assist in identifying control points and the necessary control features related to each point.

Documentation of each step in the processing cycle, together with evidence of proper reviews and credit approval, have been provided for in the present system. These control features help to ensure that sales transactions are authentic and have been accurately recorded.

The bill of lading, signed by the carrier, provides evidence of shipment. Forwarding copies of this document to billing ensures that all shipments of goods are billed to customers. By requiring all sales invoices to be accompanied by a copy of the signed bill of lading, the procedures ensure that customers will be invoiced only for goods actually shipped.

Functional responsibilities have been separated such that persons performing the order, billing, credit, and accounting functions do not have access to the goods being shipped to customers. Similarly, persons handling goods do not have access to the accounting records.

A complete audit trail has been provided in the form of file copies, together with evidence of review and approval of transactions. The audit trail permits one to trace the processing from point of origin to recording of the transaction and vice versa.

Perpetual inventory records, in combination with periodic inventory test counts and comparisons, facilitate early detection of errors or irregularities relating to inventories. In the same manner, the accounts receivable subsidiary ledger, together with monthly statements to customers and careful investigation of customer exceptions, facilitate error detection in processing sales and cash receipts.

Limited access to inventories and related documents help to prevent unauthorized use or disposition of inventories through either direct removal or by fabricating documentation permitting removal. Limiting access to customer records prevents concealing misappropriation through alteration of customer accounts.

Control Tests

As described earlier in this chapter, control testing may assume one or more of the following forms: additional observation and inquiry, reprocessing, or document examination and testing. The third form, document examination and testing, involves examining documentation underlying transactions and events and identifying errors committed during processing. This form of testing is discussed here as it relates to the processing of account sales transactions.

By identifying errors in a sample of transactions, the auditor is able to project the error to the population. Such projection permits the auditor to arrive at a better understanding of internal control and provides a basis for designing substantive audit procedures. An approach to determining proper sample size, selecting items for inclusion in the sample, examining sample items, and evaluating results of the sampling is presented in Chapter 10 as part of sampling for attributes. The present discussion is limited to describing those control testing procedures that will assist the auditor in identifying control weaknesses.

The rate of error in executing and recording transactions increases under the following conditions, all of which constitute control weaknesses:

1. Transactions are not adequately documented;
2. Documents are not prenumbered or the numeric sequence of used documents is not accounted for periodically;
3. Transactions are not reviewed for adequacy of documentation, proper approvals, and correctness of account distributions;
4. Persons reviewing documents and determining account distributions are not competent or adequately trained;
5. Accounting manuals either do not exist, or are not used in determining correctness of account distributions;
6. Write-offs of customers' accounts or returns and allowances are not properly approved.

Table 7A.2 identifies the types of errors and irregularities associated with these weaknesses and describes possible control tests. The first set of tests requires examining the documents underlying completed sales transactions for the presence of necessary controls. The second set of tests is directed toward identifying errors of *commission*—tracing recorded sales to underlying documentation—and errors of *omission*—tracing from shipping documentation to related journal entries. The purpose of these tests is to determine that recorded sales are authentic, and that all shipments of goods have been billed and recorded.

TABLE 7A.2 Control Weaknesses and Related Tests: Revenue Cycle for Sales Transactions

Control Weakness	Possible Errors	Control Tests
Inadequate documentation of sales transactions	Customers billed for goods not shipped Goods shipped and not billed	Select a sample of documented sales transactions and examine for the following characteristics: Prenumbering of documents
Lack of numeric control over the following forms: Sales orders Sales invoices Shipping orders Credit memos Bills of lading	Fictitious transactions recorded Failure to record completed sales transactions Unauthorized use of shipping orders or bills of lading to remove goods from premises	Evidence of proper reviews and approvals: Customer credit Selling prices Account distribution Inclusion of all necessary documentation: Customer order Sales order Sales invoice Shipping order Bill of lading
Customer credit approval not indicated on sales order	Goods shipped to customers whose credit has not been approved	Correctness of account distributions
Selling prices not compared with master price list	Goods billed to customers at incorrect prices	Agreement of selling prices with master price lists
Accounting manuals not used or account distribution (debit and credit effects of transactions and events) not double-checked	Transactions and events incorrectly recorded	Trace the selected transactions to journal entries and customer account postings to determine proper recording To ascertain validity of recorded sales, select a sample of recorded sales and trace to documentation, including sales invoice and bill of lading To determine that all shipments are billed and recorded, select a sample of bills of lading and trace to invoice and books of original entry
Write-off of customer accounts receivable not properly approved	Collectible accounts written off as uncollectible Customer account intentionally written off to conceal misappropriation of customer remittances	Examine all documentation underlying accounts receivable write-offs for the year Determine that the write-offs were properly recorded Determine that the write-offs were properly approved
Returns and allowances lack proper approval	Credit memos issued for unauthorized returns Credit memos issued for goods not returned Credit memos written and recorded to conceal misappropriation of customer remittances	Select a sample of credit memos processed during the year, and examine for the following characteristics: Proper approval and review Receiving report attached if credit memo involves returned goods Credit memos are prenumbered Proper recording

Design of Substantive Audit Procedures

Discovery of weaknesses in processing sales transactions should prompt the auditor to consider the following substantive audit tests (considered more fully in Chapter 12):

1. Expand confirmation of customer balances as of year end;
2. Consider confirming sales transactions, as well as receivable balances;
3. Confirm all accounts receivable write-offs with customers;
4. Expand year-end cutoff tests to obtain assurance that sales were recorded in the proper accounting period.

In addition to designing substantive audit procedures, the auditor should update the reportable conditions audit workpapers to include major weaknesses discovered during control testing.

Cash Receipts

Transactions

Cash receipts transactions included in this section are of three types:

1. Cash received from customers on account;
2. Cash sales; and
3. Miscellaneous cash receipts such as cash from disposals of plant assets or investments, dividends or interest constituting investment revenue, financing receipts (borrowing, collections on loans made to others), cash from disposals of scrap, waste, returnable containers, and so on, and other miscellaneous cash receipts.

Documents

The following documents are commonly associated with cash receipts transactions:

1. Remittance advice: The lower part of a check, usually separated from the check by a perforation, the remittance advice contains details of charges covered by the check.
2. Prelisting of incoming checks: The prelisting is prepared daily by someone independent of the cash receipts recording function and lists the checks received by mail for the day.
3. Cash receipts summary: The summary lists cash receipts contained in the daily bank deposit and is the basis for recording daily cash receipts.
4. Receipted deposit ticket: This provides evidence of the daily deposit of cash.
5. Cash register tapes: This provides evidence of cash sales for the day.

Control Features and Internal Control Flowchart

Table 7A.3 lists the main control features applicable to the processing of cash receipts. Figure 7A.2 is a flowchart describing a model set of procedures for processing and recording mail cash receipts. Although the flowchart includes only cash from customers, *all* incoming cash receipts should be similarly controlled.

TABLE 7A.3 Control Principles and Techniques: Revenue Cycle for Cash Receipts Transactions

Control Principle	Control Feature
Competence of personnel	Reconciling bank accounts Recording cash receipts Preparing deposits Opening mail and prelisting cash receipts Auditing cash registers Comparing deposit ticket with cash entries
Separation of duties	Receiving and prelisting cash Recording cash Depositing cash Reconciling bank accounts
Execution in accordance with authorization	Documentation of cash receipts Prelistings Cash register tapes Remittance advices Deposit tickets
Recording in accordance with GAAP	Chart of accounts and accounting manual Double checking of credits relating to miscellaneous cash receipts Sales coding on cash register tapes
Asset safeguards	Daily intact deposits Cash registers for cash sales Restrictive endorsements on incoming checks Prelisting of incoming checks
Periodic inventories and comparisons	Comparison of prelisting and cash register tapes with deposit ticket from bank and entry to record cash receipts Monthly bank reconciliations

Maintaining proper security and accountability during processing is the principal concern in providing effective control over cash receipts. Accountability is provided by the prelisting for mail receipts, and by locked in cash register tapes for cash sales. As indicated in the flowchart, the controller's office compares daily the receipted deposit ticket with the prelisting and register tapes to determine that all incoming cash receipts are deposited in the bank. The monthly bank reconciliation, prepared by someone having neither custodial nor cash recording responsibility, provides further accountability control over cash.

Security over mail cash receipts is provided by requiring that all incoming checks be restrictively endorsed immediately upon receipt. Security over cash sales receipts is strengthened by requiring the use of cash registers with locked in tapes. Fixing custodial responsibility over cash and requiring that cash receipts be deposited intact on a daily basis offers added security.

FIGURE 7A.2   Cash Receipts from Customers Flowchart

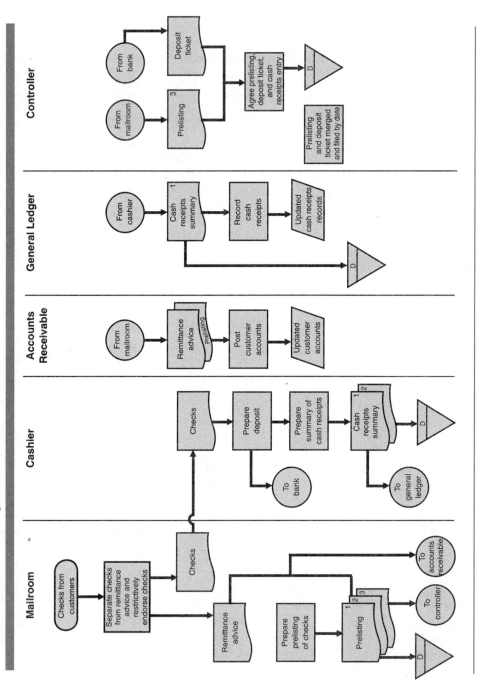

The procedures described in Figure 7A.2 provide for separating the cash custodial function from the cash recording function. The cashier, in this model, does not have access to accounting records; and the accounting personnel have no access to cash receipts. Postings are made from remittance advices and cash register tapes rather than from checks and currency. This form of separation is critical in preventing misappropriation accompanied by concealment through account alteration.

The flowchart in Figure 7A.2 also separates the function of posting customer accounts from the recording of cash receipts and the posting of the general ledger. Such separation, accompanied by agreeing the accounts receivable subsidiary ledger with the controlling account on a monthly basis, provides a double check of the recording and posting functions.

As indicated in Table 7A.3, a chart of accounts, accounting manuals and competent persons recording cash receipts are necessary controls for ensuring proper recording. Cash receipts from sources other than collections from customers are especially susceptible to recording errors. File copies of prelistings, cash receipts summaries, remittance advices, and deposit tickets provide the audit trail necessary for reconstructing transactions and tracing the processing flows.

Control Tests

In designing control tests of cash receipts transactions, the auditor is mainly interested in the adequacy of security over cash receipts and proper recording. Table 7A.4 describes several tests aimed at identifying errors in processing cash receipts. Note that the control tests are directed at detecting undeposited cash receipts, as well as recording errors.

Undeposited receipts may or may not have been recorded. If recorded, the cash receipts record will not agree with the deposit ticket. If unrecorded, the prelisting will not agree with the deposit ticket or the cash receipts record. Unrecorded cash receipts are especially difficult to detect if cash is not prelisted. Under these circumstances, auditors may elect to prepare their own prelisting on a surprise basis and compare details with the cash receipts entries and the deposit ticket. If the auditor does suspect employee *misappropriation* of cash receipts, management should be so informed.

Material *errors* in recording cash receipts from sources other than collections from customers on account are generally of two types: errors in recording miscellaneous cash receipts transactions, and errors involving credits to the wrong revenue account. First, because of the nonrecurring nature of miscellaneous receipts, recording errors are more likely to occur. A system of review and approval, as well as accounting manuals, are needed to minimize the incidence of such errors. Second, if several categories of sales revenue are present, controls are needed to ensure credits to the proper sales accounts. Cash registers programmed to record product codes and summarize sales by category assist in minimizing these errors.

If material errors of the above types have occurred, analytical procedures should have aroused the auditor's suspicions prior to performing the control tests noted in Table 7A.4. As a result, a larger sample of prelistings and cash register tapes will be selected for testing, given the higher expected error rate.

TABLE 7A.4 Control Weaknesses and Related Tests: Revenue Cycle for Cash Receipts Transactions

Control Weakness	Possible Errors	Control Tests
Bank accounts not properly reconciled	Cash receipts processing errors not located on a timely basis	Examine several months' reconciliations for possible errors
Incoming cash receipts not prelisted Cash registers and tapes not properly controlled	Recorded cash receipts are not deposited in the bank	If mail cash receipts are pre-listed, select a sample of pre-listings and cash register tapes representing several days' cash receipts
Bank deposit ticket not compared with prelisting and cash register tapes	Unrecorded cash receipts are not deposited in the bank	Trace to bank statement and cash receipts record Test postings to customers' accounts by tracing from remittance advice to subsidiary ledger If mail cash receipts are not pre-listed, select a sample of deposit tickets representing several days' cash receipts Trace from deposit ticket to cash receipts record Trace from cash receipts record to underlying documentation (cash register tapes and remittance advice) Trace from remittance advice to subsidiary ledger To test for unrecorded cash receipts, given the absence of prelistings, consider intercepting and prelisting cash receipts on a surprise basis Trace prelisting to cash receipts record and bank statement Trace prelisting to customers' accounts in subsidiary ledger
Accounting manuals not used to assist in properly recording miscellaneous cash receipts	Miscellaneous cash receipts credited to incorrect accounts	Using the same sample of cash receipts prelistings: Identify all cash receipts, other than customer payments on account
Credits arising from miscellaneous cash receipts not double-checked	Miscellaneous cash receipts credited to incorrect accounts	Trace to cash receipts record and determine that proper accounts were credited
Sales not coded on cash register tapes	Credits to wrong sales accounts	Select a sample of cash register tapes representing several days' sales Determine proper sales categories represented by each day's sales Trace to cash receipts record and determine that proper accounts were credited

Design of Substantive Audit Procedures

Control weaknesses relating to cash receipts should lead to one or more of the following audit program approaches (considered more fully in Chapter 12):

1. Expand the review of bank reconciliations to cover several months;
2. Extend accounts receivable confirmation; and
3. Increase testing of cash receipts from miscellaneous revenues, and disposals of noninventory assets (e.g., plant assets and marketable securities).

EXPENDITURE CYCLE
Purchases

Transactions

Purchases transactions, as defined here, include purchases of materials, merchandise for resale, supplies, services (other than payroll), and plant assets. Given their materiality, payroll transactions are addressed as a separate section within the expenditure cycle.

Documents

The following documents are associated with purchases transactions:

1. Purchase requisition: This form is prepared and signed by the person requesting goods or services and approved by someone authorized to do so.
2. Purchase order: This is a formal order based on the approved requisition and sent to the appropriate vendor.
3. Receiving report: Prepared by receiving department employees, this form is evidence of the receipt of purchased goods, as well as sales returns.
4. Vendor's invoice: This is the billing document received from the vendor.
5. Voucher: This form contains evidence of approval of vendors' invoices for payment.
6. Daily voucher summary: A compilation of vouchers approved for payment on a given day, the voucher summary serves as the basis for recording the daily vouchers.

Control Procedures and Internal Control Flowchart

Table 7A.5 identifies the features necessary to achieve satisfactory control over purchase transactions. Figure 7A.3 configures the model into a flowchart depicting the purchasing and vouchering functions.

The use of prenumbered documents, including requisitions, purchase orders, receiving reports, and vouchers, enhances accountability for purchases. It also provides the audit trail necessary for reconstructing purchase transactions. Approvals, account distributions, and double check of account distributions should be evidenced on the face of the appropriate documents.

Accountability is also important in the inventory purchasing and production functions, given the movement of inventory from receiving to stores, and from

TABLE 7A.5   Control Principles and Techniques: Expenditure Cycle for Purchase Transactions

Control Principle	Control Feature
Competence of personnel	Purchasing Receiving Managing stores Preparing vouchers (including account distribution) Approving vouchers Recording vouchers Maintaining accounts payable ledger
Separation of duties	Requisitioning goods and services Purchasing Receiving Custody over inventory Recording purchases

Execution in accordance with authorization	Voucher system
	Documentation of purchases
	    Requisition
	    Purchase order
	    Receiving report
	    Voucher
	Documents prenumbered
	Evidence of proper review and approval appearing on document
	Purchase order prepared only on basis of properly approved requisition
	Voucher prepared only after
	    Determining presence of all necessary documents
	    Agreeing prices, quantities, footings, and extensions on documents

Recording in accordance with GAAP	Chart of accounts and accounting manuals Account distribution on face of voucher Double-checking account distributions (and evidence of same on face of voucher)
Asset safeguards	Limited access to inventories, negotiable securities, small tools, and other valuable and portable assets Limited access to documents authorizing acquisitions of assets or services Fixed responsibility over assets and documents Documentation of asset movements for proper accountability Prenumbered documents

Periodic inventories and comparisons	Periodic count and comparison of the following on a test basis:
	    Inventories of materials, goods, tools, etc.
	    Negotiable securities
	    Plant assets
	    Supplies
	Account for numeric sequence of used documents on a regular basis
	Comparison of creditors' statements with subsidiary ledger to clear exceptions

FIGURE 7A.3 Purchases Flowchart

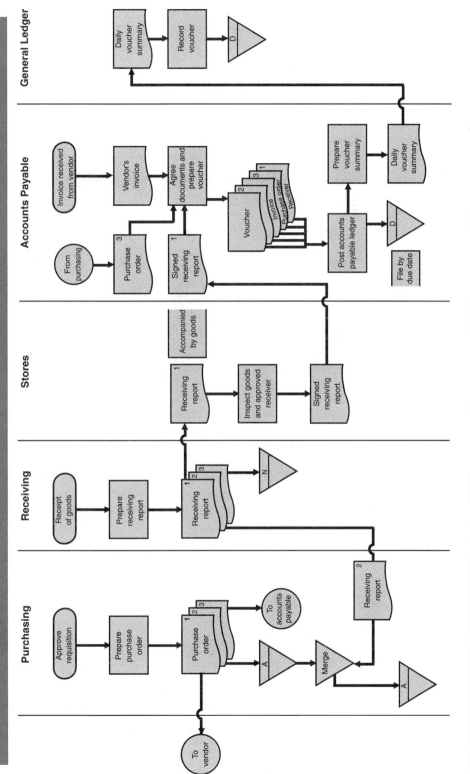

stores to production. Proper documentation increases accountability control by documenting these movements. In Figure 7A.3, for example, a copy of a signed receiving report is forwarded from stores to accounts payable. This copy serves as evidence that the goods were received by stores in satisfactory condition.

Use of a voucher system helps to ensure that only properly authorized disbursements will be made. As depicted in Figure 7A.3, vendors' invoices are paid only when all of the documents, along with evidence of review and approval, are present. Accounting manuals, along with review of account distributions, enhance the accuracy of recording purchase transactions. This is particularly critical for nonrecurring purchases of goods and services other than stock in trade.

As with cash, separation of custodial and record keeping functions is important to maintaining proper security over inventories of materials, goods, and supplies. Moreover, if the assets are portable, limited access and fixed responsibility for inventories become even more critical to effective control.

Periodic test counts and comparisons, perpetual inventory records, and annual physical inventories also support inventory security and accountability. These controls permit timely identification and investigation of abnormal losses from shrinkage. In addition, the use of perpetual inventory records leads to more effective cost control, and thereby enhances the accuracy of inventory and cost of sales amounts.

Control Tests

For purchase transactions, internal control tests are focused on the documents evidencing receipt of goods and services and approval for payment. Table 7A.6 identifies errors which are associated with purchase control weaknesses and suggests appropriate tests for evaluating the controls. Control weaknesses leading to recording errors are the most critical in terms of possible impact on the financial statements. For this reason, auditors consider tests for completeness of documentation and accuracy of account distribution to be most critical.

In obtaining an initial understanding of control structure policies and procedures, the auditor will have observed the purchasing procedures for adequacy of separation, proper asset safeguards, and periodic inventories and comparisons. The auditor also evaluates competence of personnel during the review phase. The effectiveness of this last control, however, is further tested during the document examination phase, given the decision to test controls. Frequent errors in recording or lack of agreement between receiving reports, purchase orders, and invoices is further indication of lack of competence. Inasmuch as internal control consists of people performing various functions, weaknesses involving competence are critical. Auditors, therefore, should expand substantive procedures accordingly when the client's organization is composed of individuals who are not adequately trained and not competent to review and record transactions accurately.

Design of Substantive Audit Procedures

(covered more fully in Chapter 13). Inasmuch as purchase transactions affect the inventory, plant asset, and operating expense accounts, control weaknesses should lead the auditor to expand substantive tests in these areas. Extending test counts during inventory observation, increasing inventory pricing and extension tests, and devoting greater attention to possible inventory obsolescence are possible extensions of procedures relating to inventories. Reviewing documentation for a larger

TABLE 7A.6   Control Weaknesses and Related Tests: Expenditure Cycle for Purchase Transactions

Control Weakness	Possible Errors	Control Tests
Inadequate documentation of purchases	Vendors paid for goods and services not received by the client	Select a sample of documented purchase transactions and examine for the following characteristics:
Documents not properly approved or reviewed	Unauthorized purchases	
Documents not prenumbered	Goods not ordered received and paid for	Prenumbering of documents
	Invoicing errors undetected	Evidence of proper reviews and approvals:
Accounting manuals not used	Errors in recording purchase transactions	Approval of requisition
		Approval of purchase order
Account distribution does not appear on face of voucher or is not subject to review	Errors in recording purchase transactions	Signatures on receiving report evidencing inspection by receiving and receipt by stores
		Review of account distribution on face of voucher
Creditors' statements not examined for possible errors	Undetected errors in recording purchase transactions	Inclusion of all necessary documentation:
		Purchase requisition
Lack of perpetual inventory records	Undetected errors in recording inventory transactions	Purchase order
		Receiving report
		Voucher
		Vendor's invoice
		Type of goods or services and prices appearing on purchase order agree with vendor's invoice
		Quantities and types appearing on receiving report agree with vendor's invoice
		Correctness of account distribution

proportion of plant asset additions, as well as repairs and maintenance, and recalculating depreciation expense may be adequate for extending substantive procedures related to plant assets, repairs, and depreciation. If prior application of analytical procedures indicate major changes in operating expenses, control weaknesses in the purchases subset of the expenditure cycle become even more critical. Under these conditions, the auditor should intensify substantive tests of the major components of operating expenses.

In addition to inventories, plant assets, depreciation, and operating expenses, the control weaknesses also affect accounts payable. For this reason, the auditor may consider extending auditing procedures related to accounts payable. Possibilities include reconciling vendors' accounts with year-end vendors' statements and confirming creditors' accounts on a test basis.

Payments to Vendors

Transactions

Payments to vendors for purchases of materials, supplies, merchandise, services, and other nonrecurring expenditures are considered in this section. The discussion assumes that the control procedures require a properly approved voucher for every disbursement, and that all disbursements be made by check. Given this assumption, all of the transactions involving payments to vendors will result in debits to accounts payable and credits to cash in bank.

Documents

The following documents are associated with disbursement transactions:

1. Voucher: This is an authorization to pay one or more vendors' invoices. The approved voucher should be accompanied by the invoice, purchase order, requisition, and receiving report relating to the expenditure.
2. Disbursement check: This is the payment of the approved voucher.

Control Features and Internal Control Flowchart

Table 7A.7 lists the features necessary for effective control over cash disbursements transactions. Figure 7A.4 portrays the flow of documents, the functions performed, and the separation of these functions needed in achieving proper control.

The foremost concern in designing control procedures for payments to vendors is preventing unauthorized disbursements. Requiring that all cash disbursements be made by check and that a properly approved and documented voucher be submitted as a prerequisite for check signing are the controls most critical in meeting this concern. The documents to be submitted along with the approved voucher include the vendor's invoice, the purchase order, and the receiving report if purchases of goods are involved. Review of the documentation for completeness and evidence of review and approval further strengthens control over disbursements.

Limited access to vouchers and disbursement checks and effective cancellation of paid invoices are also necessary to adequately control disbursements (prevention controls). Unlimited access to these documents can lead to the submission of fraudulent disbursement checks, supported by previously paid invoices and vouchers. In the absence of effective document cancellation, previously paid invoices might be paid a second time, intentionally or unintentionally.

As with cash receipts, the bank reconciliation, prepared by someone not having custodial or recording responsibility for cash, provides a means for identifying errors and irregularities in recording cash receipts and disbursements (a detection control). To attain maximum effectiveness, the reconciliation procedures should require careful examination of paid checks for agreement of payees and endorsements with the cash disbursements record. Also, voided checks should be examined for proper cancellation and bank statement credits should be traced to the cash receipts record.

The procedures portrayed in Figure 7A.4 provide for separation between the voucher preparation and payment. In addition to preparing the voucher, the accounts

TABLE 7A.7   Control Principles and Techniques: Expenditure Cycle for Payments to Vendors

Control Principle	Control Feature
Competence of personnel	Reviewing documents and signing checks Recording disbursements
Separation of duties	Recording disbursements Signing checks Posting creditors' accounts Reconciling bank accounts
Execution in accordance with authorization	No checks signed without adequate documentation (including approved voucher) Review of all documentation prior to signing checks All payments (except petty cash) by check
Recording in accordance with GAAP	Chart of accounts and accounting manuals Voucher system such that all debits for cash disbursements are to accounts payable
Asset safeguards	Limited access to disbursement checks Mailing of disbursement checks immediately upon signing No checks signed in advance Limited access to check signing devices Fixed responsibility for custody of checks and check signing devices Cancellation of paid invoices and vouchers
Periodic inventories and comparisons	Monthly bank reconciliations Agreement of currency, checks, and vouchers in petty cash box to authorized fund amount before reimbursing

payable function includes the posting of creditors' accounts. The treasury function is responsible for preparing and signing disbursement checks. Once signed, a disbursement check assumes the form of a financial asset. To preserve accountability and maintain adequate separation, therefore, signed disbursement checks should be mailed directly to vendors by the treasurer.

FIGURE 7A.4   Payments to Vendors Flowchart

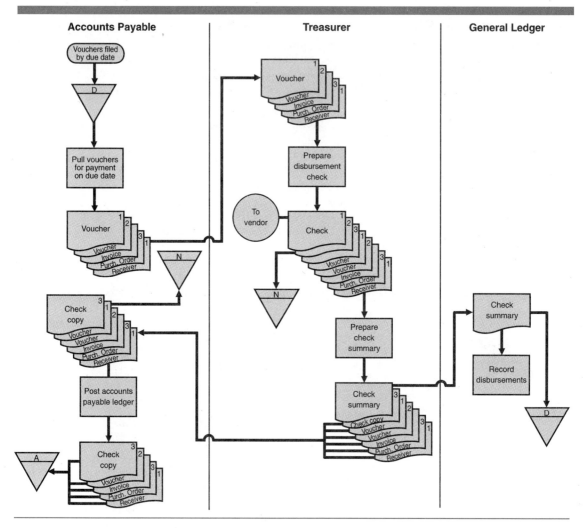

Dual signing of checks by the treasurer and someone else authorized by the board of directors is advisable to further prevent errors and irregularities. Moreover, to preserve adequacy of document review, checks should not be signed in advance. Designating three or more individuals as check signers, while requiring only two signatures, is a means for avoiding advance signing.

As with previous flowcharts, the model portrayed in Figure 7A.4 provides an audit trail in the form of file copies of disbursement documents. When combined with Figure 7A.3, the model permits expenditure transactions to be reconstructed and traced from the point of requisition to vouchering, payment, and posting of the creditor's account.

TABLE 7A.8   Control Weaknesses and Related Tests: Expenditure Cycle for Payments to Vendors

Control Weakness	Possible Errors	Control Tests
Inadequate documentation of cash disbursements	Unauthorized disbursements	Select a sample of paid invoices and examine for the following characteristics:
Disbursements not always based on approved vouchers (debits not always to accounts payable)	Errors in recording cash disbursements	Adequacy of documentation Voucher Purchase order
Access to disbursement checks not limited and responsibility not fixed	Unauthorized disbursements	Requisition Receiving report Vendor's invoice
Disbursement checks returned to accounts payable for mailing to vendors	Unauthorized disbursements	Proper review and approval of documents
Checks are sometimes signed in advance	Unauthorized disbursements	Correctness of account distribution
Documents are not effectively canceled upon payment of vendors' invoices	Unauthorized disbursements	Effective cancellation of documents

Control Tests

Table 7A.8 extends the control tests described for purchasing to include cash disbursements. Attributes of interest in examining paid invoices include adequacy of documentation, proper reviews and approvals, cancellation of used documents, and correctness in recording disbursement transactions. In addition, the auditor, through observation during the initial understanding phase, should ascertain that disbursement checks are mailed immediately upon signing and that checks are not signed in advance of the payment date.

Design of Substantive Audit Procedures

In addition to expanding bank reconciliation procedures as described, the auditor also needs to be alert to recording errors. This is especially critical in the absence of a formal voucher system. Under these circumstances, the auditor should consider extending the analysis of nontrade cash disbursements.

Payroll

Transactions

Payroll transactions include recording the payroll, vouchering net pay and the various withholdings as they become due, writing a disbursement check to transfer net pay to the payroll bank account, and issuing individual payroll checks to employees.

Documents

The following documents are necessary both for achieving proper control over payroll and for complying with the various laws requiring the maintenance of adequate payroll records:

1. Time cards: The time card is a record of the time worked by an employee. The card may be prepared manually or it may be automated by use of a time clock.

2. Employee earnings record: The employee earnings record is a document maintained for each employee, showing hours worked, gross pay, deductions, and net pay for each pay period.

3. Payroll summary: The payroll summary is a listing, by employee, of gross pay, deductions, net pay, and check number. A payroll summary is prepared for each pay period. Exhibits 7A.1 and 7A.2 illustrate the employee earnings record and payroll summary.

4. Payroll voucher: The payroll voucher is a voucher authorizing a check to be drawn on the general account for deposit in the payroll bank account. The check will equal the net pay for the payroll period.

5. Payroll checks: After the net pay has been transferred to the payroll bank account, individual payroll checks are written for each employee.

Control Features and Internal Control Flowchart

Table 7A.9 lists the features that are most important in effecting proper control over payroll transactions. Figure 7A.5 incorporates the features into a payroll processing model flowchart.

Because of the extent of calculations involved in payroll processing, error prevention becomes increasingly difficult for entities with large numbers of employees. For this reason, computer processing of payroll frequently offers the most effective control. When properly programmed to verify input data, an EDP payroll system provides consistency, accuracy, and speed in calculating and processing payroll transactions. Chapter 8 explores the impact of EDP processing on the internal control structure generally.

Error prevention in manual payroll systems is enhanced through a system of double checks attained through separation of functional responsibilities. As described in Table 7A.9 and illustrated in Figure 7A.5, the following duties should be separated:

1. Timekeeping:
   a. reviewing time cards for proper hours and approvals; and
   b. comparing control totals of time cards with copy of payroll summary received from payroll.

2. Payroll:
   a. preparing payroll on basis of time cards received from timekeeping, and current list of employees and pay rates received from personnel; and
   b. double-checking calculations of gross pay, withholdings, and net pay.

3. Personnel:
   a. maintaining current list of employees and pay rates; and
   b. authorizing hires, terminations, and pay rates.

EXHIBIT 7A.1 Employee Earnings Record

Name: Lance Bannister
Employee Number: 272 45 6809
Address: 3020 Harvest Road
Alandale, Ohio 44568

Withholding Class: Single
Exemptions: One
Department: Maintenance
Wage Rate: $8.00 per hour

Hours	Date	Paid To	Gross	FICA	FIT	Health Ins.	Union Dues	Other	Net Pay	Check Number
40	1/6/93	Lance Bannister	$ 320.00	$ 22.88	$ 39.00	$ 5.00	$ 3.00	$0.00	$ 250.12	37089
42	1/13/93	Lance Bannister	336.00	24.02	41.00	5.00	3.00	0.00	262.98	38121
38	1/20/93	Lance Bannister	304.00	21.74	39.00	5.00	3.00	0.00	235.26	40664
			. . .	. . .	. . .	. . .	. . .	. . .	. . .	
	Quarter Total		$4,300.00	$307.45	$460.00	$60.00	$36.00	$0.00	$3,436.55	

EXHIBIT 7A.2 Payroll Summary

Period Ended 1/6/93

Employee Number			Employee Name	Gross	FICA	FIT	Health Insurance	Union Dues	Other	Net Pay	Check Number
348	90	8765	Harold Allen	$ 344.00	$ 24.60	$ 42.00	$ 5.00	$ 3.00	$0.00	$ 269.40	37087
197	88	0956	Joshua Anderson	356.00	25.45	44.00	8.00	3.00	0.00	275.55	37088
272	45	6809	Lance Bannister	320.00	22.88	39.00	5.00	3.00	0.00	250.12	37089
234	98	7689	Steven Celley	383.00	27.38	48.00	8.00	3.00	0.00	296.62	37090
321	67	8854	Lawrence Dancer	266.00	19.02	25.00	8.00	3.00	0.00	210.98	37091
				. . .	. . .	. . .	. . .	. . .	. . .	. . .	
			Totals	$10,500.00	$750.75	$1,350.00	$210.00	$90.00	$0.00	$8,099.25	

**TABLE 7A.9   Control Principles and Techniques: Expenditure Cycle
for Payroll Transactions**

Control Principle	Control Feature
Competence of personnel	Timekeeping and approving time cards Calculating gross pay, deductions, and net pay Preparing payroll tax returns Reconciling payroll bank accounts Maintaining employee personnel records
Separation of duties	Authorizing hiring, termination, and pay rates Maintaining employee personnel records Reconciling bank accounts Timekeeping Preparing payroll checks Signing checks and distributing payroll
Execution in accordance with authorization	Time cards or clock cards required Time cards approved and signed by supervisor Payroll prepared on basis of current list of employees received from personnel

Recording in accordance with GAAP	Review of payroll calculations, including gross pay,
	   deductions, and net pay
	Review of payroll entries for correctness of account
	   distributions
	Standard journal entries for monthly payroll accruals

Asset safeguards	Payrolls paid by check Distribution of payroll checks immediately upon signing Use of imprest payroll bank accounts Control over unclaimed checks Limited access to time cards, clock cards, and unused payroll checks
Periodic inventories and comparisons	Payroll bank reconciliations on a monthly basis Periodic comparison of entries in payroll summary with authorized list of employees maintained in personnel

4. Treasurer:
   a. signing payroll checks after reviewing payroll summary; and
   b. distributing payroll checks immediately upon signing.
5. General Ledger: Recording payroll.

Separation of duties also helps in preventing payroll fraud. The various means through which most payroll frauds have been accomplished collectively are referred to as *payroll padding*. Payroll padding involves adding employees or hours to the payroll and misappropriating the monies associated with such padding. Separating the functions of check signing and distribution, production, payroll preparation, and accounting makes payroll padding difficult in the absence of collusion. Requiring personnel department to approve hires, terminations, and pay rates is another control device designed to prevent payroll padding.

FIGURE 7A.5 Payroll Flowchart

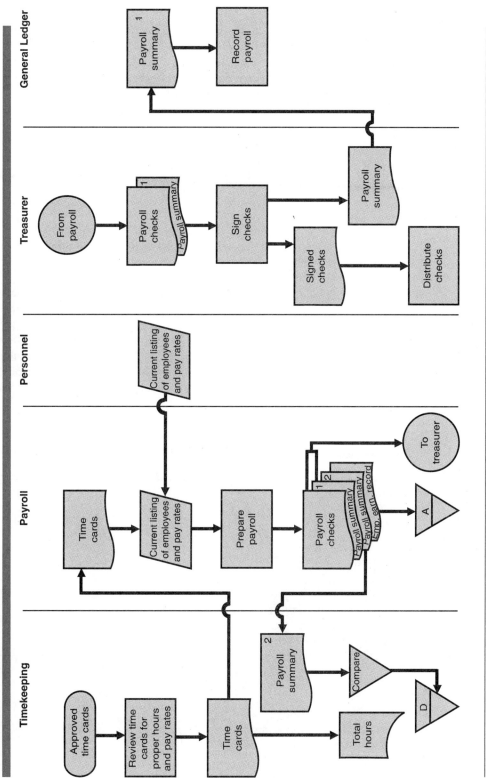

A set of standard journal entries, as illustrated in Exhibit 7A.3 helps to ensure accuracy in recording the payroll and the employer's payroll taxes. The entries can be drafted in advance for the year, one set for each month, and only the amounts for each debit and credit need be entered at the end of the month when known.

Paying the payroll by check and depositing net pay in an imprest payroll bank account also assist in preventing payroll errors and fraud. Under this type of system, payroll checks cannot be issued for more than a maximum specified amount, and unclaimed checks are returned to the treasurer for safekeeping.

Reconciliation of payroll bank accounts by persons not having responsibility for preparing, recording, or distributing payroll assists in detecting payroll processing errors and fraud.

Control Tests

In testing payroll controls for risk assessment purposes, the auditor is primarily concerned with evaluating the accuracy of payroll processing, including calculation and recording of payroll. Discovered control weaknesses that permit payroll padding should be brought to the attention of management, but these weaknesses ordinarily do not affect the financial statements as significantly as weaknesses in the accuracy controls.

Table 7A.10 relates control weaknesses to possible errors, and recommends control tests to assist the auditor in evaluating possible material misstatements resulting from such weaknesses. In performing the recommended control tests, the auditor examines the primary documentation underlying the calculation, recording, and distribu-

EXHIBIT 7A.3   Standard Journal Entries for Payroll

Journal Voucher Number 21
Payroll Distribution   Month/Year 3/93

Account Title	Debit	Credit
Direct labor	X	
Manufacturing overhead	X	
General and administrative	X	
Accrued payroll		X

Journal Voucher Number 22
Monthly Payroll Taxes   Month/Year 3/93

Account Title	Debit	Credit
FICA tax expense	X	
Workers' compensation expense	X	
State unemployment tax expense	X	
Federal unemployment tax expense	X	
Payroll taxes payable		X

TABLE 7A.10   Control Weaknesses and Related Tests: Expenditure Cycle for Payroll

Control Weakness	Possible Errors	Control Tests
Lack of care in calculating payroll and failure to review and double-check calculations	Errors in calculating gross pay, deductions, net pay, and payroll taxes	Select a sample of payroll summaries from the period under audit and perform the following procedures:
Lack of competent personnel in areas of payroll calculation, payroll tax return preparation, or reconciliation of payroll bank accounts	Errors in calculating gross pay, deductions, net pay, and payroll taxes	Examine time cards for proper approval Compare time cards with payroll summary for agreement of hours, employee name, and employee number
Standard journal entries not drafted for monthly payroll entries	Errors in recording payroll and payroll taxes	Compare pay rate with authorized list of rates maintained by personnel department
Journal entries to record payroll and payroll taxes not reviewed for correctness	Errors in recording payroll and payroll taxes	Recalculate gross pay, deductions, and net pay
Inadequate separation of duties among timekeeping, personnel, production, payroll accounting, and check distribution	Payroll padding	Trace from payroll summary to standard journal entry for correctness of payroll recording Review payroll tax returns for correctness Review payroll bank reconciliation for correctness

tion of payroll. These procedures, therefore, should assist the auditor in evaluating the materiality of errors committed by the client in calculating or recording payroll.

If inadequate separation of duties or lack of asset safeguards increase the probability of payroll padding, the auditor should consider accompanying the paymaster during the distribution of one or more payrolls. This should be done by the auditor on an unannounced basis and is a form of control test that enables the auditor to detect the presence of improper payroll checks. Checks that are unclaimed at the completion of payroll distribution are then compared with current personnel records to determine whether the employees are still on the payroll; and the ultimate disposition of unclaimed checks is ascertained. Comparison of hours and rates, as recommended in Table 7A.10, also assists in detecting payroll padding.

Design of Substantive Audit Procedures

Weaknesses in payroll control should lead the auditor to extend testing of the year-end accruals of payroll, payroll withholdings, and employer payroll tax expense. If the client is a manufacturing concern, goods in process and finished goods inventories may also be affected by payroll recording errors. The auditor should therefore determine, on the basis of the audited payroll balances, whether standard labor and overhead rates are reasonable.

Production

Transactions

The transactions that make up the production cycle are internal in nature. They are as follows (the journal entries associated with each of the transactions assume that perpetual inventory records are used to maintain accountability over the production flows):

1. Movement of materials from stores to production

   - Debit: Goods in Process
   - Credit: Raw Materials Inventory

2. Conversion of materials into finished goods

   - Debit: Goods in Process
   - Credit: Direct Labor Applied
             Manufacturing Overhead Applied

3. Transfer of finished goods to inventory

   - Debit: Finished Goods Inventory
   - Credit: Goods in Process

Documents

The following documents are usually associated with these transactions:

1. Materials requisition: This is a formal written materials request from production to stores.
2. Production order: This document authorizes and initiates the production of goods to fill a customer's order or for stock.
3. Production report: This is a summary of materials, labor, and overhead inputs and finished goods output for a given time period.
4. Monthly cost summary: This is a journal entry summarizing material, labor, and overhead inputs and finished goods output for the month.

Control Features and Internal Control Flowchart

Table 7A.11 and Figure 7A.6 identify and describe the principal components of internal control over production. Maintaining accountability as materials proceed through the production process is critical to effective control. This is accomplished through perpetual inventory records for materials, goods in process, and finished goods. Documentation of the flows, including evidence of proper authorizations at each stage of the process also promotes accountability. Perpetual inventory records, along with standard costs and variance analysis, are also helpful in identifying major errors and irregularities involving inventory.

Limiting access to inventories, fixing of custodial responsibility over inventories, and conducting periodic test counts and comparisons, enable prompt identification and follow-up in the event of major inventory shortages.

TABLE 7A.11   Control Principles and Techniques: Expenditure Cycle for Production

Control Principle	Control Feature
Competence of personnel	Setting standard costs Recording inventory cost flows Maintaining inventory records Determining overhead application rates Costing physical inventory
Separation of duties	Maintaining inventory records Custody over inventories Taking physical inventories Production Accounting for inventory cost flows
Execution in accordance with authorization	Production initiated only on the basis of properly approved production order accompanied by signed requisitions Documentation of all inventory movements
Recording in accordance with GAAP	Job order or process cost system for recording cost flows Standard costs and variances incorporated into the accounting system Maintenance of detailed manufacturing overhead ledger Standard journal entries for costing monthly production
Asset safeguards	Daily production and scrap reports Orderly arrangement of goods in warehouses Limited access to inventories and fixed responsibility Limited access to inventories of repair parts, small tools, and supplies and fixed responsibility
Periodic inventories and comparisons	Periodic test counts of inventories and comparison with perpetual records Monthly agreement of subsidiary ledgers (materials, goods in process, finished goods, and manufacturing overhead) with control accounts

Proper recording of inventory cost flows is enhanced through assignment of competent personnel to inventory accounting, the use of standard journal entries for monthly cost summaries, and monthly comparisons of perpetual inventory records with the related controlling accounts.

Control Tests

The auditor's major concern in testing the production cycle for risk assessment purposes is the adequacy of the system in accurately recording inventory cost flows. Testing the inventory costing model by recalculating standard cost for a sample of finished products and tracing a sample of production orders through the system are effective means for obtaining the necessary evidence.

FIGURE 7A.6 Production Flowchart

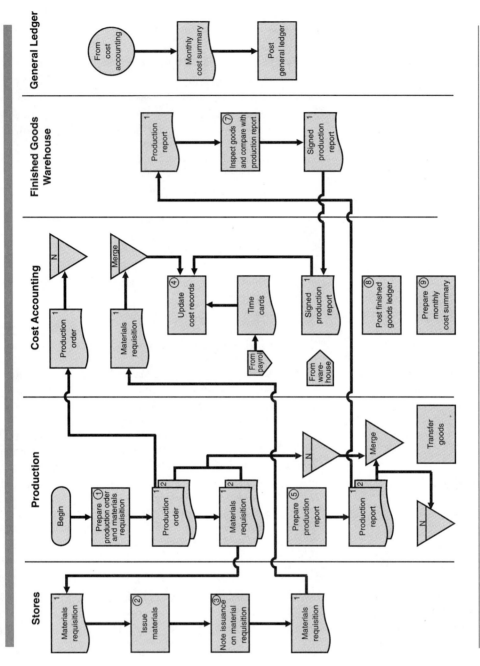

Note: Circled numbers denote sequence in which functions are performed.

Table 7A.12 suggests control tests which the auditor can use to evaluate the production control procedures. The recommended tests assume that the client has developed standard costs for finished products and uses perpetual inventory records in accounting for inventory flows.

The first set of procedures is designed to test the standard cost system for reasonableness. In applying these procedures, the auditor might proceed as follows:

Objective	Procedure
1. Determine reasonableness of types and quantities of materials used in finished product.	Examine bill of materials describing the type and amount of each material used in the finished product
2. Determine reasonableness of direct labor operations and time required to produce a unit of finished product.	Examine routing sheets describing each step in the manufacture of a given product, expressed in terms of: Labor operation Labor time and rate Material input and cost at each step in the process
3. Determine reasonableness of materials prices used to cost finished products	Trace from bill of materials to current vendors' invoices
4. Determine that proper labor rates are being used to cost finished products	Trace from routing sheets to listing of labor rates provided by personnel department
5. Determine reasonableness of overhead rates applied to finished products	Recalculate overhead rates on a test basis by relating actual overhead to base (labor hours, labor dollars, machine hours, etc.). Compare calculated rates with standard rates. Consider capacity utilization.

The second set of tests described in Table 7A.12 is concerned with the adequacy of documentation supporting inventory cost flows and the accuracy of recording the flows. These tests require the auditor to select a sample of completed production orders, examine for proper documentation, and trace the cost flows through the recording and posting process. Assuming that standard costs are incorporated into the general ledger, the auditor must determine that inventories are recorded at standard cost. This can be done by tracing the inventory debits to the audited standard cost records. The auditor should also recalculate variances on a test basis and obtain explanations for significant variances occurring in the sample of production orders.

Design of Substantive Audit Procedures

Material weaknesses in inventory and production controls should lead to extended testing of the year-end physical inventories. This is particularly important if the

TABLE 7A.12   Control Weaknesses and Related Tests: Expenditure Cycle for Production

Control Weakness	Possible Errors	Control Tests
Persons recording inventory cost flows, maintaining inventory records, determining overhead application rates, setting standard costs, or costing physical inventory not competent to do so	Errors in recording inventory cost flows Errors in costing inventory and cost of sales Errors in perpetual inventory records	Select a sample of finished products and test for the following attributes: Proper determination of material types and quantities needed to produce finished product
Inadequate documentation of inventory movements	Unauthorized issuance of materials Inaccurate inventory records	Proper determination of labor operations and times required to produce finished product
Lack of rigorous cost accounting system as evidenced by: Absence of journal entries recording cost flows Failure to incorporate standard costs and variance analysis into the accounting system Failure to maintain detailed manufacturing overhead ledger Standard journal entries not used in costing monthly production	Inventory recording errors Errors in calculating and recording cost of sales Failure to promptly locate and correct unfavorable variances	Current materials prices and labor rates used to cost products Reasonableness of rates used in applying overhead to finished products Select a sample of completed production orders and test for the following attributes: Adequacy of documentation of production flows as evidenced by Materials requisition Production order Job order cost sheet or departmental production reports Time cards
Lack of periodic test counts and comparison of physical inventory with perpetual records	Undetected inventory shrinkage or recording errors	Recording and posting accuracy (trace from requisition to materials ledger; from materials ledger to cost sheets; and from production reports to finished goods ledger)
Subsidiary inventory and overhead ledgers not agreed to controlling accounts on a regular basis	Undetected errors in recording or posting overhead accounts	Evidence of proper authorization of production orders and approval of requisitions Accuracy in posting production reports to monthly cost summary

perpetual inventory records are unreliable because of the weaknesses. Extended testing should consist mainly of expanding inventory test counts during the observation of physical inventory taking. In addition, depending on the nature of the weaknesses, the auditor may elect to recalculate direct labor and overhead included in ending goods in process and finished goods inventories.

FINANCING AND INVESTING CYCLE

Control structure policies and procedures and the auditor's tests of controls, as related to the financing and investing cycle, are discussed in this section according to the following categories of transactions:

1. Borrowing from others, excluding open trade accounts with creditors. The transactions may involve long-term or short-term notes, bonds payable, mortgages payable, or long-term financing leases.
2. Lending to others, excluding open trade accounts with customers.
3. Acquisitions and disposals of financial assets. Purchases of marketable securities such as common stocks, preferred stocks, corporate bonds, and government securities fall into this category of transactions.
4. Capital stock and dividend transactions. Stock issuance and reacquisition, stock retirement, and dividend declarations are the principal transactions involving stockholders' equity.

Borrowing from Others

Transactions

Issuance of debt instruments, accrual of interest, and repayment of debt are the transaction classes comprising borrowing activities.

Documents

The following documents are associated with borrowing transactions:

1. *Remittance advice or bank credit memo:* This evidences receipt of loan proceeds.
2. *Copy of the debt instrument (note payable, bond indenture, lease agreement):* This specifies the terms under which the debt is to be repaid.
3. *Voucher authorizing payment of interest, principal, or both:* This authorizes payment by the entity.
4. *Standard journal entry or journal voucher for monthly interest accrual:* This ensures that all interest charges will be reflected in the monthly financial statements.

Control Features

The major features in effective internal control over borrowing activities are the proper authorization of borrowing and the control of cash receipts and disbursements resulting from borrowing and repayment. Borrowing authority should be clearly defined in policy and procedures manuals in terms of the person and the maximum amount of borrowing authority delegated to that person. The control procedures should provide that amounts in excess of the specified maximum be authorized by the board of directors and recorded in the directors' minutes.

Cash receipts from borrowing should be subject to the same control procedures as those described previously for the revenue cycle. They should be included in the prelisting of cash receipts and compared with the deposit ticket and cash receipts entry related to that day's receipts.

Disbursements for interest and principal repayments should be supported by properly approved vouchers. Documentation in the form of copies of the debt instruments or calculations of interest should accompany the vouchers. Evidence of review and approval should appear on the face of the vouchers.

Control Tests

The control tests related to borrowing and repayment have already been described in the sections dealing with the revenue cycle (cash receipts) and the expenditure cycle (cash payments). In addition, as part of the initial internal control understanding phase, the auditor should review policy and procedures manuals for proper definition of borrowing authority. The auditor should also question management concerning control procedures related to miscellaneous cash receipts and disbursements.

Unlike purchases and sales, borrowing transactions are fewer in number and more likely to be individually significant. For this reason, the auditor examines the majority of these transactions during the substantive testing phase of the audit, regardless of the effectiveness of internal control. The attention devoted to control testing of the borrowing cycle, therefore, is usually less than that accorded the revenue and expenditure cycles.

Design of Substantive Audit Procedures

If the control procedures do not provide for adequate authorization and approval of borrowing transactions, the auditor should consider the following substantive procedures (covered more fully in Chapter 14):

1. Examine loan agreements for authenticity of nontrade liabilities;

2. Examine directors' minutes for recorded authorization of outstanding liabilities;

3. Inquire of management as to proper authorization of liabilities not authorized in the directors' minutes; and

4. Consider confirming all material balances in nontrade liability accounts.

Lending to Others

Transactions

Lending transactions consist of the following:

1. Transfers of cash or other assets to others in exchange for some form of debt instrument—usually a note receivable;

2. Accrual of interest on notes receivable;

3. Collections of notes receivable or interest.

Documents

The documents relating to lending transactions are:

1. *Notes receivable:* These are the debt instruments.
2. *Canceled checks:* These are evidence of the lending transactions.
3. *Supporting calculations of interest accruals by debtors.*
4. *Cash receipts listings, remittance advices, and deposit tickets:* These are evidence of receipt and deposit of interest, principal, or both.

Control Features

The system of internal control over lending transactions should contain the following features:

1. Lending transactions should be subject to proper authorization and approval. The policies and procedures manuals should clearly define authority, and the system should provide for board approval and the recording of loan authorizations in the minutes of the directors' meetings.
2. Disbursement of loan proceeds should be accompanied by a properly approved voucher and a copy of the note receivable authorizing the payment.
3. Cash receipts resulting from interest and principal remittances should be controlled in the same manner as cash receipts from customers. To this end, they should be included in the daily cash receipts listings and compared with deposit tickets and cash receipts entries.
4. Monthly interest accruals should be provided for by means of a standard journal entry or journal voucher. This control prevents inadvertent omission of necessary adjustments.

Control Tests

As with borrowing transactions, the auditor evaluates the effectiveness of internal control over the receipt and disbursement of loan proceeds during the control testing of the revenue and expenditure cycles. Reviewing the policies and procedures manuals and questioning management during the initial understanding phase complete the control testing of lending activities.

Design of Substantive Audit Procedures

As with borrowing transactions, failure to provide for proper loan authorization is the control weakness of greatest concern. Under these circumstances, the auditor should consider extending the following substantive audit procedures (covered more fully in Chapter 14):

1. Examine loan agreements for all material year-end balances in nontrade receivables;
2. Examine directors' minutes for recorded authorization of all material year-end balances in nontrade receivables;
3. Inquire of management as to authorization of those loans not recorded in the directors' minutes; and
4. Consider confirming year-end balances in nontrade receivables.

Acquisitions and Disposals of Financial Assets

Transactions

The principal transactions in this category are:

1. Purchases of marketable securities and long-term investments;
2. Sale of securities and investments.

Documents

The documents associated with asset acquisitions and disposals are:

1. *Brokers' advices and canceled checks.* These documents are evidence of the purchase of assets.
2. *Brokers' advices, receipted deposit tickets, cash receipts listings, and remittance advices:* These documents evidence the sale of financial assets.

Control Features

The following control features should be included in an effective system of internal control over the acquisition and disposal of financial assets:

1. Proper authorization of purchases and sales;
2. Review and approval of vouchers and documentation supporting purchases of financial assets;
3. Effective control over cash receipts from disposals; and
4. Provision for reviewing calculations in support of gains and losses on disposals and interest accruals.

The policies and procedures manuals should identify responsibility for purchase and sale of investment securities. Moreover, provision should be made for board of director approval of transactions exceeding given dollar amounts.

Cash receipts and disbursements associated with disposals and acquisitions should be subject to the same controls as receipts and disbursements relating to normal operating activities. Standard journal entries or journal vouchers should be drafted for monthly interest accrual. Accounting manuals should provide guidance in calculating gain or loss from disposals.

Control Tests

Control over the purchase and sale of financial assets is evaluated as part of the auditor's control tests of cash receipts transactions and payments to vendors. During the initial understanding phase of control structure, the auditor should review the policies and procedures manuals for provisions relating to authorizations for acquisition or disposal. Accounting manuals should be examined for adequacy of instructions for calculating gains and losses on disposals. In reviewing standard journal entries, the auditor should determine that provision has been made for proper interest accrual.

Design of Substantive Audit Procedures

(Covered more fully in Chapter 14). As with borrowing and lending transactions, failure of the client to provide for proper authorization of acquisitions and disposals should prompt the auditor to inquire of management as to the propriety of the transactions. The auditor may even consider confirming the more significant transactions with brokers or with buyers and sellers for transactions not processed through securities brokers.

Control weaknesses that suggest material errors in calculating gains and losses and accrued interest should lead to extended tests in computing year-end balances. The accounts affected include gain or loss on the disposal of securities, interest receivable, and interest revenue. In applying analytical procedures, the auditor should be able to evaluate the extent of possible misstatement.

Capital Stock and Dividend Transactions

Transactions

The principal transactions relating to capital stock and dividends are the following:

1. Issuance, reacquisition, and retirement of capital stock;
2. Declaration and payment of cash dividends; and
3. Stock dividends and stock splits.

Documents

The following documents are associated with stock transactions:

1. *Board of directors' minutes:* The minutes provide evidence that stock issuance and reacquisitions have been properly authorized.
2. *Remittance advices, cash receipts listings, and deposit tickets:* Cash receipts from stock issuance are evidenced by remittance advices attached to checks received from brokers or investment bankers, cash receipts listings, and bank deposit tickets.
3. *Disbursement vouchers and canceled checks:* The disbursement vouchers and canceled checks support reacquisitions of stock and dividend payments.

Control Features

The main control features related to capital stock transactions are the following:

1. All stock issuances and reacquisitions, as well as dividend declarations, should require board approval;
2. Cash receipts from stock issuance should be subject to the same control as other cash receipts;
3. Disbursements for reacquisition of stock should be controlled in the same manner as other cash disbursements; and
4. Imprest accounts should be used for paying dividends, and a single voucher and check should be written to transfer the total amount of a dividend declaration from the general to the imprest account.

Control Tests

Control tests of capital stock and dividend transactions should consist of evaluating the effectiveness of receipts and disbursements controls, and the adequacy of authorizations and approvals of stock issuance, reacquisitions, and dividends. Control testing of the revenue and expenditure cycles, as described earlier, should provide the information necessary for evaluating the effectiveness of controls over receipts and disbursements related to capital stock transactions. Examining policy and procedures manuals and examining directors' minutes for approvals should enable the auditor to determine the adequacy of authorizations and approvals.

Design of Substantive Audit Procedures

Failure to provide for proper authorization of capital stock issuance, reacquisition, and/or dividend declarations suggests that the auditor proceed as follows (covered more fully in Chapter 14):

1. Examine minutes for board of director approval of capital stock and dividend transactions;
2. Confirm with the board those transactions not recorded in the minutes; and
3. Examine stock certificates supporting treasury stock balances.

Control weaknesses affecting cash receipts and disbursements related to capital stock and dividend transactions suggests the following substantive audit procedures:

1. Examine remittance advices, brokers' advices, cash receipts listings, deposit tickets, and bank statement credits for all cash receipts arising from stock issuance;
2. Examine brokers' advices, vouchers, and canceled checks supporting stock reacquisitions; and
3. Reconcile dividend bank accounts for one or more months of the year under audit.

8

Internal Control and EDP

CHAPTER OUTLINE

I. Need for a different audit approach
    A. Auditing around vs. through the computer
    B. Audit objectives vs. audit approach
        1. Change in audit trail
        2. Combining of functions

II. Types of EDP accounting systems
    A. Processing systems
    B. File systems
    C. Hardware configurations

III. Kinds of EDP controls
    A. General controls—pervasive controls
    B. Application controls—specific controls
    C. User controls—manual controls

IV. Techniques for testing EDP–based controls
    A. Understanding the system
    B. Testing controls to reduce the assessed level of control risk
    C. Auditing through the computer to test controls

V. EDP and audit risk implications
    A. Factors affecting control risk
    B. How mitigated
    C. Managing detection risk

VI. Appendix: Effective writing in auditing

OVERVIEW

EDP accounting applications have an impact on the auditor in two ways. First, they affect the auditor's review of control structure policies and procedures; this topic is covered in this chapter. Second, they influence the nature of substantive audit testing; this aspect is addressed in Chapter 9. As shown in Figure 8.1, this chapter is concerned with the same segment of the audit process as Chapter 7. While Chapter 7 emphasized controls associated with manual processing systems, however, Chapter 8 considers EDP environments.

EDP accounting systems are diverse in practice and, for this reason, have different control features. The systems vary as to method of processing, file integration, and hardware configuration. Whatever the nature of the system, the auditor must determine that the necessary controls are properly designed and implemented.

EDP controls may be classified as to three types:

1. General controls;

2. Application controls; and

3. User controls.

General controls are more pervasive than application controls. User controls consist of manual controls (e.g., control totals) applied by departments whose transactions are processed by the computer. The purpose of user controls is to verify the completeness and accuracy of computer output.

Although many techniques exist for testing EDP controls, they may be broadly classified as to auditing "around" the computer and auditing "through" the computer. Auditing around the computer compares input with output and treats the computer as a "black box," ignoring the means by which transactions are processed. Auditing through the computer, on the other hand, directly tests the EDP controls. Most auditors use a combination of methods in further testing of EDP controls.

Auditors need to consider the impact of EDP systems on audit risk. **On-line real-time (OLRT) systems** affect audit risk in two ways. First, direct input of transactions, internal storage of files and data, and lack of complete and permanent transaction documentation pose increased risk to the auditor. Second, and offsetting the increased risk, the existence of adequate controls in the supervisory programs of such systems mitigates risk by assuring consistent and correct processing of transactions. These issues, together with methods for dealing with increased risk, are covered in the final section of the chapter.

STUDY OBJECTIVES

After reading this chapter, you should be able to:

1. Differentiate between auditing around and auditing through the computer;

2. Classify and describe the different types of EDP accounting systems;

3. Classify and define the major EDP accounting controls;

4. Develop an approach to assessing control risk through review of control structure policies and procedures, given significant EDP accounting applications; and

5. Evaluate and deal with audit risk factors uniquely associated with EDP accounting applications.

FIGURE 8.1 **The Audit Process**

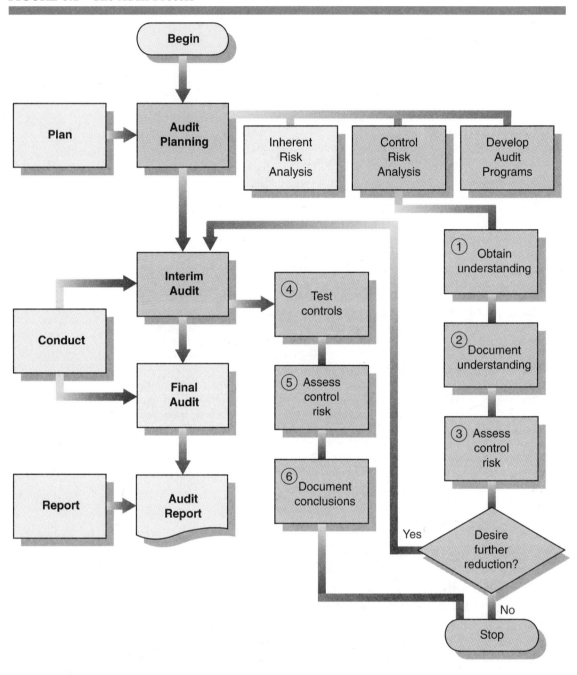

NEED FOR A DIFFERENT AUDITING APPROACH

Auditing Around vs. Through the Computer

Computers are being used to an ever-increasing extent to process transactions and to store accounting data. The systems range from simple batch processing to complex on-line real-time processing. This trend in computer use affects two aspects of audit risk:

1. Assessing control risk, given the need for EDP controls

2. Managing detection risk by substantiating transactions processed by the computer and balances stored in computer files.

The first area concerns the **phases of processing** and is the subject matter of the current chapter. The second area deals with the **results of processing** and is covered in Chapter 9.

In verifying the phases of processing (assessing control risk, given EDP accounting controls), the auditor has a choice of **auditing around the computer** or **auditing through the computer.** To illustrate, assume a company processes its payroll by computer. The auditor may choose to test payroll controls by either of the following approaches:

1. Manually calculate gross pay, withholdings, and net pay by examining time cards and employee earnings records (input). Trace these to payroll summary (output). This is an example of auditing around the computer.

2. Identify the computer controls (validity checks, reasonableness tests, etc.) used in processing payroll, and test the controls by either tracing transactions through the system or by observing the system during transaction processing. This is an example of auditing through the computer. The merits of auditing around and through the computer, as well as types of computer systems and controls, are considered in this chapter.

Audit Objectives vs. Audit Approach

Auditing objectives, as addressed in Chapter 4, are not affected by the type of accounting system encountered by the auditor. The audit approach, however, may need to be modified to accommodate EDP accounting applications. The reasons for such modification are discussed in the following paragraphs.

Change in the Audit Trail

The audit trail frequently assumes a different form when transactions are processed by computer. The more advanced computer systems produce less documentation than manual systems, but the decrease in documentation is offset by programmed controls to ensure consistent and accurate processing of transactions. Moreover, internal storage of transactions and files reduces the need for permanent retention of hard copy. Under such circumstances, the auditor needs to test computer controls more extensively and perform audit procedures more frequently—while documentation is still available.

When sales orders are input at terminal locations, for example, the computer performs most of the verification procedures involving customer number, credit limit, price, terms, and so on. Such checking by computer, as contrasted with manual checking, reduces the need for extensive documentation and also makes permanent retention of the hard copy unnecessary once all verification procedures have been performed and documented internally. The visible audit trail, under such conditions, has been transformed into a computer audit trail. Control testing may therefore shift from examination of documents to observation of control activity performed during input, inasmuch as the internal processing by computers is not visible to the human eye.

Combining of Functions

In addition to audit trail modification, computer processing of transactions permits the combining of functions which are ordinarily separated in manual systems. Returning to the sales order example, EDP processing enables the computer to validate the customer number, credit limit, price, stock number, credit terms, etc., through input editing. A manual system, on the other hand validates through visual checking followed by second-party review. In a computerized payroll system, internal computer checking of employee number to determine whether the person is a valid employee, as well as testing the correctness of labor rates and the reasonableness of hours worked, replaces the more traditional manual performance of these control procedures. Such combining of functions, like the audit trail modifications, requires a somewhat different approach to control testing by the auditor. Testing the validation controls through observation, tracing transactions through the system, or auditing around the computer is necessary given the absence of separation under such circumstances.

The modifications in audit approach introduced earlier are considered in greater depth later in the chapter. The various types of EDP systems and the kinds of controls, however, need to be examined before discussing computer auditing approaches.

TYPES OF EDP ACCOUNTING SYSTEMS

Many types of computer systems are presently in use. These systems are distinguished by the methods they use for processing transactions, by the type of filing system used for storing data, and by the hardware configuration comprising the system. This section briefly describes the more common systems to be found under each of these headings.

Processing Systems

Batch Processing Systems

In a **batch processing** system, transactions are accumulated and processed in groups. Sales orders for the day, invoices to be recorded, and daily cash receipts might each be viewed as a "batch" of transactions to be processed as a group. Control totals, consisting of adding machine tapes summing the dollar amount of transactions in a group, are usually developed and compared with output in order to ensure complete and accurate processing. Batch processing systems are distinguished by their relative simplicity and reliability. They do not process transactions as quickly as the more advanced systems, nor do they possess the potential for providing timely information concerning the files updated by transaction processing. Figure 8.2 illustrates a typical batch processing system.

FIGURE 8.2   Batch Processing System

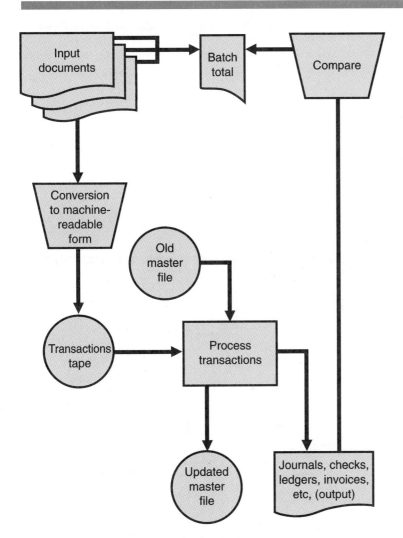

Transactions are accumulated for later processing in groups or "batches." Prior to processing, they are converted to a machine readable form. Transactions are processed against an old master file to produce an updated master file. The printed output is usually a by-product of the processing run.

Real-Time Processing Systems

In a **real-time processing** system, transactions are entered as they occur and are processed as they are entered. These systems form the heart of management information systems. Given the continuous updating of the data base as transactions are entered, the status of such files as accounts receivable, accounts payable, and inventory may be determined at any time. Although powerful in terms of information capability, real-time systems are more complex than batch processing systems. Moreover, they do not ordinarily provide the extent of audit trail documentation produced by batch systems. For this reason, they are more difficult to audit in terms of obtaining satisfaction concerning the existence of necessary controls and in designing substantive testing procedures. Notwithstanding such complexity, present generation computer systems are characterized more and more by their real-time processing capability. Figure 8.3 illustrates a real-time processing system.

FIGURE 8.3   On-Line Real-Time System

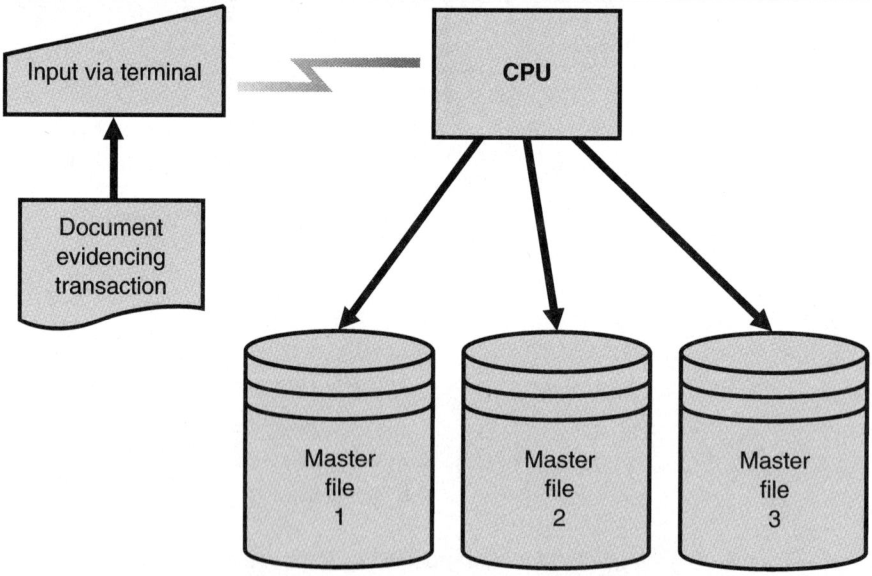

Transactions are entered as they occur, usually at a location remote from the CPU. Hard copy (the document) is retained at the location of transaction origin. Several files (e.g., sales, accounts receivable, inventory) are updated simultaneously as transactions are processed.

Time Sharing and Service Bureaus

Time sharing occurs when a computer serves more than one user. In transaction processing, time sharing occurs when a computer processes transactions for more than one entity. A savings and loan association, for example, may rent time on its computer to a mortgage investment company which uses the computer to process loan payments.

A **service bureau** is a company that processes transactions for other entities. A commercial bank, for example, may handle the complete payroll processing for small companies that, singly, do not have a sufficient number of transactions to justify acquisition of a computer.

If a client rents computer time from another entity or uses a service bureau for data processing activities, the auditor must obtain satisfaction concerning the controls over the outside processing in addition to examining the client's own internal controls.[1]

File Systems

Separate File System

In a separate file system, each file is updated individually in separate processing runs. The processing of customer orders, for example, updates the customers' accounts; the processing of vendors' invoices updates accounts payable; and the processing of inventory transactions updates the various inventory accounts. Batch processing systems are usually characterized by separate file processing.

Integrated Data Base System

These systems update many files simultaneously as transactions are processed. Processing of a sales order, for example, updates the accounts receivable control account as well as the subsidiary ledger; inventory control and the related subsidiary ledger are also updated; and the sales control and sales detail are also posted as the sales

---

[1]See Auditing Standards Board, *AICPA Professional Standards,* New York: AICPA, Section AU 324.

order is processed. **Integrated data base systems** contain a set of interrelated master files that are integrated in order to reduce data redundancy. The software used to control input, processing, and output referred to as the *data base management system* (DBMS), handles the storage, retrieval, updating, and maintenance of data in the data base.

Integrated files are most often associated with real-time systems, and, as stated earlier, pose the greatest challenge for auditors. Controls within these systems are harder to test and assess due to the danger of file destruction; and the internal storage of data in random, rather than sequential, order increases the difficulty involved in performing substantive tests.

Hardware Configuration

Punched Card or Magnetic Tape Systems

Punched card and magnetic tape systems, usually associated with batch processing systems, require the conversion of hard copy documents into machine-readable form. This is achieved by punching the data on cards that may be processed directly or converted to magnetic tape prior to computer processing. Data may also be keyed directly to tape. Given the advances in micro computer technology and related software, punched card and magnetic tape systems are gradually being replaced by floppy or hard disk systems.

On-Line Systems

On-line systems are unique in that transactions are entered by way of a communication device (such as a terminal) connected directly to the computer. Such systems do not require conversion of hard copy to machine-readable form prior to processing. Instead of punched cards or magnetic tape, on-line systems store data and files on disks. On-line systems may or may not be real-time systems, depending upon whether transactions are processed and files updated immediately as transactions are entered. Certain on-line systems allow queuing transactions for later processing in batches.

Electronic data interchange (EDI), currently being adopted by an increasing number of companies, is the computer-to-computer exchange of intercompany business documents in a "public standard format." More specifically, it is a technique whereby the company's computer system is linked to those of its suppliers and customers and transactions, such as purchases, sales, and cash receipts and payments, may be initiated automatically by the system. Documents, such as purchase orders, invoices, receiving acknowledgements, and checks are converted into public standard format such that the other company's computer can read and accept it. Public standard format, developed by the Accredited Standards Committee of the American National Standards Institute, is a set of uniform standards for electronic communications. Called ANSI X12, the standards establish rules for data transmission that specify what documents and information can be transmitted and in what format. EDI eliminates the need to re-enter data into the accounting system. This results in fewer errors and more timely information. These systems, however, also require greater attention to proper controls over input of transactions.

Two methods are available for implementing EDI. The first, referred to as the "direct" method, links the computers of Company A and Company B directly—a manufacturer and one of its parts suppliers, for example (see Figure 8.4). The second, called the "indirect" method (see Figure 8.5), utilizes a network for linking

FIGURE 8.4 Electronic Data Interchange System: Direct Approach

FIGURE 8.5 Electronic Data Interchange System: Indirect Approach

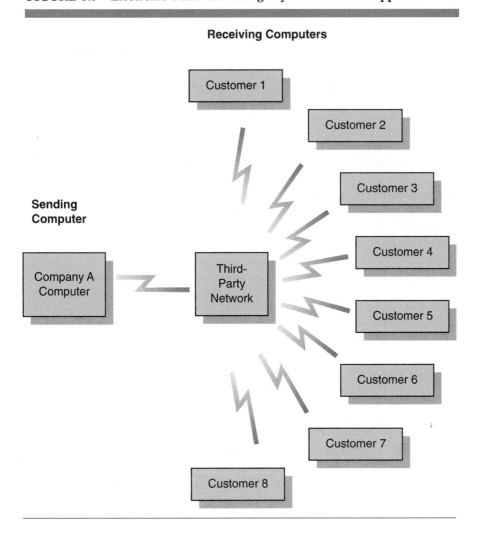

several companies' computers by providing a "mailbox" for each participant. The network, through what is called "protocol conversion," transforms the senders' messages into the format preferred by the receivers. The advantage of the indirect method is that the sender company can transmit documents to several receiver companies without having to change its document form each time a message is sent to a different receiving company. Instead, the network protocol conversion will make sure the document is received in the proper form.

Microcomputer Systems

The advances in **microcomputer** technology have enabled even the smallest firms to justify computer processing of transactions. Their relatively low cost, when combined with advanced software capable of creating and maintaining integrated data bases on hard disks, makes the microcomputer a valuable data processing and management information system tool for the small company. Microcomputer systems may consist of "stand alone" computers used by single individuals; or they may be connected to one another and/or to mainframe computers through a form of networking.

Distributed Data Processing

Many large companies also use microcomputers extensively, for both data processing and analysis. Companies with branches or divisions, for example, frequently use micro- or minicomputers for processing branch or division transactions and for transmitting them to the home office mainframe via communication links. At the same time, the micro- or minicomputer can be used by the local managers for various kinds of analysis, such as analysis of inventory status, customer history, and aging of accounts receivable.

Virtually always, such **distributed processing** systems are connected to the mainframe computer located at the home office. Additionally, they may be linked to one another through a system of **networking.** This enables the micro- and minicomputers to communicate with one another and share work loads. A division, faced with an unusually large number of transactions to be processed, for example, may decide to enlist the assistance of other microcomputers in the system to share the chore of processing. Figure 8.6 illustrates a typical distributed data processing system.

Where microcomputers are placed at remote locations and linked to the company's mainframe computer, the data security risk increases. For this reason, controls must be designed to prevent microcomputer users from initiating unauthorized or erroneous file changes.

KINDS OF EDP CONTROLS

EDP controls are frequently classified as to **general controls** and **application controls.** Control procedures which are interactive with two or more control objectives may be classified as general controls. Those which are designed to achieve specific control objectives may be classified as application controls. General controls are broader in scope than application controls and relate to all or many computerized accounting activities. They are concerned with the organizational structure of the EDP function, the safeguarding of data files and programs, and the

FIGURE 8.6   Distributed Data Processing System

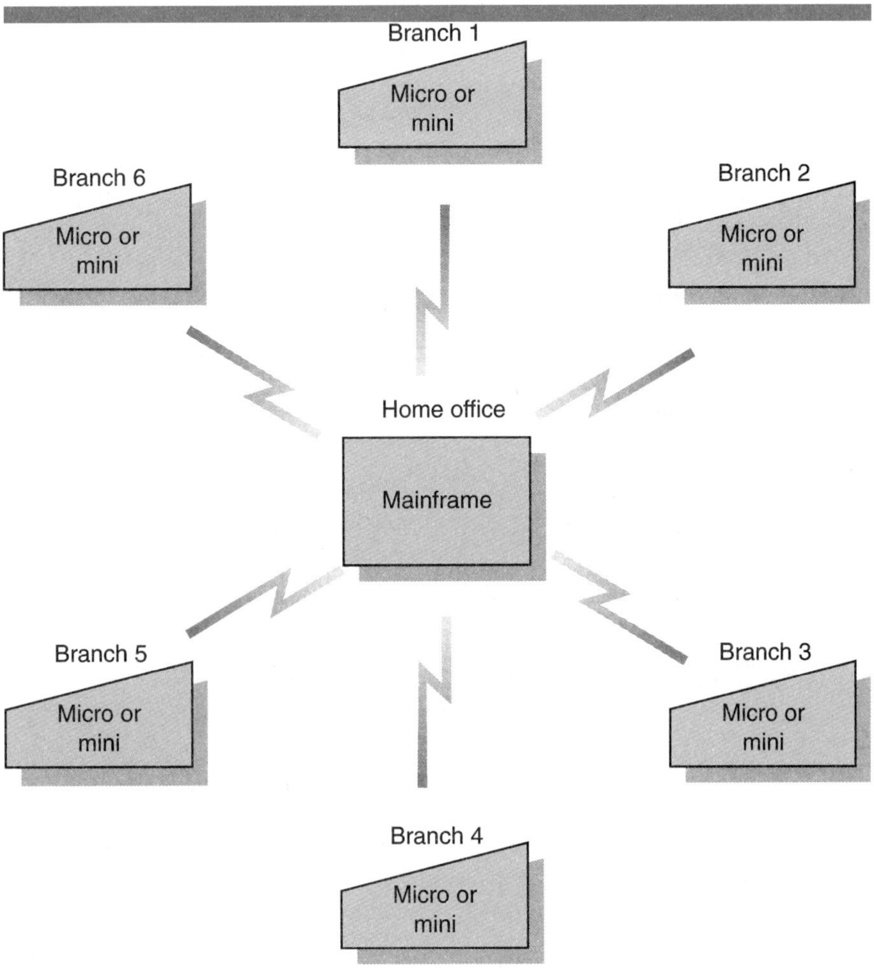

Transactions are entered at branches and processed on the home office mainframe.
Documentation is retained at the branch. Microcomputers are used as terminals
and "stand alone" computers for local processing and analysis. Microcomputers
may be networked for shared processing tasks and for communication.

adequate documentation of systems, programs, and program changes. Application
controls relate to individual computerized accounting applications and are generally
classified as to input, processing, and output controls. Inasmuch as general controls
affect all applications, auditors usually consider general control weaknesses to be
more critical than application control weaknesses.

A third category of controls, **user controls** are those controls established by
departments outside data processing whose transactions are processed by a computer. They consist of control totals to check the accuracy of data processing, as
well as provision for approval of input and review of output.

Each of these types of controls is discussed in the following paragraphs, after which the auditor's approach to control risk assessment, given EDP controls, is examined.

General Controls

Organization and Operation Controls

Because such tasks as editing, comparing, and reviewing are combined within EDP, given computer processing of transactions, care must be taken to ensure adequate separation of duties *within* the EDP function. Such separation should include at least the following employees:

1. **EDP Manager:** In overall charge of the data processing activity.
2. **Systems Analysts:** Design new systems and modify existing systems in accordance with the information needs of the users.
3. **Programmers:** Write and test programs based on the system design and/or modification.
4. **Computer Operators:** Process transactions through the system in accordance with the operator instructions for the application being updated.
5. **Input Preparation Group:** Convert input data to a machine-readable form.
6. **Librarian:** Maintains custody over master files and programs. Permits access only on the basis of proper authority.
7. **Data Control Group:** Distributes output, monitors reprocessing of errors, and compares input with output on a test basis.

Figure 8.7 is a partial organization chart showing a recommended structure for the EDP function. Note that the EDP manager reports to a sufficiently high level to ensure the necessary breadth of computer applications within the entity. Reporting to the chief accountant, or the sales manager, for example, might restrict computing goals and prevent maximum exploitation of EDP capability.

Systems Development and Documentation Controls

The processing of transactions by computer requires increased dependence on the computer systems and software for accuracy and completeness of processing. Such reliance creates a need for effective control over the definition, design, development, testing, and documentation of the systems and programs constituting each application.

In order to ensure the reliability of financial data, user groups, as well as the accounting and internal auditing staffs, should participate in the system design. To an increasing extent, especially in the design of the more complex on-line real-time systems, the independent auditors are also becoming involved in system design. The nature of independent auditor involvement is advisory and focuses on ensuring that the necessary controls are incorporated into the system.

Once a system has been designed and developed, it must be thoroughly tested before being used to process transactions on a routine basis. Such testing is usually performed by the programmers who wrote the routines to be used in the application.

FIGURE 8.7   Organization Chart for EDP Function

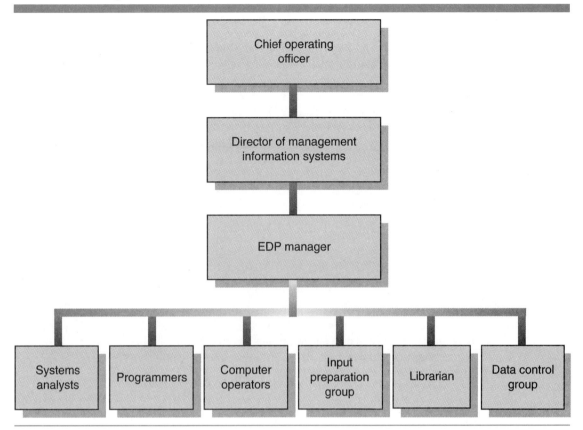

Systems and programs, as well as modifications, must be adequately docu-mented and properly approved before being used. Documentation ordinarily as-sumes the following forms:

1. System flowcharts;
2. Program flowcharts;
3. Program changes (including evidence of proper approval);
4. Operator instructions;
5. Program descriptions explaining the purpose for each part of a program.

Such documentation and approval facilitates reviewing and updating systems and programs as the environment changes. Also, good documentation makes it easier for new EDP personnel to familiarize themselves with the systems and programs in place. Finally, adequate documentation evidencing approval of changes minimizes the probability of unauthorized system and program changes that could result in loss of control and decreased reliability of financial data.

Access Controls

In order to prevent unauthorized use of files and programs, access must be limited to authorized individuals. Access controls should encompass files, programs, documentation, and hardware. In a batch processing system, such control may be achieved by fixing responsibility on a person designated as librarian. The librarian then institutes a formal "checkout" system whereby only authorized persons remove files and programs and such movements are documented by the librarian.

In an on-line system and/or EDI, access limitation is achieved through control over *passwords,* which are codes used for accessing various parts of the data base. Some of the passwords permit examining the data base (read only), whereas other codes permit updating of files (read and write capability). Data base control should include voiding the passwords of individuals leaving the employ of the company and periodic changing of passwords to ensure that only current employees with properly approved passwords may access data bases. Data base control should also provide for the fixing of responsibility over the various elements of the data base to facilitate identifying the source of any problems regarding access to and changes in data base files.

Data and Procedural Controls

This set of controls is for the purpose of controlling daily computer operations. A system of backup files stored both on and off the premises, to guard against loss of valuable files and data due to casualty or other factors, is an example of data control. Environmental controls, including temperature, humidity, and dust control are other examples of data and procedural controls.

Application Controls

A separate set of application controls is required for each computer application—for example, sales order processing, cash receipts, vouchers, cash disbursements, and payroll. Application controls are classified as to input controls, processing controls, and output controls.

Input Controls

Input controls are concerned with the accuracy and completeness of data fed into the data processing system. Examples of input controls are computer editing and recording forms.

Computer editing is the process of including programmed routines for computer checking as to validity and accuracy of input. Examples of computer editing are:

1. Tests to determine that only numeric data are entered in numeric fields, and that only alphabetic data are entered in alphabetic fields.

2. Tests for valid codes, routines that test the accuracy of code numbers entered as input into the system (e.g., customer number, product code, and employee number).

3. Tests for reasonableness, routines that cause the computer to reject input that is abnormal in amount (employee hours in excess of 50 per week is an example of a reasonableness test).

4. Completeness tests, to determine that all necessary fields contain data (e.g., name, address, and social security number for employees on the active payroll).

5. **Check digit,** a value computed by a formula when data are entered, then recomputed and compared to the original value whenever the field is used. The purpose is to verify the correctness of input or output. Account numbers, customer numbers, employee numbers, and vendor numbers are examples of check digit applications. The check digit is based on the values of the other digits in the field, and when the digit produced by the routine differs from the check digit in computer memory, an apparent input or output error has occurred.

Computer editing is a vital ingredient of the supervisory program controls in on-line real-time and EDI systems. Given the combining of functions within the supervisory programs, computer editing compensates for such controls as keypunch verification and control totals present in batch systems and manual checking in noncomputerized systems.

Recording forms are for the purpose of ensuring consistency and completeness of recurring inputs. A recording form used in recording purchases, for example, might contain the following information:

- Stock number
- Supplier number
- Quantity
- Date
- Cost per unit
- Alphabetic description

All purchases are entered on the recording form first, and then entered into the data processing stream. The audit trail is made more visible in complex EDP systems by the use of recording forms.

Processing Controls

Processing controls are those controls concerned with the manipulation of data once it is entered into the computer. An example of a processing control would be the inclusion of header and trailer label information, consisting of file name, record counts, and other data for comparison purposes. Echo checks, particularly useful in OLRT and EDI systems whereby the computer sends the message back to the sender for verification, is another example of a processing control.

Output Controls

Output controls are concerned with the verification and distribution of the computer output. Examples of output controls include: having the control group distribute printed output only to authorized recipients; adding batch totals to beginning balances and comparing with the ending balance; and maintaining an error log accessible only to the control group for the purpose of monitoring the reprocessing of errors.

Inasmuch as application controls are often dependent on general controls, the auditor may find it more efficient to review general controls before reviewing the application controls. Figure 8.8 illustrates the interdependence of general and application controls and highlights the pervasiveness of general controls. Unlimited access to data files (a general control weakness), for example, affects all applications, whereas failure to compare sales prices appearing on sales orders with master price lists affects only the sales processing application program.

User Controls

User controls are manual control procedures applied by organizational units (user groups) whose data are processed by EDP. These controls consist mainly of control totals. *Control totals* are calculated totals developed prior to submission of data for processing and later compared with the computer output. The payroll department, for example, may develop control totals for gross pay, number of checks to be processed, or total hours worked in the pay period. These totals are then compared

FIGURE 8.8   General Controls vs. Application Controls

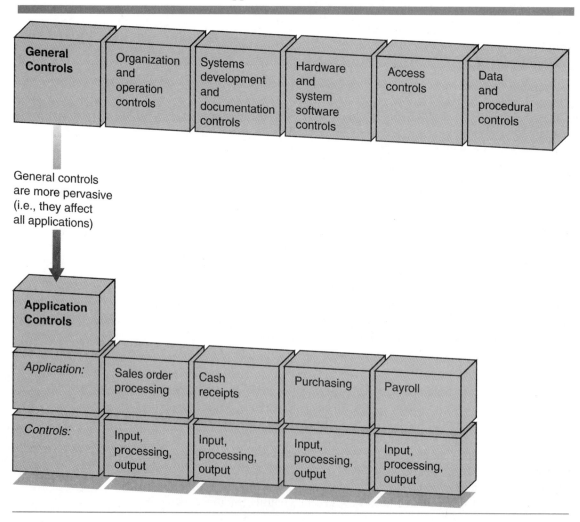

with the payroll summary output received from EDP. Accounts receivable may calculate total debits to accounts receivable, or number of sales invoices to be processed and reconcile them to the sales summary EDP output.

Control totals may consist of dollar totals (e.g., cash receipts listings), record counts (e.g., number of time cards to be processed), or *hash totals*. Hash totals have no significance other than as a control total. The sum of account numbers for those accounts to be updated, for example, may be compared with a computer generated total of account numbers actually updated in a processing run.

In designing substantive audit programs, auditors may elect to rely on user controls for the following reasons:

1. As part of the overall decision regarding evaluation of internal control structure policies and procedures, the auditor gains maximum efficiency by evaluating a mixture of EDP and user controls.

2. The EDP controls may be weak, thereby giving the auditor no alternative but to evaluate user controls for control risk assessment purposes.

3. User controls may be less costly for the auditor to test than EDP controls in more complex systems. This election may be justified only if the necessary audit objectives are attainable notwithstanding the bypassing of EDP controls. It is not justifiable on the basis of lack of auditor understanding of the EDP system.

In evaluating user controls and assessing control risk, the auditor must determine that separation of functional responsibilities within user departments is adequate; identify the controls that reconcile input with output; and obtain satisfaction that the necessary reconciliations are being made. Ordinarily, this is accomplished through observation, inquiry, and testing a sample of the documented reconciliations.

TECHNIQUES FOR TESTING EDP-BASED CONTROLS

To assess control risk for clients with EDP accounting applications, auditors must first obtain a sufficient understanding of the EDP controls to enable them to determine the significant accounting applications and to identify the essential control structure features.[2] After obtaining an understanding of the system, the auditor must identify those general and application controls for which control testing is to be performed. The next step is to test the controls as necessary. A final assessment must be made of control risk, together with documentation of the auditor's understanding of the structure and the basis for any reduction of the assessed level of control risk below the maximum level, after which substantive audit programs may be developed. The flowchart in Figure 8.9 illustrates the steps involved.

Understanding the System

The auditor can best gain an understanding of the essential accounting and control features by observing the system, asking questions of client personnel, and studying the system and program documentation.

---

[2]GAAS require that some consideration be given to a computer system when it processes significant accounting applications.

**FIGURE 8.9   Evaluating EDP Controls for Control Risk
Assessment Purposes**

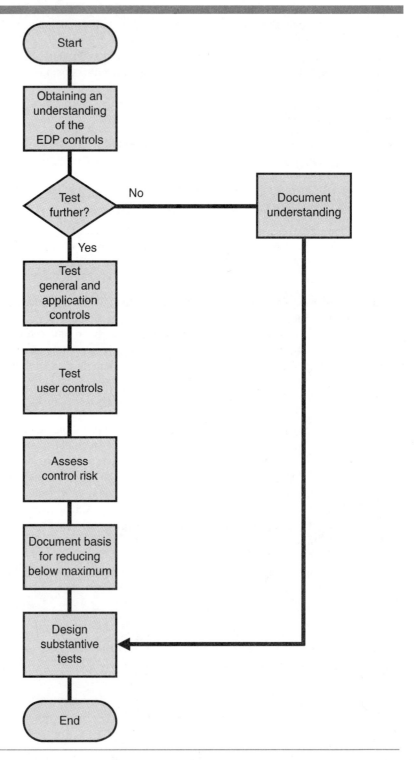

Observation and Inquiry

Observation of the system and inquiry of client personnel helps the auditor to identify and evaluate the general controls. The following specific features of the system should be covered during this phase of the review:

1. The organization and operation of the EDP function;
2. The extent to which access to data files, programs, and computer hardware is limited;
3. How new programs and program modifications are authorized, documented, and tested;
4. How systems are designed, documented, and tested;
5. The existence of hardware controls and environmental controls;
6. The extent of backup files; and
7. The functions of the data control group.

Study of Systems and Program Documentation

Narrative descriptions and flowcharts of all systems and programs should be an integral part of the documentation for each EDP application. Study of such documentation enables the auditor to identify and initially evaluate the application controls that have been included in the systems and program design. Documentation, for purposes of this phase of the review, may be classified as *systems documentation, program documentation,* and *operations documentation* (information provided to the computer operator).

The following specifications might be included by the auditor in studying the documentation for each significant accounting application:

1. Narrative descriptions of systems and programs;
2. System and program flowcharts;
3. Descriptions of input and output;
4. File descriptions;
5. Control features; and
6. Operator instructions, including a description of programs to be used, inputs and outputs required, and the sequence of cards, tapes, disks, and other files applicable to the processing run.

Control Testing to Reduce the Assessed Level of Control Risk

Through inquiry, observation, and study of documentation as just described, the auditor is able to identify the general, application, and user controls which are vital to control structure effectiveness. The next step is to perform control tests that the auditor considers cost-effective for the purpose of reducing the assessment of control risk below the maximum level. Such testing may be performed by auditing around the computer or through the computer. Figure 8.10 compares these two approaches to further testing.

FIGURE 8.10   Auditing around the Computer vs. Auditing through the Computer

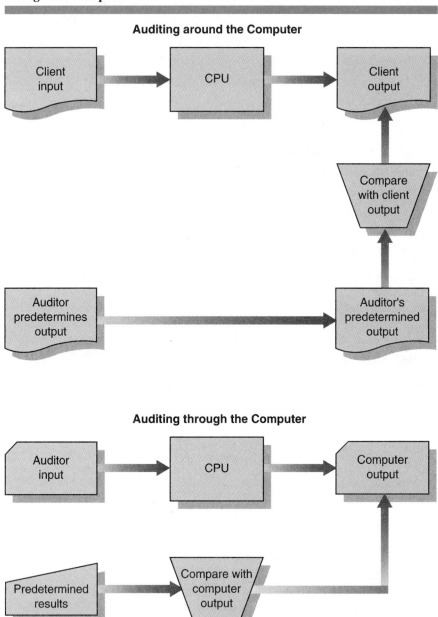

In *auditing around the computer,* the auditor concentrates on input and output, and ignores the specifics of how the computer processes data. If inputs and outputs are correct, the auditor assumes that the processing must have been accurate. In testing payroll applications, for example, the auditor might first examine selected time cards for hours and employee earnings records for rates, then trace these to the payroll summary output and compare hours, rates, and extensions. The comparison of inputs and outputs may be done manually or with the assistance of the computer. The computer assisted approach has the advantage of permitting the auditor to make more comparisons than would be possible if done manually.

Auditing through the computer involves direct testing of the programmed controls used in processing specific applications. Returning to the payroll example, the auditor identifies the controls included in the payroll application (e.g., limit tests, validity tests, and check digits) and tests them by directly observing the control functions during data processing.

Auditing around the computer has the advantage of ease of comprehension in that the tracing of source documents to output does not require any in-depth study of application programs. A major disadvantage, however, is that the auditor, not having directly tested the controls, cannot make assertions about the underlying process. Moreover, in some of the more complex EDP systems, intermediate print-outs may not be available for making the needed comparisons.

Auditing through the computer has the advantage of enabling the auditor to test EDP controls in both simple and complex systems. This approach also enables the auditor to make direct assertions about the processing of transactions. If the controls over transaction processing are determined through direct testing of the relevant controls to be reliable, the auditor may conclude that the records have an increased probability of being accurate.

Gaining adequate assurance that client programs tested are, in fact, the programs used to process client data presents a major problem in auditing through the computer. This problem is addressed in the ensuing discussion of techniques for auditing through the computer.

Techniques for Auditing Through the Computer

The following paragraphs briefly describe the more common methods used by auditors in *directly* testing EDP controls for risk assessment purposes. Each of the approaches has advantages and disadvantages. For this reason, auditors have discovered that some combination of two or more of the techniques best serves the control testing objectives.

Test Data Approach

The **test data approach** requires the preparation of simulated input data (transactions) that are processed, under the auditor's control, by the client's processing system. Some of the hypothetical transactions are valid, and some contain errors that should be detected by the controls which the auditor wishes to test. The test data should ideally contain a combination of all inputs required to execute all of the logic contained in the process. Examples of errors which might be included in testing the payroll application are the following: an employee credited with working 98 hours in a single week; an incorrect social security number; a recently terminated employee included in the current payroll. The results of the processing are then compared with the auditor's predetermined output to verify that the errors have been logged by the computer for follow-up and correction. Figure 8.11 diagrams the test data approach.

FIGURE 8.11   Test Data Approach

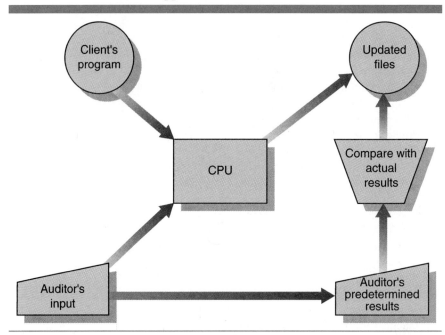

The major problems associated with the test data approach relate to the difficulty in designing test data which are sufficiently comprehensive to thoroughly test the controls for which the auditor desires further understanding, and in gaining assurance that the programs tested are the same programs used by the client in processing live transactions. The ITF approach overcomes the latter problem.

ITF Approach

The auditor, in applying the **integrated test facility approach,** creates a fictitious entity within the client's actual data files. Hypothetical data for the fictitious entity are then processed as part of the client's ongoing data processing activity. A fictitious customer account, for example, might be created and integrated into the accounts receivable ledger. The auditor introduces artificial transactions (unusual or abnormal) into the data processing system *while live data are being processed*. The company is instructed to routinely handle the business involved without actually shipping goods or mailing customer invoices to the fictitious entity.

The auditor compares the results of processing with the anticipated results as a basis for evaluating the effectiveness of accounting control over customer billings, shipments, and remittances. The ITF approach, particularly useful for testing EDI systems, is portrayed in Figure 8.12.

The principal advantage of the ITF approach is the assurance gained by the auditor that the programs tested are the same programs used by the client to process live data. The more frequently the auditor applies the test procedures during the period under audit, the stronger is such assurance. A major disadvantage, however, is the risk of damaging the client's files by failing to completely purge them of the

FIGURE 8.12   ITF Approach

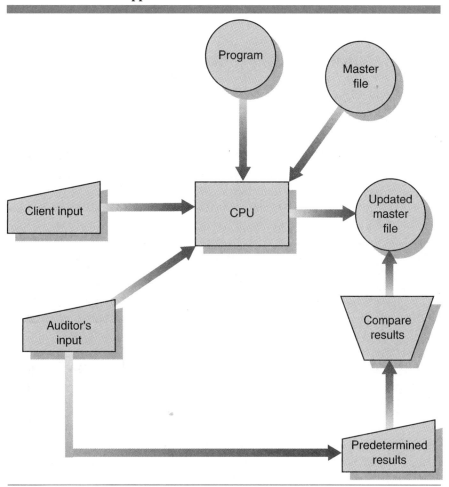

hypothetical transactions. Two alternative approaches are available for assuring that ITF transactions are promptly removed from the files. First, a "filtering" system can be used to mark the transactions, and the transactions so coded are automatically removed from the processing stream before culmination of a hypothetical transaction. A disadvantage of the filtering approach when people are inputting transactions is that it reveals the test transactions to the data processing employees. An alternative approach that retains the anonymity of test transactions is for the auditor to prepare a set of reversing journal entries for manually removing the test data at the culmination of the processing runs.

Tagging and Tracing

Tagging and tracing is a technique whereby selected transactions which pass by specific processing points are analyzed. Client programs need to be modified in order to mark or "tag" input data so that relevant information (hard copy) is displayed at key points in the processing system. The hard copy, so produced, is available only to the auditor and may describe such inputs as hours worked in a pay period in excess of 50; or sales orders processed in excess of $10,000. This enables the auditor to examine transactions at the intermediate steps in processing.

The advantage of the tagging and tracing approach lies in the use of actual data and elimination of the need for reversing journal entries. The disadvantage is that erroneous data will not necessarily be tagged. An effective combination approach may be to use the ITF approach for a few hypothetical transactions, and the tagging and tracing approach to follow live data through a complex system.

Design Phase Auditing

Most commonly associated with supervisory programs contained in on-line real-time and EDI systems, **design phase auditing** involves the auditor in the auditee's systems design. The goal is to ensure inclusion of controls that will detect exception or unusual conditions and record and log information about the initiating transactions. The special controls are intended to compensate for the loss of documentary evidence (audit trail), given on-line real-time systems and distributed processing systems.

Inasmuch as the systems associated with design phase auditing are usually complex, computer audit specialists may be needed to assist in designing the necessary controls, as well as monitoring and reviewing the control functions. A **computer audit specialist** is an employee of the CPA firm who, typically, will have served on the audit staff for a period of time, followed by specialized training in computer system design and control and EDP auditing.

Once the necessary controls have been designed and incorporated into the system, frequent visits by the auditor to the client's premises are necessary. The purpose of such visits is to determine, through observation of the data processing activity, that the controls are functioning properly.

A major advantage of design phase auditing is that it addresses the audit trail problems associated with the more complex on-line real-time systems. Lack of documentary evidence and substitution of computer checking for manual checking necessitates increased attention by the auditor to EDP accounting controls for assurance as to reliability of accounting data. This need is met by auditor participation in system design, and frequent auditor monitoring of control activity.

A possible disadvantage of design phase auditing relates to the independence issue, given auditor monitoring and review of a system which he or she helped to design. One might observe, however, that making control recommendations during the system design phase is really no different from auditor recommendations for control improvements after the fact and documented in the reportable conditions letter.

Parallel Simulation

This technique requires the auditor to create a set of application programs that simulate the processing system, and compare output from the real and simulated systems. Figure 8.13 illustrates parallel simulation.

Although a control testing technique, **parallel simulation** is, in fact, an automated version of auditing around the computer. The comparison of input with output ignores the essential characteristics of the processing system and assumes that, if the outputs are identical, the system is processing transactions accurately.

FIGURE 8.13 Parallel Simulation

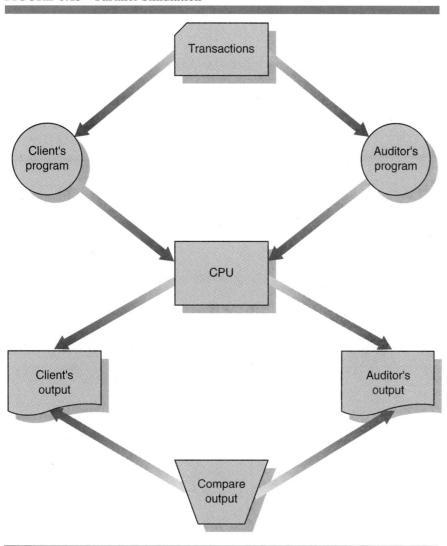

Using the computer to make such comparisons, however, significantly increases the number of data records that can be simulated. For this reason, the approach may be useful in combination with design phase auditing.

Surprise Audit

In using this technique, the auditor, on an unannounced basis—during neither the scheduled interim nor final audit phases—requests duplicate copies of client programs at the conclusion of specific processing runs. The programs are copied onto spare magnetic tape reels or disks that the auditor brings for this purpose. The "in-use" programs are then compared with the "authorized" versions which have been acquired previously by the auditor for checking purposes. Special computerized programs are available for automatically making the comparisons.

TABLE 8.1   Summary of Techniques for Auditing the Phases of Processing

Technique*	Major Feature	Advantage	Disadvantage
Test Data Approach (T)	Preparation of simulated input data processed under auditor's control	Good test of existing controls	Difficulty in designing comprehensive test data; programs tested may not be the ones used during the year
ITF Approach (T)	Fictitious entity created within client's data files; fictitious transactions processed against the entity during live processing	Tests the actual system during operation	Difficulty in removing transactions from the system
Tagging and Tracing (T)	Process of analyzing selected transactions that pass by specific processing points	Use of actual data eliminates need for reversing entries	Will not necessarily tag erroneous data
Design Phase Auditing (T)	Special controls designed to detect exceptional or unusual conditions and to record and log information about the initiating transaction	Effective method for ensuring proper controls given OLRT systems	Question of independence
Parallel Simulation (A)	Auditor creates a set of application programs that simulate processing system and compares output	Increases the number of data records that can be compared	Does not provide information concerning how transactions are processed and the controls housed in the application programs
Surprise Audit (T)	Request duplicate copies of client's programs and compare with authorized version	Discloses program modifications	Auditor may not always have a current copy of authorized version of program

*(T) indicates auditing through the computer; (A) indicates auditing around the computer.

Surprise auditing assists the auditor in determining whether client personnel are using authorized versions of programs in processing data. This approach also provides a means for assessing whether program modifications have been properly authorized and documented.

For surprise auditing to be effective, the auditor must be notified by the client whenever program changes are made. Otherwise, the auditor's copy of the client's program will not be a current copy, and the comparison will not be relevant.

Table 8.1 summarizes these techniques for testing EDP controls. Although all of the approaches have strong points, they also have weak points; and the best course for the auditor is to utilize a *combination of the methods* in order to gain satisfactory assurance as to the proper functioning of the controls.

EDP AND AUDIT RISK IMPLICATIONS

Factors Affecting Control Risk

On-line real-time (OLRT) systems and electronic data interchange (EDI) systems, as described earlier, pose increased risk to the auditor due mainly to audit trail modifications and added difficulty in control testing. OLRT systems process transactions as they occur (some automatically), and several files (e.g., sales, accounts receivable, inventory) are updated simultaneously by a single transaction input.

Some of the more common characteristics of OLRT and EDI systems are the following:

1. The use of on-line terminals for entering transactions from remote locations;
2. Integrated data bases maintained in the form of disk files;
3. Supervisory programs (DBMS) for storing programs and managing the system.
4. Absence of documentation (e.g., when EDI processes transactions directly from sending computer to receiving computer). Figure 8.14 illustrates an OLRT system.

Audit trail modification associated with OLRT and EDI systems consists mainly of decreased transaction documentation. Inasmuch as transactions are entered at remote locations and transactions and balances are stored internally, the need for the more traditional documentation is reduced. Moreover, documents used to enter information into the computer for processing may, for the reasons cited earlier, exist for only a short period. In some computer systems, input documents may not exist at all because information is directly entered into the system.[3]

Temporary, rather than long-term, retention of documents may require that the auditor visit the client's premises frequently during the year and audit transactions while the hard copy still exists. Situations in which documentation does not exist at all require increased attention to the controls housed in the supervisory programs. To justify assessing control risk below maximum, more testing needs to be performed by the auditor. Such testing is more difficult, however, given the increased vulnerability of the client's files to destruction during the testing process.

---

[3]*AICPA Professional Standards, op. cit.*, Section AU 311.09.

FIGURE 8.14   On-Line Real-Time System

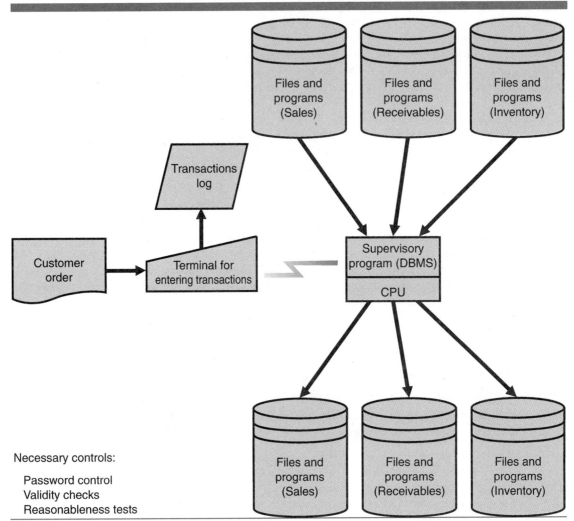

Necessary controls:

  Password control
  Validity checks
  Reasonableness tests

How Mitigated

Suggested means for *reducing the control risk* associated with OLRT systems are the following:

1. Systems, programs, and modifications should be well-documented, and modifications should be properly approved and reviewed.

2. Access to input terminals should be restricted by effective control over passwords and by assigning responsibility for elements of the data base. In distributed systems utilizing a mainframe linked to microcomputers at numerous remote locations, specially designed software has been developed to strengthen input controls. Referred to generally as the "PC-mainframe link," the software controls the flow of data between a mainframe and a PC. This is achieved by

"change controllers" within the programs that limit access to either all or specified files through a system of passwords as well as user identification codes.

3. Passwords should be changed frequently and former passwords voided.

4. Passwords assigned to former employees should be voided upon termination of employment.

5. In designing OLRT systems, careful attention should be given to input editing. Examples of input editing controls are validity tests for checking customer or employee numbers, stock numbers, prices or pay rates, vendor numbers, and so on; limit or reasonableness tests; echo checks; and balance checks (e.g., debits equal credits for each transaction entered).

6. All computer activities should be logged into a history file with user identification, terminal identification, time, and date.

7. Journal files should be maintained for backup (such files may be kept on tape or disks).

Like OLRT, EDI systems also increase audit risk. Although EDI should increase processing accuracy, lower inventory investment through reduced lead times, and provide for more timely information, this means of processing transactions poses serious control and audit challenges. First, like other on-line real-time systems, the audit trail is diminished. Moreover, given automatic initiation of certain transactions (e.g., inventory reorder when minimum levels are reached), authorizations may be difficult to verify and the risk of unauthorized persons transmitting messages increases. To compensate for these challenges, compensating controls should be in place, and the auditor needs to obtain an understanding of these controls and test them as appropriate. The following are examples of possible controls:

1. Strict identification and password controls housed in the software should permit only specified individuals to perform a given type of transaction.

2. Terminals can be limited to perform only certain transactions.

3. Software can be programmed to produce a log of transactions showing date, time, type of transaction, and operator.

4. *Data encryption* can be used, whereby an encoding key is used by the sender to "scramble" the message. The receiver must then have the corresponding key to unscramble and read the message. With data encryption, strict security must be maintained over the encoding keys.

5. The EDI software should contain input and receiving edit controls that detect errors and print them in the form of an error log. The EDP control group would then handle the reprocessing of the errors.

6. An **echo check** may also be programmed into the EDI software, whereby the receiving computer returns the message to the sending computer for confirmation that information received is the same as information sent.

Case 8.1, involving computer fraud, illustrates the importance of unique controls for OLRT and EDI systems and the need for auditor evaluation of these controls in EDP systems. In this case, the auditors either did not detect the control weaknesses, or failed to properly evaluate the full effects of those weaknesses.

CASE 8.1

San Fernando Valley Wholesalers

Case Description

San Fernando Valley Wholesalers sold furniture and appliances to retailers located in western United States, primarily California. All of the company's 200 salespersons were on a commission basis. Sales commissions were paid biweekly on the basis of a computer printout of commission checks. A commission listing register was also printed out by the computer.

San Fernando used an on-line system for processing sales orders and calculating commissions. Sales orders were entered by way of terminals located at the company's 20 regional sales offices. The computer was programmed to check for proper salesperson number, customer number, product code, price, and customer credit limit. In addition, commission rates for each product code were stored in the computer, thereby permitting automatic calculation and storage of commissions for each sales order. In printing the biweekly commission checks and listing, the computer was also programmed to print checks only for sales orders that had been shipped and billed.

Gerald Collins, the San Francisco regional sales manager, was also a trained accountant and computer programmer, and before joining San Fernando's marketing staff, he had been a computer audit specialist for a large regional CPA firm. His CPA certificate and license to practice had been revoked in 1982 upon conviction for accepting bribes from a client. After joining San Fernando, he had made it a point to become familiar with the company's sales processing system. As such, he thoroughly understood the programmed controls and knew that a sales invoice number and shipping order number were needed in order to complete a sales commission transaction. Although the regional sales managers were not entitled to earn commissions, Collins devised a scheme for paying himself fraudulent commissions. Using the employee number of one of his recently terminated salesmen, he entered fictitious sales order, shipping order, and sales invoice numbers. To conceal the overstatement of sales, he reversed the entries prior to the monthly sales printout.

Joel Harris & Associates, CPAs, had been auditing San Fernando for several years and were not aware of Collins' thefts, which had been occurring since 1988. Laura Henry, a recently promoted senior auditor for Joel Harris, was designated the in-charge auditor for the 1991 San Fernando audit. Henry decided, as part of her analytical procedures, to apply commission rates to sales by regional sales office and compare with commissions paid. This had not been done previously, and Henry wished to perform the test, given the significance of "commissions expense" in the 1991 income statement. She was also concerned with the apparent lack of control over passwords permitting access to the home office computer data base and the failure to log and periodically account for sales order and shipping order numbers. Failure to perform a record count and comparison with currently active employees at the conclusion of the commission processing computer run also troubled Henry.

Henry's test revealed that commissions paid materially exceeded the calculated commissions for the San Francisco office. Suspecting possible fraud, Henry arranged a conference with Herbert Mills, the audit manager for the San Fernando audit. They agreed that the amounts involved did not materially impact the 1991 financial statements, but that they should notify Elizabeth Stone, San Fernando's corporate controller, of the control weaknesses and possible fraud. Upon learning of the situation, Stone directed the internal audit staff to conduct an investigation. After a lengthy investigation, the internal audit manager, accompanied by Stone, confronted Collins, who admitted to stealing approximately $500,000 in fraudulent commissions since 1988. San Fernando's management and board of directors decided to sue Joel Harris & Associates for not detecting the fraud during their 1988 to 1991 audits.

What Would You Have Done?

Laura Henry was correct in relating the control weaknesses involving sales order processing to the results of her analytical procedures. The following controls for preventing errors and irregularities were absent in San Fernando's sales and commission processing system:

1. Passwords for terminated employees should be voided;
2. Only authorized persons should be permitted to enter sales orders;
3. Sales order and shipping order numbers should be controlled and periodically accounted for;
4. Sales personnel should not be able to introduce journal entries into the system;
5. The system should provide for deducting commissions on returned sales from the following period's commissions;
6. The computer should be programmed to compare the names appearing on the commission register with a listing of currently active salespersons stored in the computer.

Henry was also correct in arranging the conference with Mr. Mills, the audit manager, rather than proceeding with her own investigation. Although the fraud was significant in total, it was not considered material to San Fernando's 1991 financial statements. Under such circumstances, the independent auditors should notify the client that a fraud is suspected. The client then decides whether to investigate further. If the decision is to investigate further, the client may select either the auditors or their own employees to conduct the investigation.

What Was Done?

If the control weaknesses discovered by Laura Henry in 1991 also existed from 1988 to 1990, Henry's predecessor on the San Fernando audit may have been negligent for not detecting and evaluating the weaknesses and for not notifying management of the weaknesses. The auditors, however, should not have been expected to detect the frauds that, in this instance, did not have a material impact on the assertions contained in the financial statements. Management is responsible for designing, implementing, and monitoring a satisfactory control structure. Management cannot expect the independent auditors to discover defalcations that result from management's own negligence.

Although the characteristics of OLRT and EDI systems described in this section pose risk problems for the auditor, other aspects of these systems serve to strengthen the internal control structure. Input editing features that test transaction input for validity, reasonableness, and proper account distribution ensure that all transactions will be consistently processed. Such processing consistency virtually eliminates the occurrence of clerical errors normally associated with manual systems.[4]

Managing Detection Risk

When confronted by OLRT and EDI systems, the auditor can reduce detection risk by giving careful consideration to the following:

1. Auditors need to become more involved in system design, given the lack of transaction documentation associated with OLRT and EDI systems. Such participation is necessary in order to ensure that the supervisory programs contain the necessary controls for proper input editing. Auditor participation may also provide for tagging certain types of transaction conditions for later follow-up by the audit team and for supplying the auditor with copies of all programs and program modifications relating to significant accounting applications.

2. Greater use by the audit team of computer audit specialists may be necessary in light of the complexities associated with OLRT and EDI systems and the related danger of file destruction during testing. The primary role of the specialist is to assist in the design phase; but assistance during internal control testing is also quite common in practice.

3. Control testing by means of more frequent visits to the client's premises (quarterly or monthly) to observe the functioning of control activities may become necessary as systems become more advanced. Termed *continuous auditing,* this transition in form of control testing is necessitated by both the lack of documentation and the more temporary nature of document retention associated with OLRT systems.

4. The independent auditors may elect to rely on the internal audit staff for assistance in evaluating the design and review of control procedures. Indeed, the internal auditors may have a better understanding of the day-to-day data processing routine and may therefore be in a better position than the independent auditors to identify the necessary control points. Such reliance is warranted provided the independent auditors can determine that the internal auditors possess reasonable competence and report to a sufficiently high level within the organization to ensure an adequate degree of objectivity in the conduct of their activities.[5]

5. Computer assistance may be required in order for the auditor to analyze certain data, given internal storage of transactions and files. Commonly referred to as auditing with the computer, this topic is more fully addressed in Chapter 9.

---

[4]Such assurance, one might note, is not limited to OLRT systems, but is present whenever transactions are processed by EDP systems containing the necessary programmed control features.

[5]AICPA *Professional Standards, op. cit.,* Section AU 322.

6. Auditors must be alert to the increased potential for management fraud given computer capability for altering data bases and fabricating documentation for nonexistent transactions. Case 8.2 illustrates how a client enlisted the aid of the computer in facilitating the manufacture of fraudulent insurance policies.

CASE 8.2

Freedom Insurance Company

Case Description

Robert Mull, the partner in charge of the Freedom Insurance Company audit, could not understand how his audit team could have overlooked $133 million of fictitious insurance policies during the 1992 audit. Mull, Geneer, & Associates, CPAs, had been conducting the Freedom audit for five years, and this was the first knowledge they had of the fraud.

A business practice called *reinsurance* is common in the life insurance industry. Under reinsurance, one company sells its policies to another insurance company, receiving the discounted value of future premiums less a service charge. The buying company then collects the premiums and pays any claims resulting from death or other causes. Since 1987, Freedom, with the support and guidance of its CEO, John LaFeet, and with the aid of its latest generation computer, had been manufacturing fictitious insurance policies and selling them to other insurance companies under the guise of reinsurance. Freedom, of course, would have to remit the premiums from its own assets, inasmuch as the purported policy holders did not exist. The company also filed occasional claims based on the death of fictitious policy holders. Actuarial tables, stored in the computer, provided the information necessary to determine an appropriate number, as well as the timing of claims, for death benefits.

Freedom began the fraudulent reinsurance practice in 1987 as a means for solving a short-term liquidity problem. John LaFeet later decided to use the practice to achieve growth and leadership status in the insurance industry. By 1992, the portfolio of fictitious policies had grown to $133 million, nearly 30 percent of Freedom's outstanding policies.

Inasmuch as the buying companies did not follow the practice of confirming the policies with individual holders, the probability of detection from that source was remote. The independent auditors, on the other hand, presented a threat of detection. They followed the practice of selecting a sample of policies and examining them in detail, including the underlying documentation. They also confirmed the selected policies with the policyholders. Inclusion of one or more of the fictitious policies in the sample could lead to detection. To overcome this threat, LaFeet and his management team "rifled" the auditors' workpapers during lunch breaks until they discovered the auditors' sampling plan, including policy numbers for which documentation was to be requested. Then, Freedom employees, with the aid of the computer, manufactured all the necessary supporting documentation for all bogus policies included in the plan. Addresses of employees who were part of the fraud were used as policyholders' addresses, thus ensuring return of auditor confirmation requests. The files were then held "at the ready" until requested by the auditors.

The fraud continued for five years and only came to light when a disgruntled ex-employee granted an interview to a leading financial periodical. During the interview, the employee described the fraud and admitted his own role in John LaFeet's plan for growth.

What Would You Do?

Although the auditors may have properly questioned the rapid growth in Freedom's reinsurance business, the fabricated documentation would have removed any suspicion of fraud. The fabricated documentation was made possible in this case through management override of the control system. Management override, as described in Chapter 6, is one of the inherent limitations present even in the most effective internal control structure. Auditors, under conditions of management override, cannot be expected to detect cleverly concealed frauds.

LaFeet's use of computerized actuarial tables provided for an appropriate number of death claims proportionate to outstanding policies. Application of analytical procedures by the auditors, therefore, should not have produced any unusual findings.

What Was Done?

The one act of negligence committed by the auditors was in not properly safeguarding their audit workpapers. LaFeet's knowledge of the sampling plan provided the needed ingredient, without which concealment would have been difficult. Auditors should not leave workpapers lying unattended during periods of absence, such as lunch breaks. Access to computerized audit workpapers should be limited by use of passwords known only to the auditors. Hard copy workpapers should be returned to auditor carrying cases and locked.

Except for this carelessness, the auditors conducted an effective examination, properly relying on controls that appeared to be functioning effectively and correctly applying audit sampling methods in selecting policies for detailed examination and confirmation.

KEY TERMS

Application controls	Librarian
Auditing around the computer	Microcomputer
Auditing through the computer	Networking
Batch processing	On-line real-time system
Check digit	Output controls
Computer audit specialist	Parallel simulation
Computer operator	Phases of processing
Data control group	Processing controls
Design phase auditing	Programmer
Distributed processing	Real-time processing
Echo check	Results of processing
Electronic data interchange (EDI)	Systems analyst
General controls	Tagging and tracing
Input controls	Test data approach
Integrated data base systems	Time sharing
Integrated test facility approach	User controls

1. Define and give an example of general controls, application controls, and user controls.
2. Differentiate between auditing around and through the computer.
3. Explain why the audit approach may need to be modified, given the existence of significant EDP accounting applications.
4. In what respects does the audit trail assume a different form when transactions are processed by computer?
5. Differentiate between batch processing systems and real-time processing systems.
6. Why are real-time processing systems ordinarily more difficult to audit than batch processing systems?
7. What is an EDI system and what are its advantages and disadvantages?
8. What constitutes adequate separation of functional responsibilities within the EDP function?
9. Why are systems and program documentation important to effective internal control?
10. How does access control differ between batch systems and on-line systems?
11. What function does a "recording" form serve? What information should be included on the form?
12. Why might the auditor prefer to review general controls before reviewing application controls?
13. List three possible reasons for auditor testing of user controls.
14. Describe the sequence of steps to be followed by the auditor in studying control structure policies and procedures for clients with EDP accounting applications.
15. How does the auditor gain an understanding of the essential accounting and control features of an EDP accounting system?
16. How does the auditor review and test user controls?
17. Why do auditors prefer to apply a combination of techniques in directly testing computer controls?
18. Identify the advantages and disadvantages of each of the following "through the computer" techniques:
    a. Test data approach
    b. ITF approach
    c. Tagging and tracing
    d. Design phase auditing
19. Parallel simulation is thought to be an automated version of auditing around the computer. Explain why.
20. On-line real-time systems and EDI systems affect audit risk in two offsetting ways. Explain how.
21. Why should auditors become more involved in OLRT systems design?

1. Smith Corporation has numerous customers. A customer file is kept on disk storage. Each customer file contains name, address, credit limit, and account balance. The auditor wishes to test this file to determine whether credit limits are being exceeded. The best procedure for the auditors to follow would be to

    a. Develop test data that would cause some account balances to exceed the credit limit and determine if the system properly detects such situations.

    b. Develop a program to compare credit limits with account balances and print out the details of any account with a balance exceeding its credit limit.

    c. Request a printout of all account balances so they can be manually checked against the credit limits.

    d. Request a printout of a sample of account balances so they can be individually checked against the credit limits.

2. Which of the following is an example of a check digit?

    a. An agreement of the total number of employees to the total number of checks printed by the computer.

    b. An algebraically determined number produced by the other digits of the employee number.

    c. A logic test that ensures all employee numbers are nine digits.

    d. A limit check that an employee's hours do not exceed 50 hours per work week.

3. When an auditor tests a computerized accounting system, which of the following is true of the test data approach?

    a. Test data are processed by the client's computer programs under the auditor's control.

    b. Test data must consist of all possible valid and invalid conditions.

    c. Testing a program at year end provides assurance that the client's processing was accurate for the full year.

    d. Several transactions of each type must be tested.

4. An EDP input control is designed to ensure that

    a. Machine processing is accurate.

    b. Only authorized personnel have access to the computer area.

    c. Data received for processing are properly authorized and converted to machine-readable form.

    d. Electronic data processing has been performed as intended for the particular application.

5. Adequate technical training and proficiency as an auditor encompasses an ability to understand an EDP system sufficiently to identify and evaluate

    a. The processing and imparting of information.

    b. Essential accounting control features.

    c. All accounting control features.

    d. The degree to which programming conforms with application of generally accepted accounting principles.

6. When erroneous data are detected by computer program controls, such data may be excluded from processing and printed on an error report. This error report should be reviewed and followed up by the

    a. Computer operator.

    b. Systems analyst.

    c. EDP control group.

    d. Computer programmer.

7. Auditing by testing the input and output of an EDP system instead of the computer program itself will

    a. Not detect program errors that do not show up in the output sampled.

    b. Detect all program errors, regardless of the nature of the output.

    c. Provide the auditor with the same type of evidence.

    d. Not provide the auditor with confidence in the results of the auditing procedures.

8. After a preliminary review of a client's EDP control, an auditor may decide not to perform further tests related to the control procedures within the EDP portion of the client's internal control structure. Which of the following would not be a valid reason for choosing to omit further tests?

    a. The controls duplicate operative controls existing elsewhere in the system.

    b. There appear to be major weaknesses that would preclude further testing.

    c. The time and dollar costs of testing exceed the time and dollar savings in substantive testing if the further tests show the controls to be operative.

    d. The controls appear adequate to provide a basis for assessing control risk below the maximum level.

9. When an on-line real-time (OLRT) electronic data processing system is in use, internal control can be strengthened by

    a. Providing for the separation of duties between keypunching and error listing operations.

    b. Attaching plastic file protection rings to reels of magnetic tape before new data can be entered on the file.

    c. Making a validity check of an identification number before a user can obtain access to the computer files.

    d. Preparing batch totals to provide assurance that file updates are made for the entire input.

10. Which of the following is not a characteristic of a batch processed computer system?

    a. The collection of like transactions that are sorted and processed sequentially against a master file.

    b. Keypunching of transactions, followed by machine processing.

    c. The production of numerous printouts.

    d. The posting of a transaction, as it occurs, to several files, without intermediate printouts.

11. Which of the following computer documentation would an auditor most likely utilize in obtaining an understanding of the internal control structure?

    a. Systems flowcharts.

    b. Record counts.

    c. Program listings.

    d. Record layouts.

12. To obtain evidential matter about control risk, an auditor ordinarily selects tests from a variety of techniques, including

    a. Analysis.

    b. Confirmations.

    c. Reperformance.

    d. Comparison.

13. Which of the following audit techniques most likely would provide an auditor with the most assurance about the effectiveness of the operation of an internal control procedure?

    a. Inquiry of client personnel.

    b. Recomputation of account balance amounts.

    c. Observation of client personnel.

    d. Confirmation with outside parties.

14. An auditor wishes to perform tests of controls on a client's cash disbursements procedures. If the control procedures leave *no* audit trail of documentary evidence, the auditor most likely will test the procedures by

    a. Inquiry and analytical procedures.

    b. Confirmation and observation.

    c. Observation and inquiry.

    d. Analytical procedures and confirmation.

15. An auditor's flowchart of a client's accounting system is a diagrammatic representation that depicts the auditor's

    a. Program for tests of controls.

    b. Understanding of the system.

    c. Understanding of the types of irregularities that are probable, given the present system.

    d. Documentation of the study and evaluation of the system.

16. Which of the following statements most likely represents a disadvantage for an entity that keeps microcomputer prepared data files rather than manually prepared files?

    a. It is usually more difficult to detect transposition errors.

    b. Transactions are usually authorized before they are executed and recorded.

    c. It is usually easier for unauthorized persons to access and alter the files.

    d. Random error associated with processing similar transactions in different ways is usually greater.

17. Internal control is ineffective when computer department personnel

    a. Participate in computer software acquisition decisions.

    b. Design documentation for computerized systems.

    c. Originate changes in master files.

    d. Provide physical security for program files.

18. Which of the following most likely represents a weakness in the internal control structure of an EDP system?

    a. The systems analyst reviews output and controls the distribution of output from the EDP department.

    b. The accounts payable clerk prepares data for computer processing and enters the data into the computer.

    c. The systems programmer designs the operating and control functions of programs and participates in testing operating systems.

    d. The control clerk establishes control over data received by the EDP department and reconciles control totals after processing.

19. When EDP programs or files can be accessed from terminals, users should be required to enter a(an)

    a. Parity check.

    b. Personal identification code.

    c. Self-diagnosis test.

    d. Echo check.

20. The possibility of erasing a large amount of information stored on magnetic tape most likely would be reduced by the use of

    a. File protection rings.

   b. Check digits.

   c. Completeness tests.

   d. Conversion verification.

21. When an accounting application is processed by computer, an auditor can *not* verify the reliable operation of programmed control procedures by

   a. Manually comparing detail transaction files used by an edit program to the program's generated error listings to determine that errors were properly identified by the edit program.

   b. Constructing a processing system for accounting applications and processing actual data from throughout the period through both the client's program and the auditor's program.

   c. Manually reperforming, as of a point in time, the processing of input data and comparing the simulated results to the actual results.

   d. Periodically submitting auditor prepared test data to the same computer process and evaluating the results.

22. When an auditor tests a computerized accounting system, which of the following is true of the test data approach?

   a. Test data must consist of all possible valid and invalid conditions.

   b. The program tested is different from the program used throughout the year by the client.

   c. Several transactions of each type must be tested.

   d. Test data are processed by the client's computer programs under the auditor's control.

23. An auditor who is testing EDP controls in a payroll system would most likely use test data that contain conditions such as

   a. Deductions *not* authorized by employees.

   b. Overtime *not* approved by supervisors.

   c. Time tickets with invalid job numbers.

   d. Payroll checks with unauthorized signatures.

24. To obtain evidence that user identification and password controls are functioning as designed, an auditor would most likely

   a. Attempt to sign on to the system using invalid user identifications and passwords.

   b. Write a computer program that simulates the logic of the client's access control software.

   c. Extract a random sample of processed transactions and ensure that the transactions were appropriately authorized.

   d. Examine statements signed by employees stating that they have *not* divulged their user identifications and passwords to any other person.

25. Processing data through the use of simulated files provides an auditor with information about the operating effectiveness of control policies and procedures. One of the techniques involved in this approach makes use of

   a. Input validation.

   b. Program code checking.

   c. Controlled reprocessing.

   d. Integrated test facility.

26. Which of the following computer-assisted auditing techniques allows fictitious and real transactions to be processed together without client operating personnel being aware of the testing process?

    a. Parallel simulation.

    b. Integrated testing facility approach.

    c. Test data approach.

    d. Exception report tests.

27. Errors in data processed in a batch computer system may *not* be detected immediately because

    a. Transaction trails in a batch system are available only for a limited period of time.

    b. There are time delays in processing transactions in a batch system.

    c. Errors in some transactions cause rejection of other transactions in the batch.

    d. Random errors are more likely in a batch system than in an on-line system.

28. An auditor would most likely be concerned with which of the following controls in a distributed data processing system?

    a. Hardware controls.

    b. Systems documentation controls.

    c. Access controls.

    d. Disaster recovery controls.

29. In a computerized payroll system environment, an auditor would be *least* likely to use test data to test controls related to

    a. Missing employee numbers.

    b. Proper approval of overtime by supervisors.

    c. Time tickets with invalid job numbers.

    d. Agreement of hours per clock cards with hours on time tickets.

30. To gain access to a bank's on-line customer systems, users must validate themselves with a user identification code and password. The purpose of this procedure is to provide

    a. Data security.

    b. Physical security.

    c. Context-dependent security.

    d. Write-protection security.

31. In auditing an on-line perpetual inventory system, an auditor selected certain file updating transactions for detailed testing. The audit technique which will provide a computer trail of all relevant processing steps applied to a specific transaction is described as

    a. Simulation.

    b. Snapshot.

    c. Code comparison.

    d. Tagging and tracing.

ESSAY QUESTIONS AND PROBLEMS

8.1 Increasing use of sophisticated EDP systems has produced significant changes in the accounting environment. Some of these changes are the following:

    a. Documents that are used to enter information into the computer may exist for only a short time or only in computer-readable form. In some computer systems, input documents may not exist at all because information is entered directly into the system.

    b. Computer processing uniformly subjects like transactions to the same processing instructions.

    c. Many internal control procedures, once performed by separate individuals in manual systems, may be concentrated in systems that use computer processing.

    d. The potential for individuals to gain unauthorized access to data or assets may be greater in computerized accounting systems than in manual systems.

Required:

For each of the changes, discuss the impact on the internal control structure and the independent audit.

8.2 The importance of input editing increases with the complexity of EDP systems.

    a. What is meant by input editing?

    b. Give two examples each of input editing routines for payroll processing and sales order processing.

    c. Why does input editing become increasingly significant as the complexity of EDP systems increases?

8.3 As more and more clients install complex EDP accounting systems, independent auditors are participating to an increasing extent in systems design. At the same time, the independent auditor's use of computer audit specialists is growing.

Required:

    a. What is "design phase" auditing and why is it important?

    b. In what way does design phase auditing affect auditor independence?

    c. What function does the "computer audit specialist" serve?

    d. To what extent may the independent auditor rely on the computer audit specialist?

8.4 User controls are manual control procedures applied by organizational units (user groups) whose data is processed by EDP.

    a. Give two examples each of user controls for a payroll application and a sales order processing application.

    b. Under what circumstances might an auditor elect to test user controls?

    c. Discuss the auditor's approach to further testing of user controls.

8.5 When auditing an electronic data processing (EDP) accounting system, the independent auditor should have a general familiarity with the effects of the use of EDP on various characteristics of the control structure and on the auditor's study of such control. The independent auditor must be aware of those control procedures that are commonly referred to as *general controls* and those that are commonly referred to as *application controls*. General controls relate to all EDP activities and application controls relate to specific accounting tasks.

Required:

    a. What general controls should exist in EDP-based accounting systems?

    b. What are the purposes of each of the following categories of application controls?

       1. Input controls;

       2. Processing controls;

       3. Output controls. (AICPA adapted)

8.6 Johnson, a CPA, was engaged to examine the financial statements of Horizon, Incorporated, which has its own computer installation. During the preliminary review, Johnson found that Horizon lacked proper segregation of the programming and operating functions. As a result, Johnson intensified the study and evaluation of the internal control procedures surrounding the computer and concluded that the compensating general controls provided reasonable assurance that the objectives of the internal control structure were being met.

Required:
a. In a properly functioning EDP environment, how is the separation of the programming and operating functions achieved?
b. What are the compensating general controls that Johnson most likely found? Do not discuss hardware and application controls. (AICPA adapted)

8.7 You are reviewing the audit workpapers containing a narrative description of the Tenney Corporation's factory payroll system. A portion of that narrative is as follows:

Factory employees punch time clock cards each day when entering or leaving the shop. At the end of each week the timekeeping department collects the time cards and prepares duplicate batch-control slips by department showing total hours and number of employees. The time cards and original batch-control slips are sent to the payroll accounting section. The second copies of the batch-control slips are filed by date.

In the payroll accounting section, payroll transaction cards are keypunched from the information on the time cards, and a batch total card for each batch is keypunched from the batch-control slip. The time cards and batch-control slips are then filed by batch for possible reference. The payroll transaction cards and batch total card are sent to data processing where they are sorted by employee number within batch. Each batch is edited by a computer program that checks the validity of employee number against a master employee tape file and the total hours and number of employees against the batch total card. A detail printout by batch and employee number is produced which indicates batches that do not balance and invalid employee numbers. This printout is returned to payroll accounting to resolve all differences.

In searching for documentation, you found a flowchart of the payroll system that included all appropriate symbols, but was only partially labeled. The portion of this flowchart described by the above narrative appears as Figure 8.15.

Required:
a. Number your answer 1 through 17. Next to the corresponding number of your answer, supply the appropriate labeling (document name, process description, file order) for each numbered symbol on the flowchart.
b. Flowcharts are one of the aids an auditor may use to determine and evaluate a client's internal control structure. List the advantages of using flowcharts in this context. (AICPA adapted)

8.8 The following four topics are part of the relevant body of knowledge for CPAs having field work or immediate supervisory responsibility in audits involving a computer:
a. Electronic data processing equipment and its capabilities.
b. Organization and management of the data processing function.
c. Characteristics of computer-based systems.
d. Computer center operations.

FIGURE 8.15 **Flowchart for Problem 8.7**

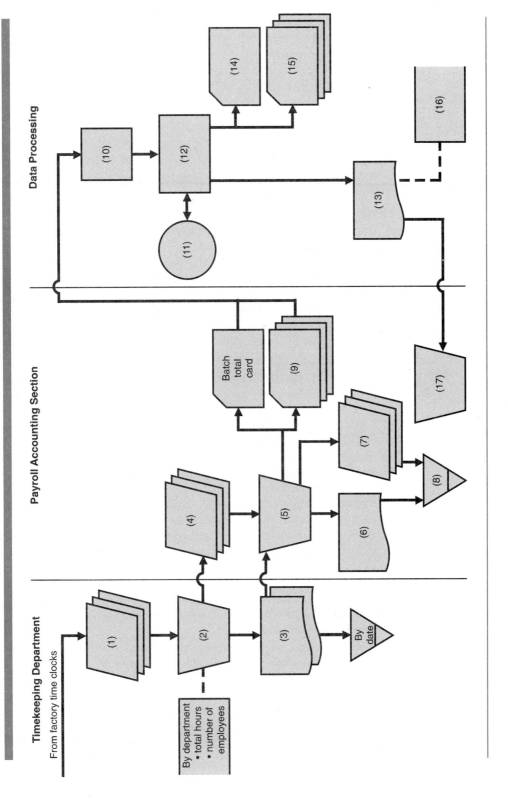

CPAs who are responsible for computer audits should possess certain general knowledge with respect to each of these four topics. For example, on the subject of EDP equipment and its capabilities, the auditor should have a general understanding of computer equipment and should be familiar with the uses and capabilities of the central processor and the peripheral equipment.

Required:

For each of the topics numbered *b* through *d*, describe the general knowledge that should be possessed by those CPAs who are responsible for computer audits. (AICPA adapted)

8.9 Programmed control procedures may be tested by using one or more of the following means: test data approach, ITF approach, tagging and tracing, and surprise audit.

Required:

a. Briefly define each of the above testing alternatives and identify the primary advantage and disadvantage of each.
b. Why is some combination of the above approaches usually advisable?
c. Differentiate between auditing around the computer and auditing through the computer.
d. Parallel simulation has been characterized as an "automated version of auditing around the computer." Explain why. Under what circumstances might the auditor elect to use parallel simulation?

8.10 Ajax, Inc., an audit client, recently installed a new EDP system to process more efficiently the shipping, billing, and accounts receivable records. During interim work, an assistant completed the review of the accounting system and the internal controls. The assistant determined the following information concerning the new EDP system and the processing and control of shipping notices and customer invoices.

Each major computerized function, i.e, shipping, billing, accounts receivable, etc., is permanently assigned to a specific computer operator who is responsible for making program changes, running the program, and reconciling the computer log. Responsibility for the custody and control over the magnetic tapes and system documentation is randomly rotated among the computer operators on a monthly basis to prevent any one person from having access to the tapes and documentation at all times. Each computer programmer and computer operator has access to the computer room via a magnetic card and a digital code that is different for each card. The systems analyst and the supervisor of the computer operators do not have access to the computer room.

The EDP system documentation consists of the following items: program listing, error listing, logs, and record layout. To increase efficiency, batch totals and processing controls are omitted from the system.

Ajax ships its products directly from two warehouses which forward shipping notices to general accounting. There, the billing clerk enters the price of the item and accounts for the numerical sequence of the shipping notices. The billing clerk also prepares daily adding machine tapes of the units shipped and the sales amount. Shipping notices and adding machine tapes are forwarded to the computer department for processing. The computer output consists of:

- A three-copy invoice that is forwarded to the billing clerk, and

- A daily sales register showing the aggregate totals of units shipped and sales amounts that the computer operator compares to the adding machine tapes.

The billing clerk mails two copies of each invoice to the customer and retains the third copy in an open invoice file that serves as a detail accounts receivable record.

Required:

a. Prepare an internal control flowchart for Ajax's shipping and billing subset of the revenue cycle.

b. Based on the narrative and your flowchart, identify the control weaknesses.

c. Describe one specific recommendation for correcting each condition in internal controls in the new EDP system and for correcting each condition or inefficiency in the procedures for processing and controlling shipping notices and customer invoices. (AICPA adapted)

8.11 A nationwide sportswear retailer is preparing to implement electronic data interchange (EDI) of invoices, purchase orders, and delivery schedules with its suppliers. The retailer has a single distribution center for all the stores which transmit sales and inventory positions daily to the distribution center. When conversion is complete, EDI will be used to transfer all business documents between the retailer and its suppliers. If EDI is really successful, management wants to implement EDI in its other lines of business.

Management has asked the director of internal auditing to plan for auditing the sportswear division to (1) compare its performance with and without EDI and (2) audit the new system after installation on a continuing basis. The director consulted the audit staff, who suggested considering the following techniques for the continuing audit:

1. Test data method

2. Integrated test facility

3. Parallel simulation

Before responding to management, the director wanted the audit staff to agree on the best approach and decided to prepare a memorandum to the audit staff as a basis for further discussion.

Required:

1. Assume the role of the director of internal audit in consulting with the internal audit staff. Specifically, you are to write a memorandum to your staff that proposes:

   a. Data which internal auditors could use to compare performance with and without EDI.

   b. The best computer audit technique of the suggested ones for the continuous audit and justification for the choice.

   c. An explanation of why the other techniques are inadequate.

2. Assume the role of independent auditor. In reviewing the work of the internal auditing staff, as part of your understanding of the client's control structure, would you be more interested in the role of the internal auditors in comparing performance with and without EDI, or would you be more interested in their continuous auditing efforts? Explain. (IIA adapted)

8.12 Auditors have various EDP audit techniques available to aid in testing computer based systems. Included in these audit techniques are: (a) test decks (data), (b) parallel simulation, (c) integrated test facility (ITF), and (d) tagging and tracing.

Required:

Describe each of the four identified audit techniques and list two situations where they are most appropriately used. Use the following format:

(a) Test Decks:
1. Description
2. Uses
   a.
   b.

(b), (c), (d)—same format as (a). (IIA adapted)

APPENDIX

EFFECTIVE WRITING IN AUDITING

NEED FOR CONSIDERATION

The purpose of this appendix is to help auditors and accounting students write more effectively. The appendix focuses on the writing requirements of the practicing auditor, the auditing student, and the CPA candidate.

A common misconception among nonaccountants is that accountants and auditors work with numbers only. Contrary to this perception, practicing accountants and accounting students do extensive writing. Consider some of the topics covered in this textbook that impose writing requirements on the auditor:

1. The engagement letter;
2. The audit report (particularly qualified opinions and explanatory paragraphs);
3. The reportable conditions letter;
4. The management letter;
5. Audit workpaper documentation;
   a. Internal control memoranda
   b. Explanation of audit procedures applied
   c. Audit conclusions based on evaluation of evidence
6. Accounting firm materials;
   a. Training manuals
   b. Policy and procedures manuals

In addition, accounting instructors, especially in the auditing course, often require students to write. This writing may take the form of solutions to end of chapter essay questions, research papers, or essay questions on examinations. This textbook contains such an exercise in the form of Trim Lawn Manufacturing Corporation, an audit practice case. Several of the case modules—particularly Module I—require extensive analysis and writing. A careful reading of this appendix should help students better plan and complete those requirements. In addition, the appendix offers a practice case, together with a recommended solution. The practice case is at the end of the appendix and requires the student to develop an outline for a reportable conditions letter and write the letter.

In addition to helping the auditing student and practitioner toward more effective writing, the appendix should assist the CPA candidate in meeting the essay requirements of the CPA examination. These requirements vary by exam part. Approximately 40 percent of the auditing portion of the exam, for example, consists of essay questions.

The first part of the appendix instructs the reader in effectively planning a written document with emphasis on preparing a detailed outline. The next section discusses how to compose a document based on the prepared outline. The appendix then addresses computer-assisted writing tools. The last part of the appendix, preceding the practice case, offers guidance to accounting students and CPA candidates in effectively answering essay questions.

HOW TO PLAN A WRITTEN DOCUMENT

To be most effective, the writer should carefully plan the document before writing it. To this end, the writer should identify the reader(s) of the document, consider the information to be conveyed, and prepare a detailed outline.

Identify Reader(s) and Information Content

Effective communication requires that the writer meet the reader's needs. Different readers have different information needs. In writing an engagement letter, for example, the reader is the client. The client is interested in the nature of the CPA's proposed service. The information content, therefore, should consist of a clear communication of the nature of the engagement. If the CPA is to perform an audit, he/she should emphasize reasonable rather than absolute assurance in the letter and clearly define the two terms for the client. If the engagement is for a review, the CPA should stress the contrast between an audit and a review.

In answering an essay question, the reader is the course instructor or the CPA examination grader. Instructors and graders are looking for certain "key points" in grading answers to essay questions. Therefore, the writer should identify as many of these points as possible before drafting an answer.

Careful thought and planning before writing helps writers identify readers and their information needs. An outline, as discussed below, can help in this regard.

Prepare an Outline

Careful attention to preparing an outline has two advantages. First, writing the document is much easier when done from an outline. Second, given the structured format of an outline, the flow of the resulting document will be more logical and the writer is less likely to overlook essential points.

Include as Much Detail as Possible

A detailed outline facilitates the writing task. This is especially true if the writer is composing a lengthy research paper.

An outline, in the form of successive levels of headings, enables the writer to think carefully about content and organization. By frequently revising the outline, the writer can improve the logical flow of the document.

For example, assume that your auditing instructor asks you to describe to the auditing class the standard audit report and its possible modifications. You might begin with two main headings:

I. Standard audit report

II. Modifications

Upon further consideration, you wish to identify the components of the report. Your outline now becomes:

I. Standard audit report
    A. Introductory paragraph
    B. Scope paragraph
    C. Opinion paragraph

II. Modifications

Since report modifications may or may not affect the audit opinion, you decide to further refine the outline as follows:

I. Standard audit report
    A. Introductory paragraph
    B. Scope paragraph
    C. Opinion paragraph

II. Modifications
    A. Modifications that affect the audit opinion
    B. Modifications that do not affect the audit opinion

Up to this point, the outline contains two levels, but you will probably add third and fourth levels as further refinements. For example, under the heading "modifications that affect the audit opinion," you might add third level headings for "qualified opinions," "adverse opinions," and "disclaimers of opinion."

Make Certain the Outline Flows Logically and Clearly

An outline has the advantage of promoting logical thinking and organization before writing. In the audit report project, preparing an outline eased the writer's task in two ways. First, the structure of the outline form helped in identifying main headings and subheadings and in determining the sequence of topics. Further, by adding second, third, and even fourth levels to the outline, the writer can provide enough detail to make the actual writing task comparatively easy.

The writer should consider the first draft of an outline just that. To refine the logical flow and completeness of the final paper, one should modify and expand the outline. The writer may identify additional main topics and/or subtopics. The writer may decide that the order of presentation can be improved by shifting the order of topics, or by converting first-level topics to second-level or vice versa.

To summarize, identifying readers and information content, followed by an outline, helps the writer to develop a paper that is clear and complete and that flows logically. Moreover, once the writer has prepared the detailed outline, he/she should find the task of drafting the finished document much easier.

HOW TO COMPOSE A WRITTEN DOCUMENT

As much as the outline eases the writing task, the writer should not let it serve as a constraint. As the writing proceeds, the outline may need to be further refined. These changes may take the form of new topics or revised orderings that occur to the writer. Also, having prepared the outline, the writer now needs to concentrate on writing style and sentence flow. The following paragraphs address the writing process.

Facilitate the Reader's Task

Most people who read reports, letters, papers, and other written communications from auditors are busy and wish to comprehend the subject matter easily and quickly. Writers can use certain techniques to help in this regard.

Maintain a Logical Order

As discussed above, the outline improves the logical flow of a document. Lengthy reports should be broadly divided into three parts: *Introduction; main body;* and *summary and conclusions*. In the introduction, the writer should identify the purpose of the report and the major points to be covered. The main body of the report should cover the detail as included in the outline. The summary and conclusions should briefly recap the main ideas included in the body of the report. The author should write the introduction, together with the summary and conclusions, in a manner that permits the busy reader to temporarily bypass the main body of the report and still grasp the essential points.

Use Headings and Subheadings

Nothing is more frustrating for the reader than to confront a long report without adequate headings and subheadings. The writer should recognize that a reader's concentration span is limited and can absorb a maximum of one or two topics at a time. Liberal use of headings and subheadings eases the strain on the reader and promotes comprehension of the main ideas.

The use of headings and subheadings should be automatic, given a carefully prepared and detailed outline. In placing the headings in the body of the document, the writer should follow a consistent format. For example, the following rules might be adopted:

- Main headings: Centered and in capital letters;
- Subheadings: Centered, but in lower case;
- Third level: To the left margin and underlined.

The writer should be careful to avoid either too few or too many heading and subheadings. A good rule is to include at least two or three paragraphs under a single heading, and to cover no more than two pages under a single heading or subheading.

Repeat Main Ideas

A writer can effectively use some repetition to reinforce main ideas, although unnecessary redundancy should be avoided. If the auditor is drafting a reportable conditions letter to the audit committee, for example, the goal is to persuade the client to correct material control structure weaknesses. An effective approach is to identify the major weaknesses early in the letter and the adverse results if not corrected. The auditor may then discuss the weaknesses in further detail in the body of the document, and repeat the possible financial statement consequences in the summary. A CPA might use a similar approach in an engagement letter to emphasize the levels of assurance provided by an agreed upon type of service.

Clarity and Conciseness are Important

Added length does not necessarily enhance the quality of a document. Indeed, the writer should convey information as concisely as possible without sacrificing completeness.

Clarity is increased by following proper rules of grammar and avoiding the use of words that are more complex than necessary. Correct spelling and punctuation also improve the clarity and flow of a document.

The following practices should help in maintaining clarity and conciseness in written communications:

1. **Keep sentences short and simple, but complete.** Consider the following sentence from a reportable conditions letter:

    In our review of internal controls over the processing of sales transactions, we discovered that input editing controls were lacking, resulting in several recording errors in journalizing sales transactions.

    This sentence is too long, making it difficult to comprehend. It can be shortened as follows without loss of content:

    A lack of input editing controls resulted in several errors in recording sales transactions.

    The writer who wishes to maintain reader interest and attention should avoid long sentences.

2. **Avoid the passive voice if possible.** The active voice is defined as a state in which the subject acts upon the verb. The passive voice is present when the subject is acted upon. Consider the following sentence written in the passive voice:

    Engagement letters are written by CPAs in order to avoid possible misunderstandings with the client as to type of service to be performed.

    This same sentence in the active voice follows:

    The CPA sends an engagement letter to the client to avoid possible misunderstandings as to the type of service the CPA is to render.

    The active voice is more spirited and provides a clearer definition of the subject and the object of the sentence. For this reason, writers should use the active voice wherever possible.

3. **Avoid uncertain modifiers and pronouns.** Nothing detracts from clarity more than doubt concerning modifiers and/or pronouns. Consider the following sentence, for example:

    When conducting an audit, GAAS must be followed.

GAAS, in this sentence, is an uncertain modifier. That GAAS must be adhered to is clear; who is conducting the audit is not clear. The sentence reads as if GAAS is conducting the audit. The sentence should be written as follows:

When conducting an audit, the auditor must follow GAAS.

4. **Avoid shifting verb tense.** A common difficulty for most writers is to maintain consistency in verb tense. For example:

   We conducted a search for subsequent events and discovered that a fire destroyed the inventory of raw materials that are stored in the Scranton warehouse.

   If the fire destroyed the materials, they are no longer there. The sentence should read:

   We conducted a search for subsequent events and discovered that a fire destroyed the inventory of raw materials that were stored in the Scranton warehouse.

5. **Keep paragraphs short and confined to one idea.** Long paragraphs burden the reader and contribute to loss of concentration. Short paragraphs are preferable. A short paragraph is one consisting of four or five sentences. The writer should begin a paragraph by introducing the main idea and limit it to that one idea.

6. **Use listings and diagrams to promote clarity.** When an idea or concept contains several subparts, listings are easier for the reader to follow than a paragraph containing the same information. For example, the steps the auditor follows in conducting a search for subsequent events are listed in Chapter 14. The listing is clearer than a long paragraph and more readily identifies the procedures for the student who is later reviewing the topic.

   Diagrams also promote clarity and build reader interest. Chapter 1 presents a diagram of the audit process in the form of a flowchart. The pictorial representation, in this instance, is clearer than a narrative because it highlights the principal steps in the process. In addition, the flowchart provides a break from reading and offers a different medium for presenting the process overview.

7. **Use positive rather than negative statements.** Positive statements are more pleasing to the reader than negative statements. For example, consider the sentence, *Because, contrary to prior assurances, you failed to provide us with an adjusted trial balance, we could not complete the audit within the preferred time frame.* This tone does not promote good auditor/client relations. A more diplomatic way of stating the same observation is: *Upon receiving the adjusted trial balance from your controller, we could proceed with the audit in a timely manner.* If writers hope to gain readers' attention and cooperation, they should avoid negative language.

8. **Use proper spelling and grammar.** Improper spelling and grammar are as disturbing to the reader as uncertain modifiers and pronouns. When in doubt as to spelling, look up the word. When uncertain as to proper grammar, consult a report writing source such as *A Manual for Writers,* by Turabian.

9. **Consider rewriting.** The first draft of a document is precisely that. The writer should consider it a rough draft to be revised and rewritten. The writer may

discover that shorter sentences or simpler words can add clarity without loss of content or meaning.

Having someone proofread the draft is also helpful. If the proofreader is an experienced writer and is knowledgeable about the subject matter, the input is particularly valuable. Major omissions, unnecessary redundancy, lack of clarity, and illogical flow are weaknesses often detected by proofreading.

COMPUTER-ASSISTED WRITING

Computer software, such as word processors, grammar checkers, outliners, and data bases have enhanced writing capability. The following paragraphs briefly address these software packages.

Word Processors

Word processors, by enabling the writer to insert, delete, and move text within the body of a document, ease the task of composing and editing. In addition, most word processors contain a spell checker and thesaurus. Words can be checked for spelling as they are entered; or the entire document can be spell-checked upon completion. The thesaurus supplies synonyms and antonyms to avoid redundant word usage.

Grammar Checkers

Authors can use grammar checkers such as "Right Writer" and "Grammatik" to edit documents for proper usage, punctuation, and clarity. Consider the sentence, *The FASB has gone to far in there efforts to please the corporate community.* Spell checking will not flag the words "to" and "there" since they are correctly spelled, although improperly used. A grammar checker, however, will signal the errors for the writer, suggesting replacement with the words "too" and "their." In addition, grammar checkers will detect punctuation errors.

The greatest advantage of grammar checkers is their ability to enhance the clarity of a document. They do this by identifying such clarity impediments as long sentences, unclear sentences, run-on sentences, uncertain modifiers, and use of the passive voice. A grammar checker also will evaluate a document by level of education needed to comprehend the document—the lower the level, presumably, the clearer the document.

Outliners

Although some word processors contain outline features, they are not as flexible as stand-alone outline programs. The stand-alone programs, such as "Max Think" and "Think Tank," permit the writer to organize thoughts while outlining. The flexibility of the programs provides this feature.

The writer may begin the outline by entering ideas at random, in the form of major headings. The major headings can then be expanded with second and third level subtopics, easily inserted wherever they relate to the major headings. The writer may decide to change the sequencing of major topics to enhance logical flow, or change one of the major topics to a subtopic of another major topic. The outliners, with the "move" feature, permit easy resequencing of topics as well as manipulation of topics from one level to another. With these features, writers are better able to develop detailed and logically constructed outlines before writing documents.

Data Bases

With a computer and a modem, several data bases are available to assist in research and writing. A data base that is particularly useful to accountants and auditors is "The National Automated Accounting Research System" (NAARS), developed jointly by the AICPA and Mead Data Central. NAARS makes it possible to research the financial statements, footnotes, and auditors' reports of approximately 4,200 companies in each file year included in the library. By entering key words or "descriptor" words, the researcher can access documents pertaining to a given topic. For example, if one wishes to find an audit report with an uncertainty paragraph relating to pending litigation, the words "uncertain" and "litigation" will retrieve audit reports containing those words. Most of the audit reports illustrated in Chapter 15 were retrieved using the NAARS data base.

In addition to NAARS, the NEXIS part of the data base provides access to magazines, newspapers, and other periodicals. As with NAARS, the use of key words to identify subjects, events, or people enables one to access news reports concerning given topics.

Most libraries, including university libraries, can now be reached by computer and modem. Researchers can thereby access data by both author and subject matter. This process enables one to identify applicable works before checking them out at the library.

To summarize, computer software has increased writing capacity, and for many persons, has made research and writing a more enjoyable experience.

HOW TO ANSWER ESSAY QUESTIONS

Much of the preceding discussion about planning and composing a document also applies to answering essay questions. The need to outline, the need for clarity, logical flow, proper grammar, and correct spelling and punctuation are important ingredients if the examinee is to satisfy the requirements of the examiner.

In addition, the examinee should read the question carefully and formulate an answer outline before beginning to write. Too often, examinees feel pressed for time and begin writing before fully reading and comprehending the question. This can actually result in spending too much time on the question, and, more important, failing to properly address the requirements of the question.

Before writing, the examinee should follow these steps:

1. *Read the requirements of the question* before reading the question. Know what the examiner is looking for; then

2. *Read the question carefully.* As you read the question, recall the requirements. This will enable you to distinguish the relevant from the irrelevant data;

3. *Address the requirements mentally and rough out an answer in outline form.* This approach serves the same purpose as outlining a document. The outline will enable you to be complete in your answer and will add to the logical flow of your answer.

Answer the Question

Although you have completed three steps before writing an answer, you have likely reduced the actual writing time while improving the quality of your answer. As you write your answer, you should observe the following rules:

1. Follow the outline to maintain the logical flow and to avoid overlooking the major points you wish to cover in your answer;

2. Be concise and address the question directly. Examiners will penalize you for unnecessary verbiage. Your ability to answer a question briefly, while covering all important aspects, will be recognized and rewarded;

3. Write clearly and legibly. Don't try to impress the examiner with your vocabulary. If a simpler word works as well, use it. Although you are not graded on penmanship, the examiner must be able to read your writing. If your writing is difficult to read, try to write more slowly, while staying within the prescribed time limit.

4. Use proper spelling and grammar. Although incorrect spelling and improper grammar do not affect the content of your answer, you display a higher degree of overall competence with correct spelling and proper grammar. Moreover, some instructors penalize students for misspelled words and incorrect grammatical usage.

5. Outline the remainder of your answer if you run out of time. Outlining the remainder of your answer shows the examiner that you identified the significant points, but simply did not have time to finish writing. If you already have a rough outline, you need only refine that portion related to the remainder of the question. Although you will receive partial rather than full credit, an effective outline should result in minimal loss of points.

SUMMARY

These tips on effective writing should help auditors, accounting students, and CPA candidates to achieve greater success in their writing efforts. Remember, in accounting, as in virtually all professions, effective writing is essential to career success. Remember, also, that no person is born an effective writer. Good writing comes with practice and proper instruction.

PRACTICE CASE—REPORTABLE CONDITIONS LETTER

Hightech University is a state university located in a large urban area and has a total enrollment of about 25,000 students. In addition to a large liberal arts program, H.U. has several professional colleges including business, education, engineering, law, nursing, and pharmacy. The university is governed by a board of trustees that includes an audit committee. The state requires that the university be audited annually by independent CPAs. The current audit is for the fiscal year ended June 30, 1994.

The auditors, Wembly & Sloan, CPAs, have completed their examination and plan to issue an unqualified audit opinion on the financial statements of H.U. As part of their audit, the firm also must draft a reportable conditions letter. As you may recall, the auditor addresses this letter to the audit committee of the board, and describes deficiencies in internal control that could have a significant effect on the reliability of accounting data.

The deficiencies described below were extracted from the ''reportable conditions'' audit workpaper. This workpaper was started at the beginning of the audit and updated by the audit team as deficiencies were discovered. The workpaper forms the basis for creating the reportable conditions letter. Jonathon Black, the in-charge senior for the Hightech audit, has discussed each of the deficiencies with Herbert Weller, university controller.

1. The university installed a new integrated computer information system (ICIS) to replace the manual system. We had previously recommended to the board that completion of system installation requires a minimum period of nine to fifteen months. This includes installing and testing software, and developing and implementing control policies and procedures. The university established a time frame of five months.

2. After the five-month implementation period, the ICIS system replaced the manual system, which was abandoned entirely at that point. Virtually all entities installing new information systems operate the old and new systems in parallel for six months to one year following start up of the new system. This practice facilitates record reconstruction in the event of a new system failure.

3. The university did not name a full-time project manager to coordinate implementation activities—a necessary step, given the short (five month) time frame. Instead, the controller assumed this role in addition to his other responsibilities.

4. Technical software problems have not yet been resolved in ICIS, and some question remains as to whether the system is yet operational. For this reason, we are concerned about the reliability of data flowing from the system.

5. A data control group does not exist for distributing output and monitoring the reprocessing of errors.

6. Departments originating transactions via ICIS terminals do not maintain transaction logs.

7. Control totals, in the form of dollar totals or transaction count totals, are not developed for later comparison with processed data.

8. Originating departments do not require authorization for data entry.

9. Data entry forms are not used by persons generating transactions in the absence of definitive source documents.

10. Users do not appear to be utilizing ICIS documentation, including user manuals, supplied by the software manufacturer. Also, the university has not written supplemental materials to provide documentation for those application aspects unique to H.U.

11. The controller has not provided users with written procedures describing consistent transaction processing steps.

12. Physical access to terminals is unlimited in many departments. Currently, it is possible for one person to approve a request for payment, create a new vendor name and address, and authorize payment.

13. General ledger cash account balances have not been reconciled with bank balances on a timely basis. Also, the student accounts receivable control has not been reconciled with the student subsidiary ledger.

14. An accountant in the controller's office prepares internal monthly and quarterly financial statements. These financial statements are then submitted to the vice president for administrative affairs without review by supervisory personnel. Although skeletal financial statements are produced automatically by ICIS, the accountant must prepare numerous manual schedules that contain various adjustments and reclassifications. As a result of this procedure, we noted numerous errors in the unaudited June 30, 1994 financial statements.

15. Journal entries are not always supported by adequate explanations.

16. H.U. has several large construction projects in progress, including the football stadium expansion and the new student recreation center. Our review of construction cost records in the Facilities Planning Office shows that the capital project files have not been reconciled with the accounting records maintained in the controller's office.

17. The controller's office has encountered difficulty in determining the nature and amounts of interfund transfers during 1994 due to numerous other transactions recorded as transfers.

18. The month-end calculation to allocate short-term investment income among the various funds is based on month-end balances only. As a result, the allocations may not be reflective of the balances of each fund throughout the month.

19. Employees are not required to take time off for vacation time earned and there are instances where little or no time is used.

Required:

Based on the above descriptions, you are to prepare an outline for a reportable conditions letter, after which you are to draft the letter. Address your completed document to the audit committee of the board of trustees. In preparing your outline, try to classify the major weaknesses, along with recommendations for improvement. You may decide that one or more of the deficiencies described above are not reportable conditions and, therefore, should not be included in the letter.

Note: The recommended solution begins on the next page of this appendix. You may wish to complete some or all of the requirements on your own before consulting the solution and solution notes.

I. Introductory paragraph
  A. Standardized (see *AICPA Professional Standards,* Section AU 325.12)
  B. Defines reportable conditions

II. Integrated computer information system (ICIS)
  A. Implementation problems
    1. Implementation period too short
      a. Five months
      b. Should be nine to fifteen months
    2. Not operated parallel with manual system
      a. Manual system abandoned completely upon installation of ICIS
      b. Difficult to recover from system failure
      c. Manual system should have continued parallel to ICIS for at least six months following installation
    3. Full-time project manager not utilized to coordinate implementation
      a. Controller assumed responsibility in addition to other duties
      b. This situation, together with the short lead time and immediate abandonment of manual system, has produced many problems with system implementation
  B. Control weaknesses resulting from improper implementation strategy
    1. H.U. does not utilize a control group
      a. Output may be distributed to unauthorized users
      b. Errors may not be detected or may not be corrected in a timely manner
      c. A data control function should be established
    2. Transaction logs are not maintained
      a. Unauthorized transactions may enter the system
      b. Transaction logs should be required
        (1) Transaction or transaction batch
        (2) Preparer's name or initials
    3. Control totals are not developed
      a. No means for comparing input with output
      b. Control totals (dollar and/or transaction count) should be developed by user and held for later comparison with recorded data
    4. Transactions may be entered without approval
      a. Unauthorized transactions may enter the system
      b. Approval mechanism should be developed
      c. Fix responsibility
      d. Assign identification codes and passwords to limit access
    5. Data entry forms are not used
      a. Lack of audit trail and inability to reconstruct transactions
      b. Prenumbered data entry forms should be designed and required for all transactions not supported by definitive source documents
        (1) Budget adjustments
        (2) Journal entries
        (3) Error corrections
        (4) Expense redistributions

6. Manufacturer supplied user manuals are not being utilized by operating personnel
   a. Increases probability of errors in processing transactions
   b. Documentation should be supplemented by university-prepared supplements tailored to unique H.U. applications
   c. Users should be trained and encouraged to use the documentation
7. Controller has not provided users with written procedures to guide in transaction processing
   a. Inadequate documentation to support transaction processing sequences may result in inconsistent processing and resultant errors
   b. Written procedures should be developed to guide processing consistency
8. Physical access to terminals is unlimited in many departments
   a. Unauthorized transactions may be entered
   b. An employee could set up a vendor, pay the vendor, and misappropriate the check
   c. Policies should be established to clearly define responsibility for transaction processing, as well as limit access to ICIS terminals
   d. User ID numbers should be given to H.U. employees only and should remain secret and changed regularly

III. **Reconciliation with general ledger**
   A. Cash balances have not been reconciled to bank statement balances, and student accounts receivable control has not been reconciled with student subsidiary ledger
   B. Undetected errors and/or irregularities may significantly distort monthly and quarterly financial statements.
   C. A system of monthly reconciliation and follow-up of reconciling items should be instituted immediately

IV. **Monthly and quarterly financial statements are prepared by a staff person and are not reviewed prior to submission to vice president for administrative affairs**
   A. Many schedules, prepared manually by staff person, may contain significant errors. This, in turn, may cause errors in the financial statements
   B. Unaudited 1994 financial statements contained numerous errors
   C. Financial statements should be reviewed by the controller before they are submitted to vice president

V. **Journal entries not supported by adequate explanation**
   A. Reconstruction and vouching of transactions may be difficult, if not impossible, under these circumstances
   B. All journal entries should be supported by documentation and explanation

VI. **Capital project files have not been reconciled with accounting records**
   A. May increase the risk of unapproved cost overruns
   B. Reconciliations should be completed monthly
   C. Contractor cost records submitted with progress billings should be reviewed prior to payment processing

VII. **Interfund transfers are commingled with other transactions incorrectly recorded as fund transfers**
   A. Difficult to determine the nature and amount of actual fund transfers
   B. Difficult to ascertain compliance with legal requirements relative to fund restrictions
   C. Instructions clearly defining the circumstances under which fund transfers are mandated and appropriate should be drafted by the controller's office

VIII. **Interest allocation is based on month-end balances**
   A. May result in inequitable income allocations among funds
   B. The allocation should be based on average monthly balances
   C. This is not a control weakness that would significantly affect the financial statement assertions. Therefore, it should not be included in the reportable conditions letter

IX. **Employees are not required to take vacation time off**
   A. Errors and irregularities may occur and go undetected
   B. Require all accounting and ICIS employees to take at least five consecutive days of vacation time each year
   C. Assign replacements qualified to detect significant errors and irregularities that may have occurred

X. **Closing paragraphs—AICPA standardized (See *Professional Standards*, Section AU 325.12)**
   A. Conditions that were described above also influenced the nature, timing, and extent of auditing procedures
   B. Distribution of letter limited to audit committee, management, and employees of the university

Reportable Conditions Letter

September 2, 1994

To: The Audit Committee
     Board of Trustees
     Hightech University

We have audited the financial statements of Hightech University for the year ended June 30, 1994, and have issued our report thereon dated August 5, 1994. In planning and performing our audit, we considered the university's internal control structure in order to determine our auditing procedures for the purpose of expressing our opinion on the financial statements and not to provide assurance on the internal control structure. However, we noted certain matters involving the internal control structure and its operation that we consider to be reportable conditions under standards established by the American Institute of Certified Public Accountants. Reportable conditions involve matters coming to our attention relating to significant deficiencies in the design or operation of the internal control structure that, in our judgment, could adversely affect the university's ability to record, process, summarize, and report financial data consistent with the assertions of management in the financial statements.

The reportable conditions noted during our audit, all of which have been discussed with the appropriate members of management, are summarized below.

INTEGRATED COMPUTER INFORMATION SYSTEM

In 1993, the university installed a new Integrated Computer Information System (ICIS) to replace the manual system. We have grave concerns about the reliability of accounting data produced by this system. These concerns are expressed in the following paragraphs.

Factors Causing Control Problems

In our opinion, the university implemented the system without an adequate implementation strategy. First, the implementation period was not long enough to make the system fully operational.

The university chose five months as the implementation period. We had recommended nine to fifteen months as a reasonable implementation period. The software manufacturer agreed with us in this recommendation.

Second, upon start-up of ICIS, the university abandoned the manual system. Common system implementation strategy suggests operating the old system parallel to the new system for at least six months. When systems are not run parallel, recovery from new system failure becomes very difficult.

Third, the university did not utilize a full-time project manager to coordinate implementation of ICIS. Instead, the controller assumed implementation and coordination responsibility in addition to his other duties.

These three factors, in our opinion, have caused internal control deficiencies that we believe raise significant questions about the reliability of accounting data produced by the system. We have described these deficiencies in the following paragraphs.

Control Deficiencies Within ICIS

Lack of Data Control Group

The university does not use a data control group. Adequate organizational structure within the data processing function requires assigning, to one or more individuals, responsibility for distributing output to authorized users and monitoring the reprocessing of errors. Absence of this control may result in undistributed system output or distribution to unauthorized users. Also, without independent monitoring of error reprocessing, errors that occur may not be detected or corrected in a timely manner. We recommend, therefore, that the university establish a data control function within ICIS. We also recommend that the person(s) so designated be independent of programmers and systems analysts.

Transaction Logs are Not Maintained

Whenever departments enter transactions from remote terminals, effective control requires some form of written transaction log. The log should identify the individual entering the transaction, the date, and the type of transaction. H.U.'s ICIS makes no provision for logging transactions. Under these conditions, unauthorized transactions may enter the system. We strongly urge the university to institute a policy requiring transaction logs.

Control Totals are Not Maintained

Originating departments do not develop control totals for batches of transactions being processed. As a result, departments originating transactions have no means for comparing the results of processing with transaction input. This condition may result in unrecorded transactions. We recommend that control totals—either dollar amounts or transaction counts—be developed by originating departments and held for later comparison with processing results.

Transactions May be Entered Without Approval

We noted that departments often enter batches of transactions, such as journal entries, adjustments, and expense reclassifications, into the system without prior approval. Under these conditions, unauthorized transactions may enter the system. We recommend that the controller's office develop a formal approval mechanism to be followed consistently. Supervisors should document all approvals to permit later review. We also recommend that the university fix responsibility for both entering and approving transactions.

Data Entry Forms are Not Used

Certain transactions, such as budget transfers, journal entries, error corrections, and expense redistributions, are not supported by definitive source documents. Without some form of documentation, an "audit trail" is lacking. Without an audit trail, auditors and others cannot reconstruct the transactions. We recommend that the controller's office design prenumbered data entry forms and require them as support for all transactions not leaving an otherwise visible audit trail. The preparer should date the form, clearly describe the transaction, and sign the form.

Manufacturer-Supplied User Manuals are Not Being Utilized by Operating Personnel

Although the software manufacturer has supplied H.U. with extensive documentation to support ICIS, operating personnel do not appear to use the manuals. This condition increases the risk of processing errors and prevents persons from fully understanding the system and realizing its capabilities. We recommend the university conduct training sessions for operating personnel and encourage them to use the manuals. We also recommend that the university prepare supplements to the manuals to tailor the materials to H.U.'s unique processing applications.

The Controller has Not Provided Users with Written Procedures to Guide in Transaction Processing

Without detailed processing instructions, transactions may be inconsistently processed and errors may result. We recommend that the controller's office write a set of detailed instructions for processing the university's recurring transaction sets, and provide instruction to those persons authorized to enter such transactions.

Physical Access to Terminals is Unlimited in Many Departments

We observed that, in some departments, administrative officers, faculty, staff, and even students may enter transactions into ICIS terminals. Under these conditions, an employee could create a vendor name, authorize payment of a nonexistent invoice, and intercept and misappropriate the signed check drawn in payment. We recommend that the university identify authority for entering transactions and fix responsibility in those individuals so identified. Moreover, the university should limit access to ICIS terminals by assigning user identification codes and passwords. These codes and passwords should be given to H.U. authorized employees only, and should remain secret and be changed regularly.

In addition to reportable conditions relating directly to ICIS, we noted other weaknesses that qualify as reportable conditions. The following paragraphs describe those weaknesses together with our recommendations.

FAILURE TO RECONCILE WITH GENERAL LEDGER

The university has not consistently reconciled general ledger cash balances with bank statement balances, and the student accounts receivable control account has not been reconciled with the student subsidiary ledger. Failure to complete these reconciliations may result in undetected errors and irregularities and significantly misstate the monthly and quarterly internal financial statements. In completing these reconciliations as part of our audit, we discovered numerous errors. We recommend that the university immediately institute a policy requiring monthly reconciliations and prompt follow-up of reconciling items.

INTERNAL FINANCIAL STATEMENTS NOT SUBJECT TO REVIEW

The controller's office submits monthly and quarterly financial statements to the Vice President for Administrative Affairs. Although ICIS automatically produces skeletal financial statements, several schedules, manually prepared, support the statements. Currently, a staff accountant in the controller's office prepares the schedules and assembles them with the statements. She then submits the statements and schedules to the vice president without review by a supervisor. As a result, the statements and schedules may contain errors. We noted several errors in the June 30, 1994 unaudited financial statements. We recommend that the controller, or other qualified supervisor in the controller's office, review the statements and schedules prior to submission to the vice president.

JOURNAL ENTRIES ARE NOT SUPPORTED BY ADEQUATE EXPLANATION

We observed many journal entries without adequate explanation. Some contained no explanation. This condition makes reconstruction or tracing transactions to source documents difficult or impossible. We recommend that all journal entries contain clear and complete explanations and refer to any documentation supporting the entries.

CAPITAL PROJECTS FILES HAVE NOT BEEN RECONCILED

The university has several large construction projects currently in progress, including the football stadium renovation and expansion and the new student recreation center. Our review of construction cost records in the Facilities Planning Office shows that the capital projects files are not reconciled with the accounting records maintained in the controller's office. Failure to reconcile increases the risk of unapproved cost overruns by contractors. We recommend that the controller's office reconcile these records monthly. We also urge that contractor cost records submitted with progress billings be reviewed before payment processing.

TRANSACTIONS INCORRECTLY RECORDED AS INTERFUND TRANSFERS

We discovered, during our analysis of interfund transfers, that several other transactions were incorrectly recorded as fund transfers. Because of this condition, we had difficulty determining the nature and amount of actual fund transfers. Moreover, commingling other transactions with interfund transfers results in incorrect fund balances. This, in turn, raises a question as to compliance with legal requirements relative to fund restrictions. We recommend that the controller's office coordinate an effort to write detailed instructions clearly defining the circumstances under which fund transfers are mandated and appropriate.

VACATION TIME OFF NOT REQUIRED

The university does not require employees to take vacation time off. As a result, several persons who execute and process transactions and who have custody over valuable assets do not use the vacation time available to them. A policy requiring all employees to take at least part of their vacation time off strengthens internal control by providing replacements for them in the interim. Qualified replacements are likely to detect significant errors and irregularities that have occurred. We recommend that the university implement a policy requiring all accounting and ICIS employees to take at least five consecutive days of vacation time off each year.

We considered these conditions in determining the nature, timing, and extent of the audit procedures applied in our audit of the 1994 financial statements, and this report does not affect our report on these financial statements. We have not considered the internal control structure since the date of our report, August 5, 1994.

This report is intended solely for the information and use of the audit committee of the board of trustees, management, and others within Hightech University.

Sincerely,

Jack Sloan
Wembly & Sloan, CPAs

The appendix offered several suggestions for more effective writing. The following notes describe how the above solution incorporates these suggestions.

The Outline

1. The outline contains considerable detail, thereby enabling the writer to concentrate on writing style rather than content in writing the final document.
2. The outline includes several levels. This encourages and facilitates liberal use of subheadings in constructing the final document.
3. The outline flows logically. Logical flow enhances the clarity and readability of the final document.
4. The outline carefully classifies the points listed in the narrative as to:
   a. Implementation problems related to ICIS;
   b. Control weaknesses resulting from improper implementation; and
   c. Control weaknesses not related to ICIS implementation.

The Document

1. The document was produced directly from the detailed outline.
2. The letter begins with an introductory paragraph, followed by a main body, and concludes with a closing paragraph.
3. The letter contains several headings and subheadings.
4. The document follows consistent placement rules for headings and subheadings.
5. The document contains minimal narrative under each heading to further promote understanding.
6. Paragraphs have been kept short, each expanding on a single idea.
7. The writing is clear and concise. Reportable conditions and recommended improvements are brief and to the point.
8. Verb tense is consistent and the document contains no uncertain modifiers.
9. Although the letter uses the passive voice occasionally, the active voice appears much more frequently. Long, technical documents must utilize the passive voice to some extent. Otherwise, the flow tends to become awkward.
10. The document emphasizes positive rather than negative statements. Since the reportable conditions letter is designed to impress upon management and the audit committee the need for effective internal control, the negative effects of control weaknesses must be stressed. For this reason, the document may appear to contain negative statements, but negativism is not used capriciously.
11. The reportable conditions letter was spell-checked with a word processor spell checker. It was checked for grammar using Right Writer, Version 4.0.

9

EDP and Substantive Audit Testing: Auditing with the Computer

CHAPTER OUTLINE

I. **Advantages of auditing with the computer**
   A. Increased audit testing capacity
   B. Assistance in performing complex tasks

II. **How to audit with the computer**
   A. Generalized audit software packages
   B. Custom-designed programs
   C. Microcomputer packages

III. **Microcomputer packages and substantive audit testing**
   A. Analytical procedures
   B. Electronic workpaper files
   C. Other substantive testing applications
      1. Accounts receivable aging analysis
      2. Inventories
      3. Audit adjustments
      4. Financial statement preparation
      5. Automated text working papers
   D. Budget and time summary

IV. **Expert systems in auditing**

OVERVIEW

In addition to internal control structure testing implications, the computer also affects substantive audit testing. The nature of this impact is addressed in this chapter. Figure 9.1 shows where the discussion fits into the audit process.

When auditing the results of processing (substantiating transactions and balances), the auditor may elect to audit *with* the computer or audit *without* the computer. The first approach uses the speed and accuracy of the computer to assist in performing various audit tasks. The second consists of manually gathering and evaluating audit evidence. In testing a client's inventory for possible obsolescence, for example, the auditor may wish to calculate turnover for those classes of inventory for which obsolescence appears most probable. If the client's inventory records are computerized, the auditor may use a computer routine to make the turnover calculations. Without the aid of the computer, the turnover calculations would have to be done manually.

This chapter discusses alternative approaches for auditing with the computer and identifies applications for which these approaches are relevant. A major part of the chapter is devoted to use of the microcomputer in substantive audit testing and demonstrates how the audit is becoming increasingly automated, given widespread use of microcomputers. The chapter also addresses the concept of expert systems in auditing. **Expert systems** are computer programs that can assist the auditor in making judgments within a specialized domain.

To provide the student with ''hands-on'' exposure to computer auditing, the chapter describes Trim Lawn Manufacturing Corporation, a computer audit software package that can be used to assist the auditor in workpaper preparation and integration, application of analytical procedures, and other audit tasks. Chapters 9 through 15 contain optional assignments of modules contained in the package. This case can also be completed without using the computer.

STUDY OBJECTIVES

After reading this chapter, you should be able to:

1. Define ''auditing with the computer'';
2. Identify the advantages of auditing with the computer;
3. Differentiate among generalized audit software packages, custom-designed programs, and microcomputer packages;
4. Describe ways in which the computer can be used to facilitate substantive audit testing, including the use of expert systems.

FIGURE 9.1   The Audit Process

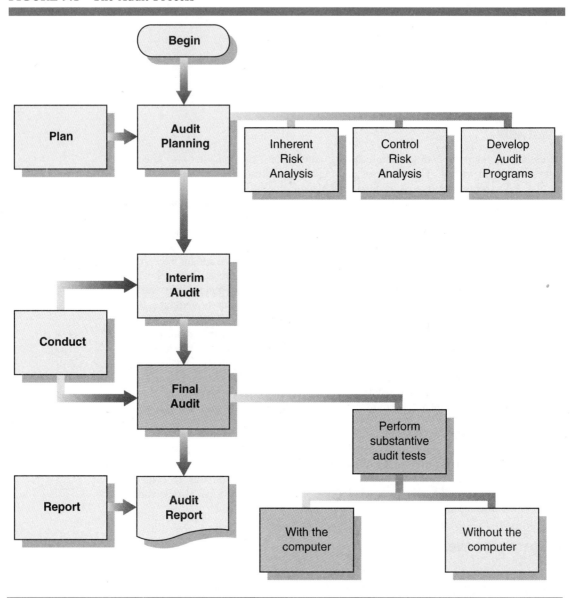

ADVANTAGES OF AUDITING WITH THE COMPUTER

As defined in Chapter 4, substantive audit testing consists of examining evidence in support of the assertions contained in the financial statements. Use of the computer to assist in gathering and evaluating audit evidence enhances the effectiveness of substantive testing by permitting the auditor to examine increased quantities of evidence in support of management's financial statement assertions. By examining larger quantities of evidence and by enlisting the aid of the computer in analyzing and evaluating evidence, the auditor is able to *more effectively manage detection risk.*

Speed and clerical accuracy are the features that make the computer especially advantageous in performing substantive audit tests. In examining inventories, for example, the auditor must gather evidence in support of the client's calculations of final inventory costs. This includes determining that the proper prices were applied to the various categories of inventory and recalculating the product of price per unit times quantity of units for a sample of inventory line items. The extended amounts must also be added on a test basis and compared with the client's totals. In applying these procedures, the auditor can harness the ability of the computer to quickly manipulate large amounts of data in an error-free manner, permitting a larger number of inventory prices, extensions, and footings to be tested.

The capacity of the computer to store large amounts of data for multiple purposes permits the auditor to expand the breadth and depth of analytical procedures. Trend and proportional analysis, as well as comparison with industry averages, can be performed quickly and accurately with computer programs designed for that purpose.

The computer can also increase the cost-effectiveness of auditing. Determining sample sizes, as well as drawing samples and evaluating sample results as described in Chapters 10 and 11, can be done more efficiently with computer assistance; and accounts and transactions may be audited more quickly. Moreover, given computerized data files and the necessary programs, the cost of using the computer in completing these audit tasks is much less than that of performing them manually with expensive audit staff hours.

Greater speed and accuracy and the ability to examine larger quantities of evidence are major advantages of auditing with the computer.

HOW TO AUDIT WITH THE COMPUTER

One or a combination of the following approaches to auditing with the computer are currently being used:

1. Generalized audit software packages;
2. Custom-designed programs;
3. Microcomputer packages.

Generalized Audit Software

Generalized software packages have been developed by auditing firms and others to perform various audit tasks. These programs are used by the auditor to perform substantive testing on the client's computer files. Such tasks as sample selection and evaluation, accounts receivable aging and confirmation, depreciation computation, inventory extensions, footings, turnover calculations, and analytical procedures may be performed more quickly and more effectively with the aid of generalized audit software packages.

The programs are designed to access the computer files of numerous clients. Many accounting firms have developed the programs "in-house" for use by the audit staff. Minimal training is required for staff people to obtain a working knowledge of the packages.

A disadvantage of the generalized packages is the inability to access the files of the more sophisticated on-line real-time systems. As more applications go "on-line," therefore, generalized audit software packages, as presently constituted, will decline in use.

Custom-Designed Programs

Custom-designed programs are written for specific audit tasks and particular clients. They may be written by the auditor or by the client. Whether written by the auditor or the client, the auditor must test the programs to determine that they adequately perform the designated tasks.

Being more expensive to develop and test, custom programs are not as efficient as generalized packages. They may be the only feasible means, however, for gathering sufficient, competent evidential matter, especially for clients with unique computer systems not amenable to audit by use of generalized software packages.

Microcomputer Packages

A significant development in auditing during recent years has been the increasing use of the microcomputer in performing various audit tasks. This has been especially pronounced as the computers have become smaller and more portable, as well as faster and more powerful. In using **microcomputer software packages** for analyzing the client's data, the auditor must first transfer accounting data from the client's files to the microcomputer. This may be done by manually entering the data into the microcomputer. A more efficient approach, if feasible, is to place the auditor's microcomputer on-line and directly download the data from the client's files. However the transfer is effected, the auditor then utilizes the power of the microcomputer to perform substantive tests on the data.

The microcomputer may be used whether or not the client's system is computerized. The tests are performed more efficiently, however, given computerized client files, inasmuch as downloading becomes relatively automated. If the client's system is manual, the auditor must arrange for manually entering client data into the microcomputer prior to performing substantive testing. This task has also been facilitated, however, by the increasing availability of *optical scanning devices*. Optical scanners can read the data and enter it into the computer without the need for "keyboarding."

In addition to the advantages cited earlier for generalized programs, the microcomputer offers the ability to automate the audit workpapers. With an electronic spreadsheet or data base package, the working trial balance, lead schedules, supporting schedules, and working copies of financial statements can be *linked*. Such linkage permits all workpapers to be updated automatically when a change is made in a supporting schedule. An audit adjustment, for example, added to a supporting schedule, also affects the lead schedule, the working trial balance, and the financial statements. Proper linkage of the workpapers provides for automatically adding the necessary changes upon entry of the adjusting data.

The remainder of this chapter discusses ways by which the auditor can use the microcomputer to assist in performing substantive testing. Included in the end-of-chapter materials for Chapters 9 through 15 are assignments from the Trim Lawn Manufacturing Corporation, an optional computer audit practice case. These assignments permit the student to apply some of the auditing procedures that can be automated with the microcomputer. Each optional assignment relates to audit procedures described in the chapter and requires little computer time. This permits the student to experience a wide variety of audit tasks currently being facilitated by the microcomputer.

PERFORMING SUBSTANTIVE AUDIT TESTS WITH THE AID OF A MICROCOMPUTER AND ONE OR MORE AUDIT SOFTWARE PACKAGES

Analytical Procedures

Exhibits 9.1 through 9.3 demonstrate how an electronic spreadsheet can help in applying analytical procedures. The important advantage of the spreadsheet module here is in automating the calculations. By saving the equations for the various ratios and storing them in the appropriate cells of the spreadsheet, only the actual client data need be entered in order for the analysis to be completed. The percentages in Exhibits 9.1 and 9.2, for example, as well as the ratios in Exhibit 9.3, will automatically adjust to changes in the financial statement components. Exhibit 9.3 compares key ratios in two ways. First, client data are compared with the prior year; second, the data are compared with industry averages where relevant.

Similar spreadsheet templates could be developed for comparing the current year's sales and cost of goods sold with the prior year, by month or by quarter, and for calculating inventory turnover by major categories of goods. By automating the calculations, the computer permits the auditor to concentrate on interpreting the results. Analytical procedures, when computerized, can also be applied more extensively than would be possible given manual calculations.

EXHIBIT 9.1   Analytical Procedures: Balance Sheet Components

			Prepared by: lfk Date: 1/6/95 Reviewed by: cck Date: 1/9/95	
		Auditee, Inc. 12/31/94		
			Percent of Total	
	12/31/93 Final	*12/31/94 G/L*	*12/31/93*	*12/31/94*
Assets				
Current assets:				
Cash	$ 392,400	$ 426,700	5.05%	4.99%
Marketable securities	52,200	74,400	0.67	0.87
Receivables (net)	1,601,400	1,715,300	20.63	20.07
Inventories	2,542,500	2,810,200	32.75	32.88
Prepaid expenses	24,900	19,500	0.32	0.23
Total current	4,613,400	5,046,100	59.43	59.04
Long-term investments	3,000	190,000	0.04	2.22
Other assets	0	0	0.00	0.00
Property, plant, and equipment (net)	3,146,500	3,310,900	40.53	38.74
Total	$7,762,900	$8,547,000	100.00	100.00
Liabilities and Stockholders' Equity				
Current Liabilities:				
Notes payable	750,000	825,000	9.66	9.65
Accounts payable	2,150,400	1,340,300	27.70	15.68
Accrued payables	210,600	180,500	2.71	2.11
Income taxes payable	150,000	1,170,000	1.93	13.69
Total current	3,261,000	3,515,800	42.01	41.13
Bonds payable	1,000,000	1,200,000	12.88	14.04
Common stock	2,400,000	2,400,000	30.92	28.08
Retained earnings	1,101,900	1,431,200	14.19	16.75
Total	$7,762,900	$8,547,000	100.00	100.00

EXHIBIT 9.2   Analytical Procedures: Income Statement Components

			Percent of Sales	
	12/31/93 Final	12/31/94 G/L	1993	1994
Sales	$2,000,000	$4,000,000	100.00%	100.00%
Cost of goods sold	1,000,000	1,500,000	50.00	37.50
Gross profit	1,000,000	2,500,000	50.00	62.50
Operating expenses:				
Wages and salaries	120,000	150,000	6.00	3.75
Utilities	80,000	120,000	4.00	3.00
Professional services	20,000	25,000	1.00	0.63
Depreciation	150,000	140,000	7.50	3.50
Taxes and fringe benefits	12,000	15,000	0.60	0.38
Repairs and maintenance	8,000	36,000	0.40	0.90
Bad debts	2,000	1,000	0.10	0.03
Insurance	4,000	2,000	0.20	0.05
Miscellaneous	1,000	3,000	0.05	0.08
	397,000	492,000	19.85	12.30
Operating income (net)	603,000	2,008,000	30.15	50.20
Other income and expense:				
Interest and dividends earned	30,000	50,000	1.50	1.25
Interest expense	150,000	170,000	7.50	4.25
	(120,000)	(120,000)	−6.00	−3.00
Income before taxes	483,000	1,888,000	24.15	47.20
Taxes	200,000	800,000	10.00	20.00
Net income	283,000	1,088,000	14.15	27.20
Retained earnings (beginning of year)	1,000,000	1,101,900		
	1,283,000	2,189,900		
Dividends	181,100	758,700		
Retained earnings (end of year)	$1,101,900	$1,431,200		

EXHIBIT 9.3   Analytical Procedures: Ratio Analysis

	12/31/93	12/31/94	Industry Averages 1994
Current ratio	1.41	1.44	1.50
Quick ratio	.63	.63	.80
Accounts receivable turnover	1.25	2.33	1.50
Inventory turnover	.39	.53	1.00
Times interest earned	4.22	12.11	10.00
Debt to equity	.29	.31	.50
Profit margin	.14	.27	.18
Asset turnover	.26	.47	.33
Return on assets	.04	.13	.06
Return on stockholders' equity	.08	.28	.14

Note: Examined and tested sales for proper year-end cutoff, given abnormal increase in sales and profit margins (See WP S.)

Electronic Workpaper Files

Exhibits 9.4 through 9.10 illustrate the linking of audit workpapers with the aid of an electronic spreadsheet. Although only the cash lead schedule and a bank reconciliation supporting schedule are included in the illustration, all schedules may be linked to the working trial balance in this manner, using **electronic workpaper files.**

Additions, deletions, or changes in audit adjustments need only be entered in the supporting schedule workpaper. The relevant cell equations housed in the template will automatically reflect the change in the lead schedule and the working trial balance. Note in Exhibit 9.8 an adjustment has been added for a year-end bank loan. This event requires an adjustment as of the balance sheet date debiting "cash in bank — general" and crediting "notes payable — current." To effect the change, the auditor simply enters the adjustment on the bank reconciliation supporting schedule. The cash lead schedule (Exhibit 9.9) and the working trial balance are automatically updated.[1]

Accounts Receivable Aging Analysis

In addition to linking the audit workpapers, spreadsheet templates can automate the preparation of the workpapers. An accounts receivable aging analysis is illustrated

---

[1]Exhibit 9.10 includes the balance sheet working trial balance only inasmuch as the income statement is not affected by the audit adjustment.

EXHIBIT 9.4 Working Trial Balance: Balance Sheet

Auditee, Inc.
12/31/94

	12/31/93 Final	12/31/94 G/L	AJEs	RJEs	12/31/94 Final	WP No.
Assets						
Current assets:						
Cash	$ 392,400	$ 426,700	$ 0	($ 10,000)	$ 416,700	A
Marketable securities	52,200	74,400			74,400	
Receivables (net)	1,601,400	1,715,300	(1,115,900)		599,400	C
Inventories	2,542,500	2,810,200	100,000		2,910,200	E
Prepaid expenses	24,900	19,500			19,500	
Total current	4,613,400	5,046,100	(1,015,900)	(10,000)	4,020,200	
Long-term investments	3,000	190,000			190,000	
Other assets	0	0	18,000	10,000	10,000	
Property, plant, and equipment (net)	3,146,500	3,310,900			3,328,900	
Total	$7,762,900	$8,547,000	($ 997,900)	$ 0	$7,549,100	
Liabilities and Stockholders' Equity						
Current Liabilities:						
Notes payable	750,000	825,000			825,000	
Accounts payable	2,150,400	1,340,300			1,340,300	
Accrued payables	210,600	180,500			180,500	
Income taxes payable	150,000	1,170,000	(400,000)		770,000	
Total current	3,261,000	3,515,800	(400,000)		3,115,800	
Bonds payable	1,000,000	1,200,000			1,200,000	
Common stock	2,400,000	2,400,000			2,400,000	
Retained earnings	1,101,900	1,431,200	(597,900)		833,300	
Total	$7,762,900	$8,547,000	($ 997,900)		$7,549,100	

EXHIBIT 9.5   Working Trial Balance: Income Statement

	12/31/93 Final	12/31/94 G/L	AJEs	RJEs	12/31/94 Final	WP No.
Sales	$2,000,000	$4,000,000	($1,000,000)		$3,000,000	S
Cost of goods sold	1,000,000	1,500,000	(100,000)		1,400,000	
Gross profit	1,000,000	2,500,000	(900,000)		1,600,000	
Operating expenses:						
Wages and salaries	120,000	150,000			150,000	
Utilities	80,000	120,000			120,000	
Professional services	20,000	25,000			25,000	
Depreciation	150,000	140,000	2,000		142,000	
Taxes and fringe benefits	12,000	15,000			15,000	
Repairs and maintenance	8,000	36,000	(20,000)		16,000	
Bad debts	2,000	1,000	115,900		116,900	
Insurance	4,000	2,000			2,000	
Miscellaneous	1,000	3,000			3,000	
	397,000	492,000	97,900		589,900	
Operating income (net)	603,000	2,008,000	(997,900)		1,010,100	
Other income and expenses:						
Interest and dividends earned	30,000	50,000			50,000	
Interest expense	150,000	170,000			170,000	
	(120,000)	(120,000)			(120,000)	
Net income before taxes	483,000	1,888,000	(997,900)		890,100	
Taxes	200,000	800,000	(400,000)		400,000	
Net income	283,000	1,088,000	(597,900)		490,100	
Retained earnings (beginning of year)	1,000,000	1,101,900			1,101,900	
	1,283,000	2,189,900	(597,900)		1,592,000	
Dividends	181,000	758,700			758,700	
Retained earnings (end of year)	$1,101,900	$1,431,200	($ 597,900)		$ 833,300	

Auditee, Inc.

in Exhibit 9.11. The auditor uses the aging analysis in evaluating the adequacy of the allowance for doubtful accounts. In automating the workpaper, cell equations may be inserted for performing the following calculations:

1. Footing and crossfooting the columns;

2. Calculating outstanding balances after applying subsequent collections;

3. Applying expected loss percentages to the various categories of receivables to assist the auditor in evaluating collectibility.

EXHIBIT 9.6   Cash Lead Schedule

Prepared by: lfk   Date: 1/23/95
Reviewed by: cck   Date: 2/5/95

Auditee, Inc.
Cash
12/31/94

WP No. A

	12/31/94 G/L	AJE	RJE	12/31/94 Final	WP
Cash in bank—general	$420,000		($10,000)	$410,000	A-1
Cash in bank—payroll	6,000			6,000	
Petty cash	700	—		700	
	$426,700	$0	($10,000)	$416,700	
				To WTB	

EXHIBIT 9.7   Bank Reconciliation before Audit Adjustment

Prepared by: lfk   Date: 1/23/95
Reviewed by: cck   Date: 2/5/95

Auditee, Inc.
Cash in Bank
General
12/31/94

WP No. A-1

12/31/94 Balance per bank		$450,000 *
Add deposits in transit		50,000 &
Total		500,000
Deduct:		
Outstanding checks	30,000 &	
Restricted balance	10,000 !	
		40,000
12/31/94 Balance per reconciliation		460,000
12/31/94 Balance per G/L		420,000
RJE No. 1: Restricted cash		(10,000)
12/31/94 Balance per reconciliation (above)		$410,000 To WPA

* Traced to bank confirmation attached
& Traced to cutoff bank statement obtained directly from bank
! Examined loan agreement (see permanent file)

EXHIBIT 9.8   Bank Reconciliation after Audit Adjustment

	Prepared by: lfk Date: 1/23/95
	Reviewed by: cck Date: 2/5/95

Auditee, Inc.
Cash in Bank
General
12/31/94

WP No. A-1

12/31/94 Balance per bank		$450,000 *
Add deposits in transit		50,000&
Total		500,000
Deduct:		
Outstanding checks	30,000&	
Restricted balance	10,000 !	
		40,000
12/31/94 Balance per reconciliation		$460,000
12/31/94 Balance per G/L		420,000
AJE No. 1: Unrecorded year-end loan receipts		50,000
RJE No. 1: Restricted cash		(10,000)
12/31/94 Balance per reconciliation (above)		$460,000 To WP A

* Traced to bank confirmation attached
& Traced to cutoff bank statement obtained from bank
! Examined loan agreement (see permanent file)

EXHIBIT 9.9   Cash Lead Schedule after Audit Adjustment

	Prepared by: lfk Date: 1/23/95
	Reviewed by: cck Date: 2/5/95

Auditee, Inc.
Cash
12/31/94

WP No. A

	12/31/94	AJE	RJE	12/31/94 Final	WP
Cash in bank—general	$ 420,000	$50,000	($10,000)	$460,000	A-1
Cash in bank—payroll	6,000			6,000	
Petty cash	700			700	
	$ 426,700	$50,000	($10,000)	$466,700	
				To WTB	

EXHIBIT 9.10 Working Trial Balance: Balance Sheet after Cash Audit Adjustment

Auditee, Inc.
Working Trial Balance
12/31/94

	12/31/93 Final	12/31/94 G/L	AJEs	RJEs	12/31/94 Final	WP No.
Assets						
Current assets:						
Cash	$ 392,400	$ 426,700	$ 50,000	($ 10,000)	$ 466,700	A
Marketable securities	52,200	74,400			74,400	
Receivables (net)	1,601,400	1,715,300	(1,115,900)		599,400	C
Inventories	2,542,500	2,810,200	100,000		2,910,200	E
Prepaid expenses	24,900	19,500			19,500	
Total current	4,613,400	5,046,100	(965,900)	(10,000)	4,070,200	
Long-term investments	3,000	190,000			190,000	
Other assets	0	0		10,000	10,000	
Property, plant, and equipment (net)	3,146,500	3,310,900	18,000		3,328,900	
Total	$7,762,900	$8,547,000	($ 947,900)	$ 0	$7,599,100	
Liabilities and Stockholders' Equity						
Current liabilities:						
Notes payable	750,000	825,000	50,000		875,000	
Accounts payable	2,150,400	1,340,300			1,340,300	
Accrued payables	210,600	180,500			180,500	
Income taxes payable	150,000	1,170,000	(400,000)		770,000	
Total current	3,261,000	3,515,800	(350,000)		3,165,800	
Bonds payable	1,000,000	1,200,000			1,200,000	
Common Stock	2,400,000	2,400,000			2,400,000	
Retained earnings	1,101,900	1,431,200	(597,900)		833,300	
Total	$7,762,900	$8,547,000	($ 947,900)		$7,599,100	

EXHIBIT 9.11 Accounts Receivable Aging Analysis

WP C

| | | | Prepared by: if | Date: 2/5/95 |
| | | | Reviewed by: c | Date: 2/15/95 |

Auditee, Inc.
A/R Aging Analysis
12/31/94

Customer	Total	Current	1–60	61–90	91–120	121+
				Past Due (days)		
Audobon, Inc.	$ 100,000	0	$ 30,000	$ 70,000		
Bando	0	0				
Crail, Ltd.	260,000	60,000	200,000			
Dorodiak, Inc.	210,000	0	100,000	30,000		80,000
Klarion Chief	40,000	20,000	20,000			
Laubers	1,080,000	80,000				
Mastalon, Inc.	30,000	0	30,000			
	$1,720,000	$160,000	$ 380,000	$100,000	$0	$80,000
% Estimated uncollectible		1.00%	5.00%	20.00%		100.00%
Estimated uncollectibile($)	$ 120,000	1,600	19,000	20,000	0	80,000

	Receivables—net		B. D. Expense	
12/31/94 balance per G/L	$1,715,300*		$ 1,000	
AJE 2	(1,000,000)			
AJE 6	(115,000)		115,000	
12/31/94 balance per audit	$ 599,400	(see WP S)	$116,900	

Confirmed all accounts (See WP C-1)   To WTB   To WTB

*Accounts receivable	$1,720,000
Allowance for bad debts	(4,700)
Accounts receivable—net	$1,715,300

Evaluated adequacy of allowance for doubtful accounts by preparing above aging analysis, analyzing subsequent collections through 2/15/95, and by discussing past-due accounts with credit manager. Based on this evaluation and given the adjusting entry above, the allowance is adequate.

Property, Plant, and Equipment

Some otherwise time-consuming tasks associated with the audit of property, plant, and equipment can be substantially automated with the assistance of the microcomputer. Some of these are agreeing the subsidiary plant ledger to the controlling accounts, recalculating depreciation and gain or loss on disposals, testing whether accumulated depreciation exceeds cost, and analyzing repairs and maintenance accounts for large debits that may require capitalization as property.[2]

Audit of Investment Portfolios

The audit of large investment portfolios has been similarly automated with the help of **electronic spreadsheets.** Exhibit 9.12 illustrates a worksheet for short-term marketable equity securities. In addition to agreeing the subsidiary ledger to the control account, the auditor can use the spreadsheet to recalculate cost for partial liquidations and gain or loss on disposals. Costs of individual securities can be automatically compared with market prices, and the adjustment, based on an aggregate portfolio comparison, can be calculated.

Amortization schedules for bonds, leases, and other long-term liabilities, as well as long-term investments in interest bearing securities, can be automated with the aid of electronic spreadsheets. Determining the effective interest rate and calculating present value are also facilitated.

A weakness of **spreadsheet systems** in auditing applications is their limited capacity to handle large amounts of data. This is because all of the data in the spreadsheet are in random access memory (RAM) storage. The maximum size of the spreadsheet, therefore, is limited by the computer's RAM storage. For this reason, auditors are using **relational data base systems** to an increasing degree to assist in performing the above tasks given the ability of these packages to handle large volumes of data. Data base systems are becoming an even more attractive alternative with the introduction of **"plug-in" hard disks.** Auditors using lap-top computers, for example, may have a separate plug-in hard disk for each client, and, with relational data base packages, can analyze large volumes of client data stored on the hard disks.

Other Substantive Testing Applications

Accounts Receivable Confirmation and Analysis

The computer can assist in determining sample size for confirmation purposes and in selecting customers' accounts to be confirmed. Confirmations for selected accounts can be printed by the computer, and final results can be evaluated. The auditor usually relies on statistical sampling software packages, spreadsheet templates, or **data base systems** in applying these procedures. A relational data base

---

[2] The substantive audit procedures and related workpapers mentioned and illustrated in this chapter are addressed more fully in Chapters 12 through 14. For this reason, students may wish to review parts of this chapter as the related topics are discussed in the later chapters.

EXHIBIT 9.12   Marketable Securities

	Auditee, Inc. Short-Term Marketable Equity Securities WP B.1 12/31/94					
	12/31/93		1994 Additions			
Security	Shares	Cost	Date	Shares	Cost	Date
American Telephone & Telegraph	400	$ 25,000√				
Burroughs Corp.	100	5,000√				2/6/92
Citi Corp.	100	2,002√				
E. I. DuPont	500	18,380√				
Eastman Kodak			2/3/92	100~	$ 7,828 ~⊗A	
Exxon Corp.	200	6,052√				4/2/92
Ford Motor co.			4/6/92	450~	7,540 ~⊗A	
IBM	400	29,004√				
ITT	400	17,693√				
Johnson & Johnson		√	8/8/92	400~	18,554 ~⊗A	
Pfizer, Inc.		√	9/12/92	400~	15,633 ~⊗A	
Southern California Edison	500	16,342√				6/8/92
Trinova	400	24,000√				
USX			11/23/92	300~	7,500 ~⊗A	
United Technologies	200	8,151√				
Wendy's International	600	7,600√	11/30/92	200~	3,000 ~⊗A	
Westinghouse Electric			12/20/92	200~	5,975 ~⊗A	
Xerox Corp.	500	21,918√				11/23/92
		$181,142			$66,030	

√ Traced to last year's workpaper
~ Vouched to broker's advice
⊗ Examined cancelled check
⋋ Traced to remittance advice and bank statement
A Examined directors' minutes for authorization

(continued)

EXHIBIT 9.12 *(continued)*

| | | | | Prepared by: | lfk | Date: 1/23/95 |
| | | | | Reviewed by: | cck | Date: 1/30/95 |

| 1994 Disposals | | | | 12/31/94 | | 1994 |
Shares	Sale Price	Cost	Gain/(Loss)	Shares	Cost	Market	Dividends
				400 E	$ 25,000	$ 23,200	$ 875 +
100~	$6,433 ~✗	$5,000 A	$1,433	0	0		130 +
				100E	2,002	5,400	220 +
				500E	18,380	38,440	1,080 +
				100E	7,828	5,525	430 +
200~	5,559 ~✗	6,052 A	(493)	0	0		140 +
				450E	7,540	24,300	960 +
				400E	29,004	52,000	1,675 +
				400E	17,693	15,880	1,230 +
				400E	18,554	26,200	2,340 +
				400E	15,633	26,800	990 +
300~	10,112 ~✗	9,805 A	307	200C	6,537	6,875	450 +
				400E	24,000	26,800	730 +
				300E	7,500	5,250	300 +
				200E	8,151	6,800	560 +
				800C	10,600	9,900	880 +
				200E	5,975	10,900	750 +
				300E	13,151	15,600	960 +
200~	9,200 ~✗	8,767 A	433				
	$31,304	$29,624	$1,680		$217,548	$299,870	$ 14,700
			*		*		*
					To WTB		To WTB

* Traced to general ledger
+ Recalculated, based on Standard & Poor's Dividend Reporter
E Examined securities
C Confirmed with broker
A Examined directors' minutes for authorization

package, for example, may be used to assist in performing the following tasks (more fully described in Chapter 12) relative to the audit of accounts receivable:

1. Select and list customer balances above a certain balance for purposes of stratifying the population of customer accounts;
2. List all accounts with credit balances for further follow-up;
3. Select balances for confirmation and print confirmation requests;
4. Sort accounts by account number, dollar balance, customer class, or location;
5. Check for valid account number;
6. Compare credit limit to the current balance for each account and list exceptions;
7. Compare cash receipts after year end to invoices at the balance sheet date;
8. Calculate ratios as part of the application of analytical procedures (e.g., turnover, returns and allowances to sales, bad debt expense to accounts receivable, and average balance per customer).

Inventories

As more fully described in Chapter 11, audit sampling software may be used to test a client's inventories. The auditor can use the programs to select items for quantity, pricing, and extension tests; for evaluating sample results; and for inventory turnover analysis.

To assist in inventory taking and auditor test counts as well as other data gathering audit tasks, a small computer called **GRiDPAD** is available. Resembling a flat screen, GRiDPAD can be programmed to display business forms or checklists—an inventory test count workpaper, for example. Instead of a keyboard, an electronic pen is used to record the auditor's test counts and comments. All the recorded data can then be downloaded into a regular computer for further analysis.

Audit Adjustments

The working trial balance, lead schedules, and supporting schedules can be automatically updated upon the single recording of an audit adjustment. Once proposed adjustments are agreed to by the client, at the close of audit fieldwork, they can be quickly entered and all relevant workpapers will be immediately updated. Workpapers are similarly updated for changed or deleted adjustments or for reclassification entries.

Financial Statement Preparation

After all adjustments and reclassifications have been entered and the workpapers updated, financial statements reflecting these adjustments and reclassifications can be automatically generated with the aid of the microcomputer. If one or more subsidiaries are to be included, the consolidation process can be likewise automated by the inclusion of relevant modules in the software package.

Automated Text Working Papers

Standard letters (engagement letter, lawyer's letter, client representation letter, and reportable conditions letter), audit programs, and the standard audit report can be included in the data base developed with the assistance of the audit software package. With **automated text workpapers,** only the modifications necessary to fit the circumstances of a specific engagement need be made by the auditor prior to the final printing of the documents.

Footnotes, which are an integral part of the financial statements, may also be created, deleted, or modified more easily if incorporated into the auditor's automated data base.

In addition to relational data base systems for facilitating text automation, **optical disk storage** technology, called CD-ROMs (for compact disk read-only memories), has made possible the storage of large volumes of data needed on a recurring basis—permanent file materials, for example. The CDs are read with lasers and the materials can even be transferred by modem to another computer at a distant location.

As the volume of data contained in auditor/client data bases grows, given the new technology, searching for specific content becomes more challenging. To assist in this regard, **hypertext,** a software technique whereby words in a file are coded, enables the auditor to conduct a search for particular words or topics. With the aid of hypertext, the auditor is also able to simplify searching the professional standards and tax laws to obtain answers to technical accounting, auditing, and tax questions.

Budget and Time Summary

As part of the audit and planning phase, the auditor prepares a budget that estimates the time to complete the various parts of the audit (see Chapter 5). The budget typically classifies the time according to task and audit staff level, inasmuch as the billing rates vary for different staff levels. As the audit work proceeds, the actual times are entered and compared with the budgeted times. Significant variances are then investigated and analyzed as to cause. Possible causes are inexperienced audit staff assistants, unanticipated weaknesses in internal control, and failure of the client to have an adjusted trial balance on a timely basis. Exhibit 9.13 contains a budget and time summary prepared with the aid of an electronic spreadsheet. The resulting template, by building calculating equations into the appropriate cells, permits easy modification of the budget as conditions change. It also provides for automatically calculating variances between budgeted time and actual time. In recurring engagements, the prior year's budget may be used as a starting point for preparing the current budget. Times can then be modified for changed conditions (e.g., changes in internal accounting control, changes in client personnel, or changes in audit personnel).

EXPERT SYSTEMS IN AUDITING

In addition to automating routine tasks and permitting fuller analysis of client data, computers are also being used to an increasing degree to assist the auditor in making various kinds of judgment decisions. Termed **expert systems,** these software packages have the ability to make expert quality decisions within specialized domains. Their advantages in facilitating financial audits are twofold. First, they allow increased accessibility to expert knowledge. Second, they assist in achieving consistency in task performance and increase the efficiency in training new decision makers.

EXHIBIT 9.13 Budget and Time Summary

Auditee, Inc.
12/31/94

Audit Module	Budgeted Audit Time					Actual Audit Time					Actual Amount (Over) Under Budget	Explanation of Variance
	Assistant	Senior	Manager	Partner	Total	Assistant	Senior	Manager	Partner	Total		
RISK ANALYSIS:												
Study of the business and the industry	7	3	1		11	9	3	1		13	(2)	New assistant
Study of the organizational structure	5	3	1		9	7	3	1		11	(2)	Ibid.
Analytical review procedures	4	6	1		11	4	4	1		9	2	No abnormal relationships
Phase I, internal control review	3	3			6	4	3			7	(1)	Control changes from prior year
Control testing and completion of Phase II	11	4	2	1	18	13	6	2	1	22	(4)	Extended procedures given control changes
SUBSTANTIVE TESTING:												
Cash in bank	2				2	2				2	0	
Accounts receivable: Confirmation	12	2			14	14	2			16	(2)	Extended procedures given control weakness

					Total					Total	
Aging analysis and evaluation of allowance for bad debts	3	1			4	3	1			4	0	
Inventory observation	20	8			28	20	8			28	0	
Inventory valuation	15	4			19	17	4			21	(2)	Inexperienced assistant
Plant assets	13	2			15	13	2			15	0	
Marketable securities	5	1			6	5	1			6	0	
Current liabilities	10	6			16	12	8			20	(4)	Extended procedures given control weaknesses
Long-term liabilities	4	6			10	5	7			12	(2)	*Ibid.*
Stockholders' equity	1	1			2	1	1			2	0	
OTHER:												
Search for subsequent events	3	2			5	3	2			5	0	
Workpaper review	6	4	1		11	6	4	1		11	0	
Draft of working financial statements and footnotes	3	1	4		8	3	1	4		8	0	
	118	61	10	6	195	130	65	11	6	212	(17)	

Expert systems consist of a body of expert knowledge and a set of decision parameters for solving problems. Experts in the specialized domain (tax experts, pension accounting specialists, bank audit specialists) develop the knowledge base portion of the software package. Formulation of the base may be completed by such techniques as verbal protocol analysis or gaming and simulation techniques. The decision parameters, known as the *knowledge representation framework,* can be purchased as an **expert system shell** package. Based on rules, frames, or logic, the expert systems shell is basically an expert system awaiting a knowledge base. Once the software has been developed, it is tested through system validation which compares the system's performance to that of other experts.

Some of the areas in which CPAs are presently making use of expert systems are predicting the likelihood of bankruptcy, developing audit strategies and generating audit programs, determining the likelihood of fraud, evaluating control structure policies and procedures and assessing control risk, and tax planning and developing tax strategies. The accounting firm of Coopers & Lybrand has developed an expert system called "Risk Advisor" for identifying and quantifying audit risk.

Although a relatively new form of computer application in auditing, expert systems hold the promise for revolutionizing auditing in years to come. The list of possible expert system applications in auditing is limited only by the imagination of the CPA.

KEY TERMS

Automated text workpapers	GRiDPAD
Custom-designed programs	Hypertext
Data base systems	Microcomputer software packages
Electronic spreadsheets	Optical disk storage
Electronic workpaper files	"Plug-in" hard disks
Expert systems	Relational data base systems
Expert system shell	Spreadsheet systems
Generalized audit software packages	

COMPUTER AUDIT PRACTICE CASE

Trim Lawn Manufacturing Corporation

As part of the end-of-chapter materials for Chapters 9 through 15, optional assignments will be made from the Trim Lawn Manufacturing audit practice case presented in the appendix following Chapter 17, (page 725). This case consists of 15 modules. Each module relates to one or more audit phases and can be completed either with or without the computer. The assignments at the end of the chapters parallel the chapter discussion and require the student to analyze files, make changes where appropriate, and draft audit adjustments and reclassifications. Several questions concerning specific audit issues must also be answered in completing the modules included in each assignment.

Completing the assignments by auditing with the computer requires the use of a data diskette containing partially completed audit workpapers. This diskette is provided free of charge by West Educational Publishing. The workpapers on the diskette may be accessed and completed by loading a Lotus 1-2-3 system disk (Version 2.01 or later, or the educational version of Lotus). Instructions for completing the workpapers as well as other requirements are contained in the Trim Lawn appendix.

As an alternative to auditing with the computer, the assignments may be completed manually by acquiring the Trim Lawn Workbook containing partially completed workpapers. The module requirements for auditing with and without the computer are essentially the same. When auditing without the computer, however, the workpapers must be manually completed and calculated.

For Chapter 9 purposes, complete the following assignments from Trim Lawn:

- Module I: Assessment of inherent risk and control risk.

- Module II: Preparation of time budget.

REVIEW QUESTIONS

1. Define *auditing with the computer.*
2. Discuss three approaches to auditing with the computer.
3. What is the major feature associated with microcomputer audit packages?
4. What is meant by *linking* audit workpapers?
5. How is the application of analytical procedures made more effective by auditing with the computer?
6. How does an electronic spreadsheet automate an accounts receivable aging analysis?
7. What is the advantage of a data base system over a spreadsheet system for substantive audit testing purposes?
8. How are audit adjustments automatically reflected in lead schedules and in the working trial balance?
9. How might the computer assist in preparing draft copies of financial statements, footnotes, and the audit report?
10. What are *expert systems?*
11. What are the components of expert systems? How are these components developed?
12. Identify two possible audit applications for expert systems.
13. Define the following terms and explain their relevance to auditing:
    GRiDPAD
    Hypertext
    CD-ROM
    ''Plug-in'' hard disk

MULTIPLE CHOICE QUESTIONS FROM CPA AND CIA EXAMINATIONS

1. The auditor typically has two roles to play in EDP environments. First, he or she may be responsible for evaluating the client's EDP systems in the course of an audit. Second, he or she may be able to
   a. Use the computer as a tool to perform the audit more efficiently or effectively.
   b. Earn extra revenue by selling hardware systems to audit clients.

    c. Provide the IRS with computer tapes of audit clients.

    d. Earn extra revenue by selling software systems to audit clients.

2. The purpose of using generalized computer programs is to test and analyze a client's computer
    a. Systems.
    b. Equipment.
    c. Records.
    d. Processing logic.

3. Which of the following is an advantage of generalized computer audit packages?
    a. They are all written in one identical computer language.
    b. They can be used for audits of clients that use differing EDP equipment and file formats.
    c. They have reduced the need for the auditor to study input controls for EDP-related procedures.
    d. Their use can be substituted for a relatively large part of the required control testing.

4. Auditors often make use of computer programs that perform routine processing functions such as sorting and merging. These programs are made available by electronic data processing companies and others and are specifically referred to as
    a. Compiler programs.
    b. Supervisory programs.
    c. Utility programs.
    d. User programs.

5. Which of the following tasks could not be performed when using a generalized audit software package?
    a. Recalculations of numbers.
    b. Retracing of transactions through calculation and classification operations.
    c. Scanning for unusual items.
    d. Computation of operating ratios.
    e. Physical counts.

6. When an EDP auditor performs control tests on an inventory file containing over 20,000 line items, that auditor can maintain independence and perform most efficiently by
    a. Employing an independent contractor to write an extraction program.
    b. Using a generalized audit software program.
    c. Obtaining a printout of the entire file and then selecting each ''nth'' item.
    d. Using the systems department's programmer to write an extraction program.
    e. Asking the console operator to print every item that cost more than $100.

7. Which of the following is not an advantage of using a generalized computer audit program? Such use
    a. Requires the auditor to have only a minimal knowledge of computer technology.
    b. Assures compatibility with data base management systems.
    c. Eliminates the requirement to develop custom audit software for each type of audit.
    d. Provides the auditor with a high level of programming independence.
    e. Permits greater reliance to be placed on the audit results than could be obtained from manual techniques.

8. An auditor would be least likely to use a generalized computer audit program for which of the following tasks?
   a. Selecting and printing accounts receivable confirmations.
   b. Listing accounts receivable confirmation exceptions for examination.
   c. Comparing accounts receivable subsidiary files to the general ledger.
   d. Investigating exceptions to accounts receivable confirmations.

9. General and special computer programs have been developed for use in auditing EDP systems. When considering the use of these computer audit programs, the auditor
   a. Should determine the audit efficiency of using a given computer program.
   b. Will find them ineffective for applications containing many records and requiring significant time for testing.
   c. Should use them on a surprise basis in order for them to be effective.
   d. Will find them economically feasible for any size EDP system.

10. The Smith Corporation has numerous small customers. A customer file is kept on disk storage. For each customer the file contains customer name, address, credit limit, and account balance. The auditor wishes to test this file to determine whether credit limits are being exceeded. Assuming that computer time is available, the best procedure for the auditor to follow would be to
    a. Develop a test deck which would cause the account balances of certain accounts to be increased until the credit limit was exceeded to see if the system would react properly.
    b. Develop a program to compare credit limits with account balances and print out the details of any account with a balance exceeding its credit limit.
    c. Ask for a printout of all account balances so that they can be manually checked against the credit limits.
    d. Ask for a printout of a sample of account balances so that they can be individually checked against the credit limits.

11. An auditor would *least* likely use computer software to
    a. Access client data files.
    b. Prepare spreadsheets.
    c. Assess EDP control risk.
    d. Construct parallel simulations.

12. An auditor using audit software probably would be *least* interested in which of the following fields in a computerized perpetual inventory file?
    a. Economic order quantity.
    b. Warehouse location.
    c. Date of last purchase.
    d. Quantity sold.

ESSAY QUESTIONS AND PROBLEMS

9.1 After determining that computer controls are valid, Hastings is reviewing the sales system of Rosco Corporation in order to determine how a computerized audit program may be used to assist in performing tests of Rosco's sales records.

Rosco sells crude oil from one central location. All orders are received by mail and indicate the preassigned customer identification number, desired quantity, proposed delivery date, method of payment, and shipping terms. Since price fluctuates daily, orders do not indicate a price. Price sheets are printed daily and details are stored in a permanent disk file. The details of orders are also maintained in a permanent disk file.

Each morning the shipping clerk receives a computer printout that indicates details of customers' orders to be shipped that day. After the orders have been shipped, the shipping details are entered in the computer which simultaneously updates the sales journal, perpetual inventory records, accounts receivable, and sales accounts.

The details of all transactions, as well as daily updates, are maintained on disks that are available for use by Hastings during the audit.

Required:

a. How may a computerized audit program be used by Hastings to perform substantive tests of Rosco's sales records in their machine readable form? Do not discuss accounts receivable and inventory.

b. After performing these tests with the assistance of the computer, what other auditing procedures should Hastings perform in order to complete the examination of Rosco's sales records? (AICPA adapted)

9.2 In the past, the records to be evaluated in an audit have been printed reports, listings, documents, and written papers, all of which are visible output. However, in fully computerized systems that daily update transaction files, output and files are frequently in machine-readable forms such as cards, tapes, or disks. Thus, they often present the auditor with an opportunity to use the computer in performing an audit.

Required:

Discuss how the computer can be used to aid the auditor in examining accounts receivable in such a fully computerized system. (AICPA adapted)

9.3 Random Mills, a wholesale yarn distributor, utilizes a minicomputer in processing inventory and payroll transactions. Accounts receivable, however, consist of manual records. A physical inventory is taken annually, and the perpetual records are adjusted accordingly. Statements are mailed to customers on a monthly basis and exceptions are promptly cleared.

Steve Yarl, a senior auditor for Hankins and Poole, CPAs, is in charge of the Random Mills examination. Internal control questionnaires and flowcharts have been completed and internal control in each of the three areas has been judged satisfactory.

Hankins and Poole have recently developed in-house a software package which automates many of the tasks performed in the typical audit. The software is used in conjunction with portable microcomputers that accompany the staff on each audit.

Required:

a. How might the software be used to assist Yarl and his audit team in the examination of Random Mills' payroll, inventory, and accounts receivable?

b. Auditing with the aid of a microcomputer software package may be applicable to both control structure testing and substantive testing and may be used whether the client's system is manual or computerized. Explain this statement as it relates to the Random Mills audit.

9.4 Talbert Corporation hired an independent computer programmer to develop a simplified payroll application for its newly purchased computer. The programmer developed an on-line data base microcomputer system that minimized the level of knowledge required by the operator. It was based upon typing answers to input cues that appeared on the terminal's viewing screen, examples of which follow:

a. Access routine:
   1. Operator access number to payroll file?
   2. Are there new employees?
b. New employees routine:
   1. Employee name?
   2. Employee number?
   3. Social security number?
   4. Rate per hour?
   5. Single or married?
   6. Number of dependents?
   7. Account distribution?
c. Current payroll routine:
   1. Employee number?
   2. Regular hours worked?
   3. Overtime hours worked?
   4. Total employees this payroll period?

The independent auditor is attempting to verify that certain input validation (edit) checks exist to ensure that errors resulting from omissions, invalid entries, or other inaccuracies will be detected during the typing of answers to the input cues.

Required:

Identify the various types of input validation (edit) checks the independent auditor would expect to find in the EDP system. Describe the assurances provided by each identified validation check. Do not discuss the review and evaluation of these controls (AICPA adapted.)

9.5 Electronic spreadsheet-based audit software packages automate the preparation and modification of workpapers. Equations, rather than numbers, are entered in certain cells of the workpaper, thereby automatically recalculating amounts when changes are made. As an example, consider Exhibit 9.13, the budget and time summary. Each line total for "budgeted audit time" is produced by the equation summing assistant time, senior time, manager time, and partner time. Similar equations are placed in the total cells for "actual audit time."

Required:

a. What form of equation is placed in the "column total" cells? In the "actual (over)/under budget" cells?
b. Consider Exhibits 9.1 through 9.3.
   1. Identify the cells in which equations are likely to be found.
   2. Describe the nature of each equation.

9.6 A medium-sized company purchased a mainframe-based payroll software package to service two plants, five distribution centers, and 10 sales offices. The old system was completely manual and was reviewed by the internal auditing department last year. The audit included the following steps:

1. A system walk-through to identify control points and to verify proper segregation of duties.
2. Performing a payoff (surprise payroll distribution).
3. Verifying the gross-to-net payroll calculations.
4. Reviewing payroll files.
5. Checking signatures.
6. Verifying completeness of documentation.
7. Footing and cross-footing departmental totals.
8. Verifying the labor distribution system journal entry to both the cost system and the general ledger.
9. Testing additions, deletions, and changes to the master payroll based on data gathered from the payroll supervisor's files.

Required:
Contrast the required audit steps performed to audit the new automated system versus the audit steps performed last year for each appropriate control objective in a payroll system. Maximize the use of computer audit-assisted techniques and take into consideration the information systems environment. Presume that a microcomputer is available, and an appropriate audit software or a "report writer" is available with the package. Use the following format for your answer:

Control	*Manual*	*Automated*
Objective	*Test*	*Test*

(IIA adapted)

10

Statistical Sampling for Testing Control Procedures

CHAPTER OUTLINE

I. **Sampling applications in auditing**
   A. Control testing
   B. Substantive testing

II. **Sampling for control testing**
   A. Forms of control testing
   B. Sampling to test controls leaving documentation

III. **Statistical vs. nonstatistical sampling**
   A. GAAS permits either
   B. Statistical sampling as a mathematical approach
   C. Nonstatistical sampling as a subjective approach

IV. **Statistical sampling and audit judgment**

V. **Statistical sampling for control testing**
   A. Sampling for attributes
   B. Choice of sampling method
   C. Calculating the sample size
   D. Case study
      1. Drawing the sample
      2. Examining the sample items
      3. Evaluating the sample results

VI. **Statistical sampling and audit risk implications**
   A. Review of audit risk and reason for quantifying
   B. How to quantify control risk
   C. How to quantify inherent risk
   D. How to quantify detection risk

VII. **Extended example**

OVERVIEW

Chapter 10 is the first of two chapters dealing with statistical sampling in auditing. The discussion in Chapter 10 is restricted to sampling as applied to the auditor's assessment of control risk. Figure 10.1 identifies that part of the audit process occupied by this discussion. Chapter 11 considers sampling applications for substantive testing purposes.

Chapter 10 begins by comparing statistical with nonstatistical sampling, noting that although both approaches are permitted by GAAS, the coverage in Chapters 10 and 11 is restricted to statistical sampling. The ability of statistical sampling to assist the auditor in evaluating audit risk, by providing a means for partially quantifying it, is the reason for limiting the discussion to this means of audit sampling.

Identifying attribute sampling as the appropriate method for control testing and control risk assessment purposes, the chapter proceeds to define sampling terms and outline the steps involved in the sampling process.

The means by which statistical sampling assists in audit risk quantification are described at length and an extended example is presented at the end of the chapter to further clarify the concepts.

STUDY OBJECTIVES

After reading this chapter, you should be able to:

1. Identify the audit areas in which sampling is appropriate;
2. Differentiate between statistical and nonstatistical sampling;
3. Define the following terms:
   a. Expected occurrence rate,
   b. Tolerable occurrence rate,
   c. Risk of underassessment,
   d. Upper occurrence limit;
4. Apply attribute sampling to a control testing example;
5. Relate attribute sampling to audit risk;
6. Quantify audit risk as an input to variables sampling for substantive testing purposes.

FIGURE 10.1   The Audit Process

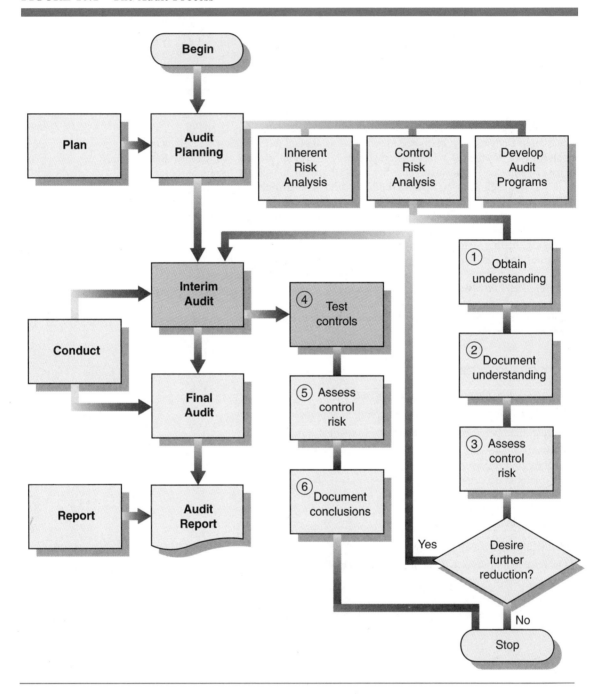

SAMPLING APPLICATIONS IN AUDITING

Virtually all independent audits are test based. A test-based audit permits the auditor to draw conclusions by examining only a portion of the transactions and events completed by the client firm. Detailed audits, requiring the examination of all transactions, were common in the early stages of auditing; but as entities grew in size, the volume of transactions became too great for a detailed audit to be cost-effective. For this reason, auditors began to recognize the importance of control structure policies and procedures for preventing and detecting material errors and irregularities; and auditing gradually evolved from detail to test basis. At the same time, audit reports shifted from guaranteeing the accuracy of the accounts to providing reasonable assurance as to overall fairness of financial presentation.

In test-based auditing, the selection of those transactions to be examined requires some sampling methodology. Such methodology may involve the use of either statistical or nonstatistical sampling. Generally accepted auditing standards permit either approach.[1]

Sampling methods are used by auditors in both control testing and substantive testing. For control testing purposes, sampling is used to estimate error rates and thereby assist in evaluating the effectiveness of internal control procedures. In substantive testing, sampling is used to estimate the dollar amount of account balances and transactions. Sampling for control testing is covered in this chapter. Sampling for substantive testing is examined in Chapter 11.

HOW SAMPLING CAN ASSIST IN CONTROL TESTING

Sampling provides a systematic approach to estimating error rates in certain kinds of populations. The error rates provide evidence of control weaknesses and assist the auditor in assessing control risk within transaction cycle subsets.

Forms of Control Testing

As presented in Chapter 7, control structure understanding and testing assumes three forms in the typical independent audit. Where there is a visible audit trail in the form of documentation, the auditor *examines documents,* as appropriate, to verify the effectiveness of internal control procedures. Evidence as to whether transactions have been executed in accordance with management's authorization and recorded in accordance with GAAP is gathered through such examination. In the absence of an audit trail, the auditor *observes* the control environment and procedures, and possibly *reprocesses* selected transactions. Management support of the control structure, adequacy of separation of duties, competence and integrity of personnel, and the existence of periodic inventories and comparisons are verified by the auditor through observation. Password security, user identification codes, and input editing controls are tested through reprocessing.

---

[1]Auditing Standards Board, *AICPA Professional Standards,* New York: AICPA, Section AU 350.03.

Sampling to Test Controls Leaving Documentation

Sampling methods are commonly applied to the first form of control testing, that is, in verifying the existence of proper reviews, approvals, and recording where there is an audit trail of documentation.[2] Observation for control effectiveness ordinarily does not require the use of audit sampling. Although transaction reprocessing may involve a form of sampling, the auditor utilizes judgment sampling rather than probability sampling in testing a few selected transactions designed to violate controls.

Sampling can assist the auditor in the following ways during the examination of documentary evidence for control testing purposes:

1. Determining the number of documents to examine in testing for a specific attribute;
2. Selecting the documents to be tested;
3. Evaluating the sample results; and
4. Further assessing the control risk.

STATISTICAL SAMPLING VS. NONSTATISTICAL SAMPLING

When confronted with a task requiring the application of sampling methods, the auditor must elect whether to apply statistical or nonstatistical sampling. As stated earlier, auditing standards permit either approach. In order to make a rational selection, the auditor must recognize the distinction between the two methods.

Statistical sampling is a mathematical approach to inference. In determining sample size, in selecting the sample, and in evaluating the sample results, a consistent and orderly approach is followed. Setting precision ranges and reliability levels, as defined and discussed in Chapter 11, are important steps in applying this approach.

Large populations providing ready access to each item are more conducive to statistical sampling methods than smaller populations or populations containing items not readily accessible by the auditor. A large population of prenumbered vouchers, for example, all of which are filed sequentially, may be tested for control effectiveness by applying statistical sampling.

Nonstatistical sampling is a more subjective approach to inference in that mathematical techniques are not consistently used in determining sample size, selecting the sample, or evaluating sample results. Instead, the auditor exercises professional judgment in making such determinations. Smaller populations, or populations containing items not so readily accessible by the auditor, are often more conducive to the application of nonstatistical sampling techniques. Given a relatively small number of customer accounts, for example, the auditor may find it cost-effective to examine a larger percentage of the accounts than would be required by the application of statistical sampling methods. Similarly, a large population of vouchers processed by an on-line real-time system may not be filed in a manner that lends itself to random selection. Under such conditions, nonstatistical sampling methods may be more appropriate.

---

[2]*Ibid.*, Section AU 350.32.

Reprocessing and document testing—two approaches to control testing.

Although both methods are permitted under GAAS, the discussion in this chapter and the next is restricted to statistical sampling. In addition to being a more consistent approach to audit sampling, statistical sampling provides the only effective means for quantifying audit risk. Therefore, it fits more neatly into the risk analysis framework of this textbook.

STATISTICAL SAMPLING AND AUDIT JUDGMENT

Although statistical sampling involves the application of mathematical techniques in determining sample size and in evaluating sample results, it does not replace audit judgment. In determining sample size, for example, the auditor must exercise judgment in selecting a tolerable rate of error beyond which the assessed level of control risk would not be reduced. Audit judgment is also required in determining an acceptable risk of incorrectly assessing control risk below the maximum level. In evaluating sample results, judgment must be exercised in assessing the materiality of control weaknesses. Statistical sampling does provide for greater *consistency* in the application of audit judgment. By providing a uniform framework for determining sample size, selecting the sample, and evaluating results, statistical sampling permits the auditor to make audit judgments within the bounds of consistent parameters.

STATISTICAL SAMPLING FOR CONTROL TESTING

The goal of control testing is to determine whether those controls which the auditor wishes to test were functioning effectively during the period under audit. Some controls are tested through observation, some are tested by transaction reprocessing, and some are tested by examining documents. Statistical sampling techniques, as discussed in the following paragraphs, are applicable to the latter.

Sampling for Attributes

Some **attributes** of interest to the auditor in testing controls by examining documents are the following:

1. Are purchase invoices properly approved for payment?
2. Are account distributions correct?
3. Do vouchers contain the necessary documentation?
4. Are proper labor rates being used to compute payroll?
5. Do time cards agree with the payroll summary as to hours?
6. Are all sales invoices properly approved and accompanied by shipping orders and bills of lading?
7. Do selling prices agree with published price lists?

Statistical sampling techniques will assist in determining the number of documents to be examined for each attribute of interest, in selecting the documents, and in evaluating the results of the sampling.

Choice of Sampling Method

For auditing applications, the following sampling methods are commonly used:

1. **Attribute sampling:** An estimate of *frequency* of events (errors or irregularities). This method is covered in the current chapter for control testing.
2. **Variables sampling:** An estimate of *amount* (account balance or dollar amount of errors). Variables sampling is used for substantive testing purposes and is covered in Chapter 11.
3. **Discovery sampling:** An orderly approach to locating a particular event. In auditing applications, this method is used to find an example of an error or irregularity when the auditor's suspicions are aroused. Related more to detection of fraud, discovery sampling is beyond the scope of this textbook.

Calculating the Sample Size

In applying statistical sampling techniques, the auditor is trying to draw conclusions about a population by looking at part of it. The question is, How much does the auditor need to examine? In applying attribute sampling to control testing, sample size is a function of the following factors.

Population Size

For attribute sampling purposes, *population size* (the number of vouchers processed during the period, the number of employee time cards submitted, the number of sales invoices written, etc.) does not have a material influence on sample size unless the population contains fewer than 1,000 items (see Table 10.1). Inasmuch as virtually all attribute sampling applications in auditing involve population sizes well in excess of 1,000, tables for determining sample size ignore population size.

Expected Occurrence Rate

The **expected occurrence rate** is the anticipated error rate. For example, an attribute of interest, for control testing purposes, is whether the proper accounts were debited for vouchers processed. The expected occurrence rate, for purposes of this test, is the estimated percentage of vouchers containing account distribution errors. The estimate may be based on the initial understanding phase of the control structure review and evaluation, on the prior year's audit if this is a recurring audit, or on a pilot sample selected for the purpose of estimating the population occurrence rate. The expected occurrence rate positively affects sample size in that a high expected rate requires a larger sample than would be appropriate were a low rate of error expected.

Tolerable Occurrence Rate

The **tolerable occurrence rate** is the maximum rate of error acceptable to the auditor, while still warranting a lowering of assessed control risk below the maximum level. It

TABLE 10.1   Effects of Population Size on Sample Size

Population Size	Sample Size
50	45
100	64
500	87
1,000	90
2,000	92
5,000	93
100,000	93

Source: AICPA, *Audit Sampling Guide* (New York: Author, 1983) page 35.

is inversely related to sample size in that the lower the tolerable rate of error, the larger is the sample size. Whether the rate is to be set high or low depends on audit judgment.

In setting the tolerable occurrence rate, the auditor considers the importance of the attribute being tested. The more critical an attribute to those control policies and procedures relevant to an audit, the lower the tolerable occurrence rate. Account distribution errors, for example, may be considered more critical to effective control than lack of initials evidencing approval of purchase requisitions. Setting a lower tolerable occurrence rate when examining vouchers for erroneous debits increases the sample size and thereby recognizes the materiality of control weaknesses involving account distribution errors.

The expected occurrence rate and the tolerable occurrence rate together define **precision,** which is the range within which the true answer most likely falls. The narrower the precision range (i.e., the closer the two rates), the larger the sample size (see Table 10.2). Given an expected occurrence rate, the lower the tolerable occurrence rate, the larger the sample size. Likewise, given a specified tolerable occurrence rate, the higher the expected occurrence rate, the larger the sample size.

Acceptable Level of Risk of Understating Control Risk

As discussed in Chapter 5, audit risk may be classified as:

1. The risk that material errors or irregularities exist (inherent risk and control risk); and

2. The risk that such material errors or irregularities will go undetected (detection risk).

The auditor studies the business and industry and applies analytical procedures (as discussed in Chapter 5) as a basis for assessing inherent risk, studies and evaluates internal control structure policies and procedures for assessing control risk, and designs substantive audit procedures to reduce detection risk to an acceptable level.

A weak control structure (maximum level of control risk) increases the overall audit risk. This, in turn, requires more substantive testing than would be required

TABLE 10.2   Precision and Sample Size

Expected Occurrence Rate	Tolerable Occurrence Rate	Precision	Sample Size
1%	4%	3%	156
1	5	4	93
1	6	5	78
1	7	6	66
1	8	7	58
2	8	6	77
3	8	5	95
4	8	4	146

given a satisfactory control structure.[3] In a test-based audit, the auditor must assess control risk by examining a sample and extending the results to the population (Chapter 10). Such assessment, when combined with the auditor's evaluation of inherent risk, will then serve as an input into calculating sample sizes for substantive testing purposes (Chapter 11).

The risk of incorrectly assessing control risk below the maximum level, also a function of audit judgment, is the risk that the sample supports the auditor's lowering of assessed control risk when the true error rate in the population does not justify such reduction. In nonstatistical terms, it is the probability that the auditor will assess control risk at a lower level than justified for a given subset of the client's control structure. **Risk of underassessment** (assessing control risk too low) relates to *reliability* or the confidence level, defined as the likelihood that the true answer falls within the range (precision) established through sampling. It is inversely related to sample size in that the lower the acceptable risk of underassessment, the larger is the required sample size. Stated differently, the greater the confidence the auditor wishes to place on the results of sampling, the larger the number of items to be included in the sample.

Risk of underassessment is similar to *beta risk,* defined in statistics as the risk of incorrect acceptance. Given that it represents a primary basis for the audit opinion, the risk of underassessment should be set at a low level. Most auditors, as a rule of thumb, accept a risk of underassessment $\leq = 10$ percent.

The expected occurrence rate, the tolerable occurrence rate, and the acceptable risk of underassessment, as just defined, are the inputs contained in the sample size tables presented in this chapter. They have the following effects on sample size:

Parameter	Effect on Sample Size
Population Size	Positive
Expected Occurrence Rate	Positive
Tolerable Occurrence Rate	Inverse
Acceptable Risk of Underassessment	Inverse

The tables provide for two possible levels of risk of underassessment of control risk: 5 percent and 10 percent.

Case Study

As a means for applying the concepts just discussed, consider the following example. In testing control structure policies and procedures relevant to the expenditure cycle, the CPA wishes to examine the client's vouchers to determine whether the necessary controls are present and functioning effectively. One of the attributes to be tested is proper documentation of transactions. With respect to a specific voucher, the absence of one or more of the following documents is considered an error:

1. Purchase requisition;
2. Purchase order;

---

[3]Overall audit risk is the joint probability of inherent risk, control risk, and detection risk. It was represented in Chapter 5 by the notation $IR \times CR \times DR$.

3. Receiving report;

4. Vendor's invoice.

Based on last year's audit and this year's preliminary control structure study and evaluation, the CPA believes the client's vouchers contain a 3 percent error rate with respect to inadequate documentation (expected occurrence rate). The CPA wishes to gain assurance, with 95 percent confidence (risk of underassessment = 5 percent), that the population error rate is ≤6 percent (tolerable occurrence rate). An upper error limit greater than 6 percent, in other words, will preclude the auditor from lowering the assessed control risk below the maximum level. Tables 10.3 and 10.4 list sample sizes based on risk of underassessment, expected occurrence rate, and tolerable occurrence rate. In Table 10.3, the sample size corresponding to the intersection of 3 percent expected occurrence rate and 6 percent tolerable occurrence rate is 195. This means that the auditor must select 195 vouchers and examine each one for completeness of documentation.

Drawing the Sample

In applying statistical sampling methods, the items to be included in the sample must be drawn on a probability basis. That is, every item in the population must have a known or equal chance of being included in the sample. Referred to as **random selection,** the following alternatives are available to the auditor: Random number tables and systematic sampling.

Random number tables (like Table 10.5) or computer-generated random numbers are most appropriate when documents are prenumbered and filed in numerical sequence for ready access by document number. Before using random number tables, two determinations are necessary. First, some form of correspondence between the document numbers and the random number tables must be established. If the documents contain four digits, for example, and the random numbers are five digit numbers, the auditor must determine which four digits of the random numbers to use, and apply the method consistently in drawing the sample. If a chosen number in the table does not conform to a document number used during the period, the auditor would discard that number and proceed sequentially to the next usable number in the table.

In addition to establishing correspondence between the random number tables and the document numbers, the auditor must determine a consistent route through the tables in order to ensure systematic movement. Such a route may be vertical, horizontal, or diagonal; but once determined, the route must be followed consistently for a particular sample.

After determining numeric correspondence and route, the first number may be selected from the table. This selection must be made at random. Thereafter, each succeeding item in the table (using the predetermined route) is drawn until the number of documents selected is equal to the sample size.

The auditor must determine whether a particular number (document) may be selected more than once (sampling with replacement) or whether a document may be drawn only once for inclusion in the sample (sampling without replacement). Although both methods are statistically acceptable, most auditors prefer to sample without replacement.

TABLE 10.3 Statistical Sample Sizes for Control Testing 5 Percent Risk of Underassessment (with number of expected errors in parentheses)

EXPECTED POPULATION DEVIATION RATE	TOLERABLE RATE										
	2%	3%	4%	5%	6%	7%	8%	9%	10%	15%	20%
0.00%	149(0)	99(0)	74(0)	59(0)	49(0)	42(0)	36(0)	32(0)	29(0)	19(0)	14(0)
.25	236(1)	157(1)	117(1)	93(1)	78(1)	66(1)	58(1)	51(1)	46(1)	30(1)	22(1)
.50	*	157(1)	117(1)	93(1)	78(1)	66(1)	58(1)	51(1)	46(1)	30(1)	22(1)
.75	*	208(2)	117(1)	93(1)	78(1)	66(1)	58(1)	51(1)	46(1)	30(1)	22(1)
1.00	*	*	156(2)	93(1)	78(1)	66(1)	58(1)	51(1)	46(1)	30(1)	22(1)
1.25	*	*	156(2)	124(2)	78(1)	66(1)	58(1)	51(1)	46(1)	30(1)	22(1)
1.50	*	*	192(3)	124(2)	103(2)	66(1)	58(1)	51(1)	46(1)	30(1)	22(1)
1.75	*	*	227(4)	153(3)	103(2)	88(2)	77(2)	51(1)	46(1)	30(1)	22(1)
2.00	*	*	*	181(4)	127(3)	88(2)	77(2)	68(2)	46(1)	30(1)	22(1)
2.25	*	*	*	208(5)	127(3)	88(2)	77(2)	68(2)	61(2)	30(1)	22(1)
2.50	*	*	*	*	150(4)	109(3)	77(2)	68(2)	61(2)	30(1)	22(1)
2.75	*	*	*	*	173(5)	109(3)	95(3)	68(2)	61(2)	30(1)	22(1)
3.00	*	*	*	*	195(6)	129(4)	95(3)	84(3)	61(2)	30(1)	22(1)
3.25	*	*	*	*	*	148(5)	112(4)	84(3)	61(2)	30(1)	22(1)
3.50	*	*	*	*	*	167(6)	112(4)	84(3)	76(3)	40(2)	22(1)
3.75	*	*	*	*	*	185(7)	129(5)	100(4)	76(3)	40(2)	22(1)
4.00	*	*	*	*	*	*	146(6)	100(4)	89(4)	40(2)	22(1)
5.00	*	*	*	*	*	*	*	158(8)	116(6)	40(2)	30(2)
6.00	*	*	*	*	*	*	*	*	179(11)	50(3)	30(2)
7.00	*	*	*	*	*	*	*	*	*	68(5)	37(3)

*Sample size is too large to be cost-effective for most audit applications.

Note: This table assumes a large population.

Source: AICPA, *Audit Sampling Guide* (New York: AICPA, 1983), page 106.

TABLE 10.4 Statistical Sample Sizes for Control Testing 10 Percent Risk of Underassessment (with number of expected errors in parentheses)

EXPECTED POPULATION DEVIATION RATE	TOLERABLE RATE										
	2%	3%	4%	5%	6%	7%	8%	9%	10%	15%	20%
0.00%	114(0)	76(0)	57(0)	45(0)	38(0)	32(0)	28(0)	25(0)	22(0)	15(0)	11(0)
.25	194(1)	129(1)	96(1)	77(1)	64(1)	55(1)	48(1)	42(1)	38(1)	25(1)	18(1)
.50	194(1)	129(1)	96(1)	77(1)	64(1)	55(1)	48(1)	42(1)	38(1)	25(1)	18(1)
.75	265(2)	129(1)	96(1)	77(1)	64(1)	55(1)	48(1)	42(1)	38(1)	25(1)	18(1)
1.00	*	176(2)	96(1)	77(1)	64(1)	55(1)	48(1)	42(1)	38(1)	25(1)	18(1)
1.25	*	221(3)	132(2)	77(1)	64(1)	55(1)	48(1)	42(1)	38(1)	25(1)	18(1)
1.50	*	*	132(2)	105(2)	64(1)	55(1)	48(1)	42(1)	38(1)	25(1)	18(1)
1.75	*	*	166(3)	105(2)	88(2)	55(1)	48(1)	42(1)	38(1)	25(1)	18(1)
2.00	*	*	198(4)	132(3)	88(2)	75(2)	48(1)	42(1)	38(1)	25(1)	18(1)
2.25	*	*	*	132(3)	88(2)	75(2)	65(2)	42(1)	38(1)	25(1)	18(1)
2.50	*	*	*	158(4)	110(3)	75(2)	65(2)	58(2)	38(1)	25(1)	18(1)
2.75	*	*	*	209(6)	132(4)	94(3)	65(2)	58(2)	52(2)	25(1)	18(1)
3.00	*	*	*	*	132(4)	94(3)	65(2)	58(2)	52(2)	25(1)	18(1)
3.25	*	*	*	*	153(5)	113(4)	82(3)	58(2)	52(2)	25(1)	18(1)
3.50	*	*	*	*	194(7)	113(4)	82(3)	73(3)	52(2)	25(1)	18(1)
3.75	*	*	*	*	*	131(5)	98(4)	73(3)	52(2)	25(1)	18(1)
4.00	*	*	*	*	*	149(6)	98(4)	73(3)	65(3)	25(1)	18(1)
5.00	*	*	*	*	*	*	160(8)	115(6)	78(4)	34(2)	18(1)
6.00	*	*	*	*	*	*	*	182(11)	116(7)	43(3)	25(2)
7.00	*	*	*	*	*	*	*	*	199(14)	52(4)	25(2)

*Sample size is too large to be cost-effective for most audit applications.
Note: This table assumes a large population.
Source: AICPA, *Audit Sampling Guide* (New York: AICPA, 1983), page 107.

TABLE 10.5   Illustration of Table of Random Numbers

	(01)	(02)	(03)	(04)	(05)	(06)	(07)	(08)
(0001)	9492	4562	4180	5525	7255	1297	9296	1283
(0002)	1557	0392	8989	6898	1072	6013	0020	8582
(0003)	0714	5947	2420	6210	3824	2743	4217	3707
(0004)	0558	8266	4990	8954	7455	6309	9543	1148
(0005)	1458	8725	3750	3138	2499	6017	7744	1485
(0006)	5169	6981	4319	3369	9424	4117	7632	5457
(0007)	0328	5213	1017	5248	8622	6454	8120	4585
(0008)	2462	2055	9782	4213	3452	9940	8859	1000
(0009)	8408	8697	3982	8228	7668	8139	3736	4889
(0010)	1818	5041	9706	4646	3992	4110	4091	7619
(0011)	1771	8614	8593	0930	2095	5005	6387	4002
(0012)	7050	1437	6847	4679	9059	4139	6602	6817
(0013)	5875	2094	0495	3213	5694	5513	3547	9035
(0014)	2473	2087	4618	1507	4471	9542	7565	2371
(0015)	1976	1639	4956	9011	8221	4840	4513	5263
(0016)	4006	4029	7270	8027	7476	7690	6362	1251
(0017)	2149	8162	0667	0825	7353	4645	3273	1181
(0018)	1669	7011	6548	5851	8278	9006	8176	1268
(0019)	7436	5041	4087	1647	7205	3977	4257	9008
(0020)	2178	3632	5745	2228	1780	6043	9296	4469

Source: Dan M. Guy, *Statistical Sampling in Auditing* (New York: John Wiley & Sons, 1982), page 24.

When documents are not prenumbered, an acceptable alternative to the use of random number tables or computer-generated numbers is systematic sampling with a random start. **Systematic sampling** involves choosing every nth item in the population until the requisite sample size is reached. Two requirements in applying this method are that the start be at random and that the entire field be covered. If, for example, the population of vouchers is 19,500 and the sample size is 195, the auditor would select the first voucher at random and every 100th voucher thereafter.

In applying random sampling methods, auditors frequently stratify populations. The purpose of **stratified sampling** is to permit the auditor to vary the intensity of examination for certain subsets of the population. Inasmuch as stratification is more appropriate for substantive testing than for control testing, it is addressed more completely in Chapter 11.

Examine the Sample Items

Having drawn the sample on a probability basis, the auditor must carefully examine each item in the sample for the chosen attribute. A prerequisite to effectively performing this step in the sampling process is a clear definition by the auditor of deviations from the attribute being tested. The absence of a receiving report, for example, may be defined as a deviation (error) if the related voucher is for goods purchased, but does not constitute an error if purchased services are the subject matter of the voucher. Similarly, lack of an approved requisition is not an error if certain inventory items are automatically reordered when the minimum stock level has been reached.

The preceding discussion was based on a single attribute—proper documentation. In examining a particular type of document, however, the auditor is usually interested in more than a single attribute. In testing vouchers, for example, the following attributes may be relevant:

1. Proper documentation;

2. Evidence of proper approvals and reviews;

3. Proper account distribution;

4. Agreement of receiver and vendor's invoice as to type and quantity of goods received and billed;

5. Agreement between the purchase order and vendor's invoice as to price; and

6. Correctness of extensions and footings on vendor's invoice.

Rather than drawing six different samples for testing these attributes, the auditor draws a single sample and tests each document for all of the attributes. Exhibit 10.1 presents a sampling plan worksheet for the purpose of testing vouchers for the six attributes just listed. Note that the sample sizes are not the same for all attributes because expected occurrence rate, tolerable occurrence rate, and precision are not the same for all attributes. These parameters are a function of the preliminary evaluation of control structure and the auditor's judgment concerning materiality, which may vary for different attributes.

In following the sampling plan outlined in Exhibit 10.1, the auditor randomly draws a sample equal to the maximum sample size presented in the worksheet (195). In examining the vouchers for errors, the auditor proceeds as follows:
The first 95 vouchers are examined for all attributes;

■ Vouchers 96–129 are examined for attributes (1), (2), (3), (4), and (6);

■ Vouchers 130–156 are examined for attributes (1), (2), (3), and (6);

■ Vouchers 157–181 are examined for attributes (1) and (2);

■ Vouchers 181–195 are examined for attribute (1).

Evaluate the Sample Results

Having examined each item in the sample for the attributes being tested, the auditor must next evaluate the sample results. Three steps are involved in this process:

1. The auditor must calculate the **upper occurrence limit** (Exhibit 10.2);

2. The upper occurrence limit is compared with the tolerable occurrence limit;

3. The impact on substantive audit programs is considered.

EXHIBIT 10.1   Attribute Sampling Plan Worksheet 1

Index	S.1
Prepared by	LFK
Date	9/3/93
Reviewed by	SEL
Date	9/15/93

XYZ Company
Voucher Testing for Control Effectiveness
12/31/93

Attribute Tested	Risk of Under-assessment	Expected Occurrence Rate	Tolerable Occurrence Rate	Precision	Sample Size	Number of Detected Errors	Upper Occurrence Limit
1. Proper documentation	5%	3%	6%	3%	195		
2. Proper reviews and approvals	5	2	5	3	181		
3. Proper account distribution	5	1	4	3	156		
4. Agreement of receiver and vendor's invoice as to type and quantity of goods received and billed	5	3	7	4	129		
5. Agreement between purchase order and vendor's invoice as to price	5	3	8	5	95		
6. Correctness of extensions and footings on vendor's invoice	5	1	4	3	156		

411

EXHIBIT 10.2   Attribute Sampling Plan Worksheet 2

Index   S.1
Prepared by   LFK
Date   9/3/93
Reviewed by   SEL
Date   9/15/93

XYZ Company
Voucher Testing for Control Effectiveness
12/31/93

Attribute Tested	Risk of Under-assessment	Expected Occurrence Rate	Tolerable Occurrence Rate	Precision	Sample Size	Number of Detected Errors	Upper Occurrence Limit
1. Proper documentation	5%	3%	6%	3%	195	3	4%
2. Proper reviews and approvals	5	2	5	3	181	3	5
3. Proper account distribution	5	1	4	3	156	5	7
4. Agreement of receiver and vendor's invoice as to type and quantity of goods received and billed	5	3	7	4	129	2	5
5. Agreement between purchase order and vendor's invoice as to price	5	3	8	5	95	2	7
6. Correctness of extensions and footings on vendor's invoice	5	1	4	3	156	1	3

The upper occurrence limit is a function of the number of errors detected in the sample relative to the sample size and the designated risk of underassessment. Tables 10.6 and 10.7 are provided for calculating the upper occurrence limit.

The point at which sample size and number of deviations intersect determines the upper occurrence limit.[4] If the upper occurrence limit exceeds the tolerable occurrence rate, the auditor should consider maintaining assessed control risk at the maximum level for that set of attributes. For all attributes except (3), the upper occurrence limit, as determined by sampling, is equal to or less than the tolerable occurrence rate, thus indicating an apparent justification for lowering assessed risk. Attribute (3), however, is indicative of a control weakness that may, in turn, require

TABLE 10.6 Statistical Sample Results Evaluation Table for Control Tests (upper limits at 5 percent risk of underassessment)

SAMPLE SIZE	ACTUAL NUMBER OF DEVIATIONS FOUND										
	0	1	2	3	4	5	6	7	8	9	10
25	11.3	17.6	*	*	*	*	*	*	*	*	*
30	9.5	14.9	19.6	*	*	*	*	*	*	*	*
35	8.3	12.9	17.0	*	*	*	*	*	*	*	*
40	7.3	11.4	15.0	18.3	*	*	*	*	*	*	*
45	6.5	10.2	13.4	16.4	19.2	*	*	*	*	*	*
50	5.9	9.2	12.1	14.8	17.4	19.9	*	*	*	*	*
55	5.4	8.4	11.1	13.5	15.9	18.2	*	*	*	*	*
60	4.9	7.7	10.2	12.5	14.7	16.8	18.8	*	*	*	*
65	4.6	7.1	9.4	11.5	13.6	15.5	17.4	19.3	*	*	*
70	4.2	6.6	8.8	10.8	12.6	14.5	16.3	18.0	19.7	*	*
75	4.0	6.2	8.2	10.1	11.8	13.6	15.2	16.9	18.5	20.0	*
80	3.7	5.8	7.7	9.5	11.1	12.7	14.3	15.9	17.4	18.9	*
90	3.3	5.2	6.9	8.4	9.9	11.4	12.8	14.2	15.5	16.8	18.2
100	3.0	4.7	6.2	7.6	9.0	10.3	11.5	12.8	14.0	15.2	16.4
125	2.4	3.8	5.0	6.1	7.2	8.3	9.3	10.3	11.3	12.3	13.2
150	2.0	3.2	4.2	5.1	6.0	6.9	7.8	8.6	9.5	10.3	11.1
200	1.5	2.4	3.2	3.9	4.6	5.2	5.9	6.5	7.2	7.8	8.4

*Over 20 percent
Note: This table presents upper limits as percentages. This table assumes a large population.
Source: AICPA, *Audit Sampling Guide* (New York: AICPA 1983), page 108.

---

[4]For those sample sizes in Exhibit 10.2 not contained in the evaluation tables, the number in the table most nearly corresponding to actual sample size was selected.

TABLE 10.7   Statistical Sample Results Evaluation Table for Control Tests (upper limits at 10 percent risk of underassessment)

SAMPLE SIZE	ACTUAL NUMBER OF DEVIATIONS FOUND										
	0	1	2	3	4	5	6	7	8	9	10
20	10.9	18.1	*	*	*	*	*	*	*	*	*
25	8.8	14.7	19.9	*	*	*	*	*	*	*	*
30	7.4	12.4	16.8	*	*	*	*	*	*	*	*
35	6.4	10.7	14.5	18.1	*	*	*	*	*	*	*
40	5.6	9.4	12.8	16.0	19.0	*	*	*	*	*	*
45	5.0	8.4	11.4	14.3	17.0	19.7	*	*	*	*	*
50	4.6	7.6	10.3	12.9	15.4	17.8	*	*	*	*	*
55	4.1	6.9	9.4	11.8	14.1	16.3	18.4	*	*	*	*
60	3.8	6.4	8.7	10.8	12.9	15.0	16.9	18.9	*	*	*
70	3.3	5.5	7.5	9.3	11.1	12.9	14.6	16.3	17.9	19.6	*
80	2.9	4.8	6.6	8.2	9.8	11.3	12.8	14.3	15.8	17.2	18.6
90	2.6	4.3	5.9	7.3	8.7	10.1	11.5	12.8	14.1	15.4	16.6
100	2.3	3.9	5.3	6.6	7.9	9.1	10.3	11.5	12.7	13.9	15.0
120	2.0	3.3	4.4	5.5	6.6	7.6	8.7	9.7	10.7	11.6	12.6
160	1.5	2.5	3.3	4.2	5.0	5.8	6.5	7.3	8.0	8.8	9.5
200	1.2	2.0	2.7	3.4	4.0	4.6	5.3	5.9	6.5	7.1	7.6

*Over 20 percent
Note: This table presents upper limits as percentages. This table assumes a large population.
Source: AICPA, *Audit Sampling Guide* (New York: AICPA, 1983), page 109.

modification of substantive audit programs. Under such conditions, the auditor must address the following questions:

1. How might the weakness affect the financial statements?
2. Is the probability of material impact on the financial statements high?
3. Do compensating controls exist?
4. If the auditor believes that the weakness is material and compensating controls do not exist, what substantive audit procedures are necessary in order to determine whether, in fact, the weaknesses have affected the financial statements, and to what extent?[5]

Applying this approach to attribute (3), assume that the auditor decides to extend substantive audit testing, given the significance of account distribution errors relating to vouchers. The form that such extension will assume may vary. For

---

[5]As discussed in Chapter 7, the auditor who plans to consider compensating controls must also examine those controls for effectiveness.

example, the auditor may elect to extend the examination of vouchers for proper account distribution by selecting all credits to accounts payable in excess of a specified dollar amount. Alternatively (or in addition), the auditor may increase the amount of analytical procedures applied to certain expense and asset accounts, comparing the balances in selected accounts with the prior year. Such comparison will highlight significant changes, which may have resulted from account distribution errors.

Before concluding this section, a "short-cut" step in evaluating sample results is presented, which frequently avoids the need for using the evaluation tables and determining the upper occurrence limit. This step involves comparing the number

FIGURE 10.2   Summary of Steps in Applying Attribute Sampling

1. Define:
   a. Sampling objectives
   b. Sampling unit
   c. Population
   d. Errors (attributes)

2. Set Parameters:
   a. Expected occurrence rate
   b. Tolerable occurrence rate (TOR)
   c. Risk of underassessment

3. Calculate sample size

4. Draw the sample on a probability basis

5. Examine the sample and list errors

6. Evaluate the sample results:
   a. Determine the observed error rate and the upper occurrence limit (UOL)
   b. Compare UOL and TOR. Is UOL $\leq$ TOR?
      1. If yes, lower assessed level of control risk
      2. If no, maintain control risk at maximum

7. Design substantive audit programs

8. Develop sampling plans for substantive testing (Chapter 11)

of expected deviations with the actual deviations. The expected number of deviations may be calculated by multiplying the expected occurrence rate by the sample size. If the number of expected deviations is greater than the number of detected errors, the auditor may conclude that the upper occurrence limit does not exceed the tolerable occurrence rate and need not proceed to the tables. To illustrate, for attribute (1), the expected number of deviations is 6 (195 × .03), while the number of detected errors is 3. Based on this comparison, the auditor may conclude that the upper occurrence limit does not exceed the tolerable rate of 6 percent and, therefore, the assessed level of control risk may be lowered.

Summary of Steps in Applying Attribute Sampling

Figure 10.2 summarizes the sampling process described in the preceding paragraphs and highlights the link between control testing and substantive testing. Defining sampling objectives, the sampling unit, the population, and what constitutes errors is critical to a successful attribute sampling plan. For example, given a choice of sampling unit between shipping orders and sales invoices, if the auditor wishes to test for unbilled shipments, he/she should choose shipping orders as the sampling unit and trace the sample to sales invoices to determine that shipments have been properly billed to customers. If the sampling objective is to determine that all invoices are accompanied by shipments to customers, the sampling unit should be the sales invoice. In applying the sampling plan in this case, the auditor will trace sales invoices to shipping orders to confirm shipment to customers.

Comparing the upper occurrence limit with the tolerable occurrence rate is vital to developing sampling plans for substantive testing purposes that reflect the auditor's control risk assessment. If the upper limit is below the tolerable rate, the auditor may elect to further reduce the assessed level of control risk. If the upper occurrence limit exceeds the tolerable rate, however, the assessed level of control risk should not be reduced, and may even be increased beyond the level based on the auditor's initial understanding. This final link between control testing and substantive testing will be described in Chapter 11.

STATISTICAL SAMPLING AND AUDIT RISK IMPLICATIONS

Statistical sampling, by offering a means for partially quantifying audit risk, provides a useful framework for risk analysis. The following paragraphs explain the approach and procedures to be applied to such quantification and analysis.

Review of Audit Risk and Reason for Quantifying

As presented in Chapter 5, three types of audit risk must be dealt with by the CPA in conducting a financial audit:

1. Inherent risk;
2. Control risk;
3. Detection risk.

Inherent risk and control risk are both considered and evaluated during the audit planning phase. The auditor's study of the business and industry and the application of analytical procedures provides an effective basis for assessing inherent risk and for budgeting added audit resources to those areas posing higher than average risk. Control risk is assessed by the auditor as a result of the study and evaluation of the client's control structure policies and procedures, and, if deemed appropriate, performance of control testing during the interim audit.

Detection risk is managed by varying the nature, timing, and extent of substantive testing. The magnitude of acceptable detection risk, therefore, is determined by:

1. The analysis of inherent risk during the planning phase; and

2. The analysis of control risk during the study and evaluation of control structure and any added control testing performed.

Although GAAS does not require the quantification of audit risk, such quantification of the risk components is necessary if the auditor wishes to design and implement statistical sampling plans for substantive audit testing purposes. The following paragraphs demonstrate how attribute sampling aids in quantifying these types of audit risk, thereby providing the inputs needed in designing variables sampling plans as discussed in Chapter 11.

How to Quantify Control Risk

Relate Upper Occurrence Limit to Qualitative Evaluation

The first step in quantifying control risk is to relate possible upper occurrence limits to a qualitative assessment of the client's control structure. Such assessment should be made for each transaction cycle segment. For example, assume the following limits and qualitative assessments have been assigned by the auditor preparatory to testing the sales order processing phase of the revenue cycle for effectiveness:

Upper Occurrence Limit	Control Structure Assessment
≤1%	Excellent
>1%≤3%	Good
>3%≤5%	Fair
>5%≤7%	Poor
>7%	Unreliable

Determining the maximum upper occurrence limit beyond which the auditor will elect not to reduce control risk assessment below the maximum level is a function of audit judgment. Significance of the attributes relative to the financial statement assertions serves as an input into the decision. Significance relates to the auditor's assessment of the importance of error types. The auditor, for example, might consider errors in processing sales orders to have little impact on the financial statements. Sales pricing errors, conversely, might be judged more critical in terms of financial statement impact. For the more critical variables, the auditor relates acceptable control structure to a lower upper occurrence limit than for the less critical variables. In the above example, a computed upper occurrence limit of 3 percent may be necessary for internal control over sales pricing to be rated as "good," while a 5 percent limit may suffice for other aspects of sales processing.

Relate Qualitative Evaluation to Quantitative Assessment of Control Risk

The qualitative evaluation of internal control can now be translated into a quantitative assessment of control risk. Continuing the above illustration, the table may be expanded as follows:

Upper Occurrence Limit	Internal Control Evaluation	Control Risk
≤1%	Excellent	10%
>1%≤3%	Good	30%
>3%≤5%	Fair	50%
>5%≤7%	Poor	70%
>7%	Unreliable	100%

The more effective the internal control structure policies and procedures relative to a given subset of a transaction cycle, the lower the auditor may justifiably set the assessed level of control risk. Excellent internal control warrants substantial reduction below the maximum level and produces a minimal control risk. Unreliable internal control, conversely, warrants no reduction, and the auditor may assume a 100 percent probability of material errors occurring under such conditions.

How to Quantify Inherent Risk

Inherent risk is the risk that, control structure aside, material errors and/or irregularities will occur. Most auditors begin with a conservative estimate of inherent risk equal to 100 percent and subsequently modify the estimate, based on the following sequence of steps:

1. Study the business and industry and identify high risk areas;
2. Apply analytical procedures to identify abnormal conditions;
3. Investigate abnormalities disclosed in step 2;
4. Design substantive audit procedures based on the results of steps 1 to 3;
5. Study and evaluate control structure policies and procedures to assess control risk;
6. Design substantive audit procedures to reflect the auditor's assessment of control risk.

As an example, assume that the auditor, in performing control tests of sales orders and invoices, discovers numerous errors of a material nature and decides to set control risk at a relatively high level (70 percent).[6] Assume further, however,

---

[6]Under conditions of unreliable internal control, control risk is set equal to 100 percent.

that analytical procedures indicate no material changes in relationships or proportions. Sales volume, both in total and by months, was essentially the same as the prior year, and appears to be justified by existing economic conditions. Moreover, no changes in the client's operations had occurred in the current year which would warrant material changes in volume. These findings give the auditor added assurance as to the absence of material errors and justify a reduction in inherent risk assessment below the initial 100 percent.

Assume that, in the present case, the auditor reduces the inherent risk estimate to 70 percent. Such a reduction reduces the extent of substantive testing which the auditor would otherwise have to perform under conditions of weak or unreliable control structure.

How to Quantify Detection Risk

Detection risk was defined in Chapter 5 as the probability that the auditor will not detect material errors that occur and are not detected by internal control procedures. The following equation for determining detection risk was presented in Chapter 5:

$$DR = \frac{AR}{CR \times IR}$$

where:

$$AR = \text{overall audit risk}$$
$$DR = \text{detection risk}$$
$$CR = \text{control risk}$$
$$IR = \text{inherent risk}$$

The weaker the control structure policies and procedures (the higher the control risk) and the more closely inherent risk, as modified by analytical procedures and study of the business and industry, approaches 100 percent, the lower will be the detection risk which the auditor is willing to assume in order to maintain an overall audit risk ≤ 10 percent.[7] Detection risk, in other words, is the one element in the equation that can be managed by the auditor and is set in response to the auditor's analysis of inherent risk and control risk.

Given the quantification of inherent risk and control risk as explained in the preceding paragraphs, the above equation may be used to express detection risk as a percentage. For example, if control risk, inherent risk, and audit risk are set at 50, 70, and 5 percent respectively, detection risk equals 14 percent. Table 10.8 displays detection risk percentages, given various combinations of control risk and inherent risk, and assumes an overall audit risk of 5 percent.

Detection risk is inversely related to the extent of substantive audit procedures to be applied to a given transaction cycle. A low detection risk, based on weak control structure policies and procedures and high inherent risk, requires extended substantive testing in order to minimize the risk of accepting a book value which is

---

[7]Recall from Chapter 5 that overall audit risk should always be set ≤ 10 percent, inasmuch as it forms the basis for the audit opinion.

**TABLE 10.8   Table for Determining Detection Risk
(5 percent audit risk assumed)**

Upper Occurrence Limit	Control Structure Evaluation	Control Risk	Inherent Risk				
			10%	*30%*	*50%*	*70%*	*100%*
≤1%	Excellent	10%	*	*	*	71%	50%
>1 to ≤3%	Good	30	*	55%	33%	24	16
>3 to ≤5%	Fair	50	*	33	20	14	10
>5 to ≤7%	Poor	70	71%	24	14	10	7
>7%	Unreliable	100	50	16	10	7	5

*The allowable level of audit risk of 5 percent exceeds the product of *CR* and *IR,* and thus, the planned substantive test of details may not be necessary.
Source: Adapted from SAS 39.

materially misstated. Stated differently, the following relationship exists between the level of detection risk and the quantity of evidence to be gathered and examined by the auditor in evaluating management's assertions:

Detection Risk	*Quantity of Evidence*
High	Minimal
Moderate	Moderate
Low	Substantial

Detection risk, as just quantified, is used in Chapter 11 as an input in calculating the sample size for substantive testing. A significant advantage of quantifying inherent risk, control risk, and detection risk is that such quantification provides a concrete link between audit planning and the design of substantive audit programs. Risk quantification does not replace audit judgment, but it promotes greater consistency in the application of professional judgment.

EXTENDED EXAMPLE

An example is presented here in order to further illustrate the concepts just discussed and to demonstrate how inherent risk assessment and control risk assessment serve as inputs to the design of substantive audit procedures. Control testing of the sales order and invoicing segment of the revenue cycle is used as a basis for the illustration.

Hotsaws, Inc. manufactures chain saws and space heaters. The products are sold directly to large retailers and wholesale hardware distributors. A staff of 40 sales representatives market the units and submit orders to the home office. A prenumbered sales invoice is prepared after the order has been examined for correctness of prices, approval of customer credit, and availability of stock. One of the staff auditors for Hawkins, CPAs, Hotsaws' independent auditors, prepared the flowchart depicted in Exhibit 10.3. Based on the flowchart and discussions with the personnel involved in the sales order, shipping, and billing process, Gerald Kolb,

EXHIBIT 10.3 Hotsaws, Inc. Customer Order, Shipping, and Billing Flowchart

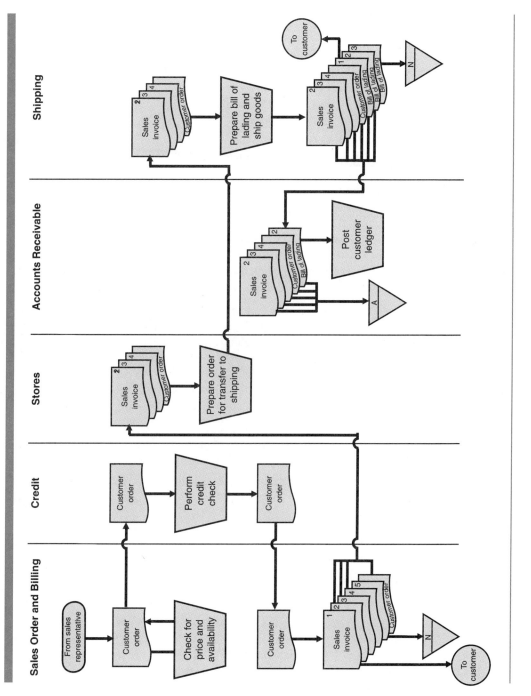

the in-charge senior auditor for the Hotsaws engagement, arrived at the following conclusions regarding control structure weaknesses and possible errors resulting from such weaknesses:

1. Customers are invoiced before billing is notified of shipment. This control weakness could result in customers being billed for goods not received. Moreover, fictitious sales may be recorded, inasmuch as evidence of shipment is not required for recording purposes.

2. Shipping does not compare the sales invoice and customer order with the goods received from stores. Customers could be shipped goods not ordered.

3. Accounts receivable does not review and compare documents before posting customers' accounts. The following errors might therefore occur that would otherwise have been detected by such review and comparison:
   a. quantities and/or types of goods appearing on customer order may not agree with sales invoice or bill of lading;
   b. extensions and/or footings on sales invoice may be in error;
   c. shipping mode or terms may not agree with customer specifications;
   d. credit and discount terms may be in violation of company policy.

Given these weaknesses and the high probability of resulting errors, Kolb tentatively plans to reduce his assessment of control risk relative to billing and shipping only slightly below the maximum level. He also decides to apply attribute sampling methods for the purpose of further testing the controls for effectiveness. The control tests should either add further support to the preliminary assessment or provide a basis for further modification of assessed control risk.

Kolb identifies the sampling unit for control testing purposes as the population of 10,000 prenumbered sales invoices processed during the fiscal year and decides to sample the invoices for the following attributes:

1. Sales invoice is accompanied by a bill of lading evidencing shipment;
2. Goods per invoice agree with bill of lading as to type and quantity;
3. Prices appearing on sales invoice agree with master price list;
4. Evidence of credit approval appears on face of invoice;
5. Proper sales accounts have been credited;
6. Extensions and footings on face of invoice are correct;
7. Credit and discount terms are in accordance with company policy;
8. Goods per invoice agree with customer order as to type and quantity.

Given an acceptable risk of underassessment of 5 percent and the expected and tolerable occurrence rates contained in Exhibit 10.4, sample sizes were determined using Table 10.3. The maximum sample size, 195, was then drawn at random from the population of 10,000 prenumbered sales invoices processed during the year. The invoices were examined in the order drawn for the following attributes:

- First through 78th: All attributes
- 79th through 127th: Attributes 1, 2, 3, 6, 7, and 8
- 128th through 146th: Attributes 1, 2, 6, and 8
- 147th through 195th: Attribute 1.

EXHIBIT 10.4 Attribute Sampling Plan Worksheet 1

Index   S.1
Prepared by LFK
Date   9/3/93
Reviewed by SEL
Date   9/15/93

Hotsaws, Inc.
Sales Orders and Invoicing
12/31/93

Attribute Tested	Risk of Under-assessment	Expected Occurrence Rate	Tolerable Occurrence Rate	Precision	Sample Size	Number of Detected Errors	Upper Occurrence Limit
1. Goods were shipped	5%	3%	6%	3%	195		
2. Goods agree with bill of lading as to type and quantity	5	4	8	4	146		
3. Invoice price agrees with master price list	5	2	6	4	127		
4. Credit approval noted on face of invoice	5	1	6	5	78		
5. Proper sales account(s) credited	5	1	6	5	78		
6. Correctness of extensions and footings on face of invoice	5	4	8	4	146		
7. Credit and discount terms agree with company policy	5	2	6	4	127		
8. Goods agree with customer order as to type and quantity	5	4	8	4	146		

EXHIBIT 10.5   Attribute Sampling Plan Worksheet 2

Index   S.1
Prepared by LFK
Date   9/3/93
Reviewed by SEL
Date   9/15/93

Hotsaws, Inc.
Sales Orders and Invoicing
12/31/93

Attribute Tested	Risk of Under-assessment	Expected Occurrence Rate	Tolerable Occurrence Rate	Precision	Sample Size	Number of Detected Errors	Upper Occurrence Limit
1. Goods were shipped	5%	3%	6%	3%	195	5	5%
2. Goods agree with bill of lading as to type and quantity	5	4	8	4	146	9	10
3. Invoice price agrees with master price list	5	2	6	4	127	3	6
4. Credit approval noted on face of invoice	5	1	6	5	78	1	6
5. Proper sales account(s) credited	5	1	6	5	78	0	4
6. Correctness of extensions and footings on face of invoice	5	4	8	4	146	1	3
7. Credit and discount terms agree with company policy	5	2	6	4	127	2	5
8. Goods agree with customer order as to type and quantity	5	4	8	4	146	10	11

Exhibit 10.5 displays the results of the sampling in terms of the number of detected errors and the upper occurrence limit for each attribute tested. For attributes 2 and 8, the upper occurrence limit exceeds the tolerable rate, which suggests that the auditor maintain assessed control risk at a high level and extend the examination of accounts receivable (substantive testing) as of the year end.

Prior to the implementation of the above sampling plan, Kolb had conducted a study of the business and discovered no change in operations that would suggest a significant change in the volume or mix of sales for the year. Analytical procedures, however, revealed that accounts receivable turnover had declined substantially from the previous year. The balance in trade receivables at year end increased dramatically from the preceding balance sheet date, and "days' sales in accounts receivable" increased from 30 days to 60 days (Hotsaws' credit terms are 2/10; net 30).

The results of analytical procedures, coupled with the control structure weaknesses revealed by the control testing, suggest to Gerald Kolb that customers' accounts receivable may contain disputed items in the form of goods shipped but not ordered and goods invoiced but not shipped. For these reasons, Gerald sets the inherent risk at 100 percent and the control risk at 70 percent (poor internal control).

Using the 100 percent inherent risk, 70 percent control risk, and a risk of underassessment of 5 percent as inputs to Table 10.8, the resulting detection risk is shown to be 7 percent. Chapter 11 will demonstrate how a low detection risk percentage, as input into the equation for determining sample size for substantive testing, increases the required sample size (i.e., greater amounts of evidence must be gathered in evaluating management's assertions). Moreover, the specific control weaknesses in the present example (goods invoiced not in agreement with bill of lading or customer order) suggest that the nature, as well as the extent, of audit procedures may require modification in order to provide adequate evidence of proper valuation of accounts receivable as of year end. These matters are also addressed in Chapter 11 and are further explored in the substantive audit testing chapters, Chapters 12 through 14.

KEY TERMS

Attribute	Risk of underassessment
Attribute sampling	Statistical sampling
Discovery sampling	Stratified sampling
Expected occurrence rate	Systematic sampling
Nonstatistical sampling	Tolerable occurrence rate
Precision	Upper occurrence limit
Random selection	Variables sampling

COMPUTER AUDIT PRACTICE CASE

Trim Lawn Manufacturing Corporation
Module III of the Trim Lawn audit practice case (in the appendix following Chapter 17) contains an exercise requiring the application of attribute sampling to the sales processing system. This exercise may be completed at this time.

REVIEW QUESTIONS

1. In what ways can sampling assist the auditor in performing tests of a client's internal control structure policies and procedures?
2. Differentiate between statistical and nonstatistical sampling.
3. Differentiate between attribute and variables sampling.
4. Define *expected occurrence rate* and *tolerable occurrence rate*, explaining how they are set and how they affect sample size.
5. Why is the risk of underassessment usually set ≤10%?
6. What is meant by *random selection* of samples?
7. How does systematic sampling result in random selection?
8. Why are sample sizes not necessarily the same for all attributes tested in a sampling plan?
9. Define *upper occurrence limit*.
10. How does the relationship between the tolerable occurrence rate and the upper occurrence limit affect the auditor's decision concerning control risk assessment?
11. Name and define the three factors comprising overall audit risk.
12. Which of the three risk factors is usually set at 100 percent, and how might it be reduced below 100 percent?
13. How does risk quantification serve as a link between audit planning and the design of substantive audit procedures?

MULTIPLE CHOICE QUESTIONS FROM CPA AND CIA EXAMINATIONS

1. Which of the following models expresses the general relationship of risks associated with the auditor's assessment of control risk (*CR*), analytical review procedures and other relevant substantive tests (*IR*), and ultimate audit risk (*AR*) that would lead the auditor to conclude that additional substantive tests of details of an account balance are not necessary?

	IR	*CR*	*AR*
a.	20%	40%	10%
b.	20%	60%	5%
c.	10%	70%	4.5%
d.	30%	40%	5.5%

2. An auditor plans to examine a sample of 20 checks for countersignatures as prescribed by the client's internal control procedures. One of the checks in the chosen sample of 20 cannot be found. The auditor should consider the reasons for this limitation and
   a. Evaluate the results as if the sample size had been 19.
   b. Treat the missing check as a deviation for the purpose of evaluating the sample.
   c. Treat the missing check in the same manner as the majority of the other 19 checks, that is, countersigned or not.
   d. Choose another check to replace the missing check in the sample.

3. In attribute sampling, a 10 percent change in which of the following factors normally will have the least effect on the size of a statistical sample?
   a. Population size.
   b. Precision (confidence interval).
   c. Reliability (confidence level).
   d. Standard deviation.

4. In estimation sampling for attributes, which one of the following must be known in order to appraise the results of the auditor's sample?
   a. Estimated dollar value of the population.
   b. Standard deviation of the values in the population.
   c. Actual occurrence rate of the attribute in the population.
   d. Sample size.

5. An advantage of using statistical sampling techniques is that such techniques
   a. Measure risk mathematically.
   b. Eliminate the need for judgmental decisions.
   c. Define the values of precision and reliability required to provide audit satisfaction.
   d. Have been established in the courts to be superior to judgmental sampling.

6. If certain forms are not consecutively numbered
   a. Selection of a random sample probably is not possible.
   b. Systematic sampling may be appropriate.
   c. Stratified sampling should be used.
   d. Random number tables cannot be used.

7. In assessing sampling risk, the risk of incorrect rejection and the risk of overassessment of control risk relate to the
   a. Efficiency of the audit.
   b. Effectiveness of the audit.
   c. Selection of the sample.
   d. Audit quality controls.

8. At times a sample may indicate that the auditor's planned lowering of assessed control risk is justified when, in fact, the true error rate does not justify such lowering. This situation illustrates the risk of
   a. Underassessment.
   b. Overassessment.
   c. Incorrect precision.
   d. Incorrect rejection.

9. In examining cash disbursements, an auditor plans to choose a sample using systematic selection with a random start. The primary advantage of such a systematic selection is that population items
   a. That include irregularities will not be overlooked when the auditor exercises compatible reciprocal options.
   b. May occur in a systematic pattern, thus making the sample more representative.
   c. May occur more than once in a sample.
   d. Do not have to be prenumbered in order for the auditor to use the technique.

10. The tolerable rate of deviations for a control test is generally
    a. Lower than the expected rate of errors in the related accounting records.
    b. Higher than the expected rate of errors in the related accounting records.
    c. Identical to the expected rate of errors in the related accounting records.
    d. Unrelated to the expected rate of errors in the related accounting records.

11. To determine the sample size for a test of controls, an auditor should consider the tolerable occurrence rate, the allowable risk of assessing control risk too low, and the
    a. Expected occurrence rate.
    b. Upper precision limit.
    c. Risk of incorrect acceptance.
    d. Risk of incorrect rejection.

12. Which of the following combinations results in a decrease in sample size in a sample for attributes?

	Risk of Assessing Control Risk Too Low	Tolerable Rate	Expected Population Error Rate
a.	Increase	Decrease	Increase
b.	Decrease	Increase	Decrease
c.	Increase	Increase	Decrease
d.	Increase	Increase	Increase

13. As a result of tests of controls, an auditor assessed control risk too low and decreased substantive testing. This occurred because the true error rate in the population was
    a. Less than the risk of assessing control risk too low based on the auditor's sample.
    b. Less than the error rate in the auditor's sample.
    c. More than the risk of assessing control risk too low based on the auditor's sample.
    d. More than the error rate in the auditor's sample.

    Questions 14 and 15 are based on the following:

    An auditor desired to test credit approval on 10,000 sales invoices processed during the year. The auditor designed a statistical sample that would provide a 1 percent risk of assessing control risk too low (99 percent confidence) that not more than 7 percent of the sales invoices lacked approval. The auditor estimated from previous experience that about 2 ½ percent of the sales invoices lacked approval. A sample of 200 invoices was examined and 7 of them were lacking approval. The auditor then determined the upper occurrence limit to be 8 percent.

14. In the evaluation of this sample, the auditor decided to increase the level of the preliminary assessment of control risk because the
    a. Tolerable rate (7 percent) was less than the achieved upper occurrence limit (8 percent).
    b. Expected occurrence rate (7 percent) was more than the percentage of errors in the sample (3 ½ percent).
    c. Achieved upper occurrence limit (8 percent) was more than the percentage of errors in the sample (3 ½ percent).

d. Expected occurrence rate (2 ½ percent) was less than the tolerable rate (7 percent).

15. The allowance for sampling risk (precision) was
   a. 5 ½ percent.
   b. 4 ½ percent.
   c. 3 ½ percent.
   d. 1 percent.

16. An auditor who uses statistical sampling for attributes in testing internal controls should increase the assessed level of control risk when the
   a. Sample rate of error is less than the expected rate of error used in planning the sample.
   b. Tolerable rate less the allowance for sampling risk exceeds the sample rate of error.
   c. Sample rate of error plus the allowance for sampling risk exceeds the tolerable rate.
   d. Sample rate of error plus the allowance for sampling risk equals the tolerable rate.

17. What is an auditor's evaluation of a statistical sample for attributes when a test of 100 documents results in 4 errors if the tolerable rate is 5 percent, the expected population error rate is 3 percent, and the allowance for sampling risk is 2 percent?
   a. Accept the sample results as support for lowering the assessed level of control risk because the tolerable rate less the allowance for sampling risk equals the expected error rate.
   b. Do not decrease the assessed level of control risk because the sample error rate plus the allowance for sampling risk exceeds the tolerable rate.
   c. Do not decrease the assessed level of control risk because the tolerable rate plus the allowance for sampling risk exceeds the expected population error rate.
   d. Accept the sample results as support for lowering the assessed level of control risk because the sample error rate plus the allowance for sampling risk exceeds the tolerable rate.

18. In performing tests of controls over authorization of cash disbursements, which of the following sampling methods would be most appropriate?
   a. Ratio.
   b. Attributes.
   c. Variables.
   d. Stratified.

19. Which of the following controls would be most effective in ensuring that recorded purchases are free of material errors?
   a. The receiving department compares the quantity ordered on purchase orders with the quantity received on receiving reports.
   b. Vendors' invoices are compared with purchase orders by an employee who is independent of the receiving department.
   c. Receiving reports require the signature of the individual who authorized the purchase.
   d. Purchase orders, receiving reports, and vendors' invoices are independently matched in preparing vouchers.

20. To determine whether accounts payable are complete, an auditor performs a test to verify that all merchandise received is recorded. The population of documents for this test consists of all
    a. Vendors' invoices.
    b. Purchase orders.
    c. Receiving reports.
    d. Canceled checks.

21. The sampling unit in a test of controls pertaining to the existence of payroll transactions ordinarily is a(an)
    a. Clock card or time ticket.
    b. Employee Form W–2.
    c. Employee personnel record.
    d. Payroll register entry.

22. Samples to test internal control structure procedures are intended to provide a basis for an auditor to conclude whether
    a. The control procedures are operating effectively.
    b. The financial statements are materially misstated.
    c. The risk of incorrect acceptance is too high.
    d. Materiality for planning purposes is at a sufficiently low level.

ESSAY QUESTIONS AND PROBLEMS

10.1 a. Attribute sampling is appropriate in testing certain types of controls to assess control risk, but is not appropriate for testing others. Explain why.

   b. Of the following controls, indicate those that might be tested by the application of attribute sampling methods. For those controls not amenable to attribute sampling, state the control objective for each and identify alternative means of testing for effectiveness.
      1. Correctness of pay rates and hours used in preparing the payroll summary;
      2. Competence of the EDP manager;
      3. Ability of the systems analyst to access programs and update transaction files;
      4. Correctness of debits resulting from the processing of vendors' invoices;
      5. Monthly reconciliation of all bank accounts;
      6. Completeness of receiving reports for incoming goods;
      7. Prenumbering of sales invoices and periodic check as to numeric sequence;
      8. Retention of voided documents;
      9. Agreement of selling prices appearing on customer invoices with company price lists;
      10. Ability of the cashier to access cash receipts records and customer accounts.

10.2 Sampling can assist the auditor in various ways during the examination of documentary evidence for control testing. Using a payroll application as an example, assume that you are interested in evaluating control structure policies and procedures relative to the processing of a client's hourly payroll. Specifically, you wish to determine the correctness of rates and hours and the genuineness of listed employees. Discuss how attribute sampling might assist you in the following phases of your payroll control testing:

1. Determining the number of payroll transactions to test;
2. Selecting the transactions for testing;
3. Evaluating the results of the payroll test;
4. Assessing audit risk associated with the payroll cycle.

10.3 Although statistical sampling involves the application of mathematical techniques in determining sample size and evaluating sample results, it does not replace audit judgment. Assuming that you are examining the revenue cycle for control risk assessment purposes and that your client is a wholesale distributor of lumber products, discuss how audit judgment enters into each of the following determinations:

a. Allowable selling price deviations from master price lists;
b. Acceptable risk of underassessment of control risk relative to the processing of sales transactions;
c. Determining the materiality of identified control weaknesses.

10.4 For each of the following attributes, identify the sampling unit and carefully define what constitutes an error:

a. Approval of purchase invoices for payment;
b. Correctness of account distributions;
c. Receiving report attached to paid vouchers;
d. Correctness of labor rates used in computing payroll;
e. Agreement of hours on time cards with payroll summary;
f. Approval of customer credit;
g. Agreement of sales prices with master price list;
h. Shipping order attached to sales invoice.

10.5 a. Explain how each of the following factors affects sample size for attribute sampling purposes:

   1. Population size;
   2. Expected occurrence rate;
   3. Tolerable occurrence rate; and
   4. Acceptable level of risk of underassessment.

 b. Explain how the auditor determines factors 2, 3, and 4.

10.6 Cloder, Inc., an audit client of Charles Lo, CPA, manufactures and sells lawn furniture, barbecue grills, and sporting goods. Products are sold direct to retailers, including some rather large chain outlets. All sales are on account and invoices are payable by the 10th of the month following the sale. A 1 percent cash discount is available for invoices paid within 10 days of the invoice date.

   Charles Lo wishes to test the sales order, invoice, and shipping procedures for control effectiveness as part of his assessment of control risk within the revenue cycle. To this end, he elects to apply attribute sampling to the population of 25,000 prenumbered sales invoices processed during 1994. Having decided upon an acceptable risk of underassessment of 5 percent, Lo plans to test for the following attributes:

a. Proper documentation of sales, as evidenced by existence of prenumbered and approved sales order, sales invoice, and shipping order;

b. Agreement of quantity and type of goods shipped on sales invoice and shipping order;

c. Agreement of price on sales invoice and company price lists;

d. Evidence of proper credit approval;

e. Correctness of credits to the various revenue accounts;

f. Correctness of extensions and footings on face of invoice.

Based on last year's audit and this year's initial understanding of Cloder's control structure, Lo believes the sales invoices to contain a 2 percent error rate with respect to attributes a, c, e, and f; and a 3 percent error rate as to attributes b and d. He is willing to accept a tolerable occurrence rate of 6 percent as a condition for lowering his assessment of control risk relative to the sales processing system.

Required:

a. Determine the sample size.

b. Discuss the audit risk factors and the audit judgment process leading to the determination of sample size in the present case. In other words, what prompted Lo to decide upon the values chosen as determinants of sample size?

c. Develop a sampling plan worksheet similar to Exhibit 10.5.

d. Assume that the following errors were discovered in examining the sample:

Attribute	Errors
a	0
b	10
c	2
d	1
e	4
f	1

Calculate the upper occurrence limit and evaluate the sample results.

e. What impact might the evaluation have on substantive audit testing?

10.7 Prior to performing substantive tests for Farmall, Inc., a large manufacturer of farm machinery, Cynthia Schwab and her audit team conducted a study of the business and industry, applied analytical procedures, and obtained an initial understanding of Farmall's control structure policies and procedures. Profits in the industry had declined during 1992 to the point where only Farmall reported net income. The remaining companies (six large manufacturers of farm machinery) reported losses ranging from minimal to substantial. One of the companies, Alice Palmers, Inc., was in receivership by year end. Analytical procedures revealed higher than normal sales in August, the last month of Farmall's fiscal year. In addition, the gross profit rate increased from 35 percent in 1991 to 47 percent in 1992. The preliminary study of control structure in the area of sales and shipments led the auditors to conclude that the controls were generally adequate to prevent unauthorized shipments or billings and, therefore, should be further tested for possible lowering of the assessed control risk.

Required:

a. Discuss the audit risk implications of the Farmall engagement;

b. How does the possibility of management override affect the auditor's determination of detection risk?

   c. How would you deal with inherent risk in the present circumstances?

   d. In what way(s) might statistical sampling assist Schwab and her audit team in quantifying the various audit risk factors confronting them in the Farmall engagement?

10.8 Jiblum, a CPA, is planning to use attribute sampling in order to determine whether the assessed level of control risk can be lowered relative to sales processing. Jiblum has begun to develop an outline of the main steps in the sampling plan as follows:

   1. State the objective(s) of the audit test (e.g., to test the effectiveness of control structure policies and procedures relative to sales processing).

   2. Define the population.

   3. Define the sampling unit (e.g., client copies of sales invoices).

Required:

   a. What are the remaining steps in the above outline that Jiblum should include in the statistical test of sales invoices? Do not present a detailed analysis of tasks that must be performed to carry out the objectives of each step. Parenthetical examples need not be provided.

   b. How does statistical methodology help the auditor to develop a satisfactory sampling plan? (AICPA adapted)

10.9 The use of statistical sampling techniques in an examination of financial statements does not eliminate judgmental decisions.

Required:

   a. Identify and explain four areas where judgment may be exercised by a CPA in planning a statistical sampling test.

   b. Assume that a CPA's sample shows an unacceptable error rate. Describe the various actions that he or she may take based upon this finding.

   c. A nonstratified sample of 80 accounts payable vouchers is to be selected from a population of 3,200. The vouchers are numbered consecutively from 1 to 3,200 and are listed, 40 to a page, in the voucher register. Describe four different techniques for selecting a random sample of vouchers for review.

(AICPA adapted)

10.10 The following factors are often identified in comparing statistical and nonstatistical sampling:

   a. Statistical sampling is a mathematical approach to inference, whereas nonstatistical sampling is a more subjective approach to inference.

   b. Statistical sampling is a more consistent approach to sampling.

   c. Statistical sampling provides a more effective means than nonstatistical sampling for quantifying audit risk.

Required:

   a. Explain each of the above statements, using examples as appropriate.

   b. Notwithstanding the advantages of statistical sampling, under what circumstances might nonstatistical sampling be appropriate?

10.11 Cleary and Luce, the independent auditors for Wiggins Hardware Wholesalers, are conducting a test of control procedures over sales processing. During the year to date (1/1/92 to 6/30/92), Wiggins had issued 11,400 prenumbered sales invoices ranging in number from 22447 to 33847. Each sales invoice is accompanied by a combination shipping order/bill of lading form signed by the carrier. These forms are also prenumbered and range from 44233 to 55833. The warehouse manager has informed Mary Lance, the in-charge auditor assigned to the Wiggins examination, that shipping orders are frequently voided and this explains the overusage of these forms relative to sales invoice forms.

Based on her initial understanding of Wiggins' control structure, Lance believes that controls over sales processing, billing, and collection are adequate to permit reducing the assessed level of control risk below the maximum level; but she is not willing to reduce her assessment without testing the controls for operating effectiveness. Specifically, she is concerned with the following attributes relating to sales to customers:

1. Proper approval of customer credit prior to shipment;
2. A sales invoice exists for every shipment;
3. The bill of lading is signed by the carrier;
4. Prices on the invoice are in accordance with official price lists;
5. The sale has been properly recorded and posted to the customer's account.

Lance asks you to develop and implement a sampling plan for determining whether the assessed level of control risk relating to sales can be reduced below maximum. Given an acceptable risk of underassessment of 5 percent, you have set the following percentages for expected occurrence rate and tolerable occurrence rate:

Attribute Number	Expected Occurrence Rate	TolerableRate
1	1%	4%
2	2%	5%
3	2%	5%
4	1%	5%
5	2%	5%

Required

a. What is the population and sampling unit for purposes of your sampling plan? (Hint: It is either the sales invoice or the shipping order/bill of lading.) Justify your answer.

b. Calculate the sample size for each of the attributes.

c. How would you draw the sample to conform to random sampling rules?

d. Assuming the following discovered errors, calculate the upper occurrence limit?

Attribute Number	Errors
1	2
2	11
3	3
4	3
5	3

e. To what extent, if any, can you advise Lance, relative to reducing the assessed level of control risk in the area of sales processing?

10.12 Sampling for attributes is often used to allow an auditor to reach a conclusion concerning a rate of occurrence in a population. A common use in auditing is to test the rate of deviation from a prescribed internal control procedure to determine whether the planned assessed level of control risk is appropriate.

Required:

a. When an auditor samples for attributes, identify the factors that should influence the auditor's judgment concerning the determination of
   1. Acceptable level of risk of assessing control risk too low,
   2. Tolerable occurrence rate, and
   3. Expected occurrence rate.

b. State the effect on sample size of an increase in each of the following factors, assuming all other factors are held constant:
   1. Acceptable level of the risk of assessing control risk too low,
   2. Tolerable occurrence rate, and
   3. Expected occurrence rate.

c. Evaluate the sample results of a test for attributes if authorizations are found to be missing on 7 check requests out of a sample of 100 tested. The population consists of 2500 check requests, the tolerable occurrence rate is 8 percent, and the acceptable level of risk of assessing control risk too low is considered to be low.

d. How may the use of statistical sampling assist the auditor in evaluating the sample results described in c, above?

(AICPA adapted)

11

Statistical Sampling for Substantive Testing

CHAPTER OUTLINE

I. **Introduction**

II. **Approaches to variables sampling**
   A. Mean per unit
   B. Difference estimation

III. **Mean per unit**
   A. Calculating sample size
   B. Equation for MPU sample size
   C. Raw materials inventory example
   D. Drawing the sample and evaluating the sample results

IV. **Difference estimation**
   A. Reasons for using and conditions to be met
   B. Steps in applying
   C. Accounts receivable example

V. **Probability proportional to size sampling**
   A. Advantages of PPS
   B. Steps in applying
   C. PPS application involving plant assets additions

VI. **Computer-assisted sampling**

OVERVIEW

Chapter 10 addressed statistical sampling for control testing purposes. Chapter 11 discusses the auditor's use of statistical sampling for substantive testing purposes. Figure 11.1 identifies the chapter subject matter within the framework of the overall audit process.

Three variations of statistical sampling are commonly used by auditors for substantive audit testing. Two of these, mean per unit and difference estimation sampling, are discussed in the first part of this chapter, and the third, probability proportional to size sampling, is covered in the last part.

Mean per unit, often referred to as classical variables sampling, calculates a mean value for a sample and extends this value to the population. The population, for substantive testing purposes, might consist of inventories, accounts receivable, plant asset additions, or some other dollar amount of transactions or balances. Difference estimation, a variation of mean per unit, compares audited value and book value for a sample and imputes the dollar difference to the population. It is usually more cost-effective than mean per unit in that the sample sizes are smaller.

Probability proportional to size sampling, a variation of attribute sampling, calculates an upper error limit (expressed in dollars rather than as a per cent) and compares it with the tolerable error as set by the auditor. Such sampling is more cost-effective than either mean per unit or difference estimation sampling and, therefore, should be used where conditions warrant.

STUDY OBJECTIVES

After reading this chapter, you should be able to:

1. Determine the appropriate sampling method to apply under varying circumstances;
2. Apply any of the three sampling methods addressed in the chapter:
   a. Mean per unit,
   b. Difference estimation,
   c. Probability proportional to size;
3. Evaluate sample results and draw conclusions:
   a. Accept book value as fairly representative of true population value, given a tolerable level of risk of incorrect acceptance (beta risk), or
   b. Reject book value as being materially misstated, given a tolerable level of risk of incorrect rejection (alpha risk).

FIGURE 11.1   The Audit Process

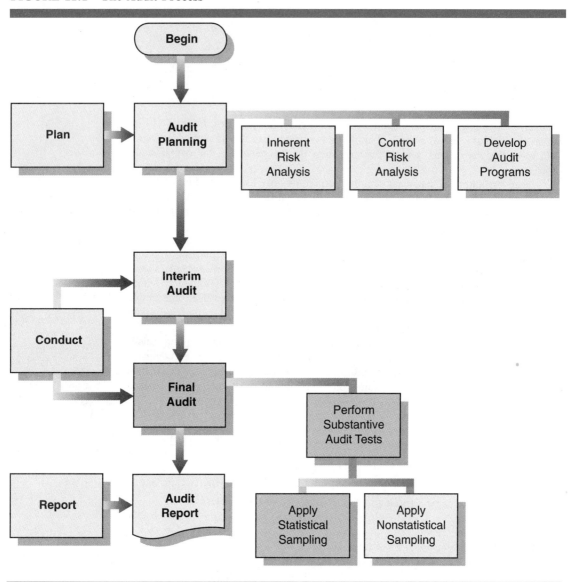

INTRODUCTION

Attribute sampling for control testing was examined in Chapter 10 as a means for assisting the auditor in estimating error *percentages* and assessing control risk. Chapter 11 explores the application of statistical sampling for substantive testing purposes, and concentrates on *dollar* estimates rather than percentages.

In performing substantive tests, the auditor's goal is to determine whether the book values appearing in the client's general ledger are fair representations of the related substance. To this end, the auditor examines, confirms, calculates, and inquires. Statistical sampling techniques can assist by providing a consistent approach to judging the fairness of those dollar representations.

The two methods most commonly used by auditors in applying sampling for substantive testing purposes are *variables sampling* and *probability proportional to size sampling*. Classical **variables sampling** is used to estimate the dollar amount of transactions or account balances by examining a sample and extending the results to the population. It is commonly applied to such balance sheet components as trade accounts receivable and inventories, given the large number of postings to these accounts. Variables sampling approaches are covered in the first part of this chapter. **Probability proportional to size sampling,** a variation of attribute sampling, is used to estimate the dollar amount of *overstatement* errors; it is discussed in the second part of the chapter.

APPROACHES TO VARIABLES SAMPLING

Two alternative approaches are available to the auditor in applying variables sampling. They are:

1. Mean per unit; and
2. Difference estimation.

Mean per unit (MPU) consists of calculating the sample mean and multiplying by the number of items in the population in order to arrive at the *audited value* of the population. **Difference estimation** involves calculating the average difference between the audited value and the client's book value and multiplying by the number of items in the population. The result is the estimated *total difference* between the audited and book values. A positive value ($AV>BV$) represents an understated book value, while a negative value ($AV<BV$) is indicative of an overstated book value.

Difference estimation often results in smaller sample sizes than MPU and is more cost-effective under those circumstances. These two variations of classical variables sampling are discussed in the following paragraphs.

MEAN PER UNIT (MPU)

In applying mean per unit sampling, the auditor must calculate sample size after giving due consideration to risk and materiality. Detection risk, an important ingredient in determining sample size for mean per unit sampling purposes, has been defined as the risk that material errors which are not prevented or detected by the client's control structure will not be discovered by the auditor. It is a function of control risk, inherent risk, and overall audit risk; it was expressed in Chapter 10 by the following equation:

$$DR = \frac{AR}{CR \times IR}$$

where:

AR = Audit risk
CR = Control risk
IR = Inherent risk

(See Table 10.8 for detection risk percentages, given various combinations of the other components of the equation.)

Detection risk is referred to as **beta risk** by statisticians. This is defined as the risk of an incorrect acceptance. For auditing applications, this means incorrectly accepting a book value which is materially in error. The opposite of beta risk is **alpha risk,** the risk of incorrect rejection (i.e., incorrectly rejecting a book value that is stated fairly).

Beta and alpha risk, as related to substantive audit testing, may be represented in terms of classical hypothesis testing as follows:

	S_0	S_1
	B.V. Correct	*B.V. Materially Misstated*
H_0 Accept book value	X	beta risk
H_1 Reject book value	alpha risk	X

The *null* hypothesis (H_0) accepts the book value as being fairly stated, whereas the *alternate* hypothesis (H_1) rejects the book value as being materially misstated. If the null hypothesis is chosen and the book value is fairly stated (true state = S_0), a correct judgment has been made. If, on the other hand, the book value is materially misstated (S_1), an incorrect decision has been made. The risk of accepting the null hypothesis when the alternate state exists is the beta risk. The risk of accepting the alternate hypothesis (H_1) when the true state is (S_0) is the alpha risk.

Recall from Chapter 10 that beta risk was equated with the risk of underassessing control risk and alpha risk was synonymous with overassessing control risk. In terms of audit effectiveness and audit efficiency, assessing control risk too low and/or assessing detection risk too high may adversely affect audit effectiveness by causing the auditor to gather insufficient evidence to support an audit opinion. The worst possible result occurs if the auditor renders an unqualified audit opinion on financial statements that are materially misstated. Conversely, assessing control risk too high and/or detection risk too low impacts audit efficiency if, as a result, the auditor gathers more evidence than is needed under the true circumstances. This adds unnecessary cost to the audit in terms of the time and effort expended in gathering and evaluating the excessive amounts of evidence. These risk combinations can be summarized as follows:

	Lowers Audit Effectiveness	*Lowers Audit Efficiency*
Beta Risk:		
Assessing control risk too low	X	
Accepting a population that is materially in error	X	
Alpha Risk:		
Assessing control risk too high		X
Rejecting a population that is reasonably stated		X

This analysis demonstrates once again the importance of exercising care in assessing risk. One might note at this point that, if the auditor is to err, a sacrifice in efficiency is less harmful than a sacrifice in effectiveness. In other words, too much evidence is preferable to insufficient evidence.

Calculating Sample Size for MPU Sampling

Both beta and alpha risk must be set by the auditor as a condition for determining sample size. As recalled from Chapter 10, beta risk (referred to as *detection risk* in that chapter) is a function of the auditor's study of the business, application of analytical procedures, and study and evaluation of control structure policies and procedures. It serves as the "link" between audit planning and substantive audit testing. Table 11.1 is a reproduction of Table 10.8 except for the substitution of the term *beta risk* for *detection risk*.

Alpha risk, the risk that the sample results will lead the auditor to improperly conclude that a materially correct book value is significantly in error, is a function of overall audit risk. Most auditors simply equate alpha risk with overall audit risk, setting it ≤10 percent.

In addition to beta and alpha risk, the other factors influencing sample size for mean per unit variables sampling are as follows.

Population Size

Population size (e.g., the number of customer accounts in the accounts receivable subsidiary ledger, or the number of line items on inventory listings) has a positive influence on sample size; that is, the larger the population, the larger is the sample size.

Standard Deviation

The **standard deviation** is a measure of population variability. More specifically, it is defined as the degree of variation of individual values about the population mean. As can be seen from Figure 11.2, the more narrowly dispersed the values in the population, the smaller the standard deviation.

TABLE 11.1   Table for Determining Beta Risk
(5 percent audit risk assumed)

Upper Occurrence Limit	Internal Control Evaluation	Control Risk	Inherent Risk 10%	30%	50%	70%	100%
≤1%	Excellent	10%	*	*	*	71%	50%
>1 to ≤3%	Good	30	*	55%	33%	24	16
>3 to ≤5%	Fair	50	*	33	20	14	10
>5 to ≤7%	Poor	70	71%	24	14	10	7
>7%	Unreliable	100	50	16	10	7	5

*The allowable level of audit risk of 5 percent exceeds the product of *CR* and *IR,* and thus, the planned substantive test of details may not be necessary.
Source: Adapted from SAS 39.

FIGURE 11.2   Normal Probability Distributions with Varying Degrees of Standard Deviation

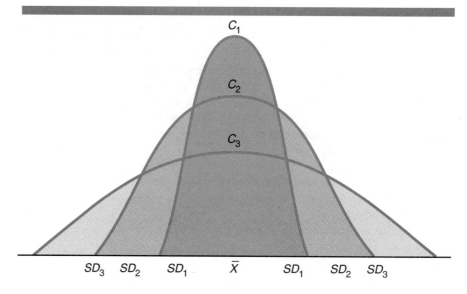

SD_1: Standard deviation for population represented by C_1 (curve no. 1).

SD_2: Standard deviation for population represented by C_2.

SD_3: Standard deviation for population represented by C_3.

Like population size, the standard deviation positively influences sample size; that is, the greater the variation, the larger is the sample size. The standard deviation of the sample may be expressed by the following equation:

$$SD = \sqrt{\frac{\Sigma\,(\bar{x} - x_i)^2}{n - 1}}$$

where:

$$\bar{x} = \text{Mean value}$$
$$x_i = \text{Individual values}$$
$$n = \text{Sample size}$$

In Figure 11.2, curve 3, which is flat and wide, denotes a large standard deviation, whereas curve 1, which is high and narrow, indicates little variation about the mean. Variables sampling attempts to describe the population in terms of its mean and standard deviation.

Precision

Precision is defined as the range (plus or minus) within which the true answer most likely falls. It is set by the auditor as a function of materiality and those levels of beta and alpha risk deemed acceptable. Precision has a negative influence on sample size. The narrower the range of precision, the larger is the sample size. A narrow precision range is associated with risk aversion and a conservative concept of materiality.

Reliability

Also referred to as confidence level, **reliability** is the likelihood that the sample range contains the true value. It is based on overall audit risk—that is, the degree of confidence the auditor wishes to place in the sampling results. As stated earlier, the overall audit risk and alpha risk are usually maintained at ≤10 percent. The **confidence level** is the complement of audit or alpha risk. An alpha risk of 5 percent, for example, is associated with a 95 percent confidence level. Like the population size and standard deviation, the confidence level also has a positive influence on sample size; that is, the greater the degree of confidence set by the auditor, the larger is the sample size.

To summarize, the parameters described above affect sample size as follows:

	Positive Effect	*Negative Effect*
Population size	X	
Standard deviation	X	
Precision (narrowing)		X
Reliability	X	
Materiality		X
Beta risk		X
Alpha risk		X

Equation for MPU Sample Size

Given the above sample size determinants, the following equation may be used to express sample size for MPU:

$$n = \left(\frac{N \times SD \times Ur}{A} \right)^2$$

where:

N = Population size (number of customer accounts, number of inventory line items, etc.)

SD = Standard deviation (can be estimated by examining a pilot sample of 30 to 40 items at random or by using the book value and a computer program for calculating SD)

Ur = Reliability factor related to the confidence level selected. Referred to as coefficients of reliability, the factors most commonly used in auditing applications are as follows:

Reliability	*Audit (Alpha) Risk*	Ur *Coefficient*
.99	.01	2.58
.95	.05	1.96
.90	.10	1.65

FIGURE 11.3   Probability Distribution Showing the Relationship between Confidence Levels and _Ur_ Factors

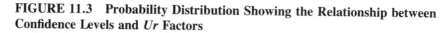

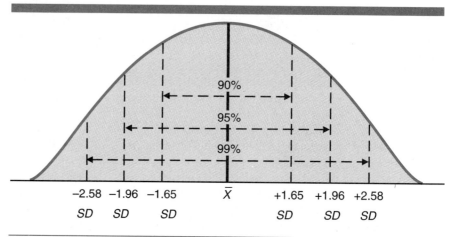

The _Ur_ factor may be understood most clearly as the number of standard deviations from the mean for a given confidence level (see Figure 11.3).

_A_ = **Desired precision,** a function of audit judgment, is based on materiality and acceptable risk levels. It may be expressed by the following equation:

$$A = M \times \frac{1}{1 + \dfrac{Zb}{Za/2}}$$

where:

M = Materiality expressed in dollars

Zb = Z value corresponding to acceptable level of beta risk (see Table 11.2)

$Za/2$ = Z value corresponding to acceptable level of alpha risk divided by 2 (see Table 11.2).

Raw Materials Inventory Example

The following example is used to illustrate and further clarify the equations just presented. In auditing the inventories of Xano, Inc., a toy manufacturer, John Halter, the in-charge senior auditor for Alright, CPAs, decides to apply MPU sampling in estimating the value of Xano's raw materials inventory. The physical inventory was taken by Xano and observed by Halter and his team of staff auditors. Several test counts were made and Halter is satisfied with the physical inventory quantities appearing on the inventory tags.

The quantities as evidenced by the tags have been translated into a computer printout of the raw materials inventory. In addition to the quantities, the printout includes prices and extended inventory costs. The costed inventory has been recorded by Xano's controller, Lonnie Mack, and posted to the general ledger. Perpetual records are not maintained for raw materials or finished goods.

TABLE 11.2   Z Values Related to Alpha and Beta Risk

Alpha/2 or Beta	Z Value	Alpha/2 or Beta	Z Value	Alpha/2 or Beta	Z Value
1.00%	2.33	17.00%	.96	34.00%	.42
2.00	2.06	18.00	.92	35.00	.39
2.50	1.96	19.00	.88	36.00	.36
3.00	1.89	20.00	.85	37.00	.34
4.00	1.76	21.00	.81	38.00	.31
5.00	1.65	22.00	.78	39.00	.28
6.00	1.56	23.00	.74	40.00	.26
7.00	1.48	24.00	.71	41.00	.23
8.00	1.41	25.00	.68	42.00	.21
9.00	1.35	26.00	.65	43.00	.18
10.00	1.29	27.00	.62	44.00	.16
11.00	1.23	28.00	.59	45.00	.13
12.00	1.18	29.00	.56	46.00	.11
13.00	1.13	30.00	.53	47.00	.08
14.00	1.09	31.00	.50	48.00	.06
15.00	1.04	32.00	.47	49.00	.03
16.00	1.00	33.00	.44	50.00	.00

In sampling terms, Halter wishes to estimate the value of the raw materials inventory by computing an average value for a sample and imputing this value to the population. The following values have been identified or set by Halter:

- *Population Size:* 20,000 line items on the computer printouts.
- *Book Value:* $20 million, as taken from the general ledger and also appearing as the total of the computer printout.
- *Materiality:* $1 million.
- *Alpha Risk and Audit Risk:* 5 percent (confidence level and the Ur factor are therefore 95 percent and 1.96 respectively).
- *Beta Risk:* 7 percent. Halter found internal control over the processing of raw materials purchases to be poor and, therefore, assesses control risk at 70 percent (see Table 11.1). Inherent risk = 100 percent.
- *Standard Deviation:* $370. This preliminary estimate of standard deviation was determined by examining a pilot sample of 40 line items, selected at random from the computer printout, and calculating the standard deviation.

Given these values, the sample size equation appears as follows:

$$n = \left(\frac{20,000 \times \$370 \times 1.96}{\$569,768}\right)^2 = 648$$

The denominator, \$569,768, is calculated by the following equation:

$$A = \$1,000,000 \times \frac{1}{1 + 1.48/1.96} = \$569,768$$

The Z values were taken from Table 11.2.

Whenever the sample size equation produces a sample size ≥ 5 percent (N), the following finite correction factor should be applied:

$$n' = \frac{n}{1 + n/N}$$

where $n' =$ sample size adjusted for the finite correction factor. The finite correction factor is necessary because the sample size equation, for purposes of simplicity, assumes sampling with replacement, and this produces larger sample sizes than more complex equations based on sampling without replacement. Inasmuch as auditors do not replace an item in the population for possible repeat selection, after selecting it once, the finite adjustment is made to larger sample sizes to reduce them to acceptable amounts.

In the present example, 648 is less than 5 percent of 20,000, and the correction factor is not needed.

Drawing the Sample and Evaluating the Sample Results for MPU Sampling

Continuing with the example, 608 additional line items need to be selected at random from the computer listings. The pilot sample, drawn for the purpose of estimating the standard deviation, may be considered part of the final sample. Assuming that Halter used a set of random number tables in drawing the pilot sample of 40, he will draw the remaining items by beginning in the random number table at the stopping point for the 40 and proceeding until 608 additional line items have been selected.

In practice, auditors often stratify populations for MPU sampling purposes by examining 100 percent of the larger dollar value items and sampling the remainder. In such cases the subsets are considered as two populations rather than one and are evaluated separately. For example, in the present case assume that the book value of the total raw materials inventory was \$30 million and consisted of the following two subsets:

- 100 line items with a total value of \$10 million; and
- 20,000 line items with a total value of \$20 million.

Under these circumstances, the audit team may elect to audit all of the 100 items comprising the \$10 million of book value, and randomly sample the second subset, inasmuch as the average value of the first subset is much higher (\$100,000) than for the second subset (\$1,000).

Having drawn the sample, the next step is to calculate its audited value and impute this value to the population. This entails examining each item carefully for the audit objectives (e.g., existence, ownership, and valuation) being tested. In the present example, Halter is interested in the following aspects of Xano's raw materials inventory:

1. The items appearing on the inventory listings were correctly transcribed as to type and quantity from the inventory tags;

2. The inventory items were costed in accordance with GAAP and on a basis consistent with the preceding year; and

3. Prices were correctly multiplied by quantities and extended amounts were correctly footed.

Having audited each item in the sample for these characteristics, the sample mean ($\bar{y}$) may be calculated by the following equation:

$$\bar{y} = \frac{\Sigma yi}{n}$$

Assuming the mean audited value of the sample is $990, the estimated population value is determined as follows:

$$Y = \bar{y} \times N = \$990 \times 20{,}000 = \$19{,}800{,}000$$

The final step in evaluating the sample results is to compute achieved precision and draw conclusions. **Achieved precision** is the calculated range within which the true value of the population most likely falls. The equation for computing achieved precision (A') is as follows:[1]

$$A' = N \times Ur \times \frac{SD}{\sqrt{n}}$$

Assuming the standard deviation of the sample is $360, the equation assumes the following form:

$$A' = 20{,}000 \times 1.96 \times \frac{360}{\sqrt{648}} = \$554{,}368$$

Achieved precision (A') must be $\leq$ desired precision (A). Otherwise, the actual beta risk is higher than that specified in the sampling plan, and further sampling would be necessary in order to reduce the risk to an acceptable level. In the present case, $554,368 < $569,768. Therefore, the beta risk is within acceptable bounds.

Having imputed the sample results to the population and having computed precision, Halter may now express the following conclusion: "I am 95 percent confident that the true value of Xano's raw materials inventory is $19,800,000 $\pm$ $554,368." This conclusion may also be expressed in terms of a range as follows:

$Y - A'$	Y	$Y + A'$
$19,245,632	.$19,800,000	..$20,354,368

---

[1]If the finite correction factor is needed in adjusting the initial sample size, this equation must be modified and becomes:

$$A' = \left(N \times Ur \times \frac{SD}{\sqrt{n}} \right)\left(\sqrt{\frac{N-n}{N-1}} \right)$$

Having calculated the precision range, Halter should next determine the *range of acceptability,* defined as the range of possible book values considered acceptable to the auditor. The lower end of the range, i.e., the lowest acceptable book value, equals the upper level of the precision range reduced by materiality (M). The upper end of the range, i.e., the highest acceptable book value, equals the lower level of the precision range increased by (M). In the present case, this range may be represented by the following continuum:

$$Y + A' - M \ldots\ldots\ldots\ldots\ldots\ldots\ldots\ldots\ldots\ldots\ldots\ldots\ldots Y - A' + M$$
$$\$19,354,368 \ldots\ldots\ldots\ldots\ldots\$20,000,000 \ldots\ldots\ldots\ldots\ldots\$20,245,632$$
$$(\$20,354,368 - \$1,000,000) \quad \text{Book Value} \quad (\$19,245,632 + \$1,000,000)$$

Inasmuch as the book value falls within the range of acceptability, Halter may accept Xano's inventory value as being fairly stated. Had the book value of the inventory fallen outside this range, an audit adjustment would be necessary in order to bring the book value to an amount no greater than the upper level of acceptability and no less than the lower level. For example, a book value of $20,500,000 would require a downward adjustment of $254,368 ($20,500,000 − $20,245,632). Conversely, a book value of $19,000,000 would necessitate an upward adjustment of $354,368 ($19,354,368 − $19,000,000).

DIFFERENCE ESTIMATION

Difference estimation, a variation of MPU, is used to project the total dollar error in a population. This is done by comparing audited value (AV) and book value (BV) for a sample, and imputing the difference to the population. If $AV - BV$ is positive, book value is understated, while a negative difference is indicative of an overstated book value.

Reasons for Using and Conditions to be Met

Where usable, difference estimation is more cost-effective than MPU, inasmuch as sample sizes are smaller. The reason for smaller sample sizes is that the standard deviation of differences is less than the standard deviation of individual item values about the mean.

The following conditions must exist in order for difference estimation sampling to be appropriate:

1. A book value must be available for each population item (e.g., customer account balances in the accounts receivable subsidiary ledger);
2. The total book value must be the sum of the individual book values (i.e., the sum of the subsidiary ledger accounts must be equal to the control account in the general ledger);
3. The sample must be large enough to produce a normal distribution; and
4. There must be a large population of nonzero differences divided approximately equally between overstatement and understatement.

In applying the difference estimation sampling approach, the following steps are necessary:

1. Sum the individual book values and compare with total book value.

2. Draw a pilot sample containing at least 30 differences and estimate the standard deviation as follows:

$$SD_d = \sqrt{\frac{\Sigma \, (d_i - \bar{d})^2}{n - 1}}$$

where:

SD_d = Standard deviation of the differences
d_i = Individual differences
$\bar{d}$ = Mean of the differences
n = Number of items in the pilot sample

Differences, for difference estimation purposes, are always calculated by the equation:

$$d_i = AV - BV$$

where:

AV = Audited value
BV = Book value

As stated above, a positive value points to understatement and a negative value to overstatement.

3. Having estimated the standard deviation of the differences between audited value and book value, the sample size may now be calculated as follows:

$$n = \left(\frac{Ur \times SD_d \times N}{A}\right)^2$$

Note that the sample size equation for difference estimation is identical to the MPU equation, except that SD_d, a lower number, is substituted for SD. As in the MPU equation, the finite correction factor,

$$n' = \frac{n}{1 + n/N}$$

is required if $n \geq 5$ percent N.

4. Randomly select the additional sample items.

5. Audit the sample, listing all differences, and calculate the mean of the differences $(\bar{d})$:

$$\bar{d} = \frac{\Sigma d_i}{n}$$

where:

$\bar{d}$ = Mean of the differences

d_i = Individual differences, as represented by $AV_i - BV_i$

6. Calculate the standard deviation of the differences (SD_d):

$$SD_d = \sqrt{\frac{\Sigma (d_i - \bar{d})^2}{n - 1}}$$

7. Calculate achieved precision (A'):

$$A' = Ur \times N \times \frac{SD_d}{\sqrt{n}}$$

8. Calculate the estimated population difference (D):

$$D = N \times \bar{d}$$

9. Calculate estimated audited value (EAV)

$$EAV = BV \pm D$$

10. State your conclusions. This is done in the same manner as for MPU, but with a smaller sample size.

Accounts Receivable Example

A case is presented to illustrate the difference estimation approach to audit sampling. Although the case involves accounts receivable, difference estimation may be applied to any account or set of transactions that meets the four conditions stated earlier.

White Wash, Inc., a large wholesale distributor of appliances and bathroom fixtures, distributes its products to retail outlets on a nationwide basis. Helen Kane, a CPA and senior auditor with Proud, Tall, and Straight, CPAs, has been assigned to the White Wash account as the in-charge auditor.

White Wash has 14,000 customer accounts with a total book value of $22.4 million. Jerry Crash, one of Kane's assistants on the audit, has determined that the sum of the book values agrees with the accounts receivable control account in the general ledger.

A study of control structure policies and procedures relative to the revenue cycle has led Kane to conclude that internal control over sales and accounts receivable is fair, and she has assessed control risk at 50 percent. Inasmuch as the application of analytical procedures produced no unusual numbers, Kane decides on an inherent risk of 50 percent. Assuming the alpha risk is set at 5 percent, beta risk becomes 20 percent (see Table 11.1).

Kane wishes to confirm a sample of customers' accounts and apply difference estimation sampling for the purpose of evaluating the fairness of White Wash's accounts receivable book value. As stated in Chapter 4, confirmation consists of a written communication from the client to the customer, requesting that the customer notify the auditor directly concerning the correctness or incorrectness of the balances as represented by the client.

Before calculating sample size, Kane must estimate the standard deviation of the differences between audited and book value. To this end, she confirms a sample of 75 customer accounts drawn at random. A careful audit of the replies produces a standard deviation of $464. Sample size may now be calculated as follows:

$$n = \left(\frac{1.96 \times \$464 \times 14,000}{A} \right)^2$$

Assuming that Kane considers $800,000 to be a material misstatement of accounts receivable, precision (A) may be calculated as follows:

$$A = M \times \frac{1}{1 + Zb/(Za/2)}$$
$$= \$800,000 \times .7$$
$$= \$560,000 \text{ (see Table 11.2 for } Z \text{ values)}$$

Substituting for A, the sample size equation becomes:

$$n = \left(\frac{1.96 \times \$464 \times 14,000}{\$560,000} \right)^2 = 517$$

To complete the sample, Kane selects 442 additional customer accounts at random for confirmation and carefully audits the replies. For customers not responding to second and third requests for confirmation, alternate procedures (e.g., examining shipping orders, bills of lading, and remittance advice) are applied in order to obtain satisfaction concerning valuation, existence, and classification.[2]

By applying the following equation to the sample results, Kane calculates a negative mean of the differences in the amount of $61.34:

$$\bar{d} = \frac{\Sigma\, d_i}{n}$$

Imputing the mean to the population by the equation

$$D = \bar{d} \times N$$

produces an estimated overstatement of accounts receivable in the amount of $858,760 ($61.34 × 14,000).

The estimated audited value (EAV) may now be computed as follows:

$$EAV = BV \pm D = \$22,400,000 - \$858,760 = \$21,541,240.$$

Assuming the standard deviation of the differences (SD_d) for the completed sample of 517 equals $410, achieved precision is determined as follows:

$$A' = 1.96 \times 14,000 \times \frac{\$410}{\sqrt{517}} = \$494,620$$

Inasmuch as $A' < A$, further sampling is not necessary.

---

[2]See Chapter 12 for a more detailed discussion of substantive audit procedures applied to trade accounts receivable.

Kane may now state, with 95 percent confidence, that the true value of the accounts receivable of White Wash, Inc. at year end is $21,541,240 ± $494,620. This conclusion may be expressed diagrammatically as follows:

$EAV - A'$	EAV	$EAV + A'$
$21,046,620	$21,541,240	$22,035,860

The range of acceptability may be represented as:

$EAV + A' - M$	$EAV - A' + M$
$21,235,860	$21,846,620
($22,035,860 − $800,000)	($21,046,620 + $800,000)
	Book Value $22,400,000

A minimum audit adjustment, therefore, of $553,380 is necessary in order to reduce the book value to an amount equal to the upper level of acceptability ($22,400,000 − $21,846,620). This adjustment may be made directly to individual customer accounts to the extent of actual errors discovered in the sample. Any remaining adjustment, in order for the total to equal $553,380, may be credited to the "allowance for doubtful accounts."

PROBABILITY PROPORTIONAL TO SIZE SAMPLING

Probability proportional to size (PPS) sampling (also known as dollar unit sampling) is a variation of attribute sampling. In applying PPS, the auditor estimates the dollar amount of error (rather than error percent) by examining a sample and calculating an upper error limit for the population, based on the sample results.

Advantages of PPS

PPS is easier to use than classical variables sampling and, therefore, more cost-effective. Some of the advantages of PPS over classical variables sampling are the following:

1. The standard deviation calculation is not required, thereby eliminating the need for pilot samples;
2. By automatically stratifying the population, large dollar errors have a higher probability of being detected; and
3. Sample size is usually smaller than either MPU or difference estimation.

A significant limitation of PPS sampling is that it is most applicable to populations for which the auditor suspects few errors, and those of *overstatement* only. The following situations, for example, are candidates for PPS sampling:

1. The auditor expects the inventory to contain few but significant overpricing errors;
2. Analytical procedures and study of the business lead the auditor to suspect that accounts receivable are materially inflated; and
3. Based on past experience with the client, the auditor believes that a substantial amount of repairs and maintenance expense has been capitalized.

Although PPS sampling can also be used where both overstatement and understatement errors exist, it is more difficult to apply and is therefore considered beyond the scope of this textbook.[3]

Given its cost-effectiveness in testing for overstatement errors, however, PPS sampling should be used whenever conditions warrant its use.

Steps in Applying

For PPS purposes, the sampling unit is the individual dollar. The sum of the dollars constitute the account balance (e.g., accounts receivable) or the total of transactions processed during the period under audit (e.g., postings to machinery and equipment). Given random selection, each dollar in the population has an equal chance of being included in the sample.

The **logical sampling unit** is the item to which the randomly selected dollar attaches. Referred to as a *hook,* the "snagged" item might assume the form of a customer account, a line item on an inventory listing, or a posting to a plant asset account.

The sequence of steps required in applying PPS sampling are presented next, followed by a case illustrating the concepts.

Calculate Sample Size

Sample size is determined by the following equation:

$$n = \frac{BV \times RF}{TE - (AE \times EF)}$$

where:

BV = Book value of the population.
RF = Reliability factor corresponding to the level of incorrect acceptance (beta risk), as set by the auditor, and assuming zero errors.
TE = **Tolerable error** acceptable to the auditor (expressed in dollars).
AE = **Anticipated error,** the amount of error expected by the auditor. Also expressed in dollars, anticipated error is a function of the auditor's judgment concerning inherent risk and control risk.
EF = Expansion factor which assumes a positive value only where errors are expected.

The denominator of the sample size equation determines desired precision and is a function of audit judgment.

Draw the Sample

The first step in drawing the sample is to calculate the **sampling interval.** The sampling interval, the distance between two consecutive sample items, is expressed by the following equation:

$$SI = \frac{BV}{n}$$

---

[3]See for example, Carmichael, D. R. and Guy, Dan, *Audit Sampling—An Introduction to Statistical Sampling in Auditing,* Second Edition, New York: John Wiley & Sons, 1986, Chapter 6.

Having determined the sampling interval, systematic sampling is applied in drawing the sample. A number between 1 and *SI* is chosen at random and forms the starting point for the sample selection. Logical units containing every *SI*th dollar thereafter are drawn for inclusion in the sample. This results in stratified sampling, in that logical units which are greater than the sampling interval have a 100 percent chance of being selected, and other logical units have a chance dependent on size.[4]

Evaluate the Sample Results

Evaluation of sample results consists of calculating the projected error and computing the precision and the upper error limit. The **projected error** relates to the errors discovered in the logical units included in the sample. A logical unit containing one or more errors is said to be "tainted." Moreover, if the book value of the logical unit is less than the sampling interval, a "tainting" percentage must be applied in order to project the error to the entire sampling interval containing the logical unit.

Computed precision and the upper error limit are determined by the following sequence of steps:

1. Compute basic precision by applying the following equation:

$$BP = RF \times SI$$

2. Calculate the incremental precision allowance (*IA*) where errors are found in logical units that are smaller than the sampling interval.
3. *BP + IA* = Allowance for Sampling Risk.
4. Calculate the upper error limit (*UEL*), which is the sum of the projected error and the allowance for sampling risk. The upper error limit should be less than the tolerable error in order for the book value to be acceptable to the auditor.

These PPS concepts are illustrated in the following case study.

PPS Application Involving Plant Asset Additions

Alice Holden, the in-charge auditor for Jole, Inc., a manufacturer of original and replacement mufflers, suspects that material amounts of repairs and maintenance charges have been capitalized in the Machinery and Equipment account. Her suspicions are founded on the results of analytical procedures showing a significant decrease in Repairs and Maintenance. This expense, as a percentage of sales, fell from 8 percent in 1992 to 4 percent in 1993. Moreover, her study of the business and industry has revealed a severe "profit squeeze" during the current year, which may have prompted the company to intentionally capitalize repairs in the plant asset accounts. Jole has always followed a policy of debiting repair and maintenance parts and supplies to expense at the point of purchase.

Internal control procedures relative to the processing of vendors' invoices have been found to be strong, and this leads Holden to believe that the problem may be one of management override rather than unintentional errors.

Holden decides to use PPS sampling in determining the extent to which such expenses have been improperly capitalized in 1993. The sampling unit for this

---

[4]This explains the term "probability proportional to size" as applied to this form of sampling.

application is the individual dollars debited to Machinery and Equipment during the year.[5] The logical sampling unit is the debit postings to the account. Inasmuch as many of the invoices from vendors contain both repair items and capital items, postings are often made to both Repairs and Maintenance and Machinery and Equipment from a single invoice.

The total of the debit postings to Machinery and Equipment for 1993 equals $3.5 million and consists of 3,980 individual postings made to the account during the year. The dollar postings ($3.5 million) represents the book value (BV) for PPS sampling purposes. Based on her evaluation of internal control procedures relative to the processing of invoices, the results of analytical procedures, and the problem of deteriorating profits, Holden decides on a 5 percent risk of incorrect acceptance, and an anticipated error of $60,000. The tolerable error, given her best judgment as to materiality, is set at $111,000. A calculated upper error limit exceeding $111,000, in other words, will be construed as a material overstatement of the Machinery and Equipment account and will require a downward adjustment. The sample size may now be calculated as follows:

$$n = \frac{BV \times RF}{TE - (AE \times EF)} = \frac{\$3,500,000 \times 3.00}{\$111,000 - (\$60,000 \times 1.6)} = 700$$

(See Table 11.3 for the reliability and expansion factors relating to a 5 percent risk of incorrect acceptance.)

TABLE 11.3 Reliability Factors and Expansion Factors for PPS Sampling (by risk of incorrect acceptance)

OVER-STATEMENT ERRORS	RISK OF INCORRECT ACCEPTANCE								
	1%	*5%*	*10%*	*15%*	*20%*	*25%*	*30%*	*37%*	*50%*
RELIABILITY FACTORS									
0	4.61	3.00	2.31	1.90	1.61	1.39	1.21	1.00	0.70
1	6.64	4.75	3.89	3.38	3.00	2.70	2.44	2.14	1.68
2	8.41	6.30	5.33	4.72	4.28	3.93	3.62	3.25	2.68
3	10.05	7.76	6.69	6.02	5.52	5.11	4.77	4.34	3.68
4	11.61	9.16	8.00	7.27	6.73	6.28	5.90	5.43	4.68
5	13.11	10.52	9.28	8.50	7.91	7.43	7.01	6.49	5.58
6	14.57	11.85	10.54	9.71	9.08	8.56	8.12	7.56	6.67
7	16.00	13.15	11.78	10.90	10.24	9.69	9.21	8.63	7.67
8	17.41	14.44	13.00	12.08	11.38	10.81	10.31	9.68	8.67
9	18.79	15.71	14.21	13.25	12.52	11.92	11.39	10.74	9.67
10	20.15	16.97	15.41	14.42	13.66	13.02	12.47	11.79	10.67
EXPANSION FACTORS									
	1.90	1.60	1.50	1.40	1.30	1.25	1.20	1.15	1.00

Source: *AICPA Audit Sampling Guide* (New York, AICPA, 1983) page 117.

---

[5]The Machinery and Equipment account is selected because the auditor suspects an overstatement resulting from debits of ordinary repairs to this account.

The sampling interval becomes:

$$SI = \frac{BV}{n} = \frac{\$3,500,000}{700} = \$5,000$$

Given the sample size of 700 and the sampling interval of $5,000, Holden now picks a number at random between 1 and 5,000 (assume 2,124), and proceeds to select every 5,000th dollar thereafter. Exhibit 11.1 displays the results of the first five invoices selected. Note that one of the invoices contained billings for repairs as well as equipment and another invoice was for repair parts only.

Exhibit 11.2 summarizes all invoices containing posting errors. The next step is to calculate the projected error. For each logical unit containing an error and having a book value of less than the sampling interval ($5,000), Holden must apply a *tainting* percentage to the sampling interval (see Exhibit 11.3), thereby extending the error projection to the entire interval.[6]

Having calculated the projected error, the final step is to calculate the allowance for sampling risk and the upper error limit. This is done as follows:

1. Calculate **basic precision (BP).**

$$BP = RF \times SI$$

    where:

    RF = Reliability factor corresponding to the risk of incorrect acceptance

    SI = Sampling interval

    $BP = 3.00 \times \$5000 = \$15,000$

2. Calculate the **incremental allowance for precision.** This calculation need be made only where errors are found in logical units which are smaller than the sampling interval. Exhibit 11.4 calculates the incremental allowance for the Jole sample. Note the ranking of projected errors from high to low. The incremental reliability factors are found in Table 11.3, beginning with an assumption of one overstatement error. The reliability factor, given one overstatement error and a 5 percent risk of incorrect acceptance, 4.75 minus the reliability factor associated with zero errors, 3.00, equals 1.75. The incremental factor is then reduced by one to arrive at the first number in column 2 of Exhibit 11.4.

3. Calculate the **allowance for sampling risk.** Basic precision plus the incremental allowance equals the allowance for sampling risk. For the Jole Machinery and Equipment account, the allowance for sampling risk is calculated as follows:

$$ASR = BP + IA$$

    where:

    ASR = Allowance for sampling risk;

    BP = Basic precision; and

    IA = Incremental allowance.

    $ASR = \$15,000 + \$7,541 = \$22,541$

---

[6]If no errors are found in the sample, the projected error is zero and the auditor may conclude that the population is not overstated by more than the tolerable error at the specified risk of incorrect acceptance.

EXHIBIT 11.1   Sample Selection: First Five Selections

$ Number	Vendor	Invoice Amount	Company Posting M&E	Company Posting Repairs	Correct Posting M&E	Correct Posting Repairs
7124	Martin Equipment	$4,257	$4,257	$0	$4,257	$0
12124	Holert, Inc.	3,112	3,112	0	3,112	0
17124	Ubba Tools	1,217	1,217	0	800	417
22124	Herol Industrial Supplies	4,985	4,985	0	0	4,985
27124	Knock Motors	2,786	2,786	0	2,786	0

EXHIBIT 11.2   Summary of Errors

		Machinery & Equipment Posting		
$ Number	Vendor	Company Posting (BV)	Correct Posting (AV)	BV − AV
17124	Ubba Tools	1217	800	417
22124	Herol Industrial Supplies	4985	0	4985
52124	Lott Industries	12863	3456	9407
962124	Jerrod Enterprises	72350	0	72350
2102124	Terry Trees	2134	1100	1034
3222124	International Hoes	3260	900	2360

EXHIBIT 11.3   Projected Error

		(1) Book Value	(2) Audited Value	(3) Error (BV − AV)	(4) Tainting % (BV − AV)/ BV	(5) Sampling Interval	(6) Projected Error (4) × (5)
17124	Ubba Tools	$ 1,217	$ 800	$ 417	34%	$5,000	$ 1,713
22124	Herol Industrial Supplies	4,985	0	4,985	100	5,000	5,000
52124	Lott Industries	12,863	3,456	9,407	N/A	N/A	9,407
962124	Jerrod Enterprises	72,350	0	72,350	N/A	N/A	72,350
2102124	Terry Trees	2,134	1,100	1,034	48	5,000	2,423
3222124	International Hoes	3,260	900	2,360	72	5,000	3,620
				$90,553			$94,513

N/A = not applicable

EXHIBIT 11.4   Incremental Allowance for Precision

$ Number	Vendor	(1) Ranked Projected Errors	(2) Incremental Reliability Factor − 1	(3) Incremental Allowance (1) × (2)
22124	Herol Industrial Supplies	$5,000	0.75	$3,750
3222124	International Hoes	3,620	0.55	1,991
2102124	Terry Trees	2,423	0.46	1,115
17124	Ubba Tools	1,713	0.40	685
				$7,541

4. Compute the **upper error limit** and compare it with the tolerable error.

$$UEL = PE + ASR$$

where:

UEL = Upper error limit;

PE = Projected error; and

ASR = Allowance for sampling risk.

In the present example the calculation is as follows:

$$UEL = \$94,513 + \$22,541 = \$117,054.$$

Inasmuch as the upper error limit ($117,054) exceeds the tolerable error ($111,000), Holden concludes that the Machinery and Equipment account is materially overstated and, conversely, that the Repairs and Maintenance Expense account is materially understated. In statistical terms, Holden may conclude, with 95 percent confidence, that the book value is not overstated by more than $117,054.

Based on the results of the sampling, she may elect to sample further in an effort to locate additional invoices containing material errors or she may recommend an audit adjustment in the amount of $90,553, the total amount of the overstatement errors contained in the sample. Such an adjustment, accompanied by a reevaluation of the adjusted book value, may bring the population within the bounds of acceptance.

COMPUTER-ASSISTED SAMPLING

Many of the statistical sampling procedures described in this chapter can be performed more efficiently with the use of computers and statistical software. Moreover, most of the software is presently available for use with microcomputers, thus significantly broadening its audit applicability. The software can be used to:

1. Calculate sample sizes;

2. Select items to be included in samples; and

3. Evaluate sampling results.

For determining sample size, most of the programs require only that the auditor specify the confidence level and precision required. For attribute sampling, precision will be expressed as a percent; for variables sampling and PPS sampling, precision will be stated in dollars.

The computer can also be used to assist in selecting the items to be included in the sample. The auditor enters the highest and lowest numbers, for example, in a group of prenumbered documents representing a given population and also enters the sample size from the sample size calculation procedure. The computer will then produce a worksheet that lists the items to be selected for examination.

After the sample items have been examined and audited, the statistical software can calculate such measures as the best estimate of population value, precision range, range of acceptability, and the upper error limit.

In addition to broadening and expediting sampling applications in auditing, statistical software offers the advantage of enabling auditors with little or no training in statistical sampling to utilize the procedures, inasmuch as the calculations are performed by the computer with limited input by the auditor. The auditor must, of course, be able to interpret the results and exercise judgment in determining the need for modifying the assessed level of control risk and/or the need for audit adjustments based on the sampling results.[7]

Statistical software—another example of auditing with the computer.

---

[7]For a listing of available software, see Viator, Ralph E. and Poe, C. Douglas, *Journal of Accountancy,* May, 1989, pp. 143–150.

KEY TERMS

Achieved precision   Logical sampling unit
Allowance for sampling risk   Mean per unit
Alpha risk   Precision
Anticipated error   Probability proportional to size sampling
Basic precision   Projected error
Beta risk   Reliability
Confidence level   Sampling interval
Desired precision   Standard deviation
Difference estimation   Tolerable error
Incremental allowance for precision   Upper error limit
                                             Variables sampling

COMPUTER AUDIT PRACTICE CASE

Trim Lawn Manufacturing Company

The Trim Lawn audit practice case contains an exercise requiring the application of probability proportional to size sampling to factory equipment additions. This exercise may be completed at this time.

REVIEW QUESTIONS

1. Differentiate between classical variables sampling and probability proportional to size sampling.
2. Identify and distinguish between the two approaches to variables sampling used by auditors.
3. What is another term for *detection risk*?
4. How does detection risk affect sample size in substantive testing?
5. What is the *standard deviation* and how does it affect sample size?
6. How does the auditor estimate the standard deviation for calculating sample size?
7. Differentiate between alpha risk and beta risk.
8. How are alpha and beta risk set by the auditor, and how do they influence sample size?
9. Define *precision* and *reliability* for variables sampling.
10. Why is stratification of populations often useful for substantive testing purposes?
11. Differentiate between achieved and desired precision.
12. Why must achieved precision be ≤ desired precision?
13. Why are sample sizes usually smaller for difference estimation purposes than MPU?
14. What conditions must be met for difference estimation sampling to be appropriate?
15. How does PPS sampling differ from attribute sampling?
16. Under what conditions may PPS sampling be used?
17. Define the following terms as used in PPS sampling:
    a. logical sampling unit
    b. sampling interval
    c. projected error

    d. basic precision

    e. incremental precision allowance

    f. allowance for sampling risk

    g. upper error limit.

18. Name three areas of computer application in sampling. How does the computer facilitate sampling in each of the areas?

MULTIPLE CHOICE QUESTIONS FROM CPA AND CIA EXAMINATIONS

1. Statistical sampling provides a technique for
   a. Exactly defining materiality.
   b. Greatly reducing the amount of substantive testing.
   c. Eliminating judgment in testing.
   d. Measuring the sufficiency of evidential matter.

2. The theoretical distribution of means from all possible samples of a given size is a normal distribution, and this distribution is the basis for statistical sampling. Which of the following statements is not true with respect to the sampling distribution of sample means?
   a. Approximately 68 percent of the sample means will be within one standard deviation of the mean for the normal distribution.
   b. The distribution is defined in terms of its mean and its standard error of the mean.
   c. An auditor can be approximately 95 percent confident that the mean for a sample is within two standard deviations of the population mean.
   d. The items drawn in an auditor's sample will have a normal distribution.

3. If the achieved precision range of a statistical sample at a given reliability level is greater than the desired range, this is an indication that the
   a. Standard deviation was larger than expected.
   b. Standard deviation was less than expected.
   c. Population was larger than expected.
   d. Population was smaller than expected.

4. What is the primary objective of using stratification as a sampling method in auditing?
   a. To increase the confidence level at which a decision will be reached from the results of the sample selected.
   b. To determine the occurrence rate for a given characteristic in the population being studied.
   c. To decrease the effect of variance in the total population.
   d. To determine the precision range of the sample selected.

5. If the auditor is concerned that a population may contain exceptions, the determination of a sample size sufficient to include at least one such exception is a characteristic of
   a. Discovery sampling.
   b. Variables sampling.

    c. Random sampling.

    d. Dollar unit sampling.

6. In the application of statistical techniques to the estimation of dollar amounts, a preliminary sample is usually taken primarily for the purpose of estimating the population

    a. Variability.

    b. Mode.

    c. Range.

    d. Median.

7. Use of difference estimation sampling techniques to estimated dollar amounts is inappropriate when

    a. The total book value is known and corresponds to the sum of all the individual book values.

    b. A book value for each sample item is unknown.

    c. There are some observed differences between audited values and book values.

    d. The audited values are nearly proportional to the book values.

8. The major reason that the difference estimation method is expected to produce audit efficiency is that the

    a. Number of members of the populations of differences or ratios is smaller than the number of members of the population of book values.

    b. Beta risk may be completely ignored.

    c. Calculations required in using difference or ratio estimation are less arduous and fewer than those required when using direct estimation.

    d. Variability of the populations of differences or ratios is less than that of populations of book values or audited values.

9. Which of the following sampling plans would be designed to estimate a numerical measurement of a population, such as a dollar value?

    a. Numerical sampling.

    b. Discovery sampling.

    c. Sampling for attributes.

    d. Sampling for variables.

10. An underlying feature of random-based selection of items is that each

    a. Stratum of the accounting population be given equal representation in the sample.

    b. Item in the accounting population be randomly ordered.

    c. Item in the accounting population should have an opportunity to be selected.

    d. Item must be systematically selected using replacement.

11. Which of the following would be designed to estimate a numerical measurement of a population, such as a dollar value?

    a. Sampling for variables.

    b. Sampling for attributes.

    c. Discovery sampling.

    d. Numerical sampling.

12. When planning a sample for a substantive test of details, an auditor should consider tolerable misstatement for the sample. This consideration should

    a. Be related to the auditor's business risk.

    b. Not be adjusted for qualitative factors.

   c. Be related to preliminary judgments about materiality levels.

   d. Not be changed during the audit process.

13. While performing a substantive test of details during an audit, the auditor determined that the sample results supported the conclusion that the recorded account balance was materially misstated. It was, in fact, not materially misstated. This situation illustrates the risk of

   a. Incorrect rejection.

   b. Incorrect acceptance.

   c. Assessing control risk too low.

   d. Assessing control risk too high.

14. In a probability proportional to size sample with a sampling interval of $10,000, an auditor discovered that a selected account receivable with a recorded amount of $5,000 had an audit amount of $2,000. The projected error of this sample was

   a. $3,000.

   b. $4,000.

   c. $6,000.

   d. $8,000.

15. When using classical variables sampling for estimation, an auditor normally evaluates the sampling results by calculating the possible error in either direction. This statistical concept is known as

   a. Precision.

   b. Reliability.

   c. Projected error.

   d. Standard deviation.

16. PPS sampling is less efficient if:

   a. Computerized account balances are being audited.

   b. Statistical inferences are to be made.

   c. The audit objective is oriented to understatements.

   d. The account contains a large number of transactions.

17. A sampling method that can be used to estimate overstatement error of an account balance but is not based on normal-curve mathematics is:

   a. Discovery sampling.

   b. Mean per unit sampling.

   c. Attributes sampling.

   d. Probability proportional to size sampling.

ESSAY QUESTIONS AND PROBLEMS

11.1 Alpha and beta risk are important ingredients in determining sample size for variables sampling.

Required:

   a. Differentiate between alpha and beta risk.

   b. Discuss the relevance of alpha and beta risk for audit hypothesis testing purposes.

   c. Identify and discuss the factors considered by the auditor in quantifying alpha and beta risk in variables sampling applications.

11.2 Standard deviation is defined as the degree of variation of individual item values from the population mean; precision is defined as the range within which the true answer most likely falls.

Required:
a. How are standard deviation and precision related?
b. What factors would you consider in specifying precision?
c. How do standard deviation and precision affect sample size?

11.3 During the course of an audit engagement, a CPA attempts to ascertain that there are no material misstatements in the accounts receivable of a client. Statistical sampling is a tool that the auditor often uses to obtain representative evidence to verify accounts. On a particular engagement an auditor determined that a material misstatement in a population of accounts would be $35,000. To obtain satisfaction the auditor had to be 95 percent confident that the population of accounts was not in error by more than $35,000. The auditor decided to use MPU sampling and took a preliminary random sample of 100 items (n) from a population of 1,000 items (N). The sample produced the following data:

Arithmetic mean of sample items, $\bar{y}$ $4,000
Standard deviation of sample items SD $200

Required:
a. Define the statistical terms *reliability* and *precision* as applied to auditing.
b. If all necessary audit work is performed on the preliminary sample items and no errors are detected, what can the auditor say about the total amount of accounts receivable at the 95 percent confidence level, and at what confidence level can the auditor say that the population is not in error by $35,000?
c. Assuming that the preliminary sample was sufficient, compute the auditor's estimate of the population total, and indicate how the auditor should relate this estimate to the client's recorded amount.

The following list of *Ur* and reliability factors may be used as needed in completing the above requirements:

Confidence Level	Ur Factor
91.086%	1.70
91.988%	1.75
92.814%	1.80
93.568%	1.85
94.256%	1.90
94.882%	1.95
95.000%	1.96
95.450%	2.00
95.964%	2.05
96.428%	2.10
96.844%	2.15

(AICPA adapted)

11.4 Joel Lewis of Howell and Howell, CPAs, is the in-charge auditor for Lazy Girl Chair Company, an audit client of Howell and Howell. In planning for the finished goods inventory audit, Lewis decides to use mean per unit sampling in evaluating the quantities, prices, and extended amounts on the inventory listings. The inventory listings consist of 12,000 line items on computer printouts. Each line item is identified by stock number and includes quantity, price, and extended amount of that specific furniture item. Lewis and his audit team observed the year-end physical inventory and were concerned about the lack of control during inventory taking. Operations continued during the physical counting; goods were moved from storeroom to production area and from production to finished goods; obvious overstocking conditions were observed by the "team"; and inventory tags were not prenumbered. With considerable effort, however, Lewis and his staff assistants were able to satisfy themselves as to physical quantities. This required counting approximately 60 percent of the finished goods. In addition to the identified control weaknesses during inventory, Lewis had observed other weaknesses in maintaining perpetual inventory records (the inventory adjustment reflected a 10 percent shrinkage factor) and in processing sales orders.

The total appearing on the printouts, $2,632,400, was traced to the general ledger by Sally Straw, one of Lewis' assistants.

Required:
a. How might the apparent lack of control over finished goods inventory affect the sampling plan in the present situation?
b. Assuming the audit team decides to assess both inherent risk and control risk at 100 percent and chooses a 10 percent risk of incorrect rejection, what is the beta risk?
c. If a pilot sample of 40 line items from the inventory listings produces a preliminary estimate of standard deviation in the amount of $90 and $110,000 is considered to be the minimum acceptable misstatement of finished goods inventory, what is the sample size?
d. What audit procedures should the "team" apply to the sample items?
e. Assuming a sample mean of $160 and a standard deviation of $85, what is the achieved precision and the estimated audited value of the population? State the conclusions to be drawn based on the audit sampling.

11.5 As a staff training exercise, Catherine Stahlman wishes to demonstrate the cost-effectiveness of difference estimation sampling by calculating and contrasting sample size for mean per unit and difference estimation. She has developed the following data and assumptions as inputs for the exercise:
1. *Application:* Trade accounts receivable
2. *Number of customer accounts:* 3,500
3. *Total book value:* $7,200,000
4. *Control risk:* 60 percent
5. *Inherent risk:* 50 percent
6. *Alpha risk:* 5 percent
7. *Preliminary estimate of standard deviation* (based on pilot sample): Standard deviation is $750; and standard deviation of differences is $380
8. *Individual item materiality:* $320,000

Required:
a. Calculate sample size for both MPU and difference estimation purposes.
b. Why do the sample sizes differ?
c. If difference estimation is more cost-effective than MPU, why would MPU ever be used in auditing applications?

11.6 The Ancient and Archaic Museum of Pello, Oklahoma, has a common endowment fund in the amount of $52 million. This fund consists of the common stocks of 1,350 publicly held companies. Jason Law, the in-charge senior for the Ancient and Archaic audit, wishes to apply difference estimation sampling in evaluating the fairness of the fund's book value. The approach will be to select a sample from the 1,350 accounts in the investment ledger, audit them carefully as to type, quantity, ownership, cost, market value, and lower of cost or market, and extend the results to the population.

One of Law's assistants has obtained a computer printout of the investment ledger and determined that the sum of the accounts equals $52 million, the control account balance in the general ledger. Jerry Strand, the museum controller, has assured Law that the securities have been valued at the lower of cost or market as of the balance sheet date.

Prior audits and the current year's testing of control procedures relative to the processing of securities transactions have led Law to believe that the population contains numerous differences divided equally between overstatement and under-statement. As a result, he concludes that internal control is poor, and assesses control risk at 70 percent for substantive testing purposes. Inherent risk and alpha risk are set at 90 percent and 5 percent respectively. A pilot sample of 40 securities drawn at random from the computer printout produces a standard deviation of the differences between audited and book value in the amount of $3,200.

Required:
a. Assuming Law and the audit team have established $800,000 as individual item materiality, calculate the sample size.
b. State the conclusions given the following sampling results: Mean of the dif-ferences, ($4,600) (negative); standard deviation of the differences, $2,800.
c. What alternatives are available to the audit team as indicated by the sample results?

11.7 Larry Charles of Charles and Charles, CPAs, is planning the merchandise inven-tory audit of L Mart, a large retail chain. Computer printouts of priced inventory, categorized by line of merchandise, have been provided to Charles for audit purposes. Inasmuch as profit declines have been an ongoing problem for L Mart during the last quarter, Charles anticipates some significant inventory overpricing errors. His suspicions are further aroused through the application of analytical procedures. Historical gross profit rates, as applied to different lines of L Mart's merchandise, produced estimated inventory figures significantly below the values booked by L Mart's controller, Huey Dewlou. Following are the results of the test:

Merchandise Line	Gross Profit Test	L Mart Book Value
Appliances and Furniture	$23,456,000	$27,478,933
Housewares	$12,600,000	$14,575,456
Sporting Goods	$16,750,000	$22,489,345
Audio-Video	$34,400,000	$41,348,990
Clothing	$56,788,000	$62,788,800

Charles decides to apply probability proportionate to size sampling (PPS) to each merchandise line in order to estimate the extent of overstatement error (if any) attributable to each. Satisfaction regarding inventory quantities has already been obtained by observing the ending inventory counts at several locations.

Internal control over the processing of inventory purchases and store security measures instituted over the years have led Charles to evaluate overall control within the purchasing and inventory cycle as good. The major concern, therefore, is one of possible management override in the form of inventory overpricing errors.

The following sampling plan has been developed for each line of merchandise:

Merchandise Line	Risk of Incorrect Acceptance	Anticipated Error	Tolerable Error
Appl. and Fur.	20%	$ 500,000	$1,300,000
Housewares	20%	$ 180,000	$1,000,000
Sporting Goods	20%	$ 230,000	$1,000,000
Audio-Video	15%	$ 900,000	$2,200,000
Clothing	15%	$2,200,000	$4,100,000

Required:
a. What is the sampling unit for purposes of the test? What is the logical sampling unit? What is the sample size for each line?
b. Calculate the sampling interval for each of the sample sizes determined in a.
c. Assuming the following sample results for the clothing line, calculate projected error, basic precision, and incremental precision allowance:

$ Number	Line	Book Value	Audited Value
590,603	Suzzanna Jackets	$ 435,980	$ 363,200
8,169,587	Glenn Browning Sport Coats	$3,476,962	$1,450,480
16,380,153	Floorshine Shoes	$1,529,800	$ 987,954
21,432,809	Fruit of the Limb Underwear	$ 211,000	$ 56,765
28,380,211	London Rain Top Coats	$1,580,327	$1,076,400
36,590,777	Roy Rogers Wallets	$ 847,000	$ 56,842
44,801,343	Bigtex Romper Suits	$ 631,000	$ 102,877
47,327,671	Pierre Cardex Suits	$5,160,000	$2,620,900
54,906,655	Spear Dress Shirts	$1,223,545	$ 478,954
61,854,057	Lee High Jeans	$4,876,544	$1,897,665

d. What conclusions can be drawn based on the sample results? Are any further procedures indicated? Explain.

11.8 In order to minimize its tax liability, Holea Manufacturing Company, a publicly held manufacturer of lawn mowers and snowblowers, has, in the past, been rather liberal in treating maintenance and repairs expenditures as ordinary expense items. Katherine Hoppel of Pete Waterhose & Co, CPAs, the in-charge auditor for the Holea engagement, decides to apply probability proportional to size (PPS) sampling to test the repairs and maintenance account for possible overstatement. Given higher than normal profits arising from heavy sales of snowblowers during the very severe winter just ended, Hoppel suspects that material amounts of capital expenditures once again have been charged to the repairs and maintenance account. Her suspicions are further supported by the application of analytical procedures. In past years, pre-audited repairs and maintenance expenditures have ranged from 8 percent to 10 percent of net sales. The audited values have been considerably lower, ranging from 4 percent to 5 percent of net sales. For the current year, the unaudited amount, $2,566,000, equals 12 percent of net sales. A total of 1,385 postings to the repairs and maintenance account constitutes the balance in the account. No credits were posted to repairs during the year. In the past, vendors' invoices have frequently included both capital and repair expenditure charges.

Given effective internal control over the processing of vendors' invoices, Hoppel believes the problem to be one of possible management override rather than weak control. She decides on a risk of incorrect acceptance of 10 percent and an anticipated error of $60,000.

Required:

a. Assuming that Hoppel is willing to accept a tolerable error of $110,000, calculate the sample size and the sampling interval.
b. What is the sampling unit in the present case? What is the logical unit? Using the sample size and sampling interval determined in a, discuss the steps required in drawing and evaluating the sample.
c. Assuming the following errors were discovered in the sample, calculate basic precision, the incremental allowance for sampling risk, the allowance for sampling risk, and the upper error limit. What conclusions can be drawn from the sampling results?

$ Number	Vendor	Book Value	Audited Value
4,531	Challenge, Inc.	$ 2,622	$1,875
71,181	Tools Unlimited	$17,344	$3,160
157,826	Triple Tier Enterprises	$ 1,360	$ 0
297,791	Buntworth Brown, Inc.	$20,231	$ 0
586,452	Johnsons Wholesalers	$14,761	$2,356
996,785	Truncated Tools, Inc.	$ 5,389	$ 890
1,363,790	Chalmers Repair Parts	$16,122	$1,088
1,793,456	Kaiser Suppliers	$ 7,988	$1,867
2,122,988	Hapworth, Ltd.	$43,668	$ 0

11.9 Paul Edwards has decided to use probability proportional to size (PPS) sampling, sometimes called dollar unit sampling, in the audit of a client's accounts receivable balance. Few, if any, errors of account balance overstatement are expected.

Edwards plans to use the following PPS sampling table of reliability factors for errors of overstatement (by risk of incorrect acceptance).

Number of Overstatement Errors	1%	5%	10%	15%	20%
0	4.61	3.00	2.31	1.90	1.61
1	6.64	4.75	3.89	3.38	3.00
2	8.41	6.30	5.33	4.72	4.28
3	10.05	7.76	6.69	6.02	5.52
4	11.61	9.16	8.00	7.27	6.73

Required:

a. Identify the advantages of using PPS sampling over classical variables sampling.

(*Note:* Requirements b and c are not related).

b. Calculate the sampling interval and the sample size Edwards should use given the following information:

Tolerable error $12.000
Risk of incorrect acceptance 1%
Number of errors allowed 0
Recorded amount of accounts receivable $250,000

c. Calculate the total projected error if the following three errors were discovered in a PPS sample:

Error	Recorded Amount	Audit Amount	Sampling Interval
1	$ 600	$ 220	$2,000
2	1,500	160	2,000
3	3,000	2,500	2,000

(AICPA adapted)

11.10 In conjunction with the potential acquisition of a manufacturing firm, the auditor has been asked to verify the book value of equipment of the company to be acquired. The auditor has decided to use a mean per unit variables sampling technique to estimate the book value.

The reported book value of the equipment is $5,550,000. An error of more than $200,000 will be considered material. The auditor has chosen to use a confidence level of 95 percent (1.96 Z factor for a two-tail test) for the sample.

The results of a pilot sample of equipment records yields a preliminary estimated standard deviation of $300. Based on the above parameters, the auditor computes a required sample size of 160 from the 3,400 items listed in the company's equipment inventory. The results of the sample were:

Sample standard deviation $280
Total audit value of sampled items $262,400

Required:

a. Identify the factors impacting sample size. Briefly explain each.
b. Using the sample data, compute the value of the equipment account based on the sample data above. Include a measure of reliability (confidence interval) achieved.
c. Briefly state whether the sample results support the reported book value.
d. Identify the two types of sampling risk that the auditor might have considered in formulating the statistical sample and briefly state how to control each.

(IIA adapted)

11.11 You are auditing a company offering both department store and catalog sales. You are designing a variables sampling plan to estimate the amount of revenue resulting from catalog sales. Company records indicate that 85,000 catalog sales were completed during the year ending December 31, 19XX. The total sales recorded for the same period were equal to $15,682,000. *Catalog sales are not separately recorded.* A pilot sample of 30 catalog sales resulted in the following:

Estimated population standard deviation = $9.00
Average billing amount = $27.50.

The appropriate statistical sampling table indicates that a desired precision of $1.38 (5 percent of average billed amount) and the pilot sample standard deviation of $9.00 will require testing a sample of 121 transactions. It is the policy of your firm to conduct such tests at the 90 percent confidence level ($Z = 1.65$)

Required:

a. Can the 30 items used as a pilot sample also be used as part of the sample of 121? Explain.

b. What are the factors that impact the precision of the estimate of a population value?

c. Given the pilot sample results, what can the auditor do to decrease the size of the sample standard deviation?

d. The standard error of the mean can be computed by dividing the population standard deviation by the square root of sample size (ignoring the finite population correction factor). Assuming no change in the estimated population standard deviation after considering all 121 items, what is the value of:

The standard error of the mean?

The achieved precision?

e. Assuming no change in the estimated average billing amount after considering all 121 items, compute estimated total catalog sales.

f. Compute the 90 percent confidence interval for estimated total catalog sales.

(IIA adapted)

12

Substantive Audit Testing: Revenue Cycle

CHAPTER OUTLINE

    I. **Introduction**

   II. **Review of the audit process**

  III. **Overview of substantive testing**
      A. Timing of substantive testing
      B. Cost benefit and substantive testing
      C. Analytical procedures and substantive testing
      D. Audit objectives, evidence, and procedures
      E. Emphasis and direction of substantive testing—need for a balanced audit approach

  IV. **Auditing the revenue cycle**
      A. Sales transactions and accounts receivable balances
      B. Cash receipts transactions and cash balances

   V. **Audit risk analysis and the revenue cycle: Some warning signs**
      A. Inflated sales or fictitious accounts receivable
      B. Inadequate loan loss reserves
      C. Early revenue recognition
      D. Proof of cash

  VI. **Appendix: Auditing objectives and procedures: Revenue cycle**

OVERVIEW

Substantive testing is the process of obtaining evidence in support of transactions and balances. Chapters 12, 13, and 14 discuss substantive testing according to transaction cycles.

In determining the nature, timing, and extent of substantive procedures to be applied in the circumstances, the auditor must consider such matters as audit risk, materiality, and cost-effectiveness. Although most substantive testing is done after the balance sheet date, a certain amount may be completed during the interim audit.

This chapter covers substantive testing of the revenue cycle in two parts:

1. Sales transactions and accounts receivable balances; and

2. Cash receipts transactions and cash balances.

For each part, specific audit objectives are identified. This is followed by a discussion of audit evidence and procedures necessary to meet the specified objectives.

The chapter concludes with a consideration of audit risk associated with the revenue cycle. Warning signs are identified that should arouse the auditor's suspicions concerning possible misstatements of financial statement components. Cases are cited and discussed to illustrate the warning signs.

STUDY OBJECTIVES

After reading this chapter, you should be able to:

1. Define substantive testing;

2. Identify specific audit objectives related to the revenue cycle;

3. Develop audit programs for the revenue cycle which relate audit procedures to audit objectives for each component of the cycle;

4. Modify audit programs, as necessary, in light of "warning signs" that surface during: a study of the business and industry, application of analytical procedures, or a study of control structure policies and procedures.

INTRODUCTION

Substantive audit testing is the process of obtaining evidence in support of transactions and balances. The nature, timing, and extent of substantive testing is a function of the auditor's judgment concerning audit risk and materiality. The substantive procedures selected by the auditor are incorporated into audit programs. Audit programs are designed at the conclusion of the audit planning phase, based on the auditor's assessment of inherent risk and control risk. They may be further modified as conditions warrant.

Substantive testing is discussed in the current and succeeding chapters according to the following transaction cycles:

- *Chapter 12: Revenue Cycle:* includes sales transactions, accounts receivable balances, cash receipts transactions, and cash balances.
- *Chapter 13: Expenditure Cycle:* includes purchases, cash payments, operating expenses, inventories, plant assets, intangible assets, and accounts payable.
- *Chapter 14: Financing and Investing Cycle:* includes borrowing and investing transactions, interest revenue and expense, dividends, notes receivable, notes payable, bonds payable, capital stock, and retained earnings.

These are the same transaction cycles that were introduced in Chapter 4 and used in Chapter 7 for discussing control testing. An appendix follows each chapter. The appendix consists of a matrix relating auditing objectives to audit evidence and procedures within each of the transaction cycles. It thereby provides a framework for applying substantive testing within the respective cycles. Although not intended to be all-inclusive, the appendix may serve as a model for developing comprehensive programs for substantive audit testing.

REVIEW OF AUDIT PROCESS

Figure 12.1, as in previous chapters, shows where the chapter material fits into the overall audit process. As can be seen, the current chapter discusses substantive testing relative to the revenue cycle. Those steps in the audit process preceding substantive testing have been covered in Chapters 5 through 11. They are as follows:

1. Inherent risk has been assessed by means of discussions with management, a study of the business and industry, and the application of analytical procedures.

2. Control structure policies and procedures have been studied and evaluated by observation of the control environment, inquiry of management and employees, completion of questionnaires, checklists, memoranda, and flowcharts, examining documents for errors, and reprocessing transactions through the accounting system; the auditor's understanding of control structure has been documented; and control risk has been assessed, along with documentation of the auditor's basis for reducing assessed control risk below the maximum level.

3. Detection risk has been analyzed in light of findings regarding inherent risk and control risk.

The next step is for the auditor to design substantive audit procedures in the form of audit programs. The programs are developed on the basis of the results of steps 1 through 3. These programs were introduced in Chapter 4 and will be elaborated upon in this and the two ensuing chapters.

FIGURE 12.1   The Audit Process

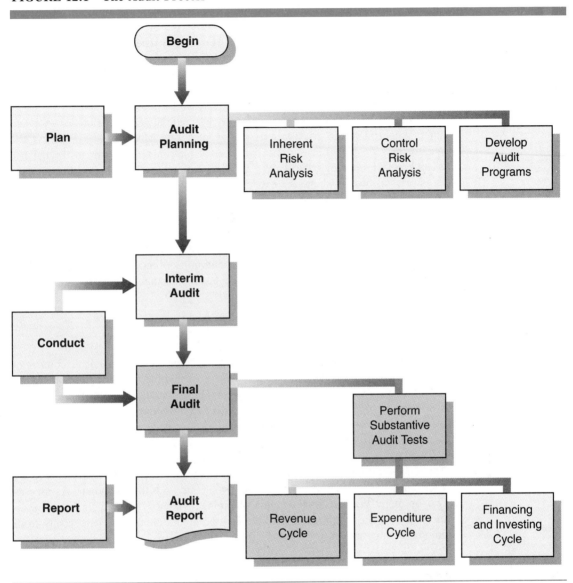

OVERVIEW OF SUBSTANTIVE TESTING

Timing of Substantive Testing

In collecting evidence in support of transactions and account balances (substantive testing), the auditor must determine the nature, timing, and extent of procedures to be applied in the circumstances. These determinations are based on audit judgment, influenced by such factors such as audit risk, materiality, and cost-effectiveness.

Although most substantive audit tests are applied as of the balance sheet date, a limited amount of substantive testing may be performed during the interim audit to conserve time on the final audit. A general rule of thumb is that the auditor performs tests of balances (e.g., confirming accounts receivable, observing inventory taking, and reconciling bank balances) as of the balance sheet date, and tests transactions (e.g., plant asset additions and disposals, research and development expenditures, operating revenues and expenses, and purchases and sales of marketable securities) during the interim audit, as well as the final audit.

An exception to this general rule may be made under conditions of excellent internal control within given transaction cycle subsets. Under these conditions, the auditor may decide to test certain balances at interim points prior to the balance sheet date. If internal control over sales processing, billing, and collection, for example, has been evaluated as excellent, the auditor may elect to confirm customers' accounts receivable at an interim date. SAS 45, however, cautions against performing excessive amounts of substantive testing during interim periods. Too much substantive testing during the interim audit may increase detection risk to an unacceptable level as of the balance sheet date.[1] A good rule, therefore, is to increase interim balance testing under conditions of good to excellent internal control and to perform minimal balance testing during the interim audit under conditions of fair to weak internal control.

Cost-Benefit and Substantive Testing

In considering cost-effectiveness, the auditor recognizes that sufficient, competent evidence must be obtained regardless of the cost involved. Given alternate means for achieving a specific audit objective, however, the auditor should choose the less costly set of procedures. To illustrate, assume that the auditor wishes to ascertain the existence and ownership of securities owned by the client. Assume further that these securities are in safekeeping at a distant location. Obviously, the objective can be satisfied by the auditor visiting the location and physically examining the securities. The objective could be met more economically, however, and just as effectively, by confirming the securities' existence and ownership with the custodian. As long as two or more alternate methods for obtaining evidence are equally effective in meeting the stated audit objective, the auditor should choose the least costly from among the alternatives.

Analytical Procedures and Substantive Testing

Chapter 5 discussed the application of analytical procedures as part of the auditor's analysis of inherent risk. The purpose was to identify unusual relationships warranting further investigation. Such further investigation has presumably been factored into the design of substantive audit programs. A material decline in accounts receivable turnover, for example, may be indicative of collection problems. This, in

---

[1]Auditing Standards Board, *AICPA Professional Standards,* New York: AICPA, 1991, Section AU 313.03.

turn, affects net realizable value and may warrant extending the confirmation of customers' accounts, expanding the analysis of customer remittances subsequent to the balance sheet date, and/or increasing attention to the adequacy of the allowance for uncollectible accounts.

In addition to applying analytical procedures during the planning phase of the audit, SAS 56 also requires that analytical procedures be applied as part of the overall audit review.[2] As part of the overall review phase, the application of analytical procedures assists the auditor in assessing conclusions and in determining the sufficiency of audit evidence.[3] Upon conclusion of the audit of inventories, for example, the auditor may estimate the ending inventory using historical gross profit rates. If the estimated inventory is materially at variance with the audited inventory, the auditor may have to audit the inventories further to resolve the reason for the disparity.

Audit Objectives, Evidence, and Procedures

Figure 12.2 summarizes the audit objectives, evidence, and procedures model, as presented in Chapter 4. In the chapters to follow, each transaction cycle is addressed within this framework. Accordingly, each part of the transaction cycle is considered in the following order:

1. The specific *audit objectives* relevant to that part of the cycle;

2. The types of *audit evidence* needed to satisfy the objectives; and

3. The *audit procedures* which can be used to collect the necessary evidence.

Emphasis and Direction of Substantive Testing

Before considering the transaction cycles in depth, a word of caution regarding the emphasis and direction of substantive testing is in order. In analyzing audit risk, auditors frequently discover conditions which lead them to suspect that assets and revenues may be overstated or that liabilities and expenses may be understated. Under such conditions, attention is directed to developing programs which will aid in detecting various types of management misrepresentation fraud. Over the past several years, a significant number of frauds of "asset/earnings inflation" have surfaced in the courts. Accordingly, considerable attention is devoted in this text to audit procedures designed to detect asset overstatements and liability understatements.

At the same time, however, the emphasis needs to be properly *balanced*. Companies that are successful in terms of profits and cash flows, for example, may seek to understate revenues or overstate expenses. The goal may be to understate the tax liability, or avoid remitting profits to the parent company. Moreover, unintentional errors resulting from internal control weaknesses may materially misstate

---

[2]*Ibid.*, Section 329.

[3]*Ibid.*

FIGURE 12.2   Substantive Audit Testing Model for Designing Audit Programs

1. Audit Objectives

Specify Audit Objectives

Existence or Occurrence	Valuation or Allocation
Completeness	Presentation and Disclosure
Rights and Obligations	

2. Audit Evidence

Identify Relevant Types of Evidence for Each Objective

Physical	Mathematical
Confirmation	Analytical
Documentary	Hearsay

3. Audit Procedures

Develop Audit Programs

Observe	Vouch	Recalculate
Examine	Inspect	Trace
Count	Inquire	Compare
Confirm	Calculate	Reconcile
Analyze		

financial statements in either direction. If, therefore, the auditor suspects material understatement, audit programs should be modified accordingly.

Table 12.1 presents a **balanced audit approach** designed to avoid overemphasizing either extreme in audit direction. By testing assets and expenses for overstatement and liabilities and revenues for understatement, the auditor is considering both directions of possible misstatement. The model presented in Table 12.1 represents a *neutral* position regarding emphasis of direction. It should be modified when specific risk analysis factors lead the auditor to strongly suspect misstatement in one specific direction. For example, assume that past experience with a client has been one of recurring attempts to overstate earnings. Assume further that analytical procedures produce unusual relationships indicative of earn-

TABLE 12.1 Audit Balance Matrix

	AUDIT EMPHASIS	
ACCOUNT	*Test for Overstatement*	*Test for Understatement*
Assets	X	
Liabilities		X
Revenues		X
Expenses	X	

ings inflation during the current year. Under these circumstances, the auditor should place more emphasis on asset overstatement and liability understatement than on revenue understatement and expense overstatement.

AUDITING THE REVENUE CYCLE

Substantive testing of the **revenue cycle** (sales revenue, cash receipts, cash balances, and accounts receivable) is discussed in the following two sections. The steps involved in processing revenue cycle transactions are diagrammed in Figure 12.3. To briefly summarize some of the significant control points as discussed in the appendix following Chapter 7, we might note the following:

1. All incoming customer orders should be properly approved for credit;
2. Sales order/sales invoice sets should be generated only on the basis of properly approved customer orders;
3. Shipments to customers should be made only on the basis of properly approved sales order/invoice sets accompanied by credit approval;
4. All shipments should be evidenced by signed bills of lading signed by the carrier;
5. Invoices should be mailed to customers only on the basis of signed bills of lading;
6. Sales should be recorded only after receipt of bill of lading evidencing shipment and sales invoice with customer order attached, evidencing order approval, credit approval, and billing;
7. Customer remittances should be restrictively endorsed and prelisted upon receipt;
8. Customer remittances, along with other cash receipts, should be deposited intact daily;
9. Cash receipts should be recorded daily by persons who are competent and who do not have access to cash or checks;
10. Receipted bank deposit tickets should be compared with prelistings and cash receipts journal entries daily;

FIGURE 12.3   Revenue Cycle—Summary of Processing Steps

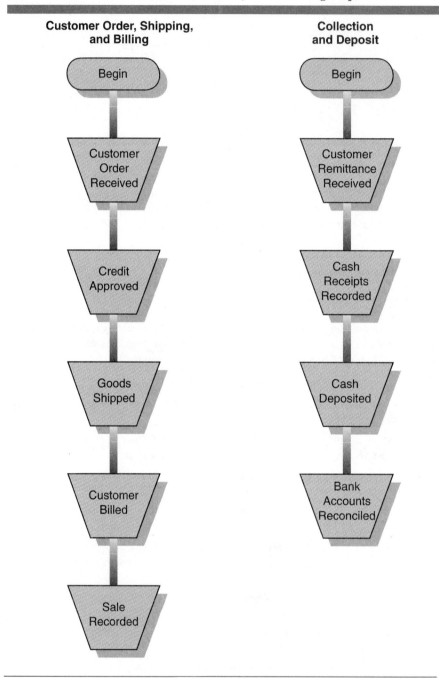

11. All bank accounts should be reconciled monthly by persons not having access to cash or accounting records;

12. Internal documents such as customer order forms, sales order/sales invoice sets, shipping orders, and bills of lading should be prenumbered and the numeric sequence of used documents should be periodically accounted for;

13. To the extent the revenue cycle is computerized, adequate input editing, processing, and output controls should be designed and implemented to provide reasonable assurance as to proper recording of transactions and security over the resulting data bases.

In designing risk-based audit programs for the revenue cycle, the auditor must keep the above control points in mind, along with specifically identified risk factors associated with each.

The first of the two sections that follow deals with sales transactions and accounts receivable balances. The second section covers cash receipts transactions and cash balances. Each section is divided further into two parts: audit objectives and audit evidence/procedures.

Sales Transactions and Accounts Receivable Balances

Audit Objectives

The audit objectives relating to sales transactions and accounts receivable balances may be classified as follows:

1. **Existence and Completeness.** The auditor needs to determine that all sales are recorded in the proper accounting period, and that all debits to accounts receivable represent actual transactions.

2. **Valuation.** The auditor must ascertain that sales are recorded at proper amounts in accordance with GAAP. This requires that only completed sales be reflected and that consignments out be excluded from sales; that sales be recognized only on the basis of revenue having been substantially earned; and that sales revenue not be recognized before realization is complete or reasonably predictable. The auditor must also determine, by evaluating the allowance for doubtful accounts, that accounts receivable balances are stated at amounts not exceeding estimated net realizable values.

3. **Presentation and Disclosure.** Credit balances in accounts receivable should be reclassified as current liabilities if material. Similarly, significant amounts of nontrade receivables and receivables from related parties should be reported separately. Related-party transactions, moreover, need to be fully disclosed in footnotes to the financial statements. If the client's accounts receivable are computerized, the auditor can utilize generalized auditing software to assist in identifying credit balances, nontrade receivables, related-party balances, and account balances exceeding approved credit limits. Pledging or assignment of accounts receivable as loan collateral must also be disclosed in the body of the financial statements or in footnotes.

Audit Evidence and Procedures

Analytical procedures, applied earlier in the audit process, will have revealed any significant changes in patterns of sales, cost of sales, or gross profit. This, along with a study of industry sales patterns and control testing of the revenue cycle, will influence the extent of application of the procedures addressed in the following paragraphs.

To obtain satisfaction that sales are recorded in the proper accounting period, the auditor should apply **sales cutoff** procedures. Such tests require examining documentary evidence supporting sales transactions for a few days before and after year end. Sales orders, sales invoices, shipping orders, and bills of lading form the necessary documentary evidence. In examining the evidence, the auditor should note shipping dates and freight terms, making certain that sales reflected in the year under audit were shipped before year end, and that sales in transit at year end were shipped F.O.B. shipping point. The auditor must also determine consistency of the current year-end sales cutoff with that of the preceding year. If cutoff is not consistent, the current year may contain a greater or fewer number of days' sales than the number of working days in the year. Cutoff is addressed more extensively in Chapter 13 as part of the inventory audit discussion.

Confirmation of accounts receivable on a test basis helps the auditor to substantiate the genuineness of receivables and to evaluate correctness of valuation of the year-end balances. Confirmation is defined in SAS 67 as ''the process of obtaining and evaluating a direct communication from a third party in response to a request for information about a particular item affecting financial statement assertions.''[4] As applied to trade accounts receivable, confirmation consists of customers replying directly to the auditor concerning the accuracy of the receivable balances, as reflected by the client. Two types of confirmation are utilized in practice. **Positive confirmation** requests the customer to respond as to agreement or disagreement with the reported balance (see Exhibit 12.1). **Negative confirmation** requests the customer to reply only in the event of disagreement (see Exhibit 12.2). A disadvantage of the negative confirmation is that nonreplies may signify agreement or simply failure to respond. For this reason, SAS 67 permits the negative form of confirmation only where the auditor has assessed the level of inherent risk and control risk as low; the auditor has no reason to believe that the recipient will not review the confirmation request; and a large number of small balances are involved.[5] If the first two conditions are met and customers' accounts include both large and small balances, auditors frequently stratify the population of customer accounts as to size, requesting positive confirmation for most of the large balances, and relying on negative confirmation for a sample of the smaller accounts.

After the subsidiary accounts receivable ledger has been compared with the general ledger control account, and the customer statements, which are to accompany the confirmation form, have been prepared, the auditor must control the mailing of the confirmation requests. To maintain control, the auditor either mails the forms directly or carefully supervises the client's mailing of the confirmations.

---

[4]Auditing Standards Board, Statement on Auditing Standards No. 67, *The Confirmation Process,* New York: AICPA, November, 1991, paragraph 4.

[5]*Ibid.,* paragraph 20.

EXHIBIT 12.1   Positive Accounts Receivable Confirmation Request

(control number)<u>108</u>

Jarol, Inc.
2334 Oak Street
Phoenix, Arizona

January 12, 1994

Roberts Discount Stores
835 Mound Street
Los Angeles, California

Gentlemen:

Our auditors, Arfol & Tick, CPAs, are making an examination of our financial statements. Please examine the accompanying statement and either confirm its correctness or report any differences to our auditors.

Your prompt attention to this request will be appreciated. An envelope is enclosed for your reply.

Very truly yours,

John Saling

John Saling
Credit Manager

EXHIBIT 12.2   Negative Accounts Receivable Confirmation Request

Trane, Inc.
4555 Pheasant Point
Julio, Texas

January 12, 1994

Links Bakeries
434 Tenth Street
Libo, Louisiana

Gentlemen:

Please examine the accompanying statement. If it does not agree with your records, please report any exceptions directly to our auditors, Rightly & Wrongly, CPAs, who are making an examination of our financial statements.

Very truly yours,

Stephen Jurs

Stephen Jurs
Credit Manager

For both positive and negative confirmation requests, a CPA firm-addressed envelope, included with the customer statement and confirmation request, ensures that customer replies are received directly by the auditor.

As the replies are received, they are logged into a control worksheet (see Exhibit 12.3), and all exceptions are cleared. Many exceptions consist of goods or remittances in transit, and, assuming proper cutoff, do not require audit adjustment. Those exceptions that are indicative of genuine disputes concerning prices, discounts, allowances, or returns need to be explored in depth and may require audit adjustment if material.

For customers not responding to the initial requests for positive confirmation, the auditor should mail second and possibly third requests. In the absence of replies to second and third requests, the auditor should apply alternate procedures. Such procedures may be in the form of examining billing and shipping documents or remittance advice (the lower part attached to the customer's check and detailing the invoices paid by the remittance) in support of subsequent collections. If customers cannot confirm balances because the sales and accounts receivable systems restrict information to transactions, the auditor should consider confirming selected transactions with these customers.

Auditors must be careful not to rely too heavily on client documentation of sales where numerous nonreplies to confirmation requests are experienced. Confirmations are a form of external evidence, and therefore provide greater assurance as to existence and valuation than internal evidence in the form of client documentation. Under conditions of significant nonreplies, therefore, the concept of due audit care should lead the auditor to consider whether an unqualified audit opinion can be

EXHIBIT 12.3 Confirmation Control Worksheet

			W.P. No.	C.3
			Prepared by:	lfk 1/15/94
			Reviewed by:	gfg 1/22/94

Jarol, Inc.
Accounts Receivable—Trade
Confirmation Control Worksheet
12/31/93

Confirmation Number	Customer	Balance	Date Returned	Comments
100	Congre Wholesalers	$ 2,688	2/6	No exception
101	Trac Two	12,357	2/3	No exception
102	House of Glass	6,654		(1)
103	General Arts	34,890	2/8	(2)
104	Uler Office Supply	4,532	3/1	No exception
105	Jolly News	1,388	2/20	No exception
106	Riker Gifts	7,760		(3)
107	Lila's Pharmacy	5,235	2/13	No exception
108	Roberts Discount Stores	66,890	2/2	(4)
109	Usher, Inc.	54,378	3/2	No exception
110	Save More	8,697	2/5	No exception

(1) No response to second and third requests.
   Examined shipping documents and subsequent collections.—No exceptions.
(2) Credit not given for returned merchandise.
   Customer has issued debit memo for $1,870.
   Credit manager indicates that CM is forthcoming.
(3) No response to second and third requests.
   Examined shipping documents and subsequent collections.—No exceptions.
(4) Remittance of $12,346 in transit at year-end.
   Traced to January cash receipts. (see WP B.2)

rendered. The case presented later in this chapter illustrates how overreliance on internal evidence can lead to significant audit risk.

An **accounts receivable aging analysis** is useful in evaluating the adequacy of the allowance for doubtful accounts (see Exhibits 12.4 and 12.5). Note that the worksheet includes post-balance sheet collections of customers' year-end balances. Subsequent remittance by the customer is the best evidence of collectibility at the balance sheet date.

In addition to completeness, existence, and valuation, the auditor must gather evidence in support of proper presentation and adequacy of disclosure relative to sales revenue and trade accounts receivable. Credit balances in customers'

EXHIBIT 12.4   Accounts Receivable Aging Analysis

WP C

Auditee, Inc.
12/31/93

Prepared by: LFK   Date: 2/5/94
Reviewed by: CCK   Date: 2/15/94

Customer	Total	Current	Past Due				Subsequent Collections (through 1/31/94)
			1–60 days	61–90 days	91–120 days	121 + days	
Audobon, Inc.	$100,000	$0	$30,000	$70,000			$40,000 &
Bando	0	0					0 &
Crail, Ltd.	260,000	60,000	200,000				60,000 &
Dorodiak, Inc.	210,000	0	100,000	30,000		80,000	100,000 &
Klarion Chief	40,000	20,000	20,000				20,000 &
Laubers	80,000	80,000					80,000 &
Mastalon, Inc.	30,000	0	30,000				0 &
12/31/93							
Total Accounts Receivable	$720,000	$160,000*	$380,000*	$100,000*	$0*	$80,000*	$300,000
Subsequent collections	300,000	160,000	130,000	10,000	0	0	
Uncollected at 1/31/94	$420,000	$0	$250,000	$90,000	$0	$80,000	
Estimated uncollectible (%)			10%	20%		100%	
Estimated uncollectible ($)	$123,000	$0	$25,000	$18,000	$0	$80,000	

& Traced to remittance advice
* Obtained from subsidiary ledger

EXHIBIT 12.5   Allowance for Doubtful Accounts

		Prepared by: ___LF
		Date: 2/5/94
		Reviewed by: CG
		Date: 2/15/94

Auditee, Inc.

WP C-1   <center>Accounts Receivable — Trade
Allowance for Doubtful Accounts
12/31/93</center>

1/1/93	Balance per ledger	$97,000&
1/1 – 12/31/93	Write-offs	(76,000)*
12/31/93	Balance per ledger	$21,000
	AJE 6	102,000 See WP C
12/31/93	Final balance	$123,000 –To WP C

AJE 6

Bad debts expense	$102,000	
Allowance for doubtful accounts		$102,000
To adjust allowance for doubtful accounts		
to amount considered reasonable in the		
circumstances.		

& Traced to WTB
* Examined documentation, and discussed with credit manager and legal counsel.

Discussed adequacy of allowance for doubtful accounts with credit manager, in light of aging analysis (see WP C). The above balance, as adjusted, appears to be adequate.

accounts, nontrade receivables, and related-party receivables are best detected through inquiry of management. Such inquiry is further corroborated by analysis of the accounts receivable subsidiary ledger as part of the confirmation process. The standard bank confirmation, as described later in the chapter, may disclose pledging or assignment of accounts receivable as collateral securing loans.

Substantive testing of trade accounts receivable provides evidence in support of operating revenue transactions. The auditor should also apply substantive procedures to miscellaneous revenues. The first step in auditing miscellaneous revenues is to apply analytical procedures. These consist of comparing balances in the accounts with the prior year, for both amount and source of revenue. Assuming no major abnormalities, substantive procedures may be limited to vouching credits on a test basis by examining underlying documentation.

If analytical procedures reveal major changes in amount or source, the auditor should consider confirming transactions. If revenues have declined significantly, transactions should be confirmed for nonexistence as well as for existence. Confirming for nonexistence requires identifying the historic sources of miscellaneous revenues and requesting the companies so identified to provide the auditors with the dollar volume of transactions with the client during the year.

Figure 12.4 summarizes the preceding discussion by presenting a model audit program for performing substantive tests of the sales and accounts receivable portion of the revenue cycle. If the auditor discovers increased or decreased audit risk as a result of analytical procedures, study of the business and industry, or the control structure study and evaluation, the program, as contained in Figure 12.4, would need to be modified.

FIGURE 12.4   Model Audit Program for Sales Transactions in Revenue Cycle

Analytical Procedures
1. Compare sales, cost of sales, and gross profit with the prior year, on a month-by-month basis, and account for major changes.
2. Compare sales patterns and gross profit rates with industry averages.
3. Calculate turnover of accounts receivable, and compare with prior year and industry average.
4. Compare sales returns and allowances and miscellaneous revenues with prior year and account for significant changes.
5. Compare sales, cost of sales, and gross profit with budgeted amounts and account for significant variances.

Other Substantive Audit Procedures
1. Perform sales cutoff procedures by examining documentary evidence for a few days before and after year end.
2. Vouch credits to miscellaneous revenue accounts on a test basis by examining underlying documentation.
3. Confirm accounts receivable balances on a test basis:
   Agree subsidiary ledger to control account in general ledger
   Consider stratifying population and confirming larger accounts and credit balances on a positive basis.
   Examine evidence of shipment and remittance advice for those customers not responding to second and third requests for positive confirmation.
4. Prepare an aging analysis of accounts receivable, and evaluate the adequacy of the allowance for doubtful accounts.
5. Examine directors' minutes, correspondence, contracts, and bank confirmation for evidence of:
   Pledging or assigning accounts receivable as collateral for loans
   Existence of related parties and related-party transactions

Cash Receipts Transactions and Cash Balances

Audit Objectives

The audit objectives related to cash receipts transactions and cash balances may be classified as follows:

1. **Existence and Completeness.** The auditor must be reasonably assured that all cash receipts and only cash receipts of the period under audit have been recorded and deposited prior to year end. The auditor must also be satisfied that all cash balances and only cash balances of the client are reflected on the ending balance sheet.

2. **Presentation and Disclosure.** The auditor should be alert to the possibility of bank overdrafts and insist upon reclassification as current liabilities if material in amount.

Restricted funds, such as sinking funds, should be classified as noncurrent assets, inasmuch as they are unavailable for payment of current obligations. When the obligation becomes current, the balances should be classified as current assets.

Loan agreements frequently require the borrower to maintain minimum levels in demand deposit accounts. Referred to as "compensating balance requirements," these restrictions, along with other restrictive covenants contained in the agreements, should be disclosed in footnotes to the financial statements.

Audit Evidence and Procedures

The **standard bank confirmation** form (see Exhibit 12.6) should be used for all bank accounts, both active and inactive.[6] The form is signed by the client, completed by the bank, and returned directly to the auditor. The bank confirmation provides evidence of the existence and valuation of the accounts. It also requests the bank to confirm outstanding loans to the company, as well as collateral securing the loans.

If the client has reconciled bank accounts as of year end, the auditor should examine such reconciliations for evidence of proper valuation and cutoff. If the client has not reconciled the accounts, the auditor should consider this a control weakness and complete the reconciliations as an extended audit procedure (see Exhibit 12.7).

The auditor should also obtain a **cutoff bank statement** directly from the bank. The client requests the bank to forward the statement to the auditor. A cutoff bank statement covering a two- or three-week period immediately following year end permits the auditor to examine evidence in support of the reconciling items appearing on the year-end bank reconciliation. Deposits in transit, outstanding checks, and other reconciling items are traced to the cutoff bank statement and to the canceled checks returned with the statement. All canceled checks dated prior to year end are traced to the list of outstanding checks appearing on the year-end

---

[6]Although inactive accounts may contain zero or nominal balances, the volume of transactions flowing through the accounts during the year may have been substantial. For this reason, auditors should guard against underauditing inactive bank accounts.

EXHIBIT 12.6   Standard Form to Confirm Account Balance Information
with Financial Institutions

AUDITEE, INC.
CUSTOMER NAME

We have provided to our accountants the following information as of the close of business on _December 31_, 19_93_, regarding our deposit and loan balances. Please confirm the accuracy of the information, noting any exceptions to the information provided. If the balances have been left blank, please complete this form by furnishing the balance in the appropriate space below.* Although we do not request nor expect you to conduct a comprehensive, detailed search of your records, if during the process of completing this confirmation additional information about other deposit and loan accounts we may have with you comes to your attention, please include such information below. Please use the enclosed envelope to return the form directly to our accountants.

Financial
Institution's
Name and
Address

FIRST NATIONAL BANK
201 MARCHAL STREET
MERIDIAN, MS

1. At the close of business on the date listed above, our records indicated the following deposit balance(s):

ACCOUNT NAME	ACCOUNT NO.	INTEREST RATE	BALANCE*
AUDITEE, INC.- GENERAL	_65-2318-431_	—	$ _450,000.00_
AUDITEE, INC. - PAYROLL	_81-6713-562_	—	_10,000.00_

2. We were directly liable to the financial institution for loans at the close of business on the date listed above as follows:

ACCOUNT NO./ DESCRIPTION	BALANCE*	DATE DUE	INTEREST RATE	DATE THROUGH WHICH INTEREST IS PAID	DESCRIPTION OF COLLATERAL
_1013864_	_$850,000_	_12/31/94_	_9½%_	_12/31/93_	_None_

John Helmil - Controller   _1/8/94_
(Customer's Authorized Signature)   (Date)

The information presented above by the customer is in agreement with our records. Although we have not conducted a comprehensive, detailed search of our records, no other deposit or loan accounts have come to our attention except as noted below.

George Kennedy   _1/15/94_
(Financial Institution Authorized Signature)   (Date)

Commercial Loan Officer
(Title)

EXCEPTIONS AND/OR COMMENTS

Please return this form directly to our accountants:

Double & Toil, CPAs
1023 Mercury Rd
Meridian, MS

*Ordinarily, balances are intentionally left blank if they are not available at the time the form is prepared.

Approved 1990 by American Bankers Association, American Institute of Certified Public Accountants, and Bank Administration Institute. Additional forms available from: AICPA—Order Department, P.O. Box 1003, NY, NY 10108-1003

EXHIBIT 12.7 Bank Reconciliation

```
                                                           Prepared by: lfk
                                                           Date: 1/23/94
       WP No. A-1                    Auditee, Inc.         Reviewed by: jrg
                                 Cash in Bank—General      Date: 2/5/94
                                      12/31/93

       12/31/93       Balance per bank                     $450,000 *
                      Add deposits in transit                50,000 &
                         Total                               500,000

                      Deduct:
                         Outstanding checks      30,000 &
                         Restricted balance      10,000 !
                                                             40,000

       12/31/93       Balance per reconciliation           $460,000

       12/31/93       Balance per general ledger           $420,000
                      AJE No. 1—bank collection of customer note   50,000 +
                      RJE No. A—restricted balance           (10,000)

       12/31/93       Balance per reconciliation           $460,000 To WPA


                      AJE 1

       Cash in bank—general                      50,000
          Notes receivable                                   50,000
       To record bank collection of customer note.

                      RJE A

       Cash in bank—restricted                   10,000
          Cash in bank—general                               10,000
       To reclassify restricted cash as a noncurrent asset.


       *  Traced to bank confirmation attached
       &  Traced to cutoff bank statement obtained directly from bank
       !  Examined loan agreement (see permanent file)
       +  Examined bank credit memo included with bank statement
```

bank reconciliation to determine that they were recorded in the proper accounting period. Payees, endorsements, and clearing dates appearing on canceled checks should all be carefully noted when examining the cutoff bank statement. Payees are compared with the cash disbursements record for agreement, and endorsements are compared with payees appearing on the face of the check. Lack of agreement may be indicative of efforts to conceal defalcations or other forms of irregularities. Late clearing dates appearing on canceled checks dated before year end may result from holding the cash disbursements record open after year end.

The auditor should also apply **cash receipts cutoff** tests to year-end cash transactions. Cash receipts on the last business day of the year should be examined by reference to cash receipts listings, remittance advices, and deposit tickets. The cash should also be traced to the bank statement, if deposited before year end. If the cash receipts were not deposited by year end, they should be traced to the bank reconciliation and to the cutoff bank statement. For deposits in transit, the auditor should determine that the bank credited the deposit within one or two working days after year end. Credits dated later than this may be indicative of faulty cutoff procedures and, possibly, inflated year-end cash balances.

If customer remittances have been misappropriated by one or more employees with access to customer accounts, a form of concealment known as *lapping* may have been applied. **Lapping** involves crediting current remittances to the accounts of customers who have remitted previously. The purpose is to keep all accounts current in order to avoid auditor suspicion and unusual customer exceptions to confirmation requests. For example, assume that Customer A remitted $2,000 on November 1, and the remittance was misappropriated by an accounts receivable clerk prior to recording. Assume further, that Customer B remitted $5,000 on December 30 and that the company closes its books on December 31. The dishonest clerk may elect to credit $2,000 of B's remittance to Customer A, and only $3,000 to Customer B's account in the subsidiary ledger. The effect is to lessen the probability of detection by transferring the fraudulent debit from a past due to a current customer's account. The auditor is less likely to be suspicious of a Customer A confirmation exception, given the current status of the account. Instead he/she could assume that the difference represents a remittance in transit.

In addition to confirming customer accounts and clearing all exceptions, an auditor who suspects lapping because of control weaknesses should consider tracing the details of year-end cash receipts to remittance advices and the accounts receivable subsidiary ledger. Any credits to accounts other than the customer remitting will thereby be detected. This procedure may also be applied to cash receipts for the first couple of days following year end. This set of procedures is another example of modifying the nature of substantive audit procedures under conditions of weak internal control.

If the client has more than one bank account, the auditor should complete an **analysis of interbank transfers** for one or two weeks before and after year end (see Exhibit 12.8). The purpose of this test is to detect errors or irregularities involving year-end checks in transit between banks.

Kiting, a type of misrepresentation fraud used to conceal bank overdrafts or cash misappropriations as well as to obtain interest-free loans, may be detected by analyzing interbank transfers. Kiting occurs when a company draws a check on one bank for deposit in another bank, but does not record the transaction, or records only a part of the transaction before year end. A journal entry is made to record the receipt, and the check is listed as a deposit in transit to conceal the overdraft. The disbursement side of the transaction is not recorded until after year end, and the check is not listed as outstanding in the reconciliation of the disbursing bank. In Exhibit 12.8, Check # 1668, drawn on Huron Bank—Duluth, for deposit in First Bank—Chicago, is apparently a form of ''kiting,'' inasmuch as the cash receipt was recorded in 1993.

EXHIBIT 12.8 Analysis of Interbank Transfers

WP A-3

Hublee Motors
12/31/93

				Prepared by:	lfk	
				Date:	2/3/94	
				Reviewed by:	jrg	
				Date:	2/10/94	

Check Number	Drawn on	Deposited in	Check Amount	Date of Check (1)	Date of Receipt (1)	Date Credited by Depository Bank	Date Debited by Payor Bank
1067	First Bank—Chicago	City Bank—Cleveland	$10,000	12/30/93	12/31/93	1/2/94*	1/5/94*
2079	1st Bank—Knoxville	Huron Bank—Duluth	22,354	12/31/93	1/3/94	1/4/94*	1/9/94*
3063	City Bank—Cleveland	1st Bank—Knoxville	30,000	12/30/93	1/2/94	1/3/94*	1/5/94*
1668	Huron Bank—Duluth	First Bank—Chicago	44,000	1/2/94	12/31/93	1/2/94*	1/4/94*

AJE 3

Cash in Bank—Duluth	$22,354	
Receivable from Knoxville Branch		$22,354

AJE 4

Cash in Bank—Knoxville	30,000	
Receivable from Cleveland Branch		30,000

AJE 5

Receivable from Duluth	44,000	
Cash in Bank—Chicago		44,000

Examined check registers and cash receipts records for the period December 15, 1993, to January 15, 1984. All interbank transfers, detected by the above examination, are listed above.

(1) Same as date recorded.

*Traced to cutoff bank statement. Compared payees and endorsements with check register.

A highly publicized check kiting case occurring in the mid-1980s involved the president and chief executive officers of Transit Mix Concrete Corporation and two large banks, Marine Midland and Citibank. The officers drew checks on the Transit Mix Concrete account at Citibank and deposited those checks in an account at Marine Midland for Water Tunnel Associates, a ''dummy'' company also operated by Mr. Halloran and Mr. Madden, the officers of Transit Mix Concrete. Of the $9.2 billion transferred between the two banks, the two officers were charged with stealing $23 million.[7]

In another case, the use of **float,** defined as the time lag for cash transfers between the disbursing bank and the payee bank, permitted the brokerage firm of E. F. Hutton to fraudulently obtain interest-free loans exceeding $8 million from some 400 banks between 1980 and 1982.[8]

In addition to analyzing interbank transfers, the auditor should also examine cash receipts and disbursements for a few days before and after the balance sheet date. This procedure assists in detecting other errors and irregularities. Repayment of officers' loans prior to year end, for example, followed by relending after year end will surface during the analysis. Checks in transit between divisions, the disbursement having been recorded but not the receipt, will also be detected.

By examining loan agreements and the bank confirmation, and through inquiry of client personnel, the auditor should be able to identify compensating balance requirements and other cash restrictions. Such restrictions require disclosure in footnotes to the financial statements.

Audit attention should also be directed toward cash receipts derived from sources other than customers. These include sales of plant assets, sale of securities or other investments, proceeds from loans obtained, collections of loans to others, proceeds from stock issuance, and so on. Cash receipts of this nature are identified in analyzing the related accounts and noting credit postings to plant assets, investment accounts, notes payable, capital stock, and notes receivable. Once identified, the cash receipts should be vouched by reference to the underlying documentation and traced to the cash receipts record and to the bank statement on a test basis.

In addition to bank accounts, other forms of cash such as petty cash funds, change funds, and various forms of undeposited cash on hand are included in ''Cash'' on the balance sheet. Although audit procedures may be applied to these items, they are usually limited, given the concepts of relative risk and materiality. Counting the funds on a test basis and comparing balances with prior years may be the extent of procedures applied.

Figure 12.5 contains a model audit program for substantive testing of cash receipts transactions and cash balances. The analytical procedures serve as input to further modification of the nature, timing and extent of the other substantive procedures.

---

[7]Marcia Chambers, ''Two Face Charges in a Bank Theft of $23 Million,'' *New York Times,* June 28, 1985, Section B, Page 3.

[8]Charles P. Alexander, ''Crime in the Suites,'' *Time,* June 10, 1985, page 56.

FIGURE 12.5   Model Audit Program for Cash Receipts Transactions and Cash Balances in the Revenue Cycle

Analytical Procedures
1. Compare cash accounts with prior years and investigate additions or deletions of accounts.
2. Compare cash receipts from miscellaneous sources with prior year and account for major changes.

Other Substantive Procedures
1. Count and list cash on hand at year end and trace to cash receipts record and bank statement.
2. Vouch significant cash receipts from sources other than customers and trace to deposit tickets and bank statements on a test basis.
3. Confirm bank balances directly with bank.
4. Compare balance on confirmation with year-end bank statement.
5. Reconcile bank accounts as of year end.
6. Obtain cutoff bank statement(s) directly from banks and trace reconciling items from bank reconcilation to cutoff statement.
7. Prepare analysis of interbank transfers for a few days before and after year end.
8. Examine loan agreements and directors' minutes for compensating balance requirements and consider reclassifying as noncurrent if significant.
9. Inquire as to status of inactive bank accounts.

AUDIT RISK ANALYSIS AND THE REVENUE CYCLE: SOME WARNING SIGNS

In the preceding discussion of audit procedures, unless otherwise noted, it was assumed that the auditor did not discover any unusual conditions which would indicate a higher than normal audit risk situation. The following paragraphs consider some "warning signs" that might cause the auditor to suspect that certain components of the revenue cycle have been intentionally misstated. Auditing procedures that the auditors might have applied, given the warning signs, are also identified.

Inflated Sales or Fictitious Accounts Receivable

If sales or accounts receivable are materially inflated, the application of analytical procedures should reveal abnormal sales patterns or reduced accounts receivable turnover or both. Moreover, if sales were inflated by holding the sales record open after year end, sales cutoff procedures should assist the auditor in detecting the misrepresentation.

In a case brought to light several years ago, a major toy manufacturer fabricated several invoices at year end in order to inflate sales and accounts receivable and thereby avoid reporting losses for the year.[9] Although other toy companies were reporting declining sales for the year, Company X enjoyed a sizable increase. January sales (the last month of the fiscal year, normally the lowest month for sales volume) reflected an especially heavy volume. The company reported $2.9 million (1.3 million pounds) of toys shipped on the last day of the fiscal year, Saturday, January 31! In this case, the auditors apparently did not pursue abnormalities that should have been brought to their attention by the application of analytical procedures. Moreover, the auditors did not adequately clear exceptions to confirmation requests returned by customers. Instead of investigating allegations of nonshipment, as evidenced by the returned confirmations, the auditors relied on management's assertions. Indeed, they accepted the fabricated sales orders, sales invoices, and bills of lading at face value, and ignored the confirmations. In essence, the auditors "went through the motions" but did not actually confirm accounts receivable.

The lesson for auditors in this case is that warning signs should be heeded, and audit resources allocated accordingly. The auditors should have performed a more thorough sales cutoff test. Also, given the presence of both external and internal evidence, accompanied by control weaknesses and/or abnormalities revealed by analytical procedures, auditors should formulate their audit conclusions on the basis of the stronger external evidence. In the present case, the auditors elected to accept management's assertions (internal evidence) and ignore the confirmation exceptions (external evidence).

Another case of year-end sales inflation assumed the form of substantial increases in selling prices above the company's list prices for all December sales, the last month of the fiscal year. Customers were told by the salespersons that pricing errors had occurred and to hold the invoices for payment until credit memos had been received in January. The auditors' suspicions were first aroused when the application of analytical procedures revealed above normal December sales. Suspicions were intensified upon the return of confirmation requests with numerous exceptions to prices appearing on December invoices. The auditors detected the fraud while performing sales cutoff tests. In examining transactions for a few days before and after year end, the auditors discovered the large number of credit memos representing price adjustments applicable to December invoices.

Inadequate Loan Loss Reserves

Commercial banks and savings and loan associations derive most of their revenue from interest on loans made to their customers. For many years relatively modest "loan loss reserves," established through debits to expense, proved adequate to absorb losses from uncollectible loans. As certain industries (agriculture and energy, for example) began to decline, however, and as the loan portfolios included increasing numbers of real estate loans and foreign loans, loan loss reserves, as traditionally maintained, were insufficient at many institutions. In several cases, the

---

[9]Alan P. Johnson, *Auditing Judgment: A Book of Cases*. Homewood, Ill.: Richard D. Irwin, 1980, pages 112–24.

losses were so great as to threaten the solvency of the bank. In some instances, such as Lincoln Savings, United American Bank of Knoxville, First Oklahoma Bancorp, and Penn Square Bank of Oklahoma City, the auditors were sued for failing to detect the problem loans.

The Lincoln Savings and Loan Association case, the most costly thrift failure ever with losses exceeding $2.5 billion, provides some important lessons for auditors. Charles Keating, a land developer, bought Lincoln in 1984 and quickly completed several real estate sales and financing transactions with related parties. The real estate was mostly Arizona desert land, but, given the existence of related parties, the inflated prices enabled Lincoln to record large "paper" gains on the sales. Moreover, the loans to finance the sales were significantly in excess of the appraised values of the properties. These transactions allowed Lincoln to record large profits and the Lincoln-backed loans provided a conduit for channeling funds from Lincoln to American Continental Corporation, Lincoln's parent company and a company also controlled by Keating. This in turn allowed cash flow to the Keating family.

The auditors in this case were accused of actually approving the related-party transactions.[10] At the very least, they did not devote adequate audit resources to examining related-party transactions. The rapid increase in the investment portfolio, the rising proportion of real estate transactions, accompanied by loan guarantees by Lincoln, and the high incidence and amount of cash transfers from Lincoln to American Continental should have alerted the auditors to the heightened risk of irregularities.

As a result of these and similar cases, auditors who examine the financial statements of commercial banks and savings and loan associations are devoting increasing attention to the loan portfolio and to evaluating the adequacy of loan loss reserves.

Such warning signs as past due interest, uncollected installments, insider loans, heavy concentrations of loans to borrowers in depressed industries, inadequate collateral, and foreign loans require careful evaluation of loan collectibility, loan collateral, and the adequacy of loan loss reserves.

In the United American Bank of Knoxville case, the major problem consisted of insider loans to the bank chairman, his family, and business associates. The financial statements for the year ended December 31, 1982 included loan loss reserves of $9.3 million and were accompanied by an unqualified opinion from the auditors. At the same time, approximately $377 million of loans were classified by the FDIC as partly or totally uncollectible.[11] Like the Lincoln Savings case, the lesson to be learned here is that auditors must be alert to the increased probability of misrepresentation fraud when significant related-party transactions and balances are present. SAS 45 provides guidance for auditors in identifying related parties, determining the existence of related-party transactions, and auditing related-party transactions and balances.[12]

---

[10]Paulette Thomas, "Auditors Say Lincoln S&L 'Sham' Deals Were Approved by Arthur Young & Co.," *Wall Street Journal,* November 15, 1989, Section A, page 2.

[11]Geoffrey Colvin, *et al.,* "Jake Butcher's Fall," *Fortune,* March 21, 1983, page 7.

[12]*AICPA Professional Standards, op.cit.,* Section AU 334.

Early Revenue Recognition

Auditors should be alert to the possibility of **early revenue recognition** when clients recognize revenue before the point of sale. Percentage of completion accounting for construction contracts and the proportional method for recognizing revenue from service contracts are acceptable alternatives to recognizing revenue at the point of sale. Certain conditions must be met, however, in order for these methods to be appropriate under the circumstances. First, the earning process must be substantially complete; second, realization must be reasonably assured; and third, the revenue and related costs must be capable of reasonable measurement. Several cases have surfaced over the years in which companies have recognized revenue without having met all of these conditions.

In the case of Frigitemp Corporation, a company engaged in manufacturing custom made refrigeration equipment for ships and hospitals, decorating hotels and casinos, and building food service systems, a method for revenue recognition referred to as "cost to cost percentage of completion" was used. Under this method, revenue was recognized in proportion to the amount of money spent on raw materials. As a result, the company purchased excessive amounts of materials in order to maximize reported profits. In one instance, a supplier gave Frigitemp an invoice for $4.2 million in deck planking, most of which was still growing in forests on the West Coast.[13]

Another case of premature revenue recognition involved National Student Marketing Corporation (NSMC), a company whose stock price had risen from $6 to $80 per share in five months. The company sold marketing programs to companies for promotions on college campuses. Management alleged that its major revenue producing activity was preparation of layout, and that firm contracts for the programs had been obtained. Revenue was therefore recognized on completion of the layout. Many of the contracts, it was later discovered, had been fabricated, and others represented unbilled receivables for commitments instead of firm contracts. As a result, profits were materially overstated in 1968.[14]

Careful examination of the contracts and commitments should have alerted the auditors to the inappropriateness of the company's method for recognizing revenue. The mailing of confirmation requests to customers, moreover, should have prompted the auditors to further investigation and subsequent detection of the fictitious nature of the more significant contracts that had been booked by NSMC.

In addition to early revenue recognition, other warning signs were present in this case that should have alerted the auditors to possible misrepresentation fraud. The rapid increase in the company's stock price, for example, and the continued efforts by NSMC management to acquire other companies in stock for stock poolings should also have aroused the auditor's suspicions.

A recent case of early revenue recognition involved Orion Pictures Corp., producer of such films as *Dances with Wolves* and *Silence of the Lambs*. Between

---

[13]John J. Fialka, "Why Arthur Andersen Fails to Detect Accounting Fraud at Frigitemp," *Wall Street Journal,* September 21, 1984, Section A, page 1.

[14]*United States v. Natelli,* F.2d (2d Cir. 1975).

1983 and 1990, Orion reported profits every year. During the same period, however, the balance in its "deferred television and movie costs," an asset, was also increasing. The rate of increase was so significant that by 1990 the balance in the account, $766 million, exceeded its 1990 revenues, $584 million. For other filmmakers, reported revenues significantly exceeded the balance in deferred assets. Paramount Pictures and Disney, for example, reported revenues during the same period that were approximately four times the balance in their respective deferred asset accounts.

Further analysis determined that Orion was not writing off failed films, thus accounting for the continued increase in the asset carrying value. Perhaps the most flagrant abuse of revenue accounting occurred in 1990 when Orion received $175 million from Columbia Pictures as an advance against future distribution abroad of Orion films, most of which had not yet been made. Although clearly unearned, Orion recorded $50 million of the advance as revenue. This allowed the company to report a $20 million pretax profit for 1990 rather than a $30 million loss.

Although accounting for revenue from the sale of television shows and movies is complex and not so structured as for other types of revenue, this was clearly a case that should have alerted the auditors to possible earnings inflation. Moreover, the auditors' suspicions should have been aroused by the application of analytical procedures. The steady increase in the deferred asset balance, the excess of the balance over 1990 revenue, and the opposite pattern for other filmmakers in the industry should have led the auditors to devote increased attention to Orion's revenue recognition policies and to carefully analyze the deferred asset account.

The warning signs just cited are examples of conditions that auditors are most likely to identify while studying the business and industry and applying analytical procedures. The audit implications of such findings make it imperative that all members of the audit team be made aware of identified high risk situations and that audit programs be modified accordingly. This is the essence of audit risk analysis and audit program modification, as presented in Chapter 5.

Proof of Cash

The auditor who determines that internal control over cash transactions is weak may elect to prepare a proof of cash for one or more months of the year under audit. This is a time-consuming and costly audit procedure and, for this reason, should be completed only under conditions of weak internal control over cash. The **proof of cash** (see Exhibit 12.9) performs the same function as the bank reconciliation and, in addition, reconciles the client's recorded receipts and disbursements with bank statement credits and debits. If cash receipts have been misappropriated or erroneously recorded, therefore, the receipts per books will not reconcile with the receipts per the bank statement. Similarly, if cash disbursements have been misrecorded, the disbursements per books will not reconcile with bank statement debits. In summary, this extended audit procedure should help to detect errors and irregularities involving cash receipts or disbursements under conditions of weak internal control. It will also aid in detecting omitted entries.

EXHIBIT 12.9   Proof of Cash

	Biochem, Inc.		Prepared by: LFK
	12/31/93		Date: 2/17/94
WP Ref. A-3			Reviewed by: CCK
			Date: 2/22/94

	6/30/93 Bank Reconciliation	Receipts	Disburse-ments	12/31/93 Bank Reconciliation
Balance per bank statement	$167,183.23	$1,234,652.16	$1,312,589.80	$89,245.59 C
Deposits in transit				
Beginning	66,839.60	(66,839.60)		
Ending		123,678.90		123,678.90
Outstanding checks				
Beginning	(125,456.98)		(125,456.98)⊗	
Ending			77,982.12⊗	(77,982.12)
Bank collection of note receivable plus interest		(22,314.50)E		(22,314.50)
Balance per books	$108,565.85	$1,269,176.96	$1,265,114.94	$112,627.87
	GL	√	~	GL
	F	F	F	F
				CF

C Traced to bank confirmation
√ Traced to cash receipts record
~ Traced to cash disbursement record
E Examined bank credit memo
F Footed
CF Crossfooted
⊗ See lists of outstanding checks attached
GL Traced to general ledger

KEY TERMS

Accounts receivable aging analysis
Analysis of interbank transfers
Balanced audit approach
Cash receipts cutoff
Confirmation of accounts receivable
Cutoff bank statement
Early revenue recognition
Float
Kiting

Lapping
Negative confirmation
Positive confirmation
Proof of cash
Revenue cycle
Sales cutoff
Standard bank confirmation
Substantive audit testing

COMPUTER AUDIT PRACTICE CASE

Trim Lawn Manufacturing Company
The Trim Lawn audit practice case contains several exercises pertaining to the revenue cycle. They are as follows and may be completed at this time:

- Module V: Union Trust bank reconciliation
- Module VI: Analysis of interbank transfers
- Module VII: Accounts receivable aging analysis and evaluation of allowance for doubtful accounts.

REVIEW QUESTIONS

1. Define *substantive testing*.
2. What factors influence the amount of substantive testing to be applied during the interim audit?
3. Define *balanced auditing* and discuss its importance.
4. How do analytical procedures assist in the evaluation and review stages of the audit?
5. How does the auditor gain assurance as to proper sales cutoff?
6. Why is consistency of cutoff important?
7. Differentiate between positive and negative forms of confirmation.
8. Distinguish between confirmation replies requiring audit adjustment and those not requiring audit adjustment.
9. What alternate procedures might the auditor apply if replies to confirmation requests are not received?
10. Of what significance to the auditor is the accounts receivable aging analysis?
11. How are miscellaneous revenues audited?
12. What is the purpose of requesting a bank confirmation?
13. Why does the auditor request a cutoff bank statement in addition to reconciling the bank account?
14. Discuss the purpose for auditing interbank transfers.
15. What kinds of documentary evidence are examined in auditing sales transactions?
16. What kinds of mathematical evidence are obtained in auditing cash receipts transactions?
17. Auditors usually analyze subsequent collections from customers as part of the audit program for accounts receivable. What audit objective(s) is served by this procedure?
18. What determines the number of positive or negative confirmation requests to be mailed to customers in a particular engagement?
19. Define *early revenue recognition*. Why is the risk of early revenue recognition greater in some industries than in others?
20. Identify the principal classification and disclosure issues pertaining to the revenue cycle.

MULTIPLE CHOICE QUESTIONS FROM CPA AND CIA EXAMINATIONS

1. Which of the following procedures is least likely to be performed before the balance sheet date?
   a. Observation of inventory.
   b. Review of internal control over cash disbursements.
   c. Search for unrecorded liabilities.
   d. Confirmation of receivables.

2. As a result of analytical review procedures, the independent auditor determines that the gross profit percentage has declined from 30 percent in the preceding year to 20 percent in the current year. The auditor should
   a. Document management's intentions with respect to plans for reversing this trend.
   b. Evaluate management's performance in causing this decline.
   c. Require footnote disclosure.
   d. Consider the possibility of an error in the financial statements.

3. The auditor will most likely perform extensive tests for possible understatement of
   a. Revenues.
   b. Assets.
   c. Liabilities.
   d. Capital.

4. In the context of an audit of financial statements, substantive tests are audit procedures that
   a. May be eliminated under certain conditions.
   b. Are designed to discover significant subsequent events.
   c. May be either tests of transactions, direct tests of financial balances, or analytical tests.
   d. Will increase proportionately with increases in assessed control risk.

5. An unrecorded check issued during the last week of the year would most likely be discovered by the auditor when the
   a. Check register for the last month is reviewed.
   b. Cutoff bank statement is reconciled.
   c. Bank confirmation is reviewed.
   d. Search for unrecorded liabilities is performed.

6. The auditor should ordinarily mail confirmation requests to all banks with which the client has conducted any business during the year, regardless of the year-end balance, since
   a. The confirmation form also seeks information about indebtedness to the bank.
   b. This procedure will detect kiting activities that would otherwise not be detected.
   c. The mailing of confirmation forms to all such banks is required by generally accepted auditing standards.
   d. This procedure relieves the auditor of any responsibility with respect to nondetection of forged checks.

7. An auditor should perform alternative procedures to substantiate the existence of accounts receivable when
   a. No reply to a positive confirmation request is received.

   b. No reply to a negative confirmation request is received.
   c. Collectibility of the receivables is in doubt.
   d. Pledging of the receivables is probable.

8. Which of the following is not a primary objective of the auditor in the examination of accounts receivable?
   a. Determine the approximate realizable value.
   b. Determine the adequacy of control structure policies and procedures.
   c. Establish validity of the receivables.
   d. Determine the approximate time of collectibility of the receivables.

9. To establish illegal "slush funds," corporations may divert cash received in normal business operations. An auditor would encounter the greatest difficulty in detecting the diversion of proceeds from
   a. Scrap sales.
   b. Dividends.
   c. Purchase returns.
   d. C.O.D. sales.

10. The negative form of accounts receivable confirmation request is particularly useful except when
   a. Control structure policies and procedures surrounding accounts receivable is considered to be effective.
   b. A large number of small balances are involved.
   c. The auditor has reason to believe the persons receiving the requests are likely to give them consideration.
   d. Individual account balances are relatively large.

Questions 11 and 12 are based on the following:

Miles Company
Bank Transfer Schedule
December 31, 1988

Check	Bank Accounts		Date disbursed per			Date deposited per	
Number	From	To	Amount	Books	Bank	Books	Bank
2020	1st Natl.	Suburban	$32,000	12/31	1/5*	12/31	1/3&
2021	1st Natl.	Capital	21,000	12/31	1/4*	12/31	1/3&
3217	2nd State	Suburban	6,700	1/3	1/5	1/3	1/6
0659	Midtown	Suburban	5,500	12/30	1/5*	12/30	1/3&

11. The audit legend "*" most likely indicates that the amount was traced to the
   a. December cash disbursements journal.
   b. Outstanding check list of the applicable bank reconciliation.
   c. January cash disbursements journal.
   d. Year-end bank confirmations.

12. The audit legend "&" most likely indicates that the amount was traced to the
   a. Deposits in transit of the applicable bank reconciliation.
   b. December cash receipts journal.
   c. January cash receipts journal.
   d. Year-end bank confirmations.

13. Cooper, CPA, is auditing the financial statements of a small rural municipality. The receivable balances represent residents' delinquent real estate taxes. The internal control structure at the municipality is weak. To determine the existence of the accounts receivable balances at the balance sheet date, Cooper would most likely
   a. Send positive confirmation requests.
   b. Send negative confirmation requests.
   c. Examine evidence of subsequent cash receipts.
   d. Inspect the internal records such as copies of the tax invoices that were mailed to the residents.

ESSAY QUESTIONS AND PROBLEMS

12.1 Exhibit 12.10, a client-prepared bank reconciliation, is being examined by Stan Kautz, a CPA, during an examination of the financial statements of Cynthia Company.

Required:
Indicate one or more audit procedures that should be performed by Kautz in gathering evidence in support of each of the items (a) through (f) as identified in the reconciliation. (AICPA adapted)

12.2 Eleanor Finney, a CPA, was engaged to conduct an audit of the financial statements of Clayton Realty Corporation for the month ending January 31, 1993. The examination of monthly rent reconciliations is a vital portion of the audit engagement.

Exhibit 12.11, a rent reconciliation, was prepared by the controller of Clayton Realty Corporation and was presented to Finney, who subjected it to various audit procedures.

Schedules A, B, and C are available to Finney but have not been illustrated Finney has conducted a study of control structure policies and procedures and found them adequate to produce reliable accounting information. Cash receipts from rental operations are deposited in a special bank account.

Required:
What substantive audit procedures should Finney employ during the audit in order to substantiate the validity of each of the dollar amounts marked by an asterisk (*)? (AICPA adapted)

12.3 The CPA firm of Wright & Co. is in the process of examining William Corporation's 1993 financial statements. The following open matter must be resolved before the audit can be completed.

No audit work has been performed on nonresponses to customer accounts receivable confirmation requests. Both positive and negative confirmations were used. A second request was sent to debtors who did not respond to the initial positive request.

Required:
What alternative audit procedures should Wright consider performing on the nonresponses to customer accounts receivable confirmation requests? (AICPA adapted)

EXHIBIT 12.10   Problem 12.1 Client-Prepared Bank Reconciliation

Cynthia Company
Bank Reconciliation—Village Bank Account 2
December 31, 1994

Balance per bank (a)		$18,375.91
Deposits in transit (b)		
12/30	1,471.10	
12/31	2,840.69	4,311.79
Subtotal		22,687.70
Outstanding checks (c)		
837	6,000.00	
1941	671.80	
1966	320.00	
1984	1,855.42	
1985	3,621.22	
1987	2,576.89	
1991	4,420.88	(19,466.21)
Subtotal		3,221.49
NSF check returned 12/29 (d)		200.00
Error Check No. 1932		5.50
Customer note collected by the bank ($2,750 plus		
$275 interest) (e)		(3,025.00)
Balance per books (f)		$ 401.99

EXHIBIT 12.11   Problem 12.2 Rent Reconciliation

Clayton Realty Corporation
Rent Reconciliation
For the Month Ended January 31, 1993

Gross apartment rents (Schedule A)	$1,600,800*
Less vacancies (Schedule B)	20,500*
Net apartment rentals	1,580,300
Less unpaid January rents (Schedule C)	7,800*
Total	1,572,500
Add prepaid rent collected (Apartment 116)	500
Total cash collected	$1,573,000*

12.4 During the year, Strang Corporation began to encounter cash flow difficulties, and a cursory review by management revealed receivable collection problems. Strang's management engaged George Stanley, CPA, to perform a special investigation. Stanley studied the billing and collection cycle and noted the following.

The accounting department employs one bookkeeper who receives and opens all incoming mail. This bookkeeper is also responsible for depositing receipts, filing remittance advices on a daily basis, recording receipts in the cash receipts journal, and for posting receipts in the individual customer accounts and the general ledger accounts. There are no cash sales. The bookkeeper prepares and controls the mailing of monthly statements to customers.

The concentration of functions and the receivable collection problems caused Stanley to suspect a systematic defalcation of customers' payments through a delayed posting of remittances (lapping of accounts receivable). Stanley was surprised to find that no customers complained about receiving erroneous monthly statements.

Required:

Identify the procedures which Stanley should perform to determine whether lapping exists. Do not discuss control structure weaknesses. (AICPA adapted)

12.5 Carijay, Inc., maintains bank accounts at the following branch locations: Minneapolis—First Minnesota Bank & Trust; Milwaukee—Second Milwaukee Bank; Chicago—Intercontinental Bank; Detroit—Motor City Bank & Trust. Interbank transfers occur among the banks in settlement of interbranch transactions. For example, goods might be shipped from Minneapolis to Detroit. Detroit pays for the goods by drawing a check on the Motor City account and the Minneapolis branch deposits the check in the First Minnesota account. Several of these and similar transactions among the branches occur during the year. In analyzing interbank transfers at the end of 1993 and the beginning of 1994, Nancy Lau, CPA, identified these checks:

Ck. No.	Date of Check	Drawn On	Deposited in	Amount
1066	12/30/93	First Minnesota	Second Milwaukee	$10,000
2033	12/31/93	Intercontinental	Motor City Bank	$35,466
3099	1/2/94	Motor City Bank	Second Milwaukee	$55,000
1067	1/3/94	First Minnesota	Intercontinental	$12,000

Checks generally require two days before being received by the payee. All checks are deposited on the date received. In examining cash receipts records, Nancy learned that check #1066 was recorded and deposited in the payee account on 1/2/94; check #2033 on 1/2/94; check #3099 was recorded by the payee (the Milwaukee branch) and deposited on 12/31/93, but not credited by the bank until 1/2/94; and check #1067 was recorded by the recipient on 1/4/94, but was credited on the bank statement as of 12/31/93.

Required:

a. Which of the checks are indicative of kiting?

b. What is the probable reason for the kiting in each instance?

c. Draft any audit adjustments necessitated by this analysis.

12.6 A customary procedure in examining cash balances is to request the client's bank(s) to send a cutoff statement directly to the auditor. The cutoff bank statement generally covers a portion of the month following the balance sheet date.

Required:
a. What is the purpose of obtaining a cutoff bank statement?
b. In tracing reconciling items to the cutoff bank statement, the auditor notes payees, endorsements, and clearing dates for checks and notes date of credit for deposits. What, specifically, is the auditor looking for in applying these procedures?
c. In tracing reconciling items to the cutoff statement, the auditor lists the following exceptions:
  1. 12/31/93 deposit in transit cleared bank on 1/9/94.
  2. Outstanding check payable to K. Burkee, Inc., in the amount of $10,000 was endorsed by Jules Lavern, client controller.
  3. Checks 1099, 1100, 1101, and 1102, recorded as of 12/31/93, did not clear the bank until 1/22/94, 1/23/94, 1/24/94, and 1/25/94 respectively.
  Discuss the possible errors or irregularities associated with each of the above items. Are any audit adjustments necessary? Explain why.

12.7 You have been engaged to audit the books of Internal Harvester, Inc., a manufacturer of farm machinery and lawn maintenance equipment. Although the industry has been suffering losses during the past few years, Internal shows unaudited income of $1.236 million for the current year. In applying analytical procedures, you discover that Internal's sales have increased by 30 percent over the preceding year, and the gross profit margin has risen from 25 percent to 33 percent.

In confirming accounts receivable, you have encountered difficulty in obtaining replies to positive requests and the replies you have received are similar to the following response.

> According to our records, we owed Internal Harvester $34,544 as of 12/31.93. We cannot seem to account for the following invoices, and request copies be sent to us for comparison with our documentation:

Invoice No.	Date	Amount
4566	12/30/93	$12,000
4567	12/31/93	14,500
4568	12/31/93	52,800

The receivable from the customer, according to Internal's records, was $122,890. Of 100 positive confirmations mailed, the following results were obtained:

Type of Response	Number	Amount
No exception	3	$ 96,000
Exception indicated	12	420,000
No reply	85	3,678,000

The 100 accounts selected for confirmation constituted 70 percent of the dollar amount of accounts receivable as of 12/31/93.

While performing sales cutoff tests, you noted that $4 million of machinery was shipped out on 12/31/93, a Saturday. Included in the shipments were 25 combines and 33 corn pickers. Much of the supporting documentation for these shipments lacks the required initials of the carrier.

Required:

a. As an auditor exercising healthy skepticism, what do you think may have accounted for Internal Harvester's robust earnings for 1993?
b. What additional evidence is needed with regard to sales and accounts receivable?
c. Identify the substantive audit procedures you would apply in completing the examination of sales and receivables.

12.8 The purpose for applying analytical procedures is to identify abnormal patterns or relationships calling for further investigation. Describe how the balanced audit approach, together with analytical procedures, promotes audit effectiveness.

12.9 As part of the audit of accounts receivable, Jerome Jay, a CPA and in-charge auditor for the Hills High engagement, requested the client to prepare an aging analysis of the receivables as of 12/31/93, Hills High's year end. The following data are taken from that analysis:

Status	Amount	Estimated Uncollectible
Current	$2,400,000	1%
1–30 days past due	1,300,000	3%
31–60 days past due	877,000	6%
61–90 days past due	560,000	10%
Over 90 days past due	1,100,000	15%

The percentages appearing in the last column have been used in the past in estimating uncollectibility of customers' accounts. The current balance in the allowance for uncollectible accounts is $80,000. The credit manager informs you that this amount is adequate in light of successful collection efforts relating to the 61–90 and the over 90 days past due accounts.

Required:

a. Why is it necessary for the auditor to address the question of adequacy of the allowance for uncollectible accounts?
b. Discuss the procedures you would apply to ascertain the adequacy of the allowance in the present instance.
c. If you discover that the allowance is inadequate, how will you convince the Hills High controller and credit manager of the need for adjustment?

12.10 In applying substantive tests to transaction cycles, auditors emphasize the importance of determining proper cutoff. Sales cutoff, purchases cutoff, cash receipts cutoff, and cash disbursements cutoff must all be tested by the auditor.

Required:

a. What is the significance of proper cutoff?
b. Design an audit program for determining the reasonableness of sales cutoff for a wholesale distributor of appliances.

    c. Under what circumstances would you extend sales cutoff procedures? Under what conditions would you restrict them?

    d. Why is consistency of cutoff important?

12.11 Regina Co., a maker of vacuum cleaners, experienced rapidly increasing profits after going public in 1985. The value of its stock tripled during this period as investors clamored to "get on the Regina bandwagon." Then, in September, 1988, KPMG Peat Marwick, Regina's auditors, withdrew its unqualified opinion on the company's financial statements for the year ended June 30, 1988. Shortly thereafter, Regina's chief executive officer quit. The new management alleged that the prior financial statements were incorrect and probably fraudulent. Stockholders, who were forced to sell their shares at substantial losses, sued the auditors.

    In conducting a new audit of Regina, Peat Marwick discovered that instead of a $10.9 million profit, as previously reported for the fiscal year, the company had actually incurred a $16.8 million loss for the 15 months ended September 30, 1988. The fraud resulted mainly from failure to record massive returns of faulty vacuum cleaners. The returned cleaners were included in ending inventory at full cost; but the company's computers were reprogrammed so as not to record the debits to sales returns and allowances. In addition, sales invoices representing purported year-end sales, along with shipping orders and bills of lading, were fabricated; research and development costs were capitalized; and depreciation charges were understated.

Required:

    a. Discuss the auditors' responsibility for detecting this type of misrepresentation fraud.

    b. What procedures, if any, should have alerted the auditors to possible irregularities?

    c. How should the auditors have followed up on the warning signals surfacing in (b)? Be specific.

12.12 Edwards, CPA, is engaged to audit the financial statements of Matthews Wholesaling for the year ended December 31, 1994. Edwards obtained and documented an understanding of the internal control structure encompassing accounts receivable and assessed control risk relating to accounts receivable at the maximum level. Edwards requested and obtained from Matthews an aged accounts receivable schedule listing the total amount owed by each customer as of December 31, 1994, and sent positive confirmation requests to a sample of the customers.

Required:

What additional substantive audit procedures should Edwards consider applying in auditing the accounts receivable? (AICPA adapted)

12.13 A company owns several shopping centers. The standard lease with all tenants requires that they pay a fixed rent plus a percentage of net sales. It also provides that the tenant get an audit opinion on the tenant's reported sales figure or allow the lessor company's internal auditor to audit the sales figure and charge them for the audit.

    A tenant restaurant owner decided to have the lessor company's internal auditor perform this service. You, as the internal auditor, have been asked by the head of the internal auditing department to verify the sales figures presented by the restaurant.

You have determined that there are 10 waiters or waitresses employed. Only food and soft drinks are served to patrons. No carry-out orders are filled. All orders are filled by the use of handwritten, prenumbered restaurant checks. All restaurant checks and cash register tapes are retained. A record of daily sales and the general ledger are maintained by the owner.

Required:
Develop four specific objectives for the audit of the tenant restaurant and at least two audit program steps for each objective. (IIA adapted)

APPENDIX

Auditing Objectives and Procedures: Revenue Cycle

SALES TRANSACTIONS AND ACCOUNTS RECEIVABLE BALANCES

Audit Objectives	Audit Evidence and Procedures
Existence, Completeness, and Valuation	*Analytical Evidence*

Are customers valid?

Are accounts receivable reported at net realizable value?

Are sales reported in the proper accounting period?

Have sales been omitted?

Analytical Evidence

- Compare sales, cost of sales, and gross profit with prior year, on a month-by-month basis, and account for major changes.
- Compare sales, cost of sales, and gross profit with budgeted amounts and investigate significant variances.
- Compare sales patterns and gross profit rates with industry averages.
- Calculate turnover of accounts receivable, and compare with prior year and industry average.
- Compare sales returns and allowances as a percentage of sales, with prior year, and account for material changes.
- Compare miscellaneous and other nonoperating revenue accounts with prior year for both source and amount, and investigate significant changes.

Documentary Evidence

- Review accounts receivable subsidiary ledger for large balances, unusual balances, credit balances, and related-party balances.
- Perform sales cutoff procedures by examining documentary evidence (e.g., shipping orders, invoices, and bills of lading) for a few days before and after year end.
- Vouch credits to miscellaneous revenue accounts on a test basis by examining underlying documentation.

Confirmation Evidence

- Confirm accounts receivable on a test basis. Use positive confirmation requests except for smaller balances where inherent risk and control risk are assessed at low levels.
- Consider stratifying population and confirming a higher percentage of larger accounts.
- Examine evidence of shipment and remittance advice for those customers not responding to second and third requests for positive confirmation.
- Confirm year-end credit balances and accounts written off during the year.
- Consider confirming miscellaneous revenue transactions, if material, or if analytical procedures indicate major changes.

Mathematical Evidence

- Agree accounts receivable subsidiary ledger to controlling account.
- Prepare an aging analysis of accounts receivable, and evaluate the adequacy of the allowance for doubtful accounts.

Presentation and Disclosure

Any credit balances?

Any receivables from related parties?

Any pledging of receivables as collateral?

Any significant non-current or nontrade receivables?

Documentary Evidence

- Examine directors' minutes, correspondence, and contracts for evidence regarding pledging or assignment of accounts receivable.
- Scan subsidiary ledger for credit balances.
- Examine SEC ''conflict of interest statements'' for possible existence of related party receivables.

Confirmation Evidence

- Examine bank confirmation for evidence of pledging or assigning receivables as collateral for loans.

Hearsay Evidence

- Inquire of management as to related-party transactions and nontrade receivables included in accounts receivable.
- Inquire of credit manager as to extended credit terms that may require noncurrent classification of certain receivables.

CASH RECEIPTS TRANSACTIONS AND CASH BALANCES

| Audit Objectives | Audit Evidence and Procedures |

Audit Objectives

Existence, Completeness, and Valuation

Do all cash accounts exist?

Have all cash transactions been properly recorded?

Have all cash receipts been deposited?

Audit Evidence and Procedures

Analytical Evidence

• Compare cash receipts from miscellaneous sources with prior year and account for major changes.

Physical Evidence

• If present for inventory observation at year end, count and list cash on hand.

Documentary Evidence

• Trace count of year-end cash on hand to cash receipts record and to bank statement.
• Determine that above cash count agrees with final entry in cash receipts record for the year.
• Vouch significant cash receipts from sources other than customers, such as sales of plant assets or investments, and loan proceeds. Trace to remittance advices, deposit tickets, and bank statements on a test basis.

Mathematical Evidence

• Reconcile bank accounts as of year end.
• Prepare proof of cash if internal control over cash is weak.
• Prepare analysis of interbank transfers to detect kiting and errors resulting in unrecorded cash.

Confirmation Evidence

• Confirm bank balances directly with banks.
• Compare balance on confirmation with year-end bank statement.
• Obtain cutoff bank statements directly from banks.
• Trace reconciling items on year-end reconciliations to cutoff bank statements, noting especially:
  • Agreement of payees appearing on returned checks with cash disbursements record.
  • Agreement of payees on face of returned checks with endorsements on back of checks.
  • Outstanding checks at year end cleared bank within reasonable period.
  • Deposits in transit at year end were credited by bank within reasonable period.

Presentation and Disclosure

Any bank overdrafts?

Any restricted cash balances?

Documentary Evidence

- Examine loan agreements and directors' minutes for compensating balance requirements, and consider reclassifying as noncurrent if significant.

Confirmation Evidence

- Examine bank confirmation for other information provided by bank, such as outstanding indebtedness.
- Consider mailing confirmation requests to banks for guarantees of indebtedness, pledging, and/or loan commitments.

Hearsay Evidence

- Inquire as to status of inactive bank accounts.

13 Substantive Audit Testing: Expenditure Cycle

CHAPTER OUTLINE

I. **Purchases, production, and inventories**
   A. Summary of processing steps
   B. Audit objectives
   C. Audit evidence and procedures
   D. Summary audit program

II. **Plant assets**
   A. Audit objectives
   B. Audit evidence and procedures
   C. Summary audit program

III. **Intangible assets**
   A. Audit objectives
   B. Audit evidence and procedures
   C. Summary audit program

IV. **Current liabilities**
   A. Audit objectives
   B. Audit evidence and procedures
   C. Summary audit program

V. **Audit risk analysis and the expenditure cycle**
   A. Idle capacity
   B. Abnormal inventory increases
   C. High technology industry
   D. Significant increase in plant asset additions
   E. Existence of related parties

VI. **Appendix: Auditing objectives and procedures: Expenditure cycle**

OVERVIEW

This chapter discusses substantive testing of the expenditure cycle. Figure 13.1 displays this part of the audit within the overall audit process. The expenditure cycle substantive audit is addressed in four parts:

1. Purchases, production, and inventories;
2. Plant assets;
3. Intangible assets; and
4. Current liabilities and operating expenses.

As in Chapter 12, the processing steps in the expenditure cycle are enumerated and a summary flowchart is presented. Audit objectives are then identified for each part of the transaction cycle. This is followed by considering audit evidence and procedures available for meeting the objectives.

Consistent with the balanced audit approach described in Chapter 12, in testing inventories, plant assets, and intangible assets, auditors will emphasize testing for overstatement, unless they have cause to suspect understatement. In testing liabilities, emphasis will be placed on testing for understatement, unless the auditor has cause to suspect overstatement. Accordingly, auditors test inventories extensively for existence, proper valuation, and cutoff.

Plant assets and intangible assets are examined, along with the repairs expense accounts and research and development expense. Such simultaneous examination helps to identify errors in classifying expenditures as to asset additions or expenses.

In testing current liabilities for understatement, the auditor concentrates on completeness (i.e., locating errors of omission). A set of procedures referred to as the "search for unrecorded liabilities" is applied to meet this objective.

The chapter concludes with a consideration of audit risk associated with the expenditure cycle. As in Chapter 12, warning signs are identified and their impact on various parts of the cycle is discussed.

An appendix, relating audit objectives to types of evidence and procedures, is presented at the end of the chapter.

STUDY OBJECTIVES

After reading this chapter, you should be able to:

1. Identify specific audit objectives related to the expenditure cycle
2. Develop audit programs for the expenditure cycle which relate audit procedures to audit objectives for each component of the cycle
3. Modify audit programs, as necessary, in light of warning signs that surface during a study of the business and industry, analytical procedures, or the study and evaluation of control structure policies and procedures.

FIGURE 13.1   The Audit Process

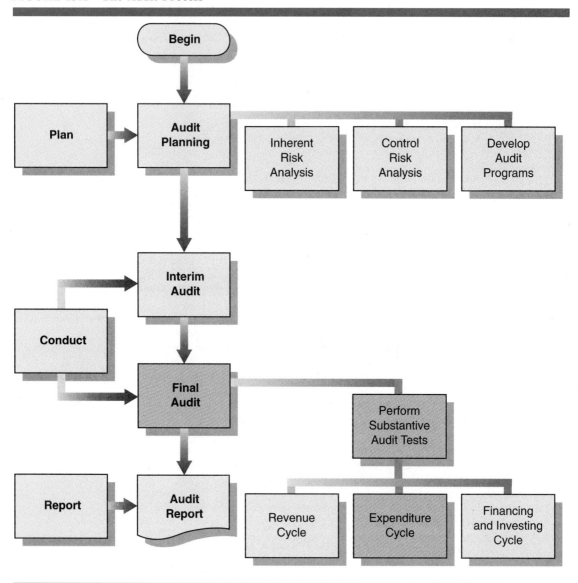

PURCHASES, PRODUCTION, AND INVENTORIES

Summary of Processing Steps

Figure 13.2 summarizes the significant processing steps included in purchases, payment of vendors' invoices, and production. The more important control points related to this part of the expenditure cycle, as more fully described in the appendix following Chapter 7, are the following:

1. Documents such as purchase orders, vouchers, receiving reports, disbursement checks, production orders, and production reports should be prenumbered and periodically accounted for;

2. For manual and batch processing systems, approvals, account distributions, and double check of account distributions should be evidenced on the face of the documents to provide for proper authorization, recording, and accountability;

3. For on-line EDP systems, proper input editing controls should provide reasonable assurance that transactions are authorized and properly recorded;

4. All movements of inventory (e.g., from receiving to stores, from stores to production, from production to finished goods, and from finished goods to shipping) should be documented to provide accountability;

5. A voucher system should be used to ensure that only properly authorized disbursements will be made;

6. Accounting manuals should be available to facilitate proper recording of unique and/or nonrecurring purchases;

7. Inventories should be physically secured, with access limited and responsibility fixed to ensure safety;

8. Perpetual inventory records should be maintained and compared with physical test counts on a recurring basis;

9. An annual physical inventory should be conducted with the independent auditors present to observe;

10. All cash disbursements should be made by check, and checks should be signed only upon submission of a properly documented and approved voucher authorizing the disbursement;

11. Access to unused vouchers and disbursement checks should be limited and responsibility for custody of these documents should be fixed;

12. Upon payment, vouchers, purchase orders, vendors' invoices', and receiving reports should be effectively canceled;

13. If check signing machines are used, they should be secured and responsibility fixed to prevent unauthorized access.

Audit Objectives

Existence and Completeness

In applying the balanced approach described in Chapter 12, the auditor tests assets for possible overstatement. Reporting nonexistent inventories on the balance sheet is one way of overstating assets. Therefore, a major part of the audit program for inventories should concentrate on determining that the inventories exist. Factors such as inventories at numerous locations, manufacturing inventories, inventories in public warehouses, and inventories out on consignment further complicate the auditor's task in verifying existence.

FIGURE 13.2   Expenditure Cycle—Summary of Processing Steps

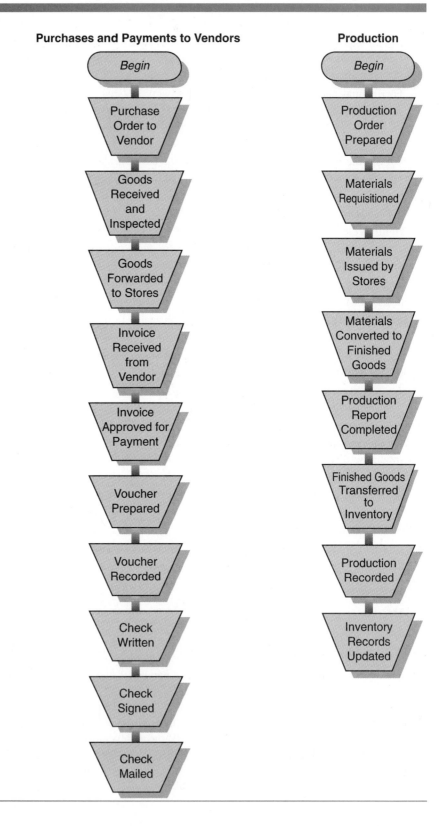

Rights and Obligations

The auditor must also determine that the client owns the inventories, as represented on the balance sheet. Inventories in transit, consigned goods, and special orders require particular attention in determining ownership.

Valuation

In auditing inventories for proper valuation, the auditor must determine the following:

1. That raw materials are valued at current vendors' prices, less applicable cash discount, and increased by an allowance for transportation;
2. That the cost accounting system is adequate in terms of assigning the proper amount of materials, labor, and overhead to finished products;
3. That the cost accounting system also permits ready identification of cost at various stages of completion to allow work-in-process valuation;
4. That the client uses an acceptable method for assigning costs to products during the acquisition, production, and disposal stages. First-in, first-out, average cost, and last-in, first-out are all acceptable valuation methods[1];
5. That slow-moving and obsolete goods, as well as other inventories, are reported on the balance sheet at amounts not to exceed net realizable value.[2]

Presentation and Disclosure

The balance sheet should disclose inventories by major classes (e.g., raw materials, work-in-process, and finished goods) and the costing method used for valuing the inventories. If inventories are pledged as collateral for outstanding loans, this fact must also be disclosed. Significant amounts of inventory, held for purposes other than manufacture or resale, should be classified separately on the balance sheet.[3]

Audit Evidence and Procedures

Inventory Observation

Observing the annual physical inventory is the most effective way for the auditor to obtain satisfaction regarding *existence*. **Inventory observation** requires that the auditor be present during the year-end inventory taking. As part of the observation, the auditor should perform test counts and evaluate the overall control exercised by the client in performing the physical inventory task.

Before the actual physical count of goods on hand, the auditor should review the inventory instructions prepared by the client (see Exhibit 13.1). The **inventory instructions** are directed to the client's personnel who will be involved in the

---

[1]Financial Accounting Standards Board, *Accounting Standards—Current Text—1990/91 Edition,* Homewood, Illinois: Irwin, 1990, Section I 78.107.

[2]*Ibid.,* Section I 78.109.

[3]*Ibid.,* Section I 78.102–103.

EXHIBIT 13.1   Inventory Instructions

Jallo, Inc.
Instructions for Physical Inventory Taking
Fiscal year ended 6/30/93

Our physical inventory will be taken in its entirety on June 29 and 30, 1993. Manufacturing operations will be halted during the inventory taking.

Raw materials and finished goods inventories are located in the warehouse at 12131 Messenger Road. A minimal amount of partially completed goods will be at various locations on the factory floor. In addition, some materials may be in the receiving area and/or in railroad cars on the company siding. Similarly, a limited amount of finished goods may be on the shipping dock, either in the shipping bays or loaded on company trucks.

The inventory will be counted by two-person count teams and double-checked by a third person. Prenumbered tags will be used for recording the counts. The tags will be issued to the count teams in packets of 100. Issued numbers will be recorded by the stores manager on a control sheet. Tags not used should be returned for proper notation on the control sheet. The teams and checkers should exercise utmost care to ensure accuracy of the counts. Obsolete materials and finished goods should be so indicated on the tags to facilitate proper pricing. The count team, as well as the checker, will initial the tags. The tags will remain on the goods until the independent auditors have completed their testing, pulled their copies of tags, and cleared the areas for resumption of operations.

Vendors have been instructed not to ship materials after June 28; and the company will not ship goods to customers after June 28. Goods will not otherwise be shipped or received during the physical inventory taking.

Similar goods should be *located together* to maximize efficiency in counting. They should also be physically arranged in a manner that facilitates ease of counting.

Consignments in and other goods not owned by Jallo should not be tagged or otherwise included in the physical inventory.

At the conclusion of the inventory, the independent auditors, along with the internal auditors, will account for all tag numbers, used and unused, and will tour the warehouse and factory to ensure that all inventory has been counted and tagged. They will then clear the area for removal of tags and authorize return to normal operations.

Joel Keller
Corporate Controller

inventory taking procedures. They cover such matters as the date and location of counts; counting procedures, including how counts will be documented and provision for double-checking of counts; arrangement of goods, including physical separation of consigned and obsolete goods; and production during inventory taking. Clear and complete inventory instructions provide the auditor added assurance concerning accuracy of counts, exclusion of consignments-in, and proper identification of obsolete and slow-moving goods.

Prenumbered **inventory tags or sheets** are used by the client for documenting the counts. If a tagging system is used, the tags (Exhibit 13.2) are physically attached to the merchandise and are removed at the instructions of the auditor after all test counting has been completed. Regardless of whether tags or sheets are used, duplicates should be provided to the auditor for control purposes.

The auditor should document the **inventory test counts** on a worksheet for later comparison with the client's final inventory listings. Exhibit 13.3 illustrates an "inventory count" worksheet. As discussed in Chapter 9, computerized techniques, such as GRiDPAD, are becoming increasingly available. By automating the documentation of client counts and auditor test counts, these applications greatly facilitate both inventory taking by the client and test counting by the auditor. Given the automated nature of the techniques, however, the auditor must carefully follow up on detected counting errors to determine that proper corrections have been made by the client.

EXHIBIT 13.2   Inventory Tag

Tag No. 21306

Inventory Class: _Finished Goods_

Location: _Warehouse #1_

Counted by: _BP_

Checked by: _RM_

Description: _Model 56A Toaster Ovens_

Quantity: _612_   Unit of Measure: _Units_

Comments: _Outdated model— write down to net realizable value_

EXHIBIT 13.3   Auditor Documentation of Inventory Counts

WP D.1

						Prepared by:	MRB
						Date:	12/31/93
						Reviewed by:	SLM
						Date:	1/12/94

Hodek Manufacturing, Inc.
Inventory Observation
Test Counts
12/31/93

Tag Number	Location	Inventory Type	Description	Client Count*	Auditor Count*	Comments
21306	Whse #1	FG	Mod. 56A Toaster Ovens	612	612	Appears overstocked. To be priced at net realizable value.
23487	Whse #1	FG	Mod. 431 Blenders	124	86	Count corrected by client.
25679	Whse #1	FG	Mod. 886 Microwave Ovens	1277	1277	
26669	Whse #2	RM	Part 345 Hinges	2344	2344	Weigh counted. Count appears reasonable.
26701	Whse #2	RM	Part 873 Oven Glass	134	123	Sheets 8 × 12 ft. Client corrected count on tag.
27333	Factory	WIP	Mod. 890 Microwave Ovens	76	76	Stamped and formed. Not assembled.

*All counts represent units.

While observing the physical inventory, the auditor must exercise control over movements within areas to be tested to prevent possible double counting. The auditor should also be alert to possible obsolescence or overstocking. Such conditions may be evidenced by signs of physical deterioration or what appear to be excessive quantities of goods. The related tags or sheets should be marked for later follow-up as to final costing.

The auditor should also inquire about obsolescence, as well as consigned-in goods, and ascertain that consignments-in are not included in the inventory. Environmental conditions such as physical arrangement of goods and security within inventory areas should be noted for possible inclusion in the reportable conditions letter.

Before concluding the inventory observation, the auditor should account for all used inventory tags (including voided tags) and sheets, as to numeric sequence, and list all unused tag or sheet numbers. This procedure is to prevent or detect the adding of nonexistent goods to tags or sheets after the counting is completed.

Inventory Confirmation

The auditor may elect to confirm goods held in public warehouses or goods out on consignment. If the amounts involved are significant, however, the auditor should arrange for physical inspection of the inventories.

Inventory Cutoff Tests

As described in Chapter 12, the purpose of **cutoff tests** is to ascertain that transactions are recorded in the proper accounting period. The auditor applies the tests to purchases, sales, cash receipts, and cash disbursements transactions. The discussion in the following paragraphs is limited to **inventory cutoff, purchases cutoff,** and **sales cutoff.** Cash receipts and disbursements cutoff were addressed in Chapter 12.

In testing purchases and sales for cutoff, the auditor must be satisfied that

1. Goods purchased before year end have been recorded as purchases, and are included in the ending inventory;

2. Goods sold by year end have been recorded as sales and excluded from the ending inventory.

The significance of errors involving inconsistencies in purchases, sales, and inventory cutoff is illustrated in Exhibit 13.4.

In determining whether a purchase or sale has occurred prior to year end, the auditor must examine documentation for evidence of passage of title. Date of receipt or shipment of goods, together with freight terms, are the principal factors determining transfer of ownership. If the freight terms are *FOB shipping point,* the title passes to the buyer upon acceptance by the shipper. If the terms are *FOB destination,* the title passes to the buyer upon receipt of goods. Receiving reports, vendors' invoices, bills of lading, freight bills, and sales invoices provide such evidence.

As part of the auditor's test for purchases and sales cutoff, attention should be directed to the shipping and receiving areas during inventory observation. The auditor should record the last document numbers (shipping order, sales invoice, receiving report, voucher) and relate them to the goods shipped or received. Later, during the final audit, these numbers should be traced to the sales and purchase records to verify their inclusion as the last sale and purchase entries of the year.

EXHIBIT 13.4   Effects of Cutoff Errors

Description of Error	Significance of Cutoff Errors Year Ended 12/31/93			
	Ending Inventory	Purchases	Sales	1993 Income Effect*
I. A 1993 purchase in the amount of $30,000 was not recorded				
A. Included in ending inventory	No Effect	Understated	No Effect	Overstated by $30,000
B. Excluded from ending inventory	Understated	Understated	No Effect	No Effect
II. A 1994 purchase in the amount of $30,000 was recorded in 1993				
A. Included in ending inventory	Overstated	Overstated	No Effect	No Effect
B. Excluded from ending inventory	No Effect	Overstated	No Effect	Understated by $30,000
III. A 1994 sale in the amount of $66,000 was recorded in 1993. Cost = $40,000				
A. Included in ending inventory	No Effect	No Effect	Overstated	Overstated by $66,000
B. Excluded from ending inventory	Understated	No Effect	Overstated	Overstated by $26,000
IV. A 1993 sale in the amount of $66,000 was recorded in 1994. Cost = $40,000				
A. Included in ending inventory	Overstated	No Effect	Understated	Understated by $26,000
B. Excluded from ending inventory	No Effect	No Effect	Understated	Understated by $66,000

Note: Consistent errors (IB, IIA, IIIB, and IVA) have less effect on income than inconsistent errors.
Rules: Recorded purchases must be included in inventory. Recorded sales must be excluded from inventory.
*Before taxes.

In addition to matching goods with documents as of year end, the auditor should also test purchase and sales transactions for a few days before and after year end. The documents to be examined for this purpose include sales invoices, shipping orders, bills of lading, receiving reports, vendors' invoices, and freight bills covering the period shortly before and after the balance sheet date. The reason for examining the documents is to determine the point at which title passed. This, in turn, identifies the period in which the transaction should be recorded. Shipping dates, receiving dates, and freight terms will assist the auditor in determining passage of title. If, for example, inventory is **in transit** from client to customer at year end and the freight terms are F.O.B. destination, the goods should be included in the client's ending inventory and the sales transaction should be reversed. Similarly, if incoming materials or goods are in transit at year end and have been shipped by the vendor F.O.B. shipping point, title has passed to the client and the goods should be included in the ending inventory and the purchase should be recorded.

In selecting the transactions to be tested, the auditor should proceed both from documents to accounting records and from accounting records to documents. This provides greater assurance of detecting errors of commission as well as errors of omission. Table 13.1 summarizes the records, documents, and substance to be examined in the test for proper sales and purchases cutoff.

TABLE 13.1   Records, Documents, and Substance for Cutoff Tests

Transaction	Records	Documents	Substance
Purchases	Voucher register	Vouchers Vendors' invoices Receivers Bills of lading Freight bills	Inventories
Sales	Sales register Customers' ledger	Sales invoices Shipping orders Bills of lading	Inventories Confirmations
Cash receipts	Cash receipts record	Remittance advice Cash receipts prelisting Cash register tapes (year end)	Cash count Bank statement Cutoff bank statement
Cash disbursements	Check register	Bank reconciliation Paid vouchers	Canceled checks Cutoff bank statement

Procedures:

1. Trace both ways (from documents to records and from records to documents) to detect errors of commission and errors of omission.
2. Examine substance at year end, record last document numbers (sales invoice, voucher, receiver, shipper, disbursement check, etc.), and determine consistency with recording of transactions.
   a. Inventory in receiving area at year end included in inventory, listed on last receiver number for the year, and recorded as last purchase in voucher register.
   b. Inventory shipped out on date of inventory excluded from inventory, billed on last sales invoice number for the year, and recorded as last sale in sales register.
   c. Trace last document numbers recorded at year end to accounting records: sales invoice to sales record; voucher and receiver to voucher register; and check to check register.

Test Pricing of Final Inventory

The auditor verifies *existence* by observing the taking of the physical inventory. *Ownership* is determined by performing cutoff tests. The auditor must also determine that the ending inventories have been properly *valued* in accordance with GAAP. Two inputs govern valuation: price and quantity. Tests of quantities have already been discussed as part of verifying existence. Satisfied as to the physical inventory, however, the auditor must next trace the quantities to the final inventory listings to ensure that the client has not committed errors in transferring the counts to the listings. In performing this procedure, the auditor should trace both quantities counted and quantities not counted. The direction of testing should proceed from the auditor's copies of tags or sheets to the final listings. As a further quantity test, the auditor should scan the client's inventory listings for large dollar amounts and trace the related quantities to the auditor's copies of tags or sheets. The purpose of this procedure is to detect material overstatements by the client, intentional or unintentional, in transferring quantities to the final inventory listings.

Before testing the prices appearing on the final inventory listings (the second input to valuation, referred to as **inventory pricing tests**), the auditor must be satisfied that the cost accounting system produces reliable inventory cost data. The auditor ordinarily tests the cost accounting system during the interim audit as part of control testing. Raw materials and purchased parts price lists, bills of material and routing sheets for manufactured goods, and perpetual inventory records should all be examined and tested for reliability. Satisfied as to prices and costing methods, the auditor can rely on the cost records as to unit prices used in valuing the final inventory.

Next, the auditor should, on a test basis, trace the prices on the final inventory listings to the audited price lists, and test extensions and footings appearing on the listings. If the inventories are computerized, the auditor may elect to use the computer to assist in these tests.

In determining whether inventories are properly valued at lower of cost or market, the auditor should test for possible obsolete or slow-moving inventory. **Tests for inventory obsolescence** may begin with analytical procedures directed at inventory turnover for various classes of goods. A significant decline in turnover relative to prior years or relative to other similar inventory items is further evidence of obsolescence. The auditor should inquire of stores personnel as to cause where turnover rates are unusually low. Turnover calculations and inquiry should also be applied to apparent overstocking noted by the auditor during inventory observation.

Summary Audit Program

Figure 13.3 presents a summary audit program for the examination of inventories. The program is not intended to be exhaustive, but rather incorporates the more significant procedures applied to the audit of inventories. Those procedures related to inventory observation (existence) and inventory pricing (valuation and ownership) are most critical to the auditor's opinion concerning inventories.

**FIGURE 13.3 Model Audit Program—Expenditure Cycle—
Inventory, Purchases, and Production**

Analytical Procedures
1. Compare purchases, inventories, and gross profit percentages with prior year and industry averages, and account for significant fluctuations.
2. Calculate inventory turnover by major classes, and compare with prior year and industry averages, and account for major fluctuations.

Other Substantive Audit Procedures
1. Review client's inventory taking instructions for completeness and adequacy.
2. Observe the taking of the client's physical inventory, and observe or confirm goods not on premises, as necessary.
3. Test for purchases and sales cutoff.
4. Determine that client has properly adjusted general ledger inventory amounts to agree with physical inventory.
5. Test the costing of the physical inventory by tracing to audited price lists and cost records.
6. Trace quantities from tags or count sheets to final inventory listings.
7. Scan inventory listings for extended amounts in excess of $10,000. Trace related quantities to auditor's copy of inventory tag.
8. Test final inventory extensions and footings.
9. Inquire as to inventory obsolescence and pledging of inventories as collateral for outstanding loans.

PLANT ASSETS
Audit Objectives

Existence and Completeness

In testing for overstated or omitted plant assets, the auditor must concentrate on such factors as whether new assets have been placed in service as of year end, whether all disposals have been recorded, and whether financing leases have been properly included among plant assets. The possibility of ''off balance sheet financing'' (failure to record financing leases) poses the greatest threat to fairness of financial presentation, given material amounts of leased assets in today's business world.

Rights and Obligations

The auditor must ascertain that the client owns the existing plant assets as of the balance sheet date. In addition, the auditor must determine that all mortgages and other outstanding indebtedness relating to the assets are included on the balance

An inspection of major additions to plant assets is one test for existence and completeness.

sheet. Financing leases with contingent rental clauses must be examined carefully for year-end accruals. If, for example, a lease contract specifies, in addition to minimum lease payments, an additional amount calculated as a percentage of net sales in excess of a specified monthly amount (contingent rentals), the auditor should recalculate the added amounts and determine that they have been properly recorded as expenses and that unpaid amounts have been reflected as current liabilities at year end.

Valuation

For valuation purposes, the auditor must determine that plant assets are properly reflected on the balance sheet at cost less accumulated depreciation. With respect to leased assets, this requires attention to the calculation of minimum lease payments and the discount rate used in determining present value. Evaluating appropriateness of depreciation methods, as well as consistency of application, are also part of the valuation objective. Proper classification of capital and revenue expenditures for costs incurred subsequent to acquisition of plant assets, and establishing correctness of computed gains or losses on disposals complete the valuation set of audit objectives.

Presentation and Disclosure

Major classes of plant assets, accumulated depreciation related to each, and depreciation methods must be clearly disclosed either in the body of the balance sheet or in footnotes thereto. Leased assets involve added disclosure as to future cash flows required under the lease agreement. Pledging of assets as security for outstanding loans must also be clearly disclosed in the body of the balance sheet or in its footnotes.

Assets removed from production for other than standby purposes, as well as assets purchased for investment purposes, must be classified separately on the balance sheet. These are nonoperating assets and therefore should not be included in plant assets.

Changes in depreciation methods for existing classes of plant assets must also be disclosed. The "cumulative effect" change, net of tax, is shown separately, after extraordinary items, on the income statement; and the nature of the change and its justification must be incorporated in a footnote.[4]

Audit Evidence and Procedures

Plant Assets Lead Schedule

To provide a focal point for applying substantive tests, the auditor should prepare or obtain a schedule of plant assets and accumulated depreciation. Exhibit 13.5 illustrates a **plant assets lead schedule.** Exhibit 13.6, "Autos and Trucks," is one of the six supporting schedules accompanying the "Plant Assets" lead schedule. The supporting schedule contains a record of the audit procedures applied and evidence gathered. Note that depreciation expense and gain or loss on disposals are analyzed, along with the related plant asset accounts. This supports the transaction cycle approach to substantive audit testing. By auditing income statement accounts in conjunction with the related balance sheet accounts, the auditor gains greater assurance as to proper matching and cutoff. The approach also enhances audit efficiency by permitting the auditor to simultaneously examine both the balance sheet and income statement effects of transactions.

After the beginning balances have been entered in the plant assets lead schedule, the auditor should reconcile the plant assets subsidiary ledger with the controlling accounts in the general ledger. Although the audit testing will be performed on the subsidiary ledger, any audit adjustments will be posted, by the client, to the controlling accounts. It is imperative, therefore, that agreement be established at the outset. This procedure is applicable, incidentally, whenever subsidiary ledgers support controlling accounts in the general ledger.

Analytical Procedures

Before vouching and recalculating, the auditor should compare depreciation and repairs and maintenance charges with the prior year and with budgeted amounts, and investigate major changes. A significant decrease in repairs, for example, could indicate errors in classifying repairs as capital expenditures. This finding should prompt the auditor to direct more attention toward vouching plant asset additions. A material increase in repairs expense, alternately, suggests possible expense overstatement and should result in added audit resources directed toward vouching debits to the repair accounts.

---

[4]*Ibid.*, Section A06.

EXHIBIT 13.5   Plant Assets Lead Schedule

WP G		Jallo, Inc. Plant Assets Lead Schedule 12/31/93			Prepared by: LK Date: 1/11/94 Reviewed by: JR Date: 1/15/94	
Description	Final Balances 12/31/92	Additions	Disposals	Final Balances 12/31/93	WP #
Assets					
Land	$ 130,000	60,000	30,000	160,000	G.1
Land improvements	50,000			50,000	G.2
Buildings	786,000	160,000	86,000	860,000	G.3
Machinery and equipment	345,000	85,000	45,000	385,000	G.4
Autos and trucks	120,000	30,000	28,000	122,000	G.5
Office furniture and equipment	86,000	12,000	6,000	92,000	G.6
	$1,517,000	347,000	195,000	1,669,000	
				WTB 1	
Accumulated Depreciation and Amortization					
Land improvements	$ 20,000	5,000		25,000	G.2
Buildings	453,000	40,000	72,000	421,000	G.3
Machinery and equipment	126,000	35,000	42,000	119,000	G.4
Autos and trucks	65,000	24,000	25,000	64,000	G.5
Office furniture and equipment	43,000	17,000	3,000	57,000	G.6
	$ 707,000	121,000	142,000	686,000	
				WTB 1	

Vouch Additions and Disposals

The auditor, on a test basis, should examine documentation supporting plant asset additions and disposals. Vendors' invoices and freight bills provide evidence supporting proper valuation and ownership of purchased assets. Work orders provide the detail covering materials, labor, and overhead applied to constructed plant assets. Materials, labor, and direct overhead charges should be traced to requisitions and time tickets on a test basis. Fixed overhead should be recalculated to support the reasonableness of the application rates. Generally accepted accounting principles require that a proportionate share of fixed overhead be applied to constructed plant assets. The auditor should also determine whether interest should be capitalized as part of the projects.

Remittance advices, deposit tickets, and bank statements should be examined in support of plant asset disposals. Control over miscellaneous cash receipts is

EXHIBIT 13.6   Plant Assets Supporting Schedule

WP G.5		Jallo, Inc. Autos and Trucks 12/31/93		Prepared by: LK Date: 1/10/94 Reviewed by: JR Date: 1/15/94
	Final *Balances* *12/31/92*	*Additions*	*Disposals*	*Final* *Balances* *12/31/93*
Assets				
Salespersons' autos	$30,000⊗			30,000
Delivery trucks	50,000⊗	30,000~	28,000	52,000
Service trucks	40,000⊗			40,000
	$120,000	30,000	28,000	122,000
	F	F	F	To WP G F
Accumulated Depreciation				
Salespersons' autos	$10,000⊗	7,000C		17,000
Delivery trucks	35,000⊗	9,000C	25,000C	19,000
Service trucks	20,000⊗	8,000C		28,000
	$65,000	24,000	25,000	64,000
	F	F	F	To WP G F

GAIN OR LOSS ON DISPOSALS

	Selling Price	Book Value	Gain (Loss)
⊗ Traced to 12/31/92 working trial balance			
F Footed and cross-footed	$6,700	$3,000	$3,700
~ Examined title and canceled check			
C Recomputed	√		
√ Traced to deposit ticket and bank statement			To WP S

evaluated during the control risk assessment phase of the audit. In applying substantive tests, the goal is to verify that material amounts of miscellaneous receipts were properly recorded and deposited intact.

As part of the vouching process, the auditor should also examine the minutes of directors' meetings for proper authorization of major acquisitions and disposals. Purchase and sale agreements should be examined for proper recording and for the existence of indebtedness, contingent liabilities, or other restrictions arising from the transactions.

Recalculate Depreciation

After evaluating the appropriateness of depreciation methods used by the client, the auditor should recalculate the depreciation charges on a test basis. Depreciation recorded on additions and disposals should be examined for consistency with company policy and the prior year. As discussed in Chapter 9, generalized audit software is available to automate a significant part of depreciation recalculation. The software may be developed in-house by an accounting firm; or it may be purchased from outside vendors.

Accelerated Cost Recovery System (ACRS) charges and Modified Accelerated Cost Recovery System (MACRS) charges for tax purposes should be recalculated on a test basis, and the temporary differences traced to the deferred tax account. In addition to depreciation charges, ACRS charges, and MACRS charges, the auditor should recalculate gains or losses on disposals of plant assets. Gains and losses for accounting and tax purposes should then be reconciled.

Vouch Repairs and Maintenance Charges

Repairs and maintenance accounts should be analyzed along with plant assets. Major expenditures should be vouched to vendors' invoices and work orders. Performing this procedure in conjunction with additions and disposals of plant assets increases the probability of locating material classification errors (i.e., ordinary repairs capitalized or extraordinary repairs expensed). The auditor should examine and evaluate company policy regarding capitalization of extraordinary repairs and should apply analytical procedures, as described above, before beginning the vouching process.

As with depreciation recalculation, generalized audit software can be used to help the auditor select debits to repairs and plant asset accounts for further analysis.

Examine Leases and Loan Agreements

The auditor must determine, by examining the contracts, whether leases have been properly classified as to financing vs. operating. For financing leases, the auditor should recalculate minimum lease payments and evaluate the appropriateness of the discount rate used in capitalizing the lease.

Loan agreements should be examined for possible pledging of plant assets as collateral. The auditor should also inquire of legal counsel and examine bank confirmations for evidence of pledging. To the extent plant assets have been pledged as security, balance sheet disclosure is required.

Summary Audit Program

Figure 13.4 summarizes the audit procedures applicable to plant asset additions, disposals, and balances. Note that the program also covers such related income statement accounts as depreciation, gain or loss on disposals, and repairs and maintenance.

INTANGIBLE ASSETS
Audit Objectives

Existence and Completeness

Intangible assets (e.g., patents, copyrights, trademarks, goodwill, and franchises) do not possess physical substance as do inventories and plant assets. Nevertheless, the auditor needs to verify the existence of recorded intangibles. As to completeness, the auditor must be satisfied that no significant amounts of purchased intangibles possessing future economic benefit have been expensed.

FIGURE 13.4 Model Audit Program for Expenditure Cycle: Plant Assets

Analytical Procedures
1. Compare depreciation expense with prior year and account for major changes.
2. Compare maintenance and repair expense with prior year, both in total and as a percentage of sales, and account for major changes.
3. Compare maintenance and repair expense with budgeted amounts and investigate significant variances as to cause.

Other Substantive Audit Procedures
1. Consider inspecting major additions to verify existence.
2. Prepare a lead schedule of plant assets and accumulated depreciation by major classes of assets.
3. Reconcile subsidiary plant ledger with controlling accounts and agree to ending balances appearing on plant assets lead schedule.
4. Examine directors' minutes and purchase and sale agreements for proper authorization and accounting for major acquisitions and disposals.
5. Vouch plant asset additions and disposals on a test basis. Be particularly alert to possible capitalization of ordinary repairs.
6. Vouch repair and maintenance expenditures on a test basis. Be particularly alert to possible expensing of plant asset additions.
7. Evaluate appropriateness and consistency of depreciation method(s).
8. Recalculate depreciation and gain or loss on disposals on a test basis.
9. For self-constructed assets, recalculate overhead allocation and interest during construction, if applicable.
10. Examine plant ledger for fully depreciated assets, and inquire as to status. Remove from accounts if disposed of or otherwise no longer in use.
11. Examine all lease agreements and determine proper classification as to financing versus operating.
12. For financing leases:
    a. Evaluate appropriateness of discount rate used in calculating net present value of minimum lease payments;
    b. Recalculate minimum lease payments;
    c. Recalculate contingent rentals, as necessary, on a test basis.
13. Examine loan agreements for possible pledges of plant assets as collateral.

Rights and Obligations

The auditor must ascertain ownership of purchased intangibles. Real and contingent liabilities arising from the intangible assets also need to be identified.

Valuation

Intangible assets should be valued at acquisition cost less accumulated amortization. Costs of developed intangibles should generally be expensed. The auditor must determine, therefore, that no research and development costs have been improperly capitalized as intangible assets.

Determining proper valuation also requires an assessment of future economic benefit to be derived from the assets. In this respect, the auditor must evaluate the reasonableness of the amortization periods selected for given classes of intangible assets.

Presentation and Disclosure

The nature of intangible assets, along with valuation and amortization methods, need to be disclosed in the financial statements. Contingent liabilities related to the intangibles also need to be disclosed.

Audit Evidence and Procedures

Analytical Procedures

In auditing intangible assets, the auditor should begin by applying analytical procedures to the current year's amortization expense and to research and development (R&D) expense. Significant abnormalities should be pursued to ascertain cause. Abnormal decreases in amortization may be indicative of disposals or writeoffs of intangibles. Unusual decreases in R&D may have been caused by improper capitalization of expenditures.

Inquiry and Examination of Underlying Documentation

The existence objective may be satisfied by examining the underlying documentation in support of purchased intangibles. Patents, copyrights, trademarks, franchise agreements, and merger agreements constitute such documentation. The auditor should also examine directors' minutes for authorization of material intangible asset purchases.

Inquiry of management and legal counsel may assist the auditor in identifying possible contingencies relating to intangible assets. Such contingencies frequently assume the form of lawsuits alleging infringement of patents, copyrights, trademarks, or franchises.

The auditor may also inquire of management as to future economic benefit accruing from recorded intangibles. Such inquiry may be further corroborated by relating copyrights, franchises, patents, trademarks, and goodwill to the revenues produced by these assets. Continued revenue producing trends are good evidence of future benefit.

Vouch Additions and Disposals

The auditor should examine correspondence, contracts and agreements, legal documents, and canceled checks related to acquisitions of intangible assets. Errors in valuing intangibles are likely to be detected by these procedures. In examining merger agreements, the auditor should evaluate the reasonableness of valuations placed on intangible assets. To the extent that any excess of cost over book value has been improperly charged to goodwill, it should be reclassified to the appropriate tangible assets.

Research and development costs should also be vouched, along with additions to intangible assets. Improperly capitalized R&D costs should be reclassified as expenses. Likewise, material amounts of purchased intangibles that have been expensed as part of R&D costs should be capitalized. Selecting debits to R&D for further analysis is another task that can be expedited with generalized audit software packages.

Credits to intangible asset accounts may represent amortization, write-offs, or disposals. In vouching disposals, the auditor should trace recorded cash receipts arising from sales of intangibles to the bank statement.

Recalculate Gains, Losses, and Amortization

Gains or losses on disposals, as well as amortization expense, should be recalculated on a test basis. If analytical procedures indicate abnormal changes in these accounts, the degree of testing may be intensified.

Summary Audit Program

Figure 13.5 summarizes these procedures in the form of a summary audit program for intangibles. Note that research and development expenditures are audited in conjunction with intangible assets as a means for detecting material classification errors.

FIGURE 13.5   Model Audit Program for Expenditure Cycle: Intangible Assets and Research and Development Expenditures

Analytical Procedures
1. Compare amortization expense with prior year and investigate material changes.
2. Compare research and development expense with prior year, both in absolute terms and as a percent of sales, and account for material changes.
3. Compare research and development expense with budgeted amounts and investigate significant variances as to cause.
4. Evaluate future economic benefit of recorded intangibles by relating assets to revenue produced by them.

Other Substantive Audit Procedures
1. Determine existence of recorded intangibles by examining underlying documentation (patents, copyrights, trademarks, franchise agreements, merger agreements, etc.).
2. Vouch additions to and disposals of intangible assets on a test basis.
3. Recalculate gain or loss on disposals.
4. Evaluate appropriateness of amortization period for recorded intangibles, and recalculate amortization on a test basis.
5. Examine minutes of directors' meetings for proper authorization of acquisitions and disposals of intangible assets.
6. Vouch research and development expenditures on a test basis and determine appropriateness of classification.
7. Inquire of management and legal counsel as to possible contingencies relating to intangible assets.

CURRENT LIABILITIES
Audit Objectives

Existence and Completeness

A common form of management misrepresentation fraud involves omitting liabilities from the balance sheet and the related expenses from the income statement. Moreover, given the large number of accruals arising at year end, together with difficulties in achieving a proper cutoff, liabilities may be unintentionally omitted from the balance sheet. For these reasons, auditing for completeness (i.e., determining that no significant amounts of liabilities have been omitted from the balance sheet) is a major goal in the audit of current liabilities. The auditor must also determine that contingent liabilities are properly disclosed in footnotes to the financial statements.

Valuation

Accruals and loss contingencies pose the greatest challenge to the auditor in verifying valuation. Examples of accruals requiring audit attention are taxes, pension liability, profit sharing and bonus accruals, and vacation pay. Another common loss contingency, requiring accrual at year-end, is the estimated allowance for doubtful accounts (already covered in Chapter 12). Other loss contingencies such as product warranty provisions and pending litigation may or may not be pertinent to a given engagement.

Many of the accruals and loss contingencies (e.g., pension liability, warranty provision, and allowance for loan losses) are based on management estimates. The auditor is responsible for evaluating the reasonableness of these estimates.[5] If the control structure supports the reliability of management's estimates, the auditor may elect to simply review and test the process used by management. Under conditions of weak control, however, the auditor may wish to develop an independent estimate.[6]

Presentation and Disclosure

The major presentation objective in the audit of current liabilities is determining that no significant classification errors between current and noncurrent liabilities have occurred. Current installments of long-term debt, for example, should be reflected in the current liability section of the balance sheet. Conversely, short-term obligations expected to be refinanced should be classified as long-term liabilities, provided the conditions set forth in Statement of Financial Accounting Standards No. 6 have been met.

Proper adherence to footnote disclosure requirements relating to leases, pensions, and contingencies must also be tested.

---

[5]Auditing Standards Board, *AICPA Professional Standards,* New York: AICPA, 1991, Section AU 342.
[6]*Ibid.*

Audit Evidence and Procedures

Search for Unrecorded Liabilities

In testing for completeness, the auditor should conduct a **search for unrecorded liabilities.** This is done by examining invoices and the voucher register for a short period after the balance sheet date. The purpose of this procedure is to determine, by reference to vouchers, invoices, and receiving reports, that recording took place in the proper accounting period. If the client has prepared year-end adjustments for accruals and other previously unrecorded liabilities, the auditor should trace invoices and vouchers, processed shortly after year-end, to the adjusting entries.

If purchases cutoff is found inadequate, the auditor should consider examining vendors' invoices, on a test basis, to the date of audit field work completion. This extended procedure should further assist the auditor in locating material amounts of unrecorded liabilities.

Analytical procedures applied to operating expenses such as interest, payroll taxes, product warranty expense, pensions, vacation pay, legal and accounting fees, rent, and so on, will also assist in locating possible omissions. In a recurring audit, examining the prior year's audit adjustments for unrecorded liabilities may likewise reveal obligations otherwise overlooked.

Confirmation

Statement of Financial Accounting Standards No. 5 sets forth the conditions under which contingent liabilities should be either recorded in the accounts or disclosed in a footnote. The criteria for making the determination are measurability of possible loss and probability of unfavorable outcome.

A type of loss contingency frequently encountered by auditors is threatened or pending litigation. Inasmuch as auditors are not legal experts, reliance is placed on the client's legal counsel for evaluating the possible outcome of litigation. Section 337 of the *Codification of Statements on Auditing Standards* describes procedures for obtaining a letter from the client's legal counsel. The auditor begins by requesting management to draft a letter to legal counsel. The letter contains a listing of pending or threatened litigation, and unasserted claims, together with management's evaluation of possible outcomes. Management may request legal counsel to provide the listing. Exhibit 13.7 illustrates the **letter of audit inquiry to the client's legal counsel.** The lawyers are requested to examine the listing and respond directly to the auditor regarding agreement or disagreement with management's listing and views. Having examined management's letter of inquiry, and the lawyer's response, the auditor may better evaluate whether the contingencies deserve recognition in the financial statements.

The auditor should also examine the bank confirmation(s) for the existence of outstanding loans which may require interest accrual and possibly disclosure of collateral securing the loans.

Mathematical Evidence

To gain assurance as to proper valuation of current liabilities, the auditor should recalculate accruals on a test basis. Examples of the more common accruals for

EXHIBIT 13.7   Letter of Audit Inquiry to the Client's Legal Counsel

Jallo, Inc.
34 Spring Street
Omaha, Nebraska 66567

January 22, 1994

Wrepre and Zent, Attorneys
8756 Whiteway Blvd.
Omaha, Nebraska 66545

Gentlemen:

In connection with an examination of our financial statements at December 31, 1993, and for the year then ended, the management of Jallo has furnished to our auditors, Went and Saw, CPAs, a description and evaluation of certain contingencies, including those set forth below involving matters with respect to which you have devoted substantial attention on behalf of Jallo in the form of legal consultation or representation. For the purpose of your response to this letter, we believe that, as to each contingency, an amount in excess of $5,000 would be material, and in total, $25,000. Your response should include matters that existed at December 31, 1993, and during the period from that date to the date of completion of their examination, which is anticipated to be on or about February 15, 1994.

PENDING OR THREATENED LITIGATION, CLAIMS AND ASSESSMENTS (EXCLUDING UN-ASSERTED CLAIMS AND ASSESSMENTS):

Product Liability Claim. The Company is a defendant in a suit brought by Piney Woods Amuse-ment Park resulting from injuries sustained by patrons during a ride on equipment installed by Jallo. The plaintiffs are seeking $3,000,000 in damages. Management is of the opinion that Jallo can find relief in the manufacturer of the equipment for any damages awarded by the court.

Nebraska Tax Assessment. An additional assessment for Nebraska income taxes has been levied as a result of a recently completed audit by the Nebraska tax division. The amount of the added assessment, applicable to 1989–1991, is $1,300,000 plus interest and penalties. The Company is appealing the finding and expects to prevail.

(continued)

which recalculation is applied are interest on notes, accrued payroll taxes and withholdings, income and property tax accruals, product warranty, pension and profit sharing, and vacation pay.

Summary Audit Program

Figure 13.6 summarizes, in the form of a model audit program for current liabilities and operating expenses, the audit procedures just described.

EXHIBIT 13.7 *(continued)*

UNASSERTED CLAIMS AND ASSESSMENTS CONSIDERED BY MANAGEMENT TO BE PROBABLE OF ASSERTION AND THAT, IF ASSERTED, WOULD HAVE AT LEAST A REASONABLE POSSIBILITY OF AN UNFAVORABLE OUTCOME:

Threatened Expropriation of Chilean Subsidiary. Due to a change in the ruling government of Chile, Jallo faces loss of its manufacturing holdings in that country. The carrying value of the properties, including inventories and equipment, is $4,600,000 at December 31, 1993. Although some recovery from the new government is expected in the event of nationalization of the facility, it is impossible to estimate the amount of recovery at this time.

Please furnish our auditors such explanation, if any, that you consider necessary to supplement the foregoing information, including an explanation of those matters on which your views may differ from those stated.

We understand that when in the course of performing legal service for us with respect to a matter recognized to involve an unasserted possible claim or assessment that may call for financial statement disclosure, if you have formed a professional conclusion that we should disclose or consider disclosure concerning such possible claim or assessment, as a matter of professional responsibility to us, you will so advise us and will consult with us concerning the question of such disclosure and the applicable requirements of Statement of Financial Accounting Standards No. 5. Please specifically confirm to our auditors that our understanding is correct.

OTHER MATTERS:
Please specifically identify the nature of and reasons for any limitations on your response.

Please indicate the amount owed to you for services and expenses, billed and unbilled, at December 31, 1993.

Very truly yours,

Harold McMillan
President

AUDIT RISK ANALYSIS AND THE EXPENDITURE CYCLE

The auditing procedures discussed in the preceding section assume no significant modifications of the initial audit programs. The implication is that neither the application of analytical procedures and study of the business and industry, nor internal control study and evaluation aroused the auditor's suspicions. This section addresses some risk factors which may be suggestive of material errors or irregularities relating to the expenditure cycle. These factors, along with extended audit procedures which might be applied in the circumstances, are discussed in the following paragraphs.

FIGURE 13.6   Model Audit Program for Expenditure Cycle:
Current Liabilities and Operating Expenses

Analytical Procedures
1. Compare year-end accruals with prior year, and account for significant changes or omissions.
2. Compare operating expenses with prior year, in terms of both absolute amount and percentage of sales, and account for major changes.
3. Compare operating expenses with budgeted amounts and investigate significant variances as to cause.

Other Substantive Audit Procedures
1. Inquire as to contingent liabilities.
2. Obtain lawyer's letter to identify contingencies requiring adjustment or footnote disclosure.
3. Search for unrecorded liabilities.
4. Recompute loss contingencies and accruals on a test basis.
5. Obtain client representation letter.

Some warning signs that should prompt further investigation and possible program modification are the following:

1. Significant amounts of idle capacity;
2. Inventory increases without comparable sales increases;
3. High technology industry causing threat of product obsolescence;
4. Significant increase in plant asset additions;
5. Existence of related parties.

Idle Capacity

Under conditions of idle capacity, the auditor must be particularly alert to the reasonableness of fixed overhead included in the ending inventories. If overhead is applied on the basis of normal volume over a multiyear operating cycle, a portion of the volume variance may be reported as a deferred charge. If the idle capacity is abnormal, however, a loss should be recognized in the current period. The auditor, therefore, should carefully evaluate the client's policy for applying overhead to inventory and ascertain that the policy is in accordance with GAAP and has been consistently followed during the current period. As part of the examination of inventories, the auditor should compare overhead as a percentage of inventory cost with the preceding year. A higher than normal percentage suggests that a capacity loss may have been capitalized.

Abnormal Inventory Increase

An unusual increase in inventory may be detected when applying analytical procedures related to comparing inventory turnover with preceding years and with industry averages. The increase may be due to expected sales increases for the upcoming year, accompanied by projected inventory supplier shortages. It may also be caused by overstocking in anticipation of current sales that never materialized. Finally, the increase may be the result of management's deliberate attempt to overstate earnings by inflating inventories.

Given an abnormal inventory increase, the auditor should inquire of management as to the cause. If management's response does not provide a satisfactory explanation of the increase, the auditor should expand the substantive testing of inventories. Extended testing in the following areas will assist in identifying the cause:

1. Search for evidence of overstocking, obsolescence, or quantity inflation during inventory observation;

2. Increase the proportion of test counts during inventory observation;

3. Expand purchases and inventory cutoff procedures;

4. Extend the tests of inventory prices and quantities appearing on the final inventory listings (prices may be inflated or quantities may have been increased in transferring from inventory tags or sheets to the final listings);

5. Arrange for observation, rather than confirmation, of significant amounts of inventory on consignment or in public warehouses.

High Technology Industry

Companies in the so-called high tech industries are often faced with a stronger threat of product obsolescence than companies in less volatile industries. This condition is attributable to the rapidity of product improvements, given the ongoing nature of the technology. The computer, electronics, and robotics industries are good examples. In addition to the obsolescence threat, the severity of competition (being the first to develop and market the latest technology) often causes liquidity problems. During the 1980s, the computer industry experienced a "shake-out" as many of the smaller companies failed due to the severity of the competition.

The auditor, under these conditions, must recognize the higher probability of obsolete or slow-moving inventory. Increased attention during inventory observation should be directed toward possible overstocking and obsolescence. Extended inventory pricing and turnover testing should also be applied during the final audit.

Efforts to increase income and earnings per share in the face of intense competition may ultimately lead to intentional overstatement of the ending inventories. Auditors must be especially alert, under these circumstances, to unusual inventory increases, and apply the procedures discussed in the preceding section.

Significant Increase in Plant Asset Additions

Companies in the rebuilding process or new and rapidly growing companies may expend large sums on capital assets. Companies in mature or declining industries, on the other hand, usually replace worn out assets, but are not expected to add heavily to the plant asset base.

Given a client in the former category, the auditor should plan to examine the underlying documentation supporting debits to plant asset accounts, evaluate the accounting for and valuation of the additions, and perhaps inspect some of the assets on a test basis. Suspicions should ordinarily not be aroused concerning asset inflation.

In the latter category, however, the auditor, upon discovering significant plant asset additions, should consider the possibility that ordinary repairs have been capitalized rather than expensed. Expanding the analysis of the repairs and maintenance accounts, in conjunction with the plant assets, should assist in determining whether the expenditures have been properly classified.

Existence of Related Parties

The existence of related parties may serve as a conduit for transferring expenses from one company to another. Research and development costs, for example, may be improperly transferred by selling the results of completed projects to related parties. In one such case, a company reported a substantial increase in earnings per share by selling an allegedly valuable patent to a "shell" company. The patent had been obtained by developing a new product internally. The sale was consummated on the basis of the parent company guaranteeing loans to the related party. The loan proceeds were then used to buy the patent from the parent.

Related-party transactions such as this often produce variances between legal form and economic substance; and when these variances occur, economic substance must take precedence. In the present case the *legal form* of the transaction was a sale at a profit. The *economic substance* of the transaction, however, was a loan from the bank to the parent company, inasmuch as the shell company had no resources to repay the loan. Because of these possible occurrences, auditors must examine related-party transactions carefully, especially if analytical procedures disclose significant improvements in profitability.[7]

KEY TERMS

Cutoff tests	Inventory in transit
Inventory confirmation	Letter of audit inquiry to the client's
Inventory cutoff	legal counsel
Inventory instructions	Plant assets lead schedule
Inventory observation	Purchases cutoff
Inventory pricing tests	Sales cutoff
Inventory tags or sheets	Search for unrecorded liabilities
Inventory test counts	Tests for inventory obsolescence

---

[7]See Chapter 14 for a description of the auditor's approach to examining related-party transactions.

COMPUTER AUDIT PRACTICE CASE

Trim Lawn Manufacturing Company
The following expenditure cycle substantive testing assignments from the Trim Lawn
audit practice case may be completed at this time:

- Module VIII: Sales and purchases cutoff tests
- Module IX: Search for unrecorded liabilities
- Module X: Estimated liability for product warranty
- Module XI: Plant asset additions and disposals

REVIEW QUESTIONS

1. How does the auditor verify the existence of inventories?
2. Why is it important for the auditor to review the client's inventory taking instructions?
3. Why is it necessary for the auditor to control inventory tags and inventory movements during the physical inventory?
4. What purpose is served in auditing cutoff?
5. How does the auditor gain assurance that quantities appearing on the final inventory listings are correct?
6. How does the auditor test inventory for obsolescence?
7. How does the application of analytical procedures assist in the audit of plant assets?
8. Identify the audit objectives and procedures concerning plant asset disposals.
9. How does the auditor ascertain proper authorization of major additions and disposals?
10. Why should the repairs and maintenance accounts be audited simultaneously with the plant asset accounts?
11. Why are lease agreements examined along with plant assets?
12. Research and development expenditures should be examined as part of the audit of intangible assets. Explain why.
13. How does the auditor ascertain the future economic benefit of recorded intangibles?
14. Briefly describe the search for unrecorded liabilities.
15. What is the purpose of the letter of audit inquiry to the client's legal counsel?
16. How might a company manipulate overhead in order to understate losses during a period of abnormally low volume operations? How should the auditor respond to such a situation?
17. How does the auditor determine whether an inventory increase is normal or abnormal?

MULTIPLE CHOICE QUESTIONS FROM CPA EXAMINATIONS

1. In a manufacturing company, which one of the following audit procedures would give the least assurance of the valuation of inventory at the audit date?
   a. Testing the computation of standard overhead rates.
   b. Examining paid vendors' invoices.
   c. Reviewing direct labor rates.
   d. Obtaining confirmation of inventories pledged under loan agreements.

2. Which of the following situations would most likely require special audit planning by the auditor?
   a. Some items of factory and office equipment do not bear identification numbers.
   b. Depreciation methods used on the client's tax return differ from those used on the books.
   c. Assets costing less than $500 are expensed even though the expected life exceeds one year.
   d. Inventory is comprised of precious stones.

3. An auditor has accounted for a sequence of inventory tags and is now going to trace information on a representative number of tags to the physical inventory sheets. The purpose of this procedure is to obtain assurance that
   a. The final inventory is valued at cost.
   b. All inventory represented by an inventory tag is listed on the inventory sheets.
   c. All inventory represented by an inventory tag is bona fide.
   d. Inventory sheets do not include untagged inventory items.

4. The accuracy of perpetual inventory records may be established, in part, by comparing perpetual inventory records with
   a. Purchase requisitions.
   b. Receiving reports.
   c. Purchase orders.
   d. Vendor payments.

5. An auditor will usually trace the details of the test counts made during the observation of the physical inventory taking to a final inventory schedule. This audit procedure is undertaken to provide evidence that items physically present and observed by the auditor at the time of the physical inventory count are
   a. Owned by the client.
   b. Not obsolete.
   c. Physically present at the time of the preparation of the final inventory schedule.
   d. Included in the final inventory schedule.

6. In verifying the amount of goodwill recorded by a client, the most convincing evidence that an auditor can obtain is by comparing the recorded value of assets acquired with the
   a. Assessed value as evidenced by tax bills.
   b. Seller's book value as evidenced by financial statements.
   c. Insured value as evidenced by insurance policies.
   d. Appraised value as evidenced by independent appraisals.

7. In violation of company policy, Lowell Company erroneously capitalized the cost of painting its warehouse. The auditor examining Lowell's financial statements would most likely detect this when
   a. Discussing capitalization policies with Lowell's controller.
   b. Examining maintenance expense accounts.
   c. Observing, during the physical inventory, that the warehouse had been painted.
   d. Examining the construction work orders supporting items capitalized during the year.

8. Which of the following is the best audit procedure for determining the existence of unrecorded liabilities?

    a. Examine confirmation requests returned by creditors whose accounts appear on a subsidiary trial balance of accounts payable.

    b. Examine unusual relationships between monthly accounts payable balances and recorded purchases.

    c. Examine a sample of invoices a few days prior to and subsequent to year end to ascertain whether they have been properly recorded.

    d. Examine a sample of cash disbursements in the period subsequent to year end.

9. An auditor who selects a sample of items from the vouchers payable register for the last month of the period under audit and traces these items to underlying documents is gathering evidence primarily in support of the assertion that

    a. Recorded obligations were paid.

    b. Incurred obligations were recorded in the correct period.

    c. Recorded obligations were valid.

    d. Cash disbursements were recorded as incurred obligations.

10. Which of the following accounts should be reviewed by the auditor to gain reasonable assurance that additions to property, plant, and equipment are not understated?

    a. Depreciation.

    b. Accounts payable.

    c. Cash.

    d. Repairs.

11. Which of the following procedures is *least* likely to be performed before the balance sheet date?

    a. Testing of internal control over cash.

    b. Confirmation of receivables.

    c. Search for unrecorded liabilities.

    d. Observation of inventory.

12. Which of the following most likely would be detected by an auditor's review of a client's sales cutoff?

    a. Unrecorded sales for the year.

    b. Lapping of year-end accounts receivable.

    c. Excessive sales discounts.

    d. Unauthorized goods returned for credit.

13. A client maintains perpetual inventory records in both quantities and dollars. If the assessed level of control risk is high, an auditor would probably

    a. Insist that the client perform physical counts of inventory items several times during the year.

    b. Apply gross profit tests to ascertain the reasonableness of the physical counts.

    c. Increase the extent of tests of controls of the inventory cycle.

    d. Request the client to schedule the physical inventory count at the end of the year.

ESSAY QUESTIONS AND PROBLEMS

13.1 Simon Pierce, an independent auditor, was engaged to examine the financial statements of Mayfair Construction, Inc., for the year ended December 31, 1993. Mayfair's financial statements reflect a substantial amount of mobile construction equipment used in the firm's operations. The equipment is accounted for in a subsidiary ledger. Pierce performed a study and evaluation of Mayfair's control structure policies and procedures and found them to be satisfactory.

Required:
Identify the substantive audit procedures that Pierce should utilize in examining mobile construction equipment and related depreciation in Mayfair's financial statements. (AICPA adapted)

13.2 Carole Taylor, a CPA, is engaged in the audit of Rex Wholesaling for the year ended December 31, 1992. Taylor performed a proper study of control structure policies and procedures relating to the purchasing, receiving, trade accounts payable, and cash disbursement cycles and has decided not to test control procedures further. Based on analytical procedures, Taylor believes that the trade accounts payable balance on the balance sheet as of December 31, 1992 may be understated.

Taylor requested and obtained a client-prepared trade accounts payable schedule listing the total amount owed to each vendor.

Required:
What additional substantive audit procedures should Taylor apply in examining the trade accounts payable? (AICPA adapted)

13.3 Charles Decker, a CPA, is performing an examination of the financial statements of Allright Wholesale Sales, Inc., for the year ended December 31, 1991. Allright has been in business for many years and has never had its financial statements audited. Decker has gained satisfaction with respect to the ending inventory and is considering alternative audit procedures to gain satisfaction with respect to management's representations concerning the beginning inventory, which was not observed.

Allright sells only one product, bottle brand X beer, and maintains perpetual inventory records. In addition, Allright takes physical inventory counts monthly. Decker has already confirmed purchases with the manufacturer and has decided to concentrate on evaluating the reliability of perpetual inventory records and applying analytical procedures to the extent that prior years' unaudited records will enable such procedures to be performed.

Required:
What audit tests, including analytical procedures, should Decker apply in evaluating the reliability of perpetual inventory records and gaining satisfaction with respect to the January 1, 1991 inventory? (AICPA adapted)

13.4 During an audit engagement, Roberta Harper, a CPA, has satisfactorily completed an examination of accounts payable and other liabilities and now plans to determine whether there are any loss contingencies arising from litigation, claims, or assessments.

Required:
What audit procedures should Harper follow with respect to the existence of loss contingencies arising from litigation, claims, and assessments? Do not discuss reporting requirements. (AICPA adapted)

13.5 Ace Corporation does not conduct a complete annual physical count of purchased parts and supplies in its principal warehouse, but uses statistical sampling instead to estimate the year-end inventory. Ace maintains a perpetual inventory record of parts and supplies and believes that statistical sampling is highly effective in determining inventory values and is sufficiently reliable to preclude a physical count of each item of inventory.

Required:
a. Identify which audit procedures should be used by the independent auditor that change or are in addition to those normally required when a client utilizes statistical sampling to determine inventory value and does not conduct a 100 percent annual physical count of inventory items.
b. List at least 10 normal audit procedures that should be performed to verify physical quantities whenever a client conducts a periodic physical count of all or part of its inventory. (AICPA adapted)

13.6 Consider the following audit objectives:
  1. Existence and completeness
  2. Rights and obligations
  3. Valuation
  4. Presentation and disclosure.

These objectives have varying degrees of importance when related to specific parts of transaction cycles. Assuming that circumstances suggest a "balanced audit" approach, as described in Chapter 12, identify the most critical objective for each of the following parts of the expenditure cycle:
a. Purchases, production, and inventories
b. Plant assets
c. Intangible assets
d. Current liabilities and operating expenses.

Justify your choice in each instance.

13.7 You are the in-charge auditor for the Joblin, Inc. examination. Joblin manufactures commercial pumps, primarily for industrial applications. In observing the taking of the year-end inventory by Joblin personnel, you noted the following:
a. All inventories, except for work-in-process which is minor, are housed in the central warehouse.
b. Inventory tags are prenumbered and show description and quantity of inventory. They were attached upon counting and removed only upon authorization by the independent auditors. The tags were issued to the two-man count teams and each number series issued was recorded by the plant superintendent on a control sheet.
c. Although the auditors did not test count one of the six finished goods bays, they walked through the area, accompanied by the plant superintendent, to ensure that all goods were tagged.
d. Inasmuch as no provision was made for auditor's copies of the inventory tags, the auditors recorded all of their test counts on inventory count sheets (part of the audit workpapers).
e. No provision was made by the client for double-checking the original inventory counts.
f. At the end of the inventory taking and observation, the auditors did not consider it feasible to account for all of the issued and unissued inventory tags. They did have the client furnish them with a copy of the control sheet maintained by the superintendent.

Required:

a. Comment on the effectiveness of the inventory taking by Joblin and the inventory observation by the auditors.

b. Consistent with your answer to (a), list any added substantive audit procedures that you would recommend.

13.8 In examining Exhibit 13.8, a worksheet for machinery and equipment, you note that the audit legends are not explained. List the legends and identify the audit procedures represented by each.

13.9 In conducting the search for unrecorded liabilities, Joel Green, senior auditor on the Grambley Wholesalers audit, performed the following procedures. He obtained the client's year-end adjustment for unrecorded invoices vouchered in the following accounting period, vouched to underlying documentation, and traced to general ledger accounts; He also obtained a client representation letter.

Required:

a. Identify the audit objective(s) served by the search for unrecorded liabilities, and discuss its overall significance.

b. Assuming the auditors judged Grambley's internal control over purchases and accounts payable to be acceptable, what added procedures should Joel Green apply? Explain the reason(s) for each procedure recommended.

EXHIBIT 13.8   Problem 13.8 Worksheet

WP C.2

Laurlee, Inc.
Machinery & Equipment
12/31/93

Prepared by: lfk
Date: 1/23/94
Reviewed by: jcf
Date: 1/29/94

	M & E	*Accum. Depr.*	*Gain/(Loss)*
12/31/92 Final Balances	$1,234,600 *	$658,900 *	
Additions:			
Stable Press	126,000 @		
Computer Controlled Welder	267,8890 @		
Disposals:			
Tracer Bed	(174,000) ^	(152,000) ^	8,000 !
1993 Depreciation		226,500 !	
12/31/93 Final Balances	$1,454,490 &	$733,400 &	$8,000&
	f	f	f
	To WP C	To WP C	To WP C

13.10 You have been engaged for the audit of Hedley Distributors for the year ended December 31, 1993. Hedley is engaged in the wholesale auto parts business. All sales are made at cost plus 50 percent of cost. Hedley maintains perpetual inventory records and adjusts the records annually after taking a physical inventory.

Shown in Exhibit 13.9 are portions of Hedley's sales and inventory accounts for tires, the single most important (35 percent of total sales) product handled by the firm.

You observed the physical inventory and are satisfied that it was taken properly. The tire inventory is located in two adjacent bays in the company's central warehouse.

When performing a sales and purchases cutoff test, you found that at December 31, 1993, the last receiving report used was #1486. Moreover, you determined that no shipments had been made on any shipping orders with numbers larger than #837.

You also obtained the following information:

a. Included in the physical inventory at December 31, 1993, were tires that had been purchased and received on receiving report #1483, but for which an invoice was not received until 1994. The cost was $12,360.

EXHIBIT 13.9   Problem 13.10 Tire Sales and Inventory Accounts

Tire Sales

Date	Reference	Amount	Date	Reference	Amount
12/31	Closing entry	$11,419,800		Balance forward	$11,250,000
			12/27	SO 834	12,300
			12/28	SO 835	32,800
			12/28	SO 836	14,600
			12/31	SO 837	43,200
			12/31	SO 838	23,800
			12/31	SO 839	34,100
			12/31	SO 840	9,000
		$11,419,800			$11,419,800

Tire Inventory

Date	Reference	Amount	Date	Reference	Amount
	Balance forward	$780,680	12/31	Adjustment to physcial	$ 127,240
12/28	RR #1482	5,600			
12/30	RR #1484	19,300			
12/31	RR #1485	9,460			
12/31	RR #1486	12,200			

b. In the warehouse at December 31, 1993, were tires that had been sold and paid for by the customer, but that were not shipped until 1994. They were all sold on sales invoice/shipping order #834. The tires were not included in the physical inventory.

c. On the evening of December 31, 1993, two cars were on the Hedley Company siding. Both cars contained tires that were not included in the 12/31/93 physical inventory: Car #SA877560 was unloaded on January 2, 1994, and received on receiving report #1486. The freight was paid by the vendor. Car #EE455621 was loaded and sealed on December 31, 1993, and, inasmuch as the freight was paid by the customer, title did not pass until the car was switched off the company's siding on January 2, 1994. The sale price was $43,200. This order was sold on sales invoice/shipping order #837.

d. Temporarily stranded on a railroad siding at December 31, 1993, were two cars of tires en route to Goodgood Tires of Omaha. They were sold on sales invoice/shipping order #835 and the terms were F.O.B. destination.

e. En route to Hedley Distributors on December 31, 1993, was a truckload of tires that was received on receiving report #1487. The tires were shipped F.O.B. destination and freight of $1,130 was paid by Hedley. However, the freight was deducted from the purchase price of $22,160.

f. Included in the physical inventory were tires damaged by excessive heat in transit and deemed unsalable. Their invoice cost was $13,050, and freight charges of $885 had been paid on the tires.

Required:

a. Calculate the corrected physical inventory at 12/31/93.

b. Draft the auditor's adjustments that are required as of 12/31/93.

c. Comment on any control weaknesses indicated by these procedures.

13.11 Kane, CPA, is auditing Star Wholesaling Company's financial statements and is about to perform substantive audit procedures on Star's trade accounts payable balances. After obtaining an understanding of Star's internal control structure for accounts payable, Kane assessed control risk at near the maximum. Kane requested and received from Star a schedule of the trade accounts payable prepared using the trade accounts payable subsidiary ledger (voucher register).

Required:

Describe the substantive audit procedures Kane should apply to Star's trade accounts payable balances. Do *not* include procedures that would be applied only in the audit of related-party payables, amounts withheld from employees, and accrued expenses such as pensions and interest.

(AICPA adapted)

13.12 Bell, CPA, was engaged to audit the financial statements of Kent Company, a continuing audit client. Bell is about to audit Kent's payroll transactions. Kent uses an in-house payroll department to compute payroll data and prepare and distribute payroll checks.

During the planning process, Bell determined that the inherent risk of overstatement of payroll expense is high. In addition, Bell obtained an understanding of the internal control structure and assessed control risk at the maximum level for payroll-related assertions.

Required:

Describe the audit procedures Bell should consider performing in the audit of Kent's payroll transactions to address the risk of overstatement. Do *not* discuss Kent's internal control structure. (AICPA adapted)

13.13 The purpose of all auditing procedures is to gather sufficient competent evidence for an auditor to form an opinion regarding the financial statements taken as a whole.

Required:

a. In addition to the example below, identify and describe five means or techniques of gathering audit evidence used to evaluate a client's inventory balance.

Technique	*Description*
Observation	An auditor watches the performance of some functions, such as a client's annual inventory count.

b. Identify the five general assertions regarding a client's inventory balance and describe one *different* substantive auditing procedure for each assertion. Use the format illustrated below.

Assertion   *Substantive Auditing Procedure*

(AICPA adapted)

13.14 Crazy Eddie, Inc., a company operating 42 electronics stores in eastern United States, had reported significant gains in sales and earnings since going public in 1984. At that time, the company raised $124 million by issuing subordinated debenture bonds and capital stock. Bear, Stearns & Co. and Salomon Brothers, Inc. were among the underwriters for these securities issues. According to Eddie Antar, the firm's founder, chief executive officer, and principal stockholder, Crazy Eddie's success resulted from rapid expansion of its electronics stores, skillful sales floor techniques, and lively commercials. An investigation by the Securities and Exchange Commission and third-party legal proceedings, however, revealed the sales and earnings growth to be, for the most part, fabricated. Reported profits of $33 million for the combined fiscal years ending February 28, 1984–1987 were followed by a loss of $109 million in 1988. The 1988 loss included items that should have been charged to prior years, but neither the new management nor the auditors could reasonably determine the years to which specific charges applied.

The fraud was effected by inflating inventories by $65 million and understating accounts payable by approximately $10 million. The inventory overstatement was accomplished by fabricating count sheets for nonexistent inventory; by including goods in inventory which had already been recorded as purchases returns and were awaiting shipment back to vendors; and by including unrecorded inventories in stores prior to physical inventory counts and auditor observation of such counts. That is, the purchases had not been recorded, but the goods were included in the ending inventory.

Sales were also inflated by including in a given store's sales goods that were shipped to other stores. Sales growth at new stores was a key success indicator emphasized by financial analysts promoting Crazy Eddie stock and debentures.

Required:

a. What, in your opinion, should the auditors' responsibility have been for detecting the Crazy Eddie fraud?

b. What procedures might the auditors have applied that would have enabled them to detect the fraud?

13.15 During the audit of the building and land accounts, you notice that one of the buildings was sold last year for a very large profit. The sale of this one property was authorized by the board of directors. The in-charge auditor did not understand why the profit was so large and, therefore, instructs you to determine which one or more of the land or building properties was sold.

You are considering the following procedures:

1. Checking the depreciation schedule to determine which properties are still being depreciated.

2. Physically inspect and photograph all properties.

3. Inspecting the tax receipts for each property.

4. Inspecting the taxing authority records for title to the properties.

5. Inspecting the property insurance policies.

Required:

Identify the one best procedure above as evidence of which property or properties were sold. Defend the choice by identifying the major strengths of your choice and the major weakness in the other procedures. Please identify your answer with 1, 2, 3, 4, and 5 corresponding to the above procedures.

(IIA adapted)

13.16 In conjunction with the initial audit of a new client, the audit team has audited the accounts payable of the company. The reported accounts payable balance was $1,750,000 and represented the cost of purchases from outside suppliers for goods and services used in regular operations.

The following tests were performed with data gathered as follows:

a. Reviewed internal controls over accounts payable. Auditors read the accounting policy manuals, familiarized themselves with the general ledger system, observed the accounts payable activity, walked several transactions through the accounting system (from purchase requisition through receipt to initial recording), and completed the internal control questionnaire after interviewing management.

b. Selected a sample of entries in accounts payable and vouched the entries to supporting documents (purchase requisition, purchase order, and receiving report).

c. Obtained a schedule of accounts payable, by supplier. Footed this schedule and agreed it to the general ledger and financial statement balances.

d. Performed a cut-off test. Verified the same cut-off for both inventory and accounts payable by tracing receipt of goods to inventory records and accounts payable subsidiary ledger.

e. Reviewed supporting documentation for selected accounts payable to ascertain whether any items were of special character requiring reclassification. Tests of authorization and valuation were also performed.

f. Confirmed accounts payable with small or zero balances. Differences were then investigated and resolved.

g. Prepared an aging schedule of accounts payable.

Required:

Using the format presented below, identify the various items of evidence (not audit steps) included in ''a'' through ''g'' and classify each item of evidence by type. Note that there may be more than one item of evidence in each of the tests listed above.

Evidence	*Classification*
Example:	Hearsay
Internal control questionnaire	

(IIA adapted)

13.17 Chambers Development Company sent its 1991 profits plummeting to $1.5 million after taking a $27 million after-tax charge against earnings. Chambers is a waste management concern in the business of obtaining landfill permits, collecting waste for deposit in the landfills, and treating the landfills. Until the special charge, Chambers had followed the practice of deferring certain indirect costs related to new landfills. Unlike other companies in the industry (Browning-Ferris Industries, Inc., Waste Management, Inc., Sanifill, Inc., and Laidlaw, Inc.), Chambers considered itself a development stage company and thereby justified deferring such costs as executive salaries related to time spent on new landfills, public relations costs, legal fees, and executive travel. For 1991, however, Richard Knight, Chambers' chief financial officer and former partner with Grant Thornton, Chambers' independent accountants, determined that the company was now an operational, rather than a development stage enterprise. Therefore, the change in accounting principle from deferral to expensing of indirect costs was made. Charles Fallon, the Grant Thornton partner in charge of the Chambers audit concurred with the change. Indeed, Grant Thornton refused to render an unqualified audit opinion unless Chambers made the change.

When the change was announced, Chambers' Class B stock fell 62 percent, from $19 to $11.50 per share. Following the drop in reported earnings, the board of directors, in a special meeting, decided to rescind all executive bonuses for 1991.

Required:

a. Comment on the appropriateness of Chambers' practice of cost deferral as a ''development stage enterprise.'' Cite appropriate authoritative pronouncements to support your position.

b. Why do you suppose the auditors agreed with the practice prior to 1991? Does this case raise any ethical issues? Explain.

APPENDIX

Auditing Objectives and Procedures: Expenditure Cycle

PURCHASES, PRODUCTION, AND INVENTORIES

Audit Objectives	Audit Evidence and Procedures

Existence and Completeness

Do inventories exist?

Documentary Evidence

- Review inventory taking instructions for such matters as:
  1. Timing and location of inventory taking.
  2. Counting procedures.
  3. How counts are documented (tags, sheets, cards, etc.).
  4. Arrangement of obsolete inventory and consignments in.
  5. Control over production during inventory.

Physical Evidence

- Observe physical inventory taking:
  1. Test count and compare with sheets or tags.
  2. Keep record of test counts for later comparison with final inventory listings.
  3. Control movements within areas to be tested.
  4. Account for numeric sequence of tags or sheets, and control auditor's copies.
  5. Note possible obsolescence or overstocking (mark tags or listings for later follow up on final audit).
  6. Note environmental conditions as to arrangement and security over areas.
  7. Note stage of completion for work in progress.
  8. Verify that consigned in goods are not inventoried.
  9. Include loading docks and receiving areas in inventory observation.

Confirmation Evidence

- Confirm goods in public warehouses and goods out on consignment.

Rights, Obligations, and Valuation

Documentary Evidence

- Test for proper cutoff:

Are inventories owned by the client?

Are inventories properly valued at lower of cost or market?

Are inventory transactions recorded in the proper accounting period?

1. During inventory observation, record document numbers of last receiving report, sales invoice, shipping order, and bill of lading.

2. During inventory observation, trace substance (goods) to receiving area or shipping area.

3. On final audit trace to purchase and sales records (should be last entry of the year).

4. Examine documents for a few days before and after balance sheet date (especially sales invoices, sales orders, shippers, and bills of lading; receiving reports, vouchers, and freight bills) and determine when title passed.

5. Trace both ways, documents to accounting records for errors of omission and accounting records to documents for errors of commission.

- Examine inventory adjustment to determine that book inventory has been properly adjusted to physical inventory.

- Test pricing of final inventory:

  1. Cost accounting system will have been examined as part of control testing during interim audit.

  2. Trace final inventory prices to audited price lists; audited materials price lists should include a charge for freight and be exclusive of discount; finished goods price lists ordinarily assume the form of audited standard cost records; and work in progress, given stage of completion, should be traced to audited routing sheets that accumulate costs by stage of production.

  3. Perform lower of cost or market value test.

  4. Determine proper valuation of goods appearing on tags or sheets marked "obsolete" or "slow moving."

- Trace auditor's copies of tags or sheets to final inventory listings:

  1. Both counted and not counted.

  2. To determine that client has not added digits, tags, or sheets.

- Scan final inventory listings for large dollar amounts and trace related quantities to auditor's copies of tags or count sheets to detect significant inventory inflation errors.

Mathematical Evidence

- Test extensions and footings:

  1. Include most large value items and sample remainder.

  2. Use computer to assist in this procedure.

Analytical Evidence

- Use the "gross profit" method to estimate ending inventory:
  1. Compare with audited inventory.
  2. Investigate further if this procedure produces wide variance.

Presentation and Disclosure

Hearsay Evidence

- Inquire about obsolescence.
- Inquire about pledging.
- Inquire about consigned goods.
- Inquire about cutoff.
- Inquire about inventory held for use or consumption rather than for manufacture or resale.

PLANT ASSETS

Audit Objectives

Audit Evidence and Procedures

Existence and Completeness

Physical Evidence

Do recorded additions exist?

Have existing additions been recorded?

Have retirements been recorded?

- Inspect major additions—especially if internal control over plant assets is weak.

Analytical Evidence

- Compare depreciation expense and maintenance and repairs with prior year and with budgeted amounts and account for major changes:
  1. Increase in depreciation may denote additions to plant assets (decrease may denote retirements).
  2. Increase in maintenance and repairs expense may be the result of plant asset additions having been erroneously expensed (decrease may be indicative of ordinary repairs having been erroneously capitalized).
  3. A favorable maintenance and repair expense budget variance also suggests possible capitalization of ordinary repairs.

Hearsay Evidence

- Examine plant ledger for fully depreciated assets:
  1. Inquire as to status.
  2. If no longer in use, or disposed of, an entry is needed to remove.

Documentary Evidence

- Vouch repairs and maintenance accounts along with plant assets:
  1. The audit objective is to locate possible misclassifications (plant assets debited to repairs expense or ordinary repairs debited to plant assets).
  2. Vouch major expenditures and test the remainder.

Valuation and Ownership

Are all assets valued at historical cost less accumulated depreciation?

Mathematical Evidence

- Prepare a lead schedule of plant assets and accumulated depreciation by major classes:
  1. Should reflect beginning balances, additions, disposals, and ending balances.
  2. Should be classified according to major categories of plant assets (e.g., land, buildings, equipment, autos and trucks, leasehold improvements, leased assets, and office equipment).

- Reconcile subsidiary ledger with controlling accounts and agree to ending balances appearing on plant assets lead schedule.
- Evaluate appropriateness and consistency of depreciation method(s).
- Recalculate depreciation and gain or loss on disposals.
- Calculate change in deferred taxes related to temporary differences between book and tax depreciation.
- For self-constructed assets, recalculate:
  1. Overhead allocation; and
  2. Interest during construction, if applicable.

Have expenditures been properly classified as to asset vs. expense?

Documentary Evidence

- Vouch plant asset additions and disposals, along with repairs and maintenance accounts, on a test basis:
  1. Examine vendors' invoices and freight bills for purchased assets.
  2. Examine work orders for constructed assets.
  3. Trace receipts from disposals to bank statement.
  4. Compare method of recording depreciation in year of acquisition and disposal with company policy for consistency.
- Examine directors' minutes and purchase and sale agreements for proper authorization and accounting for major acquisitions and disposals.

Presentation and Disclosure	Hearsay Evidence

Hearsay Evidence

- Inquire as to assets not used in production:
  1. Standby.
  2. Awaiting disposal.
  3. Held for investment purposes.

Documentary Evidence

Have financing leases been properly capitalized?

- Examine all lease agreements and determine proper classification as to financing versus operating.
- Examine loan agreements for possible pledging of plant assets as collateral.

Mathematical Evidence

- Evaluate appropriateness of discount rate used in calculating net present value of minimum lease payments.
- Recalculate minimum lease payments for financing leases.
- Recalculate contingent rentals on a test basis.

INTANGIBLE ASSETS (PATENTS, COPYRIGHTS, TRADEMARKS, FRANCHISES, GOODWILL, ETC.)

Audit Objectives	Audit Evidence and Procedures

Existence and Completeness

Documentary Evidence

Do recorded intangible assets exist?

- Examine documentation supporting intangible assets:
  1. Patents, copyrights, and trademarks.
  2. Franchise and merger agreements.
- Vouch additions and disposals:
  1. Include research and development expense.
  2. Possibility of purchased intangibles being debited to research and development expense and/or research and development expenses debited to intangible asset accounts.
- Examine minutes for proper authorization of acquisitions and disposals.

Analytical Evidence

- Apply analytical procedures to amortization expense and R&D by comparing with prior year and with budgeted amounts and investigate material changes and/or variances.

Valuation and Ownership

Are purchased intangible assets properly recorded at acquisition cost less accumulated amortization?

Documentary Evidence

- Vouch additions and disposals on a test basis:
  1. Examine agreements.
  2. Examine canceled checks.
  3. Be particularly alert to the possibility of capitalized R&D or related-party transactions.
  4. Be alert also to possible recognition of initial franchise fees as revenue before earned or realized.
  5. Trace receipts from disposals to bank statements.

Have research and development expenditures been charged to expense in accordance with GAAP?

Mathematical Evidence

- Recalculate gain or loss on disposal.
- Evaluate appropriateness of amortization period, and recalculate amortization on a test basis.

Presentation and Disclosure

Do reported intangibles possess future economic benefit?

Analytical Evidence

- Evaluate future economic benefit by relating assets to revenue produced by them.
- Compare research and development expense with prior year and investigate major changes (may be the result of errors in classifying expenditures).

Hearsay Evidence

- Inquire of management and legal counsel as to possible contingencies relating to intangible assets (e.g., patent infringement suits).

CURRENT LIABILITIES

Audit Objectives

Existence and Completeness

Audit Evidence and Procedures

Confirmation Evidence

- Obtain lawyer's letter to identify contingencies requiring adjustment or footnote disclosure.
- Examine bank confirmation for loans.

Documentary Evidence

Are all significant liabilities reflected on the balance sheet?

* Search for unrecorded liabilities:
    1. Examine paid and unpaid invoices for a short period following the balance sheet date, and determine that recording took place in the proper period.
    2. Trace to client's year-end adjustment for unrecorded liabilities.
    3. Examine loan agreements for possible existence of imputed interest.

Analytical Evidence

* Compare year-end accruals with prior year, and account for significant changes or omissions.

Hearsay Evidence

* Inquire as to contingencies.
* Obtain client representation letter.

Valuation

Are management's estimates reasonable?

Mathematical Evidence

* Recompute the following, as applicable, on a test basis:
    1. Interest accruals.
    2. Tax accruals.
    3. Liability for product warranty.
    4. Pension cost and liability.
    5. Vacation pay.
    6. Profit sharing and bonus.

Presentation and Disclosure

Documentary Evidence

* Determine that contingent liabilities are properly disclosed.

Analytical Evidence

Have significant contingencies been properly reflected?

* Examine prior year's financial statements for possible footnote disclosures required in the current year's statements.

14 Substantive Audit Testing: Financing and Investing Cycle

CHAPTER OUTLINE

I. **Introduction**
  A. Types of transactions in financing and investing cycle
    1. Investing transactions
    2. Borrowing transactions
    3. Stockholders' equity transactions
  B. Summary of processing steps in financing and investing cycle

II. **Investing transactions**
  A. Audit objectives
  B. Audit evidence and procedures
  C. Summary audit program

III. **Borrowing transactions**
  A. Audit objectives
  B. Audit evidence and procedures
  C. Summary audit program

IV. **Stockholders' equity transactions**
  A. Audit objectives
  B. Audit evidence and procedures
  C. Summary audit program

V. **Audit risk analysis and the financing and investing cycle**
  A. Search for related-party transactions
  B. Loan defaults and violations of restrictive covenants
  C. Disposal of a segment

VI. **Completing the audit**
  A. Analytical procedures as part of audit review
  B. Further materiality considerations
  C. Subsequent events
  D. Statement of cash flows
  E. Workpaper review
  F. Open items
  G. Auditor/client conference
  H. Communication with audit committee
  I. Client representation letter
  J. Communication of internal control structure related matters

VII. **Appendix: Auditing objectives and procedures: Financing and investing cycle**

OVERVIEW

This chapter discusses substantive testing of the financing and investing cycle. This part of the audit process is depicted in Figure 14.1. The discussion is presented in three parts:

1. Investing transactions;
2. Borrowing transactions; and
3. Stockholders' equity transactions

As in Chapters 12 and 13, a summary of control points is enumerated, followed by a flowchart. Audit objectives are then identified for each part of the transaction cycle. This is followed by considering audit evidence and procedures available for meeting the objectives. A more detailed consideration of audit objectives, evidence, and procedures is contained in the appendix following this chapter.

The chapter emphasizes testing investments for overstatement and liabilities for understatement. Accordingly, attention is given to such procedures as examining or confirming securities, reading loan agreements and directors' minutes, and recalculating accruals. Disclosure of details surrounding debt agreements and stockholders' equity transactions is also stressed.

The audit risk analysis section of the chapter leads off with the identification and examination of related-party transactions. Inasmuch as related-party transactions occur more frequently within the financing and investing cycle, the chapter covers this topic in depth.

The chapter concludes by addressing those steps necessary for completing the audit field work. Of particular importance, and therefore the lead topics in that section, are the need to apply analytical procedures as part of overall audit review, possible modification of materiality thresholds based on audited financial data, and the search for subsequent events.

STUDY OBJECTIVES

After reading this chapter, you should be able to:

1. Identify specific audit objectives related to the financing and investing cycle
2. Develop audit programs for the financing and investing cycle that relate audit procedures to audit objectives for each component of the cycle, and include procedures for identifying related parties and auditing related-party transactions and procedures for locating type I and type II subsequent events
3. Modify audit programs, as necessary, in light of warning signs that surface during a study of the business and industry, application of analytical procedures, or the study and evaluation of internal control structure policies and procedures.

FIGURE 14.1   The Audit Process

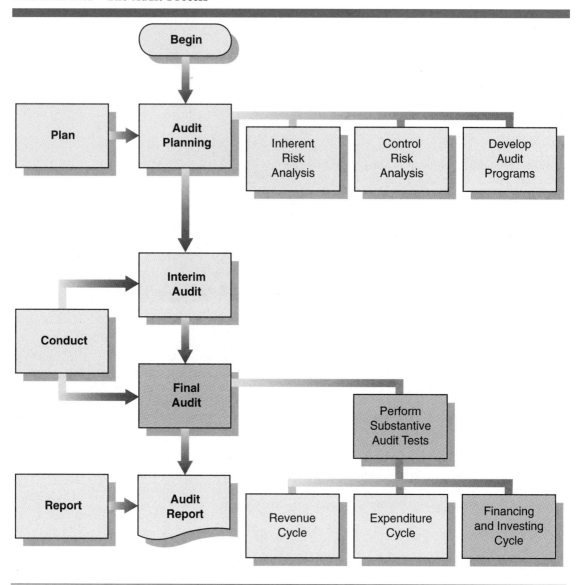

Types of Transactions in Financing and Investing Cycle

The financing and investing cycle includes the following sets of transactions:

1. Investing transactions:
   a. Lending to others, interest revenue, and notes receivable balances;
   b. Acquisitions and disposals of financial assets, including marketable equity securities (long-term and short-term), investments in bonds, interest revenue, and gain/loss on disposals;
   c. Investments in other assets (e.g., real estate) not held for operating purposes.

2. Borrowing transactions:
   a. Borrowing from others, including bonds and mortgages payable;
   b. Liability under capital leases;
   c. Deferred taxes arising from depreciation timing differences;
   d. Interest expense and liability related to borrowing transactions.

3. Stockholders' equity transactions:
   a. Cash and stock dividends, and retained earnings balances;
   b. Stock issues, stock retirements, capital stock balances, and treasury stock transactions and balances;
   c. Stock options and earnings per share.

Summary of Processing Steps in Financing and Investing Cycle

Figure 14.2 is a flowchart summarizing the processing steps typically included in the financing and investing cycle. The essential control points, as more fully described in the appendix following Chapter 7, are as follows:

Borrowing and Investing Transactions

1. Borrowing and investing transactions should be properly authorized, and authority should be clearly defined in policy and procedures manuals;

2. Control procedures should provide that borrowing and investing transactions in excess of specified amounts be authorized by the board of directors;

3. Cash receipts from borrowing and investing transactions should be subject to the same control procedures as for the revenue cycle;

4. Monthly interest accruals should be provided for by standard journal entries or journal vouchers to prevent inadvertent omission of necessary adjustments;

5. Disbursements for loans to others, and interest and principal payments should be supported by properly approved vouchers to support proper authorization and approval.

Stockholders' Equity Transactions

1. Provision should be made for board of director approval of all stockholders' equity transactions;

2. Cash receipts from stock issuance should be subject to the same control as other cash receipts;

FIGURE 14.2   Financing and Investing Cycle—Summary of Processing Steps

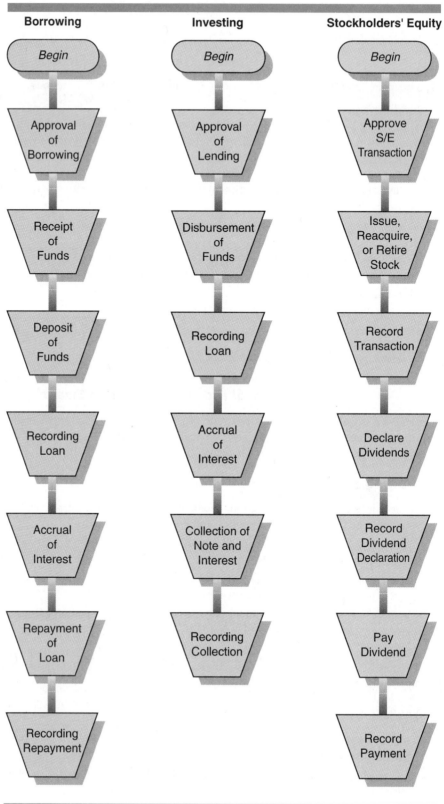

3. Disbursements for reacquisition of stock should be controlled in the same manner as other cash disbursements;

4. Imprest accounts should be used for paying dividends.

As in Chapters 12 and 13, Chapter 14 addresses audit objectives first, followed by a discussion of audit evidence and procedures. This is followed by an analysis of audit risk associated with the financing and investing cycle. Particular attention is given to locating related-party transactions, violations of restrictive covenants, and loan defaults. Attention is also directed to the increase in audit risk in the event of disposal of a segment of the client's business.

INVESTING TRANSACTIONS
Audit Objectives

Existence and Completeness

The auditor must determine that all marketable securities represented in the client's investment records exist (existence). The auditor must also verify that the client's investment records include all securities examined (completeness).

Rights and Obligations

The auditor must verify the ownership of securities included in the investment records. If the client is holding the securities as collateral for outstanding loans receivable, they are not owned and should not be represented as such. If the client *does* own the securities, but they have been pledged as collateral on outstanding loans payable, this fact needs to be disclosed in the financial statements.

Valuation

In testing financial assets for proper valuation, the auditor must determine compliance with the following measurement standards:

1. Marketable equity securities must be valued at the lower of cost or market-aggregate portfolio, as of the balance sheet date: unrealized losses and recoveries on short-term securities are to be included in the income statement; unrealized losses and recoveries on long-term securities are reported in the stockholders' equity section of the balance sheet.

2. The equity method of accounting should be applied to certain investments in unconsolidated subsidiaries.

3. Accrued interest and declared dividends on investments should be recognized as of the balance sheet date.

4. Discounts or premiums on long-term investments in bonds should be amortized. The effective interest method should be used unless straight-line amortization produces an immaterial difference.

5. Realized gains or losses on disposals should be recognized in the income statement.

6. Other securities investments should be carried at cost unless declines in market are considered permanent.

7. Notes receivable should be carried at net realizable value and estimated losses from uncollectible notes receivable should be reflected in the income statement.

Presentation

Of critical importance is how to classify securities investments in the balance sheet. In deciding whether securities are to be classified as current or noncurrent assets, the auditor should consider marketability and management intent. Both conditions must be satisfied in order for the securities to be classified as current assets; that is, they must be readily marketable, and management must intend to hold them for the short term only.

The income statement should report income from interest and dividends, except for dividends on stock accounted for under the equity method, as other income. Dividends on stock accounted for under the equity method should be reflected as an investment recovery.

Disclosure

In addition to the investment amount, the financial statements should clearly present the following information either in the body of the statements or in footnotes:

1. Method of valuation;
2. Pledging, if any;
3. Realized and unrealized gains and losses and recoveries;
4. The percent ownership of stock in affiliated companies;
5. The market value of all financial instruments.

In addition, the footnotes should clearly disclose details surrounding transactions with related parties. Finally, the annual report should include the financial position and operations of unconsolidated subsidiaries accounted for by the equity method.

The following paragraphs develop the means for acquiring evidence supporting these objectives.

Audit Evidence and Procedures

Physical Examination

The auditor usually examines securities in the client's possession to verify existence and ownership. As part of this procedure, the auditor should exercise control over all negotiable securities, cash on hand, and cash funds on the premises. Such simultaneous control prevents client substitution of cash or securities to conceal shortages.

In the **examination of securities,** the auditor should record serial numbers for later comparison with the investment records. If securities have been misappropriated, the investment records will contain securities that are no longer owned by the client. Temporary substitution of similar securities for the missing securities is one way of concealing the shortage. Comparison of serial numbers, as recorded in the investment records, with those appearing on the securities examined will reveal the substitution.

Determining that the securities are registered in the name of the client and noting evidence of pledging as loan collateral are also a necessary part of the physical examination of securities.

Confirmation

Confirmation of securities not on the premises (held in safekeeping or by a broker) is an acceptable alternative to physical examination in most instances. The auditor must request information as to name of investee, number of shares or par value of bonds, registered name of owner, and serial numbers.

If the investment in securities not on the premises is substantial, the auditor may elect to examine rather than confirm them.

In addition to confirming securities not on the premises, the auditor should confirm notes receivable with the makers of the notes. The confirmation request should cover the details of the notes as well as collateral requirements and defaults on interest or principal if applicable in the circumstances.

Documentary Evidence

The auditor should trace from the count sheets, prepared as part of the physical examination of securities, to the investment records. Comparison of serial numbers, as just noted, will assist in detecting the substitution of similar securities for missing ones. Tracing in the opposite direction, from the investment records to the count sheets, reveals shortages not covered by substitution or other means.

The auditor, on a test basis, should vouch additions and disposals of securities by reference to the underlying documentation. Brokers' advices, remittance advices, and canceled checks are representative of such documentation.

Correctness of recorded dividends may be ascertained by reference to one of the dividend reporters (*Standard & Poor's* or *Moody's*). Although the client may elect to accrue dividends that have been declared by the investee corporation, the auditor must determine, by reference to last year's working papers, that this practice has been applied consistently.

Transactions with affiliates should be carefully audited for two reasons:

1. They constitute **related-party transactions** and there may be disparities between **form vs. substance.** If so, audit adjustments or special disclosures may be necessary;
2. Intercompany and intracompany transactions occurring near year end must be carefully examined to ascertain that both sides of the transactions were recorded. Lack of **accounting symmetry** could distort assets, liabilities, or income.

For notes receivable transactions, the auditor should examine the notes for details relating to maturity date, principal amount, interest rate, and collateral. The auditor should also vouch lending transactions by reference to authorizations in the minutes, disbursement vouchers, and canceled checks. Note and interest collections should be vouched by reference to the cash receipts record, remittance advices, deposit tickets, and bank statement credits.

Mathematical Evidence

If the client maintains a subsidiary **investment ledger,** the auditor should reconcile it with the general ledger control account. As emphasized earlier, whenever the auditor plans to use a subsidiary ledger as an evidence gathering base, agreement with the related control account must be determined. This form of mathematical evidence, therefore, is often obtained before applying other procedures within a transaction cycle.

Other forms of mathematical evidence relating to investments and notes receivable include recomputation of gains and losses on disposals, interest accruals, and implicit interest where applicable. A cost or market test by reference to listed quotations as of the balance sheet date is another form of mathematical evidence supporting proper valuation of securities. If the client has already performed this procedure, the auditor need only test the client's schedule.

Hearsay Evidence

The critical areas of auditor inquiry relate to the nature of investments and notes receivable and the reasons for holding them and whether any of the investments or notes involve related parties. Responses must be further corroborated, but a logical starting point is to question management regarding these areas.

Analytical Evidence

Analytical procedures relating to investments and notes receivable involve comparing interest and dividends with the prior year. Differences not suggested by portfolio expansion, contraction, or mix changes should be investigated for possible errors.

Exhibit 14.1 illustrates a lead schedule for investments, and Exhibit 14.2 is a supporting schedule for the audit of marketable securities. The supporting schedule contains the procedures discussed in the preceding paragraphs.

EXHIBIT 14.1   Investments Lead Schedule

WP H

Jallo, Inc.
Investments—Long Term
12/31/93

Prepared by: ___ lk
Date: ___ 1/8/94
Reviewed by: ___ CK
Date: ___ 1/20/94

Description	Final Balances 12/31/92	Additions	Disposals	Final Blances 12/31/93	WP #
Investment in Alley Oops common	$750,000	150,000		900,000	H.1
Investment in Bringhall common	160,000	40,000		200,000	H.2
Investment in Bringhall preferred	55,000			55,000	H.3
Investment in Morganthal 8% debenture bonds	225,000		50,000	175,000	H.4
Investment in U.S. treasury notes	100,000	150,000	50,000	200,000	H.5
	$1,290,000	340,000	100,000	1,530,000	
				WTB 1	

EXHIBIT 14.2   Investments Supporting Schedule

		Prepared by:	LK
WP H.1	Jallo, Inc.	Date:	2/2/94
	Investments	Reviewed by:	CK
	Alley Oops Common	Date:	2/10/94
	12/31/93		

			No. of Shares
12/31/92:	Final balance	$750,000~	150,000
1/3/93:	Purchased additional shares	100,000*√	15,000
12/31/93:	Ledger balance	850,000	
	AJE #5	50,000	
12/31/93:	Final balance	$900,000	165,000
		To WP H	√

AJE #5			
Investment in Alley Oops Common	$50,000		
Dividend Revenue	50,000		
Equity in income of unconsolidated subsidiary		100,000	
To adjust investment account for excess of Jallo's share of income over dividends received, as follows:			
Dividends:			
3/1/93	(10,000)o		
6/1/93	(10,000)o		
9/1/93	(10,000)o		
12/1/93	(20,000)o		
		(50,000)	
Net income of subsidiary	303,000⊗		
Jallo's share (33%)	100,000	100,000	
		$50,000	

~ Compared with 12/31/92 workpapers
* Vouched to brokers' advice and canceled check
√ Examined minutes for directors' authorization
√ Examined stock certificates
o Traced to cash receipts record and bank statement
⊗ Examined audited income statement of Alley Oops

Summary Audit Program

Figure 14.3 summarizes the above procedures in a model audit program for the examination of investment transactions. The most critical procedures are examination of securities, recalculation of income, and vouching of acquisitions and disposals.

FIGURE 14.3   Model Audit Program for Investing Transactions

Analytical Procedures
Compare interest and dividends with prior year and investigate significant changes.

Other Substantive Audit Procedures
1. Agree subsidiary investment ledger with related general ledger control account(s).
2. Examine securities and record serial numbers for later comparison with recorded accountability (investment ledger).
3. Examine notes receivable on a test basis.
4. Confirm securities held in safekeeping.
5. Trace from count sheets or returned confirmations to investment ledger (note serial numbers to detect substitution).
6. Trace from investment ledger to count sheets or returned confirmations for evidence of missing securities.
7. Confirm notes receivable with makers on a test basis.
8. Vouch additions and disposals by reference to the following underlying documentation: broker's advice; remittance advice, cash receipts record and bank statement; and canceled checks.
9. Vouch lending transactions by reference to vouchers, canceled checks, and bank statements.
10. Vouch collections of notes and interest by reference to the cash receipts record, remittance advices, deposit tickets, and bank statements.
11. Examine minutes for proper authorization of major lending transactions and purchases and sales of investments.
12. Examine income statements of unconsolidated subsidiaries accounted for on an equity basis.
13. Verify dividends by reference to Standard & Poor's or Moody's dividend reporter.
14. Recalculate interest received or accrued.
15. Recalculate premium or discount amortization on long-term investments in interest bearing securities.
16. Recalculate gain or loss on disposal.
17. Calculate implicit interest where applicable.
18. Perform cost or market test for marketable securities.
19. Inquire of management as to nature of investments and notes receivable and reasons for holding.
20. Inquire as to related-party transactions.

Existence and Completeness

As with current liabilities, the auditor must minimize the risk that the client has failed to record material amounts of long-term liabilities (errors of omission). Treating a capital lease as an operating lease, for example, can cause the debt to equity ratio to be significantly lower than it really is. Failure to make provision for the tax impact of differences in timing between book and tax depreciation may similarly understate long-term liabilities.

Valuation

Long-term liabilities, as a general rule, should be reflected on the balance sheet at net present value. Accordingly, the auditor should determine that appropriate methods are being used to amortize premiums or discounts on long-term debt. The effective interest method more closely approximates net present value than does straight-line amortization.

A troubled debt restructuring may cause valuation problems if it requires a new implicit interest rate or produces a gain on restructuring. The auditor must determine, under such circumstances, that the resulting liability is reported in accordance with SFAS 15.

Presentation and Disclosure

Correct classification as to current or noncurrent is an important objective in the audit of liabilities. Current installments of long-term debt should be classified as current liabilities. Conversely, short-term obligations expected to be refinanced should be reclassified as long-term, if they meet the provisions of SFAS 78.

Details surrounding various aspects of long-term liabilities must be disclosed, either in the body of the financial statements or in footnotes.

Some of these are the following:

1. Defaults on bonds or violations of restrictive covenants in loan agreements;
2. Details of leases;
3. Pension disclosures;
4. Nature of tax and book temporary differences;
5. Details regarding bonds and mortgages payable (e.g., term, interest rate, collateral).

Audit Evidence and Procedures

Documentary Evidence

Most long-term liabilities (bonds, notes, leases, and mortgages payable) are supported by contracts or agreements entered into by the client. Careful **examination of debt agreements** and comparison with accounting records assists the auditor in identifying necessary accruals and disclosures. Cash flow requirements under lease agreements, for example, requires footnote disclosure. The amount and timing of

EXHIBIT 14.3   Capital Leases Audit Workpaper

WP P.2

Jallo, Inc.
Captial Leases
12/31/93

Description	Date of Agreement	Termination Date	Implicit Interest Rate	Liability 1/1/93	1993 Payments
Phoenix warehouse&	1/1/91	12/31/96	8.00%	$1,230,000*	371,400^
Memphis warehouse#&	1/1/93	12/31/98	10.00%&	2,800,000&	643,000^
Tractors and trailers&	1/1/92	12/31/95	10.00%	870,000*	349,840^
				$4,900,000	1,364,240

* Agreed to 12/31/92 workpapers and final balances.
& Examined lease agreement.
^ Examined canceled checks.

% Recomputed.
$ Agreed to 12/31/93 general ledger balance.
# Examined minutes for directors' authorization.

Minimum rentals are paid at year end on all leases
The lease agreement covering the tractors and trailers requires added rentals of $.20/mile in excess of 40,000 miles annually for each truck.

(continued)

these flows can be determined by examining the lease. Similarly, the lessor's interest rate (if stated in the lease), contingent rentals, purchase options, renewal options, and the lease term can all be identified by reading the lease.

By examining long-term debt agreements, the auditor can identify restrictive covenants (retained earnings restrictions, restrictions on the issuance of additional debt), **compensating balance requirements,** note collateral, note repayment terms, and interest rates. The auditor should also evaluate the reasonableness of interest rates and, given a low rate or no rate, consider the need for related-party disclosure, or imputed interest.

Exhibits 14.3 through 14.5 illustrate workpapers supporting the audit of leases and long-term debt, respectively. The significance of examining the lease and loan agreements is evident by the frequency of audit legends supported by that procedure.

Mathematical Evidence

Mathematical evidence is useful in evaluating accruals and apportionments commonly associated with long-term liabilities. For example, the auditor should recalculate the following, as necessary, on a test basis:

1. Premium or discount amortization;
2. Lease amortization;
3. Contingent rentals;
4. Interest accruals;

5. Gain or loss on bond redemptions;
6. Change in deferred taxes;
7. Pension liability;
8. Implicit interest.

EXHIBIT 14.3 *(continued)*

			Preapred by:	LFK
			Date:	1/13/94
			Reviewed by:	JER
			Date:	1/26/94

Interest	Principal	Liability 12/31/93	Current Portion	Noncurrent	Contingent Rentals
98,400%	273,000	957,000	294,840%	662,160	0
280,000%	363,000	2,437,000	399,300%	2,037,700	0
87,000%	262,840	607,160	289,124%	318,036	80,000%
465,000	898,840	4,001,160	983,264	3,017,890	80,000
$			$	$	

EXHIBIT 14.4 Long-Term Debt Audit Workpaper

WP P.1			Jallo Inc. 12% Mortagage Bonds Payable 12/31/93		Prepared by:	LFK
					Date:	1/21/94
					Reviewed by:	JER
					Date:	2/2/94

	Bonds Payable	Interest Payment	Interest Expense	Discount Amortization	Unamortized Discount	Issuance Price
12/31/92	0					
1/1/93	$2,000,000				213,551	1,786,449&
3/31/93		60,000$	62,526*	2,526*	211,025	
6/30/93		60,000$	62,614*	2,614*	208,411	
9/30/93		60,000$	62,706*	2,706*	205,705	
12/31/93		60,000$	62,800*	2,800*	202,905%	
	$2,000,000%		250,646%			

&Traced proceeds to cash receipts record and to bank statement.
*Per amortization schedule (See WP PF P.1 in permanent file).
%Agreed to general ledger.
$Examined canceled check payable to trustee.

EXHIBIT 14.5 Long-Term Debt, Permanent File Workpaper

		Jallo, Inc.		Prepared by: LFK
		12% Mortgage Bonds Payable		Date: 1/21/94
WP PF P.1		Amortization Schedule		Reviewed by: JER
				Date: 2/2/94

Period	Cash Credit	Interest Expense Debit	Unamortized Premium (debit) Discount (credit)	Carrying Value of Bonds
0				1,786,449.28
1	$60,000.00	62,525.72	(2,525.72)	1,788,975.00
2	60,000.00	62,614.13	(2,614.13)	1,791,589.13
3	60,000.00	62,705.62	(2,705.62)	1,794,294.75
4	60,000.00	62,800.32	(2,800.32)	1,797,095.06
5	60,000.00	62,898.33	(2,898.33)	1,799,993.39
6	60,000.00	62,999.77	(2,999.77)	1,802,993.16
7	60,000.00	63,104.76	(3,104.76)	1,806,097.92
8	60,000.00	63,213.43	(3,213.43)	1,809,311.35
9	60,000.00	63,325.90	(3,325.90)	1,812,637.24
10	60,000.00	63,442.30	(3,442.30)	1,816,079.55
11	60,000.00	63,562.78	(3,562.78)	1,819,642.33
12	60,000.00	63,687.48	(3,687.48)	1,823,329.81
13	60,000.00	63,816.54	(3,816.54)	1,827,146.35
14	60,000.00	63,950.12	(3,950.12)	1,831,096.48
15	60,000.00	64,088.38	(4,088.38)	1,835,184.85
16	60,000.00	64,231.47	(4,231.47)	1,839,416.32
17	60,000.00	64,379.57	(4,379.57)	1,843,795.90
18	60,000.00	64,532.86	(4,532.86)	1,848,328.75
19	60,000.00	64,691.51	(4,691.51)	1,853,020.26
20	60,000.00	64,855.71	(4,855.71)	1,857,875.97
21	60,000.00	65,025.66	(5,025.66)	1,862,901.63
22	60,000.00	65,201.56	(5,201.56)	1,868,103.18
23	60,000.00	65,383.61	(5,383.61)	1,873,486.79
24	60,000.00	65,572.04	(5,572.04)	1,879,058.83
25	60,000.00	65,767.06	(5,767.06)	1,884,825.89
26	60,000.00	65,968.91	(5,968.91)	1,890,794.80
27	60,000.00	66,177.82	(6,177.82)	1,896,972.62
28	60,000.00	66,394.04	(6,394.04)	1,903,366.66
29	60,000.00	66,617.83	(6,617.83)	1,909,984.49
30	60,000.00	66,849.46	(6,849.46)	1,916,833.95
31	60,000.00	67,089.19	(7,089.19)	1,923,923.13
32	60,000.00	67,337.31	(7,337.31)	1,931,260.44
33	60,000.00	67,594.12	(7,594.12)	1,938,854.56
34	60,000.00	67,859.91	(7,859.91)	1,946,714.47
35	60,000.00	68,135.01	(8,135.01)	1,954,849.48
36	60,000.00	68,419.73	(8,419.73)	1,963,269.21
37	60,000.00	68,714.42	(8,714.42)	1,971,983.63
38	60,000.00	69,019.43	(9,019.43)	1,981,003.06
39	60,000.00	69,335.11	(9,335.11)	1,990,338.16
40	60,000.00	69,661.84	(9,661.84)	2,000,000.00

(continued)

EXHIBIT 14.5 *(continued)*

```
DEBT TERMS:

    Principal                      $2,000,000E
    Term (years)                          10E
    Times interest paid/year               4E
    Nominal interest rate            12.00%E
    Per interest period               3.00%
    Effective interest rate          14.00%C
    Per interest period               3.50%C
    Interest payment                 $60,000C
    Collateral              Land and buildingsE
    Date of issuance                  1-1-93
    Due date                      12/31/2002
    Interest payment dates             3/31E
                                       6/30E
                                       9/30E
                                      12/31E
    Dividend restrictions               None
    NPV = Issuance Price      $1,786,449.28C

    E = Examine bond indenture.
    C = Computed.
```

Analytical Evidence

The auditor should compare lease amortization, interest expense, and pension liability with the prior year and investigate significant changes. Such procedures assist in identifying unrecorded liabilities resulting from overlooking necessary accruals.

Summary Audit Program

Figure 14.4 illustrates a model audit program for the audit of borrowing transactions. Analytical procedures comparing the current and prior year's expenses relating to long-term liabilities are most important for locating significant errors of omission.

STOCKHOLDERS' EQUITY TRANSACTIONS

Audit Objectives

Valuation

The valuation objective is not generally as important as presentation and disclosure in the audit of stockholders' equity transactions. The occurrence of certain transactions, however, may require some audit attention to specific valuation aspects. If

FIGURE 14.4   Model Audit Program for Borrowing Transactions

Analytical Procedures
  Compare liabilities and related expenses with prior year and investigate
  significant changes.

Other Substantive Audit Procedures
  1. Confirm bonds payable and pension plan liability with respective trustees.
  2. Examine bank confirmation for possible unrecorded liabilities or
     guarantees of indebtedness.
  3. Examine lease agreements for contingent rentals.
  4. Examine pension agreements for vesting provisions.
  5. Examine loan agreements for possible need to impute interest.
  6. Examine loan agreements, bond indentures, and pension agreements for
     the following: restrictive covenants, collateral requirements, or other
     disclosure requirements (future cash flows under lease agreements, details
     surrounding bond issues, pension provisions, etc.).
  7. Vouch the following on a test basis: interest payments, lease payments,
     and pension plan contributions.
  8. Recompute the following on a test basis: premium and discount
     amortization, lease amortization, contingent rentals, interest accruals, gain
     or loss on bond redemptions, change in deferred taxes, and pension
     liability.
  9. Compute implicit interest if applicable.

the client issues stock for noncash assets, for example, the auditor must be
satisfied as to the values assigned to the assets. Treasury stock transactions and
stock dividends also raise valuation issues. Regarding stock dividends, the auditor
must verify the appropriateness of the amount transferred from retained earnings
(market value for small stock dividends; par or stated value for large stock
dividends).

Presentation and Disclosure

The major presentation issue regarding stockholders' equity involves separation
between contributed capital and retained earnings. The most significant disclosure
question is how to calculate and present earnings per share. A complex capital
structure requires a different set of computations than a simple capital structure.

Additional disclosure questions relate to such features as restrictions on dividend availability, dividends in arrears on cumulative preferred stock, and stock
option plans.

Audit Evidence and Procedures

Documentary Evidence

Inasmuch as most stockholders' equity transactions require director approval, the auditor should examine minutes of directors' meetings for authorization of such events as stock issuance, stock reacquisition or retirement, dividends, and stock options. Satisfied that the transactions were properly approved, the auditor should vouch them by examining the underlying documentation (cash receipts entries and deposit slips for stock issuance, exercise of stock options, or sale of treasury stock; cash disbursement records and canceled checks for reacquisitions and dividends).

Stock option agreements should be examined for disclosure requirements (employees eligible, number of shares involved, option prices, and exercise dates). By examining the option agreement(s) the auditor can also identify the measurement date and determine the amount of deferred compensation, if any.

Mathematical Evidence

The auditor should recompute the following, on a test basis, where applicable:

1. Dividend declarations involving participating preferred stock;
2. Debits to retained earnings for stock dividends;
3. Debits to deferred compensation for stock option credits;
4. Earnings per share computations;
5. Gains or losses on treasury stock transactions.

Figure 14.5 presents a model audit program for stockholders' equity transactions.

AUDIT RISK ANALYSIS AND THE FINANCING AND INVESTING CYCLE

Search for Related-Party Transactions

Significant related-party transactions occur more frequently within the financing and investing cycle than within the other transaction cycles. Loans to and from related parties, repayments or refunding of these loans, stock issued for noncash assets, and stock reacquisitions are examples of transactions involved.

In accordance with Section 334 of the *Codification of Statements on Auditing Standards,* the auditor must

1. Identify related parties;
2. Identify material transactions; and
3. Examine identified material related-party transactions.[1]

The major audit risk factor associated with related-party transactions is the potential disparity between *legal form* and *economic substance*. When the two are in conflict,

---

[1] Auditing Standards Board, *AICPA Professional Standards,* New York: AICPA, Section AU 334.07-10.

FIGURE 14.5   Model Audit Program for Stockholder Equity Transactions

Analytical Procedures
1. Compare dividends with prior year and investigate significant fluctuations.
2. Compare capital stock accounts with prior year and account for all changes.
3. Compare stock option credits with prior year and account for increases.

Other Substantive Procedures
1. Confirm stock issuance and dividends with registrar and transfer agent.
2. Examine minutes of directors' meetings for dividend declarations.
3. Examine minutes of directors' meetings for proper authorization of the following: stock issuance, stock reacquisition, stock retirements, and stock options.
4. Vouch dividend declarations and payments.
5. Vouch treasury stock transactions.
6. Examine evidence of valuation where stock is issued for noncash assets.
7. Recalculate earnings per share, stock option credits and amortization, and stock dividends.
8. Examine loan agreements and directors' minutes for possible restrictions on retained earnings, and determine that appropriate disclosures have been made in the financial statements.
9. Examine stock option agreements and determine that proper disclosure has been made concerning employees participating, shares involved, option prices, and exercise dates.
10. Examine corporate charter for description of various classes of stock, and determine that proper financial statement disclosure has been made concerning participating or cumulative features of preferred stock and dividends in arrears on preferred stock.

GAAP requires that substance take precedence over form. The auditor must determine, therefore, that the financial statements clearly reflect the economic substance of material related-party transactions.[2]

In a case reported recently, the chairman of Guarantee Security Life Insurance Co., a Florida company, was able to complete related-party transactions with Guarantee's principal securities broker, Merrill Lynch & Co. Beginning in 1984, upon acquisition by Mark Sanford, subsequently appointed chairman, Guarantee offered abnormally high interest rates to purchasers of its annuities and also paid high commissions to independent agents marketing the annuities. To finance the high interest rates, the company bought high yielding junk bond investments. To conceal the risky nature of its investment portfolio, Guarantee temporarily *exchanged hun-*

---

[2]*Ibid.*, Section AU 334.02.

dreds of millions of dollars of junk bonds for U.S. Treasury securities in year-end trades with Merrill Lynch. The trades were then reversed at the beginning of the following year. This practice was followed from 1984 through 1988. Florida insurance regulators alleged that the securities swaps weren't bona fide trades, but just paper transactions. Indeed, Coopers & Lybrand, the company's auditors, said, in 1985, that the swaps couldn't be recognized under GAAP. But Coopers later relented and agreed to recognize the swaps for regulatory reporting purposes only. Accordingly, financial statements submitted to the Florida Insurance Commission reported primarily U.S. government securities rather than the junk bonds.

Given the problems encountered by companies holding junk bonds in the 1980s, Guarantee, with its top-heavy portfolio of these securities, became insolvent in August, 1991, and its 57,000 policyholders were temporarily prevented from collecting on their annuities. Subsequently, the company was seized by the State of Florida and accused of fraud in attempting to conceal the true nature of its investment portfolio. At the same time, the SEC began investigating Guarantee, Merrill Lynch, and Coopers & Lybrand. The suit filed by the Florida Insurance Commission accused Merrill Lynch of fraud and also accused Coopers & Lybrand, Guarantee's auditors, of malpractice and breach of fiduciary duty.[3]

In a similar case, United American Bank of Knoxville used other banks, all controlled by the same family, as a means for transferring problem loans, thus keeping them from being detected by the auditors. In fact, FDIC examiners reported that the "bank had about $377 million, or nearly half its total assets, in loans the FDIC classed as partly or totally uncollectible—. . .—nearly half the problem loans were made to United American's former chairman, Jake F. Butcher, his family and associates and their interests."[4]

The lesson for auditors in these cases is that when legal form and economic substance of material transactions are at variance, the *auditors must be emphatic in their insistence on the precedence of substance over form.* To do otherwise places the auditor in violation of Rule 102 of the *Code of Professional Conduct,* which states that ". . .—the member shall maintain objectivity and integrity, shall be free of conflicts of interest, and *shall not knowingly misrepresent facts or subordinate his or her judgment to others.*"[5] (emphasis added) If the year-end financial statements had reflected the true nature of the investment and loan portfolios of Guarantee and United Bank respectively, the companies would have been required to increase their loss reserves substantially. Indeed, had Guarantee done this, according to the deputy receiver, the company would have been insolvent by 1985.[6]

In addition to misrepresentation fraud, companies have also used related-party transactions as conduits for transferring assets out of the entity. In the Continental Vending Machine Corporation case (see Chapter 3), the president of Continental used a wholly owned subsidiary to obtain bank loans. The loan proceeds were transferred back and forth between the companies to "muddy" the audit trail. Finally, they were loaned to the president, who used the money to finance his

---

[3]See "Castle in the Sand," *The Wall Street Journal,* 23 December 1991.

[4]Geoffrey Colvin, *et al.,* "Jake Butcher's Fall," *Fortune,* March 21, 1983, page 7.

[5]AICPA, *Professional Standards,* Vol. 2, New York, NY: AICPA, Section ET 102.01.

[6]*Wall Street Journal,* 23 December 1991, *op. cit.*

personal transactions, mainly in the stock markets. His inability to repay the loans, together with insufficiency of collateral, forced the company into receivership.[7]

In view of the large number of significant cases involving related-party transactions, Section 334 provides extensive guidance in identifying related parties and related-party transactions, and examining the transactions for possible disparities between form and substance.[8]

Loan Defaults

If clients have significant amounts of loans outstanding, the auditor must be particularly alert to violations of restrictive covenants or failure to meet required interest or principal payments. Such failure to meet the terms of a loan agreement often makes the entire amount of the loan, together with any accrued interest, immediately due. This, in turn, may cast doubt on the ability of the firm to continue as a going concern.

Auditors should carefully read all loan agreements and extract portions covering working capital or retained earnings restrictions, maintenance of **collateral,** repayment schedules, and any other provisions relating to potential loan defaults.

If liquidity problems have prevented the client from meeting interest or principal repayment schedules, the auditor should inquire of management concerning steps taken toward restructuring the loan agreements. If **loan restructuring** has been completed before issuance of the audit report, the auditor should examine the agreements, determine whether any gain should be recognized, and whether uncertainty has been sufficiently reduced to warrant omitting the explanatory paragraph from the audit report.

Disposal of a Segment

If a client is reporting a segment disposal for the period under examination, the auditor should first determine whether the transaction meets the **"disposal of a segment"** requirements, as set forth in APBO 30.[9] If so, "gain (loss) from discontinued operations," and "gain (loss) from disposal" should be reflected "below the line" (i.e., after income from continuing operations).

In addition to determining proper classification, the auditor must verify that the amounts reported as discontinued operations do not include expenses relating to continuing operations. The application of analytical procedures by segment will usually disclose major classification errors of this type.

COMPLETING THE AUDIT

Having covered substantive audit testing in Chapters 12, 13, and 14, we now turn our attention to a few remaining, but significant, factors requiring the auditor's attention in completing the audit field work.

---

[7]*U.S. v. Simon et al.,* 425 F.2d. 796 (2d Cir. 1969).

[8]*AICPA Professional Standards, op. cit.,* Section AU 334.07-10.

[9]Financial Accounting Standards Board, *Accounting Standards—Current Text—1990/91,* Homewood, Illinois: Irwin, 1990, Section I 13.404.

Analytical Procedures as Part of Audit Review

Generally accepted auditing standards require the auditor to apply analytical procedures in the final review stages of the audit.[10] The purpose for applying analytical procedures during audit review is to ascertain that the auditor has gathered adequate evidence to resolve suspicions arising during the planning stages of the audit. For example, assume that analytical procedures applied to unaudited data during the planning stages of the audit revealed a material decline in repairs and maintenance expense, relative to the preceding year. If audit adjustments for ordinary repairs improperly capitalized have reduced the decline to insignificant proportions, analytical procedures applied as part of overall audit review will provide the needed assurance to the auditor that prior suspicions have been resolved. If, however, analytical procedures applied during audit review continue to produce abnormalities, the auditor should pursue the disparities until his/her suspicions are resolved. Such pursuit may reveal that the auditor was able to obtain a satisfactory (and documented) explanation for the abnormality; or it may require the modification of audit programs and the application of extended substantive procedures to determine the cause of the disparity.

Further Materiality Considerations

As discussed in Chapter 4, the auditor should set individual item and aggregate materiality thresholds as part of audit planning. The levels chosen are dependent on inherent risk, control risk (the quality of internal control) and the dollar amounts of unaudited financial statement components, such as net income, total assets, and net assets. Chapter 4 also suggested that the auditor may need to subsequently modify these levels, depending on the significance of proposed audit adjustments. One or more adjustments, for example, that materially reduce net income may require a decrease in both individual item and aggregate materiality thresholds. Because of the possible need for modification, therefore, the auditor should reevaluate materiality levels as part of the audit review. If the review suggests lower thresholds, the auditor should reevaluate possible audit adjustments not meeting the initial thresholds based on unaudited data and determine if they fall within the bounds of the modified thresholds based on audited income and net assets. Assume, for example, that the auditor discovered $30,000 of nonrecurring fixed overhead capacity loss improperly included in the ending inventories of goods in process and finished goods. Assume further that, based on unaudited net income of $2,000,000, the auditor established an individual item materiality threshold of 2 percent, or $40,000. Based on this criterion, the auditor would not propose an audit adjustment for the overhead capitalization error. If, however, other audit adjustments meeting the materiality threshold reduce net income from $2,000,000 to $1,000,000, the error meets the modified individual item materiality threshold based on audited income (2 percent of $1,000,000 equals $20,000 vs. the error of $30,0000.) The auditor, under these circumstances, may now elect to include the error correction in the set of proposed audit adjustments.

---

[10]*AICPA Professional Standards, op. cit.,* Section AU 329.04.

Subsequent Events

Certain events or transactions, which occur after the balance sheet date, but before the completion of audit field work, may have an impact on the audited financial statements. If the effects are material, adjustment of the statements or disclosure may be necessary.

The *Codification of Statements on Auditing Standards* classifies *subsequent events* as follows:

- **Type I subsequent events:** Those events that provide additional evidence with respect to conditions that existed at the date of the balance sheet and affect the estimates inherent in the process of preparing the financial statements.

- **Type II subsequent events:** Those events that provide evidence with respect to conditions that *did not* exist at the date of the balance sheet being reported on, but arose subsequent to that date.[11]

Type I events, if material, require adjustment of the financial statements. For example, assume that certain inventories on hand at year end and reported at full cost are believed by the auditor to be obsolete. Assume further that these inventories are sold at distress prices materially below cost after the balance sheet date, but before the end of audit field work. The distress sale provides conclusive evidence supporting obsolescence, and the inventories, therefore, should be adjusted to reflect net realizable value as of the balance sheet date.

Type II subsequent events do not require adjustment. For example, assume that uninsured inventories were destroyed by fire during the subsequent period. In this case, the conditions giving rise to the loss occurred after the balance sheet date. Although the financial statements do not require adjustment, footnote disclosure of material events of this nature may be required.

Given the adjustment and disclosure requirements associated with subsequent events, the auditor must seek to identify those of significance. Certain auditing procedures (e.g., cut-off tests and the search for unrecorded liabilities) assist in detecting subsequent events. In addition, the *Codification* lists the following procedures to be applied in the subsequent period:

---

[11]*Ibid.*, Section AU 560.02-05.

1. Read the latest available interim financial statements.

2. Inquire of and discuss with officers and other executives having responsibility for financial and accounting matters as to:
   a. Whether any substantial contingent liabilities or commitments existed at the date of the balance sheet being reported on or at the date of inquiry.
   b. Whether there was any significant change in the capital stock, long-term debt, or working capital to the date of inquiry.
   c. The current status of items in the financial statements being reported on that were accounted for on the basis of tentative, preliminary, or inconclusive data.
   d. Whether any unusual adjustments had been made during the period from the balance sheet date to the date of inquiry.

3. Read the available minutes of meetings of stockholders, directors, and appropriate committees.

4. Obtain from legal counsel a description and evaluation of any litigation, impending litigation, claims, and contingent liabilities of which he has knowledge that existed at the date of the balance sheet.

5. Obtain a letter of representations, dated as of the date of the auditor's report—. . .—as to whether any events occurred subsequent to the date of the financial statements being reported on—. . .—that in the officer's opinion would require adjustment or disclosure in these statements.

6. Make such additional inquiries or perform such procedures as he (she) considers necessary and appropriate to dispose of questions that arise in carrying out the foregoing procedures, inquiries, and discussions.[12]

Statement of Cash Flows

As part of the audit completion process, the auditor should examine the statement of cash flows. The transactions reflected in the statement have already been subjected to audit as part of the examination of the transaction cycles covered in this and the two preceding chapters. The auditor needs to determine, however, that the amounts and descriptions have been properly reflected in the statement.

---

[12]*Ibid.*, Section AU 560.12.

Audit procedures applied specifically to the statement of cash flows should include the following:

1. Reviewing the comparative balance sheets and the current year's income statement to determine that all significant cash flows have been properly calculated and reflected in the statement;

2. Determining that a proper distinction has been made among cash provided by operations, cash flows from investing transactions, and cash flows from financing transactions;

3. Identifying significant noncash financing and investing transactions, and determining that they have been properly reflected in the statement;

4. Determining that a statement of cash flows has been included for each year for which an income statement is included in the annual report.

Workpaper Review

The first standard of audit field work requires that the work is to be adequately planned and assistants, if any, are to be properly supervised. An important ingredient of supervision is the need for careful review of all audit workpapers. The in-charge senior auditor is responsible for reviewing workpapers prepared by assistants. The audit manager and the audit partner conduct an overall review of the audit workpapers.

The reviewer should ascertain that the workpapers fully describe all procedures applied and clearly display auditor conclusions and audit adjustments. The **workpaper review** should also determine that the audit procedures evidenced by the workpapers are consistent with the audit objectives specified in the audit programs for that part of the examination.

As a final step, the reviewer should examine the workpapers for completeness of indexing. As described and illustrated in Chapter 4, supporting schedules, lead schedules, and the working trial balance must be cross-indexed so that the reviewer can proceed in either direction: from supporting schedule to working trial balance or vice versa.

Open Items

As part of virtually every audit, certain questions arise during the examination which cannot be answered immediately. Information suggesting the existence of inventories out on consignment needs to be pursued further; certificates representing stock investments held in safekeeping off the premises need to be examined; certain documents cannot be located; an intercompany account has not been reconciled because the workpapers have not been received from the divisional auditors.

These questions should be listed on an **open items** workpaper and cleared as the information becomes available. Exhibit 14.6 illustrates an open items work paper. Note the initials, date, and comments of the person clearing each question.

When all of the open items have been cleared, the workpaper may be included as part of the current file; or it may be discarded, the information having been incorporated into the respective supporting schedules. Retaining the workpaper has the advantage of encouraging the auditor to fully dispose of each open item documented during the course of the examination. It also gives the audit manager an opportunity, during the workpaper review, to perform a separate evaluation of open items and their resolution by the audit team.

EXHIBIT 14.6   Open Items Workpaper

Jallo, Inc.
Open Items
WP 1   12/31/93

Description of Item	Disposition of item	Cleared
Shares represented by Treflen investment allegedly held by broker	Examined 1/14/94 See WP F.3	LFK
Conference with client's legal counsel needed in order to clarify product liability suit	Held 1/22/94 See WP P.6	JER
Examine debt restructuring agreement to be signed by client by 1/25/94. Determine if short-term obligations may be reclassified as long-term.	Examined 1/30/94 See WP P.4	JER
Ask credit manager to contact Seels, Inc. and request return of accounts receivable confirmation.	Received 1/31/94 See WP C.2	MEL
Examine and evaluate collateral securing loan to Ralph Proudsell, president.	Examined 2/1/94 See WP D.2	JER
Obtain minutes of November directors' meeting.	Legal counsel will forward	MEL
Have Detroit office visit location of Alma Motors and determine if Alma is an operating company or a "shell" company.		
Contact broker as to ask and bid price for Bool Mines stock.		

Auditor/Client Conference

Auditors ordinarily discuss proposed audit adjustments and internal control weaknesses with the client as these adjustments and weaknesses are discovered. At the close of audit field work, these discussions are summarized in a formal conference. Given the nature of the subject matter, the conference is usually attended by the audit partner, the audit manager, the in-charge senior auditor, and one or more members of the client's top management.

In addition to providing a forum for presenting and discussing audit adjustments and internal control weaknesses, the conference will also cover recommended footnote disclosures and the type of audit report to be rendered. The form of audit report, as described by the auditors, is conditional upon client acceptance of the audit adjustments and recommended disclosures.

Clients may object to the income statement effects of certain proposed audit adjustments or may deem certain footnote disclosures too "harsh." Nevertheless, proper ethical behavior requires the independent auditors to insist on fairness of financial presentation and disclosure— or take exception in their audit reports. Occasionally, compromise is possible, but compromise should not result in a sacrifice of fairness.

Communication with Audit Committee

In addition to the auditor-client conference just referred to, the auditor is required to communicate certain matters discovered during the audit to the audit committee or similar body with designated financial statement oversight authority.[13] The following are among the more important matters to be covered in the communication:

1. The auditor's responsibility for internal control structure and for the financial statements under GAAS. It is important for the audit committee to recognize that the auditor is providing *reasonable* rather than *absolute* assurance about the financial statements;

2. Selection of and changes in significant accounting policies;

3. Method of accounting for unusual transactions;

4. Significant audit adjustments;

5. Disagreements with management about matters that could be significant to the financial statements or the auditor's report;

6. Difficulties encountered in performing the audit such as delays in commencing the audit, withholding of information, undue time pressures imposed by management, unavailability of client personnel, and failure of client personnel to complete client-prepared schedules on a timely basis.[14]

Communicating these matters enables the audit committee to more effectively perform its oversight function. Such communication also assists the auditor by providing a mechanism for resolving possible disputes with management.

The communication may be oral or written. If oral, the auditor should document the communication in the workpapers.

Client Representation Letter

GAAS requires that the auditor obtain a **client representation letter** from management. The letter is dated as of the close of audit field work and should be signed by the chief executive officer and the chief financial officer of the client. Its stated purpose is to "confirm oral representations given to the auditor, indicate and document the continued appropriateness of such representations, and reduce the possibility of misunderstanding concerning the matters that are the subject of the representations."[15] The letter does not relieve the auditor from corroborating the written representations through the application of standard or extended auditing

---

[13]*Ibid.*, Section AU 380.

[14]*Ibid.*

[15]*Ibid.*, Section AU 333.02.

procedures. It does assist in making management more aware of their primary responsibility for fairness of financial presentation.

Exhibit 14.7 illustrates the recommended form. The following matters should be covered in the letter:

1. Management's acknowledgment of its responsibility for the presentation in the financial statements of financial position, results of operations, and cash flows in conformity with generally accepted accounting principles or other comprehensive basis of accounting.

2. Availability of all financial records and related data.

3. Completeness and availability of all minutes of meetings of stockholders, directors, and committees of directors.

4. Absence of errors in the financial statements and unrecorded transactions.

5. Information concerning related-party transactions and amounts receivable or payable.

6. Noncompliance with aspects of contractual agreements that may affect the financial statements.

7. Information concerning subsequent events.

8. Irregularities involving management or employees.

9. Communications from regulatory agencies concerning noncompliance with, or deficiencies in, financial reporting practices.

10. Plans or intentions that may affect the carrying value or classification of assets or liabilities.

11. Disclosure of compensating balance requirements or other arrangements involving restrictions on cash balances and disclosure of line-of-credit or similar arrangements.

12. Reduction of excess or obsolete inventories to net realizable value.

13. Losses from sales commitments.

14. Satisfactory title to assets, liens on assets, and assets pledged as collateral.

15. Agreements to repurchase assets previously sold.

16. Losses from purchase commitments for inventory quantities in excess of requirements or at prices in excess of market.

17. Violations or possible violations of laws or regulations whose effects should be considered for disclosure in the financial statements or as a basis for recording a loss contingency.

18. Other liabilities and gain or loss contingencies that are required to be accrued or disclosed by Statement of Financial Accounting Standards No. 5.

19. Unasserted claims or assessments that the client's lawyer has advised are probable of assertion and must be disclosed in accordance with Statement of Financial Accounting Standards No. 5.

20. Capital stock repurchase options or agreements or capital stock reserved for options, warrants, conversion, or other requirements.[16]

---

[16]*Ibid.,* Section AU 333.04.

EXHIBIT 14.7   Client Representation Letter

Ricks and Hanley, CPAs   February 26, 1994
1213 South Bing
Houston, Texas 73705

Attention: J. Rindley, Partner

Dear Mr. Rindley:

In connection with your audits of the balance sheets, income statements, and statements of cash flows of Jallo, Inc. as of December 31, 1993 and 1992 and for the periods then ended for the purpose of expressing an opinion as to whether the financial statements present fairly the financial position, results of operations, and cash flows of Jallo, Inc. in conformity with generally accepted accounting principles, we confirm, to the best of our knowledge and belief, the following representations made to you during your audits.

1. We are responsible for the fair presentation in the financial statements of financial position, results of operations, and cash flows in conformity with generally accepted accounting principles.

2. We have made available to you all
   a. Financial records and related data.
   b. Minutes of the meetings of stockholders, directors, and committees of directors, or summaries of actions of recent meetings for which minutes have not yet been prepared.

3. There have been no
   a. Irregularities involving management or employees who have significant roles in the internal control structure.
   b. Irregularities involving other employees that could have a material effect on the financial statements.
   c. Communications from regulatory agencies concerning noncompliance with, or deficiencies in, financial reporting practices that could have a material effect on the financial statements.

4. We have no plans or intentions that may materially affect the carrying value or classification of assets and liabilities.

5. The following have been properly recorded or disclosed in the financial statements:
   a. Related-party transactions and related amounts receivable or payable, including sales, purchases, loans, transfers, leasing arrangements, and guarantees.
   b. Capital stock repurchase options or agreements or capital stock reserved for options, warrants, conversions, or other requirements.
   c. Arrangements with financial institutions involving compensating balances or other arrangements involving restrictions on cash balances and line-of-credit or similar arrangements.
   d. Agreements to repurchase assets previously sold.

(continued)

EXHIBIT 14.7 *(continued)*

6. There are no
   a. Violations or possible violations of laws or regulations whose effects should be considered for disclosure in the financial statements or as a basis for recording a loss contingency.
   b. Other material liabilities or gain or loss contingencies that are required to be accrued or disclosed by Statement of Financial Accounting Standards No. 5.

7. There are no unasserted claims or assessments that our lawyer has advised us are probable of assertion and must be disclosed in accordance with Statement of Financial Accounting Standards No. 5.

8. There are no material transactions that have not been properly recorded in the accounting records underlying the financial statements.

9. Provision, when material, has been made to reduce excess or obsolete inventories to their estimated net realizable value.

10. The company has satisfactory title to all owned assets, and there are no liens or encumbrances on such assets nor has any asset been pledged.

11. Provision has been made for any material loss to be sustained in the fulfillment of, or from inability to fulfill, any sales commitments.

12. Provision has been made for any material loss to be sustained as a result of purchase commitments for inventory quantities in excess of normal requirements or at prices in excess of the prevailing market prices.

13. We have complied with all aspects of contractual agreements that would have a material effect on the financial statements in the event of noncompliance.

14. No events have occurred subsequent to the balance sheet date that would require adjustment to, or disclosure in, the financial statements.

Joel Adams
President and Chief Executive Officer

Jeremy Slade
Controller

Jallo, Inc.

Source: Adapted from *Codification of Statements on Auditing Standards,* Section AU 333A.05.

Communication of Internal Control Structure Related Matters

Auditing standards require that the auditor communicate any material control structure matters discovered during the audit. The communication should be to the audit committee or to individuals with a level of authority and responsibility equivalent to an audit committee in organizations that do not have one, such as the board of directors, the board of trustees, an owner in an owner-managed enterprise, or others who may have engaged the auditor.[17]

The matters required to be reported to the audit committee are referred to as **reportable conditions.** Reportable conditions are matters coming to the auditor's attention that, in his or her judgment, represent significant deficiencies in control structure that could adversely affect the entity's ability to record, process, summarize, and report financial data consistent with the assertions of management in the financial statements.[18] Such deficiencies may relate to any one or a combination of the control structure components (i.e., control environment, accounting system, or control procedures).

The report preferably should be in writing, and should state that the communication is intended solely for the information and the use of the audit committee, management, and others within the organization. The **reportable conditions letter** should:

1. Indicate that the purpose of the audit was to report on the financial statements and not to provide assurance on the internal control structure;
2. Include the definition of reportable conditions; and
3. Include the restriction on distribution.[19]

Exhibit 14.8 illustrates a recommended form for the reportable conditions letter.

In addition to ensuring proper notification of the audit committee, the letter also provides protection to the auditor. By incorporation into the audit workpapers, the letter provides evidence that the auditor discovered control structure deficiencies and suggested ways for rectifying the conditions. This can serve as an effective defense in the event of future legal actions against the auditor involving undetected errors or irregularities caused by uncorrected control weaknesses.

The **management letter,** as contrasted with the reportable conditions communication, covers all auditor-discovered weaknesses, and not just those materially affecting the financial statement assertions. The purpose of the letter is to provide constructive suggestions to management concerning improvements in the control structure. Although not required by GAAS, most auditors and their clients find the letter to be useful in contributing to maximum control effectiveness. Exhibit 14.9 illustrates a typical management letter addressed to the client's audit committee.

---

[17]*Ibid.,* Section AU 325.

[18]*Ibid.*

[19]*Ibid.*

EXHIBIT 14.8 **Communication of Reportable Conditions**

February 26, 1994

To the Audit Committee of the Board of Directors of Jallo, Inc.

In planning and performing our audit of the financial statements of Jallo, Inc. for the year ended December 31, 1993, we considered its internal control structure in order to determine our auditing procedures for the purpose of expressing our opinion on the financial statements and not to provide assurance on the internal control structure. However, we noted certain matters involving the internal control structure and its operation that we consider to be reportable conditions under standards established by the American Institute of Certified Public Accountants. Reportable conditions involve matters coming to our attention relating to significant deficiencies in the design or operation of the internal control structure that, in our judgment, could adversely affect the organization's ability to record, process, summarize, and report financial data consistent with the assertions of management in the financial statements.

Our study and evaluation disclosed the following conditions that we believe result in more than a relatively low risk that errors or irregularities in amounts that would be material in relation to the financial statements of Jallo, Inc. may occur and not be detected within a timely period. Programmed controls have not been developed for editing computer input. As a result, we found numerous posting errors during our tests of customer accounts, creditor accounts, and inventory accounts. We also noted that the company does not require data entry forms for the input of transactions into the EDP system. This weakness is compounded by a general lack of security over access to computer terminals and leads us to conclude that significant errors or irregularities could occur and go undetected given the absence of an adequate audit trail. We discussed these conditions with Elizabeth Benton, corporate controller of Jallo. Ms. Benton assured us that steps were being taken to correct the situation.

This report is intended solely for the information and use of the audit committee (board of directors, board of trustees, or owners in owner-managed enterprises), management, and others within the organization (or specified regulatory agency or other specified third party).

Source: *Codification of Statements on Auditing Standards,* Section AU 325.12.

EXHIBIT 14.9 Management Letter

March 1, 1994

Mr. Joel Adams, President
Jallo, Inc.
1010 Plaza Tower
Houston, TX 73775

Dear Mr. Adams:

We have audited the financial statements of Jallo, Inc. for the year ended December 31, 1993, and have issued our report thereon dated February 26, 1994. As part of our audit, we made a study of control structure policies and procedures only to the extent we considered necessary to determine the nature, timing, and extent of our auditing procedures.

We have submitted to Ms. Benton, corporate controller, a detailed report of our suggestions for improvements in control structure policies and procedures. Our recommendations were discussed with personnel responsible for the various areas and many of them are currently being implemented. Summarized below are our suggestions of importance which we believe warrant your attention.

COMPUTER CONTROLS

Adequate input controls over the processing of purchases and sales transactions do not exist. As a result, numerous errors are made in posting customer, creditor, and inventory accounts. We strongly urge installing such controls as validity tests, reasonableness tests, check digits, and control totals as part of the transaction editing procedure. In addition, access to computer terminals is generally unlimited and recording forms are not utilized in inputting transactions into the system. These weaknesses can result in erroneous or unauthorized transactions being processed by the system. We recommend a policy of establishing passwords and codes to insure security over computer data bases. We also suggest that the company design and require the use of recording forms for all transactions input directly into the EDP system.

INVENTORY CONTROL AT BRANCHES

Although branch managers are responsible for inventory control at their respective locations, we noted significant adjustments of the perpetual records, maintained at the home office, to the year-end physical inventories at several of the branches. We recommend that the internal audit staff be assigned the task of test counting inventories at branches during the year and comparing such counts with the perpetual records. Such periodic "spot-checking" on an unannounced basis should strengthen inventory control.

CREDIT APPROVAL

Inasmuch as Mr. Reece, credit manager, retired in January, 1993, and has not yet been replaced, customer orders have been processed without credit approval. Our aging analysis of trade accounts receivable indicated a significant increase, over the previous year end, of past due accounts. We recommend that either a new credit manager be hired or an existing staff person be assigned the responsibility for credit approval.

We appreciate the opportunity to present these comments for your consideration and we are prepared to discuss them at your convenience.

Sincerely,

Ricks and Hanley, CPAs

KEY TERMS

Accounting symmetry
Analytical procedures — (audit review)
Auditor/client conference
Client representation letter
Collateral
Communication with audit committee
Compensating balance requirements
Confirmation of securities
Disposal of a segment
Examination of debt agreements
Examination of securities
Form vs. substance

Investment ledger
Loan defaults
Loan restructuring
Management letter
Open items
Related-party transactions
Reportable conditions
Reportable conditions letter
Type I subsequent event
Type II subsequent event
Workpaper review

COMPUTER AUDIT PRACTICE CASE

Trim Lawn Manufacturing Company
As part of the audit of the financing and investing cycle, complete the following exercises contained in the Trim Lawn audit practice case:

■ Module XII: Analysis of marketable securities

■ Module XIII: Mortgage note payable and note payable to GemCorp

■ Module XIV: Working trial balance

REVIEW QUESTIONS

1. In examining investment securities, the auditor traces from investment records to count sheets and from count sheets to investment records. Why is such two-way tracing necessary?

2. As part of the examination of investment securities, the auditor should record serial numbers in the workpapers on which the counts are recorded. Explain why this is necessary.

3. What specific audit objectives can be met by examining long-term debt agreements?

4. How does the reading of directors' minutes assist the auditor in satisfying the objectives related to the audit of stockholders' equity?

5. What is the auditor's responsibility relative to related-party transactions?

6. State two ways in which financial statements might be distorted by the existence of related-party transactions.

7. Why must the auditor be concerned about restrictive covenants contained in loan agreements?

8. If the client is reporting a "disposal of a segment," the auditor must obtain satisfaction concerning two aspects of classification. Explain which aspects and why.

9. Why is it necessary for the auditor to apply analytical procedures as part of overall audit review?

10. What impact might a modification of materiality thresholds have on the audit?

11. Differentiate between a Type I and Type II subsequent event.
12. What is the auditor's responsibility for locating subsequent events?
13. How does the auditor locate subsequent events?
14. Explain the importance of the workpaper review.
15. Define the *open items workpaper* and explain its significance.
16. What topics are commonly covered during the auditor/client conference held at the close of audit field work?
17. To what extent does the client representation letter relieve the auditor of responsibility?
18. Differentiate between the reportable conditions communication and the management letter.

MULTIPLE CHOICE QUESTIONS FROM CPA EXAMINATIONS

1. Which of the following would be the least likely to be comparable between similar corporations in the same industry line of business?
   a. Earnings per share.
   b. Return on total assets before interest and taxes.
   c. Accounts receivable turnover.
   d. Operating cycle.

2. During an examination of a publicly held company, the auditor should obtain written confirmation regarding debenture transactions from the
   a. Debenture holders.
   b. Client's attorney.
   c. Internal auditors.
   d. Trustee.

3. The auditor's program for the examination of long-term debt should include steps that require the
   a. Verification of the existence of the bondholders.
   b. Examination of any bond trust indenture.
   c. Inspection of the accounts payable subsidiary ledger.
   d. Investigation of credits to the bond interest income account.

4. An audit program for the examination of the retained earnings account should include a step that requires verification of the
   a. Market value used to charge retained earnings to account for a two-for-one stock split.
   b. Approval of the adjustment to the beginning balances as a result of a write-down of an account receivable.
   c. Authorization for both cash and stock dividends.
   d. Gain or loss resulting from disposition of treasury shares.

5. All corporate capital stock transactions should ultimately be traced to the
   a. Minutes of the board of directors.
   b. Cash receipts journal.
   c. Cash disbursements journal.
   d. Numbered stock certificates.

6. Which of the following expressions is least likely to be included in a client's representation letter?
   a. No events have occurred subsequent to the balance sheet date that require adjustment to, or disclosure in, the financial statements.
   b. The company has complied with all aspects of contractual agreements that would have a material effect on the financial statements in the event of non-compliance.
   c. Management acknowledges responsibility for illegal actions committed by employees.
   d. Management has made available all financial statements and related data.

7. Which of the following auditing procedures is ordinarily performed last?
   a. Reading of the minutes of the directors' meetings.
   b. Confirming accounts payable.
   c. Obtaining a management representation letter.
   d. Testing of the purchasing function.

8. To ascertain the exact name of the corporate client, the auditor relies primarily on
   a. Corporate minutes.
   b. Bylaws.
   c. Articles of incorporation.
   d. Tax returns.

9. Which of the following statements regarding the audit of negotiable notes receivable is not correct?
   a. Confirmation from the debtor is an acceptable alternative to inspection.
   b. Materiality of the amount involved is a factor considered when selecting the accounts to be confirmed.
   c. Physical inspection of a note by the auditor does not provide conclusive evidence.
   d. Notes receivable discounted with recourse need to be confirmed.

10. For all audits of financial statements made in accordance with generally accepted auditing standards, the use of analytical procedures is required to some extent

	In the planning stage	As a substantive test	In the review stage
a.	Yes	No	Yes
b.	No	Yes	No
c.	No	Yes	Yes
d.	Yes	No	No

11. The primary objective of analytical procedures used in the final review stage of an audit is to
    a. Obtain evidence from details tested to corroborate particular assertions.
    b. Identify areas that represent specific risks relevant to the audit.
    c. Assist the auditor in assessing the validity of the conclusions reached.
    d. Satisfy doubts when questions arise about a client's ability to continue in existence.

12. An auditor's working papers should
    a. Not be permitted to serve as a reference source for the client.

b. Not contain critical comments concerning management.

c. Show that the accounting records agree or reconcile with the financial statements.

d. Be considered the primary support for the financial statements being audited.

13. An auditor would most likely verify the interest earned on bond investments by
   a. Vouching the receipt and deposit of interest checks.
   b. Confirming the bond interest rate with the issuer of the bonds.
   c. Recomputing the interest earned on the basis of face amount, interest rate, and period held.
   d. Testing the internal controls over cash receipts.

14. Which of the following documentation is required for an audit in accordance with generally accepted auditing standards?
   a. An internal control questionnaire.
   b. A client engagement letter.
   c. A planning memorandum or checklist.
   d. A client representation letter.

15. Which of the following statements ordinarily is included among the written client representations obtained by the auditor?
   a. Management acknowledges that there are *no* material weaknesses in the internal control structure.
   b. Sufficient evidential matter has been made available to permit the issuance of an unqualified opinion.
   c. Compensating balances and other arrangements involving restrictions on cash balances have been disclosed.
   d. Management acknowledges responsibility for illegal actions committed by employees.

16. An auditor searching for related-party transactions should obtain an understanding of each subsidiary's relationship to the total entity because
   a. This may permit the audit of intercompany balances to be performed as of concurrent dates.
   b. Intercompany transactions may have been consummated on terms equivalent to arm's length transactions.
   c. This may reveal whether particular transactions would have taken place if the parties had *not* been related.
   d. The business structure may be deliberately designed to obscure related-party transactions.

17. An auditor's purpose in reviewing the renewal of a note payable shortly after the balance sheet date most likely is to obtain evidence concerning management's assertions about
   a. Existence or occurrence.
   b. Presentation and disclosure.
   c. Completeness.
   d. Valuation or allocation.

18. An auditor's program to examine long-term debt most likely would include steps that require
   a. Comparing the carrying amount of the debt to its year-end market value.
   b. Correlating interest expense recorded for the period with outstanding debt.

    c. Verifying the existence of the holders of the debt by direct confirmation.

    d. Inspecting the accounts payable subsidiary ledger for unrecorded long-term debt.

19. Which of the following matters is an auditor required to communicate to an entity's audit committee?

	Significant audit adjustments	*Changes in significant accounting policies*
a.	Yes	Yes
b.	Yes	No
c.	No	Yes
d.	No	No

ESSAY QUESTIONS AND PROBLEMS

14.1 Alan Kent, a CPA who is engaged in the audit of the financial statements of Bass Corporation for the year ended December 31, 1992, is about to commence an audit of the noncurrent investment securities. Bass's records indicate that the company owns various bearer bonds, as well as 25 percent of the outstanding common stock of Commercial Industrial, Inc. Kent is satisfied with evidence that supports the presumption of significant influence over Commercial Industrial, Inc. The various securities are at two locations. Recently acquired securities are in the company's safe in the custody of the treasurer. All other securities are in the company's bank safe deposit box. All of the securities in Bass's portfolio are actively traded in a broad market.

Required:
    a. Assuming that the internal control structure policies and procedures surrounding securities is satisfactory, what are the objectives of the examination of these noncurrent investment securities?

    b. What audit procedures should be undertaken by Kent with respect to the examination of Bass's noncurrent investment securities? (AICPA adapted)

14.2 During the examination of the annual financial statements of Amis Manufacturing, Inc., the company's president, R. Alderman, and Ellen Luddy, the auditor, reviewed matters that were supposed to be included in a written representation letter. Upon receipt of the client representation letter in Exhibit 14.10, Luddy contacted Alderman to state that it was incomplete.

Required:
Identify the other matters that Alderman's representation letter should specifically confirm. (AICPA adapted)

14.3 Steve Andrews, a CPA, has been engaged to examine the financial statements of Broadwall Corporation for the year ended December 31, 1993. During the year, Broadwall obtained a long-term loan from a local bank pursuant to a financing agreement which provided that the:
    a. Loan was to be secured by the company's inventory and accounts receivable.

    b. Company was to maintain a debt to equity ratio not to exceed two to one.

    c. Company was not to pay dividends without permission from the bank.

    d. Monthly installment payments were to commence July 1, 1993.

EXHIBIT 14.10   Problem 14.2 Client Representation Letter

To E. K. Luddy, CPA

In connection with your audit of the balance sheet of Amis Manufacturing, Inc., as of December 31, 1993, and the related statements of income, retained earnings, and cash flows for the year then ended, for the purpose of expressing an opinion as to whether the financial statements present fairly the financial position, results of operations, and cash flows of Amis Manufacturing, Inc., in conformity with generally accepted accounting principles, we confirm, to the best of our knowledge and belief, the following representations made to you during your examination. There were no

1. Plans or intentions that may materially affect the carrying value or classification of assets and liabilities.

2. Communications from regulatory agencies concerning noncompliance with, or deficiencies in, financial reporting practices.

3. Agreements to repurchase assets previously sold.

4. Violations or possible violations of laws or regulations whose effects should be considered for disclosure in the financial statements or as a basis for recording a loss contingency.

5. Unasserted claims or assessments that our lawyer has advised are probable of assertion and must be disclosed in accordance with Statement of Financial Accounting Standards No. 5.

6. Capital stock repurchase options or agreements or capital stock reserved for options, warrants, conversions, or other requirements.

7. Compensating balance or other arrangements involving restrictions on cash balances.

R. Alderman, President
Amis Manufacturing, Inc.

March 14, 1994

In addition, during the year the company also borrowed amounts on a short-term basis from the president of the company, including substantial amounts just prior to year end.

Required:

a. For purposes of Andrews' audit of the financial statements of Broadwall Corporation, what procedures should Andrews employ in examining the described loans? Identify the audit objective served by each of the procedures.

b. What financial statement disclosures should Andrews expect to find with respect to the loans from the president? (AICPA adapted)

14.4 The schedule in Exhibit 14.11 was prepared by the controller of World Manufacturing, Inc., for use by the independent auditors during their examination of World's year-end financial statements. All procedures performed by the audit

EXHIBIT 14.11 Problem 14.4 Securities Schedule

World Manufacturing, Inc.
Marketable Securities
Year Ended December 31, 1992

Description of Security	Corp. Bonds %	Year Due	Serial No.	Face Value of Bonds	Gen. Ledger 1/1	Purch. in 1992	Sold in 1992	Cost	Gen. Ledger 12/31	12/31 Market	Pay Date(s)	Amount Received	Accruals 12/31
Corp. Bonds													
A	6	2002	21-7	$10,000	9,400 a				9,400	9,100	7/15	300 b,d	275
D	4	1994	73-0	30,000	27,500 a				27,500	26,220	12/1	1,200 b,d	100
G	9	2009	16-4	5,000	4,000 a				4,000	5,080	8/1	450 b,d	188
Rc	5	1996	08-2	70,000	66,000 a		57,000 b	66,000					
Sc	10	2010	07-4	100,000		100,000 e			100,000	101,250	7/1	5,000 b,d	5000
					$106,900	100,000	57,000	66,000	140,900	141,650		7,250	5563
					a,f	f	f	f	f,g	f		f	f
Stocks													
P common 1000 shares			1044		$7,500 a				7,500	7,600	3/1	750 b,d	
											6/1	750 b,d	
											9/1	750 b,d	
											12/1	750 b,d	250
U common 50 shares			8530		9,700 a				9,700	9,800	2/1	800 b,d	
											8/1	800 b,d	667
					$17,200				17,200	17,400		4,600	917
					a,f				f,g	f		f	f

Legends and comments relative to above
a = Beginning balances agreed to 1991 working papers
b = Traced to cash receipts
c = Minutes examined (purchase and sales approved by the board of directors)
d = Agreed to 1099
e = Confirmed by tracing to broker's advice
f = Totals footed
g = Agreed to general ledger

assistant were noted at the bottom "Legend" section, and it was properly initialed, dated and indexed, and then submitted to a senior member of the audit staff for review. The client's internal control was reviewed and considered to be satisfactory.

Required:

a. What information that is essential to the audit of marketable securities is missing from this schedule?

b. What essential audit procedures were not noted as having been performed by the audit assistant? (AICPA adapted)

14.5 Phoenix, Inc., a developer and producer of personal computers, printers, and other computer hardware, leases factory and office space at its only location in the Silicon Valley area of California. Quarterly lease payments of $150,000 are charged to rent expense as paid or accrued. The lease is noncancellable and was signed on January 1, 1993. The present value of the future lease payments at 1/1/93 is $3,467,215. This amount is based on the 12 percent interest rate stated in the lease agreement.

Required:

a. As in-charge auditor examining the Phoenix financial statements for the year ended 12/31/93, what additional information do you need in order to determine whether the lease is a financing or operating lease?

b. What audit procedures would you apply in gathering the information needed in (a)?

c. Assuming that the lease is considered a financing lease, and the estimated useful life and salvage value of the property are 10 years and $600,000 respectively, prepare an audit workpaper for the lease liability. Assume that the quarterly payments are due on April 1, July 1, October 1, and January 1. Include all necessary audit legends as evidence of procedures performed.

d. Draft any audit adjustments indicated by the workpaper prepared in (c).

14.6 Karen Jones, a CPA and the continuing auditor of Sussex, Inc., is beginning the audit of the common stock and treasury stock accounts. Jones has decided to design substantive tests without further testing of Sussex' internal control procedures.

Sussex has no par, no stated value common stock, and acts as its own registrar and transfer agent. During the past year, Sussex both issued and reacquired shares of its own common stock, some of which the company still owned at year end. Additional common stock transactions occurred among the shareholders during the year.

Common stock transactions can be traced to individual shareholders' accounts in a subsidiary ledger and to a stock certificate book. The company has not paid any cash or stock dividends. There are no other classes of stock, stock rights, warrants, or option plans.

Required:

What substantive audit procedures should Jones apply in examining the common stock and treasury stock accounts? (AICPA adapted)

14.7 For each of the following situations, identify the auditing procedures that should have alerted the auditor to the risk associated with the examination, and those procedures that should have assisted the auditor in locating the irregularity.

a. Chelang, Inc., a producer and distributor of auto replacement parts, has experienced difficulty in maintaining income levels due to competition from foreign producers. In a desperation move to ward off a possible proxy fight with dissident stockholders, John Long, Chelang's CEO, formed a shell company. Jongo Auto Care Centers, Inc., as the company was named, supposedly operated a regional chain of auto repair shops. Documents were fabricated in support of fictitious sales transactions with Jongo, the new customer. As a result, Chelang's earnings increased significantly over the preceding year. Others in the industry were recording declines and even losses for the same period.

b. Rosco Tanner, the president and chief executive officer of Telaney, Inc., had been living well beyond his means. As a result, he had several short positions to cover with his stockbrokers, and his creditors were becoming desperate in their attempts to collect the amounts owing them. Although Rosco could probably have "weathered the storm" by cutting back on his lavish life style, he had come to enjoy the "high living." Instead of reducing his spending, therefore, he borrowed the needed funds from the corporation. In order to confuse the auditors, he used a wholly owned subsidiary and several banks as conduits for moving the funds. The usual procedure was to have Telaney issue a note to Waxen Corp., the wholly owned subsidiary. Waxen discounted the note at one of the banks and transferred the money to Telaney. Telaney then loaned the funds to Waxen, who, in turn, loaned them to Tanner. Although Tanner pledged his stock in Telaney as collateral, the stock's intrinsic value rested upon Tanner's ability to repay the loans (the loans receivable amounts represented 35 percent of Telaney's total assets)—and Tanner was insolvent due to his continued run of "bad luck" in the stock market and his trips to Europe.

14.8 Discuss the significance of the auditor's review of subsequent events, and differentiate between Type I and Type II subsequent events. Explain how each of the following procedures assists the auditor in locating subsequent events—be specific in describing the kinds of events revealed by each set of procedures:
   a. Obtaining a letter from the client's legal counsel.
   b. Reading the minutes of the directors' meetings since year end.
   c. Reading the latest interim financial statements since year end.

14.9 Temple, CPA, is auditing the financial statements of Ford Lumber Yards, Inc., a privately held corporation with 300 employees and five stockholders, three of whom are active in management. Ford has been in business for many years, but has never had its financial statements audited. Temple suspects that the substance of some of Ford's business transactions differs from their form because of the pervasiveness of related-party relationships and transactions in the local building supplies industry.

Required:
Describe the audit procedures Temple should apply to identify related party relationships and transactions. (AICPA adapted)

14.10 Green, CPA, is auditing the financial statements of Taylor Corporation for the year ended December 31, 1993. Green plans to complete the field work and sign the auditor's report about May 10, 1994. Green is concerned about events and transactions occurring after December 31, 1993, that may affect the 1993 financial statements.

Exhibit 14.12 Problem 14.11 Schedule of Long-Term Liabilities

American Widgets, Inc.
WORKING PAPERS
December 31, 1994

Lender	Interest Rate	Payment Terms	Collateral	Balance 12/31/93	1994 Borrowings	1994 Reductions	Balance 12/31/94	Interest paid to	Accrued Interest Payable 12/31/94	Comments
φ First Commercial Bank	12%	Interest only on 25th of month, principal due in full 1/1/98; no prepayment penalty	Inventories	$ 50,000 √	$300,000 A 1/31/97	$100,000 ⊕ 6/30/94	$250,000 CX	12/25/94	$2,500 NR	Dividend of $80,000 paid 9/2/94 (W/P N-3) violated a provision of the debt agreement, which thereby permits lender to demand immediate payment; lender has refused to waive this violation
φ Lender's Capital Corp.	Prime plus 1%	Interest only on last day of month, principal due in full 3/5/96	2nd Mortgage on Park St. Building	100,000 √	50,000 A 2/29/94	—	200,000 C	12/31/94	—	Prime rate was 8% to 9% during the year
φ Gigantic Building & Loan Assoc.	12%	$5,000 principal plus interest due on 5th of month, due in full 12/31/2005	1st Mortgage on Park St. Building	720,000 √	—	60,000 θ	660,000 C	12/5/94	5,642 R	Reclassification entry for current portion proposed (See RJE-3)
φ J. Lott, majority stockholder	0%	Due in full 12/31/97	Unsecured	300,000 √	—	100,000 N 12/31/94	200,000 C	—	—	Borrowed additional $100,000 from J. Lott on 1/7/95
				$1,170,000 √ F	$350,000 F	$260,000 F	$1,310,000 T/B F		$8,142 T/B F	

Interest costs from long-term debt

Interest expense for year $281,333 T/B
Average loan balance outstanding $1,406,667 R

Five year maturities (for disclosure purposes)

Year end	
12/31/95	$ 60,000
12/31/96	260,000
12/31/97	260,000
12/31/98	310,000
12/31/99	60,000
Thereafter	360,000
	$1,310,000 F

Overall conclusions
Long-term debt, accrued interest payable, and interest expense are correct and complete at 12/31/94

Tickmark legend

F   Readded, foots correctly
C   Confirmed without exception, W/P K-2
CX Confirmed with exception. W/P K-3
NR Does not recompute correctly
A   Agreed to loan agreement, validated bank deposit ticket, and board of directors authorization, W/P W-7
φ   Agreed to canceled checks and lender's monthly statements
N   Agreed to cash disbursements journal and canceled check dated 12/31/94, clearing 1/8/95
T/B Traced to working trial balance
√   Agreed to 12/31/93 working papers
φ   Agreed interest rate, term, and collateral to copy of note and loan agreement
⊕   Agreed to canceled check and board of directors' authorization, W/P W-7

Required:

a. What are the general types of subsequent events that require Green's consideration and evaluation?

b. What are the auditing procedures Green should consider performing to gather evidence concerning subsequent events? (AICPA adapted)

14.11 Exhibit 14.12 contains a long-term debt working paper (indexed K-1). The working paper was prepared by client personnel and audited by AA, an audit assistant, during the calendar year 1994 audit of American Widgets, Inc., a continuing audit client. The engagement supervisor is reviewing the working papers thoroughly.

Required:

Identify the deficiencies in the working paper that the engagement supervisor should discover. (AICPA adapted)

APPENDIX

Auditing Objectives and Procedures: Financing and Investing Cycle

INVESTING TRANSACTIONS

Audit Objectives	Audit Evidence and Procedures
Existence and Completeness	***Physical Evidence***
Do the securities exist?	• Assume control over all negotiable securities, cash on hand, and cash funds (to prevent substitution).
	• Examine securities and record serial numbers for later comparison with recorded accountability (investment ledger).
	• Examine notes receivable.
	• Obtain receipt upon return of cash and securities.
	Confirmation Evidence
	• Confirm existence of securities not on premises.
Rights and Obligations	***Physical Evidence***
Are the securities owned by the client?	• Examine securities for evidence that client is the registered owner.
	• Examine for evidence of pledging as collateral on loans.

Confirmation Evidence

- Confirm ownership with holders of securities not on the premises.
- Confirm notes receivable with makers.

Valuation

Are securities properly valued?

- *Lower of cost or market*
- *Equity for controlling interest*
- *Net realizable value for notes receivable*

Documentary Evidence

- Perform cut-off tests:
  1. Verify dividends by reference to *Standard & Poor's* or *Moody's*.
  2. Analyze intercompany accounts, making certain both sides of intercompany transactions have been consistently recorded and look for related-party transactions.
- Trace securities examined or confirmed two ways:
  1. Trace from count sheets or returned confirmations to investment ledger (note serial numbers to detect substitution).
  2. Trace from investment ledger to count sheets or returned confirmations for evidence of missing securities.
- Vouch additions and disposals by reference to the following, as necessary;
  1. Broker's advice
  2. Remittance advice, cash receipts record, and bank statement.
  3. Canceled check.
- Examine minutes for proper authorization of major purchases and sales.
- Examine income statements of unconsolidated subsidiaries accounted for on an equity basis.
- Determine market value as of the balance sheet date.

Mathematical Evidence

- Recompute premium or discount amortization on long-term bond investments.
- Recompute gain or loss on disposal.
- Recompute interest accrual.
- Calculate implicit interest where applicable.
- Perform cost or market value test for marketable securities:
  1. Do separate analysis for long-term and short-term portfolios.
  2. Determine need for adjustment based on aggregate portfolio.

Analytical Evidence

- Compare interest and dividends with prior years and investigate significant changes.

Presentation and Disclosure

Are securities and notes receivable properly classified as to current vs. noncurrent?

Have necessary disclosures been made as to pledging, and gains and losses on transactions?

Hearsay Evidence

- Inquire of management as to nature of investments and reasons for holding them
- Inquire as to pledging of securities as loan collateral.
- Inquire as to related-party transactions.

Documentary Evidence

- Examine minutes for evidence of pledging or related-party transactions.
- Determine, by vouching, that dividends on stock reported under the equity method have been reflected as reductions in the investment account.

BORROWING TRANSACTIONS

Audit Objectives

Audit Evidence and Procedures

Existence and Completeness

Documentary Evidence

Any unrecorded liabilities?

Are liabilities properly authorized?

- Examine the following for possible failure to record long-term liabilities:
  1. Lease agreements,
  2. Pension and profit sharing plans,
  3. Directors' minutes,
  4. Bank confirmations,
  5. Bond indentures and mortgage agreements, and
  6. Directors' minutes for evidence of loan authorization,

Hearsay Evidence

- Obtain client representation letter.

Valuation

Are long-term liabilities reflected at net present value?

Confirmation Evidence

- Confirm liabilities, as appropriate.

Documentary Evidence

- Examine lease agreements for contingent rentals.
- Examine pension agreements for vesting provisions.
- Examine loan agreements for possible need to impute interest.
- Vouch the following on a test basis:
  1. Interest payments,
  2. Lease payments,
  3. Pension plan contributions.

Mathematical Evidence

- Recompute the following on a test basis:
  1. Premium and discount amortization,
  2. Lease amortization,
  3. Contingent rentals,
  4. Interest accruals,
  5. Gain or loss on bond redemptions,
  6. Change in deferred taxes,
  7. Pension liability.
- Compute implicit interest, if applicable.

Analytical Evidence

- Compare liabilities and related expenses with prior year and investigate significant changes.

Hearsay Evidence

- Obtain client representation letter.

Presentation and Disclosure

Have current portions of long-term debt been reclassified as current?

Documentary Evidence

- Examine liability agreements for the following:
  1. Restrictive covenants; consider adequacy of disclosure given violations of restrictive covenants.
  2. Collateral requirements; consider adequacy of disclosure given collateral requirements.
  3. Other disclosure requirements (future cash flows under lease agreements, details surrounding bond issues, pension provisions, etc.).

STOCKHOLDERS' EQUITY TRANSACTIONS

Audit Objectives	Audit Evidence and Procedures

Valuation

Physical Evidence

Recognize no gains or losses on stockholders' equity transactions

Examine treasury stock certificates.

Confirmation Evidence

Confirm stock issuance and dividends with registrar and transfer agent.

Documentary Evidence

Are capital stock transactions properly authorized?

- Examine minutes for dividend declarations and proper authorization of the following:
  1. Stock issuance,
  2. Stock reacquisition,
  3. Stock retirements, and
  4. Stock options.
- Vouch dividend declarations and payments.
- Vouch treasury stock transactions.
- Trace stock issuance proceeds to bank statement.
- Examine evidence of valuation where stock is issued for noncash assets.

Mathematical Evidence

- Determine whether simple or complex capital structure and recompute earnings per share.
- Recompute stock option credit.
- Recalculate debit to retained earnings for stock dividends.

Presentation and Disclosure

Documentary Evidence

Proper distinction between invested capital and earned capital?

- Examine loan agreements and directors' minutes for possible restrictions on retained earnings.
- Examine stock option agreements for details surrounding the options:
  1. Employees participating,
  2. Shares involved
  3. Option prices, and
  4. Exercise dates.

- Examine corporate charter for description of various classes of stock:
  1. Whether preferred is participating or cumulative.
  2. Dividends in arrears on cumulative preferred.
  3. Liquidation values of preferred, if different from par.

15

Audit Reports

CHAPTER OUTLINE

I. **Nature of the audit report—standard form**

II. **Components of the audit report**
   A. Title and addressee
   B. Introductory paragraph
   C. Scope paragraph
   D. Opinion paragraph
   E. Signature and date

III. **Kinds of audit opinions**
   A. Unqualified
   B. Qualified
   C. Adverse
   D. Disclaimer

IV. **Divided responsibility**

V. **Explanatory paragraph: unqualified opinion**
   A. Departure from designated principle
   B. Material uncertainty
   C. Ability of entity to continue as a going concern
   D. Change in accounting principle
   E. Emphasis of a matter

VI. **Other topics affecting audit reports**
   A. Updating the audit report
   B. Subsequent discovery of facts existing at the date of the audit report
   C. The meaning of "present fairly in conformity with GAAP"
   D. Other information in documents containing audited financial statements
   E. Supplemental information required by FASB
   F. Related-party transactions
   G. Omitted procedures discovered after the date of the audit report

OVERVIEW

The audit report is the culminating step in the audit process. Expressing an audit opinion is the auditor's overriding goal. Figure 15.1 emphasizes the placement of the audit report at the end of the audit process. The audit report concisely describes the auditor's responsibility, the nature of the examination, and the auditor's findings. Chapter 15 begins by presenting the standard audit report and describing the conditions that justify its issuance. The discussion then turns to departures from the standard report in the form of qualified opinions, adverse opinions, and disclaimers of opinion. Explanatory paragraphs, as distinguished from qualified opinions, are also considered.

The chapter concludes by considering other topics that affect audit reports. These topics are subsequent discovery of facts existing at the date of the audit report, the meaning of "present fairly in accordance with GAAP," other information in documents containing audited financial statements, supplemental information required by FASB, related-party transactions, and omitted procedures discovered after the date of the audit report.

STUDY OBJECTIVES

After reading this chapter, you should be able to:

1. Describe the standard audit report and the conditions under which issued
2. Differentiate among unqualified opinions, qualified opinions, adverse opinions, and disclaimers of opinion
3. Distinguish between an explanatory paragraph and a qualified opinion
4. Define and give examples of material scope limitations
5. Define and give examples of departures from GAAP
6. Describe situations under which an explanatory paragraph might be included in the audit report
7. Define *continuing auditor* and describe the "updating" of audit reports

FIGURE 15.1   The Audit Process

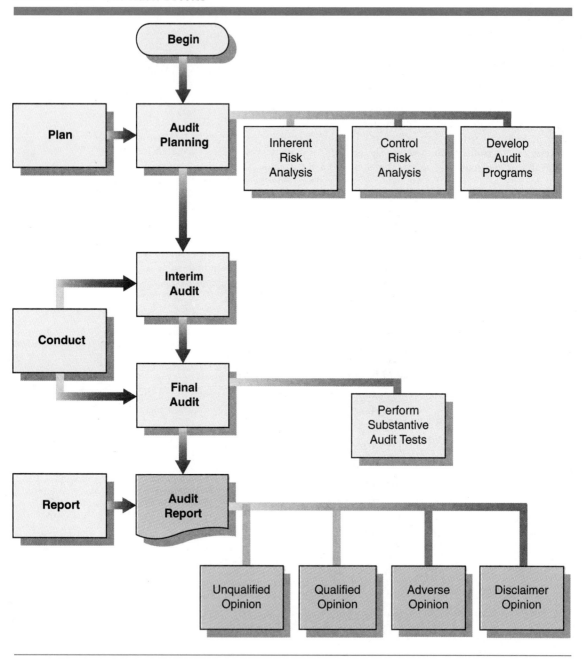

NATURE OF THE AUDIT REPORT

The audit report is the culmination of the audit process. Gathering and evaluating sufficient competent evidence to express an opinion is the auditor's overriding goal. The report cannot be drafted, nor can the opinion be formulated, until the auditor has assessed audit risk and completed all substantive tests. The report cannot be released to stockholders and others until the client has agreed to reflect the necessary audit adjustments, reclassifications, and footnote disclosures in the financial statements.

Exhibit 15.1 illustrates the **standard audit report** form recommended by the AICPA. The report contains:

1. An *introductory paragraph* which differentiates management's responsibility from that of the auditor;
2. A *scope paragraph* which describes the nature of the examination, including any limitations on the application of procedures, and acknowledges that an audit

EXHIBIT 15.1   Standard Audit Report

REPORT OF INDEPENDENT AUDITORS

To the Board of Directors and Stockholders of Microsoft Corporation:

We have audited the accompanying balance sheets of Microsoft Corporation and subsidiaries as of June 30, 1991 and 1990, and the related statements of income, stockholders' equity, and cash flows for each of the three years in the period ended June 30, 1991. These financial statements are the responsibility of the company's management. Our responsibility is to express an opinion on these financial statements based on our audits.

We conducted our audits in accordance with generally accepted auditing standards. Those standards require that we plan and perform the audit to obtain reasonable assurance about whether the financial statements are free of material misstatement. An audit includes examining, on a test basis, evidence supporting the amounts and disclosures in the financial statements. An audit also includes assessing the accounting principles used and significant estimates made by management, as well as evaluating the overall financial statement presentation. We believe that our audits provide a reasonable basis for our opinion.

In our opinion, the financial statements referred to above present fairly, in all material respects, the financial position of Microsoft Corporation and subsidiaries as of June 30, 1991 and 1990, and the results of their operations and their cash flows for each of the three years in the period ended June 30, 1991 in conformity with generally accepted accounting principles.

Deloitte & Touche
Bellevue, Washington

July 25, 1991

Source: Mead Data Central, the NAARS Service.

provides reasonable assurance that the financial statements are free of material misstatement; and

3. An *opinion paragraph* which contains an expression of *opinion* concerning the fairness of the financial statements.

Management is responsible for preparing the financial statements. The independent CPA is responsible for auditing them and expressing an opinion as to their fairness.

Scope is concerned with whether the examination was conducted in accordance with *generally accepted auditing standards* (GAAS). Failure to apply procedures considered necessary in the circumstances is labeled as a **scope restriction.** Scope restrictions, depending on materiality, may preclude the rendering of an unqualified opinion.

The audit opinion describes the auditor's findings. These findings are expressed in terms of whether the financial statements are presented in accordance with *generally accepted accounting principles* (GAAP). The audit report must contain either an expression of an opinion or an assertion to the effect that an opinion cannot be rendered and the reasons for this.

COMPONENTS OF THE AUDIT REPORT

Each part of the audit report is significant in terms of the information conveyed to the user and the responsibility assumed by the auditor. The components and their importance are addressed in the following paragraphs.

Title

The audit report *must* contain a title. Also, except when the auditor lacks independence, the title must include the word *independent*.[1]

Addressee

The audit report may be addressed to the company, the stockholders, the board of directors, or some combination of these. If the auditor is appointed by the stockholders at the annual meeting, the report should be addressed to them.

Introductory Paragraph

The **introductory paragraph** identifies the financial statements covered by the audit report and clearly differentiates management's responsibility for preparing the financial statements from the auditor's responsibility for expressing an opinion on them. Management's responsibility is direct, whereas the auditor has an indirect responsibility for exercising due care in conducting the examination and expressing an opinion on the financial statements.

---

[1]Auditing Standards Board, *AICPA Professional Standards,* New York: AICPA, Section AU 508.

Scope Paragraph

The **scope paragraph** describes what the auditor did. Specifically, it states whether or not the audit was conducted in accordance with generally accepted auditing standards (GAAS). It also states the GAAS requirement that an audit be planned to provide reasonable assurance that the financial statements are free of material misstatement. Material scope restrictions should be identified in the scope paragraph and described further in a fourth paragraph, between the scope and opinion paragraphs, of the audit report. These matters are more fully discussed below.

Opinion Paragraph

The **opinion paragraph** conveys the auditor's findings. If, in the auditor's opinion, the financial statements are presented fairly in accordance with GAAP, the standard opinion paragraph (unqualified opinion) should be rendered. Material departures from GAAP, including inadequate footnote disclosure, should prompt the auditor to depart from the standard wording. Such departures may assume the form of a qualified or adverse opinion.

Signature and Date

The report should be signed by the auditor and is usually dated as of the close of audit field work. The date is significant because it represents the time limit on the auditor's responsibility for locating Type I and Type II subsequent events. The auditor does not have responsibility to make any inquiries or to conduct any audit procedures after this date.

If a material subsequent event that occurred after this date, but prior to issuance of the audit report, comes to the auditor's attention *and* requires footnote disclosure, the auditor may elect to **dual-date the audit report.** The two relevant dates in a dual-dated report are the date of completion of audit field work and the date of the subsequent event.[2] Exhibit 15.2 illustrates a dual-dated audit report. The February 26th subsequent event, referred to in this report, involved a merger of Meditrust with another company and was significant enough, in the auditor's judgment, to warrant dual dating. The details of the merger were fully described in Note 12, to which reference was made in the dual-dating line of the audit report.

---

[2]*Ibid.*, Section AU 530.05.

EXHIBIT 15.2   Dual-Dated Audit Report

REPORT OF INDEPENDENT AUDITORS

To the Shareholders and Trustees of Meditrust:

We have audited the accompanying consolidated balance sheets of Meditrust as of December 31, 1990 and 1989 and the related consolidated statements of income, changes in shareholders' equity, and cash flows for each of the three years in the period ended December 31, 1990. These financial statements are the responsibility of the Company's management. Our responsibility is to express an opinion on these financial statements based on our audits.

We conducted our audits in accordance with generally accepted auditing standards. Those standards require that we plan and perform the audit to obtain reasonable assurance about whether the financial statements are free of material misstatement. An audit includes examining, on a test basis, evidence supporting the amounts and disclosures in the financial statements. An audit also includes assessing the accounting principles used and significant estimates made by management, as well as evaluating the overall financial statement presentation. We believe that our audits provide a reasonable basis for our opinion.

In our opinion, the financial statements referred to above present fairly, in all material respects, the consolidated financial position of Meditrust at December 31, 1990 and 1989, and the consolidated results of its operations and its cash flows for each of the three years in the period ended December 31, 1990 in conformity with generally accepted accounting principles.

Coopers & Lybrand
Boston, Massachusetts

January 18, 1991
(Except for Note 12, as to which the date is February 26, 1991.)

Source: Mead Data Central, the NAARS Service.

KINDS OF AUDIT OPINIONS

Upon completion of the audit field work, the auditor must decide whether or not an opinion can be rendered. If an opinion cannot be rendered, the auditor must clearly disclaim an opinion and give the reasons for the disclaimer. If an opinion can be rendered, the auditor must decide whether to issue an unqualified, qualified, or adverse opinion. These alternatives are discussed in the following paragraphs.

Unqualified Opinion

Exhibit 15.1 contains an **unqualified audit opinion.** For the auditor to issue an unqualified opinion, the following conditions must exist:

1. No material scope restrictions, imposed or otherwise, have prevented the auditor from collecting sufficient, competent evidence, and
2. The financial statements, including footnote disclosures, contain no material departures from GAAP.

In terms of audit risk, an unqualified opinion means that the auditor was able to effectively manage detection risk, given the assessed levels of inherent risk and control risk. That is, the auditor gathered sufficient, competent evidence to express an unqualified opinion at that level of confidence complementing the overall audit risk level required by the auditor. In addition, the evidence either supported management's assertions, or management agreed to the auditor's recommended modifications in the form of audit adjustments, reclassifications and/or footnote disclosures.

Qualified and Adverse Opinions

Whenever financial statements contain a *departure from GAAP,* the auditor must decide whether to render an unqualified opinion, a qualified opinion, or an adverse opinion. Materiality is the criterion used in deciding among these alternatives. Materiality is judged within the context of whether the departure might significantly affect investment or lending decisions based on the financial statements. A departure that does not result in a material distortion of the financial statements does not warrant a qualification of the auditor's opinion.

Qualified and **adverse opinions** include a fourth paragraph more fully describing the reason for the opinion. This paragraph is placed between the scope and opinion paragraphs of the audit report (see Exhibit 15.3). Departures from GAAP may result from the application of an accounting principle that is at variance with the one prescribed by the body designated by the AICPA to formulate accounting principles—for example, a departure from a statement issued by the Financial Accounting Standards Board or inadequate footnote disclosure. Exhibit 15.3 illustrates an opinion qualified because of a departure from a prescribed principle.

An adverse opinion is issued whenever financial statements contain departures from GAAP that are too material to warrant only a qualification. Omitting all footnotes, for example, would ordinarily require an adverse audit opinion. In rendering an adverse opinion, the auditor states that the financial statements *do not present fairly* financial position, results of operations, and cash flows in conformity with GAAP. An adverse opinion is the subject of much graver user concern than is

EXHIBIT 15.3   Qualified Opinion—Departure from GAAP

REPORT OF INDEPENDENT AUDITORS

To the Board of Directors of Honda Motor Co., Ltd.:

We have audited the accompanying consolidated balance sheets of Honda Motor Co., Ltd. and subsidiaries as of March 31, 1990 and 1991, and the related consolidated statements of income, stockholders' equity and cash flows for each of the years in the three-year period ended March 31, 1991. These consolidated financial statements are the responsibility of the Company's management. Our responsibility is to express an opinion on these financial statements based on our audits.

We conducted our audits in accordance with generally accepted auditing standards. Those standards require that we plan and perform the audit to obtain reasonable assurance about whether the financial statements are free of material misstatement. An audit includes examining, on a test basis, evidence supporting the amounts and disclosures in the financial statements. An audit also includes assessing the accounting principles used and significant estimates made by management, as well as evaluating the overall financial statement presentation. We believe that our audits provide a reasonable basis for our opinion.

The segment information required to be disclosed in financial statements under United States generally accepted accounting principles is not presented in the accompanying consolidated financial statements. Foreign issuers are presently exempted from such disclosure requirement in Securities Exchange Act filings with the Securities and Exchange Commission of the United States.

In our opinion, except for the omission of the segment information referred to in the preceding paragraph, the consolidated financial statements referred to above present fairly, in all material respects, the financial position of Honda Motor Co., Ltd. and subsidiaries as of March 31, 1990 and 1991, and the results of their operations and their cash flows for each of the three years ended March 31, 1991 in conformity with United States generally accepted accounting principles.

KPMG Peat Marwick
Tokyo, Japan

May 17, 1991

Source: Mead Data Central, the NAARS Service.

a qualified opinion. Exhibit 15.4 illustrates an adverse opinion resulting from a material departure from GAAP.

The third standard of reporting states that informative disclosures in the financial statements are to be regarded as adequate unless otherwise stated in the audit report. When disclosure is inadequate, the auditor should provide the needed information in the audit report, if practicable. The opinion should still be qualified or adverse because the information is not disclosed in the financial statements or footnotes. In addition to omitted or misrepresented footnotes, inadequate disclosure may also assume the form of omitted financial statements. Failure to include the statement of cash flows, for example, results in inadequate disclosure, and should lead to a qualified audit opinion.

EXHIBIT 15.4 Adverse Opinion

REPORT OF INDEPENDENT AUDITORS

To the Stockholders and Directors of ABC Company:

We have audited the accompanying balance sheet of ABC Company as of December 31, 1993, and the related statements of income, retained earnings, and cash flows for the year then ended. These financial statements are the responsibility of the company's management. Our responsibility is to express an opinion on these financial statements based on our audit.

We conducted our audit in accordance with generally accepted auditing standards. Those standards require that we plan and perform the audit to obtain reasonable assurance about whether the financial statements are free of material misstatement. An audit includes examining, on a test basis, evidence supporting the amounts and disclosures in the financial statements. An audit also includes assessing the accounting principles used and significant estimates made by management, as well as evaluating the overall financial statement presentation. We believe that our audit provides a reasonable basis for our opinion.

As discussed in Note X to the financial statements, the company carries its property, plant and equipment accounts at appraisal values, and provides depreciation on the basis of such values. Further, the company does not provide for income taxes with respect to temporary differences between financial income and taxable income arising because of the use, for income tax purposes, of the installment method of reporting gross profit from certain types of sales. Generally accepted accounting principles require that property, plant and equipment be stated at an amount not in excess of cost, reduced by depreciation based on such amount, and that deferred income taxes be provided. Because of the departures from generally accepted accounting principles identified above, as of December 31, 1993, inventories have been increased $_____ by inclusion in manufacturing overhead of depreciation in excess of that based on cost; property, plant and equipment, less accumulated depreciation, is carried at $_____ in excess of an amount based on the cost to the company; and allocated income tax of $_____ has not been recorded, resulting in an increase of $_____ in retained earnings and in appraisal surplus of $_____. For the year ended December 31, 1993, cost of goods sold has been increased $_____ because of the effects of the depreciation accounting referred to above and deferred income taxes of $_____ have not been provided, resulting in an increase in net income and earnings per share of $_____ and $_____ respectively.

In our opinion, because of the effects of the matters discussed in the preceding paragraph, the financial statements referred to above do not present fairly, in conformity with generally accepted accounting principles, the financial position of ABC Company as of December 31, 1993, or the results of its operations and cash flows for the year then ended.

(Signature)

(Date)

Source: *Codification of Statements on Auditing Standards,* Section AU 508.69.

Qualified Opinions and Disclaimers of Opinion

The independent auditor should either qualify or disclaim an opinion, given **material scope restrictions.** A scope restriction means that the auditor has not gathered sufficient competent evidential matter to support an audit opinion.

Scope restrictions are sometimes **client-imposed.** For example, management may not permit the auditors to examine securities purportedly held as investments;

EXHIBIT 15.5   Qualified Opinion Due to Scope Limitation

REPORT OF INDEPENDENT AUDITORS

To the Board of Directors and Shareholders of The Learning Annex, Inc.:

We have audited the accompanying consolidated balance sheets of The Learning Annex, Inc. and Subsidiaries as of June 30, 1990, and the related consolidated statements of operations, shareholders' equity (deficiency), cash flows, and the schedules listed in the Index at Item 14(a)2 for the year ended June 30, 1990. These financial statements are the responsibility of the company's management. Our responsibility is to express an opinion on these financial statements and schedules based on our audit.

Except as discussed in the following paragraph, we conducted our audit in accordance with generally accepted auditing standards. Those standards require that we plan and perform the audit to obtain reasonable assurance about whether the financial statements are free of material misstatement. An audit includes examining, on a test basis, evidence supporting the amounts and disclosures in the financial statements. An audit also includes assessing the accounting principles used and significant estimates made by management, as well as evaluating the overall financial statement presentation. We believe that our audit provides a reasonable basis for our opinion.

Because of inadequacies in the company's accounting records during the year ended June 30, 1990, it was not practicable to extend our auditing procedures to the extent necessary to enable us to obtain certain evidential matter as it relates to classification of certain items in the consolidated statements of operations.

In our opinion, except for the effects of such adjustments or disclosures, if any, related to the classification of certain items in the consolidated statement of operations as discussed in the preceding paragraph, such consolidated financial statements present fairly, in all material respects, the financial position of The Learning Annex, Inc. and Subsidiaries as of June 30, 1990, and the results of their operations and their cash flows for the year ended June 30, 1990, in conformity with generally accepted accounting principles and the schedules referred to above present fairly, in all material respects, when read in conjunction with the related financial statements, the information required to be set forth therein.

Grant Thornton
New York, New York

September 28, 1990

Source: Mead Data Central, the NAARS Service.

or management may prohibit the auditors from confirming accounts receivable. Scope restrictions can also occur without management intervention. For example, the auditors may be unable to observe the taking of the physical inventory because they were engaged by the client after year end; or the client's outside legal counsel may be unable or unwilling to respond to a letter of audit inquiry.

The auditor may or may not be able to obtain the necessary evidence by means of alternate auditing procedures. If the auditor *is* able to obtain satisfaction by other means, the audit report should not be modified. If the auditor cannot obtain satisfaction by other means, a qualified opinion or a disclaimer is in order, depending on the materiality of the limitations.

In the event of material client-imposed scope restrictions, the auditor should ordinarily disclaim an opinion on the financial statements.[3] One or more client-imposed restrictions casts a negative reflection on the overall reliability of management's assertions contained in the financial statements. The resulting increase in inherent risk is usually sufficient to preclude the rendering of an audit opinion.

Exhibit 15.5 illustrates a qualification of opinion related to a material scope restriction that was *not* client-imposed. In this instance, the auditors were unable to satisfy themselves as to proper classification of revenues and expenses. The inability to determine classification was due to inadequate accounting records. Although the scope limitation impacted classification within the income statement, it apparently did not affect net income or net assets and therefore was not serious enough to warrant a disclaimer of opinion.

Exhibit 15.6 illustrates the proper wording for a **disclaimer of opinion** resulting from a scope restriction. In this case, an initial audit (as contrasted with a recurring audit), the auditors could not gain satisfaction regarding the reasonableness of the beginning inventories or the cost of property, plant, and equipment acquired in prior years. Given the magnitude of the amounts involved, the auditors elected to disclaim an opinion.

In addition to scope restriction disclaimers, CPAs also issue disclaimers of opinion when associated with financial statements of clients for whom audits were not intended. As discussed more fully in Chapter 16, such accounting services as compilations and reviews result in unaudited financial statements. To clearly convey to users that the statements are unaudited, the CPA attaches a disclaimer of opinion.

Figure 15.2 and Table 15.1 summarize this discussion in terms of the conditions under which each type of audit report is rendered. The nature of the condition (i.e., scope restriction vs. departure from GAAP) and the auditor's judgment as to materiality of the condition's impact on lending and investment decisions are the key ingredients in deciding among the alternatives.

DIVIDED RESPONSIBILITY

Frequently, if the client has one or more subsidiaries which are included in the financial statements, other CPAs are retained to audit the subsidiaries. Under such circumstances, the principal auditor must decide whether to accept full responsibility for the audit, or whether to divide responsibility. A **principal auditor** is one

---

[3]*Ibid.,* Section AU 508.42.

EXHIBIT 15.6   Disclaimer of Opinion—Scope Restriction

REPORT OF INDEPENDENT AUDITORS

To the Board of Directors and Shareholders of X Company:

We were engaged to audit the accompanying balance sheets of X Company as of December 31, 1992 and 1991, and the related statements of income, retained earnings, and cash flows for the years then ended. These financial statements are the responsibility of the company's management.

The company did not make a count of its physical inventory in 1992 or 1991, stated in the accompanying financial statements at $_____ as of December 31, 1992, and at $_____ as of December 31, 1991. Further, evidence supporting the cost of property and equipment acquired prior to December 31, 1991, is no longer available. The company's records do not permit the application of other auditing procedures to inventories or property and equipment.

Since the company did not take physical inventories and we were not able to apply auditing procedures to satisfy ourselves as to inventory quantities and the cost of property and equipment, the scope of our work was not sufficient to enable us to express, and we do not express, an opinion on these financial statements.

(Signature)

(Date)

Source: *Codification of Statements on Auditing Standards,* Section AU 508.72.

who has examined the major portion of the combined entity. For example, assume Company A has a relatively small subsidiary, Company B. Assume also that Company A is audited by Auditor I and Company B is audited by Auditor II. Under these circumstances, Auditor I is the principal auditor. In some instances, identifying the principal auditor is not so easy, but consideration of more nebulous circumstances are deemed to be outside the scope of this textbook. **Full responsibility** means that the principal auditor accepts responsibility for all work performed on the audit. Under **divided responsibility,** the principal auditors are responsible for the components of the group audited by them, and the other auditors are responsible for the subsidiaries examined by them.[4] If responsibility is divided, the audit report must clearly identify the division.

The principal auditor may decide to accept full responsibility if the other auditor is an associated or correspondent firm or the portion examined by other auditors is not material to the overall financial statements. Regardless of whether the decision is to divide responsibility or accept full responsibility, the principal auditor must obtain satisfaction concerning the other auditors' independence and professional

---

[4]*Ibid.,* Section AU 543.03.

FIGURE 15.2 Audit Reporting Decision Analysis

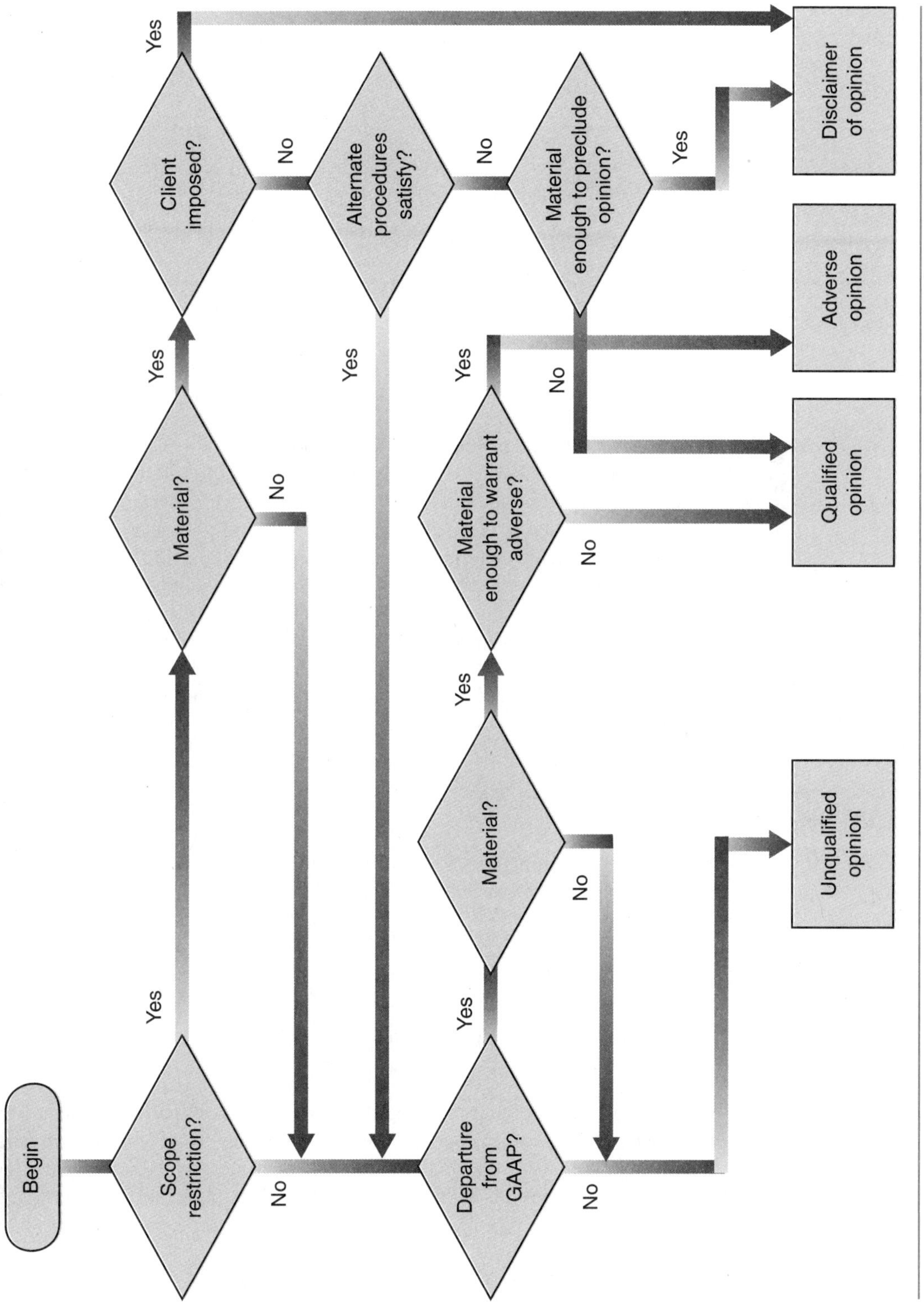

TABLE 15.1   Types of Audit Reports

	TYPE OF AUDIT REPORT			
CONDITIONS	*Unqualified*	*Qualified*	*Adverse*	*Disclaimer*
1. No material scope limitation;	X			
no material departure from GAAP	X			
2. Material scope limitation		X		X
3. Material departure from GAAP		X	X	

reputation.[5] Additionally, if the decision is to accept full responsibility, the principal auditor should consider whether it will be necessary to visit the other auditor to discuss the audit and review the audit programs and workpapers of the other auditor.[6]

If the principal auditor decides to accept full responsibility, the wording of the audit report need not be modified. A decision to divide responsibility, on the other hand, requires that reference be made to the work of the other auditors in both the scope and opinion paragraphs of the audit report. Exhibit 15.7 illustrates the proper wording for divided responsibility. Note that the magnitude of the statements audited by the other auditors, expressed as a percentage of total assets and revenues, is set forth in the scope paragraph and that the division of responsibility is stated in the opinion paragraph. Note also that division of responsibility does not constitute a qualification of the auditor's opinion. The report should not be viewed as inferior to a report that does not contain a reference to other auditors.

EXPLANATORY PARAGRAPH ADDED TO THE AUDITOR'S REPORT

Under the following conditions, an auditor may depart from the standard audit report wording *without qualifying* the opinion:

1. Departure from principle promulgated by body designated by Council;

2. Material uncertainties;

3. Ability of entity to continue as a going concern;

4. Change in accounting principle; or

5. Emphasis of a matter.

Such departures normally assume the form of an **explanatory paragraph** added *following* the opinion paragraph. This is in contrast to the explanatory paragraph placed *between* the scope and opinion paragraphs describing a qualified or adverse opinion. The conditions giving rise to an explanatory paragraph are discussed below.

---

[5]*Ibid.*, Section AU 543.10.

[6]*Ibid.*, Section AU 543.12.

EXHIBIT 15.7   Opinion Based in Part on Report of Other Auditors

---

REPORT OF INDEPENDENT AUDITORS

To the Board of Directors and Stockholders,
Gulf Resources & Chemical Corporation:

We have audited the accompanying consolidated balance sheets of Gulf Resources & Chemical Corporation and subsidiaries as of December 31, 1990 and 1989, and the related consolidated statements of operations, stockholders' equity, and cash flows for each of the years in the three-year period ended December 31, 1990. These consolidated financial statements are the responsibility of the company's management. Our responsibility is to express an opinion on these financial statements based on our audits. We did not audit the financial statements of a subsidiary, City Realties Limited, which statements reflect total assets constituting 60 percent and total revenues constituting 21 percent in 1990 of the related consolidated totals. Those statements were audited by other auditors whose report has been furnished to us, and our opinion, insofar as it relates to the amounts included for City Realties Limited, is based solely on the report of the other auditors.

We conducted our audits in accordance with generally accepted auditing standards. Those standards require that we plan and perform the audit to obtain reasonable assurance about whether the financial statements are free of material misstatement. An audit includes examining, on a test basis, evidence supporting the amounts and disclosures in the financial statements. An audit also includes assessing the accounting principles used and significant estimates made by management, as well as evaluating the overall financial statement presentation. We believe that our audit and the reports of other auditors provide a reasonable basis for our opinion.

In our opinion, based on our audits and the report of other auditors in 1990, the consolidated financial statements referred to above present fairly, in all material respects, the financial position of Gulf Resources & Chemical Corporation and subsidiaries as of December 31, 1990 and 1989, and the results of their operations and their cash flows for each of the years in the three-year period ended December 31, 1990, in conformity with generally accepted accounting principles.

KPMG Peat Marwick
Boston, Massachusetts

February 22, 1991

Source: Mead Data Central, the NAARS Service.

Departure from Designated Principle

The first condition under which an audit report modification is accompanied by an unqualified opinion is an agreed-upon departure from a principle promulgated by the body designated by Council of the AICPA. Although fairness of financial presentation is to be judged within the framework of GAAP,[7] the auditor may

---

[7]*Ibid.*, Section AU 411.03.

occasionally discover an appropriate departure from a prescribed Statement of Financial Accounting Standards, Accounting Principles Board Opinion, or Accounting Research Bulletin. The auditor may agree with the departure if it can be demonstrated that application of the prescribed standard would cause the financial statements to be materially misleading. Rule 203 of the Code of Conduct states that

> A member shall not (1) express an opinion or state affirmatively that the financial statements or other financial data of any entity are presented in conformity with generally accepted accounting principles or (2) state that he or she is not aware of any material modifications that should be made to such statements or data in order for them to be in conformity with generally accepted accounting principles, if such statements or data contain any departure from an accounting principle promulgated by bodies designated by Council to establish such principles that has a material effect on the statements or data taken as a whole. If, however, the statements or data contain such a departure and the member can demonstrate that due to unusual circumstances the financial statements or data would otherwise have been misleading, the member can comply with the rule by describing the departure, its approximate effects, if practicable, and the reasons why compliance with the principle would result in a misleading statement.[8]

If the auditor agrees with a material departure, the audit report must be modified accordingly. Exhibit 15.8 contains the proper report wording for an appropriate departure from principle. Note the added paragraph describes the departure and justifies it. If the financial statement effects of the departure can be readily determined, they should also be disclosed in the explanatory paragraph. The resulting opinion, however, is unqualified.

Material Uncertainties

In some instances, the outcome of future events which may affect the financial statements cannot be reasonably estimated by management. These are termed **uncertainties.** They may or may not be considered material. Examples of uncertainties are pending lawsuits for which legal counsel cannot predict the outcome; IRS audits in progress; and the violation of one or more restrictive covenants contained in loan agreements, which violation could result in a demand by the lender for immediate payment of principal and accrued interest.

Given the possibility of material loss resulting from the uncertainty, the auditor may elect to add an explanatory paragraph following the opinion paragraph of the audit report. In deciding whether to add the explanatory paragraph, the auditor considers the likelihood of a material loss resulting from the resolution of the uncertainty.[9] SAS 58 describes the decision parameters as follows:

■ *Remote Likelihood of Material Loss*—No explanatory paragraph is necessary;

■ *Probable Chance of Material Loss*—If a material loss is probable, but the amount is not capable of reasonable estimation, the auditor should add an explanatory paragraph;

---

[8]Auditing Standards Board, *Code of Professional Conduct.* New York: AICPA, 1988, Section II, Rule 203.

[9]Auditing Standards Board, *AICPA Professional Standards,* Section AU 508.

EXHIBIT 15.8 Departure from Designated Principle

REPORT OF INDEPENDENT AUDITORS

To the Board of Directors and Stockholders of
U.S. Healthmart, Inc.:

We have audited the accompanying consolidated balance sheets of U.S. Healthmart, Inc., and consolidated subsidiaries as of December 31, 1992 and 1991, and the related consolidated statements of income, retained earnings, and cash flows for the years then ended. These financial statements are the responsibility of the company's management. Our responsibility is to express an opinion on these financial statements based on our audits.

We conducted our audits in accordance with generally accepted auditing standards. Those standards require that we plan and perform the audit to obtain reasonable assurance about whether the financial statements are free of material misstatement. An audit includes examining, on a test basis, evidence supporting the amounts and disclosures in the financial statements. An audit also includes assessing the accounting principles used and significant estimates made by management, as well as evaluating the overall financial statement presentation. We believe that our audits provide a reasonable basis for our opinion.

In our opinion, the financial statements referred to above present fairly, in all material respects, the consolidated financial position of U.S. Healthmart, Inc., and consolidated subsidiaries as of December 31, 1992 and 1991, and the results of its operations and its cash flows for the years then ended in conformity with generally accepted accounting principles.

As explained in Note 9, the corporation's health spa subsidiaries have changed their method of recording revenues from the recognition of revenue at the time of sale to the recognition of revenue over the membership term and have applied this change retroactively in their financial statements. Accounting Principles Board (APB) Opinion Number 20, "Accounting Changes," provides that such a change be made by including, as an element of net earnings during the year of change, the cumulative effect of the change on prior years. Had APB Opinion Number 20 been followed literally, the cumulative effect of the accounting change would have been included as a charge in the 1992 statement of income. Because of the magnitude and pervasiveness of this change, we believe a literal application of APB Opinion Number 20 would result in a misleading presentation, and that this change should therefore be made on a retroactive basis. Accordingly, the accompanying consolidated financial statements for 1991 have been restated.

(Signature)

(Date)

- *Reasonable Possibility of Material Loss*—If the chances of a loss are more than remote but less than probable, the auditor should base the decision as to whether to include an explanatory paragraph on

   1. Possible loss vs. auditor's judgment concerning materiality; and
   2. Whether likelihood of occurrence is closer to remote or to probable.[10]

The greater the materiality and the higher the probability of loss, the more inclined will be the auditor to add the explanatory paragraph. Exhibit 15.9 illustrates the proper wording and placement of the paragraph.

Ability to Continue as a Going Concern

Under the requirements of SAS 59, the auditor has a responsibility to evaluate whether there is substantial doubt about a client's **ability to continue as a going concern** for a reasonable period of time, not to exceed a year beyond the date of the financial statements being audited.[11] SAS 59 also provides guidance concerning whether substantial doubt exists. The auditor's consideration of going concern ordinarily relates to the ability of the client to meet its continuing obligations as they come due. If the client can meet these obligations only by disposing of substantial portions of its assets or restructuring of its debt, going concern ability would appear to be seriously impaired. Examples of conditions and events raising doubt in the auditor's mind are the following:

1. Negative trends, such as recurring operating losses;
2. Defaults on loans or similar agreements;
3. Internal matters, such as work stoppages; and
4. External matters, such as legal proceedings, legislation, or similar matters that might impair the client's ability to operate.

The auditor's evaluation is based on the aggregate results of all audit procedures performed during planning and performance of the audit. In resolving doubt about these conditions, the auditor should obtain information concerning management's plans to deal with the conditions giving rise to uncertainty. These plans may include the following:

1. Plans to dispose of assets;
2. Plans to borrow money or restructure debt;
3. Plans to reduce or delay expenditures; or
4. Plans to increase ownership equity.

If doubt remains, an explanatory paragraph may have to be added, following the opinion paragraph of the audit report. The words *substantial doubt about the ability of the entity to continue as a going concern* must be used in the paragraph.[12] Exhibit 15.10 illustrates an explanatory paragraph describing going concern uncertainty.

---

[10]*Ibid.*

[11]*Ibid.*, Section AU 341.

[12]Auditing Standards Board, *Statement on Auditing Standards No. 64—Omnibus Statement on Auditing Standards—1990*, New York: AICPA, 1990, paragraph 12.

EXHIBIT 15.9   Uncertainty Cited in the Independent Auditor's Report

REPORT OF INDEPENDENT AUDITORS

To the Board of Directors and Stockholders of
Ocean Drilling & Exploration Company:

We have audited the accompanying consolidated balance sheets of Ocean Drilling & Exploration Company and subsidiaries as of December 31, 1990 and 1989, and the related consolidated statements of operations, stockholders equity, and cash flows for each of the years in the three-year period ended December 31, 1990. These consolidated financial statements are the responsibility of the company's management. Our responsibility is to express an opinion on these financial statements based on our audits.

We conducted our audits in accordance with generally accepted auditing standards. Those standards require that we plan and perform the audit to obtain reasonable assurance about whether the financial statements are free of material misstatement. An audit includes examining, on a test basis, evidence supporting the amounts and disclosures in the financial statements. An audit also includes assessing the accounting principles used and significant estimates made by management, as well as evaluating the overall financial statement presentation. We believe that our audits provide a reasonable basis for our opinion.

In our opinion, the consolidated financial statements referred to above present fairly, in all material respects, the financial position of Ocean Drilling & Exploration Company and subsidiaries as of December 31, 1990 and 1989, and the results of their operations and their cash flows for each of the years in the three-year period ended December 31, 1990, in conformity with generally accepted accounting principles.

As discussed in the note related to liquidation of insurance subsidiary, Mentor Insurance Limited (Mentor), a Bermuda subsidiary of Ocean Drilling & Exploration Company (Company), is currently in liquidation under the supervision of the Supreme Court of Bermuda. The liquidators of Mentor have filed suit asserting various claims against the company. The ultimate outcome of the litigation cannot presently be determined. Accordingly, no provision for any liability that may result upon adjudication has been recognized in the accompanying consolidated financial statements.

KPMG Peat Marwick
New Orleans, Louisiana

March 1, 1991

Source: Mead Data Central, the NAARS Service.

If uncertainty regarding the ability of an entity to continue as a going concern is so great as to call into question whether assets should be valued at going concern or liquidation values, the auditor may elect to disclaim an opinion due to uncertainty. During the 1980s, a number of savings and loan associations, faced with risky investments following deregulation, experienced capital declines below statutory minimums. Under these circumstances, auditors were compelled to disclaim opinions. Exhibit 15.11 illustrates such a disclaimer.

**EXHIBIT 15.10   Doubt as to Going Concern Ability Cited in Independent
Auditor's Report**

REPORT OF INDEPENDENT AUDITORS

To the Stockholders and the Board of Directors of
Tonka Corporation:

We have audited the accompanying consolidated balance sheets of Tonka Corporation and
subsidiaries as of December 29, 1990 and December 30, 1989, and the related consolidated
statements of operations and cash flows for each of the three years in the period ended
December 29, 1990. These financial statements are the responsibility of the company's management. Our responsibility is to express an opinion on these financial statements based on our
audits.

We conducted our audits in accordance with generally accepted auditing standards. Those
standards require that we plan and perform the audit to obtain reasonable assurance about
whether the financial statements are free of material misstatement. An audit includes examining,
on a test basis, evidence supporting the amounts and disclosures in the financial statements. An
audit also includes assessing the accounting principles used and significant estimates made by
management, as well as evaluating the overall financial statement presentation. We believe that
our audits provide a reasonable basis for our opinion.

In our opinion, the financial statements referred to above present fairly, in all material respects, the consolidated financial position of Tonka Corporation and subsidiaries as of December 29, 1990 and December 30, 1989, and the consolidated results of their operations and their
cash flows for each of the three years in the period ended December 29, 1990, in conformity with
generally accepted accounting principles.

The consolidated financial statements have been prepared assuming that Tonka Corporation
and subsidiaries will continue as a going concern. As more fully described in Note One, the
company has incurred significant losses in 1990, which raises substantial doubt about its ability
to continue as a going concern in its present form. Management's plans in regard to these matters
include the pending sale of the company and are also discussed in Note One. The financial
statements do not include any adjustments that might result from the outcome of this uncertainty.

Ernst & Young
Minneapolis, Minnesota

February 27, 1991

Source: Mead Data Central, the NAARS Service.

EXHIBIT 15.11   Disclaimer Due to Uncertainty Regarding Going Concern

REPORT OF INDEPENDENT AUDITORS

To the Board of Directors and Shareholders of Goldome:

We have audited the accompanying consolidated statements of condition of Goldome and subsidiaries as of December 31, 1990 and 1989, and the related consolidated statements of operations, changes in shareholders' equity and cash flows for each of the years in the three-year period ended December 31, 1990. These consolidated financial statements are the responsibility of Goldome's management. Our responsibility is to report on these consolidated financial statements based on the results of our audits.

We conducted our audits in accordance with generally accepted auditing standards. Those standards require that we plan and perform the audit to obtain reasonable assurance about whether the financial statements are free of material misstatement. An audit includes examining, on a test basis, evidence supporting the amounts and disclosures in the financial statements. An audit also includes assessing the accounting principles used and significant estimates made by management, as well as evaluating the overall financial statement presentation. We believe that our audits provide a reasonable basis for our opinion.

The accompanying consolidated financial statements have been prepared assuming that Goldome will continue as a going concern. As discussed in Notes 2 and 17 to the consolidated financial statements, Goldome's capital ratios were less than its minimum regulatory requirements and its regulatory forbearance with respect to such capital requirements expired January 31, 1990. Failure to meet capital requirements could subject Goldome to legal or further administrative action by its regulators; accordingly, its ability to continue to operate in its current manner is dependent upon increasing capital to specified levels or obtaining regulatory forbearance with respect to its minimum capital requirements. Consequently, this situation raises substantial doubt about Goldome's ability to continue as a going concern. Management's efforts with respect to meeting capital requirements are discussed in Notes 2 and 17 and include the engagement of an investment banker for such purposes. The accompanying consolidated financial statements do not include any adjustments relating to the recovery of reported asset amounts that would be necessary should Goldome be unable to continue as a going concern and have to convert non-cash assets to cash at losses and write down its intangible assets.

In our opinion, the 1989 and 1988 consolidated financial statements referred to above present fairly, in all material respects, the financial position of Goldome and subsidiaries as of December 31, 1989, and the results of their operations and their cash flows for each of the years in the two-year period ended December 31, 1989, in conformity with generally accepted accounting principles.

Because of the significance of the uncertainty discussed above, we are unable to express, and we do not express, an opinion on the 1990 consolidated financial statements.

KPMG Peat Marwick
Buffalo, New York

January 23, 1991

Source: Mead Data Central, the NAARS Service.

Change in Accounting Principle

The auditor's standard report implies that accounting principles have been consistently applied during or between periods. If there has been a material change in accounting principles or method of application between periods, the auditor should add an explanatory paragraph to the audit report. A change in accounting principle may assume any of the following forms:

1. Change in accounting principle;
2. Change in reporting entity;
3. Correction of an error in principle; or
4. Change in principle inseparable from change in estimate.[13]

EXHIBIT 15.12   Change in Accounting Principle Cited in the Independent Auditor's Report

REPORT OF INDEPENDENT AUDITORS

To the Stockholders and the Board of Directors of
General Mills, Inc.:

We have audited the accompanying consolidated balance sheets of General Mills, Inc., and subsidiaries as of May 26, 1991 and May 27, 1990, and the related consolidated statements of earnings and cash flows for each of the fiscal years in the three-year period ended May 26, 1991. These financial statements are the responsibility of the company's management. Our responsibility is to express an opinion on these financial statements based on our audits.

We conducted our audits in accordance with generally accepted auditing standards. Those standards require that we plan and perform the audit to obtain reasonable assurance about whether the financial statements are free of material misstatement. An audit includes examining, on a test basis, evidence supporting the amounts and disclosures in the financial statements. An audit also includes assessing the accounting principles used and significant estimates made by management, as well as evaluating the overall financial statement presentation. We believe that our audits provide a reasonable basis for our opinion.

In our opinion, the consolidated financial statements referred to above present fairly, in all material respects, the financial position of General Mills, Inc., and subsidiaries as of May 26, 1991 and May 27, 1990, and the results of their operations and their cash flows for each of the fiscal years in the three-year period ended May 26, 1991 in conformity with generally accepted accounting principles.

As described in note thirteen to the consolidated financial statements, the company changed its method of accounting for postretirement benefit costs in fiscal 1989.

KPMG Peat Marwick
Minneapolis, Minnesota

June 27, 1991

Source: Mead Data Central, the NAARS Service.

---

[13]Auditing Standards Board, *AICPA Professional Standards, op. cit.,* Section AU 420.06–.11.

A change in principle is material when the effect on comparability of the client's financial statements is significant.

The explanatory paragraph should identify the nature of the change and refer the reader to the footnote in the financial statements that discusses the change in detail.[14] Exhibit 15.12 illustrates the appropriate wording for a change in principle. If the change in principle is not properly accounted for or is inadequately disclosed, the auditor should consider issuing a qualified or adverse opinion.

Emphasis of a Matter

Although financial statements and the accompanying footnotes may be stated fairly, the auditor may still wish to bring a matter of importance to the reader's attention. Significant related-party transactions, or a subsequent event, for example, may be properly accounted for and adequately disclosed in a footnote to the financial statements. Yet, given the nature or magnitude of the transactions, the auditor may wish to direct the reader to the appropriate footnote to prevent possible oversight. **Emphasis of a matter,** as illustrated in Exhibit 15.13, is achieved by adding an explanatory paragraph to the audit report. Like the preceding examples, the report contains a departure from the standard wording, while the opinion remains unqualified.

The preceding paragraphs have addressed the most frequent causes for modifying the audit report or opinion. Table 15.2 summarizes the causes and the effects of each on the audit report. Figure 15.3 shows the proper placement of the fourth paragraph, depending upon whether qualified, adverse, disclaimer, or explanatory.

OTHER TOPICS AFFECTING AUDIT REPORTS

Updating the Audit Report

When financial statements of the prior year are presented together with those of the current year, a *continuing auditor* should report on the statements of the prior year, as well as the current year. A **continuing auditor** is one who has audited the financial statements of the current period and one or more consecutive periods immediately prior to the current period.[15]

Referred to as **updating the audit report,** the continuing auditor must decide whether to restate the prior report in its same form or modify it. The most frequent reasons for modification are correction of a prior departure from GAAP; resolution of a prior uncertainty; or discovery, during the current year's examination, of an uncertainty that also existed at the date of the prior audit report. If a GAAP departure in previous financial statements has been corrected for inclusion in the current year's annual report, the auditor should change the qualified opinion of the prior year to an unqualified opinion when updating. If a prior uncertainty has subsequently been resolved, the auditor should omit the explanatory paragraph from the updated report. If a prior uncertainty has subsequently come to light and is still

---

[14]*Ibid.*, Section AU 508.

[15]*Ibid.*, Section AU 508.74.

**EXHIBIT 15.13   Emphasis of a Matter in the Independent
Auditor's Report**

REPORT OF INDEPENDENT AUDITORS

To the Board of Directors and Stockholders of
Macmillan Ring-Free Oil Company:

We have audited the accompanying consolidated balance sheets of Macmillan Ring-Free Oil
Co., Inc., and subsidiary companies as of December 31, 1985 and 1984, and the related statements of income, retained earnings, and cash flows for the years then ended. These financial
statements are the responsibility of the company's management. Our responsibility is to express
an opinion on these financial statements based on our audits.

We conducted our audits in accordance with generally accepted auditing standards. Those
standards require that we plan and perform the audit to obtain reasonable assurance about
whether the financial statements are free of material misstatement. An audit includes examining,
on a test basis, evidence supporting the amounts and disclosures in the financial statements. An
audit also includes assessing the accounting principles used and significant estimates made by
management, as well as evaluating the overall financial statement presentation. We believe that
our audit provides a reasonable basis for our opinion.

In our opinion, the consolidated financial statements referred to above present fairly, in all
material respects, the consolidated financial position of Macmillan Ring-Free Oil Co., Inc., and
subsidiary companies as of December 31, 1985 and 1984, and the results of its operations and
its cash flows for the years then ended in conformity with generally accepted accounting principles.

The company is under common control with certain affiliated companies and has had significant transactions with these companies and with other related parties (see Note 3).

Touche Ross & Co., Certified Public Accountants
New York, New York

April 11, 1986

Source: Mead Data Central, the NAARS Service. (This audit report was originally issued to cover the 1984 and 1985 financial
statements of Macmillan Ring-Free Oil Company. It has been revised to conform to current audit report format requirements.)

unresolved, the auditor should add the explanatory paragraph in drafting the updated
audit report. Exhibit 15.14 illustrates an audit report updated because of the resolution of a prior uncertainty regarding the net realizable value of notes receivable.

In the event a **predecessor auditor** examined the financial statements of the
prior period, the predecessor auditor's report may or may not be included with the
comparative statements. The predecessor auditor who agrees to include the earlier
report must consider whether the previously issued report is still appropriate. Reading the statements, comparing with the prior period, and obtaining a letter of
representation from the successor auditor are means for determining the suitability
of the prior report.

TABLE 15.2   Summary of Audit Report Modifications

	MODIFICATION				Explanatory Paragraph Following Scope Paragraph	Explanatory Paragraph Following Opinion Paragraph
CONDITION	Unqualified Opinion	Qualified Opinion	Adverse Opinion	Disclaimer of Opinion		
1. No material scope limitation	X					
2. No material departure from GAAP	X					
3. Material scope limitation		X		X	X	
4. Material departure from GAAP		X	X		X	
5. Divided responsibility	X					
6. Auditor agrees with departure from designated principle	X					X
7. Material uncertainty	X			X		X
8. Doubt as to going concern ability	X			X		X
9. Change in accounting principle	X					X
10. Emphasis of a matter	X					X

If the predecessor's report is not included, the successor auditor should include the following information in the introductory paragraph of the audit report:

1. That another auditor audited the prior-period financial statements;

2. The date of the predecessor's report;

3. The type of opinion the predecessor expressed; and

4. If it was other than unqualified, the substantive reasons for this.[16]

Exhibit 15.15 illustrates the proper wording when the predecessor auditor's report is not included.

Subsequent Discovery of Facts Existing at the Date of the Audit Report

After issuing the audit report, the auditors may become aware of information that may have affected the audit report had it been known at the time. For example, assume that after the auditors have completed their field work and released the audit report, a team of management advisory services personnel from the same accounting firm are retained to develop a more effective system for processing customer

---

[16]*Ibid.*, Section AU 508.83.

FIGURE 15.3   Placement of Fourth Paragraph of Audit Report

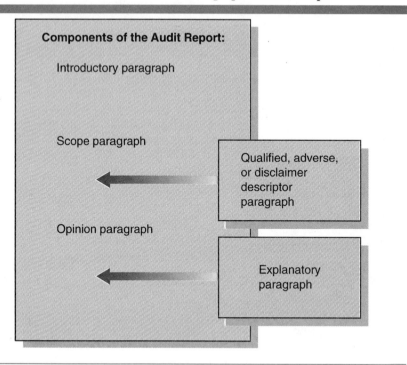

billings and collections. While performing this engagement, the team discovers that a substantial portion of reported accounts receivable were fictitious. They immediately inform the audit team. The auditors determine that the impact of the fictitious receivables is to transform a reported income of $2 million into a loss of $1.6 million. The action that the firm should take, if any, and the responsibility to third parties are the subjects addressed in the following paragraphs.

The auditors should first ascertain whether the information is reliable and whether the facts existed at the date of the audit report. If reliability and existence are affirmed, the auditors, given the significance of financial statement impact, have a duty to inform third parties known to be relying on the audit report that such reliance is no longer appropriate. This duty is satisfied by requesting the client to disclose the newly discovered facts and their impact on the financial statements.

If the client cooperates and the effects can be determined promptly, revised financial statements and audit report should be issued. The reason for the revision should be described in a footnote to the financial statements and referred to in the auditor's report. If issuance of financial statements and audit report for a subsequent period is imminent, revision can be made in such statements. If the effects cannot be determined promptly, the client should notify third persons known to be relying on the financial statements and report not to so rely on it and that revised statements and audit report are forthcoming.[17]

---

[17]*Ibid.,* Section AU 561.01–.06.

EXHIBIT 15.14   Updated Audit Report

REPORT OF INDEPENDENT AUDITORS

To the Board of Directors and Stockholders of
Customedix Corporation:

We have audited the accompanying consolidated balance sheets of Customedix Corporation as of June 30, 1990 and 1989, and the related statements of operations, stockholders' equity, and cash flows for each of the three years in the period ended June 30, 1990. These financial statements are the responsibility of the company's management. Our responsibility is to express an opinion on these financial statements based on our audits.

We conducted our audits in accordance with generally accepted auditing standards. Those standards require that we plan and perform the audit to obtain reasonable assurance about whether the financial statements are free of material misstatement. An audit includes examining, on a test basis, evidence supporting the amounts and disclosures in the financial statements. An audit also includes assessing the accounting principles used and significant estimates made by management, as well as evaluating the overall financial statement presentation. We believe that our audits provide a reasonable basis for our opinion.

In our report dated September 15, 1989, our opinion on the 1989 financial statements was qualified for the effects on those financial statements of such adjustments, if any, as might have been determined to be necessary had information been available about the net realizable value of the notes receivable discussed in Note 5(a). During the year ended June 30, 1990, additional information became available. The company determined that the continuing net realizable value of the notes is in doubt and provided an additional allowance for possible losses to fully reserve for the notes. Accordingly, our present opinion on the 1989 financial statements, as presented herein, is different from that expressed in our previous report.

In our opinion, the consolidated financial statements referred to above present fairly, in all material respects, the financial position of Customedix Corporation as of June 30, 1990 and 1989, and the results of its operations and its cash flows for each of the three years in the period ended June 30, 1990, in conformity with generally accepted accounting principles.

BDO Seidman
White Plains, New York

August 9, 1990

Source: Mead Data Central, the NAARS Service.

If the client refuses to inform third parties, the auditor must notify each member of the board of directors and also perform the following steps:

1. Notify the client that the auditor's report can no longer be associated with the financial statements;
2. Notify regulatory agencies (e.g., the SEC and stock exchange) having jurisdiction over the client that the auditors' report can no longer be relied upon;

EXHIBIT 15.15   Predecessor Audit Report not Included

REPORT OF INDEPENDENT AUDITORS

To the Board of Directors and Stockholders of
Consolidated Stores Corporation:

We have audited the accompanying consolidated balance sheets of Consolidated Stores Corporation and subsidiaries as of February 2, 1991 and February 3, 1990, and the related consolidated statements of operations, stockholders' equity, and cash flows for the fiscal years then ended. These financial statements are the responsibility of the company's management. Our responsibility is to express an opinion on these financial statements based on our audits. The consolidated financial statements of Consolidated Stores Corporation and subsidiaries for the fiscal year ended January 28, 1989, were audited by other auditors whose report thereon dated March 6, 1989, expressed an unqualified opinion on those statements.

We conducted our audits in accordance with generally accepted auditing standards. Those standards require that we plan and perform the audit to obtain reasonable assurance about whether the financial statements are free of material misstatement. An audit includes examining, on a test basis, evidence supporting the amounts and disclosures in the financial statements. An audit also includes assessing the accounting principles used and significant estimates made by management, as well as evaluating the overall financial statement presentation. We believe that our audit provides a reasonable basis for our opinion.

In our opinion, the fiscal 1990 and 1989 financial statements referred to above present fairly, in all material respects, the consolidated financial position of Consolidated Stores Corporation and subsidiaries as of February 2, 1991 and February 3, 1990, and the results of their operations and their cash flows for the fiscal years then ended in conformity with generally accepted accounting principles.

Deloitte & Touche
Dayton, Ohio

February 23, 1991

Source: Mead Data Central, the NAARS Service.

3. Notify each person known by the auditor to be relying on the financial statements that the auditor's report can no longer be relied upon.[18] If the client is publicly held, third-party notification by the auditor on an individual basis may not be possible. Under these circumstances, notifying the SEC and the stock exchange, and requesting that these agencies make appropriate third-party disclosure, usually satisfies the auditor's disclosure responsibility.

---

[18]*Ibid.*, Section AU 561.08.

The Meaning of Present Fairly in Accordance with GAAP

An unqualified audit opinion expresses the auditor's belief that the financial statements are presented fairly in conformity with GAAP. The words *presented fairly* mean free from material misstatement. The phrase *in conformity with GAAP* means that fairness has been evaluated within the framework of generally accepted accounting principles.[19] The *Codification of Statements on Auditing Standards* provides further guidance as to preferred sources of GAAP by ranking them in the following order:

I. Established Accounting Principles:
   A. FASB Statements and Interpretations, APB Opinions, GASB [Governmental Accounting Standards Board] Statements and Interpretations, and AICPA Accounting Research Bulletins;
   B. FASB and GASB Technical Bulletins, AICPA Industry Audit and Accounting Guides, and AICPA Statements of Position;
   C. Consensus positions of the FASB and GASB Emerging Issues Task Forces and AICPA Practice Bulletins;
   D. AICPA Accounting Interpretations, "Qs and As" published by the FASB and GASB staffs, as well as industry practices widely recognized and prevalent.

II. Other Accounting Literature
   A. FASB and GASB Concepts Statements;
   B. APB Statements;
   C. AICPA Issues Papers;
   D. International Accounting Standards Committee Statements;
   E. Pronouncements of other professional associations or regulatory agencies;
   F. AICPA Technical Practice Aids;
   G. Accounting textbooks, handbooks, and articles.[20]

Audit judgment determines which accounting principles should be used in any situation. In exercising such judgment, the auditor must be satisfied that the principles selected have general acceptance, that they are appropriate in the circumstances, that the financial statement components are properly classified, that disclosure is adequate, and that the economic substance of all material transactions and events have been reflected in the statements.[21]

Other Information in Documents Containing Audited Financial Statements

In addition to the financial statements and footnotes, most annual reports contain other information of interest to the shareholders. Such information may be contained in **management's discussion and analysis** (MD&A), a supplemental letter from management in the annual report to shareholders. In the letter, management elaborates on the audited financial statements by explaining the more significant changes in financial statement components occurring during the year. Exhibit 15.16

---

[19]*Ibid.,* Section AU 411.03.

[20]*Ibid.,* Section AU 411.

[21]*Ibid.*

illustrates a portion of Dana Corporation's 1990 MD&A. The president's letter, as well as the reports of divisional vice presidents, are also sources of other information, some of which may consist of financial data (e.g., segment earnings, earnings per share, and long-term debt). In expressing an opinion on the financial statements, the auditor's responsibility does not extend beyond the financial information that he or she has identified in the audit report. The auditor, therefore, has no obligation to perform any procedures to corroborate such other information.

EXHIBIT 15.16   Partial Management Discussion and Analysis

LIQUIDITY AND CAPITAL RESOURCES

Total additions to property, plant, and equipment were $229 million in 1990 compared to $228 million in 1989. These additions included new facilities in France and Brazil and expenditures to reduce manufacturing costs and improve product quality. 1991 capital expenditures are budgeted at $180 million, the majority of which was uncommitted at December 31, 1990.

Consolidated domestic and international short-term borrowings averaged $781 million during 1990 at an average interest rate of 8.8% as compared to $620 million at 9.6% during 1989. Dana funds its corporate short-term debt through the issuance of commercial paper and bank borrowings. To cover short-term working capital requirements, Dana has $300 million of credit facilities in place to back-up commercial paper issuance and $780 million in uncommitted lines available for direct borrowings with banks. At December 31, 1990, Dana's domestic and international short-term borrowings were $272 million, down from $293 million at year end 1989. Dana's financial subsidiary, Diamond Financial Holdings, Inc. (DFHI), funds short-term debt through bank borrowings. DFHI has bank lines totalling $110 million and at December 31, 1990, $110 million was borrowed against these lines. DFHI's subsidiary, Dana Credit Corporation (DCC), funds domestic and international short-term debt through commercial paper and bank borrowings. DCC has commercial paper back-up lines amounting to $250 million and uncommitted bank direct borrowing lines of $355 million. At December 31, 1990 DCC and its subsidiaries had a short-term debt position of $385 million, up from $271 million at December 31, 1989. The majority of this increase was due to financing of new business. In total, short-term debt increased during the year from $670 million to $767 million.

Long-term debt remained at approximately $1.5 billion. Maturities of medium-term notes were replaced with issuance of term notes with similar maturities.

During 1990, DFHI purchased certain assets from and made capital contributions to Diamond Savings and Loan (DSL), a wholly owned subsidiary of DFHI, under an agreement with the Office of Thrift Supervision. These transactions were financed by DFHI through short-term borrowings. On December 27, 1990, Dana announced its intention to sell DSL, preferably to an organization committed to growth and expansion in the thrift or banking industries. Accordingly, DSL has been classified as an asset held for sale.

Purchases of assets to be leased at DCC increased in 1990 due to continued growth in our middle ticket leasing markets, and include a $130 million project finance transaction for a gas co-generation facility in Michigan.

Dana Corporation anticipates that net cash flows from operating activities along with available short-term and medium-term financing capabilities are sufficient to meet its needs for 1991.

(continued)

EXHIBIT 15.16   *(continued)*

RESULTS OF OPERATIONS, 1990 vs. 1989

Total sales in 1990 were $4.95 billion compared to $4.87 billion in 1989, an increase of $87 million or 2%. Vehicular OEM and distribution sales were $3.8 billion, an increase of $57 million or 2% over 1989. Industrial sales were $1.1 billion, an increase of $33 million or 3% over 1989. Total consolidated sales include international sales of $1.4 billion, which increased $166 million or 13% over 1989.

Revenue from financial services and other income decreased $15 million to $274 million. The decrease was due primarily to a $15 million payment received in 1989 in connection with the termination of a merger agreement and reduced interest income in 1990, partially offset by increased lease financing income.

Operating income for 1990 was $336 million, a decrease of $59 million or 15% over 1989. $52 million of the decrease resulted from the operating loss of $45 million at our financial services operations, compared to operating income of $7 million in 1989. The decrease results primarily from real estate and loan loss reserves provided at Diamond Savings and Loan, as well as increased bad debt expenses at our leasing operations. Operating income in the Vehicular segment decreased $10 million or 3%, and operating income in the Industrial segment increased $3 million or 4%.

Dana's international operations had operating income of $138 million in 1990, a decrease of $10 million or 7% over 1989. This decrease was primarily due to reduced operating income at Dana's Brazilian and Canadian operations.

Equity in earnings of affiliates increased from $21 million in 1989 to $40 million in 1990, primarily due to an increase in the contribution to earnings by our South American and leasing affiliates. Foreign currency adjustments charged to earnings increased from $20 million in 1989 to $40 million in 1990, virtually all of which related to Dana's Brazilian operations.

Selling, general, and administrative expenses were $646 million, an increase of $100 million or 18% over 1989. $39 million of the increase relates to foreign affiliates (including the effects of changes in exchange rates). The remainder of the increase is attributable to costs related to expanding leasing operations and additional bad debt and loan loss reserves provided at Diamond Financial Holdings, Inc. Interest expense increased to $271 million in 1990 from $255 million in 1989, primarily due to overall higher debt levels.

Taxes on income decreased from $90 million in 1989 to $88 million in 1990 while the effective rate increased from 40.3% to 61.7%. The increase in the effective tax rate for 1990 was due to an overall increase in international rates (primarily Brazil) and certain non-deductible loan loss provisions at DFHI.

The softness in the North American light and heavy truck markets in 1990 has impacted Dana significantly. North American vehicular production is at its lowest level since the early 1980's. We expect continued softness in North American vehicle production through the first half of 1991 with a corresponding effect on operating profits. We expect that these markets will begin to recover during the second half of the year. Our industrial OE markets have been affected by a slowdown in capital spending as manufacturers are impacted by the recession. Our distribution markets are growing at a slower rate than in recent years as they are being affected by market consolidations and tight credit conditions. We currently anticipate that Dana's international sales will continue to grow, although at a slower rate than in recent years. International sales (including U.S. exports) account for 36% of Dana's consolidated sales.

Dana Corporation and Consolidated Subsidiaries

The auditor should, however, read the information and consider whether material **inconsistencies** exist between the other data and the financial statements. When inconsistencies exist, the auditor should consider whether the financial statements, the audit report, or both require revision.[22]

Supplemental Information Required by FASB

In drafting financial accounting standards, the Financial Accounting Standards Board has occasionally included requirements calling for certain supplemental information to accompany the financial statements; for example, disclosures of mineral reserves and oil and gas reserves by companies in the extractive industries. Inasmuch as FASB considers the information to be an essential part of the financial reporting of the entity, the auditor should apply certain limited procedures and should report deficiencies in or the omission of such information.[23] The limited procedures to be applied consist of the following:

1. Inquire of management as to methods used in preparing the information;
2. Compare the supplemental information for consistency with management's responses, with the audited statements, and with other knowledge obtained during the audit;
3. Consider whether representations concerning supplementary data should be included in the client representation letter;
4. Apply other procedures specifically required by FASB; and
5. Make additional inquiries if these procedures lead the auditor to suspect that the information is not properly presented within the applicable guidelines.[24]

The auditor should not refer, in the audit report, to the supplemental information or the procedures applied except when the required information is omitted or in error or the auditor is unable to complete the prescribed procedures. Reference in the audit report, under these circumstances, should be made in an explanatory paragraph following the opinion paragraph. Inasmuch as the audit opinion does not extend to the supplementary information, the opinion paragraph is not affected, and the fourth paragraph may be categorized as *emphasis of a matter*.[25]

Related-Party Transactions

Chapter 14 defined related party-transactions, gave examples, and considered the auditor's responsibility for locating and examining the transactions. Related-party transactions also have audit report implications. First, the auditor may choose to add an explanatory paragraph describing the related party and the related-party transactions and directing the reader's attention to the footnote which more fully explains the matter (see Exhibit 15.13). Second, if the transactions are not properly repre-

---

[22]*Ibid.*, Section AU 550.04.

[23]*Ibid.*, Section AU 558.06.

[24]*Ibid.*, Section AU 558.07.

[25]*Ibid.*, Section AU 558.08.

sented by management or disclosure is inadequate, the auditor should qualify or express an adverse opinion because of a departure from GAAP.[26] A less than "arms-length" transaction represented by management as "arms-length," for example, would be considered misrepresentation, and, if material, should lead to a report modification.

Omitted Procedures Discovered After the Date of the Audit Report

After release of the audit report, the auditor may discover that one or more auditing procedures, considered necessary at the date of the audit report, were omitted. CPA firms' internal inspection programs or peer review are the most frequent means for detecting **omitted procedures.**

The auditor should assess the importance of the omitted procedures in terms of support for the audit opinion. If the omitted procedures are necessary to support the opinion, and the auditor believes persons are still relying on the report, he or she should proceed as follows:

1. If the omitted procedures can be applied, they should be so applied. If they reveal facts that would have affected the audit opinion, the auditor should take those steps described in the section entitled "Subsequent Discovery of Facts Existing at the Date of the Audit Report."

2. If unable to apply omitted or alternate procedures, the auditor should consult an attorney to determine the appropriate course of action with regard to persons thought to be relying on the financial statements and audit report.[27]

KEY TERMS

Ability to continue as a going concern
Adverse opinion
Client-imposed scope restriction
Continuing auditor
Departure from designated principal
Disclaimer of opinion
Divided responsibility
Dual-dated report
Emphasis of a matter
Explanatory paragraph
Full responsibility
Inconsistency
Introductory paragraph
Management's discussion and analysis
Material scope restriction

Omitted procedures
Opinion paragraph
Predecessor auditor
Principal auditor
Qualified opinion
Scope paragraph
Scope restriction
Standard audit report
Subsequent discovery of facts
Supplemental information required by FASB
Uncertainty
Unqualified audit opinion
Updating the audit report

---

[26]*Ibid.*, Section AU 334.12.

[27]*Ibid.*, Section AU 390.05–.07.

COMPUTER AUDIT PRACTICE CASE

Trim Lawn Manufacturing Corporation
Module XV of the Trim Lawn audit practice case contains an audit report exercise. This exercise may be completed at this time.

REVIEW QUESTIONS

1. Describe the components of the audit report.
2. Define *dual-dated audit reports*.
3. List the conditions necessary for an unqualified opinion.
4. Why might an auditor decide to disclaim an opinion?
5. Define *material scope restriction*. Must a material scope restriction always lead to a modification of the audit opinion?
6. Why is a client-imposed scope restriction considered more serious than other forms of scope restrictions?
7. Differentiate between an explanatory paragraph and a qualified opinion.
8. Under what circumstances might an explanatory paragraph be added to the audit report?
9. Define the term ''principal auditor.''
10. What factors influence the auditor's decision to divide responsibility?
11. What purposes are served by a paragraph added between the scope and opinion paragraphs in the audit report?
12. What is meant by *updating the audit report?*
13. What circumstances require modification of a previously issued audit report?
14. What steps should the auditor take upon learning of information that existed at the date of the audit report?
15. Define *present fairly in accordance with GAAP.*
16. Under what circumstances might an auditor agree with a departure from a designated principle?
17. What responsibility does the auditor have for other information appearing in documents containing audited financial statements?
18. Does the audit opinion extend to the ''other information?''
19. What action should the auditor take upon discovering, after release of the audit report, that certain auditing procedures were not performed?
20. Describe the auditor's responsibility relative to the ability of the client to continue as a going concern?
21. Under what conditions should the auditor add an explanatory paragraph relating to uncertainty?
22. What steps should the auditor follow upon learning of a change in accounting principle?

MULTIPLE CHOICE QUESTIONS FROM CPA EXAMINATIONS

1. An auditor's report contains the following sentences: ''We did not examine the financial statements of B Company, a consolidated subsidiary, which statements reflect total assets and revenues constituting 20 percent and 22 percent, respectively,

of the related consolidated totals. These statements were examined by other auditors whose report thereon has been furnished to us, and our opinion expressed herein, insofar as it relates to the amounts included for B Company, is based solely upon the report of the other auditors.''

These sentences

a. Disclaim an opinion.

b. Qualify the opinion.

c. Divide responsibility.

d. Are an improper form of reporting.

2. Daniel Stone was asked to perform the first audit of a wholesale business that does not maintain perpetual inventory records. Stone has observed the current inventory, but has not observed the physical inventory at the previous year-end date and concludes that the opening inventory balance, which is not auditable, is a material factor in the determination of cost of goods sold for the current year. Stone will probably

a. Decline the engagement.

b. Express an unqualified opinion on the balance sheet and income statement except for inventory.

c. Express an unqualified opinion on the balance sheet and disclaim an opinion on the income statement.

d. Disclaim an opinion on the balance sheet and income statement.

3. If the auditor obtains satisfaction with respect to the accounts receivable balance by alternative procedures because it is impracticable to confirm accounts receivable, the auditor's report should be unqualified and could be expected to

a. Disclose that alternative procedures were used due to a client-imposed scope limitation.

b. Disclose that confirmation of accounts receivable was impracticable in the opinion paragraph.

c. Not mention the alternative procedures.

d. Refer to a footnote that discloses the alternative procedures.

4. When restrictions that significantly limit the scope of the audit are imposed by the client, the auditor generally should issue which of the following opinions?

a. ''Except for.''

b. Disclaimer.

c. Adverse.

d. ''Subject to.''

5. In which of the following circumstances may the auditor issue the standard audit report?

a. The principal auditor assumes responsibility for the work of another auditor.

b. The financial statements are affected by a departure from a generally accepted accounting principle.

c. The auditor's report covers the company's first year of operations.

d. The auditor wishes to emphasize a matter regarding the financial statements.

6. An auditor's report included an additional paragraph disclosing that there is a difference of opinion between the auditor and the client for which the auditor believed an adjustment to the financial statements should be made. The opinion paragraph of the auditor's report most likely expressed a(n)

a. Unqualified opinion.

b. Qualified or adverse opinion.

    c. Qualified or disclaimer of opinion.

    d. Disclaimer of opinion.

7. When the client fails to include information that is necessary for the fair presentation of financial statements in the body of the statements or in the related footnotes, it is the responsibility of the auditor to present the information, if practicable, in the auditor's report and issue a(n)

    a. Qualified opinion or a disclaimer of opinion.

    b. Qualified opinion or an adverse opinion.

    c. Adverse opinion or a disclaimer of opinion.

    d. Qualified opinion or an unqualified opinion.

8. When financial statements are prepared on the basis of a going concern and the auditor believes that the client may not continue as a going concern, the auditor should issue

    a. A "subject to" opinion.

    b. An "except for" opinion.

    c. An unqualified opinion with an explanatory paragraph.

    d. An adverse opinion.

9. Basic financial statements which would otherwise receive an unqualified opinion do not contain certain supplementary information that is required pursuant to a FASB pronouncement. The auditor must identify, in an additional paragraph, the supplementary information that is omitted and express a(n)

    a. "Except for" opinion.

    b. Disclaimer of opinion.

    c. Adverse opinion.

    d. Unqualified opinion.

10. The auditor's report should be dated as of the date on which the

    a. Report is delivered to the client.

    b. Field work is completed.

    c. Fiscal period under audit ends.

    d. Review of the working papers is completed.

11. It is *not* appropriate to refer a reader of an auditor's report to a financial statement footnote for details concerning

    a. Subsequent events.

    b. The pro forma effects of a business combination.

    c. Sale of a discontinued operation.

    d. The results of confirmation of receivables.

12. Does an auditor make the following representations explicitly or implicitly when issuing the standard auditor's report on comparative financial statements?

	Consistent application of accounting principles	Examination of evidence on a test basis
a.	Explicitly	Explicitly
b.	Implicitly	Implicitly
c.	Implicitly	Explicitly
d.	Explicitly	Implicitly

13. An auditor should disclose the substantive reasons for expressing an adverse opinion in an explanatory paragraph
    a. Preceding the scope paragraph.
    b. Preceding the opinion paragraph.
    c. Following the opinion paragraph.
    d. Within the notes to the financial statements.

14. In which of the following situations would an auditor ordinarily issue an unqualified audit opinion without an explanatory paragraph?
    a. The auditor wishes to emphasize that the entity had significant related-party transactions.
    b. The auditor decides to make reference to the report of another auditor as a basis, in part, for the auditor's opinion.
    c. The entity issues financial statements that present financial position and results of operations, but omits the statement of cash flows.
    d. The auditor has substantial doubt about the entity's ability to continue as a going concern, but the circumstances are fully disclosed in the financial statements.

15. An auditor may issue a qualified opinion under which of the following circumstances?

	Lack of sufficient competent evidential matter	Restrictions on the scope of the audit
a.	Yes	Yes
b.	Yes	No
c.	No	Yes
d.	No	No

16. An auditor concludes that there is substantial doubt about an entity's ability to continue as a going concern for a reasonable period of time. If the entity's disclosures concerning the matter are adequate, the audit report may include a(n)

	Disclaimer of opinion	"Except for" qualified opinion
a.	Yes	Yes
b.	No	No
c.	No	Yes
d.	Yes	No

17. When there is a significant change in accounting principle, an auditor's report should refer to the lack of consistency in
    a. The scope paragraph.
    b. An explanatory paragraph between the second paragraph and the opinion paragraph.
    c. The opinion paragraph.
    d. An explanatory paragraph following the opinion paragraph.

18. An auditor has previously expressed a qualified opinion on the financial statements of a prior period because of a departure from generally accepted accounting principles. The prior-period financial statements are restated in the current period to conform with generally accepted accounting principles. The auditor's updated report on the prior-period financial statements should

   a. Express an unqualified opinion concerning the restated financial statements.
   b. Be accompanied by the original auditor's report on the prior period.
   c. Bear the same date as the original auditor's report on the prior period.
   d. Qualify the opinion concerning the restated financial statements because of a change in accounting principle.

19. If management declines to present supplementary information required by the Governmental Accounting Standards Board (GASB), the auditor should issue a(n)
   a. Adverse opinion.
   b. Qualified opinion with an explanatory paragraph.
   c. Unqualified opinion.
   d. Unqualified opinion with an additional explanatory paragraph.

20. In which of the following circumstances would an auditor be most likely to express an adverse opinion?
   a. Information comes to the auditor's attention that raises substantial doubt about the entity's ability to continue as a going concern.
   b. The chief executive officer refuses the auditor access to minutes of the board of directors' meetings.
   c. Tests of controls show that the entity's internal control structure is so poor that it can *not* be relied upon.
   d. The financial statements are *not* in conformity with the FASB statements regarding the capitalization of leases.

21. Tread Corp. accounts for the effect of a material accounting change prospectively when the inclusion of the cumulative effect of the change is required in the current year. The auditor would choose between expressing a(n)
   a. Qualified opinion or a disclaimer of opinion.
   b. Disclaimer of opinion or an unqualified opinion with an explanatory paragraph.
   c. Unqualified opinion with an explanatory paragraph and an adverse opinion.
   d. Adverse opinion and a qualified opinion.

22. Under which of the following circumstances would a disclaimer of opinion *not* be appropriate?
   a. The auditor is engaged after fiscal year end and is unable to observe physical inventories or apply alternative procedures to verify their balances.
   b. The auditor is unable to determine the amounts associated with illegal acts committed by the client's management.
   c. The financial statements fail to contain adequate disclosure concerning related-party transactions.
   d. The client refuses to permit its attorney to furnish information requested in a letter of audit inquiry.

23. The adverse effects of events causing an auditor to believe there is substantial doubt about an entity's ability to continue as a going concern would most likely be mitigated by evidence relating to the
   a. Ability to expand operations into new product lines in the future.
   b. Feasibility of plans to purchase leased equipment at less than market value.
   c. Marketability of assets that management plans to sell.
   d. Committed arrangements to convert preferred stock to long-term debt.

24. If an auditor is satisfied that there is only a remote likelihood of a loss resulting from the resolution of a matter involving an uncertainty, the auditor should express a(n)

a. Unqualified opinion.

b. Unqualified opinion with a separate explanatory paragraph.

c. Qualified opinion or disclaimer of opinion, depending upon the materiality of the loss.

d. Qualified opinion or disclaimer of opinion, depending on whether the uncertainty is adequately disclosed.

25. An auditor includes a separate paragraph in an otherwise unmodified report to emphasize that the entity being reported upon had significant transactions with related parties. The inclusion of this separate paragraph

a. Is appropriate and would *not* negate the unqualified opinion.

b. Is considered an "except for" qualification of the opinion.

c. Violates generally accepted auditing standards if this information is already disclosed in footnotes to the financial statements.

d. Necessitates a revision of the opinion paragraph to include the phrase "with the foregoing explanation."

ESSAY QUESTIONS AND PROBLEMS

15.1 Ross, Sandler & Co., CPAs, completed an examination of the 1992 financial statements of Fairfax Corporation on March 17, 1993, and concluded that an unqualified opinion was warranted. Because of a scope limitation arising from the inability to observe the January 1, 1991 inventory, the predecessor auditors, Smith, Ellis & Co., issued a report which contained an unqualified opinion on the December 31, 1991, balance sheet and a qualified opinion with respect to the statements of income, retained earnings, and changes in financial position for the year then ended. The management of Fairfax Corporation has decided to present a complete set of comparative (1992 and 1991) financial statements in their annual report.

Required:

Prepare an auditor's report assuming the March 1, 1992, auditor's report of Smith, Ellis & Co. is not presented. (AICPA adapted)

15.2 The following report was drafted by an audit assistant at the completion of an audit engagement and submitted to the auditor with client responsibility for review. The auditor has reviewed matters thoroughly and has properly concluded that the scope limitation was not client-imposed and was not sufficiently material to warrant a disclaimer of opinion although a qualified opinion was appropriate.

To Carl Corporation Controller:

We have examined the accompanying financial statements of Carl Corporation as of December 31, 1992. Our examination was made in accordance with generally accepted auditing standards and accordingly included such auditing procedures as we considered necessary under the circumstances.

On January 15, 1993, the company issued debentures in the amount of $1,000,000 for the purpose of financing plant expansion. As indicated in Note 6 to the financial statements, the debenture agreement restricts the payment of future cash dividends to earnings after December 31, 1992.

The company's unconsolidated foreign subsidiary did not close down production during the year under examination for physical inventory purposes and took no physical inventory during the year. We made extensive tests of book inventory figures for accuracy of calculation and reasonableness of pricing. We did not make physical tests of inventory quantities. Because of this, we are unable to express an unqualified opinion on the financial statements taken as a whole. However:

Except for the scope limitation regarding inventory, in our opinion the accompanying balance sheet presents the financial position of Carl Corporation at December 31, 1992, subject to the effect of the inventory on the carrying value of the investment. The accompanying statements of income and of retained earnings present the incomes and expenses and the result of transactions affecting retained earnings in accordance with generally accepted accounting principles.

December 31, 1992

Pate & Co., CPAs

Required:
Identify all of the deficiencies in the above draft of the proposed report. (AICPA adapted)

15.3 Sturdy Corporation owns and operates a large office building in a desirable section of New York City's financial center. For many years the management of Sturdy Corporation has modified the presentation of their financial statements by reflecting a write-up to appraisal values in the building accounts, and accounting for depreciation expense on the basis of such values.

Sibyl Wyley, a successor CPA, was asked to examine the financial statements of Sturdy Corporation for the year ended December 31, 1993. After completing the examination, Wyley concluded that, consistent with prior years, an adverse opinion would have to be expressed because of the materiality of the apparent deviation from the historical-cost principle.

Required:
a. *Describe* in detail the form of presentation of the explanatory paragraph of the auditor's report on the financial statements of Sturdy Corporation for the year ended December 31, 1993, clearly identifying the information contained in the paragraph.
b. *Write a draft* of the opinion paragraph of the auditor's report on the financial statements of Sturdy Corporation for the year ended December 31, 1993. (AICPA adapted)

15.4 The CPA firm of May & Marty has audited the consolidated financial statements of BGI Corporation. May & Marty performed the examination of the parent company and all subsidiaries except for BGI—Western Corporation, which was audited by the CPA firm of Dey & Dee. BGI—Western constituted approximately 10 percent of the consolidated assets and 6 percent of the consolidated revenue.

Dey & Dee issued an unqualified opinion on the financial statements of BGI—Western. May & Marty will be issuing an unqualified opinion on the consolidated financial statements of BGI.

Required:

    a. What procedures should May & Marty consider performing with respect to Dey & Dee's examination of BGI—Western's financial statements that will be appropriate whether or not reference is to be made to the other auditors?

    b. Describe the various circumstances under which May & Marty could take responsibility for the work of Dey & Dee and make no reference to Dey & Dee's examination of BGI—Western in May & Marty's auditor's report on the consolidated financial statements of BGI. (AICPA adapted)

15.5 Devon Incorporated engaged Robert Smith to examine its financial statements for the year ended December 31, 1993. The financial statements of Devon Incorporated for the year ended December 31, 1992, were examined by Alice Jones whose March 31, 1993, auditor's report expressed an unqualified opinion. This report of Jones is not presented with the 1993–92 comparative financial statements.

    Smith's working papers contain the following information that does not appear in the footnotes to the 1993 financial statements as prepared by Devon Incorporated:

    a. One director, appointed in 1993, was formerly a partner in Jones' accounting firm. Jones' firm provided financial consulting services to Devon during 1987 and 1988, for which Devon paid approximately $1,600 and $9,000 respectively.

    b. The company refused to capitalize certain lease obligations for equipment acquired in 1993. Capitalization of the leases in conformity with generally accepted accounting principles would have increased assets and liabilities by $312,000 and $387,000, respectively; decreased retained earnings as of December 31, 1993, by $75,000; and have decreased net income and earnings per share by $75,000 and $.75 respectively for the year then ended. Smith has concluded that the leases should have been capitalized.

    c. During the year, Devon changed its method of valuing inventory from the first-in first-out method to the last-in first-out method. This change was made because management believes LIFO more clearly reflects net income by providing a closer matching of current costs and current revenues. The change had the effect of reducing inventory at December 31, 1993, by $65,000 and net income and earnings per share by $38,000 and $.38, respectively, for the year then ended. The effect of the change on prior years was immaterial; accordingly, there was no cumulative effect of the change. Smith firmly supports the company's position. After completion of the field work on February 28, 1994, Smith concludes that the expression of an adverse opinion is not warranted.

Required:

Prepare the body of Smith's report dated February 28, 1994, and addressed to the board of directors to accompany the 1993–92 comparative financial statements. (AICPA adapted)

15.6 For each of the following situations, indicate the type of audit report to be issued and the reasons for your choice. Assume the amounts involved in each case are material.

    a. Jarrel, Inc., your audit client, is being sued in a product liability action. As of the audit report date, the outcome cannot be predicted with certainty. The probability for an unfavorable decision, however, has been estimated as reasonably possible.

b. Gemco, Ltd., a Canadian mining company, has participated with Houdel, Inc., your audit client, in a joint copper exploration venture. Jason Locksmith, the chairman of Houdel, is also the principal stockholder of Gemco. Several transactions, some of them material, have occurred between Gemco and Houdel for the year under examination. You are satisfied that all of the transactions have been properly reflected in the financial statements and adequately disclosed in footnotes.

c. Laraloon Developers and Builders, another audit client, is engaged in buying land, building shopping centers, and leasing space in the centers. In an effort to raise capital, the company has been selling certain properties and leasing them back. Inasmuch as the selling prices have materially exceeded Laraloon's cost to build and develop the properties, substantial profits have been recognized and reflected in the financial statements.

d. On October 30, 1993, you were engaged to audit the financial statements of Wickso, Inc., a wholesale distributor of automotive parts and accessories. Wickso has not been previously audited and its fiscal year ends November 30, 1993. Wickso plans to take a complete physical inventory as of November 30, 1993, and agrees to provide you with all of the documentation in support of the November 30, 1992, physical inventory.

15.7 Consistent application of GAAP enhances comparability of financial statements. Auditors, therefore, must add an explanatory paragraph in their audit reports whenever GAAP are not consistently applied.

Required:
a. Identify the accounting changes that require a consistency explanation.
b. An unqualified opinion may be issued only if the auditor concurs with the change. Explain why.

15.8 Audit reports frequently contain an explanatory paragraph following the scope paragraph or the opinion paragraph.

Required:
a. Describe the conditions under which the auditor may elect to add an explanatory paragraph.
b. Describe the conditions under which an explanatory paragraph is mandatory.
c. Draft an explanatory paragraph for each of the following situations:
  1. John Growl, the chief executive officer of Layman Brothers, Inc., furniture manufacturers, also owns a large furniture outlet, Cherished Woods. Several material transactions have been consummated between Layman Brothers and Cherished Woods, and a sizeable receivable from Cherished appears on Layman's balance sheet. As auditor, you have concluded that the transactions have been properly reflected in the financial statements, and adequately described in Note 4 to the financial statements.
  2. Carnival Rides, Inc., an audit client, is being sued by persons injured in the collapse of one of its amusement park rides. The amusement park is also suing. At the date of the audit report, legal counsel is unable to predict the outcome of the lawsuits with any degree of certainty. You have concluded that the loss could be material. Note 3 to the financial statements adequately describes the litigation.

15.9 Carla Fuller, CPA, is the continuing auditor for Carol Fabrics, Inc. The current year end is January 31, 1994. Last year's audit report contained an explanatory paragraph because of uncertainty regarding the ability of Carol Fabrics to continue as a going concern. The company had defaulted on two major loan agreements and appeared to be losing the race to develop "space age" fabrics. Since the date of last year's audit report, however, company management has changed. Significant new products, which have already proven successful in the markets served by Carol Fabrics, have been developed. Creditors have agreed to major debt restructuring agreements, and the company appears to be "out of the woods."

Required:
Assuming the company presents comparative financial statements for 1994 and 1993, present the audit report. Remember, you are updating—not reproducing—last year's audit report.

15.10 In accordance with GAAP, Generchek, Inc., a large audit client, discloses certain information regarding oil and gas reserves.

Required:
a. What procedures would you apply to the supplemental data required by the pronouncement?
b. What effect would omitted or improperly presented information have on your audit report? On your audit opinion?
c. Draft the audit report assuming Generchek refuses to include the required supplemental information.

15.11 The auditor's report below was drafted by a staff accountant of Turner & Turner, CPAs, at the completion of the audit of the financial statements of Lyon Computers, Inc., for the year ended March 31, 1989. It was submitted to the engagement partner who reviewed matters thoroughly and properly concluded that Lyon's disclosures concerning its ability to continue as a going concern for a reasonable period of time were adequate. Early application of Statement on Auditing Standards No. 59, "The Auditor's Consideration of an Entity's Ability to Continue as a Going Concern," was chosen by Turner & Turner.

To the Board of Directors of Lyon Computers, Inc.:

We have audited the accompanying balance sheet of Lyon Computers, Inc., as of March 31, 1989, and the other related financial statements for the year then ended. Our responsibility is to express an opinion on these financial statements based on our audit.

We conducted our audit in accordance with standards that require that we plan and perform the audit to obtain reasonable assurance about whether the financial statements are in conformity with generally accepted accounting principles. An audit includes examining, on a test basis, evidence supporting the amounts and disclosures in the financial statements. An audit also includes assessing the accounting principles used and significant estimates made by management.

The accompanying financial statements have been prepared assuming that the company will continue as a going concern. As discussed in Note X to the financial statements, the company has suffered recurring losses from operations and has a net capital deficiency that raises substantial doubt about its ability to continue as a going concern. We believe that management's plans in regard to these matters, which are also described in Note X, will permit the company to continue as a going concern beyond a reasonable period of time. The financial statements do not include any adjustments that might result from the outcome of this uncertainty.

In our opinion, subject to the effects on the financial statements of such adjustments, if any, as might have been required had the outcome of the uncertainty referred to in the preceding paragraph been known, the financial statements referred to above present fairly, in all material respects, the financial position of Lyon Computers, Inc., and the results of its operations and its cash flows in conformity with generally accepted accounting principles applied on a basis consistent with that of the preceding year.

Turner & Turner, CPAs

April 28, 1989

Required:
Identify the deficiencies contained in the auditor's report as drafted by the staff accountant. Group the deficiencies by paragraph. Do *not* redraft the report. (AICPA adapted)

16 Other Accounting Services And Reports

CHAPTER OUTLINE

I. **Attestation standards**
   A. Attestation defined and levels of assurance
   B. Preconditions for attestation services
   C. Attestation standards as contrasted with auditing standards

II. **Audited statements prepared on a basis other than GAAP**
   A. Reasons for "other basis"
   B. Form of report

III. **Unaudited financial statements**
   A. Public entity
   B. Nonpublic entity—compilations and reviews
   C. Lack of independence
   D. Agreed-upon procedures
   E. Letters for underwriters

IV. **Reporting on internal control**
   A. Scope of study
   B. Form of report

V. **Review of interim financial information**
   A. Presented as a note to audited financial statements
   B. Presented alone

VI. **CPA's association with prospective financial statements**
   A. Forecast vs. projection
   B. Three alternate levels of service

VII. **Summary table**

OVERVIEW

In addition to audits of financial statements prepared in accordance with GAAP, CPAs conduct other kinds of audits and also perform other services, such as compilations and reviews. Except for operational and compliance auditing, discussed in Chapter 17, these other audits and services are explored in this chapter in terms of the reporting requirements, necessary procedures, and level of assurance associated with each type of engagement.

The chapter begins by presenting the 11 attestation standards. These standards define the quality of such services and complement the 10 generally accepted auditing standards. The remaining sections of the chapter address the following types of engagements:

1. Audited statements prepared on a comprehensive basis of accounting other than GAAP;

2. Compilations and reviews;

3. Application of agreed-upon procedures;

4. Letters for underwriters;

5. Reporting on internal control;

6. Review of interim financial information;

7. Association with prospective financial statements (forecasts and projections)

A table summarizing these services concludes the chapter.

STUDY OBJECTIVES

After reading this chapter, you should be able to:

1. Define *attestation* and identify the two levels of assurance that may be associated with attestation services;

2. Recognize the 11 attestation standards and their general applicability;

3. Describe the reporting requirements, types of procedures, and level of assurance associated with a variety of nonaudit services covered by the attestation standards.

ATTESTATION STANDARDS

In addition to audits of financial statements prepared in accordance with generally accepted accounting principles, most accounting firms conduct other kinds of audits and perform other services, culminating in reports to their clients: financial statements prepared on a comprehensive basis other than GAAP, compilations, reviews, reports on internal control structure policies and procedures, examinations involving agreed-upon procedures, letters for underwriters, and prospective financial statements. These topics are addressed in this chapter.

Attestation Defined and Levels of Assurance

Many of the nonfinancial services (e.g., reports on internal control) require some form of attestation (opinion) by the accountant. **Attestation,** as defined by the AICPA in *Attestation Standards,* results in a "written communication that expresses a conclusion about the reliability of a written assertion that is the responsibility of another party."[1] The statement sets forth 11 standards covering two levels of attestation. **Positive assurance:** Reports that express conclusions on the basis of an "examination" (audit) provide positive assurance. **Negative assurance:** Reports that express conclusions on the basis of a review provide negative (limited) assurance.[2] A report on a client's internal control structure, for example, may contain an expression of an opinion on the effectiveness of the structure (positive assurance). A report on interim financial information, on the other hand, may simply state that nothing came to the accountant's attention to indicate that the information is not fairly presented (negative assurance).

Preconditions for Attestation Services

A joint project of the Auditing Standards Board and the Accounting and Review Services Committee of the AICPA, the attestation standards require five preconditions for attest services to be performed (see Table 16.1 — General Standards):

1. The practitioner has adequate *training and proficiency* in the attest function;
2. The practitioner has adequate *knowledge* of the subject matter;
3. There are reasonable *measurement and disclosure criteria* concerning the subject matter;
4. The assertions are *capable of reasonably consistent estimation or measurement* using such criteria; and
5. The practitioner is *independent*.

Attestation Standards as Contrasted with Auditing Standards

The attestation standards do not supersede the 10 generally accepted auditing standards. Rather, they complement them in that the attestation standards are broader in scope and are meant to maintain quality in the performance of the services they cover.

---

[1]*AICPA Professional Standards,* New York: AICPA, Section AT 100.01.

[2]Accountants also issue reports that provide *no assurance;* for example, a compilation report. Inasmuch as these reports do not involve attestation, they are not covered by the standards.

TABLE 16.1   Attestation Standards Contrasted with Auditing Standards

ATTESTATION STANDARDS	AUDITING STANDARDS
General Standards	*General Standards*
1. The engagement shall be performed by a practitioner or practitioners having adequate technical training and proficiency in the attest function.	1. The audit is to be performed by a person or persons having adequate technical training and proficiency as an auditor.
2. The engagement shall be performed by a practitioner or practitioners having adequate knowledge in the subject matter of the attestation.	N/A
3. The practitioner shall perform an engagement only if he or she has reason to believe that the following two conditions exist: A. The assertion is capable of evaluation against reasonable criteria that either have been established by a recognized body or are stated in the presentation of the assertion in a sufficiently clear and comprehensive manner for a knowledgeable reader to be able to understand them. B. The assertion is capable of reasonably consistent estimation or measurement using such criteria.	N/A
4. In all matters relating to the engagement, an independence in mental attitude shall be maintained by the practitioner or practitioners.	2. In all matters relating to the engagement, an independence in mental attitude is to be maintained by the auditor or auditors.
5. Due professional care shall be exercised in the performance of the engagement.	3. Due professional care is to be exercised in the performance of the audit and the preparation of the report.
Standards of Field Work	*Standards of Field Work*
1. The work shall be adequately planned and assistants, if any, shall be properly supervised.	1. The work is to be adequately planned and assistants, if any, are to be properly supervised.
N/A	2. A sufficient understanding of the internal control structure is to be obtained to plan the audit and to determine the nature, timing, and extent of tests to be performed.
2. Sufficient evidence shall be obtained to provide a reasonable basis for the conclusion that is expressed in the report.	3. Sufficient competent evidential matter is to be obtained through inspection, observation, inquiries, and confirmations to afford a reasonable basis for an opinion regarding the financial statements under audit.

(continued)

TABLE 16.1   *(continued)*

ATTESTATION STANDARDS	AUDITING STANDARDS
Standards of Reporting	*Standards of Reporting*
1. The report shall identify the assertion being reported on and state the character of the engagement.	N/A
N/A	1. The report shall state whether the financial statements are presented in accordance with generally accepted accounting principles.
N/A	2. The report shall identify those circumstances in which such principles have not been consistently observed in the current period in relation to the preceding period.
N/A	3. Informative disclosures in the financial statements are to be regarded as reasonably adequate unless otherwise stated in the report.
2. The report shall state the practitioner's conclusion about whether the assertion is presented in conformity with the established or stated criteria against which it was measured.	4. The report shall either contain an expression of an opinion regarding the financial statements taken as a whole, or an assertion to the effect that an opinion cannot be expressed. When an overall opinion cannot be expressed, the reasons therefore should be stated. In all cases where an auditor's name is associated with financial statements, the report should contain a clearcut indication of the character of the auditor's work, if any, and the degree of responsibility the auditor is taking.
3. The report shall state all of the practitioner's significant reservations about the engagement and the presentation of the assertion.	N/A
4. The report on an engagement to evaluate an assertion that has been prepared in conformity with agreed-upon criteria or an engagement to apply agreed-upon procedures should contain a statement limiting its use to the parties who have agreed upon such criteria or procedures.	N/A

N/A: nonapplicable
Source: *AICPA Professional Standards*. New York: AICPA, 1991.

Table 16.1 presents both the attestation standards and auditing standards for comparison. Note that the general attestation standards, like the general auditing standards, require *adequate training and proficiency, independence,* and *due care.* In addition, given the broader spectrum of services covered, the attestation standards require that the CPA have adequate *knowledge of the subject matter* and ascertain that the *assertions are capable of attestation.*

The field work standards for attestation, like the auditing field work standards require that the CPA *properly plan the engagement, supervise the work,* and *gather sufficient competent evidence in support of the assertions.* The assertions covered under the attestation standards, unlike the financial statement assertions covered under GAAS, are not dependent on internal control for reliability. Therefore, unlike the auditing standards, the attestation standards do not require the CPA to obtain an understanding of internal control.

The attestation reporting standards are similar to GAAS reporting standards in requiring the CPA to clearly state any reservations (qualifications) regarding presentation of the assertions. They are different from reporting standards under GAAS in other respects. First, the attestation standards say nothing about GAAP, inasmuch as GAAP is not the standard used to measure the reasonableness of assertions covered by the attestation standards. Second, given the diversity of assertions and types of engagements covered by the attestation standards, the standards require that the CPA identify the assertions being reported upon, as well as the nature of the engagement. Finally, as discussed later, professional standards prohibit general distribution of some forms of attestation reports. Therefore, the attestation reporting standards require the CPA to state applicable restrictions on distribution.

AUDITED STATEMENTS PREPARED ON A BASIS OTHER THAN GAAP

Some entities elect to prepare financial statements using an accounting basis not in conformity with generally accepted accounting principles. Regulatory bodies having jurisdiction over certain industries, for example, require that the financial statements be prepared in accordance with rules they prescribe. Transportation companies regulated by the Interstate Commerce Commission and insurance companies regulated by state insurance commissions are two such industries. Other examples not involving specific industries are financial statements prepared on a tax basis or on a cash basis.

This type of engagement is similar to an audit except that fairness is evaluated within the framework of the "other basis" rather than GAAP. Control tests and substantive tests are performed as deemed necessary, and an opinion is expressed as to whether the financial statements are fairly presented in accordance with the appropriate basis.

Exhibit 16.1 illustrates the recommended form of report to be issued by the CPA for a client using a **comprehensive basis other than GAAP.** The following characteristics that distinguish this report from the standard audit report should be noted. First, in the introductory paragraph, the terms balance sheet, income statement, and statement of retained earnings are not used inasmuch as these terms imply that the financial statements were prepared in accordance with GAAP. Instead, other titles that are more descriptive of the basis are used. Second, a paragraph referring the reader to the footnote that describes the basis other than GAAP is inserted between the scope and opinion paragraphs. Third, the opinion paragraph states whether the auditor believes the financial statements are fairly presented in accordance with the described basis. Finally, when the statements are prepared in accordance with the requirements of a regulatory body, a fifth paragraph, restricting the use of the financial statements to management, the board of directors, and the regulatory agency, must be added.

EXHIBIT 16.1 Report on Comprehensive Basis of Accounting Other than GAAP

INDEPENDENT AUDITOR'S REPORT

To the Board of Directors of
XYZ Insurance Company:

We have audited the accompanying statements of admitted assets, liabilities, and surplus—statutory basis of XYZ Insurance Company as of December 31, 19X2 and 19X1, and the related statements of income and cash flows—statutory basis and changes in surplus—statutory basis for the years then ended. These financial statements are the responsibility of the company's management. Our responsibility is to express an opinion on these financial statements based on our audits.

We conducted our audits in accordance with generally accepted auditing standards. Those standards require that we plan and perform the audit to obtain reasonable assurance about whether the financial statements are free of material misstatement. An audit includes examining, on a test basis, evidence supporting the amounts and disclosures in the financial statements. An audit also includes assessing the accounting principles used and significant estimates made by management, as well as evaluating the overall financial statement presentation. We believe that our audits provide a reasonable basis for our opinion.

As described in Note X, these financial statements were prepared in conformity with the accounting practices prescribed or permitted by the Insurance Department of *[State],* which is a comprehensive basis of accounting other than generally accepted accounting principles.

In our opinion, the financial statements referred to above present fairly, in all material respects, the admitted assets, liabilities, and surplus of XYZ Insurance Company as of (at) December 31, 19X2 and 19X1, and the results of its operations and its cash flows for the years then ended, on the basis of accounting described in Note X.

This report is intended solely for the information and use of the board of directors and management of XYZ Insurance Company and for filing with the *[name of the regulatory agency]* and should not be used for any other purpose.

(Signature)

(Date)

Source: Auditing Standards Board, *Codification of Statements on Auditing Standards,* New York: AICPA, Section AU 623.08.

UNAUDITED FINANCIAL STATEMENTS

Public Entity

A CPA who is associated with **unaudited financial statements** of a *public entity* (i.e., an entity whose shares are publicly held) should disclaim an opinion and each page of the statements should be marked *unaudited.*[3] A state of *association* exists whenever:

---

[3]*AICPA Professional Standards.* New York: AICPA, Section AU 504.05.

1. *The CPA's name is used* in a document containing the statements; or

2. *The CPA has prepared or assisted in preparing* the statements.[4]

The general form of disclaimer accompanying unaudited statements is as follows:

> The accompanying balance sheet of X Company as of December 31, 19X1, and the related statements of income, retained earnings, and cash flows for the year then ended were not audited by us and, accordingly, we do not express an opinion on them. (Signature and date)[5]

If the financial statements are known by the CPA to contain a material departure from GAAP, the client should be encouraged to revise the statements accordingly. If the client refuses, the disclaimer must additionally describe the departure and state the effects on the financial statements if practicable. If the client doesn't agree to this, the CPA should refuse to be associated with the statements.[6]

Compilations and Reviews

Nonpublic entities—generally, those whose securities are not traded in a public market—may request the CPA to compile or review their financial statements. Such requests often occur when entities are applying for loans or attempting to attract outside investors. The potential lenders or investors, in reaching credit or investment decisions, may want more than the basic unaudited financial statements, but are willing to accept less than an audit. Compilations and reviews are designed to fill this need. Standards governing compilations and reviews for nonpublic entities are contained in **Statements on Standards for Accounting and Review Services** (SSARS) issued by the Accounting and Review Services Committee of the AICPA. We should note that these statements prohibit a CPA member from being associated with the unaudited financial statements of a nonpublic entity unless he/she has at least compiled or reviewed the statements, or includes a statement that he/she has not compiled or reviewed the statements and assumes no responsibility for them.[7]

The following paragraphs define compilations and reviews and are based on the SSARSs.

Compilation

In compiling financial statements for a client, the CPA presents information that is the representation of management without undertaking to express any assurance on the statements.[8] To perform a **compilation,** the CPA must possess a level of knowledge of the accounting principles and practices of the client's industry that will result in compiled financial statements appropriate to that industry.[9] A general understanding of the nature of the entity's business transactions, accounting records, the qualifications of the accounting personnel, and the accounting basis on

---

[4]*Ibid.,* Section AU 504.03.

[5]*Ibid.,* Section AU 504.05.

[6]*Ibid.,* Sections AU 504.11-.13.

[7]*Ibid.,* Section AR 100.06.

[8]*Ibid.,* Section AR 100.04.

[9]*Ibid.,* Section AR 100.10.

which the financial statements are to be presented are the necessary requirements for a compilation. Such procedures as inquiry, observation, confirmation, vouching, reconciling, and recalculating, ordinarily associated with audits, are *not required* in compilations.

The following form of report is recommended as being appropriate for a compilation:

> We have compiled the accompanying balance sheet of XYZ Company as of December 31, 19XX, and the related statements of income, retained earnings, and cash flows for the year then ended, in accordance with standards established by the American Institute of Certified Public Accountants.
>
> A compilation is limited to presenting in the form of financial statements information that is the representation of management. We have not audited or reviewed the accompanying financial statements and, accordingly, do not express an opinion or any other form of assurance on them. (Signature and date)[10]

Note that the second paragraph of the report clearly disclaims an opinion on the financial statements. Attestation is not involved in a compilation and, therefore, no form of assurance is given by the CPA.

The CPA should encourage the client to correct the financial statements for known errors or departures from GAAP. If the client refuses, the compilation report should disclose the information. If the client declines to permit disclosure in the compilation report, the CPA should refuse to be associated with the statements.

Review

More than a compilation but less than an audit, a **review** consists mainly of performing inquiry and analytical procedures. Such procedures provide the CPA a basis for expressing limited assurance concerning conformance with GAAP. A review does not contemplate a study and evaluation of internal control, confirmation, or other tests of accounting records performed in an audit.

The inquiry and analytical procedures should include the following:

1. Inquiries concerning the entity's accounting principles and practices and the methods followed in applying them.
2. Inquiries concerning the entity's procedures for recording, classifying, and summarizing transactions and accumulating information for disclosure in the financial statements.
3. Analytical procedures designed to identify relationships and individual items that appear to be unusual.
4. Inquiries concerning actions taken at meetings of stockholders, board of directors, committees of the board of directors, or comparable meetings that may affect the financial statements.
5. Reading the financial statements to consider—. . .—whether they appear to conform with generally accepted accounting principles.

---

[10]*Ibid.*, Section AR 100.17.

6. Obtaining reports from other accountants, if any, who have been engaged to audit or review the financial statements of significant components of the reporting entity.

7. Inquiries of persons having responsibility for financial and accounting matters concerning:
   a. conformity with GAAP;
   b. changes in activities or accounting principles and practices;
   c. matters as to which questions have arisen in applying the foregoing procedures; and
   d. events subsequent to the date of the financial statements that would have a material effect on the financial statements.[11]

The following form of standard report is appropriate for a review:

> We have reviewed the accompanying balance sheet of XYZ Company as of December 31, 19XX, and the related statements of income, retained earnings, and cash flows for the year then ended, in accordance with standards established by the American Institute of Certified Public Accountants. All information included in these financial statements is the representation of the management of XYZ Company.
>
> A review consists principally of inquiries of company personnel and analytical procedures applied to financial data. It is substantially less in scope than an audit in accordance with generally accepted auditing standards, the objective of which is the expression of an opinion regarding the financial statements taken as a whole. Accordingly, we do not express such an opinion.
>
> Based on our review, we are not aware of any material modifications that should be made to the accompanying financial statements in order for them to be in conformity with generally accepted accounting principles.[12]

Unlike a compilation, the review report includes, after the disclaimer, a paragraph expressing limited assurance on the financial statements. Inasmuch as limited assurance is a form of attestation, the CPA, in performing reviews, is subject to the attestation standards described earlier in the chapter.

The review report should be modified to disclose any known and uncorrected deficiencies in the financial statements. If management does not agree to the disclosure, the CPA should refuse to be associated with the statements.

To summarize, a *compilation* offers *no assurance;* a *review* offers *limited assurance;* and an *audit* offers *reasonable assurance* regarding fairness of the financial statements. Although less than the reasonable assurance offered by an audit, many lending officers accept the review report as adequate for loan application purposes.

Table 16.2 displays the range of services, the principal procedures, and the level of assurance, if any, related to various forms of association by the CPA with a client's financial statements. Note the absence of any form of assurance, in a compilation.

---

[11]*Ibid.,* Section AR 100.27.

[12]*Ibid.,* Section AR 100.35.

TABLE 16.2 Range of Services of a CPA Associated with Financial Statements

No Assurance	Limited Assurance	Positive Assurance
Compilation:	Review:	Audit:
Read financial statements Understand industry accounting practices	Inquiry Analytical procedures	Study and evaluate internal control Observe, examine, confirm, reconcile, calculate, and vouch

Lack of Independence

A CPA who lacks independence with respect to the client may not conduct an audit or a review, but may perform a compilation.[13] When a CPA is associated with financial statements but is not independent and has not compiled the statements, the accompanying disclaimer should be modified to indicate the lack of independence. The following report form is recommended:

> We are not independent with respect to XYZ Company, and the accompanying balance sheet as of December 31, 19X1, and the related statements of income, retained earnings, and cash flows for the year then ended were not audited by us and, accordingly, we do not express an opinion on them. (Signature and Date)[14]

For compiled statements, lack of independence should be disclosed in a final paragraph stating, "We are not independent with respect to XYZ Company."[15]

Agreed-Upon Procedures

The CPA may be asked to report on the application of **agreed-upon procedures** to specified elements of the financial statements. In most cases, application of the agreed-upon procedures does not provide sufficient evidence to support an opinion on the specified elements. Examples of this type of engagement are bank directors' examinations, examinations for credit union examining committees, examinations for proposed acquisitions, and examinations for creditors' committees or trustees in bankruptcy proceedings.

The CPA may accept such an engagement on the conditions that the parties involved have a clear understanding of the procedures to be performed, and distribution of the report is to be restricted to the named parties involved.[16] Moreover, the report (see Exhibit 16.2) should clearly set forth the following:

1. The specified elements to which the agreed-upon procedures were applied;
2. The intended distribution of the report;

[13]*Ibid.*, Section AR 100.22.
[14]*Ibid.*, Section AU 504.10.
[15]*Ibid.*, Section AR 100.22.
[16]*Ibid.*, Section AU 622.02.

EXHIBIT 16.2 Report on the Application of Agreed-Upon Procedures

Trustee
XYZ Company

At your request, we have performed the procedures enumerated below with respect to the claims of creditors of XYZ Company as of May 31, 1993, set forth in the accompanying schedules. Our review was made solely to assist you in evaluating the reasonableness of those claims, and our report is not to be used for any other purpose. The procedures we performed are summarized as follows:

a. We compared the total of the trial balance of accounts payable at May 31, 1993, prepared by the company, to the balance in the company's related general ledger accounts.

b. We compared the claims received from creditors to the trial balance of accounts payable.

c. We examined documentation submitted by the creditors in support of their claims and compared it to documentation in the company's files, including invoices, receiving records, and other evidence of receipt of goods or services.

Our findings are presented in the accompanying schedules. Schedule A lists claims that are in agreement with the company's records. Schedule B lists claims that are not in agreement with the company's records and sets forth the differences in amounts.

Because the above procedures do not constitute an audit made in accordance with generally accepted auditing standards, we do not express an opinion on the accounts payable balance as of May 31, 1993. In connection with the procedures referred to above, except as set forth in Schedule B, no matters came to our attention that caused us to believe that the accounts payable balance might require adjustment. Had we performed additional procedures or had we made an audit of the financial statements in accordance with generally accepted auditing standards, other matters might have come to our attention that would have been reported to you. This report relates only to the accounts and items specified above and does not extend to any financial statements of XYZ Company, taken as a whole.

(Signature and Date)

Source: Auditing Standards Board, *Codification of Statements on Auditing Standards*. New York: AICPA, Section AU 622.06.

3. The procedures performed; and

4. A statement of the accountant's findings.

The report disclaims an opinion on the financial statements because the procedures are less extensive than those applied in an audit. The disclaimer is followed, however, by limited assurance, inasmuch as the procedures are considered adequate for that purpose.

Letters for Underwriters: Reporting on Unaudited Data

Most publicly held companies are required, by law, to register new securities offerings with the Securities and Exchange Commission (SEC). A registration statement and prospectus must be completed by the company and approved by the SEC.

The primary purpose of the registration statement and prospectus is to provide prospective investors with financial and other information concerning the registrant.

Financial statements must be included as part of the documentation. In addition to the most recent audited financial statements, unaudited financial statements as of a date within 90 days of the filing date must be included if the most recent audited statements do not fall within that period.

Although not required by the SEC, a **comfort letter** from the auditors is frequently provided for in the agreement between the underwriters and the registrant.[17] The comfort letter is a letter issued by the auditor at the request of the underwriter to assist the underwriter in conducting a due-diligence review. The following matters are commonly covered in the comfort letter:

1. The independence of the accountants;
2. Compliance, in all material respects, of the audited statements with SEC requirements;
3. Unaudited financial statements;
4. Changes in financial statement items since the date of the latest financial statements included in the registration statement; and
5. Tables, statistics, and other financial information included in the registration statement.[18]

If limited procedures have been applied to the unaudited data, the CPA may give negative assurance, in the comfort letter, with respect to the data. Negative assurance relative to comfort letters is synonymous with that described earlier with respect to financial statement reviews. Like reviews, therefore, the procedures applied to the unaudited interim data consist mainly of inquiry and analytical procedures. Exhibit 16.3 illustrates a partial comfort letter covering unaudited data which have been reviewed by the CPA.

A CPA should not give negative assurance with respect to unaudited financial statements without having obtained knowledge of the client's accounting and financial reporting practices and its internal control structure policies and procedures relating to the preparation of financial statements.[19] Given this requirement, a CPA who has not previously audited the client's financial statements ordinarily should not give negative assurance in the comfort letter.

REPORTING ON THE INTERNAL CONTROL STRUCTURE

A CPA may be asked to report on a client's internal control structure policies and procedures as a special engagement for the purpose of expressing an opinion on internal control. The scope of the examination and reporting requirements are discussed in the following paragraphs.

The Auditing Standards Board considered establishment of guidelines relating to reports on internal control necessary in light of requirements contained in the

---

[17]The underwriter is responsible for issuing the registrant's securities upon approval of the SEC.

[18]*AICPA Professional Standards,* Section AU 634.06.

[19]*Ibid.,* Section AU 634.19.

EXHIBIT 16.3 Partial Comfort Letter: Negative Assurance with Respect to Unaudited Data

With respect to the three-month periods ended March 31, 1994 and 1993, we have—

a. Read the unaudited consolidated condensed balance sheet as of March 31, 1994, and unaudited consolidated condensed statements of income, retained earnings, and cash flows for the three-month periods ended March 31, 1994 and 1993, included in the registration statement; and

b. Made inquiries of certain officials of the company who have responsibility for financial and accounting matters regarding (1) whether the unaudited consolidated condensed financial statements referred to in (a) comply in form in all material respects with the applicable accounting requirements of the (Securities) Act and the related published rules and regulations and (2) whether those unaudited consolidated condensed financial statements are in conformity with generally accepted accounting principles applied on a basis substantially consistent with that of the audited consolidated financial statements included in the registration statement.

The foregoing procedures do not constitute an audit made in accordance with generally accepted auditing standards. Also, they would not necessarily reveal matters of significance with respect to the comments in the following paragraph. Accordingly, we make no representations regarding the sufficiency of the foregoing procedures for your purposes.

Nothing came to our attention as a result of the foregoing procedures, however, that caused us to believe that the unaudited consolidated condensed financial statements described above do not comply in form in all material respects with the applicable accounting requirements of the (Securities) Act and the related published rules and regulations and that the unaudited consolidated condensed financial statements are not in conformity with generally accepted accounting principles applied on a basis substantially consistent with that of the audited consolidated financial statements.

This letter is solely for the information of the addressees and to assist the underwriters in conducting and documenting their investigation of the affairs of the company in connection with the offering of the securities covered by the registration statement, and it is not to be used, circulated, quoted, or otherwise referred to within or without the underwriting group for any other purpose, including but not limited to the registration, purchase, or sale of securities, nor is it to be filed with or referred to in whole or in part in the registration statement or any other document, except that reference may be made to it in the underwriting agreement or in any list of closing documents pertaining to the offering of the securities covered by the registration statement.

(Signature and Date)

Adapted from Auditing Standards Board, *Codification of Statements on Auditing Standards*. New York: AICPA, Section AU 634.49.

Foreign Corrupt Practices Act of 1977. Such requirements mandated that public companies establish and maintain adequate systems of internal control. The guidelines are embodied in two SASs. SAS 60, discussed in Chapter 14, requires that auditors communicate reportable conditions (material weaknesses in internal control) discovered as part of the audit. SAS 30 provides the vehicle for expressing an opinion on internal control as part of a special study and evaluation.

Engagements for the purpose of expressing an opinion on internal control differ in two ways from the SAS 60 requirement that auditors communicate reportable conditions to the audit committee. First, in an engagement to express an opinion, the CPA is examining and reporting on controls as of a specified date. This differs from the financial audit in which controls are tested for effectiveness over the period covered by the financial statements. Second, engagements for the purpose of expressing an opinion are more extensive than a study of internal control made as part of an audit. The CPA, in an engagement to express an opinion, must gather sufficient evidence to provide reasonable assurance to management concerning the control environment, the accounting system, and internal control procedures. The study and evaluation made as part of an audit, on the other hand, is an intermediate step in evaluating the reliability of the financial statements. Inasmuch as an engagement to express an opinion is more extensive than that made as part of an audit, no restrictions need be placed on the use of the resulting report.

The standard form (see Exhibit 16.4) used to report on internal control, given an engagement to express an opinion, should include the following:

1. A description of the scope of the engagement;

2. The date to which the opinion relates;

3. A statement that the establishment and maintenance of the control structure is the responsibility of management;

4. A brief explanation of the broad objectives and inherent limitations of internal control; and

5. The accountant's opinion on whether the structure taken as a whole was sufficient to meet the broad objectives of internal control insofar as those objectives pertain to the prevention or detection of errors or irregularities in amounts that would be material in relation to financial statements.[20]

Note that the report expresses an opinion as of a particular point in time and is limited to evaluating the effectiveness of the structure in preventing and detecting errors and irregularities having a material impact on the financial statements. The report should be modified if material weaknesses are found or if scope limitations were encountered.

REVIEW OF INTERIM FINANCIAL INFORMATION

Interim financial information may be defined as financial statements or condensed information covering less than a year. Interim financial information may be presented alone or as a note to audited financial statements. Public companies are required by the Securities and Exchange Commission to provide interim financial information to their shareholders, and to include the information in the annual report to shareholders.[21] In addition, the independent auditors are often asked to apply limited procedures to the data. The information is usually presented in the annual

---

[20]*Ibid.*, Section AU 642.38.

[21]*Ibid.*, Section AU 722.24.

EXHIBIT 16.4   Report on Internal Control Based on Engagement to Express an Opinion

To the Board of Directors of XYZ Company:

We have made a study and evaluation of the internal control structure of XYZ Company and subsidiaries in effect at (date). Our study and evaluation was conducted in accordance with standards established by the American Institute of Certified Public Accountants.

The management of XYZ Company is responsible for establishing and maintaining the internal control structure. In fulfilling this responsibility, estimates and judgments by management are required to assess the expected benefits and related costs of control procedures. The objectives of the structure are to provide management with reasonable, but not absolute, assurance that assets are safeguarded against loss from unauthorized use or disposition, and that transactions are executed in accordance with management's authorization and recorded properly to permit the preparation of financial statements in accordance with generally accepted accounting principles.

Because of inherent limitations in any internal control structure, errors or irregularities may occur and not be detected. Also, projection of any evaluation of the structure to future periods is subject to the risk that procedures may become inadequate because of changes in conditions, or that the degree of compliance with the procedures may deteriorate.

In our opinion, the internal control structure of XYZ Company and subsidiaries in effect at (date), taken as a whole, was sufficient to meet the objectives stated above insofar as those objectives pertain to the prevention or detection of errors or irregularities in amounts that would be material in relation to the consolidated financial statements.

(Signature and Date)

Note: If the auditor has discovered material weaknesses, the opinion paragraph would be modified as follows:

Our study and evaluation disclosed the following conditions in the control structure of XYZ Company and subsidiaries in effect at (date), which, in our opinion, result in more than a relatively low risk that errors or irregularities in amounts that would be material in relation to the consolidated financial statements may occur and not be detected within a timely period.

Source: Auditing Standards Board, *Codification of Statements on Auditing Standards*. New York: AICPA, Section AU 642.39.

report in the form of a footnote and should be clearly marked as *unaudited*.[22] If limited procedures have not been applied, the audit report must be modified to include a statement that such procedures were not applied to the interim financial information. Such modification would assume the form of an explanatory paragraph following the opinion paragraph and would *not* constitute a qualification of the audit opinion.

[22]*Ibid.*, Section AU 722.26.

The objective of reviewing interim financial information is to determine whether any material modifications are necessary in order for the information to conform to GAAP. The review does not contemplate a study and evaluation of internal control or tests of the accounting records through inspection, observation, or confirmation.[23] Like reviews, therefore, it is considerably more limited in scope than an audit.

The procedures to be applied in the review consist primarily of inquiry and analytical procedures concerning accounting matters relating to the interim information. Recommended procedures are as follows:

1. Inquiry concerning the accounting system and any significant changes in internal control;

2. Application of analytical procedures to the interim information;

3. Reading the minutes of stockholders' and directors' meetings;

4. Reading the interim financial information; and

5. Inquiry of and obtaining written representations from management concerning its responsibility for the financial information and other matters.[24]

EXHIBIT 16.5   Report on Review of Interim Financial Information or Statements Presented Alone

(Addressee)

We have made a review of (describe the information or statements reviewed) of ABC Company and consolidated subsidiaries as of September 30, 1993, and for the three-month and nine-month periods then ended, in accordance with standards established by the American Institute of Certified Public Accountants.

A review of interim financial information consists principally of obtaining an understanding of the system for the preparation of interim financial information, applying analytical procedures to financial data, and making inquiries of persons responsible for financial and accounting matters. It is substantially less in scope than an audit in accordance with generally accepted auditing standards, the objective of which is the expression of an opinion regarding the financial statements taken as a whole. Accordingly, we do not express such an opinion.

Based on our review, we are not aware of any material modifications that should be made to the accompanying financial (information or statements) for them to be in conformity with generally accepted accounting principles.

(Signature and Date)

Source: Auditing Standards Board, *Codification of Statements on Auditing Standards*. New York: AICPA, Section AU 722.18.

---

[23]*Ibid.*, Section AU 722.03.

[24]*Ibid.*, Section AU 722.06.

Knowledge of a client's internal control structure policies and procedures (including knowledge of the accounting system) and its financial reporting practices is considered vital to performing a review of interim financial information. Such knowledge is usually obtained by having audited the most recent annual financial statements of the company. For this reason, CPAs are advised to carefully consider whether to accept an engagement of this kind without having previously performed an audit.[25]

If interim financial information, which has been reviewed, is presented alone (rather than in an unaudited footnote to the annual financial statements), a review report must accompany the statements. Exhibit 16.5 illustrates the recommended form of the report. The report contains a statement that the review was made in accordance with standards established by the American Institute of Certified Public Accountants. It identifies the interim financial information or statements reviewed and describes the review procedures. The report provides limited (negative) assurance by stating that the accountant is not aware of any material modifications that should be made to the interim information in order for it to conform to GAAP.

If the interim information is known by the accountant to contain a departure from GAAP, the report must be modified to disclose this. The modification should describe the nature of the departure and, if practicable, should state the effects on the interim information.[26]

THE CPA'S ASSOCIATION WITH PROSPECTIVE FINANCIAL STATEMENTS

A CPA who is associated with **prospective financial statements** that are expected to be used by a third party should either compile, examine, or apply agreed-upon procedures to the statements.[27] Prospective financial statements may assume one of two forms:

1. **Forecast:** Presents the entity's expected financial position, results of operations, and cash flows reflecting *conditions expected to exist*.

2. **Projection:** Presents financial position, results of operations, and cash flows given one or more *hypothetical assumptions*.

A forecast is appropriate for general distribution to third parties with whom the client is not in direct negotiation. A projection, however, is more tentative, and it should be restricted to those parties with whom the client is negotiating directly, and who may therefore ask questions concerning the assumptions. If the client proposes to prepare financial projections for general use, the CPA should refuse to be associated with them.[28]

---

[25]*Ibid.*, Section AU 722.09.

[26]*Ibid.*, Section AU 722.21.

[27]*Ibid.*, Sections AT 200.01-.02.

[28]*Ibid.*, Section AT 200.09.

EXHIBIT 16.6 Compilation Report for Association with a Financial Forecast

(Addressee)

We have compiled the accompanying forecasted balance sheet, statements of income, retained earnings, and cash flows of XYZ Company as of December 31, 1992, and for the year then ending, in accordance with standards established by the American Institute of Certified Public Accountants.

A compilation is limited to presenting in the form of a forecast information that is the representation of management and does not include evaluation of the support for the assumptions underlying the forecast. We have not examined the forecast and, accordingly, do not express an opinion or any other form of assurance on the accompanying statements or assumptions. Furthermore, there will usually be differences between the forecasted and actual results, because events and circumstances frequently do not occur as expected, and those differences may be material. We have no responsibility to update this report for events and circumstances occurring after the date of this report.

(Signature and Date)

Source: Auditing Standards Board, *Codification of Statements on Auditing Standards*. New York: AICPA, Section AT 200.17.

EXHIBIT 16.7 Compilation Report for Association with a Financial Projection

(Addressee)

We have compiled the accompanying projected balance sheet, statements of income, retained earnings, and cash flows of XYZ Company as of December 31, 1992, and for the year then ending, in accordance with standards established by the American Institute of Certified Public Accountants.

The accompanying projection and this report were prepared for (state special purpose, for example, "the DEF National Bank for the purpose of negotiating a loan to expand XYZ Company's plant") and should not be used for any other purpose.

A compilation is limited to presenting in the form of a projection information that is the representation of management and does not include evaluation of the support for the assumptions underlying the projection. We have not examined the projection and, accordingly, do not express an opinion or any other form of assurance on the accompanying statements or assumptions. Furthermore, even if (describe hypothetical assumption, for example, "the loan is granted and the plant is expanded") there will usually be differences between the projected and actual results, because events and circumstances frequently do not occur as expected, and those differences may be material. We have no responsibility to update this report for events and circumstances occurring after the date of this report.

(Signature and Date)

Source: Auditing Standards Board, *Codification of Statements on Auditing Standards*. New York: AICPA, Section AT 200.18.

Compilation of Prospective Financial Statements

Exhibit 16.6 illustrates a standard compilation report which a CPA would issue in conjunction with a financial forecast. Exhibit 16.7 is a compilation report accompanying a financial projection. In neither case is any form of assurance provided by the CPA. Procedures to be applied in compiling prospective financial statements should include the following:

1. Establish an understanding with the client, preferably in writing, regarding the services to be performed;

2. Inquire about the accounting principles used in the preparation of prospective financial statements;

3. Ask how the key factors are identified and how the assumptions are developed;

4. Obtain a list of significant assumptions and consider whether there are any omissions or inconsistencies;

5. Test the mathematical accuracy of the computations which translate the assumptions into prospective financial statements; and

6. Read the statements and determine that they conform to AICPA presentation guidelines in all material respects.[29]

Examination of Prospective Financial Statements

An examination of prospective financial statements, like an audit, requires a form of attestation and is more extensive than a compilation. The examination involves evaluating the preparation of the prospective statements, the support underlying the assumptions, and whether the presentation is in conformity with AICPA guidelines.[30]

In a report on the examination of prospective financial statements, the CPA *expresses an opinion* as to whether the statements are presented in conformity with AICPA guidelines and whether the assumptions provide a reasonable basis for the forecast or projection. Exhibits 16.8 and 16.9 illustrate the proper form of report on the examination of financial forecasts and financial projections respectively.[31]

Applying Agreed-upon Procedures to Prospective Financial Statements

Companies experiencing financial difficulties may be asked by their creditors to submit prospective financial statements to which certain agreed-upon procedures have been applied. Companies involved in acquisition or merger negotiations may

---

[29]*Ibid.*, Section AT 200.68.

[30]*Ibid.*, Section AT 200.27.

[31]*Ibid.*, Sections AT 200.32-.33.

EXHIBIT 16.8   Report on Examination of a Financial Forecast

(Addressee)

We have examined the accompanying forecasted balance sheet, statements of income, retained earnings, and cash flows of XYZ Company as of December 31, 1992, and for the year then ending. Our examination was made in accordance with standards for an examination of a forecast established by the American Institute of Certified Public Accountants and, accordingly, included such procedures as we considered necessary to evaluate both the assumptions used by management and the preparation and presentation of the forecast.

In our opinion, the accompanying forecast is presented in conformity with guidelines for presentation of a forecast established by the American Institute of Certified Public Accountants, and the underlying assumptions provide a reasonable basis for management's forecast. However, there will usually be differences between the forecasted and actual results because events and circumstances frequently do not occur as expected, and those differences may be material. We have no responsibility to update this report for events and circumstances occurring after the date of this report.

(Signature and Date)

Source: Auditing Standards Board, *Codification of Statements on Auditing Standards*. New York: AICPA, Section AT 200.32.

EXHIBIT 16.9   Report on Examination of a Financial Projection

(Addressee)

We have examined the accompanying projected balance sheet, statements of income, retained earnings, and cash flows of XYZ Company as of December 31, 1992, and for the year then ending. Our examination was made in accordance with standards for an examination of a projection established by the American Institute of Certified Public Accountants and, accordingly, included such procedures as we considered necessary to evaluate both the assumptions used by management and the preparation and presentation of the projection.

The accompanying projection and this report were prepared for (state special purpose) and should not be used for any other purpose.

In our opinion, the accompanying projection is presented in conformity with guidelines for presentation of a projection established by the American Institute of Certified Public Accountants, and the underlying assumptions provide a reasonable basis for management's projection (describe the hypothetical assumption, for example, "assuming the granting of the requested loan for the purpose of expanding XYZ Company's plant as described in the summary of significant assumptions"). However, even if (describe hypothetical assumption, for example, "the loan is granted and the plant is expanded") there will usually be differences between the projected and actual results, because events and circumstances frequently do not occur as expected, and those differences may be material. We have no responsibility to update this report for events and circumstances occurring after the date of this report.

(Signature and Date)

Source: Auditing Standards Board, *Codification of Statements on Auditing Standards*. New York: AICPA, Section AT 200.33.

similarly request their CPA to apply certain procedures to prospective financial information. A CPA may accept an engagement to apply agreed-upon procedures provided:

1. The specified users involved have participated in establishing the nature and scope of the engagement and take responsibility for the adequacy of the procedures to be performed;

2. Distribution of the report is to be restricted to the specified users involved; and

3. The prospective financial statements include a summary of significant assumptions.[32]

Exhibit 16.10 illustrates a report that might be issued when agreed-upon procedures have been applied. This is a form of review report and, therefore, includes a disclaimer of opinion accompanied by limited assurance.

SUMMARY TABLE

Table 16.3 summarizes accounting services other than audits, as discussed in this chapter. Regardless of whether the service involves compiling, reviewing, or examining (similar to auditing) third-party assertions, the 11 attestation standards must be observed. CPAs who examine or review third-party assertions must be independent of their clients. Independence is not a requirement for compilations.

---

[32]*Ibid.*, Section AT 200.49.

**EXHIBIT 16.10   Report on Prospective Financial Statements Given
Application of Agreed-upon Procedures**

ABC Trustee
XYZ Company

   At your request, we performed the agreed-upon procedures enumerated below with respect to the forecasted balance sheet, statements of income, retained earnings, and cash flows of XYZ Company as of December 31, 1992, and for the year then ending. These procedures, which were specified by ABC Trustee and XYZ Company, were performed solely to assist you, and this report is solely for your information and should not be used by those who did not participate in determining procedures.

   a. We assisted the management of XYZ Company in assembling the prospective financial statements.

   b. We read the prospective financial statements for compliance in regard to format with the presentation guidelines established by the American Institute of Certified Public Accountants for presentation of a forecast.

   c. We tested the forecast for mathematical accuracy.

   Because the procedures described above do not constitute an examination of prospective financial statements in accordance with standards established by the American Institute of Certified Public Accountants, we do not express an opinion on whether the prospective financial statements are presented in conformity with AICPA presentation guidelines or on whether the underlying assumptions provide a reasonable basis for the presentation.

   In connection with the procedures referred to above, no matters came to our attention that caused us to believe that the format of the forecast should be modified or that the forecast is mathematically inaccurate. Had we performed additional procedures or had we made an examination of the forecast in accordance with standards established by the American Institute of Certified Public Accountants, matters might have come to our attention that would have been reported to you. Furthermore, there will usually be differences between the forecasted and actual results because events and circumstances frequently do not occur as expected, and those differences may be material. We have no responsibility to update this report for events and circumstances occurring after the date of this report.

(Signature and Date)

Source: Auditing Standards Board, *Codification of Statements on Auditing Statements*. New York: AICPA, Section AT 200.57 — Exhibit 2.

TABLE 16.3 Summary Table of Nonaudit Services

Nature of Service	Type of Report	Level of Assurance	Distribution of Report	Principal Procedures
Compilation: Nonpublic entity	Compilation	None	General	Understand industry accounting practices Read the financial statements
Review: Nonpublic entity	Review	Limited	General	Inquiry Analytical procedures
Comprehensive basis of accounting other than GAAP	Opinion	Positive*	General	Control structure study Substantive testing
Agreed-upon procedures	Review	Limited	Restricted	As specified by agreement
Letters for underwriters	Review	Limited	Underwriters	Inquiry—as specified by agreement Read the financial statements
Report on internal control as part of audit	Disclaimer	Limited	Management or other specified third party	Study and evaluation as part of the audit
Report on internal control to express an opinion	Opinion	Positive	General	Identify control objectives and procedures Perform tests of controls as necessary
Review of interim financial information	Review	Limited	General	Inquiry Analytical procedures
Association with prospective financial statements:				
Compilation	Compilation	None	Forecast, general Projection, restricted	Inquire as to accounting principles Test mathematical accuracy of computations Read prospective statements Evaluate assumptions
Examination	Opinion	Positive**	Forecast, general Projection, restricted	Examination of evidence supporting assumptions Determine whether assumptions provide a reasonable basis for the forecast or projection Evaluate preparation and presentation of prospective data
Application of agreed-upon procedures	Review	Limited	Limited to specified users	As agreed

*Regarding other basis.

**Regarding reasonableness of assumptions but not achievability of results.

KEY TERMS

Agreed-upon procedures   Negative assurance
Attestation   Positive assurance
Attestation standards   Projection
Comfort letter   Prospective financial statements
Compilation   Review
Comprehensive basis other than GAAP   Statements on Standards for Accounting
Forecast   and Review Services (SSARS)
Interim financial information   Unaudited financial statements

REVIEW QUESTIONS

1. Define the following terms:
   a. *Attestation*
   b. *Positive assurance*
   c. *Negative assurance*
2. What conditions determine whether a CPA is "associated" with financial statements?
3. What are the minimum reporting requirements for a CPA associated with a non-public client's financial statements?
4. What steps should a CPA associated with a client's unaudited financial statements take upon learning of a material departure from GAAP?
5. What is the major difference between the 11 attestation standards and the 10 auditing standards?
6. Differentiate among the following:
   a. Compilation
   b. Review
   c. Audit
7. What are the major procedures applied in a review? In a compilation?
8. Give an example of financial statements prepared on a comprehensive basis of accounting other than GAAP.
9. What type of report is rendered by the CPA when a client's financial statements are prepared on a comprehensive basis of accounting other than GAAP?
10. What type of accounting service may be performed by a CPA who lacks independence?
11. Under what conditions may a CPA accept an engagement to report on the application of agreed-upon procedures to specified elements of the financial statements?
12. Why do underwriters request a "comfort letter" from the auditors?
13. Name three matters commonly covered in comfort letters.
14. Why should a CPA, who has not previously audited the client's financial statements, ordinarily not give negative assurance in the comfort letter?
15. Identify the major difference between a report on internal control as part of the audit engagement, and one resulting from a special engagement to report on internal control.
16. What type of assurance may be given when interim financial information is presented alone?

17. If limited procedures have not been applied to interim financial information included in the annual report, must the audit report be modified? If so, in what way? Does this constitute a qualified opinion?
18. Differentiate between a "forecast" and a "projection."
19. Why is the distribution of projections to third parties more limited than forecasts?
20. What are the major procedures applied in compiling prospective financial statements?

MULTIPLE CHOICE QUESTIONS FROM CPA EXAMINATIONS

1. The statement that "nothing came to our attention that would indicate that these statements are not fairly presented" expresses which of the following?
   a. Disclaimer of opinion.
   b. Negative assurance.
   c. Negative confirmation.
   d. Piecemeal opinion.

2. A CPA is associated with client-prepared financial statements, but is not independent. With respect to the CPA's lack of independence, which of the following actions by the CPA might confuse a reader of such financial statements?
   a. Stamping the word "unaudited" on each page of the financial statements.
   b. Disclaiming an opinion and stating that independence is lacking.
   c. Issuing a qualified auditor's report explaining the reason for the auditor's lack of independence.
   d. Preparing an auditor's report that included essential data that was not disclosed in the financial statements.

3. When an independent CPA is associated with the financial statements of a publicly held entity but has not audited or reviewed such statements, the appropriate form of report to be issued must include a(an)
   a. Negative assurance.
   b. Compilation opinion.
   c. Disclaimer of opinion.
   d. Explanatory paragraph.

4. During a review of the financial statements of a nonpublic entity, the CPA finds that the financial statements contain a material departure from generally accepted accounting principles. If management refuses to correct the financial statement presentations, the CPA should
   a. Disclose the departure in a separate paragraph of the report.
   b. Issue an adverse opinion.
   c. Attach a footnote explaining the effects of the departure.
   d. Issue a compilation report.

5. A modification of the CPA's report on a review of the interim financial statements of a publicly held company would be necessitated by which of the following?
   a. An uncertainty.
   b. Lack of consistency.
   c. Reference to another accountant.
   d. Inadequate disclosure.

6. When reporting on financial statements prepared on a comprehensive basis of accounting other than generally accepted accounting principles, the independent auditor should include in the report a paragraph that
    a. States that the financial statements are not intended to be in conformity with generally accepted accounting principles.
    b. Justifies the comprehensive basis of accounting being used.
    c. Refers to the authoritative pronouncements that explain the comprehensive basis of accounting being used.
    d. States that the financial statements are not intended to be examined in accordance with generally accepted auditing standards.

7. A financial forecast is an estimate of financial position, results of operations, and cash flows that, to the best of management's knowledge, is
    a. At the midpoint of a given precision range.
    b. At the low point of a given precision range.
    c. Conservative.
    d. Most probable.

8. In which of the following reports should a CPA not express negative or limited assurance?
    a. A standard compilation report on financial statements of a nonpublic entity.
    b. A standard review report on financial statements of a nonpublic entity.
    c. A standard review report on interim financial statements of a public entity.
    d. A standard comfort letter on financial information included in a registration statement of a public entity.

9. Compiled financial statements should be accompanied by a report stating all of the following except
    a. The accountant does not express an opinion or any other form of assurance on them.
    b. A compilation has been performed.
    c. A compilation is limited to presenting in the form of financial statements information that is the representation of management.
    d. A compilation consists principally of inquiries of company personnel and analytical procedures applied to financial data.

10. A CPA's report on a forecast should include all of the following except
    a. A description of what the forecast information is intended to represent.
    b. A caveat as to the ultimate attainment of the forecasted results.
    c. A statement that the CPA assumes no responsibility to update the report for events occurring after the date of the report.
    d. An opinion as to whether the forecast is fairly presented.

11. An auditor's report on financial statements prepared in accordance with another comprehensive basis of accounting should include all of the following *except*
    a. An opinion as to whether the basis of accounting used is appropriate under the circumstances.
    b. An opinion as to whether the financial statements are presented fairly in conformity with the other comprehensive basis of accounting.
    c. Reference to the note to the financial statements that describes the basis of presentation.
    d. A statement that the basis of presentation is a comprehensive basis of accounting other than generally accepted accounting principles.

12. When reporting on financial statements prepared on the same basis of accounting used for income tax purposes, the auditor should include in the report a paragraph that
   a. Emphasizes that the financial statements are *not* intended to have been examined in accordance with generally accepted auditing standards.
   b. Refers to the authoritative pronouncements that explain the income tax basis of accounting being used.
   c. States that the income tax basis of accounting is a comprehensive basis of accounting other than generally accepted accounting principles.
   d. Justifies the use of the income tax basis of accounting.

13. Accepting an engagement to compile a financial projection for a publicly held company most likely would be inappropriate if the projection were to be distributed to
   a. A bank with which the entity is negotiating for a loan.
   b. A labor union with which the entity is negotiating a contract.
   c. The principal stockholder, to the exclusion of the other stockholders.
   d. All stockholders of record as of the report date.

14. An accountant may accept an engagement to apply agreed-upon procedures to prospective financial statements provided that
   a. Distribution of the report is to be restricted to the specified users involved.
   b. The prospective financial statements are also examined.
   c. Responsibility for the adequacy of the procedures performed is taken by the accountant.
   d. Negative assurance is expressed on the prospective financial statements taken as a whole.

15. When an accountant examines a financial forecast that fails to disclose several significant assumptions used to prepare the forecast, the accountant should describe the assumptions in the accountant's report and issue a(an)
   a. "Except for" qualified opinion.
   b. "Subject to" qualified opinion.
   c. Unqualified opinion with a separate explanatory paragraph.
   d. Adverse opinion.

16. Which of the following professional services would be considered an attest engagement?
   a. A management consulting engagement to provide EDP advice to a client.
   b. An engagement to report on compliance with statutory requirements.
   c. An income tax engagement to prepare federal and state tax returns.
   d. The compilation of financial statements from a client's accounting records.

17. Which of the following procedures would most likely be included in a review engagement of a nonpublic entity?
   a. Preparing a bank transfer schedule.
   b. Inquiring about related-party transactions.
   c. Assessing the internal control structure.
   d. Performing cut-off tests on sales and purchases transactions.

18. Performing inquiry and analytical procedures is the primary basis for an accountant to issue a
   a. Report on compliance with requirements governing major federal assistance programs in accordance with the Single Audit Act.

    b. Review report on prospective financial statements that present an entity's expected financial position, given one or more hypothetical assumptions.

    c. Management advisory report prepared at the request of a client's audit committee.

    d. Review report on comparative financial statements for a nonpublic entity in its second year of operations.

19. Before issuing a report on the compilation of financial statements of a nonpublic entity, the accountant should

    a. Apply analytical procedures to selected financial data to discover any material misstatements.

    b. Corroborate at least a sample of the assertions management has embodied in the financial statements.

    c. Inquire of the client's personnel whether the financial statements omit substantially all disclosures.

    d. Read the financial statements to consider whether the financial statements are free from obvious material errors.

20. If requested to perform a review engagement for a nonpublic entity in which an accountant has an immaterial direct financial interest, the accountant is

    a. Independent because the financial interest is immaterial and, therefore, may issue a review report.

    b. Not independent and, therefore, may *not* be associated with the financial statements.

    c. Not independent and, therefore, may *not* issue a review report.

    d. Not independent and, therefore, may issue a review report, but may not issue an auditor's opinion.

21. A CPA in public practice must be independent in fact and appearance when providing which of the following services?

	Preparation of a Tax Return	*Compilation of a Financial Forecast*	*Compilation of Personal Financial Statements*
a.	Yes	No	No
b.	No	Yes	No
c.	No	No	Yes
d.	No	No	No

ESSAY QUESTIONS AND PROBLEMS

16.1 For the year ending December 31, 1993, Novak & Co., CPAs, audited the financial statements of Tillis Ltd. and expressed an unqualified opinion dated February 27, 1994. For the year ended December 31, 1994, Novak & Co. were engaged to review Tillis Ltd.'s financial statements; that is, "look into the company's financial statements and determine whether there are any obvious modifications that should be made to the financial statements in order for them to be in conformity with generally accepted accounting principles."

    Novak made the necessary inquiries, performed the necessary analytical procedures, and performed certain additional procedures that were deemed necessary to achieve the requisite limited assurance. Novak's work was completed on March 3, 1995, and the financial statements appeared to be in conformity with generally accepted accounting principles that were consistently applied. The report was prepared on March 5, 1995. It was delivered to Jones, the controller of Tillis Ltd., on March 9, 1995.

Required:

Prepare the properly addressed and dated report on the comparative financial statements of Tillis Ltd., for the years ended December 31, 1993 and 1994. (AICPA adapted)

16.2 In order to obtain information that is necessary to make informed decisions, management often calls upon the independent auditor for assistance. This may involve a request that the independent auditor apply certain audit procedures to specific accounts of a company that is a candidate for acquisition and report upon the results. In such an engagement, the agreed-upon procedures may constitute a scope limitation.

At the completion of an engagement performed at the request of Uclean Corporation, which was limited in scope as just explained, the following report was prepared by an audit assistant and was submitted to the audit manager for review:

To: Board of Directors of Ajax Corporation

We have applied certain agreed-upon procedures, as discussed below, to accounting records of Ajax Corporation, as of December 31, 1992, solely to assist Uclean Corporation in connection with the proposed acquisition of Ajax Corporation.

We have examined the cash in banks and accounts receivable of Ajax Corporation as of December 31, 1992, in accordance with generally accepted auditing standards and, accordingly, included such tests of the accounting records and such other auditing procedures as we considered necessary in the circumstances.

In our opinion, the cash and receivables referred to above are fairly presented as of December 31, 1992, in conformity with generally accepted accounting principles. We therefore recommend that Uclean Corporation acquire Ajax Corporation pursuant to the proposed agreement.

Signature

Required:

Comment on the proposed report describing those assertions that are:
a. Incorrect or should otherwise be deleted.
b. Missing and should be inserted. (AICPA adapted)

16.3 On March 12, 1994, Brown & Brown, CPAs, completed the audit engagement of the financial statements of Modern Museum, Inc., for the year ended December 31, 1993. Modern Museum, presents comparative financial statements on a modified cash basis. Assets, liabilities, fund balances, support, revenues, and expenses are recognized when cash is received or disbursed, except that Modern includes a provision for depreciation of buildings and equipment. Brown & Brown believes that Modern's three financial statements, prepared in accordance with a comprehensive basis of accounting other than generally accepted accounting principles, are adequate for Modern's needs and wishes to issue an auditor's

special report on the financial statements. Brown & Brown has gathered sufficient competent evidential matter in order to be satisfied that the financial statements are fairly presented according to the modified cash basis. Brown & Brown
audited Modern's 1992 financial statements and issued the auditor's special report expressing an unqualified opinion.

Required:

Draft the auditors' report to accompany Modern's comparative financial statements. (AICPA adapted)

16.4 Young and Young, CPAs, completed an examination of the financial statements
of XYZ Company, Inc., for the year ended June 30, 1993, and issued a standard
unqualified auditor's report dated August 15, 1993. At the time of the engagement,
the board of directors of XYZ requested a special report attesting to the adequacy
of the provision for federal and state income taxes and related accruals and deferred
income taxes as presented in the June 30, 1993, financial statements. Young and
Young submitted the appropriate special report on August 22, 1993.

Required:

Prepare the special report that Young and Young should have submitted to XYZ
Company, Inc. (AICPA adapted)

16.5 For each of the following engagements, indicate the nature of the service performed (i.e., audit, review, compilation, etc.), the type of report to be issued
(i.e., opinion, review, compilation), and the principal procedures to be applied.

   a. A nonpublic client asks the CPA to prepare financial statements from the
      client's records, without auditing or reviewing the statements.

   b. The board of directors of ABC Corporation request the CPA to examine
      certain elements of the financial statements of XYZ Co., a candidate for
      acquisition by ABC.

   c. Mell & Mell, Investment Bankers, have requested the CPA to issue a comfort
      letter relative to the registration of securities of Emhart, Inc., with the Se-
      curities and Exchange Commission. The comfort letter is to cover the unau-
      dited financial statements for the three months ending February 28, 1994.

   d. The board of directors of Herr, Inc., has requested the CPA to examine the
      projected financial statements for the upcoming year. The statements are to be
      used by First National Bank as part of a loan application to be submitted by
      Herr.

16.6 You have been asked by Jerrol Industries to review its financial statements for the
year ending December 31, 1994. Jerrol has requested a substantial loan from
Midcontinent Bank & Trust Co. In the past you have compiled Jerrol's financial
statements but have never audited or reviewed them.

Required:

   a. Differentiate among audits, reviews, and compilations in terms of procedures
      to be applied, and level of assurance provided.

   b. Assuming you completed your field work on February 14, 1995, and did not
      find any material cause for modification of the financial statements, draft the
      review report.

   c. Assuming you discover that Jerrol reports plant assets at appraisal values: What
      modifications should you make to the standard review report? What should you
      do if management and the board do not agree to these modifications?

16.7 Tom Fox, CPA, issued the following report on the forecasted financial statements for Burnlee, Inc.:

Trustee in Receivership
Burnlee, Inc.

At your request, I performed the agreed-upon procedures enumerated below with respect to the forecasted balance sheet, statements of income, retained earnings, and cash flows of Burnlee, Inc., as of December 31, 1995.

a. I assisted the management of Burnlee, Inc., in assembling the prospective financial statements.
b. I read the prospective financial statements for compliance in regard to format with the presentation guidelines established by the American Institute of Certified Public Accountants for presentation of a forecast.
c. I tested the forecast for mathematical accuracy.
d. I applied other auditing procedures that we considered necessary in the circumstances.

In my opinion, the accompanying forecast is presented in conformity with guidelines for presentation of a forecast established by the American Institute of Certified Public Accountants, and the underlying assumptions provide a reasonable basis for management's forecast.

March 11, 1995
Tom Fox, CPA

Required:
Comment on the above report. Indicate corrections where appropriate.

16.8 a. Contrast the scope and reporting requirements for a report on internal control as part of an audit engagement and a report on internal control as part of a special engagement to express an opinion.
b. In performing an engagement to express an opinion on Demingtree Industries' internal control structure, J. Johnson, a CPA, discovered material control weaknesses within the company's vouchering and disbursement functions. What steps should Johnson take with regard to the weaknesses? Don't forget to address the reporting implications.

16.9 One of your public clients is required by the Securities and Exchange Commission to include unaudited interim financial information in its annual report to shareholders. You have been asked to review the information.

Required:
a. What is the purpose for reviewing interim financial information?
b. Why do you suppose the SEC requires that interim financial information be included in the annual report to stockholders?
c. How should your audit report be modified if limited review procedures have not been applied to the interim information?

16.10 Analytical procedures are applied by CPAs for a variety of purposes. They are applicable to both audit and nonaudit services.

Required:
a. What is the overriding purpose for applying analytical procedures?
b. Give seven examples of situations calling for the application of analytical procedures.

17 Operational and Compliance Auditing

CHAPTER OUTLINE

I. **Introduction**

II. **Operational auditing—focuses on activities**
   A. Operational auditing defined
   B. Management auditing
      1. A special type of operational auditing
      2. Measures effectiveness
   C. Evolution of internal auditing
      1. Internal auditing began as fraud detection device
      2. Compliance auditing and operational auditing evolved to meet needs arising from increased regulation, diversification, and decentralization
      3. Foreign Corrupt Practices Act of 1977
   D. Operational auditing today—goal is to assist managers in improving activity performance
      1. Planning the audit
      2. Performing the audit fieldwork
         a. Preliminary survey
         b. Develop the audit program
         c. Perform the audit
         d. Appraise activities
         e. Evaluate findings
         f. Develop conclusions and recommendations
      3. Reporting findings and recommendations

III. **Compliance auditing**
   A. Compliance auditing defined
   B. Auditor's responsibility under generally accepted auditing standards
   C. Auditor's responsibility under the General Accounting Office's "yellow book" *Governmental Auditing Standards*
   D. Auditor's responsibility under the federal Single Audit Act of 1984
   E. Auditor's responsibility under Circular A-133
   F. Audit risk analysis and compliance auditing

IV. **Appendix. Standards for the Professional Practice of Internal Auditing**

OVERVIEW

This chapter considers operational auditing and compliance auditing. Operational auditing is a subset of internal auditing. It assists managers by reviewing and evaluating their activities and recommending improvements. The audits focus on efficiency and effectiveness of operations. Compliance auditing involves testing and reporting on compliance with various laws and regulations. These two forms of auditing have assumed greater importance in recent years, given decentralization of entity operations and the increasing number of laws and regulations affecting both profit and not-for-profit entities.

The first section of this chapter addresses operational auditing and describes how it developed over several years as a monitoring device for top management. A case study is then presented to describe how a typical operational audit is planned and performed. The importance of developing specific audit objectives and identifying appropriate evaluation criteria is emphasized in the case study. An audit program is prepared as part of the case and the various steps in performing the audit field work are identified and described. An audit report is also presented. The report contains the auditors' findings and recommendations.

The second part of the chapter focuses on compliance auditing as applied by the independent auditor when engaged in audits of state and local governmental units and other not-for-profit entities that are the recipients of federal financial assistance. The auditor, within this context, must observe governmental auditing standards as defined in the General Accounting Office's "yellow book," as well as comply with generally accepted auditing standards. Additionally, if the amount of financial assistance exceeds specified minimum levels, the auditor must also comply with the requirements of the federal Single Audit Act of 1984. Finally, for colleges, universities, and other nongovernmental not-for-profit entities receiving more than specified minimum levels of federal financial assistance, the auditor must meet the requirements set forth in Circular A-133 issued by the Office of Management and Budget.

STUDY OBJECTIVES

After reading this chapter, you should be able to:

1. Define operational auditing as a subset of internal auditing.
2. Differentiate between efficiency and effectiveness auditing.
3. Describe how operational auditing developed to fulfill specific management needs.
4. Recognize that operational auditing exists to assist managers in improving their performance.
5. List and describe the steps in planning and performing an operational audit, including:
   a. Identifying audit objectives and establishing evaluation criteria;
   b. Developing and applying the audit program;
   c. Appraising efficiency and effectiveness;
   d. Formulating conclusions and recommendations; and
   e. Reporting findings.
6. Describe compliance auditing as applied to the audits of state and local governmental units and other not-for-profit entities receiving federal financial assistance.
7. Define auditor responsibility under "yellow book" standards and the Single Audit Act of 1984.
8. Define auditor responsibility under Circular A-133.

INTRODUCTION

Internal auditing was described in Chapter 1 as a service function established within an organization to examine and evaluate its activities. Internal audits may focus on financial reporting (financial audits), compliance with policies, procedures, laws, or regulations (compliance audits), fraud detection (fraud audits), or operational efficiency and effectiveness (operational audits). Most internal audit staffs engage in all of these endeavors (see Figure 17.1).

To guide the practice of internal auditing, the **Institute of Internal Auditors** has established general and specific standards. These standards are presented in an appendix following this chapter. Although not enforceable in the same sense as the AICPA auditing and attestation standards, they do provide helpful guidance for the internal auditor concerning such matters as maintaining necessary independence, required proficiency, audit scope, performing the audit, and administering the internal audit function.

Although an important subset of internal auditing, operational audits are also performed by the **General Accounting Office** (GAO) and by the management consulting units of accounting firms. The first part of this chapter addresses operational auditing within the context of the internal auditing function. The second part describes compliance auditing as applied by independent auditors during audits of state and local governmental entities and other not-for-profit entities. Compliance auditing, within this context, involves testing and reporting on an entity's compliance with laws and regulations relating to federal financial assistance programs where the state or local governmental entity, or other not-for-profit entity, is a recipient of such assistance.

FIGURE 17.1   Internal Auditing—A Management Service Function

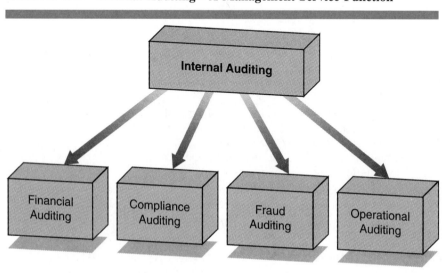

OPERATIONAL AUDITING

Operational Auditing Defined

Operational auditing, a subset of internal auditing, reviews an entity's activities for *efficiency* and *effectiveness* and may evaluate any type of activity at any level within the organization. Unlike financial auditing, operational auditing focuses on activities rather than financial statement assertions. The audited activities may be related to a function—e.g., why is employee turnover so high?—or they may be part of an organizational unit—e.g., why is the Omaha plant producing a high percentage of defective parts? The one aspect that is common to all operational audits is *maximizing organizational welfare*.

Management Auditing—A Special Type of Operational Audit

Management auditing is a subset of operational auditing that attempts to measure the *effectiveness* with which an organizational unit is administered. It concentrates more on effectiveness than efficiency. Efficiency and effectiveness, as used to describe operational auditing, are distinct terms (see Figure 17.2). **Efficiency** may be viewed as an input measure. It relates to cost control and is concerned with performing recurring functions at a minimum of cost to the entity. **Effectiveness** is output oriented and is a measure of productivity in utilizing the firm's resources. Effectiveness may also be viewed in terms of long-run profitability. As one audits at progressively higher levels within an entity, efficiency becomes less important relative to effectiveness.

Inasmuch as management audits are about management effectiveness, they can be potentially dangerous to the internal auditor. In performing these audits, the auditor must avoid disrupting the harmonious working of the management team and must take care to maintain cooperative relations between auditor and auditee. Obtaining the auditee's input, participation, and support also increases the probability of implementation of the auditor's recommendations. A partnership approach is most important in management audits.

Evolution of Internal Auditing

As first conceived, **internal auditing** focused on asset safeguards and fraud detection. Later, as laws, regulations, and policies became more numerous, compliance auditing was added to the internal auditor's responsibilities.

With the growth and diversification of companies, management encountered increasing difficulty in monitoring operations and activities that were often far removed from central headquarters. At first, decentralization and divisional autonomy relieved corporate management of the need to administer the entire breadth and depth of operations. Product managers, regional vice presidents, and divisional managers emerged as firms' chief line operating managers. Distancing top management from much of the operating activity, however, created a need for a monitoring device. Although elaborate systems of budgeting and performance reporting provided some degree of control, corporate management needed to more closely monitor the activities of the divisions and product lines. Operational auditing, as part of the internal audit function, emerged to fill this need.

FIGURE 17.2   Management Auditing—A Subset of Operational Auditing

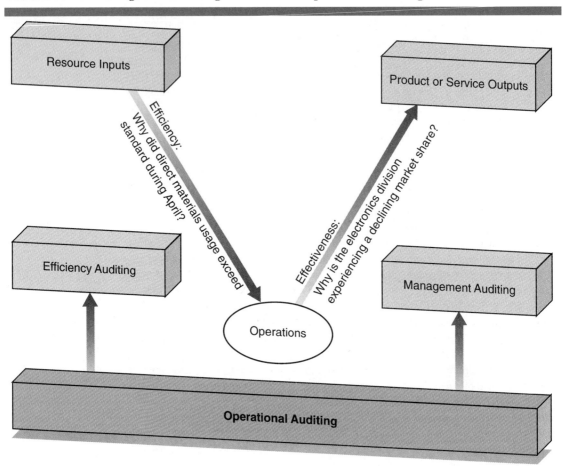

The **Foreign Corrupt Practices Act of 1977** (FCPA) also played an important role in increasing the resources devoted to internal auditing by publicly held companies. Congress passed the FCPA in response to a 1976 SEC report on investigations into questionable and illegal corporate payments and practices. The report was submitted to the Senate Committee on Banking, Housing, and Urban Affairs, and recommended legislation to prevent bribes and other illegal payments to foreign officials by public companies as a means for obtaining business. As such, the act contains provisions requiring companies to maintain accounting records that are adequate to fairly and accurately reflect transactions. The act also requires companies to develop and implement internal controls that permit preparation of financial statements in accordance with GAAP and maintain accountability over assets.

Given the severity of penalties imposed for violation of FCPA provisions, companies began to enlarge their internal audit staffs as a means for monitoring FCPA compliance. At the same time, the reporting level was raised such that many internal auditors presently report to the chief executive officer and the audit committee of the board of directors.

Operational Auditing Today

Operational auditing has only recently emerged as an integral part of internal auditing. As it exists today, operational auditing has become an important part of top management's monitoring effort. With the addition of the operational auditing function to their management service role, internal auditors are frequently referred to as the "eyes and ears of management."

Operational audits typically answer such questions as:

- Are specified employees functioning efficiently?
- Are current approaches still effective in achieving the entity's goals in light of changing conditions?

Until recently, operational auditing followed a practice of performing recurring efficiency and effectiveness audits on different functions or units in a company. The audits were conducted whether or not the auditors were aware of special problems. The emphasis has now begun to shift away from recurring audits to focus more on management's special problems and means of solving them. For example, instead of auditing the personnel function every three years, the internal audit team, at management's request, may investigate as to why the company has experienced increasing employee turnover in the appliance division within the past year. One might view this approach as **risk-based operational auditing.** Other possible problem areas targeted for operational audits might include inability to meet production quotas, unfilled customer back orders, cost overruns, low rate of return on products, a reporting system not providing management with adequate information for decision-making purposes, and possible violation of pollution control laws.

Given its wide breadth of focus, operational auditing requires other forms of expertise in addition to accounting and auditing. Many operational audit engagements now include industrial engineers, economists, statisticians, mathematicians, data processing specialists, and lawyers, as well as accountants. While these experts are not necessarily a permanent part of the internal audit staff, they are often borrowed from other units in the organization when performing operational audits requiring their particular skills.

Currently, the scope of operational auditing is virtually unlimited and may cover all functional areas and all levels of the organization. Table 17.1 lists possible operational audits by functional area.

As a byproduct of their upgraded role, internal auditors have also enhanced their image in the eyes of the independent auditors. Most public accounting firms consider the internal auditors vital to an effective independent audit and will hesitate to accept a large client audit engagement without an audit committee and a capable internal audit staff. Indeed, as discussed in Chapters 5 through 7, the independent auditor, after obtaining satisfaction concerning competence and objectivity, frequently utilizes the work of the internal auditors in completing the audit.

Operational Audit Approach

Operational auditing focuses on helping management to improve the way entity activities are performed. In this section, a hypothetical internal audit engagement is used to illustrate the various steps in planning and performing an operational audit. A sample **operational audit report** is presented at the conclusion of the exercise.

TABLE 17.1   Functional Areas Typically Covered by Operational Audits

PURCHASING
    Proper determination of the entity's needs
      for goods and services
    Selecting vendors
    Receiving goods
    Emergency purchases
    Controlling vendor influence

TRANSPORTATION
    Reviewing freight costs
    Processing claims against carriers

PERSONNEL
    Adequacy of job analysis, job descriptions,
      and compensation
    Recruitment practices
    Screening procedures
    Training programs
    Adequacy of personnel records
    Benefits
    Affirmative action
    Computerization
    Exit interviews

FINANCIAL MANAGEMENT
    Separation between controller and treasurer
    Flexible budgeting
    Budget coordination
    Performance reporting by cost and profit center
    Cash control
    Working capital management
    Investment policy

ELECTRONIC DATA PROCESSING
    Range of computer usage:
      Many firms underutilize their computers
      Manual rather than computerized reports
      Failure to place data bases on computer (e.g.,
        customers, creditors, inventories, and payroll)
    Organizational status for computer head (should
      be fairly high—otherwise range is too narrow)
    Effectiveness in serving management's needs
    Adequacy of documentation (systems analysis,
      programs, modifications, and operator instructions)
    Proper controls

Vector, Inc., is a diversified manufacturing company consisting of the following three divisions:

- EZ Parts—Automobile replacement mufflers and exhaust pipes
- Excel—Sporting goods
- Staywell—Infant products

The divisions are autonomous and are accountable to corporate headquarters on the basis of divisional budgets, monthly performance reports, and annual headquarters meetings requiring formal presentations by divisional managers. A partial organization chart is presented in Figure 17.3.

The internal audit staff consists of 25 members, most of whom are accountants, and is headed by Thomas Layne, Vector's internal audit director. Layne's reporting responsibility extends to the board of directors (see Figure 17.3). Audit teams visit the divisions on a recurring basis and examine such functions as financial controls, budgeting and profit planning, production control, receiving and distribution, and data processing. The cycling is such that each function within each division is audited every three years. In addition, Layne assigns audit teams to special problem engagements as requested by headquarters management. John Sparks, the corporate controller, is currently concerned that selling prices within the sporting goods division are not producing adequate profits and so informs Jacquelyn Shoemaker, Vector's marketing vice-president. Shoemaker, in turn, requests Layne to conduct a special investigation.

FIGURE 17.3   Vector, Inc. Partial Organization Chart

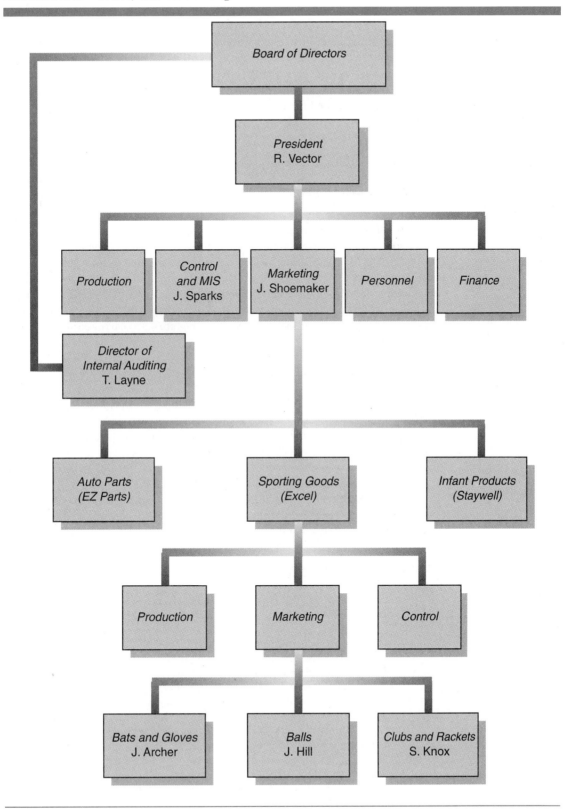

The sporting goods division operates under the trade name of Excel and manufactures and sells baseballs, golf balls, baseball bats, baseball gloves, golf clubs, footballs, tennis rackets, basketballs, soccer balls, and tennis balls. These products are divided into three lines and a product manager is responsible for pricing his/her line. The three lines and the product managers are as follows:

Line	Product Manager
Baseball bats and gloves	Jeffrey Archer
Baseballs, basketballs, soccer balls, footballs, golf balls, and tennis balls	Jennifer Hill
Golf clubs and tennis rackets	Susan Knox

Kenneth Johns has been designated the in-charge field auditor for the Excel "selling price audit." He is being assisted by Donald Krause, who has been on the staff for two years and Marjory Mason, a newly hired member of Vector's internal audit staff. Krause is a CPA and was previously employed as a staff auditor by a regional accounting firm. Mason has recently earned her baccalaureate degree in accounting and this is her first position. Johns is a CPA and has been with Vector for three years, having spent the preceding four years with a "big six" accounting firm as a senior staff auditor.

Planning the Audit

As in any type of audit, the first step in performing an operational audit is the planning phase. To properly plan the audit, audit objectives and evaluation criteria must be established. In the Vector engagement, Johns has identified the audit *objectives* as determining whether product prices are set in such a way as to promote Vector's overall profitability, and whether prices being charged to customers are in accordance with company policy.

Evaluation criteria define the process or activity being audited. Identifying evaluation criteria is necessary if the auditor is to ultimately determine the cause of discovered inefficiencies. For the Vector sales price audit, Johns has established the following criteria:

How do product managers set selling prices?
    Is market analysis undertaken?
    Does market analysis include demand analysis?
    Does market analysis include consideration of competitor pricing strategies?
    Is cost analysis performed?
    Are Vector's cost accountants involved in the process?
    Is a contribution margin approach applied?
    Are indirect costs considered in the decision?
How frequently are selling prices reviewed for adequacy?
    Are selling prices subject to approval by the marketing vice-president?
    Once selling prices are set, how does the company assure that customers are charged correctly?
    Does Excel maintain official price lists by product line?
    Are the price lists stored in the computer?
    What is the process for updating price lists to reflect modifications by product managers?

> Do computer programs contain proper input editing controls that reject quoted prices not in conformity with official prices?

The listing of evaluation criteria is similar to the internal control structure questionnaire described in Chapter 7. Instead of serving as a risk assessment device, however, it provides a focal point for developing the audit program.

As a final step in the planning phase, the auditor should discuss the timing and scope of the audit with the official to whom the auditee reports and should review the audit itself with the auditee. In the Excel sales price audit, the three product managers constitute the auditee. Jacquelyn Shoemaker, Vector's marketing vice-president, is the officer to whom they report. Johns will need to determine, in conjunction with Shoemaker, whether all product lines and all products within each line, or only a sample, are to be tested. All product lines and products are chosen in the present instance given the small number of products and the significance of each to total revenue. With regard to timing, Johns and Shoemaker agree that July will be selected for performing the audit field work. July is usually a slow sales period and the product managers will have ample time to work with the audit team.

In reviewing the audit with Excel's three product managers, Johns should make every effort to gain their cooperation. Cooperation of the auditee is critical to a successful operational audit. A harmonious relationship is necessary if everyone is to work toward promoting the best interests of the entity. Auditees frequently feel threatened and may view the internal audit as a policing exercise when, in fact, the internal auditor is trying to help the auditee to better perform his/her assigned role. In gaining the product managers' cooperation, Johns explains the nature and scope of the audit with each of them. He also discusses their participation in the audit. The product managers' role will consist mainly of answering questions, explaining and illustrating the pricing process, and providing necessary documentation. Involving operating management in the audit develops trust and creates a problem solving partnership rather than an adversarial relationship.

Performing the Audit Field Work

The field work for an operational audit engagement consists of the following steps which are addressed in the ensuing sections:

1. Conduct a preliminary survey of the activity or functional unit to be audited;

2. Develop the audit program;

3. Perform the audit;

4. Appraise the efficiency and effectiveness of the activity or unit; and

5. Evaluate the findings and develop conclusions and recommendations.

Conduct a Preliminary Audit Survey

The purpose of the **preliminary audit survey** is to familiarize the audit team with the unit or activity being audited and the auditee's perception of those operations being reviewed. Sources of information include policies and procedures manuals, discussions with the auditee, organizational charts, written mission statements, minutes of meetings, job descriptions, and reports issued by and to the auditee.

In the Excel sales price audit, the preliminary survey has consisted mainly of discussions between Johns and each of the product managers. Krause and Mason, Johns' assistants on the audit, have obtained copies of pricing analyses, divisional price lists for the sporting goods division, and organizational charts. The documentation and discussions have produced the following preliminary findings:

1. Product prices are initially based on the product manager's evaluation of the market;

2. Although the prices must be set to cover "full" cost, Excel's cost accountants have not been involved in the process and contribution margin is not considered;

3. The marketing vice-president reviews and approves all selling prices and modifications of existing prices;

4. Selling prices are reviewed on a quarterly basis;

5. Official price lists are included in the computer data base and are updated on the basis of change authorizations approved by the marketing vice-president;

6. The computer will not accept customer orders containing selling prices at variance with official prices.

Develop the Audit Program

The audit program consists of those procedures necessary to satisfy the audit objectives and produce sufficient and competent evidence to corroborate or refute the auditor's preliminary findings. Exhibit 17.1 contains the audit program developed by Johns for the Vector sales price audit. Procedures 1 through 8 test the preliminary findings and provide further insight into the price setting process. These audit procedures also determine whether the process complies with company policy. Step 9 tests the process in terms of its effectiveness in maximizing Vector's profits. Step 10 assists the auditor in formulating preliminary findings and recommendations to be discussed with each of the auditees.

Perform the Audit

The auditor carries out the audit program by:

1. Gathering and evaluating factual evidence; and

2. Comparing the facts against established evaluation criteria.

Like financial auditing, the audit evidence must be sufficient to support the auditor's findings and recommendations, and the evidence must be valid and relevant to the stated audit objectives. For the Excel Division sales price audit, evidence gathering consists of conducting interviews with the auditees and examining underlying documentation (pricing analyses, cost data, change authorizations, official price lists, and quarterly price reviews). It also involves independent calculations and analyses performed by the auditors (profitability analysis).

The evidence should be evaluated in terms of whether it is sufficient and competent relative to the evaluation criteria set by the auditor. Johns, for example, will need sufficient competent evidence to determine the following:

1. Is the market analysis and the cost analysis performed by the product managers adequate to enable them to set optimum selling prices?

2. Are all selling prices reviewed quarterly in accordance with company policy?

EXHIBIT 17.1 Audit Program for Excel Division Sales Price Audit

1. Conduct interviews with each of the product managers regarding the analysis and thought processes leading to the pricing decision;

2. Examine pricing analyses within each product manager's line to obtain further insight into the decision process and to substantiate the information obtained in the interviews
   a. Obtain cost data for each product from cost accounting
   b. Determine that sales price covers cost plus markup;

3. Trace prices from pricing analyses to change authorizations noting agreement of prices and signature of marketing vice-president denoting approval;

4. Compare latest price change authorization with computer printout of official price lists and determine agreement;

5. Examine the current year's quarterly price reviews for each line
   a. Establish that prices are being reviewed quarterly in compliance with company policy;
   b. Determine the process followed in conducting the review;

6. Prepare customer orders containing incorrect selling prices and enter them into the computer to determine proper functioning of input controls;

7. Inquire of product managers as to procedures followed when computer rejects customer order. Are specially priced orders subject to product manager approval?

8. Based on the results of 6 and 7, select a sample of sales invoices and trace billed prices to the computer printout of prices existing at the dates of the respective sales. Determine proper product manager approval of exceptions.

9. Perform independent profitability analysis to determine whether current prices are producing satisfactory margins:
   a. Select two products from each of the three product lines for testing;
   b. With assistance from the market economist, determine demand elasticity for each product;
   c. Have market economist describe major competitors' pricing strategies, including probable reaction to price changes within the industry;
   d. Calculate contribution margin per unit at varying selling prices after establishing reasonableness of unit cost data inputs;
   e. Apply cost-volume-profit analysis on basis of (b) to (d) above and determine optimum price;
   f. Compare "best" price obtained from (e) with official price list. Discuss exceptions with product managers.

10. Summarize exceptions and evaluate findings.

3. Are new product selling prices and selling price changes approved by the marketing vice-president?

4. Does the computer price list include the latest change authorizations?

5. Does the computer reject customer orders containing selling prices not in agreement with the official price list?

6. Does the product manager review all customer orders rejected by the computer?

Appraise the Efficiency and Effectiveness of the Activity or Unit

Efficiency and effectiveness appraisal generally involves evaluating reports submitted by auditees; assessing the goal setting process; determining the extent to which goals are being achieved and the degree of goal congruence (similarity of individual and entity goals); appraising the effectiveness of resource utilization within the unit or activity; and ascertaining whether fraud control is effective. For the Excel pricing engagement specifically, Johns must evaluate the following:

1. Reasonableness of the pricing strategy in terms of profit maximization;

2. Effectiveness of the control structure in preventing fraudulent and erroneous customer billing.

In evaluating the reasonableness of the existing pricing strategy, Johns will compare the established prices against the profitability analyses developed by the audit team. The quality of the existing control structure will be determined by the results of document examination and control tests as described above.

Evaluate Findings

To evaluate findings, the auditor needs to answer these questions: How well is the activity presently being performed? How might it be improved? The first question can be answered by considering the results of the efficiency and effectiveness appraisal described above. The second question needs to be carefully addressed in consultation with the auditee.

Assume that Johns arrives at the following conclusions regarding Vector's selling price strategy as practiced by the Excel Division:

1. Pricing decisions are not systematic and the resulting prices often fail to maximize Vector's profits. Product managers generally set prices in the absence of formal demand analysis, cost analysis, and competitor actions. Neither Vector's economists nor the cost accountants are involved in the process.

2. The existing control structure provides adequate assurance that customers are being billed at official prices.
    a. Selling prices are reviewed on a quarterly basis and the marketing vice-president approves all selling prices and modifications of existing prices.
    b. Official price lists contained in the computer reflect the most current prices, and input controls are effective in rejecting prices not in agreement with official prices.
    c. Sales invoices containing prices other than official prices, and rejected by the computer, are subject to approval by the respective product managers.

Although Johns is convinced that the price setting process in the sporting goods division could be improved through demand analysis and cost-volume-profit analysis, he wants to obtain the input of the product managers and gain their cooperation and commitment to any suggested change in methodology. To this end, he conducts additional meetings with each of the product managers. At these meetings, Johns emphasizes the control structure strengths which help to ensure that customers are charged correctly and that only authorized prices are included in the computer data base. He then addresses the price setting weaknesses by illustrating several examples where profitability could have been improved by setting higher or lower prices. He also assists the product managers in developing alternate strategies that consider supply and demand factors, competitors' pricing strategies, and marginal cost analysis. In the process of suggesting and assisting, Johns emphasizes the impact that the increased profitability will have on the product managers' annual bonus and profit sharing. Each product manager agrees and is appreciative of the audit team's assistance in improving their respective pricing strategies.

Develop Audit Conclusions and Recommendations

Audit conclusions and recommendations are the culmination of the audit field work. They should be developed only after the auditor has collected and evaluated all necessary evidence and discussed the findings with the auditee. Hopefully, the auditee has agreed with the findings and suggested improvements. The absence of such agreement, however, should not preclude the auditor from recommending appropriate courses of action. The formal conclusions and recommendations should be presented to the auditee before being incorporated into the audit report.

Having discussed the audit team's findings with each of the product managers, and having assisted them in developing appropriate pricing strategies, Johns decides to formally present the auditors' conclusions and recommendations in the form of a conference at Vector's headquarters offices. The presentation is scheduled as an all-day meeting to be conducted by the audit team in one of the company's meeting rooms. The following persons will be in attendance: Excel's three product managers, the audit team, Jeremy Jiles—Excel's chief cost accountant, and Judy Smolen—Vector's market economist. The audit team, with the assistance of the cost accountant and market economist, plan to present an actual pricing case applicable to each product line and demonstrate how a different price would have improved profits. To support the presentation, Johns and his assistants, with the help of Jiles, Smolen, and one of Vector's EDP specialists, have developed a computer simulation in the form of a game based on different assumptions regarding supply and demand and competitors' pricing strategies. Additionally, marginal cost and revenue data are included in the simulation.

At the end of the presentation, the following conclusions and recommendations, also to be included in the audit report to the marketing vice-president, are summarized for the product managers:

1. Controls are effective in ensuring that proper prices are being charged customers. The controls include required approval of prices by the marketing vice-president, quarterly review of existing product prices, and computerization of Vector's official price list, together with strict controls preventing unauthorized modification of prices included in the data base.

2. Current pricing strategies for Vector's sporting goods division are not producing selling prices that maximize the company's profitability. Neither cost coverage nor market demand is considered adequately in reaching pricing decisions.

3. The following approach to setting and modifying selling prices is recommended:
   a. Direct costs of producing and selling products should be identified;
   b. Demand analysis should be conducted to estimate the market for the product at varying prices;

  c. Vector's share of market should be estimated on the basis of demand analysis and predicted competitor pricing strategies;
  d. The computer simulation should be utilized to view the profit effects of various combinations of cost, price, demand, and market share;
  e. The cost accounting staff and the market economist should be utilized to assist in cost, demand, and market share analysis.

Report Audit Findings and Recommendations

The audit report is the culmination of the audit process. Assuming that the audit team has discussed all findings with the auditee and has obtained the auditee's concurrence with the resulting conclusions and recommendations, the audit report should contain no unknown surprises for the auditee. At the same time, however, the auditors should not compromise findings to assuage the auditee's feelings. Instead, the audit process and the resulting report should be viewed by all parties as a means of assisting responsible managers at the field level to take the necessary corrective action.

To avoid any misunderstandings resulting from the formal audit report, auditors follow the practice of reviewing the report draft with the auditee at a post-audit meeting prior to the release of the audit report. Johns has prepared the first draft of a proposed audit report and discussed it with each of the product managers during post-audit meetings. He has gained their concurrence and is now ready to release the final audit report as contained in Exhibit 17.2.

Unlike an independent financial audit, an operational audit report is not constrained to a single standard reporting format. To be effective, however, the report should exhibit certain characteristics. First, the audit report should be *clear and concise* and should not contain any unnecessary technical language. The audit report should be *constructive* by suggesting ways to help the auditee in improving operations where necessary. The reporting style should be *positive and unbiased*. It should neither praise nor criticize, but rather, should *focus on results*. Auditors should avoid using personal pronouns (e.g., he, she, him, her) or proper nouns (e.g., John, Kenneth, Susan, Jacquelyn).

If the auditors' findings are to be implemented, results and conclusions must be presented convincingly. Differences between actual and expected conditions should be presented as to *cause* (reason for the difference) *and effect* (risk or exposure produced by the difference). *Auditee efforts* toward improvement should be presented along with the auditors' recommendations. Lastly, *the audit report should be reviewed by the director of internal auditing* before issuance.

Most operational audit reports contain the following components (see Exhibit 17.2):

1. Letter of transmittal (including summary of findings and recommendations);

2. Scope of the audit;

3. Findings and conclusions; and

4. Recommendations.

EXHIBIT 17.2   Operational Audit Report for the Vector Sales Price Audit

April 19, 1994

To: Ms. Jacquelyn Shoemaker,
     Vice President—Marketing

From: Kenneth Johns,
       Senior Internal Auditor

Subject: Audit Report—Vector Sales Price Audit, Excel Division

Attached is your copy of the audit report on our examination of the sales price setting process as practiced in the Excel Division. The purpose of our audit was to determine whether established selling prices for the sporting goods lines are optimal in terms of maximizing Vector's profitability. We previously discussed a draft of this report with you.

Although the existing control structure provides adequate assurance that customers are being billed at established prices, those prices are less than optimal in maximizing profits. More attention by the product managers to demand and cost analysis will greatly improve pricing decisions. The product managers agree and are committed to appropriate revision in their approach to price setting. Our findings and conclusions, along with recommendations agreed to by the product managers, are described in the body of this report.

_____

                                        Signature

cc: Mr. Raymond Vector, President and CEO
     Members of the Audit Committee of the Board:
         Joel Haynes, Chairman
         Lucille Jones
         Harold Allen
         James Todd
     Product Managers—Excel Division:
         Jennifer Hill: Balls
         Jeffrey Archer: Bats and Gloves
         Susan Knox: Golf Clubs and Tennis Rackets

(continued)

EXHIBIT 17.2 *(continued)*

SCOPE OF THE AUDIT

Our audit was limited to two areas within the sporting goods division:

1. Determining whether prices are set such that company profits are maximized; and
2. Determining whether prices charged customers are in compliance with established company prices.

In satisfying the above requirements, we conducted extensive interviews with the product managers who are responsible for the price setting process; we examined documentation supporting the analysis leading to the setting of specific product prices; we examined the quarterly selling price reviews on a test basis; with the assistance of the product managers, along with Jeremy Jiles, Excel's chief cost accountant and Susan Smolen, market economist, we developed a set of optimum prices for specific products for comparison with actual prices in terms of profitability; and we compared actual prices appearing on sales invoices with established prices for a random sample of sales invoices.

FINDINGS AND CONCLUSIONS

Selling prices within the sporting goods lines are not maximizing profitability

We have found that current pricing strategies are not producing selling prices that maximize profitability within the Excel Division. Product managers presently set selling prices on the basis of the following inputs:

- Best estimate of total demand and market share at varying prices
- Total product cost as supplied by cost accounting

Little attention has been devoted to contribution margin analysis (i.e., selling price minus variable manufacturing and selling costs), demand analysis (including demand elasticity), competitor reactions to price changes, and economic conditions. In our opinion, the resulting prices are not optimal in terms of maximizing Vector's profitability.

Controls are adequate to provide reasonable assurance that prices charged customers are in compliance with official company prices

Our tests of the internal control structure related to customer billing suggest that customers are being billed in accordance with company policy. All product prices and product price modifications must be approved by the marketing vice-president and the product pricing analyses must be signed by the marketing vice-president as evidence of such approval. Approved prices are forwarded to EDP for updating of the computerized price list. Updated price lists are forwarded by EDP to marketing at the beginning of each month for review. As part of our audit, we obtained the latest printout of product prices for the sporting goods division and compared with the pricing analyses provided by marketing. We found no exceptions.

We also established that all product prices are reviewed quarterly. Although these reviews were found to be rather cursory, the product managers have assured us that economic analysis, demand analysis, and cost analysis will be applied in future reviews.

(continued)

EXHIBIT 17.2 *(continued)*

Our audit included selecting a random sample of sales invoices and tracing the billed prices to the computer printout of selling prices existing on the date of sale. The billed prices agreed with the official price list in all cases. We also introduced test data consisting of hypothetical customer orders containing incorrect selling prices. The computer rejected such orders and intervention by the EDP control group was necessary for removal of the orders from the system.

RECOMMENDATIONS

We recommend the following approach to sales price setting within the Excel Division. This approach has been developed during our audit with the help and support of the product managers, and with the assistance of the cost accounting staff, the market economist, and the EDP systems and programming personnel. It has the full support of the product managers and is presently being implemented by Susan Knox in pricing the new golf club line.

The first step in the process is information gathering. Cost accounting will provide detailed cost data regarding the product being priced, including:

- Variable manufacturing cost per unit
- Direct fixed manufacturing cost related to the product
- Direct selling expense related to the product
- Share of indirect manufacturing, selling, and administrative overhead

The market economist will assist the product manager in gathering and developing marketing data, including the following:

- Projected total market demand for the product
- Demand elasticity (market sensitivity to price changes)
- Excel's projected share of market given varying levels of advertising and promotion
- Predicted competitor reactions to price changes

The information so developed will serve as input into the "Marketing Strategy" computer program developed as a result of our sales price audit. Having received cost and market inputs, the program predicts contribution margin given varying assumptions regarding:

- Selling price
- Market demand
- Demand elasticity
- Market share
- Level of advertising
- Competitors' pricing strategies

The best selling price, in terms of profitability, under each combination of demand elasticity, advertising level, and competitor reaction is then provided by the program. The product manager is responsible for selecting the best price among the alternatives. The decision will be based generally on the product manager's judgment as to which combination is most realistic.

Summary of What Operational Auditing Does

Operational auditing assists operating managers in identifying and solving problems. It does this by setting audit goals and collecting evidence relating to the evaluation criteria. The auditor evaluates the activity in light of the evidence, consults with the auditee, and recommends corrective action. Consulting and recommending are an ongoing process occurring throughout the audit field work as necessary. At the conclusion of the field work, an audit report addressed to the person to whom the auditee is responsible is drafted and discussed with the auditee before being released. The report serves the purpose of informing management as to problem areas relating to specific activities, the auditors' recommendations for solving the problems, and the auditee's progress in implementing the recommendations. Perhaps most important is the need for auditees to perceive that the internal auditor exists to assist and not to police the auditee's operations.

COMPLIANCE AUDITING

Compliance Auditing Defined

Compliance auditing may be defined as testing and reporting on conformity with laws and regulations.[1] As used in this chapter, the term refers to the independent auditor's responsibility for determining compliance with laws and regulations when engaged in audits of state and local governmental units, as well as other entities that are the recipients of federal financial assistance. Following a General Accounting Office study that identified a large number of substandard audits of federal financial assistance, the Auditing Standards Board, in 1989, issued Statement on Auditing Standards No. 63, entitled "Compliance Auditing Applicable to Governmental Entities and Other Recipients of Governmental Financial Assistance." SAS No. 68, issued in 1992, supersedes SAS 63 by adding institutions of higher education and other not-for-profit entities receiving federal financial assistance to the compliance auditing "umbrella." SAS 68 is intended to strengthen this form of compliance auditing.

The independent auditor's compliance auditing responsibility is a function of the type of engagement, but may encompass any or all of the following:

1. Responsibility under generally accepted auditing standards (GAAS);
2. Responsibility under **Governmental Auditing Standards** as set forth in the General Accounting Office's "yellow book";
3. Responsibility under the federal *Single Audit Act of 1984* as defined in *Circular OMB A-128;*
4. Responsibility under *Circular OMB A-133, Audits of Institutions of Higher Education and Other Nonprofit Organizations,* issued by the U.S. Office of Management and Budget.

---

[1]Auditing Standards Board, *Codification of Statements on Auditing Standards,* New York: AICPA, Section AU 801.01.

Responsibility under GAAS

As discussed previously, two SASs implicitly address compliance issues. SAS 54 defines the auditor's responsibility for detecting and reporting on illegal acts perpetrated by clients. SAS 53 describes the auditor's responsibility for detecting material errors and irregularities. Additionally, SAS 68 provides explicit "how to" guidance in meeting these responsibilities when auditing state and local governmental units and other entities that are the recipients of federal financial assistance. Assistance may assume the forms of contracts, grants, loans, and/or interest rate subsidies. The reason compliance auditing is necessary in this type of environment is that *federal assistance* is accompanied by *federal requirements*. SAS 68 identifies the kinds of laws and regulations to which these entities may be subject, and provides guidance as to the proper audit approach in determining compliance with the various requirements. In addition, the statement recommends adding the following items to the client representation letter obtained at audit completion:

1. Management is responsible for the entity's compliance with laws and regulations applicable to it; and
2. Management has identified and disclosed to the auditor all laws and regulations that have a direct and material effect on the determination of financial statement amounts.[2]

Yellow Book Responsibility

When auditing state and local governmental entities that are recipients of federal financial assistance, auditors must, in addition to GAAS, comply with governmental auditing standards, as defined in the GAO's "**yellow book**." These standards assign greater responsibility to the auditor than is required under GAAS. For example, under yellow book standards, auditors must *report on the entity's compliance with laws and regulations* imposed by the assistance program, and must also report on the entity's internal control structure *regardless of whether material weaknesses are found*. Under generally accepted auditing standards, the auditor need only include, in the reportable conditions letter, material weaknesses that are discovered in the course of the audit. Also, when reporting on compliance with laws and regulations, the auditor must *give positive assurance on items tested, negative assurance on items not tested, and must describe material instances of noncompliance*. Given these requirements, SAS 68 provides guidance to the auditor in meeting them.[3]

Single Audit Act Responsibility

If the auditee is a state or local government entity and receives $100,000 or more in **federal financial assistance** in a single fiscal year, it must, in addition to GAAS and yellow book standards, be audited in accordance with the **Single Audit Act of 1984.** The major provisions of this act, are interpreted and explained in **Circular A-128,**

---

[2]*Ibid.*, Section AU 801.16.
[3]*Ibid.*, Section AU 801.17-39.

issued by the U.S. Office of Management and Budget. Under the act, the auditor must carefully *evaluate internal controls over federal financial assistance, audit compliance with specific requirements,* and *report on compliance with laws and regulations that may have a material effect on each major federal financial assistance program.* SAS 68 provides guidance in performing compliance audits under these circumstances and covers topics such as how to identify major programs, how to determine materiality, how to assess audit risk relative to undetected noncompliance, and how to evaluate the results of auditing procedures.[4]

As with yellow book requirements, SAS 68 recommends added topics to be covered in the client representation letter, given applicability of the Single Audit Act. These topics relate to such matters as management identification of all sources of federal financial assistance, as well as requirements under the programs, management compliance with reporting requirements, adequate documentation of information contained in financial reports, and notification of the independent auditor as to noncompliance, as well as appropriate action in instances of non-compliance.[5]

Responsibility Under Circular A-133

Circular A-133, "Audits of Institutions of Higher Education and Other Nonprofit Organizations," was issued by the U.S. Office of Management and Budget (OMB) in 1991. While Circular A-128 applies to state and local governmental entities, this circular applies to colleges, universities, and other not-for-profit entities. The circular sets forth requirements relative to compliance audits of those types of entities receiving over $100,000 of federal financial assistance in a single fiscal year. Assistance may include interest subsidies, insurance, direct loans, loan guarantees, contracts, and grants. Like the Single Audit Act requirements, the auditor must *test the internal control structure for each of the recipient's major programs,* and any other program receiving more than $100,000. The auditor must also *express an opinion about the specific compliance* features of the programs tested. Specifically, an A-133 audit must answer the following three questions:

1. Are the financial statements presented fairly under generally accepted accounting principles?
2. Does the control structure provide reasonable assurance of compliance with federal regulations?
3. Has the recipient complied with applicable laws and regulations?

In meeting these objectives, OMB requires a *coordinated effort* between the college or university's external auditors and the resident state or federal auditor. The external auditor is responsible for reporting on the financial statements and control structure policies and procedures as they affect the financial statements. The resident auditor is responsible for reporting on controls and compliance related to the institution's major programs.

---

[4]*Ibid.,* Section AU 801.40-88.

[5]*Ibid.,* Section AU 801.67.

Compliance Auditing and Audit Risk

The three components of audit risk, as addressed in Chapter 5, are essentially the same for all kinds of audits performed by CPAs. For compliance audits related to major federal financial assistance programs, however, SAS 68 expands upon the components of audit risk as follows:

> *Inherent risk.* The risk that material noncompliance with requirements applicable to a major federal financial assistance program could occur assuming there are no related internal control structure policies or procedures.
>
> *Control risk.* The risk that material noncompliance that could occur in a major federal financial assistance program will not be prevented or detected on a timely basis by the entity's internal control structure policies and procedures.
>
> *Detection risk.* The risk that an auditor's procedures will lead him or her to conclude that noncompliance that could be material to a major federal financial assistance program does not exist when in fact such noncompliance does exist.[6]

As discussed in Chapter 5, as part of the audit planning phase, the auditor must carefully evaluate and assess inherent risk and control risk, and then set detection risk such that overall audit risk is maintained at a low level. In assessing inherent risk for entities receiving federal financial assistance, the auditor must gain a thorough understanding of the programs, and the laws and regulations applicable to them. The auditor should also assess the probability of management override as a possible attempt to circumvent program requirements. In assessing control risk, the auditor must study and evaluate those controls that prevent and/or detect noncompliance with the laws and regulations applicable to the major programs. Audit programs should then emphasize those areas where major noncompliance is most likely to occur.

In a case reported in 1991, Stanford University was alleged to have inflated overhead charges to the federal government as part of government reimbursement to Stanford under various research grants. The government appropriates billions of dollars each year for universities to spend on various kinds of approved research. Stanford's share of this was nearly $250 million per year and was covered under some 1,700 contracts and research grants. Under most of the contracts and grants, the government allows the universities to add a fixed percentage of the direct costs to cover indirect costs applicable to all of the contracts and grants. Examples of indirect costs are utilities, building maintenance, libraries, and staff support. The problem at Stanford arose as the result of negotiations with the government permitting increases above the standard indirect cost percentage, until, by 1990, Stanford was adding 74 percent to each contract, and government indirect cost reimbursement had grown to 28 percent of the university's operating budget. In the 10 years preceding 1991, GAO auditors estimated that Stanford may have "overcharged" the government nearly $500 million in improper indirect costs. Some of these charges included salaries and other expenses from a university owned shopping center, a share in a Lake Tahoe retreat for the Stanford board of trustees and

---

[6]*Ibid.,* Section AU 801.54.

guests, and a shower curtain and two window shades for the university president's official residence. Although Stanford denied deliberate overcharging, the school did repay approximately $2 million in acknowledged inappropriate charges, including depreciation on a school yacht, and the cost of flowers, parties, and furniture at the university president's home.[7]

The lesson for auditors in this case is the need for tailoring risk analysis to the specific needs of the audit engagement. In auditing Stanford's government contracts and research grants, the auditors should have been concerned with the constant increase in indirect cost reimbursement as a percentage of the operating budget. Given this concern, the auditors should have devoted considerable resources to analyzing the contract charges for compliance with the provisions of the applicable grants and contracts. Inquiring of university officials, reading the contracts and agreements, examining documentation supporting the charges, and confirming a sampling of major reimbursement charges with the reimbursing agencies are some of the procedures that should have been applied under these circumstances.

In today's environment of increasing federal financial assistance programs, compliance auditing is assuming ever increasing importance. Auditors must therefore continue to expand their efforts in the areas of risk analysis and audit program development for compliance auditing purposes.

KEY TERMS

Audit conclusions
Audit findings and recommendations
Circular A-128
Circular A-133
Compliance auditing
Effectiveness
Efficiency
Evaluation criteria
Federal financial assistance
Foreign Corrupt Practices Act of 1977
General Accounting Office (GAO)

Governmental auditing standards
Institute of Internal Auditors
Internal auditing
Management auditing
Operational auditing
Operational audit report
Preliminary audit survey
Risk-based operational auditing
Single Audit Act of 1984
Yellow book

REVIEW QUESTIONS

1. Differentiate between operational auditing and internal auditing.
2. Differentiate between efficiency and effectiveness as they relate to operational auditing.
3. What is management auditing? Why must internal auditors exercise particular care in performing management audits?

---

[7]See *Wall Street Journal*, "Stanford Braces for U.S. Debt of $480 Million," 2 January 1992.

4. What is "risk-based" operational auditing?
5. How has the Foreign Corrupt Practices Act influenced internal auditing?
6. Internal auditors are frequently referred to as the "eyes and ears" of management. Explain.
7. Why does operational auditing require a broader base of expertise than accounting and auditing?
8. Describe the steps in planning an operational audit.
9. What are evaluation criteria as related to operational auditing, and how does their identification assist in conducting the examination?
10. Why is the cooperation of the auditee critical to a successful operational audit?
11. What is the nature of the preliminary survey as it relates to operational auditing? What purpose does it serve?
12. How are sufficiency and competence of evidence determined in operational audits?
13. How does the auditor appraise efficiency and effectiveness in an operational audit?
14. What two questions must the auditor answer to evaluate operational audit findings?
15. The auditor should discuss operational audit findings with the auditee before making formal recommendations. Explain.
16. What course of action should the auditor pursue if the auditee disagrees with the audit findings and preliminary recommendations?
17. The audit report should contain no unknown surprises for the auditee. Explain.
18. Why is it essential that auditees view the operational audit as a device for assisting them?
19. What is the purpose of the post-audit meeting? How does it differ from the pre-audit meeting?
20. Describe the attributes of a good operational audit report.
21. Define compliance auditing.
22. How does compliance auditing relate to entities receiving federal financial assistance?
23. How is risk analysis different within the context of compliance auditing as contrasted with financial auditing?

MULTIPLE CHOICE QUESTIONS FROM CIA AND CPA EXAMINATIONS

1. The primary difference between operational auditing and financial auditing is that in operational auditing
   a. The auditor is not concerned with whether the audited activity is generating information in compliance with financial accounting standards.
   b. The auditor is seeking to help management use resources in the most effective manner possible.
   c. The auditor starts with the financial statements of an activity being audited and works backward to the basic processes involved in producing them.
   d. The auditor can use analytical skills and tools that are not necessary in financial auditing.

2. Select, in chronological order, the proper sequencing of field audit procedures.
   a. Preliminary survey, gathering and examining data, writing report, following up.
   b. Gathering and examining data, preliminary survey, writing report, following up.

    c. Assigning audit personnel, gathering auditee's view about audit conclusions, testing, following up.

    d. Establishing audit objectives, determining that corrective action was taken, presenting reports, reviewing and approving final reports.

3. Internal auditing standards state that, "internal auditors should possess the knowledge, skills, and disciplines essential to the performance of internal audits." If you were assigned to supervise an audit to determine the cost efficiency of a complex computerized information system, this would suggest that you

    a. Are a computer expert.

    b. Only audit computer operations.

    c. Should use special staff assistance if necessary.

    d. Specialize in efficiency audits.

4. The internal audit staff has been asked to conduct an audit of the purchasing department. Top management feels that there have been some production bottlenecks recently because of out-of-stock situations. What is the primary objective of the auditors in this assignment?

    a. To appraise the economy with which resources are employed.

    b. To review the reliability and integrity of financial and operating information.

    c. To review the means of safeguarding assets and verifying the existence of such assets.

    d. To ascertain whether results are consistent with established objectives and whether operations are being carried out as planned.

5. The best description of the scope of internal auditing is that it encompasses

    a. Primarily financial auditing.

    b. Primarily operational auditing.

    c. Primarily the safeguarding of assets and verifying the existence of such assets.

    d. Both financial and operational auditing.

6. During an operational audit, the auditor compares the current staffing of a department with established industry standards in order to

    a. Assess the adequacy of the controls over payroll processing for the department.

    b. Assess the current performance of the department and make appropriate recommendations for improvement.

    c. Evaluate the adequacy of the established internal controls for the department.

    d. Determine whether the department has complied with all laws and regulations governing its personnel.

7. Auditors can usually achieve better relations with auditees if they

    a. Emphasize their role as management advisors.

    b. Concentrate on uncovering errors made by lower-level employees.

    c. Concentrate on uncovering frauds and embezzlements.

    d. Emphasize their role as an insurance policy against potential frauds and embezzlements.

8. The best source of information for planning the audit approach and developing the audit program would probably be

    a. Information contained in prior audit reports.

    b. Audit procedures found in the permanent audit files.

c. The results of a preliminary survey.

d. The long-range audit plan as it applies to this specific audit.

9. A car rental agency has branch offices throughout the world. Each branch is organized into three separate departments: maintenance, operations, and accounting. What information would be most useful in establishing the objectives for an operational audit?

a. The objectives of each department.

b. The most recent financial data for each department.

c. Activity reports showing rental information for the different branches.

d. A complete listing of the perpetual inventory for the branch to be audited.

10. When management agrees with a finding and has agreed to take corrective action, the appropriate treatment is to

a. Report that management has agreed to take corrective action.

b. Omit the finding and recommendation.

c. Report that management has already taken corrective action.

d. Include the finding and recommendation, irrespective of management's agreement.

11. Disclosure of irregularities to parties other than a client's senior management and its audit committee or board of directors ordinarily is not part of an auditor's responsibility. However, to which of the following outside parties may a duty to disclose irregularities exist?

	To the SEC when the client reports an auditor change	To a successor auditor when the successor makes appropriate inquiries	To a government funding agency from which the client receives financial assistance
a.	Yes	Yes	No
b.	Yes	No	Yes
c.	No	Yes	Yes
d.	Yes	Yes	Yes

12. Because of the pervasive effects of laws and regulations on the financial statements of governmental units, an auditor should obtain written management representations acknowledging that management has

a. Implemented internal control policies and procedures designed to detect all illegal acts.

b. Documented the procedures performed to evaluate the governmental unit's compliance with laws and regulations.

c. Identified and disclosed all laws and regulations that have a direct and material effect on its financial statements.

d. Reported all known illegal acts and material weaknesses in internal control structure to the funding agency or regulatory body.

13. A governmental audit may extend beyond an examination leading to the expression of an opinion on the fairness of financial presentation to include

	Program results	Compliance	Economy & efficiency
a.	Yes	Yes	No
b.	Yes	Yes	Yes
c.	No	Yes	Yes
d.	Yes	No	Yes

14. The GAO standards of reporting for governmental financial audits incorporate the AICPA standards of reporting and prescribe supplemental standards to satisfy the unique needs of governmental audits. Which of the following is a supplemental reporting standard for government financial audits?

    a. A written report on the auditor's understanding of the entity's internal control structure and assessment of control risk should be prepared.

    b. Material indications of illegal acts should be reported in a document with distribution restricted to senior officials of the entity audited.

    c. Instances of abuse, fraud, mismanagement, and waste should be reported to the organization with legal oversight authority over the entity audited.

    d. All privileged and confidential information discovered should be reported to the senior officials of the organization that arranged for the audit.

15. Kent is auditing an entity's compliance with requirements governing a major federal financial assistance program in accordance with the Single Audit Act. Kent detected noncompliance with requirements that have a material effect on that program. Kent's report on compliance should express a(an)

    a. Unqualified opinion with a separate explanatory paragraph.

    b. Qualified opinion or an adverse opinion.

    c. Adverse opinion or a disclaimer of opinion.

    d. Limited assurance on the items tested.

Use the following information for questions 16 through 21: Each audit objective listed in questions 16-21 is independent of the other audit objectives. Fill in the blank space with the letter designating the *single* best audit technique for meeting the audit objective specified. Make your selection from the audit techniques listed below.

Audit Techniques
   a. Inspection of documents
   b. Observation
   c. Inquiry
   d. Analytical procedures

16. ____ Ascertain the reasonableness of the increases in rental revenue resulting from operating costs passed on to the lessee by the landlord. The auditor has already inspected the lease contract to determine that such costs are allowed.

17. ____ Identify the existence of personality conflicts which are detrimental to productivity.

18. ____ Determine whether research and development projects were properly authorized.

19. ____ Ascertain compliance with city ordinance forbidding city purchasing from vendors affiliated with elected city officials.

20. ____ Determine whether planned rate of return on investment in international operations has been achieved.

21. ____ Determine whether mail room staff is fully utilized.

17.1 The internal audit staff of a consumer products company recently completed an audit of the company's centralized marketing department. The audit objective was to assess the effectiveness of the marketing department in contributing to company profitability. The company's three divisions manufacture and distribute consumer-oriented electronics, sporting goods/recreational products, and small household appliances. All three divisions are dependent upon aggressive marketing to retain their market share in a highly competitive environment. The audit field work identified, and management agrees with, the following:

Sales Promotion

1. The procurement of outside printing services is subject to competitive bidding if the dollar amount is greater than $4,000 and deadlines permit. Otherwise, the media manager selects the printer based on past experience. The contract is handled via the phone and the media manager informs the accounts payable supervisor that payment to the printer is authorized.
2. Prior year advertising expenditures for the past year have exceeded the budgeted amount by 8 percent in all three divisions. An overall advertising strategy for the company's products has not been developed. Consequently, each divisional director plans its own advertising activities.
3. Advertising activities are not studied for overall cost/sales effectiveness. The marketing managers believe that the time between placing ads and seeing any response is too long to be a useful measure.

Distribution Channels

4. Although each product line is distributed through several channels, distribution costs are accumulated by product line. The product line manager decides what the appropriate channels are for each product within the line.
5. The company uses multiple warehouse facilities and each product line uses an expediter to release products from each warehouse. To date, no storage or transportation studies have been done to ensure product delivery at the lowest possible cost.
6. Product prices are determined by each division subject to committee approval from headquarters. Pricing strategy usually focuses on competitors' pricing; other pricing determinants are seldom examined.

Required:
For each of the above situations, prepare the finding and the audit recommendation section of the audit report. (IIA adapted)

17.2 The preliminary meeting between the auditor and auditee management prior to the start of an audit enables the parties to exchange information.

Required:
a. Prepare the auditor's memorandum to the auditee proposing an agenda of topics to be discussed at a preliminary meeting.
b. How might the exchange of information on the topics you described in Part (a) affect the audit? (IIA adapted)

17.3 The results of a preliminary survey of the personnel function are as follows:

Audit Area	Survey Results
I. Personnel Projections	Policies and procedures for developing personnel projections appeared to be lacking. There was no evidence of communications from top management on new or expanded business opportunities which might affect personnel projections. There was no indication of operating managers having any input regarding projections. Tests for reasonableness of projections based on economic trends were not evident.
II. Securing New Personnel	Each department recruits for its open positions without regard to other departments. Policies and procedures pertaining to selection of personnel were not evident. User department satisfaction with the personnel function was not known.
III. Position Descriptions	Dates of revisions and signatures of approval did not appear on position descriptions sampled in the survey. There was no evidence of job analysis nor were criteria established to permit subsequent maintenance of descriptions.
IV. Compensation	No evidence indicating a review of compensation levels for soundness or compliance with established industry standards was found. Compensation levels did not appear to be related to performance. Compensation levels within job classifications were not reviewed or evaluated by the personnel department.

Required:

Develop audit objectives for each audit area in the preliminary survey described above. For each objective you develop, give two audit steps which would be appropriate to follow up on the results of the preliminary survey, and give one additional audit step that could apply to each audit area. Use the format below for your answer.

Objective	Audit Steps
I.	
II.	
III.	
IV.	

(IIA adapted)

17.4 As an audit supervisor, you are about to assign a less experienced auditor to the task of developing an audit program for the purchasing department. The purchasing department has been audited five times in the last 10 years. Prior audits were limited to the financial aspects of the department's operations, but the current audit is to be directed toward operating efficiency and effectiveness.

Thus, some preliminary research will be necessary to determine the scope of the audit and the audit methodology. You want the audit to be done efficiently and to be properly focused. You are especially interested in identifying potential risk areas and in evaluating controls over them.

Required:
a. Prepare guidelines for the auditor to follow in gathering the necessary information and writing the audit program.
b. For each guideline listed in part (a), indicate its objective.
  Use the following format for your answer:

  Guidelines   Objectives

  (IIA adapted)

17.5 The quality control (QC) group in a large manufacturing company reports directly to the manager of the production department. The QC group's objective is to enforce quality standards established by management. The director of QC has the authority to reject completed production and to interrupt the production process as necessary to correct quality problems. The company views QC in terms of a four-part control cycle as follows:

1. Design engineering establishes acceptable quality levels for components and finished products. In this part of the cycle, the QC group's responsibility is to make sure that specified ranges of quality levels have been established and have been determined on a reasonable basis considering all pertinent factors.

2. The QC group determines how quality assurance will be achieved. The control group's responsibilities in this part of the cycle include establishing programs for preventive measures and determining needs for facilities, equipment, and personnel to operate the programs.

3. The QC group performs its programs and makes quality decisions based on inspection of parts and products as necessary.

4. The QC group evaluates the results of monitoring activities. In this part of the cycle, the group analyzes the extent of deviations from acceptable quality levels, studies implications, and takes appropriate corrective actions.

Required:
a. State the objectives for an audit of this function.
b. List the audit steps to achieve these objectives.
  (IIA adapted)

17.6 Your company's management is concerned with the purchasing function. The company has experienced rapid growth created by expansion of their product lines and acquisition of several subsidiaries. Each subsidiary and company operating plant has its own purchasing department. The company deals with many vendors. Supplies are warehoused in multiple locations. Senior management has asked you to do a special study of the function. They have concerns over the apparent inefficient use of resources. These concerns are based on such factors as 1) increasing inventories, 2) growing vendor lists, 3) increasing number of sole source of procurement items, and 4) an increasing average cost per purchase order.

Required:
a. What are the main components of an operational audit?
b. Explain the difference between a special and a recurring operational audit.

c. Based upon the case description, list the steps you would take to complete the special audit. Relate these steps to the case situation by giving possible examples of the steps in the context of the case. (IIA adapted)

17.7 To speed up tax return processing and reduce data entry costs, a state tax agency has installed a new feature which permits taxpayers to transmit tax returns and inquire about return processing status electronically. Taxpayers still submit payment and receive refund checks by mail. Taxpayers using the new system must request its use. The agency authorizes its use by sending them user codes, passwords, and directions for formatting their electronic tax returns. Taxpayers are responsible for using the system to inquire about the status of their returns and to submit additional information for incomplete returns.

Required:

Explain the audit objectives of an audit to determine if the new electronic processing feature is a) effective and b) efficient. For each audit objective, describe appropriate audit procedures. Identify objectives in the left-hand column and the corresponding audit procedures in the right-hand column as shown below. Indicate by each objective whether it applies to effectiveness or efficiency, or to both.

Audit Objective Category	*Audit Procedures*

(IIA adapted)

17.8 As the director of auditing for a municipality, you have received the following draft audit report from a member of your staff. The report is intended to present the results of an audit of the city's civic center operations. The report is to be presented to the city manager only. The city manager has no familiarity with civic center operations, having only recently moved to his current position from another city.

To: City Manager
From: Director of Auditing
Subject: Civic Center Operations

Finding:	The civic center is poorly managed. One piece of equipment valued at $112 could not be readily located. The civic center entered into legal contracts without review by the city attorney.
Recommendation:	Civic center management should be improved. We recommend that you fire the present civic center manager.
Recommendation:	If it has not already been done, someone should locate the missing equipment.
Recommendation:	Civic center contracts should be reviewed by the city attorney.
Conclusion:	The above information is based on standard audit procedures and included all appropriate tests. We did not audit maintenance operations.

The auditor has the following information:

1. The civic center manager entered into contracts valued at $2.8 million for goods and services of the year audited.
2. The civic center manager is responsible for equipment valued at $970,000.

3. An inventory of equipment valued at $656,000 was performed by the auditor.
4. The city attorney is paid a salary of $85,000 per year.
5. City policy requires prior review and approval by the city attorney of all contracts obligating the city.
6. Contracts valued at $480,000 were breached by suppliers. These contracts were found to be invalid and unenforceable by the city attorney subsequent to the breach.
7. Unable to require specific performance on the breached contracts, the city suffered a loss of $225,000.
8. The city policy on contracting was never formally communicated to the civic center management.

Required:
a. Identify and briefly describe the appropriate parts of an audit report.
b. Identify five deficiencies in the draft audit report and explain why they are deficiencies. (IIA adapted)

17.9 The audit department of a large manufacturing company has just completed an audit of the company's Centralized Computer Support Services (CCSS). CCSS is responsible for all data processing, except for special analysis programs run on personal computers in the R&D, engineering, marketing, and accounting departments. CCSS is responsible for coordinating the acquisition and maintenance of all equipment, however, including personal computers and associated equipment and software.

The audit of CCSS was limited to a review and evaluation of its responsiveness to the needs of the various personal computer users. This audit was requested by the vice-president of operations as a result of frequent complaints by the various departments about CCSS's unresponsiveness. Specifically, the various departments charged that CCSS failed to acquire requested personal computers in a timely fashion, even when funds were readily available. As a result, the various departments were frequently unable to do desired analytical work.

Using questionnaires, interviews, and tests of transactions, the auditors discovered that CCSS's role is limited to monitoring corporate usage of personal computers and consolidating departmental requests for personal computers before sending the requests to the purchasing department. The purchasing department actually ordered the computers and worked with the vendor. The audit revealed that CCSS took as long as five months (past the due date of a request) waiting on various requests for similar equipment so that one large request could be sent to purchasing. Once the purchase request was received by purchasing, the order was properly placed and the ordered equipment promptly received.

Required:
Write a short report based on the data given. Your report should be classified as to the main elements of an operational audit report. (IIA adapted)

17.10 Internal auditing can be classified as to financial auditing, compliance auditing, fraud auditing, and operational auditing. Operational auditing may be further categorized as to efficiency auditing and effectiveness auditing.

Required:

Classify each of the following audits as to compliance, financial, fraud, or operational. If operational, indicate whether it is an efficiency audit or an effectiveness audit.

a. Determining the cause of excessive employee turnover in a division's manufacturing operations.

b. Recalculating royalties resulting from an existing franchise agreement which calls for payment of sales related royalties.

c. Searching for the cause of a major branch's decline in profitability and making recommendations for improvement. The auditor's recommendations could lead to closing the branch.

d. Auditing travel expenditures at the company's 35 branches located throughout the United States to determine whether personal expenditures are being charged as company travel.

e. Spot-checking inventory at the company's eastern warehouse and comparing with perpetual records for possible major shrinkage.

f. Reviewing the year end adjustments to the general ledger. These adjustments had been drafted by the general accounting staff preparatory to drafting the unaudited financial statements.

g. Evaluating the adequacy of EDP controls related to transaction processing. More specifically, the auditors are interested in determining that the controls provide for accurately processing only properly approved transactions.

h. Determining the extent to which the internal reporting system is supporting the management decision process.

i. Examining existing loan agreements for possible violations of restrictive covenants.

j. Ascertaining why sewage costs have nearly doubled in the past year.

k. The director of internal auditing of a savings and loan association has been requested by management to evaluate the adequacy of the loan loss reserve.

l. An audit of the purchasing function in terms of adequacy of supply sources, reasonableness of vendor prices and whether competitive bids are required where appropriate, and quality and cost of transportation services.

17.11 Discuss the auditor's compliance auditing responsibility under each of the following sets of standards:

a. Generally accepted auditing standards;

b. GAO yellow book;

c. Single Audit Act of 1984; and

d. Circular A-133.

17.12 The College of Agriculture at Watertown State University, a large university located in the midwest, received a $2 million grant from the U.S. Department of Agriculture in July, 1992. The purpose of the grant is to further research into developing chickens producing mainly white meat. Direct costs permitted under the grant consist of compensation of faculty while on leave and assigned to the project; fringe benefits related to these faculty; graduate assistants' stipends and other support staff cost; travel directly associated with the research; telephone and fax costs applicable to the grant; and other direct costs such as computer software, chickens used in the research, and postage. In addition to the direct costs, the grant permits the university to add 25 percent of direct costs to billings submitted to the Department of Agriculture to reimburse for such indirect costs as utilities, building space, and administration.

The firm of Orens and Smead, CPAs, has been retained to audit the financial statements of Watertown State for the fiscal year ended June 30, 1993. In addition to the financial audit, the engagement letter requests the firm to audit for compliance as necessary. Although the university has several contracts and grants from the federal government, you have been assigned to perform the compliance audit for the "chicken grant." You requested and obtained the following analysis from Dr. Leghorn, the faculty member in charge of the research project:

Watertown State University
College of Agriculture
Poultry Research Grant Analysis
For the year ended June 30, 1993

7/11/92	Grant award		$2,000,000
7/11-6/30	Direct costs:		
	Faculty salaries	$300,000(1)	
	Faculty fringes	60,000(2)	
	Support staff + fringes	72,000(3)	
	Graduate assistants	48,000(4)	
	Travel	6,000	
	Telephone, postage, fax	1,400	
	Computer simulation	2,000	
	Chickens and feed	3,000	
	Total direct costs	$492,000	
	Indirect costs(25%)	123,000	
	Total billings		$615,000
6/30/93	Unexpended portion of grant: ($2,000,000-$492,000)		$1,508,000

(1) Five faculty at $60,000 each
(2) 20% of salaries
(3) Two secretaries at $30,000 + 20% fringes
(4) Four at $12,000

Required:
a. In addition to generally accepted auditing standards, cite the other source(s) of auditor responsibility in performing the compliance audit relative to the "chicken grant." Assuming Watertown State has a resident federal auditor, is the responsibility for performing the compliance audit that of the resident auditor or the independent auditor?
b. Identify internal control structure policies and procedures that should serve to prevent and/or detect noncompliance with the terms of the grant.
c. Develop an audit program that will provide reasonable assurance of detecting material instances of noncompliance with the terms of the grant.

17.13 An internal auditor with a landscaping company is preparing an audit program for the billing and accounts receivable functions. It was determined that the following objectives should be met by the appropriate operating department:
   a. Customer credit reviewed and approved before orders are accepted.
   b. Sales billed promptly and in the correct amount.
   c. Accounts receivable recorded promptly and accurately.
   d. Uncollectible accounts identified in a timely manner and processed properly.
   e. Customer discounts approved and accurately recorded.

Required:

Develop three audit procedures for each of the above listed objectives to determine whether the billing and accounts receivable functions are accomplishing those objectives. Use the following format:

Objective	*Procedure*
a.	1.
	2.
(IIA adapted)	3.

APPENDIX

Summary of General and Specific Standards for the Professional Practice of Internal Auditing*

100 **INDEPENDENCE**—INTERNAL AUDITORS SHOULD BE INDEPENDENT OF THE ACTIVITIES THEY AUDIT.

   110 **Organizational Status**—The organizational status of the internal auditing department should be sufficient to permit the accomplishment of its audit responsibilities.
   120 **Objectivity**—Internal auditors should be objective in performing audits.

200 **PROFESSIONAL PROFICIENCY**—INTERNAL AUDITS SHOULD BE PERFORMED WITH PROFICIENCY AND DUE PROFESSIONAL CARE.

   The Internal Auditing Department
   210 **Staffing**—The internal auditing department should provide assurance that the technical proficiency and educational background of internal auditors are appropriate for the audits to be performed.
   220 **Knowledge, Skills, and Disciplines**—The internal auditing department should possess or should obtain the knowledge, skills, and disciplines needed to carry out its audit responsibilities.
   230 **Supervision**—The internal auditing department should provide assurance that internal audits are properly supervised.

The Internal Auditor

240 **Compliance with Standards of Conduct**—Internal auditors should comply with professional standards of conduct.

250 **Knowledge, Skills, and Disciplines**—Internal auditors should possess the knowledge, skills, and disciplines essential to the performance of internal audits.

260 **Human Relations and Communications**—Internal auditors should be skilled in dealing with people and in communicating effectively.

270 **Continuing Education**—Internal auditors should maintain their technical competence through continuing education.

280 **Due Professional Care**—Internal auditors should exercise due professional care in performing internal audits.

300 **SCOPE OF WORK**—THE SCOPE OF THE INTERNAL AUDIT SHOULD ENCOMPASS THE EXAMINATION AND EVALUATION OF THE ADEQUACY AND EFFECTIVENESS OF THE ORGANIZATION'S INTERNAL CONTROL AND THE QUALITY OF PERFORMANCE IN CARRYING OUT ASSIGNED RESPONSIBILITIES.

310 **Reliability and Integrity of Information**—Internal auditors should review the reliability and integrity of financial and operating information and the means used to identify, measure, classify, and report such information.

320 **Compliance with Policies, Plans, Procedures, Laws, and Regulations**—Internal auditors should review the systems established to ensure compliance with those policies, plans, procedures, laws, and regulations which could have a significant impact on operations and reports and should determine whether the organization is in compliance.

330 **Safeguarding of Assets**—Internal auditors should review the means of safeguarding assets and, as appropriate, verify the existence of such assets.

340 **Economical and Efficient Use of Resources**—Internal auditors should appraise the economy and efficiency with which resources are employed.

350 **Accomplishment of Established Objectives and Goals for Operations or Programs**—Internal auditors should review operations or programs to ascertain whether results are consistent with established objectives and goals and whether the operations or programs are being carried out as planned.

400 **PERFORMANCE OF AUDIT WORK**—AUDIT WORK SHOULD INCLUDE PLANNING THE AUDIT, EXAMINING AND EVALUATING INFORMATION, COMMUNICATING RESULTS, AND FOLLOWING UP.

410 **Planning the Audit**—Internal auditors should plan each audit.

420 **Examining and Evaluating Information**—Internal auditors should collect, analyze, interpret, and document information to support audit results.

430 **Communicating Results**—Internal auditors should report the results of their audit work.

440 **Following Up**—Internal auditors should follow up to ascertain that appropriate action is taken on reported audit findings.

500 **MANAGEMENT OF THE INTERNAL AUDITING DEPARTMENT—** THE DIRECTOR OF INTERNAL AUDITING SHOULD PROPERLY MANAGE THE INTERNAL AUDITING DEPARTMENT.

510 **Purpose, Authority, and Responsibility**—The director of internal auditing should have a statement of purpose, authority, and responsibility for the internal auditing department.

520 **Planning**—The director of internal auditing should establish plans to carry out the responsibilities of the internal auditing department.

530 **Policies and Procedures**—The director of internal auditing should provide written policies and procedures to guide the audit staff.

540 **Personnel Management and Development**—The director of internal auditing should establish a program for selecting and developing the human resources of the internal auditing department.

550 **External Auditors**—The director of internal auditing should coordinate internal and external audit efforts.

560 **Quality Assurance**—The director of internal auditing should establish and maintain a quality assurance program to evaluate the operations of the internal auditing department.

*Source: Institute of Internal Auditors, *Standards for the Professional Practice of Internal Auditing.*

Trim Lawn Manufacturing Corporation—An EDP Audit Practice Case

Although this practice case is designed to be used with a microcomputer, it can also be completed without using the computer. The case provides the student an opportunity to apply auditing concepts to a "real-life" audit client. The client, Trim Lawn Manufacturing Corporation, operates within a unique business climate and control environment, and the student must assess inherent risk and control risk accordingly. The student is also asked to evaluate materiality and set individual item and aggregate materiality thresholds. In addition, the case contains modules involving sampling applications, audit program design, audit workpaper completion, audit adjustments, and an audit report upon completion of the 1993 examination.

The second purpose served by the practice case is to enable the student to utilize the microcomputer as an audit assist device. The student may use the computer in the Trim Lawn case to both automate the audit fieldwork and assist in audit decision making.

The case consists of modules. At the end of each module are two sets of requirements. If the first set, "Auditing With the Computer," is elected, the student will need an IBM compatible microcomputer containing at least 256K, a Lotus 1-2-3 System Disk-Version 2.01 or later, and the free data diskette provided by West Educational Publishing. If the second set of requirements, "Auditing Without the Computer," is chosen, the student will need to complete the workpapers contained in the Trim Lawn Workbook.

The modules parallel the phases of a financial audit. Many of the modules require both qualitative and quantitative analysis. Based on narrative material and on partially completed audit workpapers, the student will be asked to complete the workpapers, arrive at audit conclusions, and/or answer questions relating to auditing standards and interpretations. The following modules make up the Trim Lawn case:

Module I Assessment of inherent risk and control risk

Module II Preparation of time budget

Module III Control testing the sales processing subset of the revenue cycle

Module IV PPS sampling—factory equipment additions

Module V Union Trust bank reconciliation

Module VI Analysis of interbank transfers

Module VII Accounts receivable aging analysis and adequacy of allowance for doubtful accounts

Module VIII Sales and purchases cutoff tests

Module IX Search for unrecorded liabilities

Module X Estimated liability for product warranty

Module XI Plant asset additions and disposals

Module XII Analysis of marketable securities

Module XIII Mortgage note payable and note payable to GemCorp

Module XIV Working trial balance

Module XV Audit report

For maximum learning benefit, the modules should be completed as follows:

Modules I & II Following Chapter 9

Module III Following Chapter 10

Module IV Following Chapter 11

Modules V, VI, & VII Following Chapter 12

Modules VIII, IX, X, & XI Following Chapter 13

Modules XII, XIII, & XIV Following Chapter 14

Module XV Following Chapter 15

For purposes of this case, the income tax effects of audit adjustments have been ignored.

Before writing the narrative analysis required by several of the modules, the student should carefully review the "Effective Writing in Auditing" appendix following Chapter 8. Studying this appendix will enable students to better plan and compose their responses to the writing requirements. Proper planning, clarity and conciseness of written matter, and liberal use of headings and subheadings will produce a more complete and logical paper than might otherwise result. Module I, in particular, demands rigorous analysis and assessment of inherent risk and control risk. An adequate response to this requirement should result in a written narrative of 5–8 pages (double-spaced) in length. Prior reading of the appendix, therefore, should significantly ease the writing task in this module.

DESCRIPTION OF THE COMPANY

Trim Lawn was incorporated in 1955 to manufacture power lawn mowers. Snowblowers were added to the product line in 1973, and a garden tiller in 1984. Presently, the company makes the following products:

- Model 100 Lawn Mower (push-type)
- Model 200 Lawn Mower (self-propelled)
- Model 300 Riding Lawn Mower
- Big Orange Snowblower
- All Terrain Garden Tiller

All of these products are manufactured in one plant, which is located in central Ohio. The factory employs 1,200 workers. It was refurbished and updated in 1991, and is now quite automated. Trim Lawn's administrative offices are located in another building in the same complex. The company has 10 regional sales offices, each headed by a regional sales manager, located in various parts of the United States and Canada.

Products are shipped upon completion, and finished goods inventories are kept at a minimum. Engines are purchased from outside vendors. These and other purchased parts comprise the major part of Trim Lawn's inventory. All products carry a full one-year warranty covering parts and labor. The company is known for the quality of its products and for its strong service support.

Products are shipped directly to retailers who are licensed to sell Trim Lawn products. The dealer network consists of approximately 100 outlets located throughout the United States and Canada. As of the end of 1993, the company had a total of 60 customer accounts ranging in amount from $2,200 to approximately $900,000. The cumulative total of accounts receivable at December 31, 1993 was $10 million.

Trim Lawn experienced steady growth in sales and profitability of all product lines from the date of incorporation until the beginning of 1989. From early 1989 until the present time, imported lawn mowers and snowblowers have had a significant impact on Trim Lawn's revenue. This trend has continued through the present year (see Table TL.1).

Our firm, Solo and Wiggins, CPAs, has audited Trim Lawn since its incorporation in 1955. Elizabeth Hawkins is presently the partner in charge of the engagement, and John Matthews is the audit manager. The audit team consists of Mary Sondem, senior auditor in charge of the Trim Lawn audit; John Julius, assistant auditor in his third year with the firm and his third year on the Trim Lawn audit; Harvey Jensen, assistant auditor in his second year with the firm and his second year on the Trim Lawn audit; and student (you), assistant auditor, newly hired. Trim Lawn will be your first audit.

Sondem has been in charge of the Trim Lawn audit fieldwork for the past two years. Prior to that time, she had been a part of the Trim Lawn audit team as an assistant. She is very familiar with the client's operations and control structure and works well with the client personnel.

Marcy Mancura, the corporate controller of Trim Lawn, has been with the company since receiving her MBA in 1968. Mancura is also a CPA and was a staff accountant with Solo and Wiggins from 1963 to 1966. Other Trim Lawn personnel are Joshua Ravena, president and chief executive officer; Jerry Fabish, vice-president, production; Charles Gibbons, vice-president, marketing; Lawrence McKee, treasurer; Jennifer Lane, director of human resources; John Dandura, chief accountant; Jack Morrissey, director of internal auditing; and Jason Lupine, director of information systems and data processing. Figure TL.1 provides an overview of Trim Lawn's organization structure.

Trim Lawn closes its general ledger on a calendar year basis. Unaudited financial statements are prepared quarterly and are reviewed by Solo and Wiggins. The accounting system, including the general ledger, inventories, receivables, payables, and plant assets has been computerized since 1988. Payroll was placed on the computer in 1990, and after extensive "debugging," the system seems to be functioning smoothly at present. The company employs approximately 1,200 production workers, 150 salaried administrative employees, including the corporate management staff, and 75 salespersons. Hourly employees are paid weekly and salaried employees are paid biweekly.

TABLE TL.1 Trim Lawn Manufacturing Corporation—Comparative Income Statements, 1984–1993 (in thousands of dollars)

	1993	1992	1991	1990	1989	1988	1987	1986	1985	1984
Sales	$180,000	206,000	245,000	288,900	312,400	309,760	297,500	288,650	277,540	266,000
Cost of goods sold	131,256	145,606	171,500	196,452	203,060	201,344	193,375	187,623	188,727	180,880
Gross profit	48,744	60,394	73,500	92,448	109,340	108,416	104,125	101,027	88,813	85,120
Operating expenses	26,170	25,035	24,556	23,890	23,200	22,456	21,677	20,900	20,770	19,900
Operating income	22,574	35,359	48,944	68,558	86,140	85,960	82,448	80,127	68,043	65,220
Other expenses (net)	6,077	3,720	3,600	3,450	3,890	3,900	4,350	5,350	5,230	5,100
Income before taxes and extraordinary items	16,497	31,639	45,344	65,108	82,250	82,060	78,098	74,777	62,813	60,120
Income taxes	5,092	9,492	13,603	19,532	24,675	24,618	23,429	22,433	18,844	18,036
Income before extraordinary items	11,405	22,147	31,741	45,576	57,575	57,442	54,669	52,344	43,969	42,084
Extraordinary gain (loss)— net of tax	0	(1,540)	0	3,400	0	0	0	0	(1,235)	0
Net income	$ 11,405	20,607	31,741	48,976	57,575	57,442	54,669	52,344	42,734	42,084

*Unaudited.

FIGURE TL.1 Trim Lawn Manufacturing Corporation Organization Chart

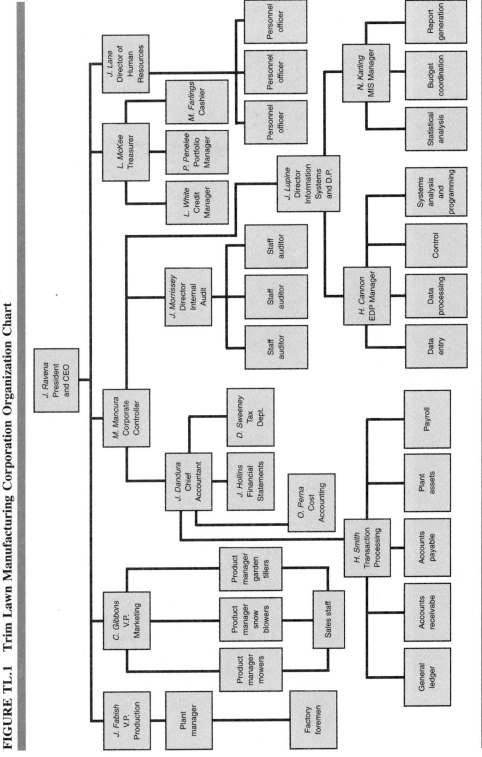

All bank accounts have been reconciled on a monthly basis, including the December 31, 1993 reconciliation. The company has provided us with a year-end adjusted trial balance and a complete set of financial statements, together with supporting schedules (see Exhibits TL.1–TL.5). Mary Sondem and her audit team were present at Trim Lawn's year-end physical inventory.

MODULE I: ASSESSMENT OF INHERENT RISK AND CONTROL RISK

In this module, you will be asked to assess inherent risk and control risk after you have done the following:

1. Applied analytical procedures to Trim Lawn's financial data;
2. Studied Trim Lawn's business operations and the lawn and garden equipment industry generally; and
3. Obtained a basic understanding of Trim Lawn's control structure, including the control environment, the accounting system, and the control procedures.

In addition, you will be asked to set individual item and aggregate materiality thresholds. These thresholds will be used in deciding whether potential audit adjustments are to be:

1. Proposed;
2. Accumulated in an aggregate materiality workpaper for later consideration; or
3. Ignored.

In completing this assignment, you may assume that Sondem has decided on the following initial risk assessments:

- Inherent risk—100 percent
- Control risk—maximum
- Audit risk—5 percent

Study of the Business, the Industry, and the Control Environment

As part of her continuing study of Trim Lawn's operations, Sondem has extracted the following data from the permanent file working paper entitled ''Business, Industry, and Control Environment.''

1. Herbert Ravena founded Trim Lawn in 1955 and successfully led the company during the ensuing 35 years. He retired in 1989 and his only son, Joshua, assumed control of the company. The Ravena family presently owns 10 percent of the outstanding Trim Lawn common stock. The remaining 90 percent is publicly held.
2. Trim Lawn has been known for the quality of its products and its strong after-sale service support. (All products are under 100 percent parts and labor warranty for one year following sale.) These attributes led to many years of steadily increasing sales and profits.

EXHIBIT TL.1   Trim Lawn Manufacturing Corporation Adjusted Trial Balance as of December 31, 1993

	Account Number	Debit *(in thousands of dollars)*	Credit
GemCorp Demand Deposit	1001	$ 6,754	
Union Trust Demand Deposit	1002	3,457	
Union Trust Payroll Account	1008	10	
Petty Cash	1012	5	
Investments in Marketable Securities	1101	3,000	
All. for Decline in Market Value of Securities	1102		$ 0
Accounts Receivable—Trade	1201	10,000	
Notes Receivable—Trade	1202	2,000	
Allowance for Doubtful Accounts	1250		400
Raw Materials Inventory	1310	1,800	
Engines Inventory	1320	6,100	
Purchased Parts Inventory	1330	3,300	
Goods in Process—Model 100 Lawn Mowers	1350	890	
Goods in Process—Model 200 Lawn Mowers	1351	1,025	
Goods in Process—Model 300 Lawn Mowers	1352	450	
Goods in Process—Snow Blowers	1361	300	
Goods in Process—Garden Tillers	1365	1,135	
Finished Goods—Model 100 Lawn Mowers	1371	500	
Finished Goods—Model 200 Lawn Mowers	1372	2,000	
Finished Goods—Model 300 Lawn Mowers	1373	1,000	
Finished Goods—Snowblowers	1376	300	
Finished Goods—Garden Tillers	1379	1,200	
Indirect Materials	1385	1,600	
Repair Parts Inventory	1390	1,400	
Prepaid Insurance	1410	400	
Deferred Taxes—Warranty	1440	200	
Land	1510	2,000	
Factory Building	1520	200,000	
Accumulated Depreciation—Building	1525		90,200
Factory Equipment	1530	150,000	
Accumulated Depreciation—Factory Equipment	1535		50,000
Office Building	1540	25,000	
Accumulated Depreciation—Office Building	1545		10,000
Office Fixtures and Equipment	1550	10,000	
Accumulated Depreciation—Office Fixtures and Equipment	1555		5,000
Autos and Trucks	1560	1,000	
Accumulated Depreciation—Autos and Trucks	1565		620
Patents	1610	3,500	
Copyrights	1620	500	

	Account Number	Debit *(in thousands of dollars)*	Credit
Deposits	1710	180	
Cost of Goods Sold—Model 100 Lawn Mower	5100	14,754	
Cost of Goods Sold—Model 200 Lawn Mower	5200	81,259	
Cost of Goods Sold—Model 300 Lawn Mower	5300	9,234	
Cost of Goods Sold—Snowblowers	5400	20,384	
Cost of Goods Sold—Garden Tillers	5500	5,625	
Direct Labor	6100	27,130	
Direct Labor Applied	6200		27,130
Indirect Labor	7201	3,200	
Depreciation—Factory Building	7205	8,200	
Depreciation—Factory Equipment	7206	13,400	
Real Estate Taxes	7210	1,900	
Personal Property Taxes	7211	1,200	
Manufacturing Supplies	7220	14,300	
FICA Tax Expense	7230	2,150	
State Unemployment Tax Expense	7231	600	
Health Insurance Premiums	7234	1,500	
Employee Pension Expense	7235	2,100	
Repairs and Maintenance Expense	7236	342	
Utilities Expense	7241	8,260	
Miscellaneous Factory Expense	7242	1,014	
Manufacturing Overhead Applied	7250		58,916
Sales Commissions	8310	2,000	
Sales Salaries	8320	800	
Bad Debts Expense	8325	600	
Product Warranty	8330	670	
Advertising	8340	3,000	
Miscellaneous Selling Expense	8350	370	
Administrative Salaries	9410	8,000	
Research and Development Costs	9420	4,000	
FICA Tax Expense	9431	856	
State Unemployment Tax Expense	9432	224	
Federal Unemployment Tax Expense	9433	120	
Workers' Compensation Premiums	9434	100	
Health Insurance Premiums	9435	500	
Employee Pension Expense	9436	100	
Employee Profit Sharing Expense	9437	100	
Depreciation—Office Building	9440	1,000	
Depreciation—Office Fixtures and Equipment	9445	1,200	
Depreciation—Autos and Trucks	9449	220	
Accounting Fees	9450	280	
Legal Fees	9451	370	
Other Professional Services	9452	20	
Supplies Expense	9460	200	
Insurance Expense	9470	450	

	Account Number	Debit *(in thousands*	Credit *of dollars)*
Printing and Copying Expense	9480	235	
Postage Expense	9481	285	
Gain/Loss on Disposal of Plant Assets	9485	250	
Miscellaneous Administrative Expense	9490	220	
Interest Expense	9701	7,000	
Loss on Decline in Market Value of Securities	9702	0	
Federal Income Tax Expense	9990	3,512	
State Income Tax Expense	9991	923	
City Income Tax Expense	9992	657	
Notes Payable—Trade	2010		1,977
Accounts Payable—Trade	2020		9,000
Interest Payable	2030		590
Sales Salaries Payable	2041		80
Administrative Salaries Payable	2042		320
Factory Wages Payable	2043		890
FICA Payable	2051		190
State Income Taxes Withheld	2052		70
City Income Taxes Withheld	2053		30
Unemployment and Workers' Compensation Premiums Payable	2054		110
Accrued Profit Sharing Payable	2055		50
Federal Income Taxes Payable	2061		1,400
State Income Taxes Payable	2062		400
City Income Taxes Payable	2063		200
Estimated Product Warranty Liability	2070		900
Accrued Commissions Payable	2080		145
Mortgage Note Payable	2110		40,000
Deferred Tax Liability—Depreciation	2120		10,600
12% Note Payable to GemCorp Bank and Trust	2130		25,000
10% Preferred Stock	3110		80,000
Common Stock	3120		50,000
Additional Paid—in Capital	3130		20,000
Treasury Stock	3140	3,949	
Retained Earnings	3150		40,378
Dividends	3160	5,000	
Sales—Model 100 Lawn Mower	4100		20,760
Sales—Model 200 Lawn Mower	4200		112,168
Sales—Model 300 Lawn Mower	4300		13,000
Sales—Snowblowers	4400		27,178
Sales—Garden Tillers	4500		6,894
Interest Earned	4901		300
Dividends Earned	4902		223
Gain on Disposal of Investments	4903		400
		$705,519	$705,519

EXHIBIT TL.2 Trim Lawn Manufacturing Corporation—Income Statements for the Years Ended December 31, 1992 and 1993 (in thousands of dollars)

	Year Ended 12/31/93*		Year Ended 12/31/92
Sales revenue		$180,000	206,000
Cost of goods sold:			
Beginning inventories	3,000		3,501
Cost of goods manufactured (Schedule 1)	133,256		145,105
Cost of goods available for sale	136,256		148,606
Ending inventories	5,000		3,000
Cost of goods sold		131,256	145,606
Gross profit on sales		48,744	60,394
Operating expenses (Schedule 3)		26,170	25,035
Operating income		22,574	35,359
Financial income and expense:			
Interest expense	7,000		5,820
Interest and dividends earned	523		2,000
Gain (loss) on disposal of investments	400		100
Loss on decline in market value of securities	0		0
Net financial expense		6,077	3,720
Income before taxes and extraordinary items		16,497	31,639
Income taxes		5,092	9,492
Income before extraordinary items		11,405	22,147
Extraordinary loss from warehouse fire (net of tax)			1,540
Net income		$ 11,405	20,607

Schedule 1: Cost of Goods Manufactured

Beginning work in process inventories		$ 4,000	2,502
Manufacturing costs:			
Direct materials:			
Beginning inventories of materials and purchased parts	12,000		10,200
Purchases	46,210		61,375
Available for production	58,210		71,575
Ending inventories of materials and purchased parts	11,200		12,000
Cost of materials used in production	47,010		59,575
Direct labor	27,130		27,425
Manufacturing overhead (Schedule 2)	58,916		59,603
Total manufacturing costs		133,056	146,603
Total work in process		137,056	149,105
Ending work in process inventories		3,800	4,000
Cost of goods manufactured		$133,256	145,105

EXHIBIT TL.2   *(concluded)*

	Year Ended 12/31/93*	Year Ended 12/31/92
Schedule 2: Manufacturing Overhead		
Indirect labor	$ 3,200	3,200
Depreciation of factory building	8,200	8,200
Depreciation of factory equipment	13,400	12,800
Property taxes	3,100	2,900
Manufacturing supplies	14,300	14,650
Payroll taxes and fringe benefits	7,100	7,250
Utilities	8,260	9,140
Repairs and maintenance	342	563
Miscellaneous	1,014	900
	$58,916	59,603
Schedule 3: Operating Expenses		
Selling Expenses:		
Sales commissions	$2,000	2,300
Sales salaries	800	700
Bad debts expense	600	800
Product warranty	1,000	1,150
Advertising	3,000	2,800
Miscellaneous selling	40	38
	7,440	7,788
General expenses:		
Administrative salaries	8,000	7,500
Research and development	4,000	3,800
Payroll taxes and fringe benefits	2,000	2,000
Depreciation—office building	1,000	1,000
Depreciation—office fixtures and equipment	1,200	1,300
Depreciation—autos and trucks	220	180
Accounting and legal fees	650	770
Other professional services	20	18
Supplies	200	280
Insurance	450	240
Printing and postage	520	115
Loss on disposal of plant assets	250	
Miscellaneous administrative	220	44
	18,730	17,247
	$26,170	25,035

*Unaudited.

EXHIBIT TL.3   Trim Lawn Manufacturing Corporation—Balance Sheets as of December 31, 1992 and 1993 (in thousands of dollars)

		12/31/93*		12/31/92
Assets				
Current assets:				
Cash on hand and in banks		$ 10,226		12,400
Investments in marketable securities		3,000		4,200
Accounts and notes receivable—trade	12,000		13,200	
Less allowance for doubtful accounts	(400)		(700)	
		11,600		12,500
Inventories:				
Materials and purchased parts	11,200		12,000	
Goods in process	3,800		4,000	
Finished goods	5,000		3,000	
Indirect materials and repair parts	3,000		2,800	
		23,000		21,800
Prepaid expenses		400		380
Deferred tax assets—warranty		200		320
Total current assets		48,426		51,600
Property, plant, and equipment:				
Land		2,000		2,000
Factory building	200,000		200,000	
Less accumulated depreciation	(90,200)		(82,000)	
		109,800		118,000
Factory equipment	150,000		130,000	
Less accumulated depreciation	(50,000)		(60,000)	
		100,000		70,000
Office building	25,000		25,000	
Less accumulated depreciation	(10,000)		(9,000)	
		15,000		16,000
Office fixtures and equipment	10,000		9,000	
Less accumulated depreciation	(5,000)		(4,000)	
		5,000		5,000
Autos and trucks	1,000		900	
Less accumulated depreciation	(620)		(400)	
		380		500
Total property, plant, and equipment		232,180		211,500
Investments and other assets:				
Patents and copyrights				
(net of accumulated amortization)	4,000		4,200	
Deposits	180		180	
Total investments and other assets		4,180		4,380
Total assets		$284,786		267,480

EXHIBIT TL.3   *(continued)*

	12/31/93*		12/31/92
Liabilities			
Current liabilities:			
Notes payable	$ 1,977		11,340
Accounts payable	9,000		10,200
Interest payable	590		620
Salaries and wages payable	1,290		1,460
Payroll withholdings	290		380
Taxes and fringe benefits payable	160		150
Income taxes payable	2,000		1,800
Estimated product warranty liability	900		1,200
Accrued commissions payable	145		152
Total current liabilities		16,352	27,302
Long-term liabilities:			
Mortgage note payable	40,000		40,000
Deferred tax liability-depreciation	10,600		9,800
12% note payable to GemCorp Bank and Trust	25,000		
Total long-term liabilities		75,600	49,800
Total liabilities		$ 91,952	$ 77,102
Stockholders' Equity			
Invested Capital:			
Preferred stock, $100 par value,			
10% cumulative, 10,000,000 shares			
authorized, 800,000 shares			
issued and outstanding	$ 80,000		80,000
Common stock, $10 par value,			
90,000,000 shares authorized,			
5,000,000 shares issued, of which			
130,000 shares are in the treasury	50,000		50,000
Paid-in capital in excess of par value			
of capital stock	20,000		20,000
Total invested capital		150,000	150,000
Retained Earnings		46,783	40,378
Total		196,783	190,378
Less cost of 130,000 shares of treasury stock		(3,949)	
Total stockholders' equity		192,834	190,378
Total Liabilities and Stockholders' Equity		$284,786	267,480

*Unaudited.

**EXHIBIT TL.4   Trim Lawn Manufacturing Corporation—
Statements of Retained Earnings for the Years Ended
December 31, 1992 and 1993 (thousands of dollars)**

	Year Ended 12/31/93*	Year Ended 12/31/92
Retained earnings—beginning of year	$40,378	29,771
Net income	11,405	20,607
Dividends	(5,000)	(10,000)
Retained earnings—end of year	$46,783	40,378
*Unaudited.		

3. Imports of lawn mowers and snowblowers have significantly increased industry competition, especially since 1988. Domestic manufacturers, including Trim Lawn, have experienced declining sales and profits as a result. In response to the foreign competition, Trim Lawn has increased its efforts to develop and incorporate the latest technology into its products. To date, these efforts have only mitigated the foreign manufacturers' increasing market share.

4. Declining sales also prompted Trim Lawn management to update its manufacturing operations. To this end, the factory was completely refurbished in 1990, and automation was effected by incorporating the latest manufacturing technology. As a result of the automation, Trim Lawn decreased its factory labor force from 1,800 in 1989 to 1,200 in 1993. The company also reduced its sales force from 100 to 75 salespersons in response to declining sales volume.

   Jerry Fabish, production vice-president, observed that the factory refurbishing has enabled the company to significantly increase the productivity of its production employees. Charles Gibbons, marketing vice-president, agrees, and predicts a reversal of the declining sales trend by mid-1994. Marcy Mancura, corporate controller, on the other hand, is concerned about the decline in the operating income margin as a percent of sales. She attributes the decline to the increased proportion of fixed overhead to total manufacturing costs, given increased automation and declining sales.

5. In 1993, in the face of declining sales and profitability, Trim Lawn also experienced liquidity problems. Cash inflows slowed and payment of trade accounts payable within the specified credit term became increasingly difficult. After much discussion with Daryl Moore, the president of GemCorp Bank and Trust Company, and GemCorp's lending officers, Mr. Ravena was able to negotiate a 10-year 12 percent note payable for $25 million. The note is unsecured and is payable in equal annual installments, together with interest,

**EXHIBIT TL.5 Trim Lawn Manufacturing Corporation—
Statement of Cash Flows for the Year Ended
December 31, 1993 (thousands of dollars)**

Cash Provided by Operating Activities:		
Net income	$ 11,405	
Add (deduct):		
Increase in inventories	(1,200)	
Decrease in accounts and notes receivable	900	
Increase in prepaid expenses	(20)	
Increase in deferred tax liability	800	
Decrease in deferred tax asset	120	
Decrease in accounts payable	(1,200)	
Decrease in interest payable	(30)	
Decrease in salaries and wages payable	(170)	
Decrease in payroll withholdings	(90)	
Increase in taxes and fringe benefits payable	10	
Increase in income taxes payable	200	
Decrease in estimated product warranty liability	(300)	
Decrease in accrued commissions payable	(7)	
Depreciation and amortization	24,220	
Gain on sale of marketable securities	(400)	
Loss on disposal of plant assets	250	
Total		34,488
Cash Provided (used) by Investing Activities:		
Disposal of plant assets	6,500	
Purchase of plant assets	(51,450)	
Sale of marketable securities	3,467	
Purchase of marketable securities	(1,867)	
Purchase of treasury stock	(3,949)	
Total		(47,299)
Cash Provided (used) by Financing Activities:		
Issuance of 12% note payable to GemCorp	25,000	
Payment of dividends	(5,000)	
Payment of mortgage note installment	(10,000)	
Issuance of notes payable	637	
Total		10,637
Increase (Decrease) in Cash		($ 2,174)

beginning March 1, 1994. The loan contains restrictive covenants. Those relevant to the Trim Lawn audit are the following:

   a. A minimum balance of $6 million must be maintained in Trim Lawn's demand deposit account with GemCorp Bank and Trust;

   b. Further borrowing is prohibited until the GemCorp note has been amortized below $10 million; and

   c. Dividends may be declared only from retained earnings in excess of $45 million.

6. In April, 1993 Mr. Ravena borrowed $1 million from the company in exchange for an unsecured note. The transaction resulted in a debit to Account 1203 — Notes Receivable, Officers. According to Ms. Mancura, Mr. Ravena plans to repay this note prior to December 31, 1993.

7. Legal action was initiated against the company by Snoro, a competitor, in late 1992. The suit alleges that Trim Lawn infringed on a process already patented by Snoro. The process, according to Snoro's attorneys, prolongs the life of the clutch assembly on the riding lawn mower model by using a plateless, air-driven clutch that has virtually eliminated friction during gear changing. Trim Lawn has responded to the action by demonstrating the unique characteristics of its patented clutch assembly. By July, 1993, the suit had neither been heard by the court nor settled outside by the litigants. Snoro is suing Trim Lawn for $30 million.

8. For many years, our audit team has observed a conscientious effort by Mr. Ravena and Ms. Mancura to establish and implement a sound control structure. As a result, financial records have been quite reliable and financial statements have conformed to generally accepted accounting principles in all material respects. Mr. Ravena's concern for proper accounting and adequate asset safeguards is well known throughout the organization.

9. Trim Lawn's internal audit staff, directed by Jack Morrissey, is viewed by our firm as quite competent. Because the company does not have an audit committee, Mr. Morrissey reports directly to Ms. Mancura, the controller. He also holds monthly meetings with the Executive Committee, consisting of Mr. Ravena, Ms. Mancura, Mr. Fabish, Mr. Gibbons, Mr. McKee, Ms. Lane, and certain members of Trim Lawn's board of directors. The purpose of these meetings is to discuss any control structure problems encountered by the internal audit staff and to inform the participants of current projects in progress by the internal auditors. The meetings also permit members of the Executive Committee to identify possible future audit tasks for Mr. Morrissey and his team. In the past, our audit team has utilized Mr. Morrissey and his three staff auditors extensively to assist in various phases of the Trim Lawn audit.

The Accounting System and Control Procedures

Trim Lawn's computerized batch processing accounting system has been in operation since the beginning of 1988. By early 1989, the system had been adequately perfected to permit discontinuing the old manual system. Some of the more significant features of the system are the following:

Computerized Ledger

A general ledger software package, installed as part of the 1988 computerization project, contains the following integrated modules: accounts receivable, accounts payable, inventories, plant assets, payroll, and general ledger.

Sales Processing

Prenumbered sales orders, including evidence of proper credit approval, are based on customer orders, approved by the regional sales manager, received from the regional sales offices via remote terminals, and reviewed by one of the three product managers. These orders are sent to accounting for a completeness review, including evidence of credit approval. After reviewing the orders, accounting prepares an input recording form. The recording form contains customer number, sales representative number, stock number, and quantity of each stock item ordered by the customer. The recording forms are then forwarded daily to EDP where they form the basis for entry into the system. A copy of the sales order is forwarded by EDP to shipping to trigger processing of the shipment to the customer. The computer prepares the sales invoice set after editing the order for the customer number, existence of customer credit approval, customer credit limit vs. existing customer balance, stock number, and availability of products. As part of the sales processing, the computer inserts the customer's name and address, product descriptions and prices, and extensions and footings. Terms of payment and discount availability are also determined by the computer and included on the invoice. For each order processed, the computer records the transaction, including costing the sale, and updates the accounts receivable and inventory modules. EDP then forwards the invoice sets to accounting where they are filed awaiting notification from shipping that the goods were shipped to the customer. Upon receipt of the shipping order and signed bill of lading from shipping, accounting reviews all documents (sales invoice, sales order, shipping order, and bill of lading) for completeness and agreement, and mails the invoice to the customer. Figure TL.2 describes the sales processing function in the form of a flowchart.

Cash Receipts

All mail is centrally received in the mailroom, opened, and distributed. Checks from customers are restrictively endorsed and prelisted before being forwarded to Mary Farlings, cashier. Ms. Farlings prepares the deposit and deposits each day's remittances intact. Remittance advices and a copy of the prelisting are sent by the mail room to the data entry section of the EDP department for entry into the computer system. A second copy of the prelisting is sent to Ms. Mancura, the controller, for comparison with the receipted deposit ticket obtained directly from the bank. The prelisting is also used by the controller's office as a control total. The total is compared with the cash receipts summary obtained from EDP as a result of computer processing of cash receipts.

Cash receipts are processed daily by the data entry section of EDP. Each remittance advice is converted to a recording form by the data entry section. The recording form contains the following information: customer number, invoice numbers paid by the customer's check, discount taken, and net amount remitted. The

FIGURE TL.2   Sales Processing Flowchart

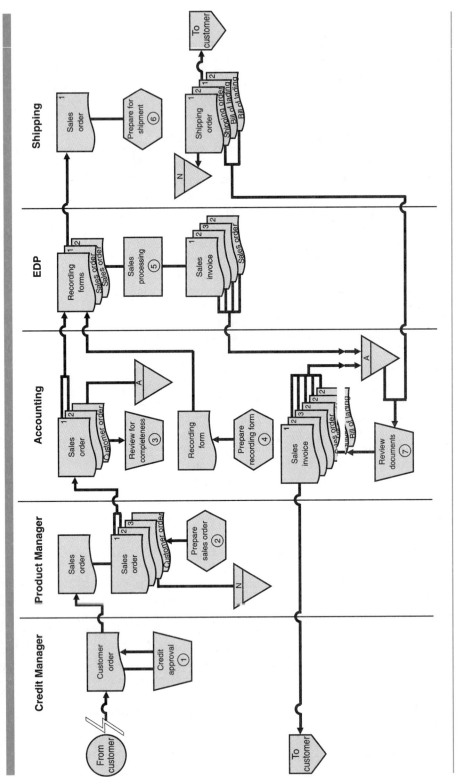

data processing section uses the recording forms as a basis for entry into the computer. Input is effected by means of input terminals. The accounts receivable module of the general ledger software package edits each customer remittance for the following characteristics: valid customer number, valid invoice number, whether discount was deducted properly, and correctness of net amount remitted. The computer, after editing, updates the customers' ledger and produces a summary cash receipts listing. The data control section of EDP delivers the listing to the controller's office for comparison with the prelisting obtained previously from the mailroom.

Miscellaneous cash receipts are processed in a fashion similar to that accorded customer remittances. The recording form for miscellaneous cash receipts, however, is prepared by the general ledger section of the transaction processing department rather than by data entry. Prepared from the remittance advice, the recording form contains the date, amount remitted, account number(s), and amount(s) to be credited. The recording forms are forwarded daily to data processing for entry into the system. A copy is retained by general ledger for later comparison with the computer output.

Purchases and Accounts Payable

Trim Lawn buys its mower, blower, and tiller engines from three unrelated vendors. Other materials and purchased parts are purchased from various vendors. All materials and purchased parts are ordered on the basis of purchase orders generated by the computer as reorder points are reached. Trim Lawn does not have a separate purchasing department within its corporate organization. Rather, Mr. Fabish, the production vice-president, performs this function.

Prices, as agreed upon by Mr. Fabish and the respective vendors, also appear on the purchase order. Purchase orders are mailed to the vendor after being reviewed and approved by the controller's office. A copy of the purchase order is sent to accounts payable and also to the receiving department for later comparison with incoming goods. When goods are received, they are counted and inspected by employees in the receiving department and a receiving report is prepared. A copy then accompanies the goods to stores where quantities and types of goods are compared with the receiving report. The stores manager then signs the receiving report and forwards it to accounts payable.

When the vendor's invoice is received, an accounts payable clerk compares it with the purchase order and receiving report and prepares a recording form for processing the invoice. The recording form contains the vendor number, vendor invoice number, stock number, quantities, price, and terms. The recording forms, along with a control tape of daily totals of vendors' invoice amounts, are forwarded to EDP for daily processing of vendors' invoices. During the input of invoices, via a terminal, the accounts payable software module of the general ledger package edits for the following characteristics: valid vendor number, valid stock number, price in agreement with vendor price stored in the computer, and terms in agreement with discount and payment terms stored in the computer. During the processing run, the computer updates the accounts payable ledger, the manufacturing overhead detail, the operating expense detail, and the perpetual inventory records for materials and purchased parts. The computer also performs a record count and compares output with input at the end of the processing run. Lastly, the due date of the invoice

FIGURE TL.3 Purchases Processing Flowchart

is stored in the computer for purposes of generating daily disbursement checks for invoices to be paid on that date.

Computer output consists of a purchases summary that is forwarded to accounts payable for review and filing. Figure TL.3 is a flowchart depicting the documents and procedures just described.

Payments to Vendors

The daily computer check writing process produces a two-part check-voucher set. A remittance advice, indicating invoice number(s) being paid, gross amount, discount, and net amount of the check constitutes the lower part of the set. The check-voucher set is sent to accounts payable for comparison with the documents contained in the alphabetic vendors' invoice file. If the amounts appearing on the remittance advice agree with the vendor's invoice, the accounts payable clerk initials the voucher, attaches the purchase order, vendor's invoice, and receiving report, and forwards the documents to the treasurer. The treasurer examines the documentation received from accounts payable for agreement among the invoice, purchase order, and receiving report as to type, quantities, and prices. If everything is in agreement and the documents include initials evidencing proper approvals, the check is approved for signature. The checks are then signed by a check signing machine and mailed directly to the vendor by the treasurer's office. The documents are effectively canceled to prevent reuse and are returned to accounts payable for filing in a numeric paid voucher file.

Responsibility for operating the check signing machine is assigned to one individual. The machine is locked at all times when not being used to sign checks, and the key is in the custody of the check signer. Figure TL.4 is a flowchart describing the payment process.

Payroll

Hourly production employees are paid weekly. Nonproduction employees are salaried and are paid biweekly. Salespersons are also paid biweekly, on a combination salary and commission compensation basis. The confidential executive payroll is prepared and disbursed by Mr. Ravena's assistant from a separate account maintained for that purpose.

The total time worked is accumulated for hourly employees by a time clock located at the factory entrance. The employee's name, social security number, and department number appear on the time card. Factory supervisors approve the time cards on a daily basis for employees working in their respective departments.

Each Monday morning, the timekeepers summarize and assemble the clock cards by department number and forward the packets to payroll. The clock cards are examined in payroll for proper approval and a tape is run of total hours by department. The clock cards, along with a copy of the tape, are then forwarded to EDP for processing.

A data entry clerk enters the employee number, the department number, and the hours worked via a terminal. Input editing consists of checking for valid employee number, valid department, and reasonableness of hours worked. The employee files housed in the computer contain current pay rates, as well as employee and department numbers. Adjustments to the employee data base for pay rate

FIGURE TL.4   Payment Processing Flowchart

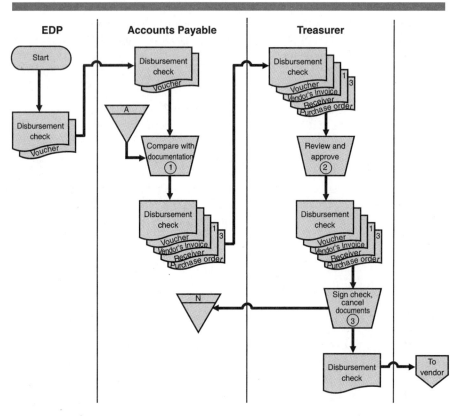

changes, additions of new employees, and deletions of terminated employees are made only on the basis of authorization slips obtained from Jennifer Lane, director of human resources. Withholding information is also included in the data base and is updated on the basis of authorization received from the human resources division.

The computer calculates gross pay, withholdings, and net pay. The employer's taxes (e.g., FICA, unemployment, and workers' compensation premium) are also calculated by the payroll module of the accounting software package. A record count is performed by the computer and compared with employee records updated at the end of the run. A register also accumulates hours by department for comparison with the adding machine tape received from payroll.

Output consists of prenumbered payroll checks, a payroll summary, and a cost distribution summary. The control group is responsible for distributing the output. The checks, along with the summaries, are forwarded to the treasurer for signature and distribution. A check for the total amount of net pay is first drawn upon the general account for deposit in the payroll account. The treasurer signs this check and forwards it to the cashier for deposit.

The individual payroll checks are signed with the aid of a check signing machine after being compared with the payroll summary on a test basis. After the checks have been signed, they are placed in a vault until Friday, at which time they are distributed by treasury personnel. Unclaimed checks are returned to the vault in the treasurer's office.

The payroll summary is forwarded to the payroll department as a basis for comparing total hours by department with the control tape and for completing the various payroll tax returns and reports. The cost summary is sent to Oliver Perna, director of cost accounting, for review and filing. Figure TL.5 is a flowchart describing the production payroll process.

As part of the integrated software package, the payroll data serves as input for updating the goods in process inventory accounts. To complete updating the goods in process and finished goods inventory, production reports and materials requisitions are entered into the system on a weekly basis. In addition to the perpetual inventory ledgers, the data base includes a manufacturing overhead detail and an operating expense ledger. Current standard costs are also incorporated into the data base. This enables the computer to calculate and print out daily, weekly, and monthly variance reports for analysis by Perna and Norman Karling, Management Information Systems Manager.

The salaried payroll is prepared in a similar fashion. EDP updates the employee data base as written authorizations are received from human resources. As with production employees, the authorizations relate to changes in employees' salaries, new employees, and terminated employees. Any overtime for salaried employees must be approved in writing by the respective department heads and routed to EDP through payroll. The payroll department reviews the overtime for proper authorization and for reasonableness before transmitting the information to EDP.

Other Accounting System Features

Monthly financial statements consist of a balance sheet, an income statement, and a statement of cash flows. These statements are generated automatically by the computer. Month-end adjustments for accruals (payroll, taxes, warranty, commissions, pension, profit sharing, interest, and fringe benefits) and apportionments (depreciation, insurance, bad debts, and amortization) are determined by John Dandura, Trim Lawn's Chief Accountant, and submitted to EDP on standard recording forms. EDP enters the data and invokes the command for printing out the financial statements. In addition to the financial statements, the adjusting entries are printed out. These are forwarded by the control group to Mr. Dandura for comparison with his copy of the adjustments as originally submitted to EDP. Exhibit TL.6 contains the December 31, 1993 adjustments for inventories (perpetual records adjusted to year-end physical inventory) and unrecorded liabilities. Exhibits TL.7–TL.10 contain beginning and ending entries in the December, 1993 transaction registers.

All documents generated by Trim Lawn in support of transactions and events are prenumbered, safeguarded, and under the responsibility of designated individuals. Used documents are canceled to prevent reuse. The internal auditing staff periodically accounts for the numeric sequence of used documents. All voided documents are retained according to Trim Lawn's document retention policy.

Within the EDP department, duties are separated among the following functions:

1. Systems analysis and programming;
2. Data entry;
3. Data processing; and
4. Control.

FIGURE TL.5   Production Payroll Processing Flowchart

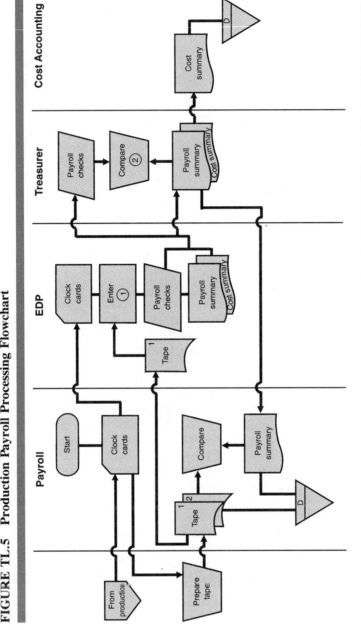

EXHIBIT TL.6 Trim Lawn Manufacturing Corporation—Selected Client Adjusting Entries, December 31, 1993

Unrecorded Invoices

7210 Real estate taxes	$722,000	
7241 Utilities expense	823,000	
7234 Health insurance premiums—factory	95,360	
9435 Health insurance premiums—administrative	32,320	
1320 Engines inventory	566,842	
1390 Repair parts inventory	87,600	
7220 Manufacturing supplies	887,000	
9450 Accounting fees	80,000	
9451 Legal fees	70,000	
2020 Accounts payable		3,364,122

Client's entry to adjust for unrecorded invoices at 12/31/93

Inventory Adjustment

5200 Cost of goods sold—Model 200 lawn mower	$223,500	
1310 Raw materials inventory	24,330	
1330 Purchased parts inventory	123,980	
1376 Finished goods—snowblowers	34,112	
1385 Indirect materials	89,900	
1390 Repair parts inventory	160,487	
1320 Engines inventory		112,390
1371 Finished goods—Model 100 lawn mowers		22,112
1372 Finished goods—Model 200 lawn mowers		334,576
1373 Finished goods—Model 300 lawn mowers		98,531
1379 Finished goods—garden tillers		88,700

Client's entry to adjust perpetual inventory records to physical inventory taken as of 12/31/93.

EXHIBIT TL.7   Trim Lawn Manufacturing Corporation—Voucher Register, December 1993

Date	Voucher No.	Vendor	Accounts Payable— Credit	Raw Materials Debit	Engines Debit	Purchased Parts Debit	Indirect Materials Debit	Repair Parts Debit	Other Account No.	Other Debit	Other Credit
Dec. 1	10112	Eastway Small Engine Mfg.	$ 237,000		237,000						
Dec. 1	10113	Geotech Steel Supply	122,350	122,350							
Dec. 1	10114	Lonsway Manufacturing	90,551			67,888	22,663				
. . .											
Dec. 30	10226	Hubbel Engine Manufacturing	331,000		331,000						
Dec. 30	10227	Geotech Steel Supply	99,600	99,600							
Dec. 31	10228	Lonsway Manufacturing	126,754			53,210	35,898	37,646			
Dec. 31	10229	Jameel Advertising	23,466						8340	23,466	
Dec. 31	10330	Premium HMO, Inc.	12,333						9435	12,333	
Dec. 31	10331	Solo and Wiggins, CPAs	56,000						9450	56,000	
Dec. 31	10332	Westman and Associates	110,000						9451	110,000	
Dec. 31	10333	ABC Janitorial Supplies	3,477						9460	3,477	
Dec. 31	10334	Jon Manufacturing Supply	936,789			936,789					
Dec. 31	10335	Jones Small Engine Manufacturers	788,000		788,000						
			$7,987,565	800,678	3,015,400	1,322,458	253,211	257,900		2,337,916	

EXHIBIT TL.8 Trim Lawn Manufacturing Corporation— Sales Journal, December 1993

Date	Invoice No.	Customer	Accounts Receivable— Debit	Sales—Credit				
				Mower Model 100	Mower Model 200	Mower Model 300	Snow- blower	Garden Tiller
Dec. 1	20331	Jocal Hardware and Lawn Outlets	$ 85,000	6,675	31,244	5,790	32,554	8,737
Dec. 1	20332	J Mart Department Stores	236,790	22,356	98,754	35,897	44,678	35,105
Dec. 30	20896	New England Lawn and Garden Supply	124,670		12,344		77,890	34,436
Dec. 30	20897	Roe and Searbuck	675,889	77,690	266,321	112,342	156,877	62,659
Dec. 30	20898	Leemer Hardware	2,063		450		1,316	297
Dec. 31	20899	Jamby, Inc.	97,860	7,950	45,000	5,660	18,800	20,450
Dec. 31	20900	Ginny Lou Midwest Sales	436,985	31,800	135,000	28,300	131,600	110,285
Dec. 31	20901	Howell Stores	273,460	19,557	84,375	28,300	131,600	9,628
Dec. 31	20902	Scramble Gogmo Stores	166,800	7,950	27,675	16,980	75,200	38,995
Dec. 31	20903	Nationwide Hardware Stores	866,320	31,800	270,000	84,900	319,600	160,020
Total			$21,656,900	2,356,700	9,234,500	1,329,800	7,988,600	747,300

EXHIBIT TL.9 Trim Lawn Manufacturing Corporation— Cash Receipts Record, December 1993

Date	Received from	Cash— Debit	Sales Discounts— Debit	Accounts Receivable— Credit	Miscellaneous Account No.	Miscellaneous Debit	Miscellaneous Credit	Deposits
Dec. 1	Midwest Hardware Supply	$ 33,840	342	34,182				
Dec. 1	J Mart Department Stores	127,890	1,292	129,182				
Dec. 1	New England Lawn and Garden Supply	65,791	665	66,456				227,521
Dec. 29	Jocal Hardware and Lawn Outlets	47,655	481	48,136				
Dec. 29	Leemer Hardware	1,423	14	1,437				
Dec. 29	Jewel Enterprises	23,414	237	23,651				72,492
Dec. 30	Kaiser and Peabody Brokerage	246,800			4902		246,800	
Dec. 30	Crandall Stores	12,313	124	12,437				259,113
Dec. 31	Howell Appliance Outlet	8,900		8,900				
Dec. 31	Jackson Builders	2,312	23	2,335				
Dec. 31	J. Ravena	1,000,000			1203		1,000,000	
Dec. 31	Arley Supply	34,589	349	34,938				
Dec. 31	Garrold Outfitters	26,549	268	26,817				
Dec. 31	Jamby, Inc.	56,741	573	57,314				1,129,091
Total		$17,733,484	152654	15,988,652		63,546	1,961,032	17,733,484

**EXHIBIT TL.10 Trim Lawn Manufacturing Corporation—
Check Register, December 1993**

Date	Payee	Voucher No.	GemCorp Check No.	Union Trust Check No.	Accounts Payable—Debit	Purchases Discounts—Credit	GemCorp Credit	Union Trust Credit
Dec. 1	Hubbel Engine Manufacturing	9887		33556	$ 435,600	4,356		431,244
Dec. 1	Lonsway Manufacturing	9889		33557	118,900	1,189		117,711
Dec. 1	Premium HMO, Inc.	9896	210612		13,600		13,600	
. . . .	. . . .							
Dec. 30	Uncle John's Discount Hardware	10088		33708	346,790	3,468		343,322
Dec. 30	Jack and Lou Wholesale Supply	10075		33709	133,457	1,335		132,122
Dec. 30	Consolidated Utilities	10096	218996		655,890		655,890	
Dec. 31	General Bell Telephone Company	10097	218997		36,880		36,880	
Dec. 31	Eastway Small Engine Manufacturing	10112		33710	237,000	2,370		234,630
Dec. 31	Geotech Steel Supply	10113		33711	122,350	1,224		121,127
Dec. 31	Lonsway Manufacturing	10114		33712	90,551	906		89,645
Dec. 31	ABC Janitorial Supplies	10092	218998		4,260		4,260	
Dec. 31	Jolly Roger Paints	10083		33713	178,800	1,788		177,012
Dec. 31	Jackson Parts Manufacturing	10081		33714	211,300	2,113		209,187
Total					$14,566,000	132,662	1,780,000	12,653,338

Systems analysts and programmers provide extensive documentation of all programs and systems, as well as program changes. Complete instructions are provided for the computer operators who enter data as part of the various processing modules.

All program changes must be approved in writing by Jason Lupine, director of information systems and data processing, as well as by affected user departments. Current back-up programs and data files are maintained in a location outside data processing. The internal auditors have current copies of the programs and periodically test transaction processing on an unannounced basis, using these programs. The tests are performed while transactions are being processed, and the auditors' output is compared with the actual company output.

All computer output is distributed by the control group to authorized recipients. Any errors occurring during processing runs are logged into the console and are accessible only by the control group. The control group then monitors the reprocessing of the errors after satisfying themselves that the errors were unintentional. Data processing personnel have no access to the error log and must contact the control group inasmuch as processing cannot continue until the error is corrected.

An accounts receivable aging analysis is produced monthly by the computer. This analysis is used by Lawrence White, the credit manager, and John Dandura, chief accountant, for determining the monthly adjustment to the allowance for doubtful accounts. Mr. White also performs extensive follow-up of customers whose accounts are past due.

Control Procedures Outside the Accounting System

In addition to the accounting system, other policies and procedures support Trim Lawn's control structure:

1. Jennifer Lane, director of human resources, instituted a program for completely updating job descriptions after the data processing system was installed in 1988. This program is now finished and training programs have been developed for data processing, as well as for new and existing employees in other functional areas.

2. Inventories of materials, purchased parts, and finished goods are secured and inventory managers have been assigned responsibility for their safekeeping. The internal audit staff perform frequent test counts and comparisons with the perpetual records on an unannounced basis.

3. Directors and department heads are responsible for making hiring recommendations. The human resources division, however, screens and investigates all applicants for proper background and required education, training, and experience for the positions. In addition, final hiring and termination authority rests with the human relations director.

Requirement: Assuming Auditing With the Computer

1. Using your data disk and the Lotus 1-2-3 program, load the file titled "Analy1." Scroll through the file and locate the following workpapers:
   a. WP A.1 — Comparative income statements;

b. WP A.2 — Sales and cost of goods sold by product line;

c. WP A.3 — Comparative schedules of manufacturing overhead and operating expenses;

d. WP A.4 — Inventories.

2. After scrutinizing the workpapers, perform the following:

a. Using the "Comparative Income Statements" data in WP A–1, calculate the percent of each income statement component to sales for 1993. (Hint: Scroll to 1992 cells for guidance as to appropriate equations for 1993.)

b. Using the "Sales and Cost of Goods Sold — by Product Line" data in WP A.2, calculate the cost per unit as a percent of sales price for 1993 by product line. (As in [art (a)', refer to 1992 equations.)

c. Using the product line data from subitem (b) and the "Inventories" data from WP A.4, calculate finished goods inventory turnover for 1993 by product line. Calculate materials and purchased parts turnover for 1993 by component. (Again, refer to 1992 equasions.)

d. Print the results of your analytical procedures. (You may want to compress the print, use a wide carriage printer, or use the Sideways Printer program if it is available in your computer lab.)

3. Using your data disk and the system disk, load the file titled "Budget." Examine the worksheet carefully and locate the following schedules:

a. WP A.6 — Budgeted vs. actual income statements for 1993;

b. Schedule 1 — Cost of goods manufactured;

c. Schedule 2 — Operating expenses.

Compare with the results of requirement 2. Do any of the variances, when considered in relation to the results of requirement 2, raise warning signals? Print the budget. (Again, as in requirement 2, you will need to compress print size or otherwise accommodate a wide workpaper.)

4. Using your data disk and the system disk, load the file titled "Analy2" and locate the following in WP A.5:

a. Comparative percentage balance sheets for 1993 and 1992;

b. Comparative ratios:
1993 vs. 1992
Industry ratios for 1993

After reviewing the workpaper, perform the following:

a. Using the "Balance Sheets" data, calculate the percent of each asset component to total assets for 1993, and calculate the percent of each liability and stockholders' equity component to total liabilities and stockholders' equity for 1993. (Note: This has been done for 1992 and, as in requirement 2, you should refer to the 1992 equations for guidance.)

b. Using the "Balance Sheets" and "Comparative Income Statements" data, calculate the following ratios for 1993:

1. current ratio;

2. quick ratio;

3. times interest earned; and

4. return on stockholders' equity.

(*Note:* The 1992 calculations have already been done for you)

    c. Compare pertinent ratios with industry averages. (These are located next to the 1992 Trim Lawn ratios.) Are there any significant disparities between Trim Lawn's ratios and the industry averages?

    d. Print the results of your analytical procedures.

5. What is the purpose of performing analytical procedures during the planning phase of the audit? What is the purpose for including budgets and performance reports in the application of analytical procedures? Based on your analytical procedures performed in items 2, 3, and 4, what, if any, concerns do you have? Relate your concerns to management's assertions contained in the financial statements (i.e., existence or occurrence, completeness, rights and obligations, valuation, and presentation and disclosure). Can you suggest some specific audit procedures to allay your concerns?

6. Given the description of the company, the industry, the control environment, accounting system, and control procedures, identify strengths and weaknesses in the control structure. Relate the strengths and weaknesses to management's assertions contained in the financial statements.

7. Based on analytical procedures and study of the business and industry, in what specific transaction areas are you willing to reduce inherent risk below 100 percent? In deciding whether or not to reduce inherent risk, consider audit complexity and the probability of management misrepresentation.

8. Based on your review of the accounting system and existing control procedures, in what specific transaction areas are you willing to assess control risk below the maximum level? For purposes of this requirement, consider the probability of material financial statement errors caused by control weaknesses.

9. Assuming Mary Sondem has established materiality criteria of 3 percent of net income and 1/2 percent of net assets, calculate the individual item materiality thresholds for audit adjustments and reclassifications respectively. How did Sondem arrive at the above percents? Will auditor suspicion of earnings inflation affect the materiality thresholds? In what way? Assuming Sondem wishes to tentatively draft potential adjustments of 10 percent of individual item materiality or greater for later consideration, calculate the aggregate materiality threshold. What factors did Sondem consider in arriving at the 10 percent figure? How does internal control structure affect aggregate materiality thresholds?

Requirement: Assuming Auditing Without the Computer

Turn to the Module I workpaper "Analytical Procedures—Audit Planning" in your Trim Lawn Workbook and scan the following workpapers:

    a. WP A.1 — Comparative income statements;

    b. WP A.2 — Sales and cost of goods sold by product line;

    c. WP A.3 — Comparative schedules of manufacturing overhead and operating expenses;

    d. WP A.4 — Inventories.

1. After scrutinizing the workpapers, perform the following:

    a. Using the "Comparative Income Statements" data in WP A–1, calculate the percent of each income statement component to sales for 1993.

b. Using the "Sales and Cost of Goods Sold—by Product Line" data in WP A.2, calculate the cost per unit as a percent of sales price for 1993 by product line.

c. Using the product line data from subitem (b) and the "Inventories" data from WP A.4, calculate finished goods inventory turnover for 1993 by product line. Calculate materials and purchased parts turnover for 1993 by component.

2. Turn to the "Budgeted vs. Actual Income Statements" (WPA.6). Examine the worksheet carefully and locate the following schedules:

   a. WP A.6—Budgeted vs. actual income statements for 1993;
   b. Schedule 1—Cost of goods manufactured;
   c. Schedule 2—Operating expenses.

   Compare with the results of requirement 2. Do any of the variances, when considered in relation to the results of requirement 2, raise warning signals?

3. Using the "Balance Sheets" data, calculate the percent of each asset component to total assets for 1993, and calculate the percent of each liability and stockholders' equity component to total liabilities and stockholders' equity for 1993.

4. Using the "Balance Sheets" and "Comparative Income Statements" data, calculate the following ratios for 1993:

   1. current ratio;
   2. quick ratio;
   3. times interest earned; and
   4. return on stockholders' equity.

   (*Note:* The 1992 calculations have already been done for you.)

   Compare pertinent ratios with industry averages. (These are located next to the 1992 Trim Lawn ratios.) Are there any significant disparities between Trim Lawn's ratios and the industry averages?

5. What is the purpose of performing analytical procedures during the planning phase of the audit? What is the purpose for including budgets and performance reports in the application of analytical procedures? Based on your analytical procedures performed in items 2, 3, and 4, what, if any, concerns do you have? Can you suggest some specific audit procedures to allay your concerns?

6. Given the description of the company, the industry, the control environment, accounting system, and control procedures, identify strengths and weaknesses in the control structure. Relate the strengths and weaknesses to management's assertions contained in the financial statements (i.e., existence or occurrence, completeness, rights and obligations, valuation, and presentation and disclosure).

7. Based on analytical procedures and study of the business and industry, in what specific transaction areas are you willing to reduce inherent risk below 100 percent? In deciding whether or not to reduce inherent risk, consider audit complexity and the probability of management misrepresentation.

8. Based on your review of the accounting system and existing control procedures, in what specific transaction areas are you willing to assess control risk below the maximum level? For purposes of this requirement, consider the probability of material financial statement errors caused by control weaknesses.

9. Assuming Mary Sondem has established materiality criteria of 3 percent of net income and 1/2 percent of net assets, calculate the individual item materiality thresholds for audit adjustments and reclassifications respectively. How did Sondem arrive at the above percents? Will auditor suspicion of earnings inflation affect the materiality thresholds? In what way? Assuming Sondem wishes to tentatively draft potential adjustments of 10 percent of individual item materiality or greater for later consideration, calculate the aggregate materiality threshold. What factors did Sondem consider in arriving at the 10 percent figure? How does internal control structure affect aggregate materiality thresholds?

MODULE II: TIME BUDGET FOR THE 1993 AUDIT

A time budget is a planning device by which the auditor estimates the time required to complete the various audit phases and the number and level of staff persons required for each phase. When used in conjunction with the recording of actual time consumed for comparative purposes, the time budget serves as an effective means for controlling the resources consumed in an audit. In this module, you will be asked to work with Solo and Wiggins' time budget for the Trim Lawn audit.

Requirement: Assuming Auditing With the Computer

1. Using your data disk and the system disk, retrieve the file titled "Time." Examine the 1992 time budget, noting particularly the relationship between budgeted and actual times consumed in the various phases of the audit.

2. Can you identify areas, based on the 1992 variances, which may need to be budgeted differently for 1993?

3. Can you identify areas, based on Module I, that may need to be budgeted differently in 1993?

4. Copy the 1992 time budget to a blank space on the worksheet, and perform the following procedures:
   a. Erase the actual times;
   b. Revise the 1992 budgeted times to reflect your best estimate of 1993 time requirements;
   c. At the bottom of your worksheet, justify the changes you have made relative to the 1992 time budget;
   d. Retitle the time budget as the 1993 budget, and print it.

Requirement: Assuming Auditing Without the Computer

1. Turn to Module II, "Time Budget" in your workbook, and examine the 1992 time budget. Note particularly the relationship between budgeted and actual times consumed in the various phases of last year's audit.

2. Based on the 1992 variances, can you identify areas that may need to be budgeted differently for 1993?

3. Can you identify areas, based on Module I, that may need to be budgeted differently in 1993?

4. Prepare a 1993 time budget to reflect your best estimate of 1993 audit time requirements. Justify the changes you have made relative to the 1992 time budget.

MODULE III: CONTROL TESTING—SALES PROCESSING

In this module you will be asked to apply attribute sampling to Trim Lawn's prenumbered sales orders to evaluate whether sales orders have been processed properly. Your sampling objective is to determine that sales have been properly documented and approved prior to shipment. As discussed previously in the case, prenumbered sales orders are prepared in the product managers' division. The sales orders are based on customer orders from the regional sales offices, together with evidence of proper credit approval. Mary Sondem has asked you to complete the sampling plan worksheet that she began earlier. Sondem has defined the sampling unit as the prenumbered sales order and the relevant attributes as:

1. Customer order attached;

2. Evidence of credit approval on face of customer order;

3. Sales order signed by product manager(s); and

4. Shipping order and bill of lading included in the document packet, and bill of lading signed by the carrier.

The population, for attribute sampling purposes, is the numeric file of sales orders. During 1993, 12,200 sales orders were processed, with document numbers ranging from 8704–20903. For each sales order drawn at random and included in the sample, you will request the client to supply the corresponding sales order, sales invoice, customer order, shipping order, and bill of lading packet from the alphabetic file maintained in accounting. You will then examine the packets for these attributes. Assume that you have already satisfied yourself as to proper pricing, extensions, and footings appearing on customer invoices by developing simulated transactions and tracing them through the EDP sales processing system.

Requirement: Assuming Auditing With the Computer

1. Using your system and data diskettes, retrieve the file titled "Attrib." Using the sample size and sample evaluation tables in Chapter 10 and the following data, complete the attribute sampling plan Worksheet (round sample sizes up to the nearest 100 items):
   a. A 5 percent risk of underassessment has been decided upon for all attributes;
   b. Errors have been defined, and expected error rates set for each attribute as follows:
      1. Customer order not attached to packet— 1 percent
      2. Credit approval lacking— 1 percent
      3. Sales order not approved by product manager— 2 percent
      4. Shipping order and bill of lading not attached or bill of lading not signed by carrier— 1 percent
   c. Tolerable occurrence limits of 5 percent have been set for all attributes;
   d. The following errors were discovered in examining the sample:

Sales Order Number	Error
9642	Bill of lading not signed by carrier
12803	Credit approval missing from customer order
16112	Product manager approval missing from sales order
18466	Customer order missing
19770	Bill of lading missing

2. Print your completed workpaper. (As before, you will need to compress print size or otherwise accommodate a wide workpaper.)

3. What is the purpose of further control testing, as performed in the above exercise? What conclusions can you draw based on your completed sampling plan worksheet? What impact might your findings have on the substantive audit programs for Trim Lawn? Based on the results of your testing, should the aggregate materiality threshold be changed for any part of the revenue cycle? Be as specific as you can in answering this question.

Requirement: Assuming Auditing Without the Computer

Turn to the Module III workpaper, "Attribute Sampling Plan Worksheet" in your workbook, and complete the following requirements:

1. Using the sample size and sample evaluation tables in Chapter 10 and the following data, complete the attribute sampling plan worksheet:
   a. A 5 percent risk of underassessment has been decided upon for all attributes;
   b. Errors have been defined, and expected error rates set for each attribute as follows:
      1. Customer order not attached to packet—1 percent
      2. Credit approval lacking—1 percent
      3. Sales order not approved by product manager—2 percent
      4. Shipping order and bill of lading not attached or not signed by carrier—1 percent
   c. Tolerable occurrence limits of 5 percent have been set for all attributes;
   d. The following errors were discovered in examining the sample:

Sales Order Number	Error
9642	Bill of lading not signed by carrier
12803	Credit approval missing from customer order
16112	Product manager approval missing from sales order
18466	Customer order missing
19770	Bill of lading missing

2. What is the purpose of further control testing, as performed in the above exercise? What conclusions can you draw based on your completed sampling plan worksheet? What impact might your findings have on the substantive audit programs for Trim Lawn? Based on the results of your testing, should the aggregate materiality threshold be changed for any part of the revenue cycle? Be as specific as you can in answering this question.

MODULE IV: PPS SAMPLING—FACTORY EQUIPMENT ADDITIONS

Mary Sondem suspects that certain expenditures for repair parts, manufacturing supplies, and repairs and maintenance expense have been erroneously debited to the factory equipment account. Her suspicions are based on the results of past audits. The same vendor's invoice frequently contains charges for parts and supplies as well as equipment, and the Trim Lawn employees preparing the recording forms often fail to distinguish among the charges and simply indicate "factory equipment" as the debit.

Mary decides to use PPS sampling in determining the extent to which such errors have occurred during 1993. She has asked you to develop and implement a sampling plan for this purpose.

Requirement: Assuming Auditing With the Computer

1. What is the sampling objective for purposes of this exercise? What is the sampling unit?

2. Using your system and data diskettes, retrieve the file labeled "PPS." Locate the following workpapers in the file:
   a. WP11.3A—Probability proportional to size sampling plan;
   b. WP11.3B—Probability proportional to size sampling plan-projected error;
   c. WP11.3C—Probability proportional to size sampling plan-computed precision and upper error limit.

Scroll to WP 11.3A, "Probability Proportional to Size Sampling Plan." Calculate sample size and sampling interval assuming Mary has set the following parameters:
   a. Risk of incorrect acceptance   5%
   b. Anticipated error $50,000
   c. Tolerable error $300,000

3. What factors did she consider in setting these parameters? Print the workpaper.

4. Scroll to WP 11.3B, "Probability Proportional to Size Sampling Plan—Projected Error." This workpaper summarizes all invoices containing posting errors and calculates the projected error. Note the equations which have been incorporated into the workpaper template.
   a. Change the book value of the Delma Stamping debit from $366,500 to $456,300. Note how the template recalculates the sample results, including the upper error limit.
   b. Now change the book value of the Delma Stamping debit back to $366,500.
   c. What factor determines whether a "tainting percent" appears in Column 4?
   d. Print the workpaper. (Compress print size or otherwise accommodate a wide workpaper.)

5. Scroll to WP 11.3C, "Probability Proportional to Size Sampling Plan—Computed Precision and Upper Error Limit." Complete the "Incremental Allowance for Sampling Risk" schedule by ranking the projected errors as appropriate. (Hint: If you forgot how to do this, refer to Chapter 11 and the PPS application presented at the end of the chapter. Also, refer to Exhibit 11.4, which is a completed schedule calculating the incremental allowance.)

6. Print the workpaper.

7. Explain the meaning of the following amounts:
   a. Basic precision;
   b. Incremental allowance for sampling risk;
   c. Allowance for sampling risk; and
   d. Upper error limit.

8. Evaluate the sampling results. Do they support Sondem's sampling objectives? Note the audit adjustment based on errors discovered while examining the sample. Is this adjustment adequate to bring the population into acceptable bounds? If not, what alternate actions might you choose to pursue, based on the sampling results?

Requirement: Assuming Auditing Without the Computer

1. What is the sampling objective for purposes of this exercise? What is the sampling unit?

2. Turn to Module IV "PPS Sampling—Factory Equipment Additions" in your workbook. Using the partially completed workpaper, WP 11.3A, "Probability Proportional to Size Sampling Plan," calculate sample size and the sampling interval.

3. What factors did Sondem consider in setting these parameters?

4. Turn to WP 11.3B, "Probability Proportional to Size Sampling Plan—Projected Error." This workpaper summarizes all invoices containing posting errors and calculates the projected error. Complete the workpaper according to the instructions at the top of each column. (Hint: If you have forgotten how to do this, refer to Chapter 11 and the PPS application presented at the end of the chapter. Also, refer to Exhibit 11.3 which is a completed schedule computing the projected error.) What factor determines whether a "tainting percent" appears in Column 4?

5. Turn to WP 11.3C, "Probability Proportional to Size Sampling Plan—Computed Precision and Upper Error Limit." Complete the "Incremental Allowance for Sampling Risk" schedule by ranking the projected errors as appropriate. (Hint: If you forgot how to do this, refer to Chapter 11 and the PPS application presented at the end of the chapter. Also, refer to Exhibit 11.4, which is a completed schedule calculating the incremental allowance.)

6. Explain the meaning of the following amounts:
   a. Basic precision;
   b. Incremental allowance for sampling risk;
   c. Allowance for sampling risk; and
   d. Upper error limit.

7. Evaluate the sampling results. Do they support Sondem's sampling objectives? Note the audit adjustment based on errors discovered while examining the sample. Is this adjustment adequate to bring the population into acceptable bounds? If not, what alternate actions might you choose to pursue, based on the sampling results?

MODULE V: UNION TRUST BANK RECONCILIATION

Trim Lawn maintains two general demand deposit accounts and a payroll account. One of the general demand deposit accounts, as well as the payroll account, are with Union Trust, a local bank. The second demand deposit account is with GemCorp, the Chicago bank from whom Trim Lawn obtained the $25 million loan referred to previously. As part of the cash audit, Sondem has asked you to reconcile all three of the bank accounts for December, 1993 and do an analysis of interbank transfers between Union Trust and Gemcorp. Recall that Trim Lawn has reconciled all bank accounts for each of the 12 months. You will begin, therefore, with the company's December, 1993 reconciliations.

Requirement: Assuming Auditing With the Computer

1. Load your system and data diskettes and retrieve the file labeled "Bank." Briefly examine the following workpapers in this file:
   a. WP 1 — Cash on hand and in banks;
   b. WP1.B — Bank reconciliation–Union Trust;
   c. WP1.C — Interbank transfer schedule.

Scroll to WP 1.B, "Bank Reconciliation, Union Trust." Does the Union Trust account reconcile for December? What are the possible causes for nonreconciliation?

2. In tracing cash disbursements from the December check register to the bank statement, you learn that check number 33551, in the amount of $117,600, was incorrectly recorded as $115,600. Incorporate this error into the appropriate section of the bank reconciliation. Does the account reconcile after making this correction? Assuming check 33551 was in payment of real estate taxes for the first half of 1993, draft the necessary audit adjustment at the bottom of your workpaper.

3. Print the bank reconciliation workpaper.

4. Scroll to WP 1 and record the audit adjustment in the "audit adjustments" column of the lead schedule.

5. The deposit in transit, as well as all checks outstanding at December 31, cleared with the bank cutoff statement. What specific audit objectives are supported by obtaining a cutoff statement directly from the bank? If the cutoff bank statement covered the period 1/1/94 through 1/21/94 and the deposit in transit was credited 1/12/94, would you be concerned? If so, why? What additional procedures would you apply to allay your concerns? Assume, for purposes of completing this and the following modules, that the deposit cleared 1/2/94.

Requirement: Assuming Auditing Without the Computer

1. Turn to your workbook section entitled "Modules V and VI— Cash on Hand and in Banks." Examine workpaper WP 1.B, "Bank Reconciliation, Union Trust." Does the Union Trust account reconcile for December? What are the possible causes for nonreconciliation?

2. In tracing cash disbursements from the December check register to the bank statement, you learn that check number 33551, in the amount of $117,600, was incorrectly recorded as $115,600. Incorporate this error into the appropriate section of the bank reconciliation. Does the account reconcile after making this correction? Assuming check 33551 was in payment of real estate taxes for the first half of 1993, draft the necessary audit adjustment at the bottom of your workpaper.

3. Turn to WP 1 and record the audit adjustment in the "audit adjustments" column of the lead schedule.

4. The deposit in transit, as well as all checks outstanding at December 31, cleared with the bank cutoff statement. What specific audit objectives are supported by obtaining a cutoff statement directly from the bank? Assuming the cutoff bank statement covered the period 1/1/94 through 1/21/94, and the deposit in transit was credited 1/12/94, would you be concerned? If so, why? What additional procedures would you apply to allay your concerns? Assume, for purposes of completing this and the following modules, that the deposit cleared 1/2/94.

MODULE VI: ANALYSIS OF INTERBANK TRANSFERS

Requirement: Assuming Auditing With the Computer

1. Load your system and data diskettes and once again retrieve the file labeled "Bank." Scroll to WP 1.C, "Interbank Transfer Schedule." This workpaper was prepared by John Julius, a member of the Solo and Wiggins audit team. As part of your audit training, Mary Sondem asks that you examine and review the workpaper and determine the need for possible audit adjustments and reclassifications. What is the purpose for analyzing interbank transfers for a short period before and after the balance sheet date? Identify possible audit adjustments and reclassifications by examining WP 1.C. Assume that GemCorp check 221344 is dated December 31, 1993 and was credited by Union Trust on December 31, 1993. As noted previously, Mr. Ravena had borrowed $1 million from Trim Lawn in April and planned to repay the loan before December 31. Did he really repay the loan in December? Do you think the check drawn on GemCorp was reflected as an outstanding check in the 12/31/93 GemCorp reconciliation? Do you think the check was recorded as a December disbursement? If not, why not? (Hint: Remember, the loan agreement with GemCorp requires a $6 million compensating balance at all times.)

2. Draft "Audit Reclassification A" at the bottom of WP 1.C.

3. Print the interbank transfer workpaper. (You will need to compress print size or otherwise accommodate a wide workpaper.)

4. Scroll to WP 1. Record Reclassification A from item 2 in the reclassification column of the lead schedule. Does the reclassification place Trim Lawn in

default on the loan agreement? If so, what further audit procedures might you elect to apply at this time?

5. Print the lead schedule.

Requirement: Assuming Auditing Without the Computer

1. Turn to WP 1.C, "Interbank Transfer Schedule" in workbook section "Modules V and VI—Cash on Hand and in Banks." This workpaper was prepared by John Julius, a member of the Solo and Wiggins, audit team. As part of your audit training, Mary Sondem asks that you examine and review the workpaper and determine the need for possible audit adjustments and reclassifications. What is the purpose for analyzing interbank transfers for a short period before and after the balance sheet date? Identify possible audit adjustments and reclassifications by examining WP 1.C. Assume that GemCorp check 221344 is dated December 31, 1993 and was credited by Union Trust on December 31, 1993. As noted previously, Mr. Ravena had borrowed $1 million from Trim Lawn in April and planned to repay the loan before December 31. Did he really repay the loan in December? Do you think the check drawn on GemCorp was reflected as an outstanding check in the 12/31/93 GemCorp reconciliation? Do you think the check was recorded as a December disbursement? If not, why not? (Hint: Remember, the loan agreement with GemCorp requires a $6 million compensating balance at all times.)

2. Draft "Audit Reclassification A" at the bottom of WP 1.C.

3. Turn to WP 1. Record Reclassification A from item 2 in the reclassification column of the lead schedule. Does the reclassification place Trim Lawn in default on the loan agreement? If so, what further audit procedures might you elect to apply at this time?

MODULE VII: ACCOUNTS RECEIVABLE AGING ANALYSIS

Mary Sondem has asked you to review the accounts receivable aging analysis and the allowance for doubtful accounts and recommend any audit adjustments or reclassifications you consider necessary. Harvey Jensen had prepared the aging analysis and the allowance for doubtful accounts workpaper before being temporarily transferred to the Orrin Hills audit. He should be back early next week; but Sondem would like to "wrap up" accounts receivable this week.

Based on the aging analysis prepared by Jensen, you decided to confirm all large accounts and a sampling of the smaller accounts, using positive confirmations.

Requirement: Assuming Auditing With the Computer

1. Load your system and data diskettes and retrieve the file labeled "AR." Locate the following workpapers in this file:
   a. WP3 —Accounts and notes receivable–trade;
   b. WP3.A—Accounts receivable aging analysis;
   c. WP3.C—Allowance for uncollectible accounts.

Scroll to WP 3.A, "Accounts Receivable Aging Analysis."

  a. What proportion of total dollar amount of accounts receivable have you included in your confirmation requests?

  b. What procedures should you apply in the event of no reply to requests for positive confirmation?

  c. What is the purpose for analyzing subsequent collections?

  d. Change the percentages of estimated uncollectible as follows:

> Current: 1/2 percent
> 1–30 days past due   5 percent

Note the effect on "estimated uncollectible—dollars"

Now change the percentages back to 1 and 10 percent respectively.

  e. Draft the suggested Reclassification Entry B

2. Scroll to WP 3.C, "Allowance for Uncollectible Accounts."

  a. What type of correspondence would you examine to satisfy yourself as to the accounts receivable write-offs?

  b. Draft the suggested Audit Adjustment 3. Are you satisfied that the balance in the allowance is adequate after your recommended adjustment?

  c. Scroll to WP 3, "Accounts and Notes Receivable—Trade" (lead schedule). Post Reclassification Entry B and Audit Adjustment 3 to the appropriate locations in the lead schedule.

3. Print workpapers 3, 3.A, and 3.C. (For workpaper 3.A, you will need to accommodate a wide workpaper.)

Requirement: Assuming Auditing Without the Computer

1. Turn to Module VII in your workbook and workpaper "WP 3.A, Accounts Receivable Aging Analysis."

  a. What proportion of total dollar amount of accounts receivable have you included in your confirmation requests?

  b. What procedures should you apply in the event of no reply to requests for positive confirmation?

  c. What is the purpose for analyzing subsequent collections?

  d. Draft the suggested Reclassification Entry B.

2. Turn to WP 3.C, "Allowance for Uncollectible Accounts."

  a. What type of correspondence would you examine to satisfy yourself as to the accounts receivable write-offs?

  b. Draft the suggested Audit Adjustment 3. Are you satisfied that the balance in the allowance is adequate after your recommended adjustment?

  c. Turn to WP 3, "Accounts and Notes Receivable—Trade" (lead schedule). Post Reclassification Entry B and Audit Adjustment 3 to the appropriate locations in the lead schedule.

MODULE VIII: SALES AND PURCHASES CUTOFF TESTS

You, along with Mary Sondem and the rest of the audit team, observed Trim Lawn's December 31, 1993 physical inventory. Sondem is satisfied with the inventory taking procedures and has considerable confidence in the reliability of the ending inventory quantities and valuation. She is concerned, however, with possible errors relating to sales and purchases cutoff. To allay these concerns, she has asked you to examine the appropriate books of original entry and underlying documentation for a few days before and after the balance sheet date. Specifically, you are interested in the following:

1. Were purchases and sales recorded in the proper accounting period?

2. Were purchases recorded at year end included in the physical inventory?

3. Were all materials, purchased parts, and engines included in inventory recorded as purchase?

4. Were the finished goods inventory accounts properly relieved for all recorded sales?

Using your microcomputer, you were able to "download" Trim Lawn's December voucher register and sales journal. These are partially reproduced in Exhibits TL.7 and TL.8 referred to in Module I. Using these as a focal point, you requested the client to provide you with the documentation supporting certain of the recorded transactions. You are now prepared to record any necessary audit adjustments and reclassifications.

Requirement: Assuming Auditing With the Computer

1. Load your system and data diskettes and retrieve the file labeled "Cutoff." Study WP 6.4, "Inventory Cutoff," and compare with the voucher register and sales journal portions reproduced in Exhibits TL.7 and TL.8. Comment on any cutoff errors that you detect and determine their effect on net income. Do the errors appear to be intentional or unintentional? Explain.

2. Draft any audit adjustments suggested by the analysis performed in 1 above. (Remember Trim Lawn maintains perpetual inventory records and adjusts its perpetual inventory to the physical inventory through the appropriate "Cost of Goods Sold" accounts.)

3. Print the completed workpaper with the proposed cutoff audit adjustments.

Requirement: Assuming Auditing Without the Computer

1. Turn to Module VIII in your workbook. Study WP 6.4, "Inventory Cutoff," and compare with the voucher register and sales journal portions reproduced in Exhibits TL.7 and TL.8. Comment on any cutoff errors that you detect and determine their effect on net income. Do the errors appear to be intentional or unintentional? Explain.

2. Draft any audit adjustments suggested by the analysis performed in 1 above. (Remember Trim Lawn maintains perpetual inventory records and adjusts its perpetual inventory to the physical inventory through the appropriate "Cost of Goods Sold" accounts.)

MODULE IX: SEARCH FOR UNRECORDED LIABILITIES

An important part of every audit is examining vendors' invoices processed after year end. Related to cutoff, as discussed in Module VIII, the purpose of this set of procedures is to determine that no significant invoices pertaining to the year being audited have been omitted from recorded liabilities. Sondem has asked that you examine the workpaper prepared by Harvey Jensen, entitled "Search for Unrecorded Liabilities," and review it for necessary adjustments.

Requirement: Assuming Auditing With the Computer

1. Load your system and data diskettes and retrieve the file labeled "Liab." Comment on the adequacy of the procedures performed by Jensen.
2. Draft Audit Adjustment 7 at the bottom of WP 15.1.
3. Print the workpaper.

Requirement: Assuming Auditing Without the Computer

1. Turn to Module IX in your workbook and examine WP 15.1, "Search for Unrecorded Liabilities." Comment on the adequacy of the procedures performed by Jensen.
2. Draft Audit Adjustment 7 at the bottom of WP 15.1.

MODULE X: ESTIMATED LIABILITY FOR PRODUCT WARRANTY

All Trim Lawn products are sold under a one-year warranty covering all parts and labor. Repairs are performed locally, either by the dealer who sold the product or by local entities licensed as official Trim Lawn repair shops. Trim Lawn reimburses the dealers and shops for labor and parts. Reimbursement is based on work orders submitted by the repairing agency. The work orders are signed by the customer, and the serial number of the product repaired or replaced also appears on the work order. Defective parts or products replaced must be returned with the accompanying work order. The parts and products are received and logged in on color-coded receiving reports designed for returns.

At the end of each month, the following standard journal entry is posted as an adjustment to estimated product warranty.

8330	Product Warranty Expense	
2070		Estimated Product Warranty Liability

For 1993, the company applied 0.5 percent to cost of goods sold in determining the amount of the monthly adjustment. Debits to account 2070 are for reimbursements and for product and parts replacements. Defective parts and products are "zero valued" and placed in the rework department. Sondem has asked you to analyze product warranty and determine the appropriate balance in the liability account. She has already provided you with a partially completed workpaper and a client-prepared analysis of returns over the past four years. You have completed the workpaper and are now ready to evaluate the adequacy of the balance.

Requirement: Assuming Auditing With the Computer

1. Load your system and data diskettes and retrieve the file labeled "Warranty." Examine the workpaper carefully and comment on its adequacy and completeness. (Note that the 12/31/93 audited balances appear to be unreasonable because you have not yet selected an appropriate provision percentage based on the "data from client-prepared analysis of warranty claims.")

2. What comprises the documentation examined by the auditor (audit legend E) supporting the debits to Account 2070?

3. How would you audit the client-prepared analysis of warranty claims? (See "Year of Claim/Year of Sale" analysis in middle of WP 20.)

4. Enter equations in cells C44, D44, and E44 that will calculate the percentage of warranty claims to cost of goods sold for each of the three years 1990–1992.

5. Note the percentage that now appears in cell B46 and the resulting adjustment to product warranty expense.

6. Draft AJE No. 8 on the workpaper.

7. Print the workpaper.

8. John Julius, the other assistant auditor on the engagement, asks why you didn't adjust the prior years' overprovision through beginning retained earnings. What is your response?

Requirement: Assuming Auditing Without the Computer

1. Turn to the Module X workpaper in your workbook and examine WP 20, "Estimated Liability for Product Warranty." Comment on its adequacy and completeness.

2. What comprises the documentation examined by the auditor (audit legend E) supporting the debits to Account 2070?

3. How would you audit the client-prepared analysis of warranty claims? (See "Year of Claim/Year of Sale" analysis in middle of WP 20.)

4. In the "Warranty claims as a percent of cost of goods sold" 1993 column, enter what you consider to be an appropriate warranty provision percentage. Justify your selected percentage.

5. Draft AJE No. 8 on the workpaper.

6. John Julius, the other assistant auditor on the engagement, asks why you didn't adjust the prior years' overprovison through beginning retained earnings. What is your response?

MODULE XI: PLANT ASSET ADDITIONS AND DISPOSALS

In Module IV, you applied PPS sampling procedures in evaluating the reasonableness of the balance in the "Factory Equipment" account. In Module XI, you will analyze the changes in "Office Fixtures and Equipment" and complete the "Plant Assets" lead schedule. Inasmuch as the additions and disposals pertaining to office fixtures and equipment are few in number, you decide to audit them in full, rather than apply sampling procedures.

Requirement: Assuming Auditing With the Computer

1. Load your system and data diskettes and retrieve the file labeled ''Plant.'' Locate the following workpapers in this file:
   a. WP11—Plant assets and accumulated depreciation—lead schedule;
   b. WP11.5—Office furniture and equipment—additions and disposals.

Scroll to WP 11.5, ''Office Fixtures and Equipment—Additions and Disposals.'' What is the nature of the ''underlying documentation'' referred to in the explanation of audit legend E?

2. In recording the April, 1993 disposal, Janel James, Trim Lawn's plant assets accountant, miscalculated the accumulated depreciation on the assets sold and thereby overstated the loss on disposal by $10,000. Draft audit adjustment 9 at the bottom of WP 11.5 to correct for this error. In addition, James did not change the standard journal entry for monthly depreciation to reflect additions and disposals during the year. As a result, depreciation expense for the year is understated. Trim Lawn depreciates office fixtures and equipment on a straight-line basis over a five-year estimated useful life with zero salvage value. One-half year's depreciation is taken on all additions and disposals. Draft Audit Adjustment 10 at the bottom of WP 11.5 to reflect the depreciation understatement. *Note:* Don't forget to enter audit adjustments 9 and 10 in body of workpaper to arrive at correct adjusted balances.

2. Scroll to WP 11, ''Plant Assets and Accumulated Depreciation—Lead Schedule.'' Post Audit Adjustments 9 and 10 to the lead schedule.

3. Print workpapers 11 and 11.5.

Requirement: Assuming Auditing Without the Computer

1. Turn to Module XI—Plant Asset Additions and Disposals in your workbook and examine WP 11.5. What is the nature of the ''underlying documentation'' referred to in the explanation of audit legend E?

2. In recording the April, 1993 disposal, Janel James, Trim Lawn's plant assets accountant, miscalculated the accumulated depreciation on the assets sold and thereby overstated the loss on disposal by $10,000. Draft audit adjustment 9 at the bottom of WP 11.5 to correct for this error. In addition, James did not change the standard journal entry for monthly depreciation to reflect additions and disposals during the year. As a result, depreciation expense for the year is understated. Trim Lawn depreciates office fixtures and equipment on a straight-line basis over a five-year estimated useful life with zero salvage value. One-half year's depreciation is taken on all additions and disposals. Draft Audit Adjustment 10 at the bottom of WP 11.5 to reflect the depreciation understatement.

   Note: Don't forget to enter audit adjustments 9 and 10 in body of workpaper to arrive at correct adjusted balances.

3. Turn to WP 11, ''Plant Assets and Accumulated Depreciation—Lead Schedule.'' Post Audit Adjustments 9 and 10 to the lead schedule.

MODULE XII: ANALYSIS OF MARKETABLE SECURITIES

The addition of snowblowers to the product line in 1973 helped considerably in increasing Trim Lawn's late summer and early fall revenues. Business remains somewhat seasonal, however, producing large amounts of idle funds to be invested temporarily after the spring and summer lawn mower sales season has ended. Larry McKee, the Trim Lawn treasurer, usually invests in marketable securities in mid-September and holds them until late January. They are sold in February, March, April, and May to finance spring inventories of mowers and garden tillers. Mr. McKee's goals in acquiring short-term investments are to maximize return while minimizing risk of loss from wide temporary price fluctuations. For this reason, the portfolio is limited to debt securities rated AA and above and common stocks of "blue chip" companies.

As of December 31, 1993, the portfolio consisted of the following holdings:

Security	Cost	Market Value
Jolson, Inc. common stock	$448,000	$450,000
Watershoals, Inc. common stock	502,500	496,700
Holly Mines common stock	517,000	493,000
General Department Stores common stock	527,000	532,900
Pedio Corporation 10% debenture bonds	156,000	162,600
National Paper 8% convertible bonds	529,500	472,600
Trimotors 11% debenture bonds	320,000	332,000

Requirement: Assuming Auditing With the Computer

1. Load your system and data diskettes and retrieve the file labeled "Securiti." What determines whether marketable securities are to be classified as current or noncurrent on the balance sheet?

2. What are the objectives in the audit of marketable securities? Examine the audit legends at the bottom of workpaper 2. Have the objectives been satisfied?

3. Enter the cost and market data for each security held at December 31, 1993.

4. Add an audit legend (and explain it at the bottom of the worksheet) regarding how market was determined.

5. Draft Audit Adjustment 11 at the bottom of WP 2 to recognize the loss on decline of market below cost. For this adjustment, use account 9702, Loss on Decline of Market Value of Securities and 1102, Allowance for Decline of Market Value of Securities.

6. Print your workpaper. (You will need to compress print size or otherwise accommodate a wide workpaper.)

Requirement: Assuming Auditing Without the Computer

1. Turn to Module XII in your workbook and examine WP 2, "Investments in Marketable Securities." What determines whether marketable securities are to be classified as current or noncurrent on the balance sheet?

2. What are the objectives in the audit of marketable securities? Examine the audit legends at the bottom of workpaper 2. Have the objectives been satisfied?

3. Enter the cost and market data for each security held at December 31, 1993.

4. Add an audit legend (and explain it at the bottom of the worksheet) regarding how market was determined.

5. Draft Audit Adjustment 11 at the bottom of WP 2 to recognize the loss on decline of market below cost. For this adjustment, use account 9702, Loss on Decline of Market Value of Securities and 1102, Allowance for Decline of Market Value of Securities.

MODULE XIII: MORTGAGE NOTE PAYABLE AND NOTE PAYABLE TO GEMCORP

In addition to a deferred tax liability relating to temporary book and tax depreciation differences, Trim Lawn's long-term liabilities consist of the following:

1. 10 percent mortgage note payable to Union Trust—$40 million; and

2. 12 percent note payable to GemCorp Bank and Trust—$25 million.

In 1990, Trim Lawn upgraded its manufacturing facilities at a cost of $120 million. The project was financed by issuing two million shares of common stock at $25 per share, and by issuing a $70 million 10 percent mortgage note payable to Union Trust. The mortgage agreement requires repayment in seven annual installments of $10 million each. Interest on the unpaid principal is payable on the first day of each month. The principal installments are due on January 1. The next payment is due on 1/1/94.

The 12 percent note payable to GemCorp was issued to alleviate the effects of the liquidity crisis of 1993. This note is unsecured and requires repayment in 10 equal annual installments. As with the Union Trust loan, interest is payable monthly. The first principal installment is due 3/1/94. This note contains restrictive covenants, as described earlier, relating to a $6 million compensating balance requirement and restrictions regarding further borrowing and dividend payments.

Sondem has asked that you analyze the long-term notes payable, being particularly alert to any violations of the restrictive covenants contained in the GemCorp loan agreement.

Requirement: Assuming Auditing With the Computer

1. Load your system and data diskettes and retrieve the file labeled "Notes." Locate the following workpapers in this file:
   a. WP14—Notes payable and accrued interest—lead schedule;
   b. WP14.3—Notes payable—long-term.

Scroll to WP 14.3, "Notes Payable—Long-Term." What are the audit objectives in the examination of long-term notes payable? Have they been achieved by the evidence provided in the workpaper?

2. Determine and enter the reclassification for the current portion of both notes as of 12/31/93. Now scroll up to WP 14, the lead schedule for notes payable and interest. Post your reclassifications to the lead schedule.

3. Print workpapers 14 and 14.3.

4. What is the probable nature of the downward adjustment of "interest expense" appearing in the adjustments column of the lead schedule?

Requirement: Assuming Auditing Without the Computer

1. Turn to Module XIII in your workbook and examine WP 14.3, "Notes Payable—Long-Term." What are the audit objectives in the examination of long-term notes payable? Have they been achieved by the evidence provided in the workpaper?

2. Determine and enter the reclassification for the current portion of both notes as of 12/31/93. Now turn to WP 14, the lead schedule for notes payable and interest. Post your reclassifications to the lead schedule.

3. What is the probable nature of the downward adjustment of "interest expense" appearing in the adjustments column of the lead schedule?

MODULE XIV: WORKING TRIAL BALANCE

Upon completion of substantive audit testing, the auditor should post all audit adjustments and reclassification entries to the working trial balance and extend the audited balances. The extended balances then form the nucleus for the audited financial statements.

Selected analytical procedures should also be applied at the conclusion of the audit field work. The results may be compared with those developed during the audit planning phase. This approach provides added support for audit conclusions contained in the workpapers.

Sondem has asked you to post the adjustments and reclassifications and perform the review phase analytical procedures.

Requirement: Assuming Auditing With the Computer

1. The instructor's diskette contains a file labeled "AJE" (adjusting journal entries). It contains all of the audit adjustments and reclassifications that you developed in prior modules of this practice case. At this time, your instructor will supply you with a printout of this file (or will copy the file onto your diskette). Review the adjustments. Some of these adjustments meet or exceed the individual item materiality threshold. These adjustments will be presented to the client as proposed audit adjustments. Other adjustments fall below the individual item materiality threshold and must be separately analyzed as to whether they are

to be considered as potential audit adjustments in the aggregate, or ignored. As you may recall, Mary Sondem set the following materiality thresholds in Module I:

Individual item materiality—income statement	$342,150
Aggregate materiality consideration	$ 34,215
Ignore as immaterial	<$ 34,215
Individual item materiality—balance sheet	$946,000

In light of the earnings overstatements revealed in previous modules, Sondem has decided to reduce the materiality thresholds for the income statement as follows:

Individual item materiality—income statement	$200,000
Aggregate materiality consideration	$ 20,000
Ignore as immaterial	<$ 20,000

She has elected to maintain the individual item balance sheet materiality threshold at $946,000. Given the revised thresholds and referring to the proposed audit adjustments and reclassifications, perform the following:

   a. Identify those adjustments falling between the aggregate and individual item materiality thresholds.

   b. Determine whether the potential adjustments that you identified in (a) above equal or exceed the individual item threshold in the aggregate. For aggregate purposes, treat income overstatements and income understatements separately. Do not net understatements against overstatements. That is, if aggregate overstatements are $500,000 and aggregate understatements are $400,000, the adjustments should be proposed to Trim Lawn management inasmuch as both exceeded the individual item materiality threshold.

   c. Decide which audit adjustments you wish to have reflected in the audited financial statements. Did you omit any of the 12 adjustments originally proposed? Why? Did you include any adjustments that failed to meet the individual item materiality threshold? Why?

   d. Decide which of the audit reclassifications you wish to have reflected in the audited financial statements. Do all three of the proposed reclassifications meet the individual item balance sheet materiality threshold?

2. Retrieve the file labeled "WTB." Post the adjustments and reclassifications to the working trial balance. Observe the following rules in making your postings:

   a. Post account increases as positive amounts, and post account decreases as negative amounts.

   b. Postings are in "thousands of dollars," whereas the adjustments and reclassifications are rounded to the nearest dollar. Therefore, in posting the adjustments and reclassifications, round to the nearest $1,000.

   c. Post all manufacturing overhead adjustments and reclassifications (the 7000 series of accounts) to "Cost of Goods Sold."

   d. Do not foot the adjustments and reclassifications columns (they will automatically be reflected in the audited column as you post them).

3. Save your file under the title "WTB." Print it after saving it.

4. Retrieve the file labeled "AUDBS." Using your printout of the working trial balance, enter the amounts from the audited column in the 1993 balance sheet. Calculate the percentages of individual balance sheet items and components relative to totals for 1993.

5. Calculate the new ratios for 1993 based on the audited financial statements. What is the purpose for applying analytical procedures in the evaluation and review phase of the audit?

6. Print the comparative audited balance sheets together with the related ratios. Compare them with the balance sheets and ratios which you developed and printed in item 4b of Module I. What conclusions can you draw regarding the comparison?

7. Retrieve the file labeled "Budget" which you reviewed as part of your assignment in Module I. You will recall that the purpose for this review was to identify significant budget variances that could be the result of under- or overbudgeting, errors in recording data, or intentional misstatement. The auditor, of course, is concerned with the latter two possibilities.

a. Substitute the audited amounts from your adjusted working trial balance for the unaudited figures in the "Actual 12/31/93" column.

b. Do significant variances still exist? If so, are you satisfied that the audit has resolved the causes of the significant variances? (Hint: Compare the variances resulting from this analysis with those calculated in Module I.)

c. If you continue to have concerns about certain of the variances, what additional evidence gathering and evaluation procedures do you suggest?

Requirement: Assuming Auditing Without the Computer

1. Turn to Module XIV in your workbook and refer to WP D, Audit Adjustments and Reclassifications. Review the adjustments. Note that these are the audit adjustments you developed in prior modules of this practice case. Some of these adjustments meet or exceed the individual item materiality threshold. These adjustments will be presented to the client as proposed audit adjustments. Other adjustments fall below the individual item materiality threshold and must be separately analyzed as to whether they are to be considered as potential audit adjustments in the aggregate, or ignored. As you may recall, Mary Sondem set the following materiality thresholds in Module I:

Individual item materiality—income statement	$342,150
Aggregate materiality consideration	$ 34,215
Ignore as immaterial	<$ 34,215
Individual item materiality—balance sheet	$946,000

In light of the earnings overstatements revealed in previous modules, Sondem has decided to reduce the materiality thresholds for the income statement as follows:

Individual item materiality—income statement	$200,000
Aggregate materiality consideration	$ 20,000
Ignore as immaterial	<$ 20,000

She has elected to maintain the individual item balance sheet materiality threshold at $946,000. Given the revised thresholds and referring to the proposed audit adjustments and reclassifications, perform the following:

a. Identify those adjustments falling between the aggregate and individual item materiality thresholds.

b. Determine whether the potential adjustments that you identified in (a) above equal or exceed the individual item threshold in the aggregate. For aggregate purposes, treat income overstatements and income understatements separately. Do not net understatements against overstatements. That is, if aggregate overstatements are $500,000 and aggregate understatements are $400,000, the adjustments should be proposed to Trim Lawn management inasmuch as both exceeded the individual item materiality threshold.

   c. Write out your proposed audit adjustments. Did you omit any of the 12 adjustments originally proposed? Why? Did you include any adjustments that failed to meet the individual item materiality threshold? Why?

   d. Turn to the audit reclassifications workpaper. Do all three of the proposed reclassifications meet the individual item balance sheet materiality threshold?

   e. Write out the reclassifications that you wish to propose to Trim Lawn management for reflecting in the audited balance sheet. Did you omit any of the reclassifications? Why?

2. Now turn to the partially completed "Working Trial Balance." Post the adjustments and reclassifications from the "Audit Adjustments and Reclassifications" workpaper to the working trial balance. Observe the following rules in making your postings:

   a. Post account increases as positive amounts, and post account decreases as negative amounts.

   b. Postings are in "thousands of dollars," whereas the adjustments and reclassifications are rounded to the nearest dollar. Therefore, in posting the adjustments and reclassifications, round to the nearest $1,000.

   c. Post all manufacturing overhead adjustments and reclassifications (the 7000 series of accounts) to "Cost of Goods Sold."

   d. Calculate the extended amounts in the 12/31/93 audited column of the worksheet.

   e. Foot the extended 1993 audited column for the income statement portion of the working trial balance. Now carry the audited "Ending Retained Earnings" figure to "Retained Earnings" in the 1993 audited column of the balance sheet portion of the "Working Trial Balance." Foot the extended 1993 audited column for the balance sheet portion.

3. Turn to the "Comparative Percentage Balance Sheets" contained in Module XIV of your workbook. Using the "Adjusted Working Trial Balance," enter the amounts from the "audited" column in the 1993 balance sheet. Calculate the percentages of individual items and components relative to totals for 1993.

4. Calculate the new ratios for 1993 based on the audited financial statements. What is the purpose for applying analytical procedures in the evaluation and review phase of the audit?

5. Compare the ratios calculated in 4 with the balance sheets and ratios that you developed in item 4b of Module I. What conclusions can you draw regarding the comparison?

6. Turn to WP A.6, "Budgeted vs. Actual Income Statements," which you reviewed as part of your assignment in Module I. You will recall that the purpose for this review was to identify significant budget variances that could be the result of under- or overbudgeting, errors in recording data, or intentional misstatement. The auditor, of course, is concerned with the latter two possibilities.

a. Substitute the audited amounts from your adjusted working trial balance for the unaudited figures in the "Actual 12/31/93" column.
b. Do significant variances still exist? If so, are you satisfied that the audit has resolved the causes of the significant variances? (Hint: Compare the variances resulting from this analysis with those calculated in Module I.)
c. If you continue to have concerns about certain of the variances, what additional evidence gathering and evaluation procedures do you suggest?

MODULE XV: AUDIT REPORT

The Solo and Wiggins audit team completed its audit field work on February 15, 1994. A conference was held on that date between members of the audit firm and Trim Lawn management. Participants in the conference were Elizabeth Hawkins, partner in charge of the Trim Lawn engagement; John Matthews, audit manager; Mary Sondem, in-charge auditor; Joshua Ravena, Trim Lawn's CEO; Marcy Mancura, Trim Lawn's controller; and Lawrence Mckee, Trim Lawn's treasurer. The Trim Lawn representatives agreed to all of the audit adjustments proposed by the audit team and agreed to reflect them in the December 31, 1993 financial statements. They also agreed to modify and/or add footnote disclosures as recommended by the audit team.

At the conclusion of the conference, the audit team obtained a client representation letter from Trim Lawn management, and presented management with a copy of the "reportable conditions" letter outlining discovered control structure weaknesses. The original of this letter was sent to Trim Lawn's board of directors. (You will recall that Trim Lawn does not have an audit committee.)

The legal action initiated against Trim Lawn by Snoro, a competitor, for alleged patent infringement was not yet settled as of February 15. Because the letter obtained by Mary Sondem from Trim Lawn's outside legal counsel was noncommittal as to the probable outcome of this action, Sondem requested an informal conference with the attorney handling Trim Lawn's case. This conference was convened on February 12, and the participants were Joel Haskins, the attorney, Marcy Mancura, Mary Sondem, and John Matthews. Mr. Haskins exhibited a degree of pessimism that produced considerable uncertainty as to the probable outcome of the litigation. Inasmuch as the amount of loss could be quite substantial and the probability of an unfavorable outcome was more than remote but less than likely, the audit team decided to add an uncertainty paragraph to the standard audit report.

No scope restrictions were encountered during the audit, either imposed or otherwise. Moreover, Trim Lawn did not change accounting principles in either 1992 or 1993.

Requirement: Assuming Auditing With the Computer

1. Load your system and data diskettes and retrieve the file labeled "Report."
2. Complete the report by adding:
   a. an appropriate title;

        b. an addressee (Solo and Wiggins were appointed by Trim Lawn's board of directors. Therefore, appropriate addressees may be the stockholders or board of directors);

        c. an explanatory fourth paragraph covering the uncertainty regarding the litigation (assume that the litigation is fully described in Footnote 3);

        d. an appropriate date for the audit report.

3. Print the audit report.

4. Sign the audit report.

Requirement: Assuming Auditing Without the Computer

1. Turn to Module XV in your workbook and examine the standard audit report contained on that page.

2. Complete the report by adding:

        a. an appropriate title;

        b. an addressee (Solo and Wiggins were appointed by Trim Lawn's board of directors. Therefore, appropriate addressees may be the stockholders or board of directors);

        c. an explanatory fourth paragraph covering the uncertainty regarding the litigation (assume that the litigation is fully described in Footnote 3);

        d. an appropriate date for the audit report; and

        e. a signature.

Answers to Selected Multiple-Choice Questions

Chapter 1

2. (d) Validity and relevance are the two components comprising competence. (a) is incorrect because external evidence may be valid but not relevant. (b) is incorrect because good internal control promotes validity, but not relevance. (c) is incorrect because hearsay evidence is often valid and relevant.

7. (d) An adverse opinion conveys the auditor's view that the financial statements do not fairly present financial position, results of operations, and cash flows. (a) is incorrect because a qualified opinion would be too mild in this situation. (b) is incorrect because special reports are not related to material departures from GAAP. (c) is incorrect because disclaimers are warranted when material scope restrictions are encountered by the auditor.

10. (c) The engagement letter summarizes the agreement between the auditor and the client and clarifies the type of engagement to be undertaken by the auditor. (a) is incorrect because the management letter is issued by the auditor to the client at the end of the engagement and contains suggestions for improving the information system. (b) is incorrect because the scope paragraph is a brief description of what the auditor did in completing the audit engagement (d) is incorrect because the introductory paragraph of the audit report is a brief summary of the respective responsibilities of management and auditor relative to the financial statements.

Chapter 2

1. (d) The SASs are defined as interpretations of the auditing standards and are binding upon the CPA, who must justify any departures from them.

3. (c) A significant goal of the public accounting profession is to narrow the expectations gap between accountants' and users' perceptions. A major factor in achieving this goal is maintenance of public confidence in the profession.

10. (b) Due care requires the CPA to perform all professional services in a diligent manner. This general standard, when combined with the first standard of field work (planning and supervision), suggests that supervisory personnel carefully oversee and review the work of each person assigned to the audit engagement. Moreover, an important element of proper review is to consider all of the factors influencing audit judgment at each level of the engagement.

Chapter 3

6. (a) Hall, Inc. is a specifically identified third party and is known by Locke to be the primary beneficiary of the audited financial statements. For this reason, Locke is liable for possible breach of contract as well as for negligence.

8. (b) Under breach of contract actions, the plaintiff (client) must prove negligence. In the present case, the fact that the fraud was *highly sophisticated and novel* relieves the auditor of detection responsibility, and, therefore, the accountants were not negligent.

15. (a) Under the law of contract, the CPA is liable to his/her client for ordinary negligence, gross negligence, and fraud. Therefore, the best defense in breach of contract actions is to demonstrate due care, i.e., the audit was conducted in accordance with GAAS.

Chapter 4

2. (d) By definition, evidence must be valid and relevant to be competent. (a) is incorrect because evidence gathered outside the enterprise may or may not be reliable, depending on the source of the evidence. (b) is incorrect because evidence gathered under satisfactory conditions of internal control may be more reliable, but not necessarily more relevant than evidence gathered under conditions of weak internal control. (c) is incorrect because oral representations of management possess greater or lesser validity as a function of management's competence, knowledge, and integrity.

5. (c) As defined in the chapter, substantive tests are tests of transactions and balances, and analytical procedures represent a form of substantive audit testing. (a) is incorrect because the concept of a "minimum audit" requires that some substantive testing be performed even when audit risk is low. (b) is incorrect because it states only one goal of substantive testing. (d) is incorrect because if internal control is strong, substantive tests will decrease—not increase.

11. (c) Although choice (a) appears correct, one must remember that a line on the financial statements consists of an aggregation of items. Choice (c), however, begins with the accounting records (a debit posting to the machinery and equipment subsidiary ledger, for example) and traces backward to the supporting evidence (the machine on the factory floor, for example). (b) is incorrect as a test for completeness for the same reason that (a) is incorrect as a test for existence. (d) is incorrect because this direction of vouching results in a test for completeness-not existence.

Chapter 5

1. (b) Although the successor auditor should attempt to communicate with the predecessor auditor, permission must be obtained from the client first. (d) is incorrect because even if the successor is aware of all the relevant facts, audit efficiency and effectiveness may be enhanced by reviewing the predecessor's audit workpapers. Moreover, the successor's awareness may be "clouded" by the fact that the information was obtained from the client rather than from the predecessor auditor, a more objective source.

3. (a) Earnings per share is a function of number of shares outstanding, par or stated value per share, and relative proportions of debt and equity comprising the capital structure. Inasmuch as these parameters may vary from company to company in the same industry, EPS is not an appropriate measure for comparison among companies. Rather, it is an effective measure of changes in profitability over time for a given company.

13. (d) Answer (d) is virtually a direct quote from SAS 53 which requires the auditor to plan the audit to provide reasonable assurance of detecting material errors and irregularities.

Chapter 6

4. (b) If a purchase has been recorded twice, the balance in the vendor's account will exceed the amount appearing on the vendor's monthly statement. The failure to reconcile should lead to detection of the error. (a) is incorrect because footing the purchase journal only proves the equality of debits and credits, and this equality is not affected by recording the same transaction twice. (c) is incorrect because tracing postings will determine agreement between the journal and ledger accounts, but will not detect the duplicate recording. (d) is incorrect for three reasons. First, the vendor may or may not acknowledge the error. Second, quarterly confirmations will not result in *timely* detection. Third, reconciliation of account and statement is a more *efficient* approach than confirmation.

5. (a) By requiring a sales invoice for every shipment, and accounting for the transaction by comparing invoice and bill of lading, the probability of failure to invoice is greatly reduced. (b) and (c) are important controls from the standpoint of proper recording, but they will not prevent unbilled shipments. (d) is incorrect because, although it provides assurance that all billings are for goods actually shipped, it does not preclude some shipments from being billed.

11. (c) The completeness assertion for inventory should provide reasonable assurance that all incoming goods are recorded and posted to perpetual inventory records. By requiring prenumbered receiving reports for all incoming goods, paying only those vendors' invoices accompanied by a properly completed receiving report, and periodically accounting for the numeric sequence of used receiving reports, completeness is reasonably assured. (a) is incorrect because reconciling the work in process account with such subsidiary records as production reports and materials requisitions helps to assure existence or occurrence, but not completeness. (b) is incorrect because proper separation of duties does not preclude custodians of inventory from performing the receiving function, provided receipts are properly documented on prenumbered receiving reports and accounted for. (d) is incorrect because a separation between payroll and inventory accounting adds no assurance concerning the recording of incoming inventory.

Chapter 7

7. (d) Unless conditions have changed since the interim study, the auditor need not perform added control tests at year-end.

10. (a) To reduce control risk below maximum, the auditor must obtain knowledge about the operating effectiveness of internal controls. Such knowledge is usually obtainable only through control testing. (b) is incorrect because it implies the present tense only, whereas operating effectiveness encompasses the period under audit. Moreover, (b) doesn't address the question of documentation of the reduced assessment and the reasons therefore.

21. (b) GAAS defines reportable conditions as "matters coming to the auditor's attention, relating to control structure deficiencies, which could adversely affect the entity's ability to record, process, summarize, and report financial data consistent with management's assertions contained in the financial statements."

Chapter 8

1. (b) Choice (b) is most cost effective in achieving the stated objective of determining whether the system prevents customers from exceeding their credit limits. Generalized audit software programs are available to assist the auditor in making the comparisons. (a) may determine whether the control works at present, but doesn't provide assurance for the period under audit. (c) and (d) meet the stated objective, but are more costly and time consuming than (b), and therefore less cost effective. In addition, (d) will not detect those balances that are significantly in excess of authorized credit limits unless those accounts are included in the random sample.

7. (a) The beginning narrative of this question describes "auditing around the computer," and, as discussed in Chapter 8, this form of control testing has the disadvantage of not permitting the auditor to arrive at any conclusions about specific programmed controls. (a) is correct, therefore, because agreement of output with predetermined results does not necessarily mean that all significant controls are working. (d) is incorrect because the auditor can obtain some assurance that the programs are producing reliable results if computer output agrees with predetermined output. If auditing around the computer produces no confidence in the auditing results, the procedure would not be an acceptable alternative, under any circumstances, to auditing through the computer.

8. (d) (d) is a justification for further control tests. If controls appear effective, the auditor may be able to further reduce the assessed level of control risk if control testing can verify operating effectiveness. (a), (b), and (c) are all valid reasons for not performing control tests. (a) is incorrect because if controls are duplicative, the auditor may decide on testing the other controls because of cost effectiveness. (b) is incorrect because major weaknesses remove any cost effectiveness advantage of testing for control effectiveness. (c) is incorrect because cost/benefit analysis is a vital part of the decision whether to test further.

Chapter 9

1. (a) As discussed in Chapters 8 and 9, computer auditing involves understanding the client's EDP applications—evaluating the means of processing; and using the computer to assist in performing substantive tests—evaluating the results of processing. Choice (a) accomplishes the second of these. (b) and (d) are incorrect because they are not part of the audit process. (c) is incorrect because providing IRS with client data is not permitted without the client's permission or a valid subpoena issued by a court.

7. (b) As stated in Chapter 9, the principal disadvantage of generalized audit software packages is its incompatibility with on-line-real-time systems, of which a DBMS is an example. Choices (a), (c), (d), and (e) all express advantages of generalized audit software programs.

9. (a) The primary justification for using the computer in performing substantive testing is increasing efficiency and effectiveness. Efficiency and effectiveness are enhanced through the computer's ability to manipulate large quantities of data and to perform complex computations quickly. (b) is incorrect because this is an advantage—not a disadvantage—of computer audit applications. (c) is incorrect because the element of surprise is occasionally necessary, but does not enhance the effectiveness of computer programs. (d) is incorrect because some EDP systems are not amenable to computer audit programs. On-line-real-time systems, for example, are not capable of being accessed by most computer audit programs.

Chapter 10

1. (a) If the joint probability of inherent risk (IR) times control risk (CR) is less than overall audit risk (AR) set by the auditor, further substantive testing is not necessary. That is, the product of the two risk factors has reduced audit risk below the specified maximum. Only in choice (a) is this condition true.

2. (b) This question illustrates the importance of correctly defining ''error'' with regard to each attribute tested by the auditor. Inasmuch as the auditor cannot establish existence of a proper countersignature, a missing check must be considered a deviation. Choices (a) and (d) are incorrect because they ignore the presence of a possible error. (c) is incorrect because the dominant condition relative to the other 19 checks is not relevant to the missing check.

8. (a) The risk of underassessment, by definition, is the risk that the auditor may lower the assessed level of control risk when, in fact, the true state of internal control does not warrant such a lowering. (b) is incorrect because overassessment is the opposite of underassessment. Choice (c) is incorrect because precision is a calculated amount and is a function of materiality, sample error, and auditor judgment, and is not dependent on over or underassessment of control risk. (d) is incorrect because incorrect rejection is another way of expressing overassessment of control risk.

Chapter 11

6. (a) To calculate sample size for mean-per-unit and difference estimation purposes, the auditor must estimate population variability. This can be done by drawing a pilot sample of 40 to 50 items at random and calculating a standard deviation for the sample. The calculated standard deviation is then used in the equation for sample size and compared later with the standard deviation of the sample.

12. (c) Tolerable occurrence limit is the maximum misstatement allowable by the auditor while accepting the book value as reasonably stated. The auditor's judgment concerning materiality will be the major factor in setting this limit. (a) is incorrect because inherent risk, as well as control risk, will influence the desired precision level but does not enter into the determination of tolerable misstatement. (b) is incorrect because materiality considerations encompass both quantitative and qualitative factors. (d) is wrong because all parameters used in statistical sampling are subject to change as additional information comes to the auditor's attention.

16. (c) As explained in Chapter 11, PPS sampling is most useful where the auditor suspects a few significant overstatement errors. If the auditor believes understatement as well as overstatement errors are present, some other sampling method, e.g., mean-per-unit or difference estimation should be applied. (a), (b), and (d) are incorrect because none of these conditions affect the efficiency of PPS sampling.

Chapter 12

6. (a) In addition to confirming balances, the standard bank confirmation also confirms outstanding indebtedness to the bank. (b) is incorrect because banks do not confirm details that would assist in detecting kiting. (c) is wrong because GAAS recommends, but does not require, mailing confirmations to banks. (d) is incorrect because bank confirmations do not assist in detecting forged checks. Also, the auditor is not responsible for detecting forged checks.

7. (a) A positive confirmation requests the customer to reply regardless of agreement or disagreement with the balance. Therefore, a nonreply is indicative of possible nonexistence of the account. (b) is wrong because a nonreply to a negative request indicates customer agreement, but not nonexistence. (c) is wrong because doubt as to collectibility affects valuation but not the existence assertion. (d) is incorrect because pledging of receivables affects disclosure, but is not related to the existence assertion.

13. (a) If internal control were strong and customers were likely to respond to confirmation requests, Cooper might elect to mail negative requests. But, in this case, control is weak and, under conditions of weak internal control over receivables, the positive form of confirmation requests should be used. (a) therefore, is correct and (b) is incorrect. (c) is incorrect because, although analysis of subsequent receipts does provide evidence of existence, it is not a substitute for confirmation. (d) is incorrect because, under conditions of weak internal control, internal documentation possesses less validity than under strong internal control.

Chapter 13

3. (b) Since the inventory sheets are prepared from the tags, tracing from tags to sheets provides assurance that the transcription was done correctly and that there are no material errors of omission. (a) is incorrect because inventory tags contain quantities but not cost data. (c) is incorrect because the auditor determines that inventory appearing on an inventory tag is bona fide by observing the physical inventory. (d) is incorrect because evidence concerning existence of inventory appearing on the sheets is obtained by tracing from sheets to tags—not from tags to sheets.

7. (d) Construction work orders describe the nature and costs associated with all internal expenditures capitalized by companies. In reviewing these, the auditor should detect the erroneous charge. (a) is incorrect because discussing capitalizing policies will not ordinarily elicit information concerning specific projects undertaken during the year. (b) is incorrect because, having been capitalized, the charge for painting will *not* appear in the maintenance expense account. (c) is wrong because observing that the warehouse had been painted may prompt the auditor to examine for proper treatment of the charge, but will not provide evidence as to how the charge was treated in the accounts.

9. (c) This is a test for existence and validity of recorded liabilities. By proceeding from an entry in the voucher register to the underlying documentation, including the vendor's invoice, the auditor obtains satisfaction that the credit to vouchers payable represents a valid expenditure. (a) and (d) are incorrect because tracing from the voucher register to voucher and invoice provides no evidence as to payment. (b) is wrong because the auditor must also examine vouchers and cash disbursements in the subsequent period to obtain evidence as to recording in the proper accounting period.

Chapter 14

6. (c) (a), (b), and (d) are incorrect because the subject matter of each of these statements affects management's assertions contained in the financial statements, and should therefore be covered in the representation letter. Acknowledging responsibility for employee's illegal acts, however, has no bearing on the fairness of financial presentation.

9. (a) Confirmation with the holder of the note (*e.g.*, a bank that has discounted the note) is an acceptable alternative to inspection; but not confirmation with the debtor. (b) is incorrect because, in a test based audit, materiality is always a consideration in selecting items to be tested. (c) is incorrect because inspecting a negotiable note does provide conclusive evidence of existence, but not evidence that the holder is a holder in due course. (d) is incorrect because confirmation of discounted notes with recourse is the only alternative to examining the note, and is therefore necessary, given the contingent liability associated with discounting.

10. (a) Analytical procedures in the planning stage are necessary to provide guidance as to the direction of auditing and is important to risk-based auditing. Analytical procedures in the review stage are vital to the auditor's evaluation as to the adequacy of evidence obtained. Therefore, *AICPA Professional Standards* require the auditor to apply the procedures in the planning and review stages of the audit.

Chapter 15

1. (c) The material enclosed in quotation marks is the standard wording used by auditors who wish to divide responsibility.

3. (c) Whenever the auditor is able to obtain satisfaction by other means, no mention need be made of the scope restriction. The third standard of field work requires the auditor to obtain sufficient, competent evidence to support an opinion on the financial statements. The availability and application of alternate means for satisfying audit objectives meets the requirements of this standard and precludes a need for any modifying language in the audit report.

6. (b) A material departure from GAAP requires a qualified or adverse opinion. (a) is incorrect because if the departure was not sufficiently material to warrant a qualification, an additional paragraph describing the departure is unnecessary. (c) and (d) are wrong because a disclaimer relates to a scope restriction—not a departure from GAAP.

Chapter 16

3. (c) A disclaimer must accompany financial statements whenever the CPA is associated with them and has not audited the statements. (a) is wrong because negative assurance is the appropriate form of reporting when financial statements have been reviewed. (b) is wrong because an "opinion" is not rendered for a compilation. (d) is incorrect because an explanatory paragraph would be added only when the CPA determines that significant financial data has been omitted from unaudited statements.

16. (b) Attestation occurs when the CPA expresses an opinion on the reliability of a written assertion by a third party. Only choice (b) results in an opinion related to an assertion. (a) is wrong because EDP advice does not constitute an opinion as to the reliability of third party assertions. (c) is incorrect because the CPA is attempting to comply with the tax laws in preparing the returns, but is not expressing an opinion on another's compliance. (d) is wrong because a compilation, by definition, offers no assurance, and is therefore not a form of attestation.

18. (d) The CPA's review of a nonpublic entity consists mainly of making inquiries of management and employees and performing analytical procedures. (a) is wrong because a compliance report is a form of attestation and therefore encompasses a broader spectrum of procedures than inquiry and analytical procedures. (b) is wrong because a review of prospective financial statements is not permitted by AICPA guidelines. (c) is incorrect because a management advisory report is associated with a consulting engagement and is covered by AICPA guidelines for consulting engagements, rather than guidelines for accounting and review services.

Chapter 17

10. (a) If the auditor properly enlists the cooperation of the auditee, obtaining agreement as to audit conclusions will likely lead to a commitment by the auditee to take corrective action, and the audit report should state this. (b) and (c) are wrong because they are untrue and represent improper compromises by the auditor. (d) is incorrect because, as stated above, if management has agreed with the auditor's conclusions and recommendations, this should be stated in the audit report.

14. (a) The GAO "yellow book" standards specifically require that the auditor report on the entity's compliance with laws and regulations imposed by applicable assistance programs, and on the entity's internal control structure. (b), (c), and (d) are not contained in the yellow book standards.

15. (b) Since a principal objective of the audit is to determine compliance with laws governing the assistance programs, detection of material noncompliance requires a qualified or adverse opinion. (a) is incorrect because of the materiality of the particular noncompliance. (c) is wrong because a disclaimer is appropriate only where the auditor has not obtained sufficient evidence to determine compliance. (d) is incorrect because limited assurance is not permitted in compliance audits under the Single Audit Act.

Glossary

Numbers in parentheses denote chapter(s) in which the term is used.

Ability to continue as a going concern (15)   The ability of an entity to continue to meet its obligations as they mature.

Access controls (8)   Controls, in an EDP system, limiting access to files, programs, documentation, and hardware.

Account (4)   A reference to financial statement components as representations of the underlying substance to which they relate.

Accountability controls (6)   Control procedures which fix responsibility for the custody of assets, documents, or accounting records.

Accounting and Review Services Committee (2)   A committee of the AICPA charged with promulgating standards and interpretations governing nonattest engagements, such as compilations and reviews.

Accounting estimates developed by management (4)   Of particular concern to the auditor, these estimates relate to such financial statement components as product warranty, bad debts, pensions, and compensated absences. Auditing standards outline auditor requirements in evaluating the reasonableness of the estimates.

Accounting manual (6)   A set of instructions and definitions that describes the kinds of transactions affecting the debit and credit sides of each of an entity's accounts, and gives instructions for the proper recording of unique transactions. The accounting manual, together with the chart of accounts, facilitates proper recording of an entity's transactions and events.

Accounting symmetry (14)   A state whereby both sides of a transaction have been consistently recorded in accordance with GAAP. Auditors are concerned with symmetry when examining intercompany and intracompany transactions.

Accounting system (6)   The methods and records established to identify, assemble, analyze, classify, and disclose components of financial statements.

Accounts receivable aging analysis (12)   A schedule displaying customers' account balances by length of time outstanding. As an audit tool, the aging analysis facilitates evaluation of the adequacy of the client's allowance for uncollectible accounts.

Accuracy controls (7)   Controls that support the reliability of recorded transactions. Examples of accuracy controls are assignment of competent persons to tasks involving account distribution and cost allocation, and a system of double-check.

Achieved precision (11)   The calculated range within which the true value of the population most likely falls.

Adverse opinion (15)   An audit opinion issued whenever financial statements contain departures from GAAP which are too material to warrant only a qualification.

Aggregate materiality (4)   The total effect of two or more errors, each of which, by itself, is not material.

Agreed-upon procedures (16)   A situation in which the CPA and the client have agreed that procedures be applied to specified elements of the financial statements. In most cases, application of the agreed upon procedures does not provide sufficient evidence to support an opinion on the specified elements. Examples are bank directors' examinations, examinations for proposed acquisitions, and examinations for creditors' committees or trustees in bankruptcy proceedings.

AICPA/FTC Consent Agreement of 1991 (2)   An agreement entered into by the AICPA and the Federal Trade Commission whereby the Institute agrees to permit greater latitude to members regarding form of organization, advertising, firm name, referral commissions, and contingent fees.

Allowance for sampling risk (11)   A statistical sampling term meaning the sum of basic precision plus the incremental allowance for sampling risk. Also referred to as "achieved precision" or "computed precision."

Alpha risk (11)   The risk of incorrect rejection of a population based on the results of sampling.

Analysis of interbank transfers (12)   An examination of cash transfers between two or more bank accounts for a few days before or after the balance sheet date. The purpose of the analysis is to assist in detecting year-end kiting and other forms of errors or irregularities.

Analytical evidence (4 and 5)   Audit evidence obtained through the application of analytical procedures.

Analytical procedures (4 and 5)   Substantive tests of financial information performed by studying and comparing relationships among data.

Anticipated error (11)   A term used in PPS sampling, the amount of error expected by the auditor.

Application controls (8)   Control procedures designed to achieve specific control objectives. Application controls relate to individual computerized accounting applications.

Assertions (1)   Representations of management as to the fairness of the financial statements.

Assessed level of control risk (7)   That level of control risk used by the auditor in determining the detection risk to accept for a financial statement assertion and, accordingly, in determining the nature, timing, and extent of substantive tests.

Asset safeguards (6)   Procedures, which are part of the overall control structure, designed to protect the entity's assets. Safeguards may be further classified as to "limited access" controls and "accountability" controls.

Attestation (1 and 16)   Any service performed by a CPA resulting in a written communication that

expresses a conclusion about the reliability of a written assertion that is the responsibility of another party.

Attestation standards (2)   Standards defining the quality of attest services other than audits; for example reports on internal control or compliance with contractual requirements.

Attribute (10)   A characteristic of interest in sampling. In auditing applications, attributes usually assume the form of types of errors having a material impact on control risk assessment.

Attribute sampling (10)   A sampling approach that estimates the frequency of events. As used for control testing purposes, this method estimates the upper error limit, expressed as a percentage, for specified attributes related to a population of documents.

Audit adjustments (4)   Journal entries proposed by the auditor to the client. The purpose of the entries is to correct the financial statements for material errors discovered during the examination.

Audit committee (1, 2, 3, and 6)   A committee of the board of directors comprised mainly of outside directors having no management ties to the organization.

Audit evidence (1 and 4)   The underlying accounting data and all corroborating information available to the auditor.

Audit field work (1)   That part of the audit performed mainly on the client's premises.

Auditing (1)   A systematic process of objectively obtaining and evaluating evidence regarding assertions and communicating the results to interested users.

Auditing around the computer (8)   Assessing control risk by comparing input and output and ignoring the specifics of how the computer processes data.

Auditing through the computer (8)   Identifying and testing programmed controls used in processing specific applications.

Auditing with the computer (9)   Using the computer to assist in gathering and evaluating audit evidence.

Auditing without the computer (9)   Manually gathering and evaluating audit evidence.

Audit objectives (4)   Goals to be attained in completing an audit. Audit objectives may be classified as information system objectives and transaction and balance objectives.

Audit of information systems (4)   That part of the audit which concentrates on assessing inherent risk and control risk through study of the business and industry, analytical review, and study and evaluation of control structure policies and procedures pertaining to an audit.

Audit of transactions and balances (4)   That part of the audit which concentrates on gathering and evaluating audit evidence in support of recorded transactions and events. (Also referred to as substantive audit testing.)

Audit planning (1 and 5)   The process of assessing audit risk, identifying audit resources, and developing audit programs.

Audit program (1 and 4)   An audit plan containing the procedures designed to achieve the audit objectives developed during the planning phase of the audit. Audit programs are usually classified according to transaction cycles.

Audit reclassifications (4)   Entries to assure proper presentation of items in the financial statements. The reclassifications are not posted by the client to the accounts, but, rather, are displayed only in the auditor's working trial balance—usually in a column separate from audit adjustments.

Audit report (1)   The mechanism for communicating the results of the audit to interested users. The standard audit report contains three paragraphs: an introductory paragraph, a scope paragraph, and an opinion paragraph.

Audit risk (1, 4, and 5)   The probability of rendering an unqualified opinion on financial statements that are materially misstated.

Audit risk analysis (5)   A methodical approach to identifying and assessing the components of audit risk, and allocating audit resources to those subsets of transaction cycles presenting the highest risk levels.

Auditing standards (1)   Define the quality of the audit and consist of three general standards, three field work standards, and four reporting standards.

Audit trail (4 and 6)   A "stream" of evidence which permits one to trace a transaction or event forward from its inception to the appropriate ledger account(s) or, conversely, backward from the ledger account to the inception of the transaction.

Audit workpapers (4)   The record of the evidence that the auditor has gathered and evaluated in support of the audit opinion.

Auditor/client conference (14)   A meeting with the top officers of the client entity, the auditor/client conference is convened by the auditor. The purpose of the meeting is to present the client with a set of proposed audit adjustments and reclassifications, along with suggested footnote disclosures. Reportable conditions (internal control weaknesses) are also covered during this meeting.

Auditor independence (2)   A state of separation between the auditor and client management. Independence consists of two aspects— independence in fact, which is a state of mind; and independence in appearance, which precludes the auditor from serving in any capacity that would convey to the public an apparent compromise of independence (such as serving on the client's board of directors).

Automated text working papers (9)   Standard letters (engagement letter, lawyer's letter, client representation letter, and reportable conditions letter) and the standard audit report form included in a data base developed with the assistance of audit software. These documents are then modified as needed to fit the circumstances of a particular engagement.

Balanced audit approach (12)   An approach to substantive audit testing designed to avoid overemphasizing either overstatement or understatement at the expense of the other. This approach tests assets and expenses for overstatement, and liabilities and revenues for understatement.

Basic precision (11) $SI \times RF$. Used in probability proportional to size sampling to represent the precision range assuming zero errors.

Batch processing (8)   An EDP system in which transactions are accumulated and processed in groups, as contrasted with a real-time system in which transactions are processed as they occur.

Beta risk (10 and 11)   The risk of incorrectly accepting a population value based on the results of sampling.

Budget and time summary (1, 5, and 9)   An audit planning and control device that classifies projected and actual time according to audit staff level.

Business risk (5)   Also known as "inherent risk," business risk is the risk that, in the absence of internal control, material errors or irregularities will occur and escape detection.

Cash receipts cutoff (12)   A set of procedures to ensure that cash receipts have been recorded in the proper accounting period. The procedures include counting and listing cash at year-end; tracing ending cash to the cutoff bank statement; examining cash receipts listings, journal entries, and bank deposit tickets for a few days before and after the balance sheet date; and confirming bank balances directly with banks.

Chart of accounts (6)   A listing of account numbers and titles for all accounts appearing in the general ledger, as well as in the detail ledgers. The chart of accounts, together with the accounting manual, facilitate proper recording of transactions and events.

Check digit (8)   A value computed by a formula when data are entered into an EDP system, then recomputed and compared to the original value whenever the field is used.

Chief accountant of the SEC (2)   An appointed official of the Securities and Exchange Commission, the chief accountant is responsible for investigating alleged ''audit failures,'' overseeing financial reporting practices of public companies, and monitoring the activities of the Financial Accounting Standards Board, as well as the peer review programs of the SEC Practice Section of the Division for CPA Firms.

Circular OMB A-128 (17)   Entitled ''Audits of State and Local Governments,'' this circular was issued by the U.S. Office of Management and Budget. It prescribes policies, procedures, and guidelines to implement the Single Audit Act of 1984.

Circular OMB A–133 (17)   Entitled ''Audits of Institutions of Higher Education and Other Nonprofit Organizations,'' this circular was issued by the U.S. Office of Management and Budget in 1991. It sets forth requirements relative to compliance audits of colleges and universities and other not-for-profit entities receiving over $100,000 of federal financial assistance in a single fiscal year.

Civil liability (3)   Liability to third parties who are not parties to a contractual agreement. Under common law, auditors are liable to third party financial statement users for gross negligence and fraud in the conduct of an examination.

Client acceptance (5)   A decision process relating to a CPA's determination of whether to continue servicing an existing client or accept a new client. Inputs to the process include evaluating management integrity, as well as the CPA's competence to complete the engagement.

Client-imposed scope restriction (15)   *See* scope restriction.

Client representation letter (14)   A letter obtained by the auditor from the client confirming the fairness of the representations and the adequacy of informative disclosures contained in the financial statements.

Code of Professional Conduct (2)   Principles and rules of conduct formulated by the AICPA to provide guidance to the CPA in the performance of all types of professional accounting and auditing services.

Collateral (14)   Security for loans or other forms of indebtedness. In conducting an audit, the CPA must determine that the value of collateral is adequate to prevent material loss from loan defaults.

Collusion (6)   One of the limitations inherent in a given control structure, collusion involves two or more individuals working together to effect misappropriation and concealment.

Comfort Letter (16)   A letter issued by the CPA at the request of the underwriter to assist the underwriter in conducting a due-diligence review. The letter commonly covers such matters as the independence of the CPA, compliance of the audited statements with SEC requirements, and unaudited financial statements. If limited review procedures have been applied to the unaudited data, the CPA may give negative assurance, in the comfort letter, with respect to the data.

Communication with audit committee (14)   A GAAS requirement that compels the auditor to convey to the audit committee, preferably in writing, certain specified matters discovered in the course of the audit.

Communication with predecessor auditor (2 and 5)   Occurs when an entity changes auditors and the new (successor) auditor initiates contact with the prior (predecessor) auditor. The successor auditor may contact the predecessor only with the client's permission. Matters to be discussed might include reasons for the change in auditors, management integrity, prior disagreements between management and auditors, and difficulties encountered in conducting audits in the past.

Compensating balance requirements (14)   Provisions in loan agreements requiring the borrower to maintain minimum cash balances with the lending institution.

Competence of audit evidence (1 and 4)   Determines the adequacy of audit evidence and is a function of validity and relevance.

Compilation (16)   A professional service in which the CPA presents information that is the representation of management without undertaking to express any assurance on the statements.

Completeness (4 and 6)   A state in which the financial statements contain the results of all transactions that have occurred since the inception of the entity.

Compliance auditing (1 and 17)   An audit conducted for the purpose of attesting to an entity's conformity with laws, regulations, and/or contract provisions.

Comprehensive basis other than GAAP (16)   An accounting basis not in conformity with generally accepted accounting principles; for example, financial statements prepared to conform to the financial reporting requirements of a regulatory body, financial statements prepared on a tax basis, and financial statements prepared on a cash basis.

Computer audit specialist (8)   An employee of the CPA firm, who, typically, will have served on the audit staff for a period of time, followed by specialized training in computer system design and control and EDP auditing.

Computer editing (8)   The process of including programmed routines for computer checking as to validity and accuracy of input.

Computer operators (8)   Persons within the EDP function who process transactions through the system in accordance with the operator instructions for the application being updated.

Confidence Level (11)   Synonymous with reliability, confidence level is the likelihood that the sample range contains the true value. It is based on the degree of confidence the auditor wishes to place in the sampling results.

Confirmation evidence (4)   Audit evidence obtained directly from third parties, external to the client.

Confirmation of accounts receivable (12)   The act of obtaining evidence of existence, ownership, or valuation directly from third parties external to the client.

Confirmation of securities (14)   Determining, by obtaining direct verification from the holder, that securities purported to be owned by the client at the balance sheet date exist and are indeed owned by the client. The holder may be a bank, a brokerage firm, or a lender holding the securities as collateral for an existing loan.

Consistency (15)   A state of using the same accounting principles during the current period as were used in the immediately preceding period.

Constructive fraud (3)   (*See also Ultramares v. Touche* in the appendix following Chapter 3.) Negligence so gross as to border on intentional deceit. Invoked by the law when the auditor appears to ignore that which was obvious, or if the auditor has no reason to believe that the financial statements fairly present financial position, results of operations, and cash flows.

Continuing auditor (15)   One who has examined the financial statements of the current period and one or more consecutive periods immediately prior to the current period.

Continuing professional education (2)   A means for CPAs to keep abreast of changes occurring within the profession.

Continuous auditing (1 and 8)   An auditing approach whereby the auditor tests controls and transactions at frequent intervals throughout the year. Especially applicable to clients with complex EDP accounting applications.

Contractual liability (3)   Liability to the client resulting from the contractual agreement between the CPA and the client. Contractual liability encompasses ordinary negligence, as well as gross negligence and fraud.

Contributory negligence (3)   A defense frequently invoked in breach of contract cases involving employee fraud, whereby the auditor counters the client's charges of negligence by claiming that the client's own negligence gave rise to the misappropriation and concealment.

Control environment (6)   The collective effect of various factors on establishing, enhancing, or mitigating the effectiveness of specific policies and procedures.

Control point (7)   The point at which an error or irregularity could occur in capturing and processing data or at which assets need to be safeguarded against loss from theft or other causes.

Control procedures (6)   Policies and procedures in addition to the control environment and accounting system that management has established to provide reasonable assurance of achieving specific entity objectives.

Control risk (5 and 7)   The risk that material errors or irregularities are not prevented or detected by the internal control structure.

Control testing (7)   An approach to further reducing the assessed level of control risk by testing a sample of transactions and estimating pertinent error rates. Control testing may assume the form of observation, reprocessing, or document testing.

Control total (8)   A calculated total to be compared with output.

Corroborating information (4)   Audit evidence consisting of such documentation as canceled checks, bank statements, sale invoices, vendors' invoices, vouchers, time cards, requisitions, purchase orders, bills of lading, and shipping orders. Auditor developed evidence, such as confirmations, reconciliations, calculations, and observation are also considered corroborating information.

Cost-benefit (4)   The process of determining that the benefit of an act or series of acts exceeds the cost of performing the act(s). In auditing, cost-benefit analysis is applied in selecting among alternate procedures for achieving stated audit objectives. It is also applied in determining whether to test control procedures for the purpose of lowering the assessed level of control risk.

Current file (4)   Those audit workpapers which support the period currently being examined.

Custom-designed programs (9)   Computer programs written for specific audit tasks and for particular clients. They may be written by the auditor or by the client. If written by the client, the auditor must test the programs.

Cutoff (12)   The act of recording transactions in the proper accounting period.

Cutoff tests (12 and 13)   Substantive tests performed by the auditor to determine that transactions were recorded in the proper accounting period. These tests are applied to cash receipts and disbursements, sales, and purchases transactions. In performing the tests, the auditor examines substance, documents, and journal entries for agreement.

Cutoff bank statement (12)   A bank statement covering a two- or three-week period immediately following year-end. If mailed directly to the auditor by the bank, the statement permits the auditor to examine evidence in support of the reconciling items appearing on the year-end bank reconciliation.

Data and procedural controls (8)   Controls designed to manage daily computer operations. A system of backup files, as well as environmental controls are examples.

Data base management system (8)   The software used by integrated data base systems to control input, processing, and output.

Data control group (8)   Persons within the EDP function who distribute output, monitor reprocessing of errors, and compare input with output on a test basis.

Data encryption (8)   An electronic data interchange control whereby an encoding key is used by the sender to "scramble" a message. The receiver must then have the corresponding key to unscramble and read the message.

Defense Contract Audit Agency (DCAA) (1)   A federal agency that examines the records of entities fulfilling defense contracts for the federal government to determine that only those costs pertaining to the fulfillment have been charged to the contracts and that the entities have conformed to the contract terms.

Departure from designated principal (15)   A departure from an accounting standard or principal promulgated by the body (currently FASB) designated by Council of the AICPA.

Design phase auditing (8)   Involvement of the auditor in designing the client's data processing system. The goal is to ensure inclusion of controls that will detect exception or unusual conditions and record and log information about the initiating transactions.

Desired precision (11)   The range of precision specified by the auditor in developing a particular sampling plan. The desired range is a function of materiality and acceptable risk levels.

Detection controls (6)   Internal controls that provide for a double-check to locate significant errors and/or irregularities after the fact.

Detection risk (5)   The risk that errors or irregularities that are not prevented or detected by the control structure are not detected by the independent audit.

Difference estimation (11)   A variables sampling method that calculates the average difference between the audited value and the client's book value and multiplies by the number of items in the population. The result is the estimated total difference between the audited and book values.

Direct evidence (4)   Evidence that permits the auditor to draw conclusions. Observing inventory, for example, provides the auditor with direct evidence as to the existence objective.

Disclaimer of opinion (15)   Inability to render an audit opinion because of lack of sufficient evidence or lack of independence.

Discovery sampling (10)   An orderly approach to locating a particular event. Used in auditing to find an example of an error or irregularity when the auditor's suspicions are aroused.

Distributed processing (8)   Processing transactions at remote locations by microcomputers or terminals and transmitting to a home office mainframe via communication links. Additionally, the microcomputers may be linked to one another through a system of networking, thereby facilitating communication and permitting the sharing of workload among locations.

Divided responsibility (15)   An audit reporting situation in which the principal auditors accept responsibility for the components audited by them and other auditors are responsible for the subsidiaries examined by them.

Division for CPA Firms (2)   A body created by the Securities and Exchange Commission and monitored by the Public Oversight Board, for the purpose of promoting quality and consistency in the rendering of professional services by CPAs.

Document examination and testing (7)   The process of testing control procedures by selecting and examining documents and transactions for errors, and projecting error rates based on such examination and testing.

Documentary evidence (4)   Evidence consisting of the accounting records and all of the underlying documentation supporting the transactions and events recorded in these records.

Dual-dated audit report (15)   An audit report containing a second date following the date of completion of audit field work. The second date pertains to a specific event which occurred subsequent to the completion of field work, and of which the auditor has become aware prior to the release of the audit report. For the report to be dual-dated, the event must be adequately disclosed in a footnote to the financial statements.

Due audit care (2)   The act of exercising reasonable diligence in the conduct of auditing and other accounting and review services.

Echo check (8)   A computer processing control whereby the computer sends the message back to the sender for verification. As used in electronic data interchange environments, the receiving computer returns the message to the sending computer for confirmation that information received is the same as information sent.

Economic substance (14)   The "real" nature of a transaction, as opposed to its legal form. For example, in a sale and leaseback transaction, the gain on sale by the lessee to the lessor may not have been realized in an "arms-length" transaction, notwithstanding conformity with the legal definition of a sale. Whenever legal form and economic substance are in conflict, economic substance should prevail.

Effectiveness (17)   A term related to management auditing, effectiveness is output oriented and is a measure of productivity in utilizing an entity's resources.

Efficiency (17)   A term related to operational auditing, efficiency is input oriented and measures cost control in performing recurring functions within an entity.

Electronic data interchange (EDI) (8)   A technique whereby a company's computer system is linked to those of its suppliers and customers, and transactions, such as purchases, sales, and cash receipts and payments, may be initiated automatically by the system.

Electronic spreadsheets (9)   A software package which enables workpapers to be automatically recalculated and linked through a set of equations, referred to as a *template*.

Electronic workpaper files (9)   Audit workpapers prepared with the assistance of the computer. Such workpapers are typically oriented to spreadsheet or data base software packages, and can be linked by using these packages.

Emphasis of a matter (15)   A fourth paragraph, added after the opinion paragraph of the audit report, whenever the auditor wishes to bring a matter of importance, which has already been adequately disclosed in the financial statements or footnotes, to the financial statement reader's attention.

Engagement letter (1)   A letter from the CPA to the client—signed by the client—clearly stating the mutual understanding of the nature of the engagement.

Environmental changes (6)   Changes in the operating conditions of an entity which may or may not be accompanied by adaptation of the control structure to the new environment. Environmental changes are classified as one of the inherent limitations of any set of control structure policies and procedures.

Errors (5)   Unintentional mistakes. Errors may be further classified as to errors of omission and errors of commission.

Errors of commission (4)   Inclusion of nonexistent items in the financial statements. Errors of commission result in overstatement of financial statement components.

Errors of omission (4)   Errors resulting in understatements of financial statement components.

Ethics rulings and interpretations (2)   Issued by the Executive Committee of the Professional Ethics Division of the AICPA, these rulings and interpretations represent further clarification of the principles and rules contained in the *Code of Professional Conduct*.

Evaluation criteria (17)   A term associated with operational auditing, evaluation criteria define the process or activity being audited. Identifying evaluation criteria is necessary if the auditor is to ultimately determine the cause of discovered inefficiencies.

Existence or occurrence (4 and 6)   A state in which all of the transactions reflected in the financial statements have actually occurred at or prior to the current year end.

Expectations gap (2)   The disparity between users' and CPAs' perceptions of professional services, especially audit services, rendered by CPAs.

Expected occurrence rate (10)   Used in attribute sampling, the expected occurrence rate is the anticipated error rate.

Expenditure cycle (12 and 13)   That transaction cycle comprising purchases, payroll, cash payments, operating expenses, inventories, plant assets, intangible assets, and accounts payable.

Expert systems (9)   Software packages that extend to the computer the ability to make expert quality decisions within specialized domains.

Explanatory paragraph (15)   A paragraph added after the opinion paragraph of the audit report for the purpose of elaborating on one or more of the following conditions: departure from a principle promulgated by the body designated by the AICPA council, material uncertainties, ability of the entity to continue as a going concern, a change in accounting principle, or emphasis of a matter.

External auditing (1)   *See* independent auditing.

Factual evidence (4)   *See* direct evidence.

Field work   *See* audit field work.

Field work standards (1 and 2)   Those auditing standards which relate to the audit process.

Final audit (1)   Those audit procedures performed after the balance sheet date, consisting primarily of tests of transactions and balances.

Financial statement auditing (1)   A historically oriented evaluation for the purpose of attesting to the fairness of financial statement presentation.

Financing and investing cycle (12 and 14)   That transaction cycle comprising borrowing from others, lending to others, interest expense, interest revenue, dividend revenue, notes payable, bonds payable, notes receivable, capital stock, and retained earnings.

Finite correction factor (11)   A downward adjustment of sample size applied whenever the initial sample size exceeds a specified percentage of the population size.

Float (12)   A term associated with kiting, float is defined as the time lag for cash transfers between the disbursing bank and the payee bank.

Forecast (16)   A forecast is a form of prospective financial statements that presents the entity's expected financial position, results of operations, and cash flows reflecting conditions expected to exist.

Foreign Corrupt Practices Act of 1977 (17)   An act passed by Congress to prevent bribes and other illegal payments to foreign officials by public companies as a means for obtaining business. As such, the Act contains provisions requiring companies to maintain accurate accounting records and adequate internal control structures.

Form vs. substance (14)   Form refers to the legal nature of a transaction or event; substance refers to the economic aspects of the transaction or event. When form and substance are in conflict relative to material transactions or events, substance should take precedence over form. Auditors are particularly alert to possible conflicts between form and substance when auditing related party transactions.

Fraud (3)   Intent to deceive.

Full responsibility (15)   As contrasted with divided responsibility, when one or more subsidiaries are audited by other CPAs, the principal auditor, after obtaining satisfaction as to the other CPAs' independence, professional status, and quality of work, may elect to assume responsibility for all work performed on the audit, including that of the other CPAs.

General Accounting Office (GAO) (1)   A federal agency reporting directly to Congress on the efficiency, effectiveness, and compliance of other government agencies, projects, and functions.

General controls (8)   Procedures designed to contribute to the achievement of specific control objectives through their interdependence with specific control procedures. General controls are broader in scope than application controls and relate to all or many computerized accounting activities.

General standards (1 and 2)   Those auditing standards that relate to the character and competence of the auditor.

Generalized audit software packages (9)   Programs developed by auditing firms and others to assist in performing substantive testing of a client's computer files.

Generally accepted auditing standards (2)   The set of standards developed by the Auditing Standards Board of the AICPA that define the quality of independent audits.

GRiDPAD (9)   A small computer that resembles a flat screen. GRiDPAD can be programmed to display business forms or checklists. An electronic pen is then used to record data in the forms or checklists. The recorded data can then be downloaded into a regular computer for further analysis. An audit application of GRiDPAD is documenting inventory test counts.

Gross negligence (3)   Failure to exercise minimum care.

Hash total (8)   A user control consisting of a meaningless sum (e.g., the sum of customer account numbers) to be compared with a computer generated total to determine that all records have been updated in a given computer processing run.

Header and trailer label information (8)   A computer processing control whereby the file name, record counts, and other data are included for comparison purposes.

Hearsay Evidence (4)   Evidence consisting of answers to questions posed by the auditor to client personnel. This is the weakest form of audit evidence and must usually be further corroborated.

Hypertext (9)   A software technique whereby words in a file are coded to aid in searching large data bases for specific content. Hypertext can be used by auditors in searching the professional standards and tax laws to obtain answers to technical accounting, auditing, and tax questions.

Inconsistency (1 and 15)   A change in accounting principle from one period to the next requiring an explanatory paragraph following the opinion paragraph of the auditor's report.

Incorporation by reference (3)   Directs the reader's attention to information included in the annual report to shareholders rather than reporting such information in Form 10–K.

Incremental allowance for precision (11)   Used in probability proportional to size sampling to express the increase in the precision range, given logical units containing error and having book values less than the sampling interval. The increment recognizes the increased standard error when projecting sample results to a larger interval.

Independence in fact vs. appearance (2)   Independence in fact is a state of mind. Independence in appearance requires the auditor to avoid situations which appear to compromise auditor independence (such as serving on the client's board of directors.)

Independent auditing (1)   An examination conducted by auditors who are independent of the persons whose assertions are being evaluated.

Indexing (4)   A system of classifying and integrating audit workpapers according to a predetermined schemata.

Indirect evidence (4)   Evidence that permits the auditor to infer certain states by examining the evidence but that does not permit the auditor to draw conclusions from the evidence. For example, the existence of inventory on the client's premises provides conclusive evidence of existence, but only inferential evidence of ownership. Further evidence, in the form of documentation, must be obtained by the auditor to further support the ownership objective.

Individual item materiality (4)   The impact of a single error or irregularity on the financial statements.

Inferential evidence (4)   *See* indirect evidence.

Information system (1)   The system that produces the data appearing on the financial statements.

Information system testing (1)   The act of assessing inherent risk and control risk by examining and testing the client's information system. The information system may be tested by studying the business and industry, performing analytical procedures, and studying and evaluating control structure policies and procedures relevant to an audit.

Inherent limitations (6)   Limitations causing an otherwise effective control structure to provide reasonable, rather than absolute, assurance of preventing and detecting errors and irregularities.

Inherent risk (5)   Sometimes called *business risk,* inherent risk relates to the susceptibility of an account balance or class of transactions to error that could be material, assuming that there were no related internal controls.

Initial audit (4)   A first-time examination. The client's financial statements may or may not have been examined in prior years by other CPAs.

Input controls (8)   Controls concerned with the accuracy and completeness of data fed into the data processing system.

Input preparation group (8)   Persons within the EDP function who convert input data to a machine readable form.

Integrated data base system (8)   A system that updates many files—for example, sales, accounts receivable, and inventory—as transactions are entered into the system.

Integrated disclosure (3)   An SEC provision that permits companies registered with the SEC to incorporate data by reference from the annual report to stockholders to Form 10–K filed with the SEC.

Integrated test facility approach (8)   A means for auditing through the computer whereby the auditor creates a fictitious entity within the client's actual data files. Hypothetical data are then processed as part of the client's regular data processing activity. The auditor then compares the results with the anticipated results as a basis for evaluating control effectiveness.

Interim audit (1)   Procedures applied prior to the client's year-end, primarily for the purpose of lowering the assessed risk level.

Interim financial information (16)   Financial statements or condensed information covering less than a year.

Internal auditing (1 and 17)   An independent appraisal function established within an organization to examine and evaluate its activities as a service to the organization.

Internal control checklist (7)   A listing of controls necessary to assure effectiveness of control structure within a given transaction cycle subset.

Internal control flowchart (7)   A means for documenting the auditor's understanding of control structure, the flowchart represents a pictorial presentation of the processing steps within a transaction cycle subset. Actions, documents, and people performing the control procedures are depicted in the flowchart.

Internal control memorandum (7)   A narrative description of a transaction cycle, together with a statement describing control strengths and weaknesses.

Internal control questionnaire (7)   A list of questions designed to cover all pertinent control points in a transaction cycle subset. Yes answers denote strengths; no answers denote weaknesses.

Internal control structure (6)   The policies and procedures established to provide reasonable assurance that specific entity objectives will be achieved.

Internal evidence (4)   Audit evidence, mainly documentary, obtained from within the client entity. Its validity is a function of existing internal control.

Introductory paragraph (15)   The first paragraph of the standard audit report, the introductory paragraph identifies the financial statements covered by the audit report and clearly differentiates management's responsibility for preparing the financial statements from the auditor's responsibility for expressing an opinion on them.

Inventory confirmation (13)   Evidence of inventory existence obtained directly by the auditor from third parties having custody of the client's inventory. This audit procedure is typically applied to inventory on consignment and to inventories in public warehouses.

Inventory cutoff (13)   The state of consistency among the physical inventory, recorded sales, and recorded purchases whereby recorded purchases have been received and included in the physical inventory, and recorded sales have been shipped and excluded from the physical inventory.

Inventory cutoff tests (13)   Substantive tests performed by the auditor to determine that purchases and sales transactions were recorded in the proper accounting period.

Inventory instructions (13)   A set of directions for the purpose of ensuring a reliable physical inventory. The instructions are written by the client and reviewed by the auditor. They cover such matters as location and timing of inventory taking; procedures for counting, double-checking counts, and documenting the counts; and the auditors' participation as observers of the inventory.

Inventory observation (13)   Performing test counts, controlling the auditor's copies of the physical inventory documentation, and otherwise evaluating the year-end inventory taking by the client. Inventory observation requires that the audit team be present during the client's annual physical inventory.

Inventory pricing tests (13)   A set of audit procedures designed to ascertain whether the client has properly costed the ending inventories.

Inventory tags or sheets (13)   Instruments for documenting the physical inventory. The tags or sheets should be prenumbered and provide for a description of the inventory item, stock number, location, and condition.

Inventory test counts (13)   Counts of the client's inventory performed by the auditor following the client's original counts and double-checks.

Investment ledger (14)   A subsidiary ledger containing the detail supporting the investment account in the general ledger.

Irregularities (5)   Misstatements of financial statements caused by intentional acts. Irregularities may be further classified as to misappropriation and misrepresentation.

Kiting (12)   A type of misrepresentation fraud used to conceal bank overdrafts or cash misappropriations, kiting occurs when a company draws a check on one bank for deposit in another bank but does not record the transaction or records only a part of the transaction before year-end.

Lapping (12)   A form of concealment that involves crediting current customer remittances to the accounts of customers who have remitted previously. The purpose is to keep all accounts current in order to avoid auditor suspicion.

Lawyer's letter (4 and 13)   *See* letter of audit inquiry to client's legal counsel.

Lead schedule (4)   A schedule that lists all of the general ledger accounts comprising a single line item on the financial statements.

Legal form (14)   The nature of a transaction as defined in the law. Legal form may be at variance with the ''real'' nature (economic substance) of the transaction. When this occurs, substance should take precedence over form in the financial statements. (*See also* Continental Vending Machine Corporation [*U.S. v. Simon*] case in the appendix following Chapter 3.)

Letter of audit inquiry to client's legal counsel (4 and 13)   A letter obtained directly by the auditor from the client's outside legal counsel. The purpose of the letter is to provide evidence regarding pending litigation and the possible need for journal entries or footnotes relating to asserted and unasserted claims.

Librarian (8)   A person within the EDP function who maintains custody over master files and programs and permits access only on the basis of proper authority.

Limited access controls (6)   Control procedures that prevent other than authorized personnel from gaining access to specified assets, documents, and/or data base elements.

Loan defaults (14)   Violations of loan agreements which could result in loan principal and interest becoming immediately due. Such defaults may assume the form of either violations of restrictive covenants or failure to meet principal or interest payments when due.

Loan restructuring (14)   Revision of loan terms for the purpose of enabling the borrower to continue amortizing the obligation in a manner mutually acceptable to the lender and borrower. The restructuring may include extending the payment date for the loan, reducing the interest rate, reducing principal, forgiving accrued interest, or settling all or part of the obligation by the transfer of noncash assets.

Logical sampling unit (11)   A term used in PPS sampling to describe the item to which the randomly selected dollar attaches (for example, a customer account, a line item on an inventory listing, or a posting to a plant asset account).

Magnetic tape system (8)   A computerized data processing system that requires conversion of hard copy documents into machine-readable form-as contrasted with on-line systems.

Management advisory services (2)   Consulting services rendered for clients by CPAs; for example, installing EDP systems, performance reporting systems, and inventory control systems.

Management auditing (1)   An examination and evaluation of the activities of management. Also referred to as effectiveness or performance auditing.

Management's discussion and analysis (15)   A supplemental letter from management in the annual report to stockholders, the letter elaborates on the audited financial statements by explaining the more significant changes in financial statement components occurring during the year.

Management letter (14)   A letter from the auditor to the client covering all auditor-discovered weaknesses in the client's control structure. The purpose of the letter is to provide constructive suggestions to management concerning improvements in the control structure.

Management override (6)   One of the limitations inherent in a given control structure, management override involves management circumvention of the control structure for the purpose of perpetrating one or more irregularities.

Management's assertions (6)   Management's representations concerning data contained in the financial statements, the assertions include existence or occurrence, completeness, rights and obligations, valuation or allocation, and presentation and disclosure.

Materiality (4 and 5)   As used in financial auditing, materiality relates to the impact of errors or irregularities on the decisions of financial statement users.

Materiality threshold (4)   The smallest aggregate level of errors or irregularities that could be considered material to any one of the financial statements.

Mathematical evidence (4)   Audit evidence consisting of calculations, recalculations, and reconciliations performed by the auditor. Mathematical evidence is a direct form of audit evidence.

Maximum level of control risk (7)   A high assessed level of control risk suggesting a primarily substantive audit approach.

Mean per unit (11)   A method of sampling for variables whereby a sample mean is calculated and extended to the population.

Microcomputer systems (8)   Data processing systems utilizing microcomputers. A microcomputer is a small computer, ordinarily used by a single individual. Microcomputers may be used as a "stand alone" computer or they may be connected to mainframe computers through a form of networking.

Microcomputer audit packages (9)   Software packages, either generalized or custom-designed, used to analyze client data and generally automate the audit. These packages assist the auditor in performing substantive testing.

Minimum audit (6)   The concept that requires the application of some minimum degree of substantive audit testing regardless of the effectiveness of the client's internal control structure. The concept of a minimum audit recognizes that effective internal control provides reasonable, but not absolute, assurance concerning the reliability of the financial statements.

Minimum care (3)   The least amount of diligence expected of the CPA in performing accounting and auditing services, below which reckless misconduct may be construed.

Misappropriation (5)   The fraudulent transfer of assets from the firm to one or more dishonest employees. The transfer is either preceded or followed by some form of concealment involving alteration of accounts or substance.

Misrepresentation (1, 5, and 6)   Deliberate attempts by management to misstate the financial statements by omitting significant information from the records, recording transactions without substance, or intentionally misapplying accounting principles.

Negative assurance (16)   A report that expresses conclusions on the basis of a review.

Negative confirmation (12)   A form of accounts receivable confirmation that requests the customer to respond only in the event of disagreement with the reported balance.

Nonstatistical sampling (10)   A subjective approach to inference, in that mathematical techniques are not used consistently in determining sample size, selecting the sample, or evaluating sample results. Smaller populations, or populations containing items not so readily accessible by the auditor, are often more conducive to testing through nonstatistical sampling techniques.

Observation (7)   A means of control testing whereby the auditor is present during transaction processing and observes for proper functioning of pertinent controls at the input stage of transaction processing.

Omitted procedures (15)   Necessary procedures not applied by the auditor, the term is used in the context of auditor discovery of the omission after the date of the audit report.

On-line-real-time system (8)   An EDP system that processes transactions as they occur (some automatically), and several files (e.g., sales, accounts receivable, inventory) are updated simultaneously by a single transaction input.

Open items (14)   Questions that have arisen during the audit for which answers were not immediately available. All open items should be cleared prior to completion of audit field work.

Operating effectiveness (7)   Part of the auditor's assessment of control risk where control tests are performed, operating effectiveness reflects how well controls functioned during the period under audit.

Operational auditing (1 and 17)   A future-oriented, independent, and systematic evaluation performed by the internal auditor for management of the operational activities controlled by top-, middle, and lower-level management for the purposes of improving organizational profitability and increasing the attainment of the other organizational objectives. A subset of internal auditing, operational auditing reviews an entity's activities for efficiency and effectiveness.

Opinion paragraph (15)   The paragraph in the audit report that reflects the auditor's findings.

Optical disk storage (9)   A computer technology made possible with the use of CD-ROMs (compact disk read-only memory), optical disk storage has made possible the storage of large volumes of data needed on a recurring basis-permanent file materials, for example. The CDs are read with lasers and the materials can even be transferred by modem to another computer at a distant location.

Optical scanning devices (9)   A computer hardware device that can read hard copy data and enter it into the computer without the need for "keyboarding."

Ordinary negligence (3)   Failure to exercise reasonable care.

Output controls (8)   Controls that are concerned with the verification and distribution of computer output.

Parallel simulation (8)   A control testing technique that requires the auditor to create a set of application programs that simulate the processing system, and compare output from the real and simulated systems.

Passwords (8)   A form of control over access to data bases, passwords are codes used for accessing various parts of the data base. Some passwords permit read only capability, while others permit updating of files (read and write capability).

Peer review (2)   The examination of one professional's work by others in the same profession. The purpose is to promote quality in the performance of professional services through self-regulation.

Periodic inventories and comparisons (6)   The act of comparing accounts and related substance on a recurring basis.

Permanent file (4)   The file containing those audit workpapers which have ongoing significance.

Phases of processing (8)   The steps required to process a given subset of a transaction cycle; for example, cash receipts from customers.

Physical evidence (4)   Audit evidence consisting of everything than can be counted, examined, observed, or inspected. It provides, through direct evidence, primary support for the existence objective.

Planning and supervision (2)   The act of predetermining the audit approach and directing and reviewing the activities of assistants assigned to the audit. The major tasks involved in planning and supervision are usually assigned to the in-charge senior auditor.

Plant assets lead schedule (13)   An audit lead schedule workpaper listing the components of the "plant assets" line item appearing on the working trial balance.

"Plug-in" hard disks (9)   A storage device that can be attached to a computer. Auditors can attach the hard disk to a lap top computer, for example, and thereby analyze large volumes of data contained in relational data bases.

Policy and procedures manual (6)   Documents assembled by entities which describe firm policies relating to such matters as customer relations, employee relations, purchasing, selling, and adherence to control structure policies and procedures. Existence of policy and procedures manuals is considered by auditors to be an essential ingredient of an effective set of control structure policies and procedures relevant to an audit.

Positive assurance (16)   A report that expresses conclusions on the basis of an examination.

Positive confirmation (12)   A form of accounts receivable confirmation that requests the customer to respond as to agreement or disagreement with the reported balance.

Preaudit conference (1, 4, and 5)   A meeting of the audit team prior to commencing field work for the purpose of increasing the effectiveness of the audit by discussing the results of risk analysis with the staff assigned to the audit.

Precision (10 and 11)   A statistical sampling term defined as the range within which the true answer most likely falls.

Predecessor auditor (15)   One who has examined the financial statements of one or more consecutive periods immediately prior to the current period, but who has not examined the financial statements of the current period.

Preliminary audit programs (5)   Initial audit programs prepared after the auditor's study of the business and industry, application of analytical procedures, and preliminary assessment of control risk. These programs may be further modified on the basis of further control structure testing.

Presentation and disclosure (4 and 6)   A state in which all of the financial statement components have been properly classified and in which disclosure, in the form of footnotes or in the body of the statements, is adequate so as not to make the financial statements misleading.

Prevention controls (6)   Internal controls that avoid the occurrence of errors and/or irregularities.

Primarily substantive audit approach (7)   An audit approach that emphasizes substantive testing rather than some combination of control testing and substantive testing. This approach is usually followed for transaction cycle subsets where control risk is assessed at maximum.

Principal auditor (15)   Where two or more auditing firms have participated in the audit of an entity, the principal auditor is the firm that has examined the major portion of the combined entity. The decision of which firm is principal auditor is necessary for a proper division of responsibility.

Private Companies Practice Section (2)   That section of the Division for CPA Firms comprising CPAs with non-SEC clients.

Privity of contract (3)   (*See also Ultramares v. Touch* and *Rhode Island Hospital Trust National Bank v. Swartz* in the appendix following Chapter 3.) Limitation of liability to the parties to a given contract. Under privity, the CPA is not liable to third parties for ordinary negligence.

Probability proportional to size sampling (11)   A variation of attribute sampling, PPS is used to estimate the dollar amount of errors in a population. Applicable only to populations for which the auditor suspects a few errors of overstatement.

Procedures driven audit (5)   An audit approach that utilizes standard audit programs regardless of varying levels of audit risk. This approach is no longer considered acceptable in today's audit environment.

Processing controls (8)   Those controls concerned with the manipulation of data once it is entered into the computer.

Programmers (8)   Persons within the EDP function who write and test programs based on the system design and/or modification.

Projected error (11)   Related to probability proportional to size sampling, the projected error is the estimated population overstatement error as calculated from the sample.

Projection (16)   A form of prospective financial statements that presents financial position, results of operations and cash flows given one or more hypothetical assumptions.

Proof of cash (12)   A form of bank reconciliation that agrees recorded receipts and disbursements for a given time period with bank statement credits and debits. As an audit procedure, the proof of cash helps to detect errors in recording cash receipts or disbursements.

Prospective financial statements (16)   Financial statements containing nonhistorical data. Prospective financial statements usually assume the form of forecasts or projections.

Public Oversight Board (2)   A body of the AICPA, consisting mainly of nonaccountants, that supervises the activities of the SEC Practice Section of the Division for CPA Firms.

Punched card system (8)   A computerized data processing system that requires the conversion of hard copy documents into machine-readable form-as contrasted with on-line systems.

Purchases cutoff (13)   The process whereby purchases are recorded in the proper accounting period.

Qualified opinion (15)   An audit opinion rendered under circumstances of one or more material scope restrictions or departures from GAAP.

Random selection (10) A term used to describe the process of selecting items to be included in a sample on a probability basis. Given random selection, every item in the population has a known or equal chance of being included in the sample.

Real-time processing (8) In a real-time system, transactions are entered into the computer as they occur and are processed as they are entered.

Reasonable care (3) The act of exercising reasonable diligence in the conduct of auditing and other accounting and review services. That degree of care exercised by the "prudent" CPA in conducting an examination of financial statements or other accounting services.

Recording forms (8) Input forms used to assure consistency and completeness of recurring inputs such as purchases and sales.

Recurring audit (4) A repeat examination of the financial statements of a client whose prior financial statements were also examined by the same auditing firm.

Related party transactions (4 and 14) Transactions between the client and persons or entities related to the client through family ties, common stock ownership, or other means. Related party transactions often produce variances between legal form and economic substance. When the two are in conflict, GAAP requires that substance take precedence over form.

Relational data base systems (9) Software packages that permit multi-classifications of large volumes of data. Having greater storage capacity than spreadsheets, these packages are being used to an increasing extent by auditors in audit workpaper preparation and linking.

Relevance of audit evidence (1 and 4) The usefulness of audit evidence in satisfying stated audit objectives.

Reliability (10 and 11) Synonymous with confidence level, reliability is a statistical sampling term meaning the likelihood that the sample range contains the true value.

Reportable conditions (7 and 14) Matters coming to the auditor's attention that, in (his or her) judgment, should be communicated to the audit committee because they represent significant deficiencies in the design or operation of the internal control structure.

Reporting standards (1 and 2) Those auditing standards that relate to the attest function.

Reprocessing (7) A form of control testing whereby the auditor introduces hypothetical transactions into the client's accounting system to test the system's ability to identify and correct errors in the capturing and processing of data. Reprocessing may be done separately or during live processing of client data.

Results of processing (8) The output, in the form of recorded transactions and balances, of a given transaction cycle; for example, sales revenue and accounts receivable balances.

Revenue cycle (12) The transaction cycle comprising sales revenue, cash receipts, cash balances, and accounts receivable.

Review (16) More than a compilation, but less than an audit, a review consists of applying procedures, mainly in the form of inquiry and analytical procedures, adequate to provide the CPA a basis for expressing limited assurance concerning the conformance of a set of financial statements with GAAP.

RICO (3) The Racketeer Influenced and Corrupt Organizations Act of 1970, a bill passed by Congress as an effort to eradicate organized crime in the United States. CPAs have been exposed to increased liability (referred to as "civil RICO") under the provisions of this act.

Rights and obligations (4 and 6) A state in which all assets reflected in the balance sheet are owned by the client at the balance sheet date and in which all liabilities reflected in the balance sheet are obligations of the client at the balance sheet date.

Risk analysis matrix (5) A diagrammatic means for matching "warning signs" with the sources of information available to the auditor for identifying the warning signs. See Table 5.1 for a comprehensive example of a risk analysis matrix.

Risk-based operational auditing (17) An operational audit focus that responds to efficiency and effectiveness problem areas within the entity as they arise.

Risk driven audit (5) An audit approach that carefully analyzes audit risk, sets materiality thresholds based on audit risk analysis, and develops audit programs that allocate a larger proportion of audit resources to high risk areas. The risk driven audit is the preferred approach in today's financial environment and, therefore, is the main focus of this textbook.

Risk of underassessment (10) The risk that the sample supports the auditor's lowering of assessed control risk when the true error rate does not justify such reduction. In nonstatistical terms, it is the probability that the auditor will assess control risk at a lower level than justified for a given subset of the client's control structure.

Rules of conduct (2)   That part of the *Code of Professional Conduct* which governs the performance of auditing and other services rendered by CPAs. The Code contains principles and rules. The principles provide a framework, while the rules are concerned with proper adherence to the principles.

S–1 review (3)   (*See also Escott v. Bar Chris Construction Corporation* in the appendix following Chapter 3.) An auditor's review of subsequent events up to the effective date of a registration statement pursuant to the Securities Act of 1933 involving new securities offerings.

Safeguard controls (7)   Controls designed to protect assets against misappropriation or other forms of loss, examples include restricted access, cash registers, and separation of duties.

Sales cutoff (12 and 13)   The process for ensuring that sales are recorded in the proper accounting period.

Sampling for attributes (10)   An estimate of frequency of occurrence of events (errors or irregularities.) In auditing, attribute sampling is frequently used to further test control procedures.

Sampling interval (11)   A term used in PPS sampling to describe the distance between two consecutive sample items.

Sampling unit (10 and 11)   A defined population item (e.g., a line item in an inventory listing, or a bill of lading evidencing shipment of goods) representing the focal point for sampling applications.

Scienter (3)   Intent.

Scope paragraph (15)   That paragraph of the audit report that tells what the auditor did. Specifically, it states whether or not the audit was conducted in accordance with GAAS.

Scope restriction (15)   A failure by the auditor to apply auditing procedures considered necessary in the circumstances. Scope restrictions may be imposed by management, or they may be unimposed–e.g., when the auditor is engaged after fiscal year end and cannot observe the year end physical inventory.

Search for unrecorded liabilities (13)   A set of auditing procedures designed to locate errors of omission involving unrecorded year-end liabilities.

SEC Practice Section (2)   That section of the Division for CPA Firms consisting of CPAs with SEC clients.

Self-regulation (2)   The state whereby the accounting profession regulates its own activities and performance without intervention by public bodies, such as Congress or the SEC.

Separate file system (8)   An EDP file system whereby each file is updated individually in separate processing runs, as contrasted with an integrated data base system.

Service bureau (8)   A company (e.g., a commercial bank) that processes transactions (e.g., payroll) for other entities.

Single Audit Act of 1984 (17)   An act of Congress applicable to the audits of state and local government units and other not-for-profit entities receiving $100,000 or more of federal financial assistance in a fiscal year. The act requires the auditor to evaluate internal controls over federal financial assistance, audit compliance with specific requirements, and report on compliance with laws and regulations that may have a material effect on each major federal financial assistance program.

Standard audit report (15)   The form of audit report recommended by the Auditing Standards Board of the AICPA. This report is rendered at the conclusion of an audit in which the auditor encountered no material scope limitations, and the financial statements conform to GAAP in all material respects.

Standard bank confirmation (12)   A confirmation form recommended by the AICPA, by which the bank provides information directly to the auditor concerning bank balances and outstanding loans relative to a specified client.

Standard deviation (11)   A measure of population variability, standard deviation may be defined as the degree of variation of individual item values about the population mean.

Standard journal entries (6)   A set of predetermined journal entries for recording recurring month-end transactions and events. Standard journal entries provide control by preventing oversights in the form of omitted accruals and/or apportionments.

Statements on auditing standards (2)   Pronouncements of the Auditing Standards Board of the AICPA that constitute interpretations of the ten generally accepted auditing standards.

Statements on responsibilities in tax practice (2) Pronouncements issued by the Committee on Federal Taxation of the AICPA, they provide guidance for CPAs in performing tax services and in representing clients before the Internal Revenue Service.

Statements on standards for accounting and review services (2) Pronouncements of the Accounting and Review Services Committee of the AICPA which establish the framework for performing compilations and review services for clients.

Statements on standards for consulting services (2) Pronouncements of the AICPA Management Advisory Services Executive Committee which provide guidance for maintaining standards of quality in the performance of consulting services for clients.

Statistical sampling (10) A mathematical approach to inference. In determining sample size, in selecting the sample, and in evaluating the sample results, a consistent and orderly approach is followed.

Statutory liability (3) Legal liability imposed by statutes. CPAs are liable to third parties under the Securities Act of 1933 and under Section 10B5 of the Securities and Exchange Act of 1934 for negligence and fraud.

Stratified sampling (10 and 11) A statistical sampling approach whereby a population is divided into two or more subsets, the parameters for each to be set differently. Used primarily in variables sampling, stratification permits the auditor to examine larger items in the population more intensively than less significant items.

Subsequent discovery of facts (15) Discovery by the auditor, after issuing the audit report, of facts existing at the date of the auditor report. The facts may or may not have changed the audit report had they been known at the date of the report.

Subsequent events (14) Events or transactions occurring after the balance sheet date, but before the completion of audit field work. Subsequent events may have a material impact on the audited financial statements and may require adjustment or disclosure.

Substance (4) That which is represented by an account. The inventory in the warehouse, for example, is the substance represented by the account, Finished Goods Inventory.

Substantive audit testing (1, 4, and 12) The process of obtaining evidence in support of transactions and balances.

Successor auditor (15) An auditor engaged to conduct an audit for a client whose financial statements have been previously examined by other auditors.

Sufficiency of audit evidence (1 and 4) Enough evidence to support the auditor's opinion on the financial statements.

Supporting schedule (4) A schedule containing evidence of substantive tests performed by the auditor, together with the results of those tests and the auditor's conclusions.

Surprise audit (8) A control testing procedure for EDP systems whereby the auditor, on an unannounced basis, requests duplicate copies of client programs, at the completion of data processing runs, for comparison with the auditor's copies of "authorized" versions.

Systematic sampling (10) A random selection means whereby the sample is drawn by selecting every nth item in the population until the required sample size is reached. In applying systematic selection, the starting point must be at random and the entire field must be covered.

Systems analyst (8) A person within the EDP function who designs new systems and modifies existing systems in accordance with the information needs of the users.

Systems development and documentation controls (8) Associated with EDP systems, these are controls over the definition, design, development, testing, and documentation of the systems and programs constituting each application.

Tagging and tracing (8) A control testing technique whereby selected transactions, which pass by specific processing points, are analyzed. Client programs need to be modified in order to mark or "tag" input data such that relevant information (hard copy) is displayed at key points in the processing system.

Tainting (11) A logical unit containing one or more errors is said to be "tainted". If the book value of the logical unit is less than the sampling interval, a "tainting" percentage must be applied in order to project the error for the entire sampling interval containing the logical unit.

Tainting percentage (11) $(BV - AV)/BV$, calculated
for any logical unit $\leq$ sampling interval and
containing error.

Temporary breakdown (6) One of the limitations
inherent in a given control structure, a temporary
breakdown relates to the occasional failure of the
control structure to prevent or detect an error or
irregularity. Such failures are due to oversight by
individuals responsible for performing control
procedures.

Test-based audit (2) An audit of a sampling of
transactions as contrasted with a detailed audit
requiring the examination of all transactions. A
test-based audit is designed to provide reasonable,
but not absolute, assurance as to fairness of
presentation.

Test data approach (8) A means for auditing
through the computer whereby the auditor
prepares simulated input data (transactions) that
are processed, under the auditor's control, by the
client's processing system. The test data should
contain a combination of all inputs required to
execute all of the logic contained in the process.

Tests for inventory obsolescence (13) Audit
procedures applied for the purpose of determining
whether inventories should be written down to
reflect a decline in value below cost. Causes of
obsolescence might be overstocking, changes in
technology, physical deterioration due to
improper storage, and style changes.
Obsolescence tests may assume the form of
inquiry, observation, and turnover tests.

Time budget (1, 5, and 9) *See* budget and time
summary.

Time sharing (8) Time sharing occurs when a
computer serves more than one user. In
transaction processing, time sharing occurs when
a computer processes transactions for more than
one entity.

Tolerable occurrence rate (10) Used in attribute
sampling, the tolerable occurrence rate is the
maximum rate of error acceptable to the auditor,
while still warranting a lowering of assessed
control risk below the maximum level.

Transaction cycle (4) A group of related
transactions affecting essentially the same set of
general ledger accounts.

Transaction documentation (6) An important
ingredient of the audit trail, transaction
documentation requires some form of underlying
document supporting any given transaction or
event. Documentation may assume the form of

vendors' invoices, sales invoices, time cards,
production reports, journal vouchers, transaction
logs, and workpaper analyses supporting
adjusting journal entries.

Transaction review (6) An examination of
transaction documentation and approvals after
completion to ensure that the transaction was
properly approved, executed, and recorded.
Transaction review should be performed by
someone who was not involved in the approval,
execution, or recording of the transaction.

Transaction testing (1) That part of the auditor's
study of control structure policies and procedures
which encompasses examination of transactions
on a test basis. The purpose of such testing is to
enable the auditor to project an upper error rate
as input into the assessment of control risk and
design of audit programs. Transaction testing may
assume the form of observation, reprocessing, or
document testing.

Type I subsequent events (14) Events occurring
between the balance sheet date and close of audit
field work that provide additional evidence with
respect to conditions that existed at the date of
the balance sheet and affect the estimates inherent
in the process of preparing the financial
statements–require adjustment if material.

Type II subsequent events (14) Events that provide
evidence with respect to conditions that did not
exist at the date of the balance sheet, but arose
subsequent to that date—may require disclosure.

Unaudited financial statements (16) Financial
statements that have not been audited. Whenever
associated with unaudited financial statements of
a public entity, a CPA should disclaim an opinion
and mark each page of the statements as
unaudited. When associated with the financial
statements of a nonpublic entity, the CPA should
at least compile the statements.

Uncertainty (15) A situation in which the outcome
of future events that may affect the financial
statements cannot be reasonably estimated by
management.

Underlying accounting data (4) Internal audit
evidence consisting of books of original entry,
ledgers and supporting work sheets.

Understanding of control structure (7) Knowledge
obtained by the auditor relative to the client's
control structure policies and procedures relevant
to an audit. The understanding so obtained must

be sufficient for the auditor to assess control risk as a basis for designing substantive audit programs.

Unqualified audit opinion (15)   An audit opinion not qualified for any material scope restrictions or departures from GAAP.

Updating the audit report (15)   The act of a continuing auditor reporting on financial statements of prior years that are presented together with those of the current year.

Upper error limit (11)   The sum of the projected error and the allowance for sampling risk. Represents the maximum overstatement error at the reliability level specified by the auditor.

Upper Occurrence Limit (10)   The calculated maximum error rate based on the results of sampling.

User Controls (8)   Manual control procedures applied by organizational units (user groups) whose data is processed by EDP. These controls consist mainly of control totals developed prior to submission of data for processing.

Validity of audit evidence (1 and 4)   A measure of the quality of audit evidence. Validity is enhanced by an effective internal control structure.

Valuation or Allocation (4 and 6)   A state in which all components of the financial statements have been properly valued in accordance with GAAP.

Variables Sampling (11)   An estimate of amount (account balance or dollar amount of errors). In auditing, variables sampling is used for substantive testing. More specifically, it is used to estimate the dollar amount of transactions or account balances by examining a sample and extending the results to the population.

Vouching (4)   The act of tracing transactions or events backward from journal entries and postings to underlying documentation and forward from documents to journal entries and postings.

Warning Signs (5)   Signals or "flags" produced by the application of analytical procedures, study of the business and industry, or by other means that are indicative of significant audit risk.

Working Trial Balance (4)   The focal point of the current file, the working trial balance may be thought of as a table of contents showing unaudited balances, adjustments and reclassifications, audited balances, and the workpapers in which the accounts are analyzed.

Workpaper review (14)   The process whereby audit workpapers for a given engagement are reviewed by those not preparing the workpapers. Workpapers completed by assistants are usually reviewed by the in-charge senior auditor; the senior auditor's workpapers are reviewed by the audit manager; and the workpapers as a whole are reviewed by the audit partner on an aggregate basis.

Yellow book (17)   Written by the General Accounting Office, the "yellow book" sets forth auditing standards to be followed in auditing recipients of federal financial assistance.

Index

Ability to continue as a going concern,
    auditor's responsibility to evaluate (*See
    also* audit report), 49–50
Account distribution—defined, 242
Account vs. substance (*See* audit evidence)
Accounting and Review Services Committee, 37
Accounting estimates (*See* substantive audit
    testing)
Accounting profession, investigation of, 30
Accounting symmetry (*See* substantive testing)
Accounts receivable confirmation (*See*
    substantive audit testing)
Account vs. substance (*See* audit evidence)
Alpha risk (*See* statistical sampling)
Analysis of interbank transfers (*See* substantive
    audit testing, cash)
Analytical procedures (*See also* substantive
    audit testing)
  during audit planning, 118, 167
  during overall review, 119, 477, 583
  examples, 119
Assertions, management, 4
Asset safeguards
  accountability controls, 206
  as a component of effective control, 206
  limited access controls, 206
Association with financial statements (*See also*
    unaudited financial statements)
  lack of independence, 666
  range of services, 666
Attestation
  defined, 4
  preconditions, 658
  standards
    contrasted with auditing standards, 658
    defined, 36
    enumerated, 659
Audit adjustments

defined, 135
illustrated, 136
Audit committee, 8
Audit evidence
  account vs. substance, 113
  characteristics of, 106
  competence, 107
  defined, 4
  evaluating audit evidence, 12
  external vs. internal, 484
  factual vs. inferential, 106
  objectively obtaining, 4
  reliability and relevance, 120
  sufficiency, 107
  underlying accounting data and
        corroborating information, 106
  validity and relevance, 107
Audit evidence and procedures
  analytical evidence, 118
  confirmation evidence, 116
  documentary evidence, 116
  hearsay evidence, 120
  mathematical evidence, 118
  physical evidence, 115
Audit field work (*See* substantive audit testing)
Audit objectives
  defined, 107
    information system, 107
    transactions and balances, 110
  completeness, 112
  existence or occurrence, 112
  presentation and disclosure, 113
  related to evidence and procedures, 110
  rights and obligations (ownership), 112
  valuation or allocation, 113
Audit opinion, types of, 13
Audit planning
  as related to risk analysis, 157

classifying business and industry
information, 159
inherent risk analysis, 157
preaudit conference, 18, 137, 180
preliminary, 14
time budget
as part of audit planning, 180
computerized, 385
defined, 14
Audit process
described, 14, 179
flowchart, 152, 199, 232, 368, 475, 516, 612
reviewed, 474
Audit programs
defined, 18, 127
developing, 128
as a function of the client's business, 129
as a function of internal control, 128
as a function of materiality, 128
illustrated, 128
summary audit programs for given
transaction cycles:
borrowing transactions, 577
cash receipts transactions, 495
current liabilities, 540
intangible assets, 535
inventories, 527
investing transactions, 572
plant assets, 533
sales transactions, 488
stockholders' equity transactions, 580
Audit reclassifications, 135
Audit report
ability to continue as a going concern, 628, 630
adverse opinion, 617, 619
change in accounting principle, 632
client imposed scope restriction, 620
communication mechanism, 6
comprehensive basis other than GAAP, 661, 662
continuing auditor-updating, 633, 637
decision flowchart, 623
departure from designated principle, 625, 627
disclaimer of opinion—scope restriction, 621, 622
disclaimer of opinion—uncertainty, 631
divided responsibility, 621, 625
dual-dating, 616
emphasis of a matter, 633, 634
explanatory paragraph following opinion
paragraph, 624
meaning of present fairly in conformity with
GAAP, 639
ranking of GAAP, 639

omitted procedures discovered after date of
audit report, 643
other information in documents containing
audited financial statements, 639
management discussion and analysis
(MD&A), 640
predecessor auditor—omission of report, 634, 638
qualified report
departure from GAAP, 617, 618
inadequate disclosure, 618
middle paragraph, 618
scope restriction, 620
standard audit report
components, 614
defined, 12, 613
illustrated, 13, 613
introductory paragraph, 614
opinion paragraph, 615
scope paragraph, 615
subsequent discovery of facts, 635
summary of audit report modifications, 635
summary of types of audit reports, 624
uncertainty, 626, 629
unqualified opinion—conditions for
rendering, 617
updating, 633, 637
Audit risk (See also substantive testing—audit
risk)
as related to audit evidence and materiality, 125
components of, 153
control risk (See also control risk), 154
defined, 16, 108, 153, 232
detection risk (See also detection risk), 154
equation for audit risk, 155
inherent risk (See also audit planning), 153
management character and attitude as risk
determinants, 246
quantification of audit risk, 155, 419
related to efficiency and effectiveness, 440
Audit risk analysis
incorporating into audit programs, 177
risk analysis matrix, 173
study of business and industry, 159, 197
summary diagram, 247
warning signs, 171
Audit risk, audit evidence, and materiality, 125
Audit sampling (See also statistical sampling)
statistical vs. nonstatistical sampling, 400
Audit trail
as a component of effective control, 203
defined, 117
vouching, 117
Audit workpapers
classified as to current and permanent, 130

current file, 131
defined, 131
guidelines for preparing, 136
indexing, 133, 135
interconnected, 133, 135
lead schedule, 131, 133
permanent file, 131
supporting schedule, 133, 134
working trial balance, 131, 132
Auditing
compliance auditing, 9, 706
contrasted with accounting, 9
defined, 4, 706
financial auditing, 8
independent auditing, 6
why necessary, 10
internal auditing, 6
management auditing, 7, 691
operational auditing, 6, 691
performance auditing, 8
systematic process, 5
Auditing around vs. through the computer (*See*
EDP)
Auditing standards
due audit care, 34
enumerated, 6
field work standards, 35
general standards, 33
independence, 34
planning and supervision, 35
reporting standards, 36
training and proficiency, 34
Auditing with the computer (*See* EDP)

Balanced audit approach (*See* substantive audit
testing)
Bank confirmation (*See* substantive audit
testing—cash)
Bank reconciliation (*See* substantive audit
testing—cash)
Beta risk (*See* statistical sampling)
Budgets as a component of effective control
(*See* internal control)

Chart of accounts as a component of control
(*See* internal control)
Client acceptance
as part of audit planning and risk analysis,
159
communication with predecessor auditor, 53,
167
Client representation letter (*See* completing the
audit)
Code of professional conduct (*See also* rules of
conduct)

principles and rules, 36–48
recent changes, 30–31
Comfort letter (*See* legal liability,
underwriters, letters for)
Commissions and referral fees (*See* rules of
conduct)
Committee on Federal Taxation of the AICPA
(TXs), 38
Communicating internal control structure
related matters (*See* completing the
audit; *see also* internal control
structure, reportable conditions)
Communication with audit committee (*See*
completing the audit)
Communication with predecessor auditor, 53,
167
Competence of personnel, as a control
element, 204
Compilation (*See* unaudited financial
statements)
Completing the audit
client representation letter, 588
communicating internal control structure
related matters, 592
communicating with audit committee, 588
conference with client, 587
management letter, 592
resolving open items, 586
workpaper review, 586
Compliance auditing, 706
audit risk aspects, 709
defined, 706
responsibility under Circular A-133, 708
responsibility under GAAS, 707
SAS 68, 706
Single Audit Act responsibility, 707
Yellow Book responsibility, 707
Confidentiality of client information (*See also*
rules of conduct), 43
Confirmation of accounts receivable (*See*
substantive audit testing)
Contingencies (*See* substantive audit testing)
Contingent fees (*See* rules of conduct)
Contingent rentals, 528
Continuous auditing, 18
Control point (*See* internal control structure)
Control risk (*See also* audit risk)
assessing, 110, 132
documenting conclusions, 243
flowchart as an assessment device (*See also*
flowcharting), 234
maximum level vs. below maximum, 235
obtaining an understanding, 232
documenting understanding, 236–241
internal control flowchart, 238
internal control memorandum, 237
internal control questionnaire, 237

quantifying control risk, 417
reduction through further testing, 241
surprise payroll distribution as a control test, 289
testing standard costs, 293
Control testing, forms of, 242, 399
document testing, 242, 399
observation, 242, 399
reprocessing, 242, 399
Cost/benefit and auditing (*See also* substantive audit testing), 129
Current file (*See* audit workpapers)
Cutoff (*See* substantive audit testing, inventories)
Cutoff bank statement (*See* substantive audit testing)

Defense Contract Audit Agency, 8
Departure from designated principle—auditor agreement, 42
Detailed vs. test based audits, 399
Detection risk (*See also* audit risk)
determining required level, 179
equation, 246
quantifying, 419
Divided responsibility (*See* audit report)
Division for CPA Firms (*See* quality control)
Due care (*See* auditing standards)

Early revenue recognition (*See* substantive audit testing, audit risk)
Effective writing in auditing, 348–356
case illustration, 356–365
EDP
application controls, 316
input, 316–317
output, 317
processing, 317
auditing with the computer, 368
batch processing systems, 306
CD-ROMs-optical disk storage, 385
control risk assessment
auditing around the computer, 305, 322
auditing through the computer, 305, 323
design phase auditing, 326
ITF approach, 324
parallel simulation, 326
surprise audit, 327
tagging and tracing, 325
techniques, summary, 328
test data approach, 323
understanding the system, 319
distributed processing, 312
electronic data interchange (EDI), 310
direct approach, 310

indirect approach, 310
factors affecting control risk, 329
flowchart for assessing control risk, 320
general controls, 314
data and procedural, 316
limited access, 316
organization and operation, 314
systems development and documentation, 314
GRiDPAD, 384, 521
Hypertext, 385
integrated data base systems, 309
managing detection risk, 334
microcomputer systems, 312
optical disk storage, CD-ROMs, 385
phases of processing vs. results of processing, 305
real-time processing systems, 308
relational data base systems, 381
spreadsheet systems, 371
substantive audit testing
analytical procedures, 371
automated text working papers, 384
budget and time summary, 385
custom designed programs, 370
electronic workpaper files, 374
generalized audit software, 370
microcomputer packages, 370
optical scanning devices, 371
''plug-in'' hard disks, 381
temporary control breakdowns minimized, 219
time sharing and service bureaus, 308
user controls, 318
Engagement letter, 16, 17
Errors and irregularities
auditor's detection responsibility, 153
defined and classified, 153
related to materiality, 153
Errors
commission, 112
omission, 112
Ethics (*See* Code of Professional Conduct)
Expectations gap
as related to audit risk analysis, 155
defined, 48
diagram, 49
self-regulation, 48
Expert systems, 385
Extensions and footings defined, 242

Final audit, 18
Flowcharting
rules, 240
symbols, 240
FTC/AICPA Consent Agreement, 44

Foreign Corrupt Practices Act of 1977, 692
Form vs. substance of transactions (*See* related
          party transactions)

General Accounting Office, 8
Generalized audit software (*See* EDP,
          substantive testing)
Generally accepted auditing standards (*See*
          auditing standards)

House Energy and Commerce Oversight and
          Investigations Subcommittee, 30

Independence in rendering professional
          services (*See also* rules of conduct), 40
Independent auditing (*See* auditing)
Inflated sales (*See* substantive audit testing,
          audit risk)
Information systems, 5
Inherent risk (*See also* audit risk)
     assessing, 157
     diagram, 170
     quantifying, 418
Initial vs. recurring audits, 137
Integrated disclosure (*See* Securities Exchange
          Act of 1934)
Interim audit, 18
Interim financial information (*See* unaudited
          financial statements)
Internal auditing, 690
     efficiency vs. effectiveness auditing,
               691
     evolution of internal auditing, 691
     management auditing—a form of internal
               auditing, 691
     operational auditing, 691
          appraising efficiency and effectiveness,
                    700
          approach, 693
          audit report, illustration of, 703
          case study, 693
          conducting the field work, 698
          developing the audit program, 698
          formulating conclusions and
                    recommendations, 701
          functional areas, 694
          performing the audit, 697
          planning the audit, 696
          preliminary audit survey, 697
          reporting findings, 702
          risk-based operational auditing, 693
     organization chart, 695
Internal control for a small business, 220
Internal control structure

accounting system
     defined, 198
     factors comprising, 202
asset safeguards as a component of control
          structure
     accountability controls, 204
     limited access controls, 202
budgeting as a component of control
          structure, 205
chart of accounts as a control device, 202
competence of personnel as a control
          element, 204
control environment
     defined, 198
     factors comprising, 198
control point, 241
     accuracy control, 241
     safeguard control, 241
control procedures
     defined, 198
     factors comprising, 204
control structure/management assertions
          matrix (*See* policies and procedures
          relevant to an audit)
defined, 198
expenditure cycle
     control points, 517
     payments to vendors, 280
     payroll, 283
     payroll padding, 286
     processing steps, 518
     production, 290
     purchases, 275
expression of an opinion, 668
financing and investing cycle
     acquisitions and disposals of financial
               assets, 298
     borrowing from others, 295
     capital stock and dividend transactions,
               299
     control points, 565
     lending to others, 296
     processing steps, 566
inherent limitations
     collusion, 217
     environmental changes, 219
     management override, 217
     temporary breakdown, 219
internal auditing as a component of control
          structure, 201
management assertions
     completeness, 211
     existence or occurrence, 208
     presentation and disclosure, 216
     rights and obligations, 212
     valuation or allocation, 214
payroll padding, 286

periodic inventories and comparisons as a
        component of control, 206
policies and procedures manuals as a
        component of control, 205
policies and procedures relevant to an audit,
        207
    control structure/management assertions
        matrix, 209
reportable conditions
    communication of, 248
    defined, 248
    example of letter, 250
reporting on, 202, 668
revenue cycle
    cash receipts and cash balances, 270
    control points, 479
    processing steps, 480
    sales and accounts receivable balances,
        265
standard journal entries as a component of
        control, 202
    illustrated, 288
transaction documentation as a component
        of control, 203
transaction review as a component of
        control, 203
Inventory observation (*See* substantive audit
        testing)

Kiting (*See* substantive audit testing, cash)

Lapping (*See* substantive audit testing, cash)
Lawyer's letter (*See* substantive audit testing)
Lead schedule (*See* audit workpapers)
Legal cases
    *1136 Tenants Corporation v. Max
            Rothenberg & Co.,* 80
    Cedars of Lebanon Hospital v. Touche, 75
    Cenco v. Seidman & Seidman, 71, 74
    Continental Vending (*See U.S v. Simon*)
    Ernst & Ernst v. Hochfelder, 78, 89
    *Escott v. Bar Chris Construction
            Corporation,* 11, 34, 77, 85
    *ESM Government Securities v. Alexander
            Grant & Co.,* 79, 90
    Fisher v. Kleitz, 86
    McKesson & Robbins, Inc., 83
    National Student Marketing (*See U.S. v.
            Natelli*)
    *Rhode Island Hospital Trust National Bank
            v. Swartz,* 74, 84
    Rusch Factors, Inc. v. Levin, 74, 84
    Ultramares v. Touche, 71, 75, 84
    United States v. Natelli, 71, 89
    United States v. Simon, 68, 71, 87
    Yale Express (*See Fisher v. Kleitz*)

Legal liability
    civil liability, 75
    constructive fraud, 71, 84
    contributory negligence, 74
    dealing with, 82
    flowchart, 73
    form vs. substance of transactions, 87
    preventing, 81
    privity of contract
        defined, 74, 84
        extension, 74, 84
    related party transactions, 87
    sources of liability
        civil RICO, 79, 90
        common law, 72
        contract law, 74
        statutory law, 72, 76
    sources and types summary, 72
    subsequent discovery of facts, 86
    types of liability
        fraud, 68, 87
        gross negligence, 68, 84
        ordinary negligence, 68
        types, summary, 80
    unaudited statements, 80
    underwriters, letters for
        described, 77, 667
        illustrated 669
Lincoln Savings and Loan, 497

Management assertions (*See* internal control
        structure)
Management auditing (*See* internal auditing)
Management Consulting Services Executive
        Committee, 37
Management discussion and analysis (MD&A),
        640
Management letter (*See* completing the audit)
Management misrepresentation fraud, 16, 69,
        153
Management's estimates (*See* substantive audit
        testing)
Materiality
    adjusting thresholds based on risk analysis, 243
    aggregate materiality workpaper, 123–124
    as related to auditing, 121
    defined, 121
    individual and aggregate, 122
    qualitative considerations, 122
    review of thresholds as part of audit review,
        583
    thresholds
        as related to projected error, 125
        revising, 125
        setting, 122
Meaning of present fairly in conformity with
        GAAP (*See* audit report)

Minimum audit
  defined, 217
  need for, 217
Misappropriation, 153

Omitted procedures (*See* audit report)
Open items workpaper (*See* substantive audit
  testing)
Operational auditing (*See* internal auditing)
Orion Pictures Corp., 498
Other accounting services, 656
  summary table, 679
Other information in documents containing
  audited financial statements, 639

Payroll padding (*See* internal control structure)
Periodic inventories and comparisons (*See*
  internal control structure)
Permanent file (*See* audit workpapers)
Preaudit conference (*See* audit planning)
Primarily substantive audit approach, 235
Private Companies Practice Section (*See*
  quality control)
Proof of cash (*See* substantive audit testing,
  cash)
Prospective financial statements
  applying agreed upon procedures, 675, 678
  compilation, 675
  compilation report
    forecast, 674
    projection, 674
  examination, 675
  examination report
    forecast, 676
    projection, 676

Quality control
  Chief Accountant of the SEC, 52
  Division for CPA Firms, 52
  maintenance of quality, 32, 48–55
  peer review, 52
  Private Companies Practice Section, 52
  Public Oversight Board, 52
  quality defined, 32–33
  SEC Practice Section, 52
  state boards of accountancy, 51
Quality Control Standards Committee of the
  AICPA, 53

Racketeer Influenced and Corrupt
  Organizations Act, 79
Related party transactions (*See also* substantive
  audit testing, audit risk)
  auditing, 579

audit report implications, 633, 642
case illustration, 161, 580
form vs. substance, 580
Reportable conditions (*See* internal control
  structure)
Reports on internal control (*See* internal
  control structure, reporting on)
Review (*See* unaudited financial statements)
Risk (*See* audit risk)
Risk driven vs. procedures driven audits, 177
Rules of Conduct
  accounting principles, 42
  acts discreditable, 44
  advertising, 45
  commissions and referral fees, 45
  confidential client information, 43
  contingent fees, 44
  form of practice and name, 46
  general standards, 41
  independence, 40
  integrity and objectivity, 41

Search for unrecorded liabilities (*See*
  substantive audit testing, current
  liabilities)
Securities Act of 1933
  auditor liability and registration statement, 76
  subsequent events review, 77, 85
Securities Exchange Act of 1934
  annual report (Form 10K), 78
  integrated disclosure and incorporation by
    reference, 78
  quarterly report (Form 10Q), 78
SEC Practice Section (*See* quality control)
Service bureaus (*See* EDP)
Standard cost, testing (*See* control risk)
Statement of cash flows (*See* substantive audit
  testing)
Statements on Responsibilities in Tax Practice,
  38
Statements on Standards for Accounting and
  Review Services, 36
Statements on Standards for Consulting
  Services, 37
Statistical sampling
  and audit judgment, 401
  as contrasted with nonstatistical sampling,
    400
  attribute sampling for control testing, 402
    calculating sample size, 403
    defined, 402
    drawing the sample, 406
    evaluating the sample results, 410
    examples of attributes, 402
    examining sample items for errors, 409
    quantifying control risk, 417
    summary of steps, 415, 416

computer assisted sampling, 458
discovery sampling defined, 402
variables sampling for substantive testing
    alpha risk, 440
    beta risk, 440
    defined, 439
    difference estimation, 448–452
    mean per unit, 439–448
    probability proportional to size (PPS),
        452–458
    precision, 442
    range of acceptability, 448
    reliability, 443
    sampling for variables defined, 402
    standard deviation, 441
    stratified populations, 409, 446
Study of business and industry (*See* audit
    planning)
Subsequent discovery of facts (*See* audit
    report)
Subsequent events (*See* substantive audit
    testing)
Substantive audit programs
    qualitative approach, 245
    quantitative approach, 245
Substantive audit testing
    accounting estimates, 118
    accounting symmetry, testing for, 569
    accounts receivable aging analysis, 486
    allocations and accruals, 118
    analytical procedures
        described, 476
        errors of omission, 120
        examples, 119
        overall audit review, 119, 477, 583
        planning, 119
    audit evidence, objectives, and procedures
        described, 477
        expenditure cycle, 554
        financing and investing cycle, 605
        revenue cycle, 510
    audit risk
        abnormal inventory increase, 541
        disposal of a segment, 582
        early revenue recognition, 498
        high technology industry, 541
        idle capacity, 540
        inadequate loan loss reserves, 496
        increase in plant assets, 541
        inflated sales, 495
        loan defaults, 582
        related parties, 542, 579
    balanced audit approach, 477–478
    borrowing transactions
        audit evidence and procedures, 573
        audit objectives, 573
        summary audit program, 577

cash
    analysis of interbank transfers, 492
    bank reconciliation, 491
    inactive bank accounts, 489
    kiting, 492
    lapping, 492
    proof of cash, 499
    standard bank confirmation form, 489–490
cash receipts transactions
    audit evidence and procedures, 489
    audit objectives, 489
    cutoff tests, 492
    float, 494
    nonrevenue cash receipts, 494
    summary audit program, 495
confirmation of accounts receivable
    as external evidence where risk is high,
        484
    described, 482
    positive vs. negative confirmation
        requests, 483
contingencies, 536–538
cost/benefit, 476
current liabilities
    audit evidence and procedures, 537
    audit objectives, 536
    contingent rentals, 528
    search for unrecorded liabilities, 537
    summary audit program, 540
cutoff bank statement, 489
defined, 19, 111, 474
emphasis and direction, 477
financing and investing cycle
    described, 565
    audit objectives and procedures, 567
intangible assets
    audit evidence and procedures, 519
    audit objectives, 532
    summary audit program, 535
interim application and related risk, 245,
    476
inventories
    audit evidence and procedures, 519
    audit objectives, 517
    confirmation, 523
    cutoff tests, 523, 525
    documentation of counts, 521–522
    inventory instructions, 520
    observation, 19, 519
    obsolescence tests, 526
    pricing tests, 526
    significance of cutoff errors, 524
    summary audit program, 527
investing transactions
    audit evidence and procedures, 568
    audit objectives, 567
    confirmation of securities, 569

examination of securities, 568
lead schedule, 570
summary audit program, 572
supporting schedule, 571
kiting, 492
lapping, 492
lawyer's letter, 116, 537
management's estimates, 118, 536
miscellaneous revenue transactions, 487
open items workpaper, 586
qualitative approach, 245
quantitative approach, 245
plant assets
audit evidence and procedures, 529
audit objectives, 527
contingent rentals, 528
lead schedule, 530
summary audit program, 533
supporting schedule, 531
vouching additions, disposals, and
repairs, 530
reconciliations, 118
related party transactions, audit of, 579
sales transactions
audit evidence and procedures, 482
audit objectives, 481
summary audit program, 488
statement of cash flows, 585
stockholders' equity transactions
audit evidence and procedures, 579
audit objectives, 577
summary audit program, 580
subsequent events
defined, 584
procedures for locating, 585

Type I and Type II, 584
timing of substantive tests, 475
Supplemental information required by FASB,
642
Supporting schedule (See audit workpapers)

Test based vs. detailed audits, 399
Time budget (See audit planning)
Transaction cycle
approach to substantive testing illustrated,
529
classification of, 127, 264
defined, 127
Treadway Report, 30

Unaudited financial statements
agreed upon procedures, 666, 667
compilation, 663
lack of independence, 666
public entity, 662
review, 664
review of interim financial information, 670,
672
type of disclaimer when associated, 663
when associated, 662
Use of client personnel, 158

Vouching (See audit trail)

Warning signs (See audit risk analysis)
Workpaper review, 586

IMPORTANT: PLEASE READ BEFORE OPENING THIS PACKAGE
THIS PACKAGE IS NOT RETURNABLE IF SEAL IS BROKEN.

West Services, Inc.
620 Opperman Drive
P.O. Box 64779
St. Paul, Minnesota 55164-0779

Student Data Disk for Trim
Lawn Manufacturing Corp.
LIMITED USE LICENSE

Read the following terms and conditions carefully before opening this diskette package. Opening the diskette package indicates your agreement to the license terms. If you do not agree, promptly return this package unopened to West Services for a full refund.

By accepting this license, you have the right to use this Software and the accompanying documentation, but you do not become the owner of these materials.

This copy of the Software is licensed to you for use only under the following conditions:

1. PERMITTED USES
You are granted a non-exclusive limited license to use the Software under the terms and conditions stated in this license. You may:

    a. Use the Software on a single computer.
    b. Make a single copy of the Software in machine-readable form solely for backup purposes in support of your use of the Software on a single machine. You must reproduce and include the copyright notice on any copy you make.
    c. Transfer this copy of the Software and the license to another user if the other user agrees to accept the terms and conditions of this license. If you transfer this copy of the Software, you must also transfer or destroy the backup copy you made. Transfer of this copy of the Software, and the license automatically terminates this license as to you.

2. PROHIBITED USES
You may not use, copy, modify, distribute or transfer the Software or any copy, in whole or in part, except as expressly permitted in this license.

3. TERM
This license is effective when you open the diskette package and remains in effect until terminated. You may terminate this license at any time by ceasing all use of the Software and destroying this copy and any copy you have made. It will also terminate automatically if you fail to comply with the terms of this license. Upon termination, you agree to cease all use of the Software and destroy all copies.

4. DISCLAIMER OF WARRANTY
Except as stated herein, the Software is licensed "as is" without warranty of any kind, express or implied, including warranties of merchantability or fitness for a particular purpose. You assume the entire risk as to the quality and performance of the Software. You are responsible for the selection of the Software to achieve your intended results and for the installation, use and results obtained from it. West Services does not warrant the performance of nor results that may be obtained with the Software. West Services does warrant that the diskette(s) upon which the Software is provided will be free from defects in materials and workmanship under normal use for a period of 30 days from the date of delivery to you as evidenced by a receipt.

Some states do not allow the exclusion of implied warranties so the above exclusion may not apply to you. This warranty gives you specific legal rights. You may also have other rights which vary from state to state.

5. LIMITATION OF LIABILITY
Your exclusive remedy for breach by West Services of its limited warranty shall be replacement of any defective diskette upon its return to West at the above address, together with a copy of the receipt, within the warranty period. If West Services is unable to provide you with a replacement diskette which is free of defects in material and workmanship, you may terminate this license by returning the Software, and the license fee paid hereunder will be refunded to you. In no event will West be liable for any lost profits or other damages including direct, indirect, incidental, special, consequential or any other type of damages arising out of the use or inability to use the Software even if West Services has been advised of the possibility of such damages.

6. GOVERNING LAW
This agreement will be governed by the laws of the State of Minnesota.

You acknowledge that you have read this license and agree to its terms and conditions. You also agree that this license is the entire and exclusive agreement between you and West and supersedes any prior understanding or agreement, oral or written, relating to the subject matter of this agreement.